Queen S0-AWQ-374

This monument is located within the grounds of a temple built to honor Queen Hatshepsut near Deir el-Bahri. The monument shows the ancient Egyptian ruler as an Egyptian god. Ancient Egyptian artists carved the figure from limestone. Find out more about Queen Hatshepsut at: www.harcourtschool.com

LOCATE IT

EGYPT

Deir el-Bahri

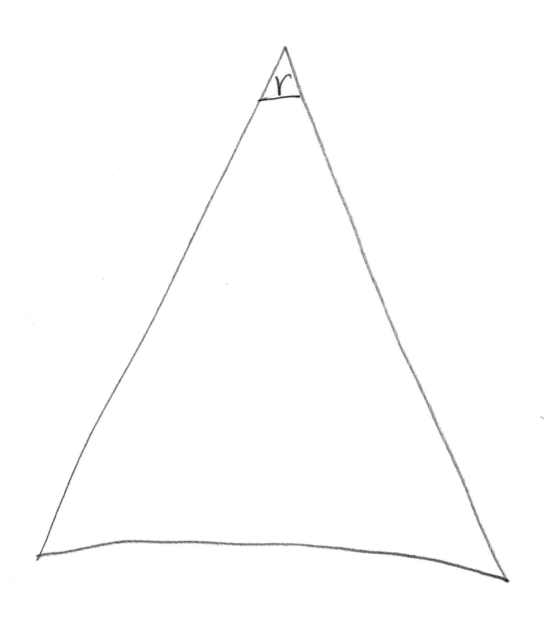

Reflections

CALIFORNIA
SERIES

Ancient Civilizations

Harcourt
SCHOOL PUBLISHERS

Orlando Austin New York San Diego Toronto London
Visit *The Learning Site!* www.harcourtschool.com

MAPQUEST. ®   TIME FOR KIDS ®

HARCOURT SCHOOL PUBLISHERS

Reflections
ANCIENT CIVILIZATIONS

Senior Author

Dr. Priscilla H. Porter
Professor Emeritus
School of Education
California State University,
  Dominguez Hills
Center for History–Social Science
  Education
Carson, California

Series Authors

Dr. Michael J. Berson
Associate Professor
Social Science Education
University of South Florida
Tampa, Florida

Dr. Margaret Hill
History–Social Science Coordinator
San Bernardino County Superintendent
  of Schools
Director, Schools of California Online
  Resources for Education:
  History–Social Science
San Bernardino, California

Dr. Tyrone C. Howard
Assistant Professor
UCLA Graduate School of Education &
  Information Studies
University of California at Los Angeles
Los Angeles, California

Dr. Bruce E. Larson
Associate Professor
Social Science Education/
  Secondary Education
Woodring College of Education
Western Washington University
Bellingham, Washington

Dr. Julio Moreno
Assistant Professor
Department of History
University of San Francisco
San Francisco, California

Series Consultants

Martha Berner
Consulting Teacher
Cajon Valley Union School District
San Diego County, California

Dr. James Charkins
Professor of Economics
California State University
San Bernardino, California
Executive Director of California Council
  on Economic Education

Rhoda Coleman
K–12 Reading Consultant
Lecturer
California State University,
  Dominguez Hills
Carson, California

Dr. Robert Kumamoto
Professor
History Department
San Jose State University
San Jose, California

Carlos Lossada
Co-Director Professional Development
  Specialist
UCLA History–Geography Project
University of California, Los Angeles
Regional Coordinator, California
  Geographic Alliance
Los Angeles, California

Dr. Tanis Thorne
Director of Native Studies
Lecturer in History
Department of History
University of California, Irvine
Irvine, California

Rebecca Valbuena
Los Angeles County Teacher of the
  Year—2004–05
Language Development Specialist
Stanton Elementary School
Glendora Unified School District
Glendora, California

Dr. Phillip VanFossen
Associate Professor,
  Social Studies Education
Associate Director, Purdue Center for
  Economic Education
Department of Curriculum
Purdue University
West Lafayette, Indiana

Grade-Level Author

Dr. André J. Branch
Assistant Professor of Education
School of Teacher Education
San Diego State University
San Diego, California

Content Reviewers

Anti-Defamation League
Education Policy & Advocacy
New York, New York

Dr. Henry E. Chambers
Professor of History
Department of History
California State University, Sacramento
Sacramento, California

Dr. Brian Fagan
Emeritus Professor
Department of Anthropology
University of California, Santa Barbara
Santa Barbara, California

Dr. Charles W. Hedrick, Jr.
Professor
Cowell College
University of California, Santa Cruz
Santa Cruz, California

Dr. Cathleen A. Keller
Associate Professor of Egyptology
Department of Near Eastern Studies
University of California, Berkeley
Berkeley, California

Dr. Samuel A. Oppenheim
Professor Emeritus/Half-Time Professor
Department of History
California State University, Stanislaus
Turlock, California

Dr. Richard Pierard
Stephen Phillips Professor of History
Gordon College
Wenham, Massachusetts

Dr. Cheryl A. Riggs
Professor and Chair
History Department
California State University,
  San Bernardino
San Bernardino, California

Dr. Terry Rugeley
Associate Professor
Department of History
University of Oklahoma
Norman, Oklahoma

Dr. David Smith
Professor
History Department
California Polytechnic University Pomona
Pomona, California

Dr. Stuart Tyson Smith
Associate Professor
Department of Anthropology
University of California, Santa Barbara
Santa Barbara, California

Dr. Miriam Raub Vivian
Department Chair and Professor of
  Ancient History
California State University, Bakersfield
Bakersfield, California

Dr. Arlene Wolinski
Professor
Mesa College
San Diego, California

Dr. Stanley Wolpert
Professor
University of California, Los Angeles
Los Angeles, California

Dr. Ping Yao
Associate Professor
Department of History
California State University, Los Angeles
Los Angeles, California

Classroom Reviewers and Contributors

Haroon Abdul-Mubaarik
Teacher
Holly Drive Leadership Academy
San Diego, California

Michael L. Jarman
Teacher
Manchester Gate Elementary School
Fresno, California

Tom Snyder
Teacher
Baird Middle School
Fresno, California

Stephen J. Squire
Teacher
Ocotillo School
Palmdale, California

Cynthia E. Thomas
Teacher
Palmyra Elementary School
Orange, California

SCHOOL PUBLISHERS

Maps
researched and prepared by

Readers
written and designed by

Copyright © 2007 by Harcourt, Inc.

All rights reserved. No part of this publication may be reproduced or transmitted in any form or by any means, electronic or mechanical, including photocopy, recording, or any information storage and retrieval system, without permission in writing from the publisher.

Requests for permission to make copies of any part of the work should be mailed to:

School Permission's and Copyrights
Harcourt, Inc.
6277 Sea Harbor Drive
Orlando, Florida 32887-6777
Fax: 407-345-2418

REFLECTIONS is a trademark of Harcourt, Inc. HARCOURT and the Harcourt Logos are trademarks of Harcourt, Inc., registered in the United States of America and/or other jurisdictions. TIME FOR KIDS and the red border are registered trademarks of Time Inc. Used under license. Copyright © by Time Inc. All rights reserved.

Acknowledgments appear in the back of this book.

Printed in the United States of America

ISBN 0-15-338504-9

2 3 4 5 6 7 8 9 10 048 15 14 13 12 11 10 09 08 07 06

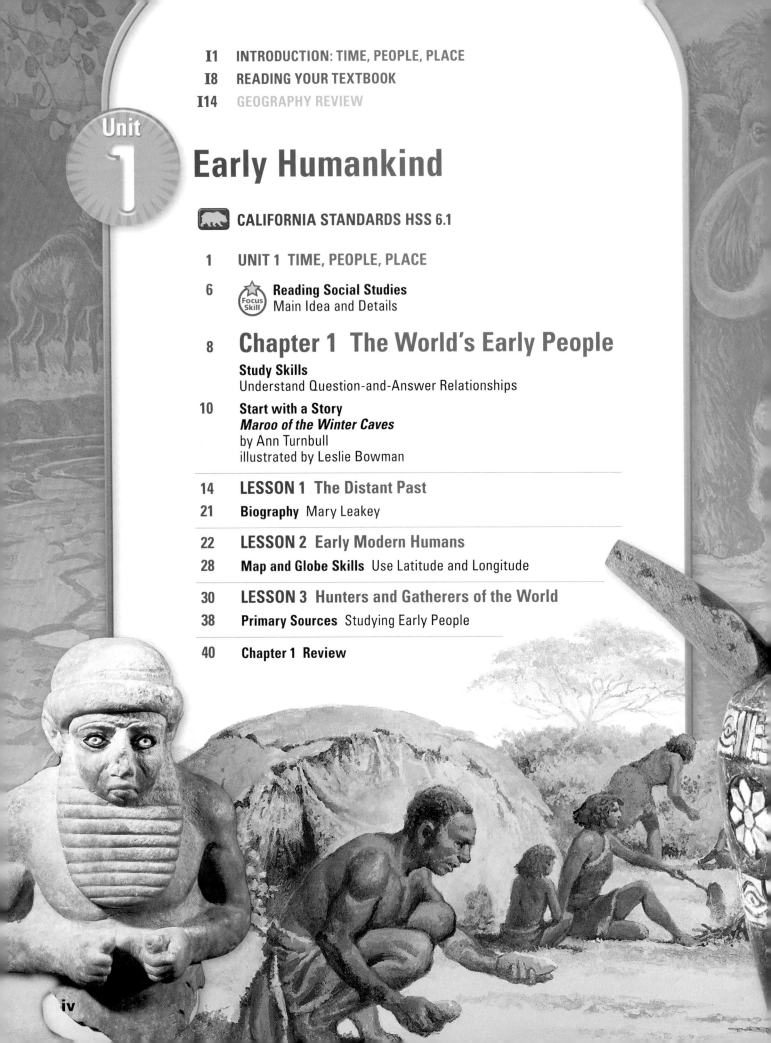

Unit 1

Early Humankind

CALIFORNIA STANDARDS HSS 6.1

iv

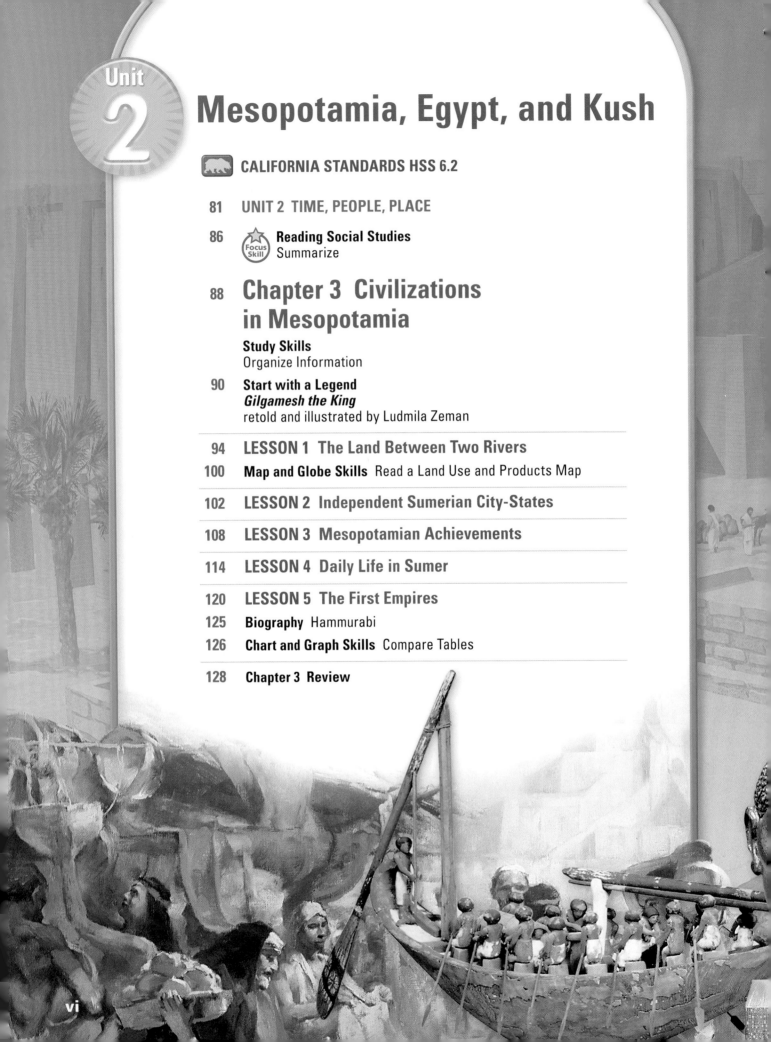

Unit 2

Mesopotamia, Egypt, and Kush

CALIFORNIA STANDARDS HSS 6.2

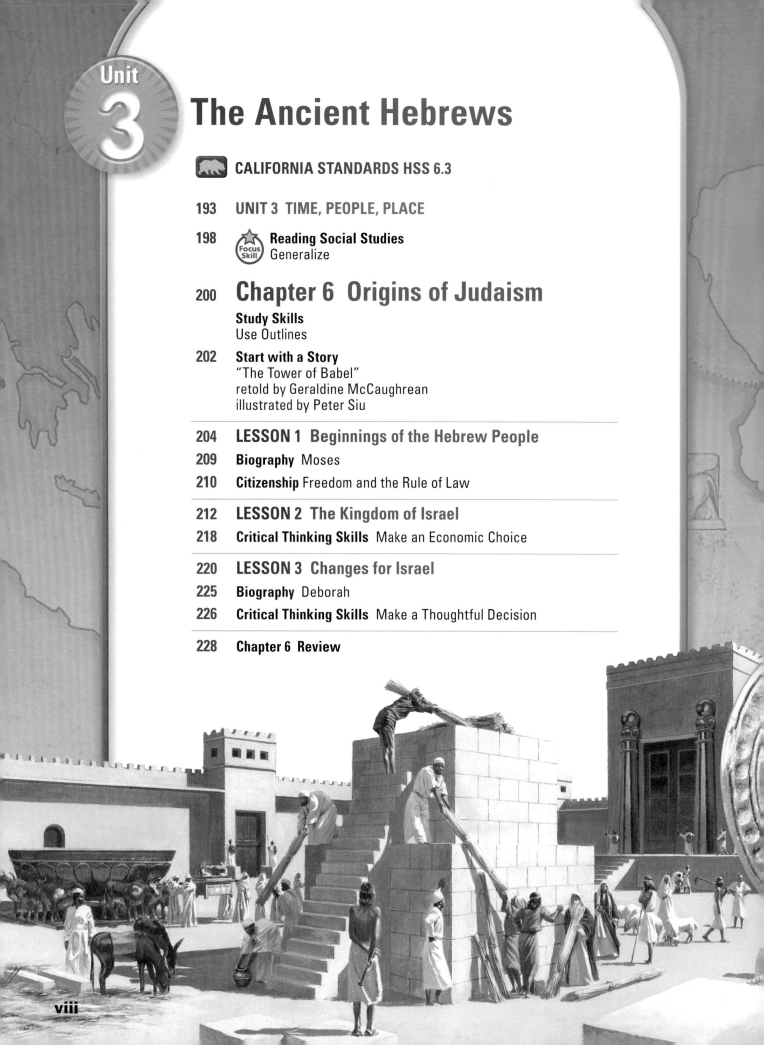

Unit 3

The Ancient Hebrews

CALIFORNIA STANDARDS HSS 6.3

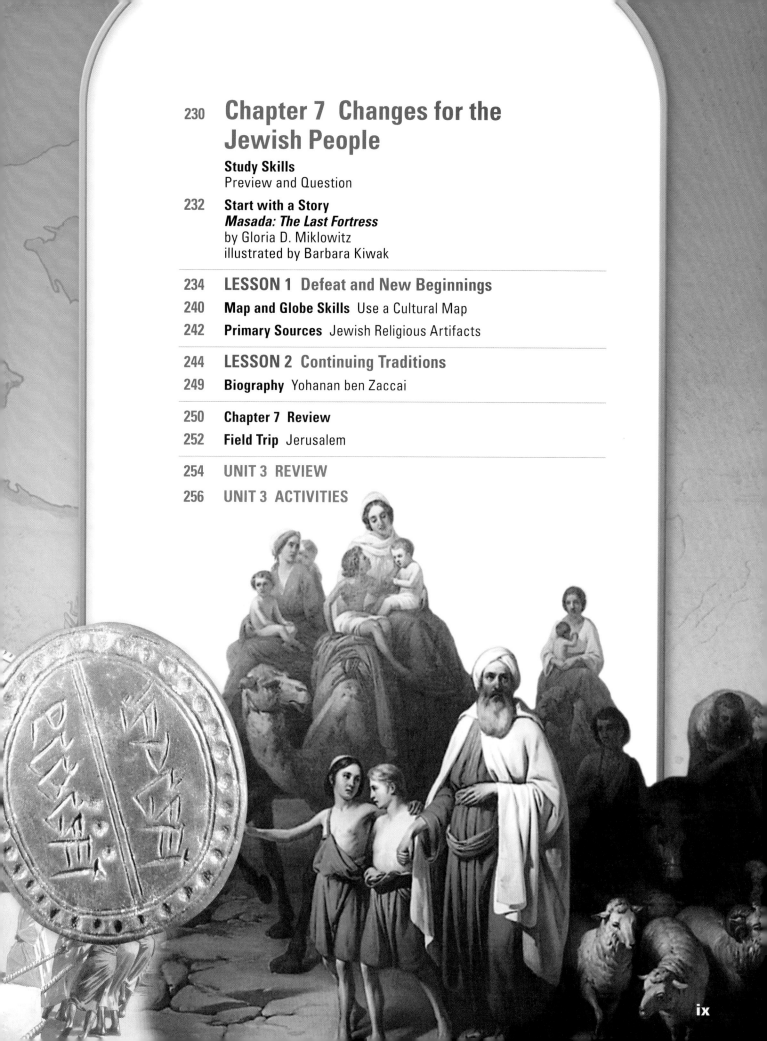

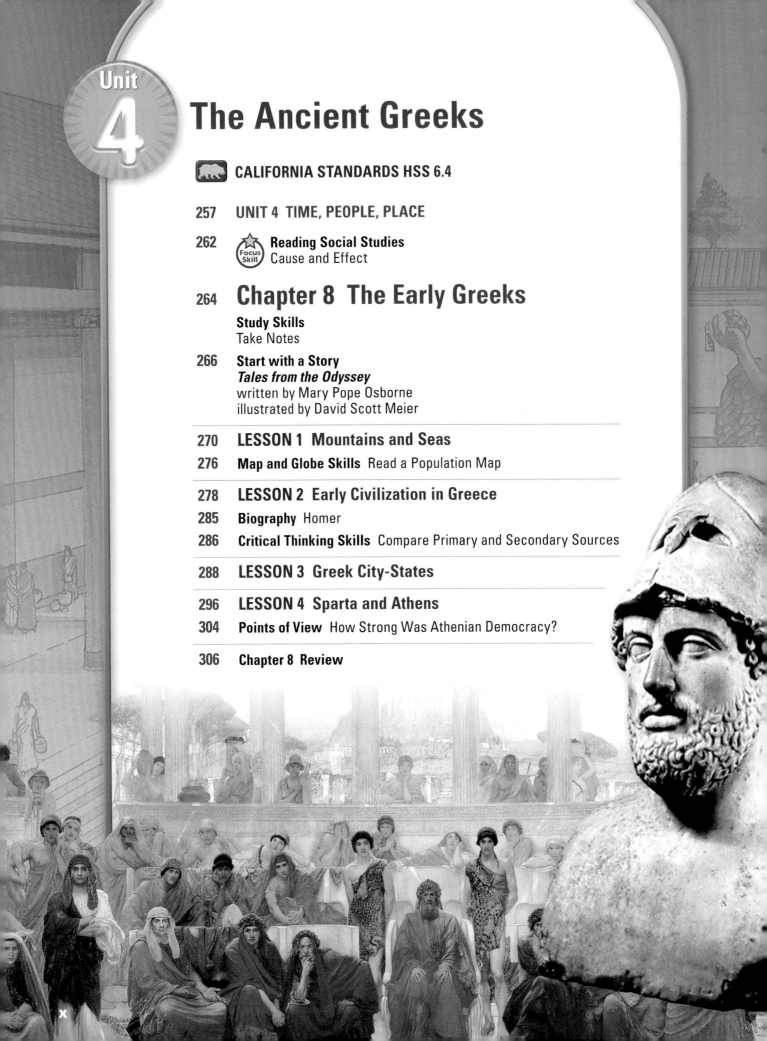

Unit 4 The Ancient Greeks

CALIFORNIA STANDARDS HSS 6.4

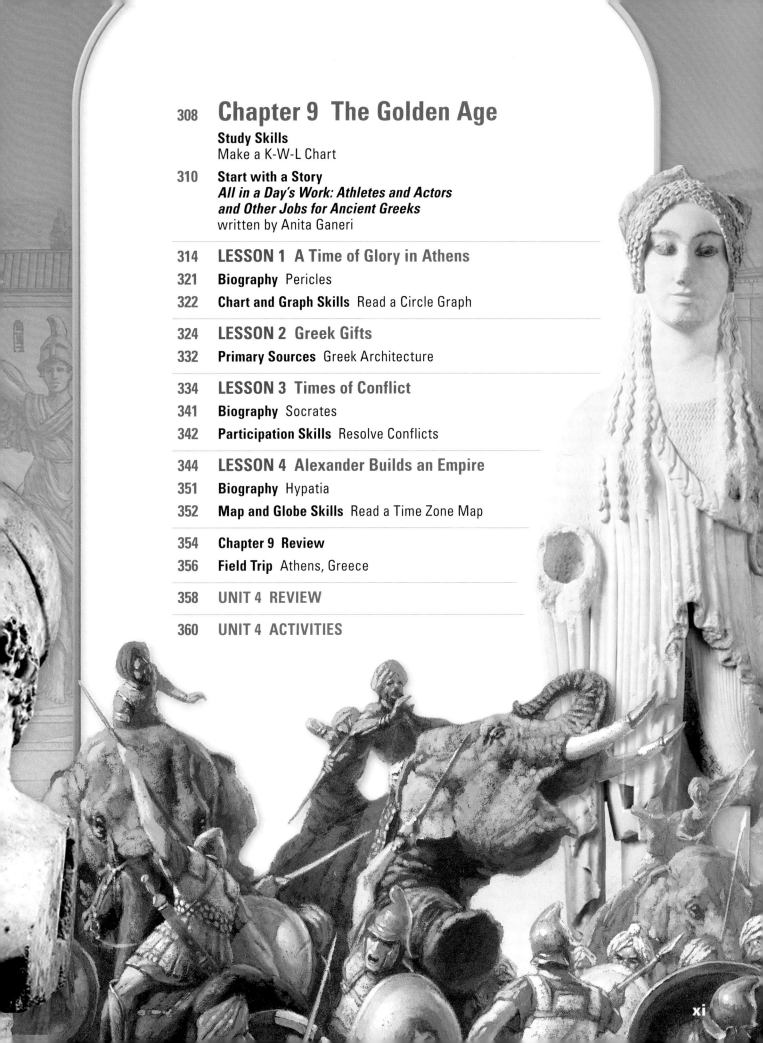

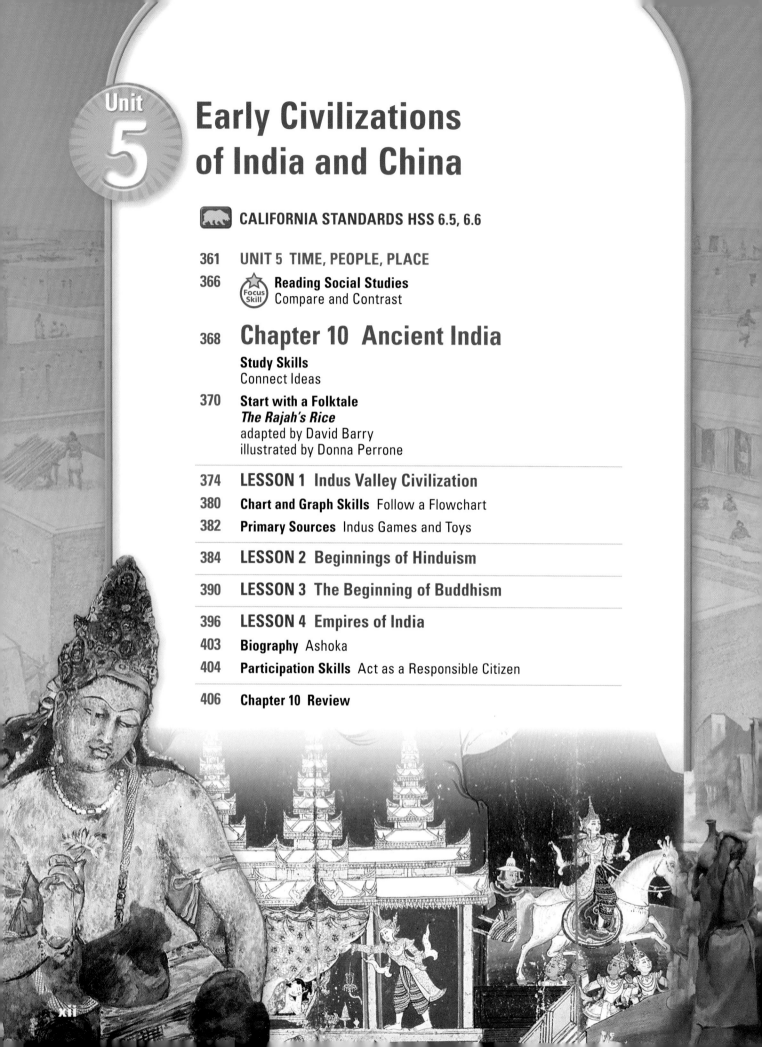

Unit 5

Early Civilizations of India and China

CALIFORNIA STANDARDS HSS 6.5, 6.6

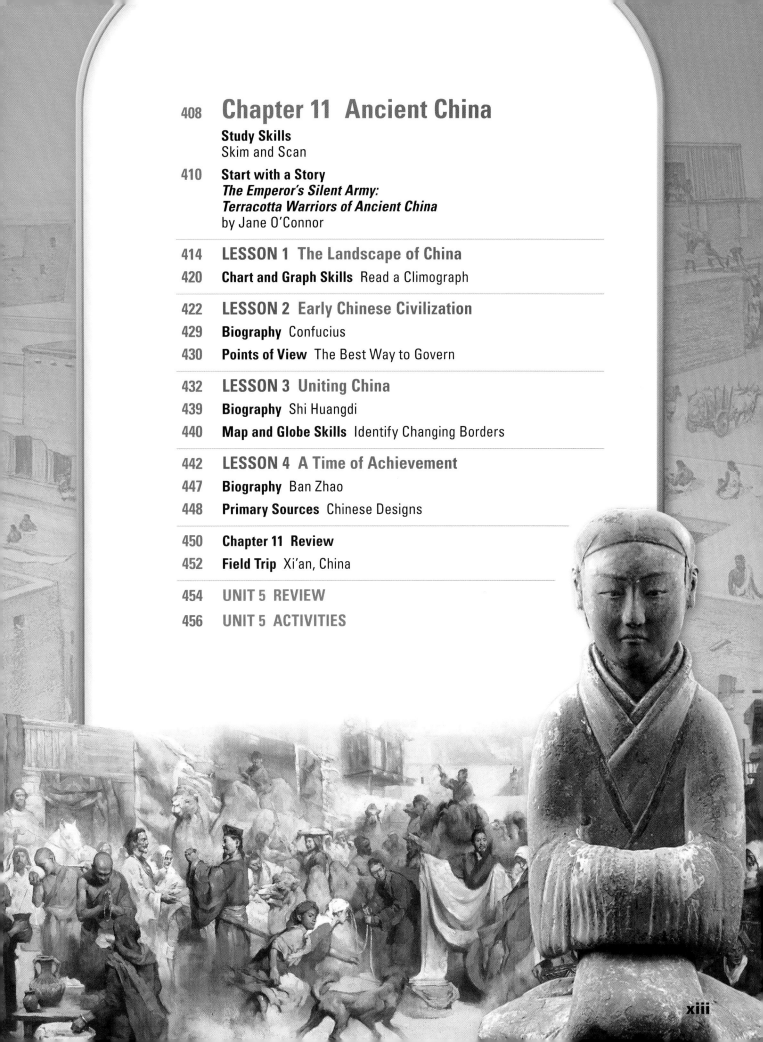

Unit 6

The Development of Rome

CALIFORNIA STANDARDS HSS 6.7

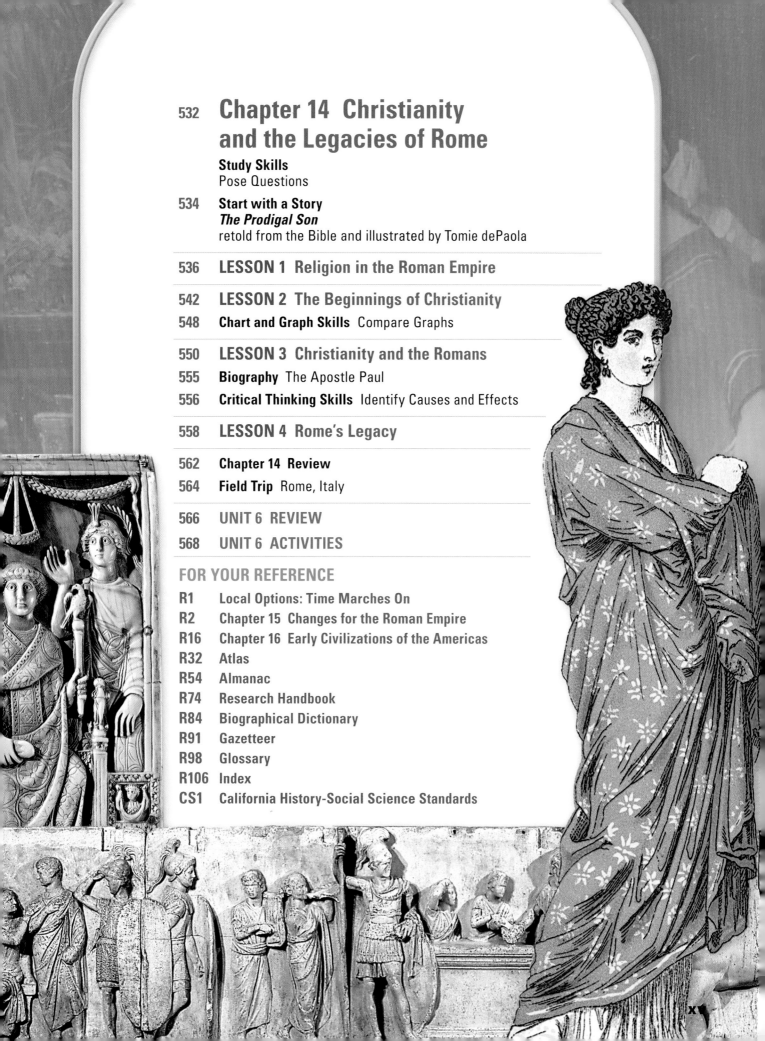

Features

Time Lines

The Story Well Told

"Study the past and use it to understand the present."*

Confucius

Have you ever wondered how ancient civilizations came to be and how they affect the world today? This year, you will be studying ancient civilizations and world geography. You will read about what it was like to live during the **time** of various ancient civilizations. You will also learn about some of the **people** who lived in those civilizations and about the **place** in which each civilization was located.

*Source: Confucius, as quoted in the *Analects*

Time People Place

Ancient Civilizations

The Story of
Ancient Civilizations is about  Time

Studying history helps you see how the present and the past are connected. It helps you identify both similarities and differences between the past and the present. It also helps you see how some things change over time while other things stay the same. As you learn to recognize these links, you will begin to think more like a historian—a person who studies the past.

Historians **research**, or investigate, the time in which events happened by searching for clues in the objects and documents that people left behind. They read journal entries, letters, newspaper articles, and other writings by people who experienced the events. They look at photographs, films, and artwork. They also listen to oral histories—the stories told aloud by people who lived at the time. By examining such **evidence**, or proof, historians are better able to piece together the historical context for the events and to understand what the world was like at the time. This helps them **interpret** the past and explain why events happened as they did.

To interpret the past accurately, historians must look closely at how events are connected to one another. They can better see such connections by studying the **chronology**, or time order, in which events happened. One way historians do this is by using time lines. A time line allows historians to place in chronological order key events and people from the historical era. A time line can also suggest how one event may have led to another.

The Story of
Ancient Civilizations is about  People

Historians research the people who lived during different times in the past. Using the evidence they collect, historians try to imagine what life was like for those people. They try to explain why people did the things they did and how various events affected their feelings and beliefs.

Historians also study people's points of views. A person's **point of view** is how he or she sees things. A point of view is shaped by a person's background and experiences. It can depend on whether a person is old or young, a man or a woman, or rich or poor. People with different points of view may see the same event very differently.

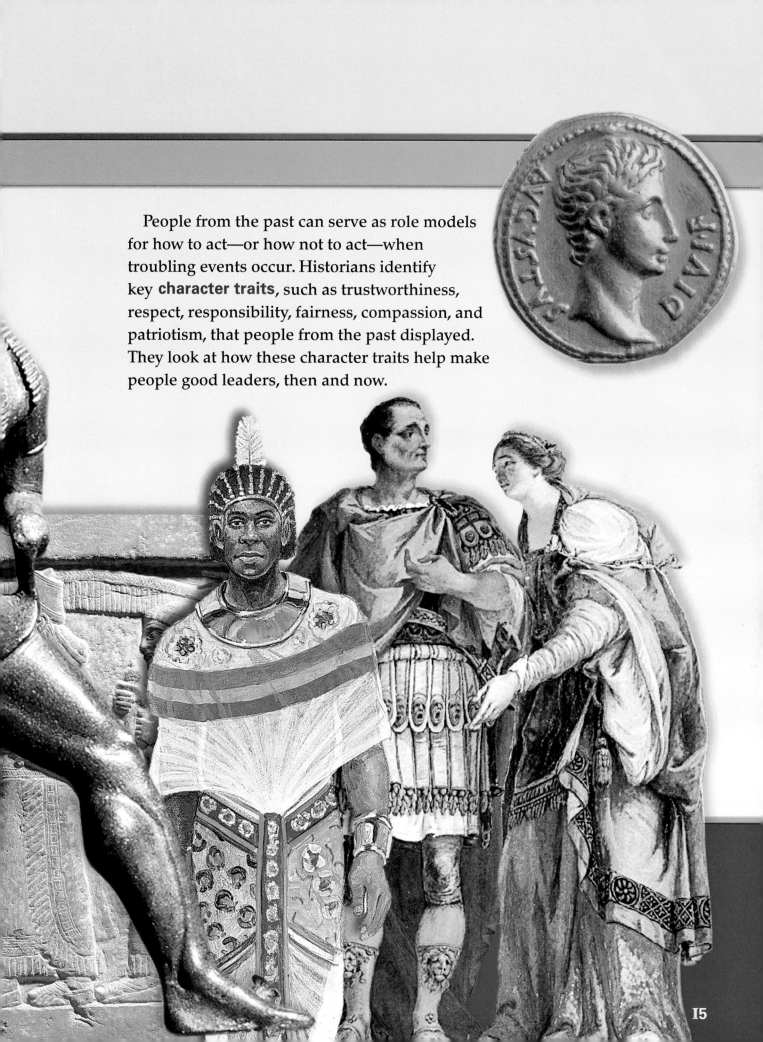

People from the past can serve as role models for how to act—or how not to act—when troubling events occur. Historians identify key **character traits**, such as trustworthiness, respect, responsibility, fairness, compassion, and patriotism, that people from the past displayed. They look at how these character traits help make people good leaders, then and now.

The Story of
Ancient Civilizations is about

 **Place**

In addition to looking at the time in which events took place and the people who took part in them, historians must also consider the place in which those events occurred. Every place on Earth has features that set it apart from all other locations. Often, these features affected what kind of events occurred. They may also have affected why the events unfolded as they did.

Maps and globes help historians to better understand the unique features of a particular place. All maps show a place's location, but some also tell about the land and the people who lived there—the routes people followed, where they settled, and how they used the land.

Maps, like other evidence, help historians more accurately tell the story of the past. They are just one valuable tool historians use to better understand how time, people, and place are connected.

Reading Your Textbook

GETTING STARTED

Unit Title •

• Your textbook is divided into six units.

• Each unit begins with the California History–Social Science Standards covered in the unit.

• The BIG IDEA tells you the key idea you should understand at the end of the unit.

• These questions help you focus on The Big Idea.

• To show that you understand the California History–Social Science Standards and The Big Idea, your teacher may have you complete one or more of these.

LOOKING AT TIME, PEOPLE, AND PLACE

• TIME pages identify important events and tell you when those events took place. You will read about these events in the unit.

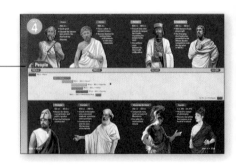

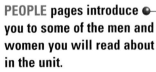
PEOPLE pages introduce • you to some of the men and women you will read about in the unit.

• PLACE pages show where some of the events in the unit took place.

READING SOCIAL STUDIES

The Reading Social Studies Focus Skill will help you better understand the events you read about and make connections among them.

This statement describes the Focus Skill.

The Focus Skill is modeled for you, and you are asked to practice it.

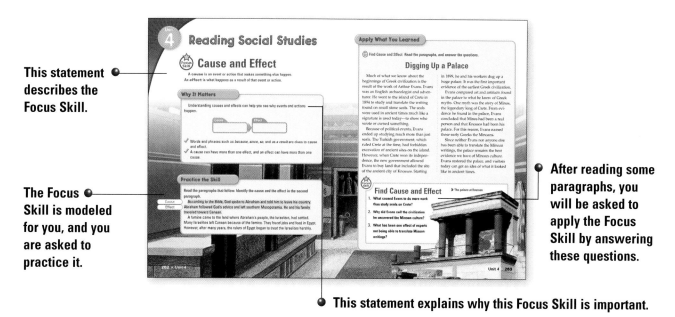

After reading some paragraphs, you will be asked to apply the Focus Skill by answering these questions.

This statement explains why this Focus Skill is important.

BEGINNING A CHAPTER

Each unit is divided into chapters, and each chapter is divided into lessons.

This Study Skill provides you with a strategy that you can use to remember and organize what you read.

Each chapter has the California History–Social Science Standards covered in the chapter.

Chapter title and number

Each chapter begins with a song, poem, journal, story, or other special reading selection.

READING A LESSON

This question helps you focus on the lesson's main idea.

These statements tell you what you should be able to do at the end of the lesson.

Some of the people and places you will read about are listed.

Remember to apply the Reading Social Studies Focus Skill as you read the lesson.

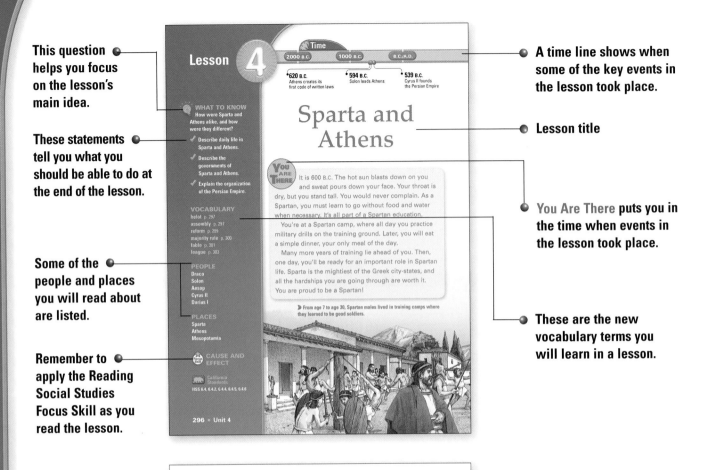

A time line shows when some of the key events in the lesson took place.

Lesson title

You Are There puts you in the time when events in the lesson took place.

These are the new vocabulary terms you will learn in a lesson.

Key people and places are boldfaced.

Some lessons have special features where you can read about Citizenship, Children in History, Geography, Primary Sources, and Points of View.

This question provides an opportunity to apply an Analysis Skill.

Vocabulary terms are highlighted in yellow.

Each short section concludes with a `READING CHECK` **question, which helps you check whether you understand what you have read. Be sure that you can answer this question correctly before you continue reading the lesson.**

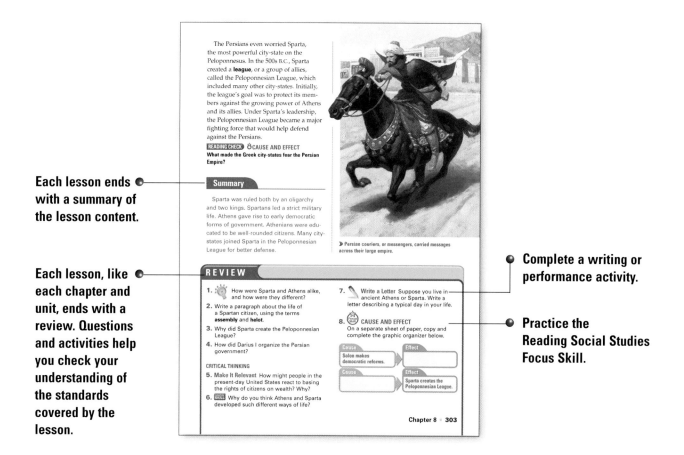

The Persians even worried Sparta, the most powerful city-state on the Peloponnesus. In the 500s B.C., Sparta created a **league**, or a group of allies, called the Peloponnesian League, which included many other city-states. Initially, the league's goal was to protect its members against the growing power of Athens and its allies. Under Sparta's leadership, the Peloponnesian League became a major fighting force that would help defend against the Persians.

READING CHECK Ŏ CAUSE AND EFFECT
What made the Greek city-states fear the Persian Empire?

Summary

Sparta was ruled both by an oligarchy and two kings. Spartans led a strict military life. Athens gave rise to early democratic forms of government. Athenians were educated to be well-rounded citizens. Many city-states joined Sparta in the Peloponnesian League for better defense.

▶ Persian couriers, or messengers, carried messages across their large empire.

REVIEW

1. How were Sparta and Athens alike, and how were they different?

2. Write a paragraph about the life of a Spartan citizen, using the terms **assembly** and **helot**.

3. Why did Sparta create the Peloponnesian League?

4. How did Darius I organize the Persian government?

CRITICAL THINKING

5. **Make It Relevant** How might people in the present-day United States react to basing the rights of citizens on wealth? Why?

6. Why do you think Athens and Sparta developed such different ways of life?

7. **Write a Letter** Suppose you live in ancient Athens or Sparta. Write a letter describing a typical day in your life.

8. CAUSE AND EFFECT
On a separate sheet of paper, copy and complete the graphic organizer below.

Cause
Solon makes democratic reforms.

Effect

Cause

Effect
Sparta creates the Peloponnesian League.

Chapter 8 ▪ 303

Each lesson ends with a summary of the lesson content.

Each lesson, like each chapter and unit, ends with a review. Questions and activities help you check your understanding of the standards covered by the lesson.

Complete a writing or performance activity.

Practice the Reading Social Studies Focus Skill.

LEARNING SOCIAL STUDIES SKILLS

Your textbook has lessons that help you build your Participation Skills, Map and Globe Skills, Chart and Graph Skills, and Critical Thinking Skills.

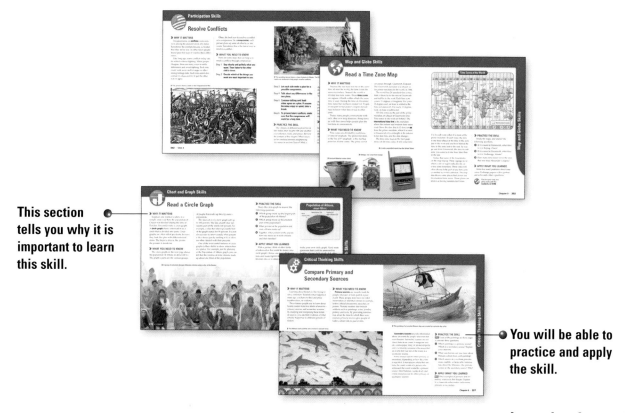

This section tells you why it is important to learn this skill.

You will be able to practice and apply the skill.

SPECIAL FEATURES

Biographies give in-depth background about some of the people who lived at the time.

Each biography focuses on a trait that the person showed.

A time line shows when the person was born and died and some key events in his or her life.

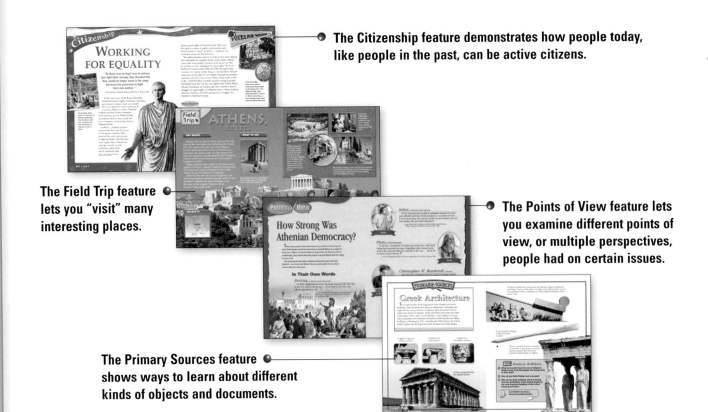

The Citizenship feature demonstrates how people today, like people in the past, can be active citizens.

The Field Trip feature lets you "visit" many interesting places.

The Points of View feature lets you examine different points of view, or multiple perspectives, people had on certain issues.

The Primary Sources feature shows ways to learn about different kinds of objects and documents.

FOR YOUR REFERENCE

At the back of your textbook, you will find different reference tools. You can use these tools to look up words or to find out information about people, places, and other topics.

Almanac
facts about the countries of the world

Atlas
maps that show places in California, in the United States, and around the world

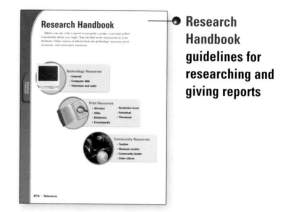

Research Handbook
guidelines for researching and giving reports

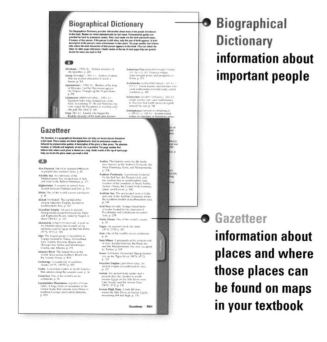

Biographical Dictionary
information about important people

Gazetteer
information about places and where those places can be found on maps in your textbook

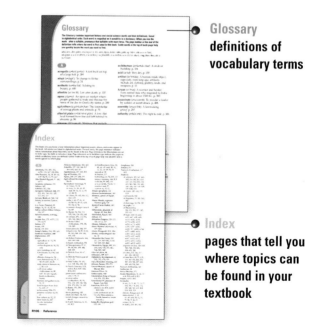

Glossary
definitions of vocabulary terms

Index
pages that tell you where topics can be found in your textbook

The Five Themes of Geography

Learning about places is an important part of history and geography—the study of Earth's surface and the way people use it. Geographers often think about five main themes, or topics, when they study Earth and its geography. Keeping these themes in mind as you read will help you think like a geographer.

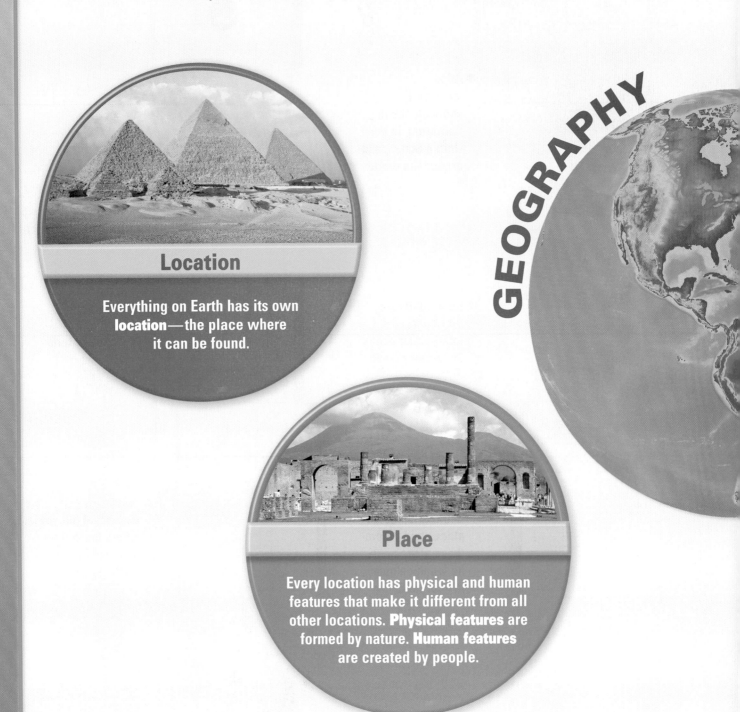

Location

Everything on Earth has its own **location**—the place where it can be found.

Place

Every location has physical and human features that make it different from all other locations. **Physical features** are formed by nature. **Human features** are created by people.

GEOGRAPHY

Human-Environment Interactions

People and their surroundings interact, or affect each other. People's activities may **modify**, or change, the environment. The environment may affect people, requiring them to **adapt**, or adjust, to their surroundings.

Movement

Each day, people in different parts of the state and country and around the world exchange products and ideas.

THEMES

Regions

Areas of Earth with main features that make them different from other areas are called regions. A **region** can be described by its physical features or its human features.

Looking at Earth

A distant view from space shows Earth's round shape. You probably have a globe in your classroom. A globe is also a sphere. It is a model of Earth that shows Earth's major bodies of water and its seven **continents**, or largest land masses. Earth's continents, from largest to smallest, are Asia, Africa, North America, South America, Antarctica, Europe, and Australia.

Because of its shape, you can see only one half of Earth at a time when you look at a globe. Halfway between the North Pole and the South Pole on a globe is a line called the **equator**.

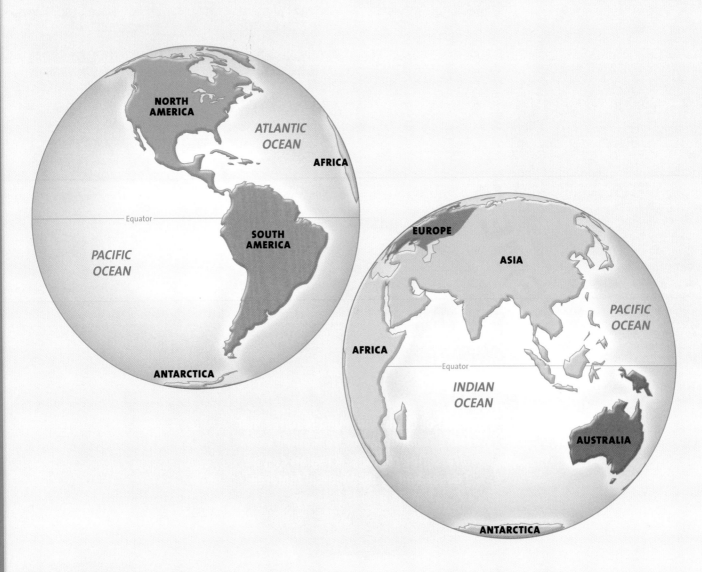

The equator divides Earth into two equal halves, or **hemispheres**. The Northern Hemisphere is north of the equator, and the Southern Hemisphere is south of it. Another line, the **prime meridian**, runs north and south, dividing Earth into the Western Hemisphere and the Eastern Hemisphere.

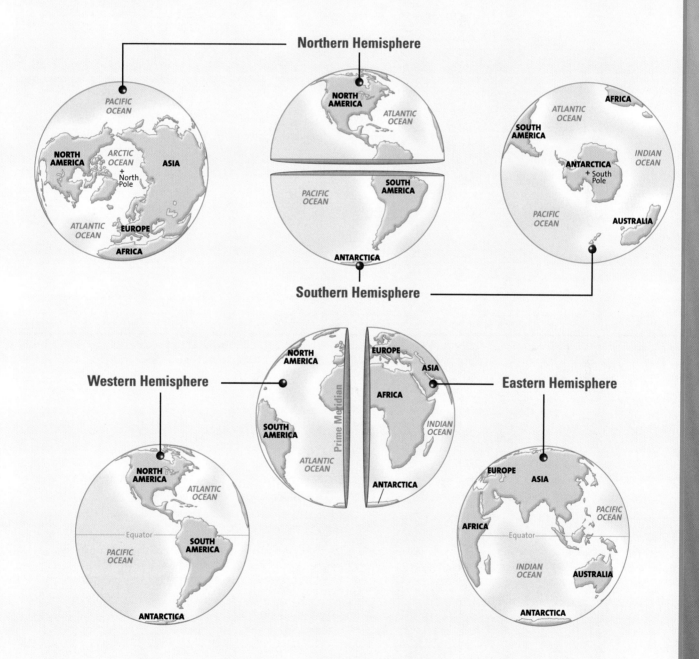

GEOGRAPHY REVIEW

Geography Terms

1. **basin** bowl-shaped area of land surrounded by higher land
2. **bay** an inlet of the sea or some other body of water, usually smaller than a gulf
3. **bluff** high, steep face of rock or earth
4. **canyon** deep, narrow valley with steep sides
5. **cape** point of land that extends into water
6. **cataract** large waterfall
7. **channel** deepest part of a body of water
8. **cliff** high, steep face of rock or earth
9. **coast** land along a sea or ocean
10. **coastal plain** area of flat land along a sea or ocean
11. **delta** triangle-shaped area of land at the mouth of a river
12. **desert** dry land with few plants
13. **dune** hill of sand piled up by the wind

14. **fall line** area along which rivers form waterfalls or rapids as the rivers drop to lower land
15. **floodplain** flat land that is near the edges of a river and is formed by silt deposited by floods
16. **foothills** hilly area at the base of a mountain
17. **glacier** large ice mass that moves slowly down a mountain or across land
18. **gulf** part of a sea or ocean extending into the land, usually larger than a bay
19. **hill** land that rises above the land around it
20. **inlet** any area of water extending into the land from a larger body of water
21. **island** land that has water on all sides
22. **isthmus** narrow strip of land connecting two larger areas of land
23. **lagoon** body of shallow water
24. **lake** body of water with land on all sides

25 **marsh** lowland with moist soil and tall grasses
26 **mesa** flat-topped mountain with steep sides
27 **mountain** highest kind of land
28 **mountain pass** gap between mountains
29 **mountain range** row of mountains
30 **mouth of river** place where a river empties into another body of water
31 **oasis** area of water and fertile land in a desert
32 **ocean** body of salt water larger than a sea
33 **peak** top of a mountain
34 **peninsula** land that is almost completely surrounded by water
35 **plain** area of flat or gently rolling low land
36 **plateau** area of high, mostly flat land
37 **reef** ridge of sand, rock, or coral that lies at or near the surface of a sea or ocean
38 **river** large stream of water that flows across the land

39 **riverbank** land along a river
40 **savanna** area of grassland and scattered trees
41 **sea** body of salt water smaller than an ocean
42 **sea level** the level of the surface of an ocean or a sea
43 **slope** side of a hill or mountain
44 **source of river** place where a river begins
45 **strait** narrow channel of water connecting two larger bodies of water
46 **swamp** area of low, wet land with trees
47 **timberline** line on a mountain above which it is too cold for trees to grow
48 **tributary** stream or river that flows into a larger stream or river
49 **valley** low land between hills or mountains
50 **volcano** opening in the earth, often raised, through which lava, rock, ashes, and gases are forced out
51 **waterfall** steep drop from a high place to a lower place in a stream or river

Geography Review

Reading Maps

Maps can provide you with many kinds of information about Earth and the world around you. A map is a drawing that shows all or part of Earth on a flat surface.

To help you read maps more easily, mapmakers add certain features to most of their maps. These features usually include a title, a map legend, a compass rose, a locator, and a map scale.

Sometimes mapmakers need to show certain places on a map in greater detail, or they must show places that are located beyond the area shown on the map. Find Alaska

A **map title** tells the subject of the map. It may also identify the kind of map.
- A political map shows cities, states, and countries.
- A physical map shows kinds of land and bodies of water.
- A historical map shows parts of the world as they were in the past.

A **map legend**, or key, explains the symbols used on a map. Symbols may be colors, patterns, lines, or other special marks.

An **inset map** is a smaller map within a larger one.

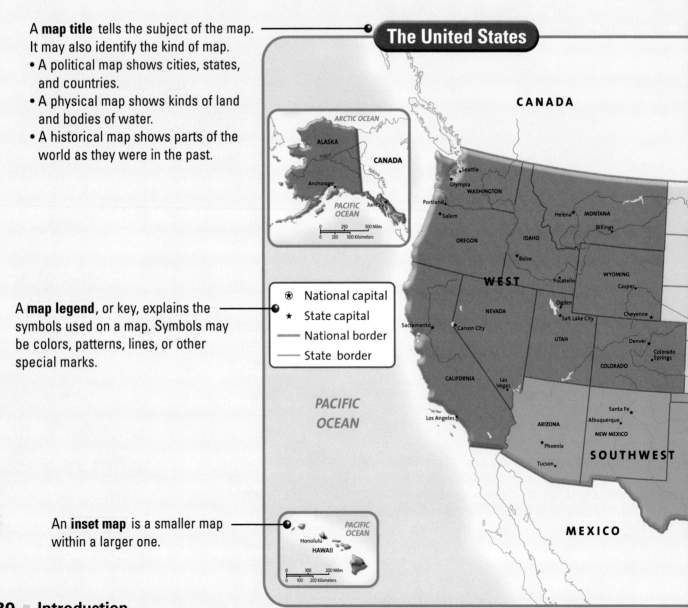

The United States

⊛ National capital
★ State capital
── National border
── State border

and Hawaii on the map of the Americas: Political on page R42. The map there shows the location of those two states in relation to the location of the rest of the country.

Now find Alaska and Hawaii on the map below. To show this much detail for these states as well as the rest of the country, the map would have to be much larger. Instead, here Alaska and Hawaii are each shown in a separate inset map, or a smaller map within a larger map.

A **locator** is a small map or globe that shows where the place on the main map is located within a larger area.

A **map scale** compares a distance on the map to a distance in the real world. It helps you find the real distance between places on a map.

A **compass rose**, or direction marker, shows directions.
• The **cardinal directions** are north, south, east, and west.
• The **intermediate directions**, or directions between the cardinal directions, are northeast, northwest, southeast, and southwest.

Finding Locations

To help people find places on maps, mapmakers sometimes add lines that cross each other to form a pattern of squares called a **grid system**. Look at the map of Egypt below. Around the grid are letters and numbers. The columns, which run up and down, have numbers. The rows, which run from left to right, have letters. Each square on the map can be identified by its letter and number. For example, the top row of squares on the map includes square A-1, square A-2, square A-3, and so on.

Egypt

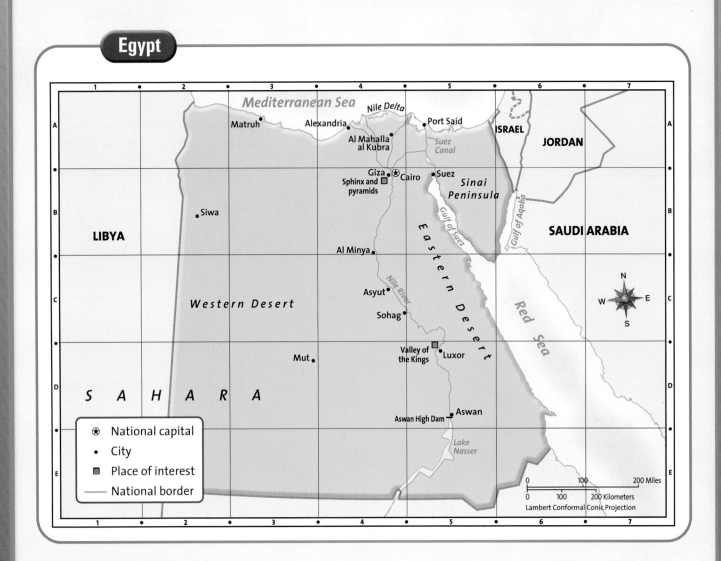

Early Humankind

 **START WITH THE STANDARDS**

California History-Social Science Standards

6.1 Students describe what is known through archaeological studies of the early physical and cultural development of humankind from the Paleolithic era to the agricultural revolution.

The Big Idea

ENVIRONMENT

Early people adapted to their environment to survive.

What to Know

- ✔ How did hunter-and-gatherer societies survive, using the resources available to them?
- ✔ Where did early people settle, and how did their environment affect them?
- ✔ How did climatic changes affect early people?
- ✔ How did people modify their physical environment?

Show What You Know

- ★ Unit 1 Test
- ✎ Writing: A Summary
- 🖌 Unit Project: A Research Notebook

Time

| Early Humankind | **12,000** years ago • The last Ice Age ends and people adapt to different environments, p. 31 | **10,000** years ago • People begin to tame animals and adapt plants, p. 50 |

14,000 years ago

11,000 years ago

| At the Same Time |  **12,000** years ago • The first Californians hunt and gather | **10,000** years ago • Most large Ice Age animals in the Americas die out |

Early Humankind

8,000 years ago
Early farmers develop
the plow and irrigation,
p. 59

5,500 years ago
The earliest
cities form,
p. 70

8,000 years ago

5,000 years ago

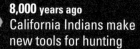

8,000 years ago
California Indians make
new tools for hunting

4,000 years ago
California Indians
begin to live in
villages all year

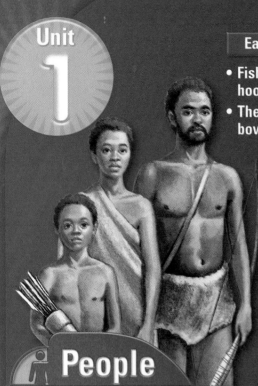

Early Africans

- Fished using nets and hooks
- The first to use the bow and arrow

Early Southwestern Asians

- Tamed dogs to help with hunting
- Livestock became their main source of meat

People

225,000 years ago

150,000 years ago

200,000 years ago • Early Africans first appear

Early North Americans

- Carried a tool kit with bone, cord, stone, and wood
- Made shelters of animal bones and hides

People of Early Pastoral Societies

- Herded goats, sheep, horses, and cattle
- Traded their surplus of skins and meat

Early Eastern Asians

- Found new ways to store grain
- Used clay containers for carrying water and storing food

Early Europeans

- Improved hunting weapons with new kinds of points and blades
- Sailed the sea because of new tools they invented

75,000 years ago

Present Day

90,000 years ago • Early southwestern Asians first appear

65,000 years ago • Early eastern Asians first appear

35,000 years ago • Early Europeans first appear

12,000 years ago • Early North Americans first appear

10,000 years ago • Pastoral societies first appear

10,000 years ago • Early farmers first appear

5,500 years ago • Early people form cities

Early Farmers

- Knowledge of farming was passed from one person to another
- Agriculture brought about permanent settlements

People in Early Cities

- People lived closer together than in towns
- Had specialized jobs, such as merchants, craftspeople, and traders

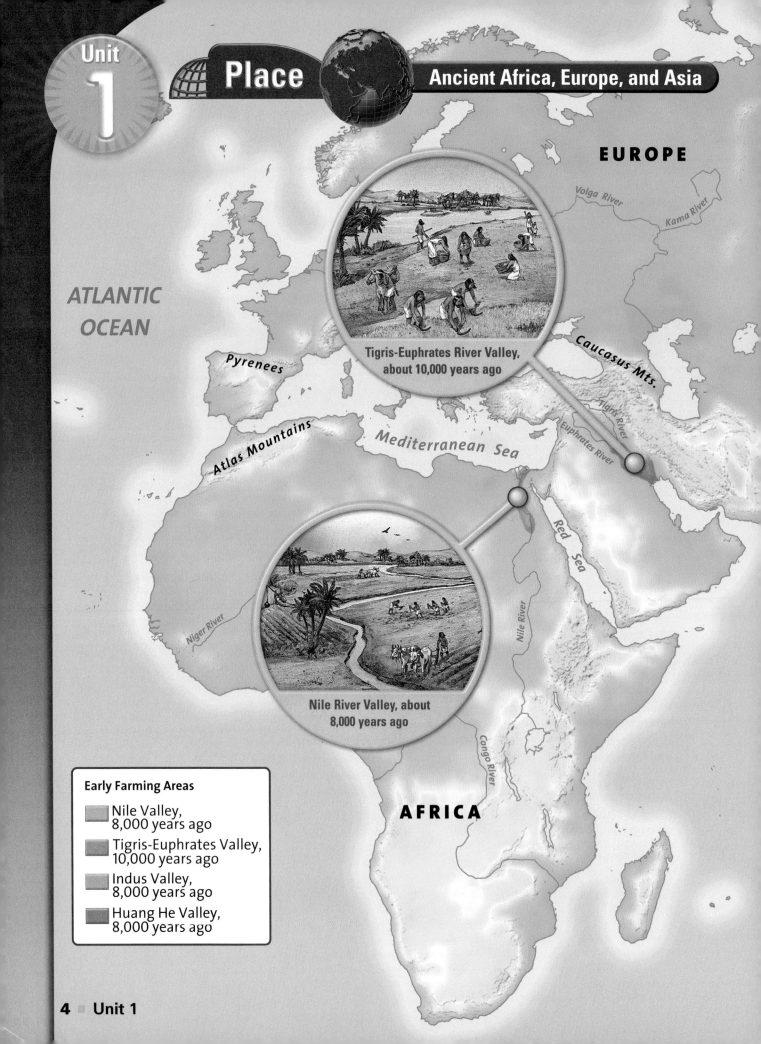

Place

Ancient Africa, Europe, and Asia

EUROPE

Volga River

Kama River

ATLANTIC OCEAN

Tigris-Euphrates River Valley, about 10,000 years ago

Pyrenees

Caucasus Mts.

Atlas Mountains

Mediterranean Sea

Euphrates River

Tigris River

Red Sea

Niger River

Nile River

Nile River Valley, about 8,000 years ago

Congo River

AFRICA

Early Farming Areas

Nile Valley, 8,000 years ago

Tigris-Euphrates Valley, 10,000 years ago

Indus Valley, 8,000 years ago

Huang He Valley, 8,000 years ago

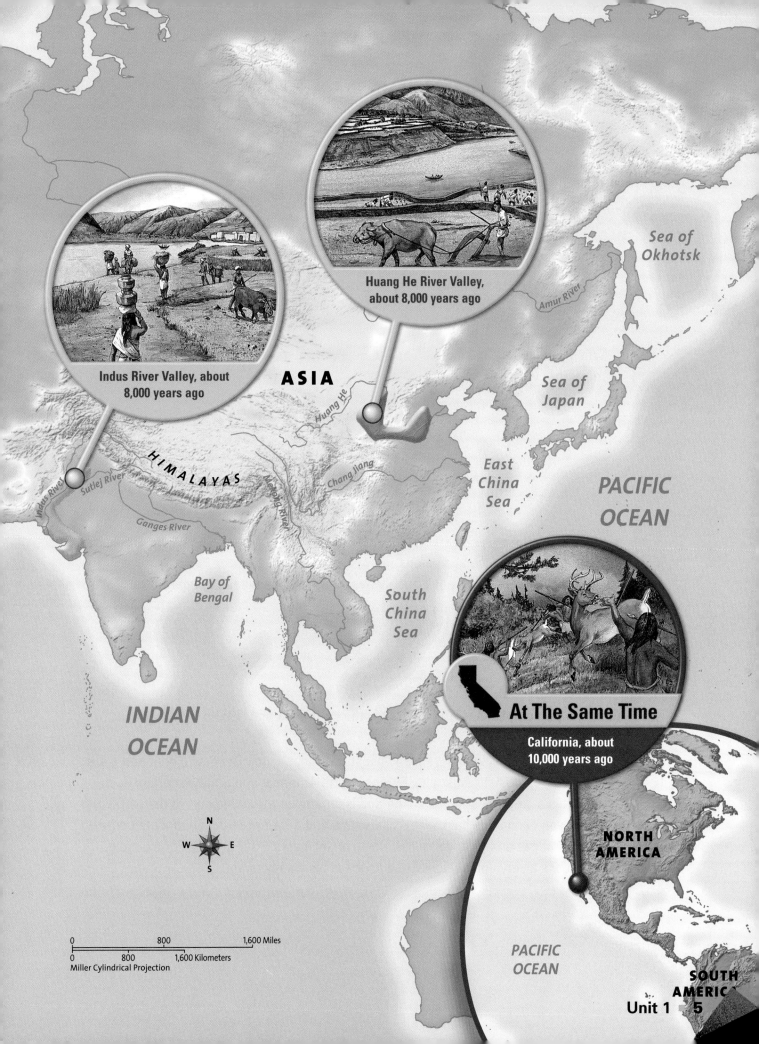

Indus River Valley, about
8,000 years ago

Huang He River Valley,
about 8,000 years ago

ASIA

HIMALAYAS

Indus River

Sutlej River

Ganges River

Huang He

Chang Jiang

Mekong River

Amur River

Sea of
Okhotsk

Sea of
Japan

East
China
Sea

PACIFIC
OCEAN

Bay of
Bengal

South
China
Sea

INDIAN
OCEAN

At The Same Time

California, about
10,000 years ago

NORTH
AMERICA

SOUTH
AMERIC

PACIFIC
OCEAN

N
W   E
S

0   800   1,600 Miles
0   800   1,600 Kilometers
Miller Cylindrical Projection

Reading Social Studies

Focus Skill

Main Idea and Details

The **main idea** is the most important idea in a passage. **Details** give information that supports the main idea.

Why It Matters

When you identify and understand the main idea and details, you are more likely to remember what you read.

> **Main Idea**
>
> **Details** ⬆

✓ In a long article, each paragraph has a main idea and details. The whole article also has a main idea and details.

✓ The main idea is usually, but not always, at the beginning of each paragraph.

Practice the Skill

Read the paragraphs that follow. Identify the main idea and details for the second paragraph.

Main Idea
Details

Our world is made up of seven landmasses, or continents. The seven continents are Africa, Antarctica, Asia, Australia, Europe, North America, and South America. Each continent is a different size and shape and is located in a specific part of the world.

The seven continents have many similarities and differences. All continents contain mountain ranges and a variety of life. However, climates differ greatly. For example, Antarctica is a very cold region, while Africa stays mainly warm.

Find the Main Idea and Details Read the paragraphs, and answer the questions.

In Search of the First Cook

Certain questions about early humans have puzzled scientists for centuries. They want to know how the very first humans lived and why humans moved to various places. They also want to know when and how humans developed language. Another very important thing scientists want to know is how cooking changed the lives of early humans.

No one knows for certain the answers to these questions. The evidence about early humans is limited. Each scientist may interpret evidence in his or her own way and may reach a different conclusion. However, scientists do agree on one thing—rarely was there a group of people who did not cook.

Even in ancient times, people realized that cooking food over a fire made their lives better in several ways. Cooking makes food safer by killing germs. Cooking breaks down the ingredients in food that are good for people so that they can digest them easier.

Find the Main Idea and Details

1. What is the main idea of the first paragraph?

2. What is the main idea of the article?

3. What are two important details that support this main idea?

Study Skills

UNDERSTAND QUESTION-AND-ANSWER RELATIONSHIPS

Knowing that different kinds of questions ask for different kinds of information will help you write proper responses.

▶ Questions that include the words *who, what, where, when,* and *how* often require you to use details in your answers.

▶ Questions that ask about relationships, such as comparisons or causes and effects, require that you make connections in your answers. You may also need to give details.

Questions About Details	Questions About Connections
Question: What is archaeology? Answer:	Question: What was the effect of settlement on early people? Answer:
Question: Where did early humans first live? Answer:	Question: Why did early Africans and early Asians use different resources? Answer:

Apply As You Read

As you read this chapter, look for the answers to the questions above. When you read the Reading Check and Lesson Review questions, think about the kind of answer that would be best for each question.

California History-Social Science Standards, Grade 6

6.1 Students describe what is known through archaeological studies of the early physical and cultural development of humankind from the Paleolithic era to the agricultural revolution.

The World's Early People

▶ Archaeologists search for evidence of early people in Colorado.

Maroo of the Winter Caves

by Ann Turnbull illustrated by Leslie Bowman

Early people depended on the resources around them for their survival. For food, they hunted wild animals. They also gathered plants that grew in the area. Early people used such resources as trees, mud, and grass to build homes. For clothing, they sewed animal skins. The fictional story that follows will help you see how the early people lived. The story features Maroo, a young girl, and her family as they go about life long ago.

Maroo woke hungry. She lay for a moment with her eyes shut, imagining biting into tough, hot meat, savoring the charred, smoke-tasting outer part and then the salty blood within. There had been no meat for a long time, but today the hunters should return. They had left yesterday on the track of a herd of bison.

Usually they came back by nightfall, but sometimes if they had hunted all day without luck, they would make camp and try again the next morning.

She opened her eyes. It was still dark in the cave, but she could see fur-wrapped shapes stirring: her mother, brother, and sister.

Nimai, the little sister, sat up and put her thumb in her mouth. Maroo reached to a niche in the cave wall and took out two dried roots. She gave one to Nimai and put one in her own mouth. The root was tough and tasteless, but it stilled the hunger pains.

Maroo found her boots and pulled them on. They were made of soft leather, trimmed with white fox fur. She tucked her deerskin trousers inside them and tied them in place with leather thongs.

niche an open space in a wall

thongs strips of material

The place where they slept was a <u>recess</u> in the wall of the inner cave. Skins were piled across the entrance to keep out drafts. There were recesses and sleeping platforms all around. Hardly any floor space was left in the small cave. More people lived here than Maroo could count using all her fingers twice.

"Maroo!"

Nimai had followed her out, thumb in mouth and boots untied. Maroo tied the boots and said, "We'll go outside and look for herbs."

They turned the corner into the outer cave. At once the air felt cold. A misty gray dawn showed in the cave mouth. Old Mother was squatting there, scraping away the ash from last night's fire. Maroo watched as Old Mother put her face close to the blackened wood in the hearth-place and blew gently. Her warm breath woke the sleeping fire; a thread of scarlet quivered in one of the pieces, then vanished. Old Mother blew again. Smoke rose from the embers, then little yellow flames sprang from the wood and joined to make bigger flames. The children squatted beside their grandmother. Old Mother brought small pieces of the precious wood from her <u>store</u> and fed the hungry flames. They grew fat and red, and their warmth beat upon the girls' faces.

The fire was built inside a circle of boulders surrounded on three sides by large, flat stones where people could sit. The flames were leaping up brightly now, and points of fire shone in Old Mother's dark eyes. There was a bone dish beside the fire full of small, smooth, round stones. The old woman dropped them gently into the heart of the fire. When they were hot she would put them into a bowl of water to make warm drinks.

Old Mother patted Maroo's hand. "Find something good to drink."

Maroo nodded. She knew her grandmother liked hot water flavored with herbs. "Will the hunters come home today, Old Mother?" she asked. "Will we have meat?"

"Will the snow melt? Will the grass grow?" Old Mother pretended despair at the questions. "You should ask the spirits such things, not an old woman." She chuckled. "They will come today. I feel it, here"—she struck her chest— "and we shall have full bellies tonight, eh, little one?" She patted Nimai's stomach. Nimai squirmed and giggled.

recess a hidden place

store place where supplies are kept

"Be off with you," said Old Mother, "and find me some good herbs."

Outside the cave the land sloped gently down a pebbly hillside scattered with stunted trees toward the lake. The spring thaw had made the scree slippery; the pebbles rolled under their feet as they started down, and Nimai would not go alone but clung timidly to Maroo's hand. The path was running with water, and the sound of water was all around, from the dripping, close by, of snow from the cave roof where the fire was melting it, to the distant roar of countless streams. From far away on the river, beyond the lake, farther than the children could see, came the faint crashing of ice floes.

They stopped at the bottom of the slope.

"Hear the river," said Nimai.

Maroo imagined the unseen river, liberated after the long winter, rushing and tumbling down from the mountains, carrying rocks, bones, broken trees, drowned animals, and smashed-up ice to the sea. The sea was harder to imagine, for she had never seen it, though some of her kinsmen had, and had brought back the shells that decorated her jacket. If only . . . Maroo thought of the coming summer, and wished: if only this summer we could go to the sea. She had wished it before, but either they had never gotten so far or they had taken a different way, up into the mountains. Perhaps this year they would go.

Maroo loved the summer with its uncertainty about where they would be from one day to the next. All winter they had scarcely left the cave, hemmed in by blizzards that blew for days on end, and a cold so intense that an unprotected finger or toe could freeze and drop off. But soon—perhaps in a few days' time if the hunters were lucky—they would leave the caves and spend the summer wandering, until the cold weather and the migrations of the reindeer brought them back to the autumn hunting grounds.

Maroo did a little dance of excited anticipation. Nimai laughed and jumped about.

"We'll go soon," said Maroo. "We'll follow the deer!"

Nimai grinned. "Fish!" she said. "Honey!"

Nimai was old enough to remember the pleasures of last summer.

Maroo led Nimai down to the shore of the lake where green shoots were showing through the melting snow. They began to search for berries and plants with thick roots that could be eaten. They found a patch of the shrub they called "drops of blood" with its little sour red berries, and

herbs plants used for flavoring foods

scree loose stones at the bottom of a hill

soon filled a small basket. Nimai kept eating the berries, and Maroo scolded her, though she furtively ate a few herself. Nearby they found a plant with strongly scented leaves. Maroo squatted down to gather a handful, glad that she could please Old Mother. Nimai wandered to the water's edge.

"Come away!" Maroo shouted.

"See my spirit!" said Nimai.

Maroo came to look. The ice that had covered the lake all winter was melting, revealing large stretches of still gray water. Nimai's small, smiling spirit form was looking up at her from the lake. The spirit of Maroo came up and stood beside it. The gently moving shape had a round face framed by brown wolverine fur and two dark plaits of hair hanging down on its chest. She put up a hand to stroke the fur, and the spirit copied her.

A stone hit the water with force and smashed the image. Both girls jumped in fright.

Maroo sprang round. "Otak!"

Her younger brother stood grinning at her, the sling loose in his hand. Maroo jumped on him and punched him. "You drove my spirit away!"

But she was laughing; she knew it would come back. They fought playfully. Nimai knelt by the water, watching the spreading rings.

my spirit Here, Nimai means her reflection.

Maroo and Otak began quarreling over the berries.

"Don't you eat those!" she said sharply. "Stay here and watch Nimai while I take the basket to Old Mother."

"That's girl's work—" Otak began.

But Maroo ignored him and ran back to the cave. When she returned, Otak was skimming a flat stone across the water. It jumped twice, to Nimai's delight.

"Again!" the little girl said.

She darted about, fetching Otak stones, always the wrong shape. Maroo found him a better one. He was poised for a throw when Nimai began to shout:

"Men, hunters!"

Otak dropped the stone and they all stared where she was pointing. Far away, along the lake shore, Maroo saw a movement. Could it be the hunters, or was it animals? Nimai was already jumping up and down.

The next moment Maroo knew. "Yes!" she exclaimed. "They're coming!"

Response Corner

1 Why do you think Maroo and Nimai were so excited to see their "spirits" in the water?

2 Imagine that you lived in the cave with Maroo and her family. What kinds of activities would you do during the winter months to keep you busy?

The Distant Past

WHAT TO KNOW
How do people today learn about the distant past?

✓ Describe what is known about the early humans through archaeological studies.

✓ Tell about the achievements of scientists who have studied the ancient past.

VOCABULARY
prehistory p. 15
archaeology p. 15
artifact p. 15
fossil p. 15
theory p. 15
hominid p. 17
Paleolithic era p. 18
migrate p. 20

PEOPLE
Mary Leakey
Louis Leakey
Richard Leakey
Donald Johanson
Tim White

PLACES
Africa
Olduvai Gorge
Lake Turkana

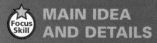
MAIN IDEA AND DETAILS

California Standards
HSS 6.1, 6.1.1

YOU ARE THERE

It's hot—so hot that sweat runs down your neck. Glare from the blazing sun hurts your eyes. Your legs ache from kneeling for hours at a time. Your hands are blistered from working in the dirt all day.

The year is 1959, and you're in eastern **Africa** with scientists **Mary Leakey** and **Louis Leakey**. For weeks, you have been at a site in **Olduvai** (OHL•duh•vy) **Gorge**, in Tanzania. You have helped dig through hundreds of pounds of earth and sifted through large mounds of soil. You have carefully dusted and labeled each clue you have found.

Suddenly, you hear a woman shout excitedly that she's found something. Everyone rushes to see Mary Leakey's discovery. It's the remains of life of long ago.

❯ Scientists, like Mary Leakey, study clues such as this footprint to learn about early life.

LOCATE IT

Laetoli

TANZANIA

▶ Dr. Dennis Stanford displays part of the huge artifact collection at the Smithsonian Institution in Washington, D.C.

Uncovering the Past

People have been living on Earth since long before written history. The period of time before people began to write is called **prehistory**. Without writing, no records could be kept, and no stories could be recorded.

Without written records, how do we learn about the distant past? One way to learn about ancient times is through scientific study. Scientists from different branches of science study evidence from the distant past. These clues help the scientists learn what happened at a place in the past.

What evidence exists from the distant past? Scientists who work in **archaeology** (ar•kee•AH•luh•jee) study things that earlier people left behind. Archaeologists study the remains of ancient campsites, shelters, and other buildings. They also learn from **artifacts**, objects made by people. Artifacts include such items as art, clothing, pottery, tools, and weapons.

Other evidence from the distant past includes **fossils**. Some scientists study remains, such as bones, of once living animals and humans. Fossils can also be footprints preserved in what is now rock.

Much information can be learned from artifacts and fossils. Artifacts help us learn how early humans lived from day to day. Fossils can provide clues to help us imagine what early humans looked like.

By comparing the artifacts and fossils of early humans from different time periods, scientists can see how their ways of life and physical features changed over time. From this, they develop **theories**, or accepted explanations, about life in the distant past.

It is not every day that scientists dig up complete artifacts or fossils. Usually, they find only small pieces of them—or nothing at all. Because of this, huge gaps exist in what we know about life long ago. Still, even small discoveries can change how we interpret, or understand, the distant past.

READING CHECK ☼MAIN IDEA AND DETAILS
What information can artifacts and fossils provide?

▶ Archaeologists (above) excavate a site on Hog Island, Alaska.
A notebook, brush, and pick (left) are important tools for their work.

Excavating Sites

Scientists excavate archaeological sites by digging up artifacts and fossils. A site might be a place where prehistoric people once sat around a campfire to work, cook, and eat. It also could be a larger area, such as the ruins of an early village. Some sites are inside caves or near where rivers once flowed, while others lie beneath present-day villages and cities. Many sites are found after years of careful study and research, but others are found by chance.

When excavating a site, scientists divide it into a grid of squares. They dig up each plot separately so that they can keep track of exactly where each artifact or fossil was found. To remove the soil from around the objects, scientists use such tools as shovels, brushes, and small picks.

Scientists work carefully as they excavate a site. They do not want to break or damage what might turn out to be an ancient

tool or a piece of bone. As they dig, scientists sift through the soil. Carefully, they search for important evidence of what once went on in that place in the past. They clean, label, and pack everything they find. Later, they send their finds to laboratories.

In the laboratories, scientists carry out archaeological studies on the evidence. For example, they perform special tests on it to tell how old it is. One such test, known as radiocarbon dating, tells how much carbon remains in something that was once alive. When an animal or a plant dies, its radioactive carbon begins to decrease. Scientists can estimate the age of evidence, such as a piece of wood or bone, by measuring the amount of carbon left in it.

Radiocarbon dating can be used only for artifacts and fossils 40,000 years old or younger. Other tests help scientists date older artifacts and fossils.

READING CHECK ⏾ **MAIN IDEA AND DETAILS**
How are sites of artifacts and fossils found?

African Beginnings

For more than 75 years, archaeologists and other scientists have worked at sites in eastern Africa. There they have found traces of early **hominids**, or humans and species with humanlike characteristics.

Scientists such as the Leakey family (Louis, Mary, and **Richard Leakey**), **Donald Johanson**, and **Tim White** have found fossils of bones of several kinds of early hominids. One of the earliest hominid groups is made up of australopithecines (aw•stray•loh•PIH•thuh•synz), which may have lived in Africa between about 4.5 million and 1 million years ago.

In 1974, Donald Johanson discovered bones from a female australopithecine that became known as "Lucy." This female was about 20 years old and about 4 feet tall when she died. This discovery showed that early australopithecines could walk on two legs, leaving their hands free to hold things.

Some australopithecines lived in forests. They ate mostly plants, especially fruit, and perhaps small animals.

Other australopithecines learned to live on open grasslands. They ate different plants and perhaps more meat than those living in forests. They also moved over longer distances in search of food. This diet and movement caused them to become different from other australopithecines. Their brain size increased, and they grew larger and stronger. Their legs became longer, helping them travel more quickly.

Fossils of the earliest hominids have been found in Africa. These discoveries provide strong evidence that human life may have begun there.

READING CHECK ○ **MAIN IDEA AND DETAILS**
What two kinds of surroundings did australopithecines live in?

⚡ **FAST FACT**

Scientists often name their paleontological discoveries, or finds of prehistoric life. Donald Johanson (right) named "Lucy" (far right) after the title of a song.

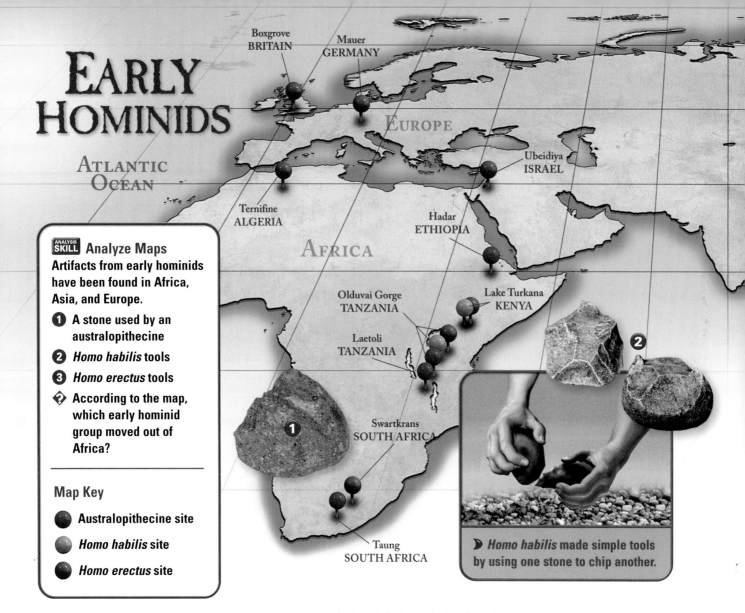

EARLY HOMINIDS

Boxgrove
BRITAIN

Mauer
GERMANY

EUROPE

ATLANTIC
OCEAN

Ubeidiya
ISRAEL

Ternifine
ALGERIA

Hadar
ETHIOPIA

AFRICA

Olduvai Gorge
TANZANIA

Lake Turkana
KENYA

Laetoli
TANZANIA

Swartkrans
SOUTH AFRICA

Taung
SOUTH AFRICA

ANALYSIS SKILL Analyze Maps

Artifacts from early hominids have been found in Africa, Asia, and Europe.

1 A stone used by an australopithecine

2 *Homo habilis* tools

3 *Homo erectus* tools

◆ According to the map, which early hominid group moved out of Africa?

Map Key

● Australopithecine site

● *Homo habilis* site

● *Homo erectus* site

▶ *Homo habilis* made simple tools by using one stone to chip another.

The Paleolithic Era Begins

By 2.5 million years ago, *Homo habilis* (HOH•moh HAB•uh•luhs) lived in Africa. The Leakey family first discovered bones from this kind of hominid in 1960 in Olduvai Gorge. Soon scientists found more *Homo habilis* bones in other parts of eastern Africa.

Like australopithecines, *Homo habilis* walked upright. However, it had a larger brain in a rounder skull, and its face and jaw were smaller.

Near *Homo habilis* bones, scientists have found simple stone tools, making this hominid the first known toolmaker. In fact, the name *Homo habilis* means "handy person." *Homo habilis* chipped stones to make tools, which they used to chop, scrape, and do other simple tasks.

The appearance of the first chipped stone tools began what is known as the **Paleolithic** (pay•lee•uh•LIH•thik) **era**, or Old Stone Age. This period began about 2.5 million years ago and ended about 10,000 years ago.

Homo habilis lived only in Africa, mainly in grassy areas near water sources and trees. *Homo habilis* ate mostly plants and some meat. Experts believe that *Homo habilis* got meat by hunting or by eating pieces left behind by animals.

ASIA

Zhoukoudian
CHINA

PACIFIC
OCEAN

INDIAN
OCEAN

Trinil
INDONESIA

AUSTRALIA

❸

> *Homo erectus* learned to make fire by striking flint stones together.

About 1.9 million years ago, another kind of hominid appeared in Africa. Today, it is known as *Homo erectus* (HOH•moh ih•REK•tuhs), meaning "upright person." The first discoveries of *Homo erectus* were made near **Lake Turkana**, in Kenya.

Homo erectus was larger and stronger than earlier hominids. It also had shorter arms and longer legs. Its brain was much larger, too. Flexible hands allowed *Homo erectus* to make better tools, including stone hand axes for chopping and for digging up roots to eat. Later, *Homo erectus* made spears from wood for hunting.

Homo erectus is the first-known hominid to master the use of fire. Perhaps earlier hominids used fires caused by lightning or volcanoes. Yet, *Homo erectus* learned to start fires. With fire, *Homo erectus* cooked food, kept away wild animals, and stayed warm in colder places. Archaeologists have found the remains of fires made by *Homo erectus* at several sites. Figuring out the ages of the fires is difficult.

Earlier hominids communicated with hand and arm movements and simple sounds. With a larger brain, *Homo erectus* may have developed some speech. With speech, *Homo erectus* could live and work better and travel farther in groups. Members of these small groups hunted together, shared food, and solved problems.

READING CHECK ☼ **MAIN IDEA AND DETAILS**
In what ways did *Homo erectus* use fire?

Beyond Africa

About 2 million years ago, Earth's climate turned colder and drier. This change transformed Africa's forests into vast grasslands. In search of food and water, *Homo erectus*, as well as wild animals, began to **migrate**, or move from one place to another.

Homo erectus is the first-known hominid to migrate and settle outside Africa. Bones and stone tools of *Homo erectus* have been found in parts of Asia and Europe.

To survive in these new surroundings, *Homo erectus* learned to change its ways of life, just as earlier hominids had done in Africa. *Homo erectus* was better at survival, however, and after many years, it was the only surviving hominid.

READING CHECK ○ **MAIN IDEA AND DETAILS**
What archaeological evidence tells us that *Homo erectus* migrated to Asia and Europe?

▶ A boy explores an archaeological site near Beijing, China, where fossils of *Homo erectus* were found.

20

Summary

Using artifacts and fossils, archaeologists and other scientists can tell us about how early hominids may have lived and what they may have looked like. Beginning with australopithecines, there were several kinds of hominids. *Homo habilis* made the first chipped stone tools. In time, *Homo erectus*, the only surviving hominid, spread from Africa into Asia and Europe.

REVIEW

1. How do people today learn about the distant past?

2. Use the terms **prehistory** and **artifact** to explain the meaning of **archaeology**.

3. What early hominid groups first lived in Africa?

CRITICAL THINKING

4. **ANALYSIS SKILL** How might an archaeological site be found by chance?

5. **ANALYSIS SKILL** How might the uncovering of *Homo habilis* artifacts in Asia change our interpretation of these hominids?

6. **Write a Journal Entry** Imagine you are a member of Johanson's team on the day of Lucy's discovery. Write a journal entry that describes the excitement when Lucy was found.

7. **Focus Skill** **MAIN IDEA AND DETAILS**
On a separate sheet of paper, copy and complete the graphic organizer below.

Main Idea

Details

| developed stone hand ax as a tool | first to master the use of fire | first to migrate out of Africa |

Mary Leakey

*"Whatever finds I have made would have been valueless without the close cooperation and unstinted help of my colleagues . . ."**

Trustworthiness

Respect

Responsibility

Fairness

Caring

Patriotism

In 1959, Mary Leakey made a discovery that changed many scientists' ideas about the ancient past. At Olduvai Gorge in Tanzania, Africa, she discovered the prehistoric hominid *Zinjanthropus boisei*, an australopithecine. The specimen she found became known as Zinj. This early hominid lived about 1.7 million years ago, long before hominids of its kind were thought to exist.

The discovery was especially important for Mary Leakey. Her husband, Louis Leakey, was already a well-known archaeologist. Mary Leakey was an artist who illustrated other scientists' findings. Until this discovery, many people did not consider her to be

▶ **Mary Leakey examines artifacts in a laboratory in the early 1960s.**

a serious scientist, despite her knowledge of archaeology. The discovery helped Mary Leakey earn the respect of those who worked in her field. Through her many accomplishments as a well-known archaeologist, Mary Leakey in turn showed respect to her fellow archaeologists by recognizing their contributions to her work.

*Mary Leakey. *Disclosing the Past: An Autobiography.* Doubleday, 1984.

Why Character Counts

❓ **How did Mary Leakey show respect for her fellow archaeologists?**

Bio Brief

1913 — Born

1948 Mary Leakey discovers *Proconsul africanus*, an early hominid species

1959 Mary Leakey finds the australopithecine Zinj in Olduvai Gorge

1978 Mary Leakey discovers a set of early hominid footprints in Laetoli, Tanzania

1996 — Died

Interactive Multimedia Biographies
Visit **MULTIMEDIA BIOGRAPHIES** at
www.harcourtschool.com/hss

Time

200,000 YEARS AGO	15,000 YEARS AGO

200,000 years ago
Early modern humans appear

50,000 years ago
Early humans improve language

15,000 years ago
Earth begins to warm

WHAT TO KNOW

Why did early humans move from place to place?

✓ Describe how early humans found food and shelter.

✓ Describe how early humans populated major regions of the world.

VOCABULARY

humankind p. 23
technology p. 23
adapt p. 24
environment p. 24
extinct p. 24
hunters and gatherers p. 25
consequence p. 25

PLACES

Africa
Asia
Europe
Australia
North America
South America

MAIN IDEA AND DETAILS

California Standards
HSS 6.1, 6.1.1, 6.1.2, 6.1.3

Early Modern Humans

YOU ARE THERE

"It's time to move on," your father calls into the family brush shelter. You groan. You're not happy to be traveling again because you enjoy this seasonal campsite. After all, your group has found plenty of wild roots and berries to eat. The hunters have been successful, too.

The weather is changing, however, and the animals have moved on. You know that you and your people need to move on also. Still, you don't look forward to the long hike to the next camp.

Then your father tells you that you'll be heading to the forestland along the winding river. Your mouth waters for the taste of the wild berries that grow there.

Humankind Begins

Like earlier hominids, *Homo sapiens*, or early modern humans, probably first lived in **Africa**. Most experts believe that *Homo sapiens* had appeared in tropical Africa by 200,000 years ago, which represents the beginning of **humankind**. *Homo sapiens* and *Homo erectus* probably lived side by side until *Homo erectus* died out.

The physical development of early humans was superior to that of earlier hominids. With fingers and hands like ours, early humans could handle things with more skill. Also, their bigger, rounder skulls held larger brains, giving them greater intelligence. In fact, the name *Homo sapiens* means "wise person."

Using their greater intelligence, early humans advanced the development of tools with new **technology**, or ways to make and do things. They developed more complex tools for specific purposes. They made tools from antler, bone, wood, and stone for cutting and scraping. They also crafted bone needles for sewing animal skins into clothing. Early humans designed weapons such as stone points attached to wood spears as well as spear throwers.

Early humans also used their greater intelligence in other ways. About 50,000 years ago, the development of language began to accelerate, or speed up, which greatly improved communication. Better communication allowed early humans to plan and organize better as well as to more easily share new ideas and new knowledge. Early humans went on to create jewelry, cave paintings, and sculptures and to form religious beliefs. They began to change their lives in ways never before possible or imagined.

READING CHECK **MAIN IDEA AND DETAILS**
How was the physical development of early humans superior to that of earlier hominids?

CITIZENSHIP

Democratic Values

Working for the common good is an important responsibility of United States citizens today.

Most experts believe that early humans worked together for the common good of their group. The members of a group worked together to set up camp, where they rested and cooked their meals. Families helped each other build shelters. They made tents from the bones and skins of animals. Early humans used campfires and weapons to help protect and defend their groups from wild animals.

Early humans used their intelligence to find better ways to survive. They made advances in building shelters, toolmaking, and communication.

Adapting to the Environment

Imagine a land without apartments, houses, stores, or even streets. Can you picture wild animals roaming through woods and storms or floods hitting without warning? What if you had to find all your own food? Such a land would be like the land in which early humans had to survive.

Like earlier hominids, early humans survived by living in groups. Each group was made up of related family members, with a total of about 30 people. Grandparents, parents, aunts, uncles, and children lived and worked together. These groups of humans found new ways to **adapt** to, or change to fit, the surroundings. By learning to adapt, they had a better chance of survival.

Groups of early humans lived in a wide variety of shelters. Some used caves and rock ledges. Others built temporary shelters out of resources available in their local **environments**, or surroundings. They used dried mud, tree branches, or whatever resources they could find.

For food, the women gathered wild grasses, nuts, and seeds. They also dug up plant roots and picked fruit from bushes and trees. They took these foods back to their group's site to share with and feed all members.

The men hunted wild animals, including animals that are now **extinct**, or no longer found on Earth. Giant sloths, saber-toothed cats, and elephantlike mammoths and mastodons are animals that once lived but are now extinct.

The men also hunted smaller animals such as deer and bison. They caught turtles, birds, reptiles, and rodents. Like the giant animals, some of these smaller animals provided not only meat for food but also bones for tools and skins for shelters and clothing.

READING CHECK SUMMARIZE

How did early humans adapt to the environment?

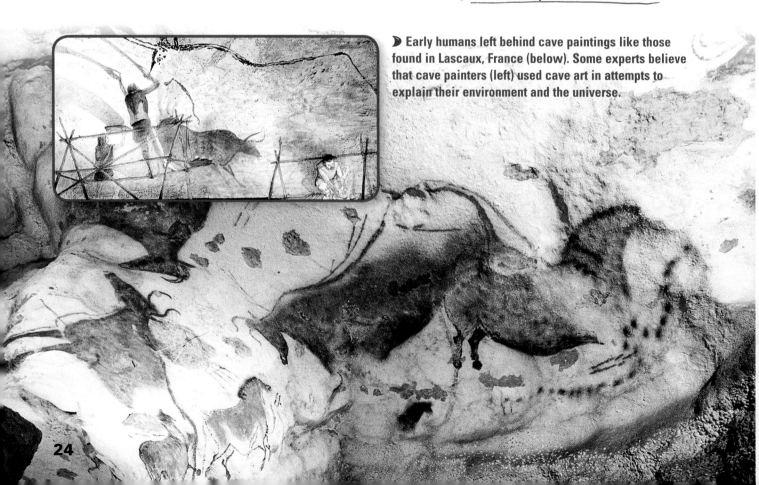

➤ Early humans left behind cave paintings like those found in Lascaux, France (below). Some experts believe that cave painters (left) used cave art in attempts to explain their environment and the universe.

▶ Early humans hunted and gathered food to survive, traveling in a wilderness environment. This painting shows some of the animals that early humans encountered, such as saber-toothed cats, mastodons, and giant sloths. These animals are now extinct.

On the Move

Groups of early humans survived by hunting and gathering. For this reason, they can be called **hunters and gatherers**. They spent many hours each day searching for food, yet hunting and gathering did not take up all their time. These early humans probably spent less time working than most people do today.

Groups of hunters and gatherers were always on the move, which meant they had no permanent home. Instead, they lived in different places in different seasons. As the weather changed and food could no longer be found in one place, they moved on to the next place. Hunters and gatherers followed animal migrations, too.

Early humans gathered plants in an area about as far as they could walk out and back in a day. Once they had gathered and eaten the useful plants in an area, they moved on. Following animal migrations required them to move even more often.

Like earlier hominids, early humans had to learn the **consequence**, or result, of an action. For example, if they learned that eating a certain plant made them sick, they avoided eating that plant. This skill helped them survive. As their populations grew, early humans began to travel into new areas in search of food. They used this skill and others as they spread across the world.

READING CHECK ☼ MAIN IDEA AND DETAILS
Why were hunters and gatherers always on the move?

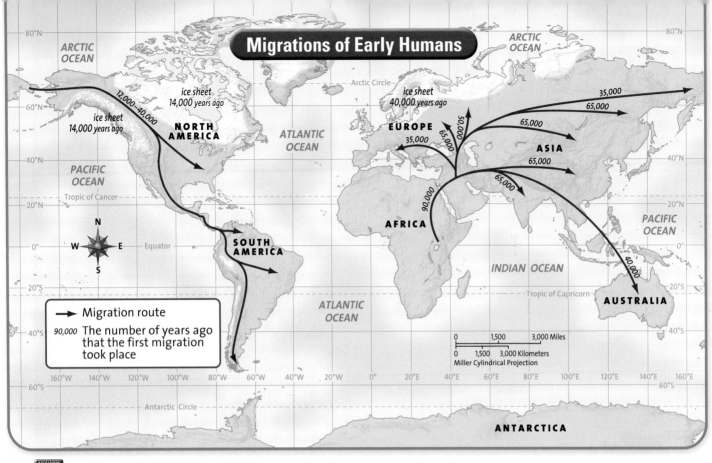

Migrations of Early Humans

ARCTIC OCEAN

ARCTIC OCEAN

Arctic Circle

ice sheet 14,000 years ago

ice sheet 14,000 years ago

ice sheet 40,000 years ago

12,000–40,000

NORTH AMERICA

ATLANTIC OCEAN

PACIFIC OCEAN

Tropic of Cancer

Equator

SOUTH AMERICA

ATLANTIC OCEAN

EUROPE

35,000

50,000

65,000

65,000

35,000

65,000

65,000

ASIA

65,000

AFRICA

90,000

90,000

65,000

INDIAN OCEAN

40,000

PACIFIC OCEAN

Tropic of Capricorn

AUSTRALIA

ANTARCTICA

Antarctic Circle

N
W   E
S

→ Migration route

90,000 The number of years ago that the first migration took place

0   1,500   3,000 Miles
0   1,500   3,000 Kilometers
Miller Cylindrical Projection

ANALYSIS SKILL Analyze Maps

◆ **Regions** Which continent did early humans reach first, Asia or Australia?

Moving Across Continents

Most experts believe that early humans began to migrate out of Africa to other continents in search of food. How they traveled to the different continents is still unknown. According to the most widely accepted theory, a change in climate made this possible.

At different times in the past, Earth has had long periods of freezing cold called Ice Ages. During the last Ice Age, Earth's climate became so cold that glaciers formed. These huge sheets of ice covered large parts of Earth. So much of Earth's water was frozen in glaciers that the level of the oceans dropped by as much as 300 feet. This caused "bridges" of dry land to be uncovered between the different continents.

Early humans arrived in southwestern **Asia** from Africa over a land bridge about 90,000 years ago. By 65,000 years ago, they lived in eastern **Europe** and much of Asia. After crossing land bridges into southeastern Asia, they may have drifted across the ocean to reach **Australia** about 40,000 years ago. Soon after, others were moving into western Europe and northeastern Asia.

As Earth's climate warmed about 15,000 years ago, glaciers that had blocked a land bridge between Asia and **North America** began to melt. This may have allowed early humans to settle North and **South America**.

As these humans migrated, they saw other prehistoric peoples. Neanderthals (nee•AN•der•tawlz) and Cro-Magnons (kroh•MAG•nuhnz) lived in Europe and Asia during part of the time when others were migrating there. Neanderthals and Cro-Magnons—both skilled toolmakers— developed highly advanced ways of life.

Neanderthals may have been the first to bury their dead. By 30,000 years ago, Cro-Magnons in Europe had created the first known art. They left behind rock and bone carvings and cave paintings. Most experts believe that Neanderthals lived until about 35,000 years ago. They do not know exactly how Cro-Magnons are related to people living today.

READING CHECK SUMMARIZE
What was the last Ice Age like?

▶ Many early humans had to follow their food supply, often facing harsh climates and difficult landscapes.

Summary

Using their intelligence, early humans were able to use a wide range of resources from the environment. They were almost constantly on the move, gathering food plants and hunting wild animals. Over time, early humans migrated to almost every continent of the world.

REVIEW

1. Why did early humans move from place to place?

2. Write a synonym and an antonym for the term **extinct**.

3. Which prehistoric people developed some of the earliest known art?

CRITICAL THINKING

4. **Make It Relevant** What are three reasons that a person of today might move?

5. **ANALYSIS SKILL** How might events have differed if land bridges between continents had not formed?

6. **Make a Time Line** Using the map titled "Migrations of Early Humans," make a time line that shows when early humans first arrived on the different continents. Be sure to label your time line.

7. **Focus Skill** **MAIN IDEA AND DETAILS** On a separate sheet of paper, copy and complete the graphic organizer below.

Main Idea

By about 65,000 years ago, early humans lived on several different continents.

Details

Use Latitude and Longitude

▶ WHY IT MATTERS

When you are studying geography, it is useful to know exactly where places in the world are located. Mapmakers have to show absolute, or exact, locations. They draw lines, forming grids, on maps and globes. These lines make it possible for people to describe exact locations, such as the places where early humans lived.

▶ WHAT YOU NEED TO KNOW

Lines that run east and west on a map or globe are called lines of latitude. **Latitude** is the distance north or south of the equator. Lines of latitude are also called parallels, because they are parallel to each other. That means that they are always the same distance apart and that they never meet. Latitude is measured in degrees.

The equator is the line on the globe that circles halfway between the North and South Poles. The equator divides Earth into the Northern and Southern Hemispheres and is marked 0°.

The lines of latitude, other than the equator, are marked with an *N* or *S*, which shows whether they are north or south of the equator. For example, 60°S refers to the line of latitude that is 60 degrees south of the equator, in the Southern Hemisphere.

Lines that run north and south are called lines of longitude. **Longitude** is the distance east or west of the prime meridian, which is 0°. The **prime meridian** is the line that runs north and south through Greenwich, England, near the city of London. Lines of longitude are also called meridians. Longitude is also measured in degrees.

Each meridian runs from the North Pole to the South Pole. The meridians meet at Earth's poles, and they are farthest apart from each other at the equator. They are marked *E* or *W* to show whether they are east or west of the prime meridian. East and west longitude meet at the 180° meridian, which runs exactly opposite to the prime meridian.

You can use latitude and longitude to describe the exact location of any place on Earth. First, pick a place on a map or globe. Next, find the parallel closest to that place. Then, find the meridian closest to the same place. Describe the place as being at that latitude (north or south) and that longitude (east or west).

Prime Meridian

Equator

▶ This image of Earth shows the locations of the equator and the prime meridian.

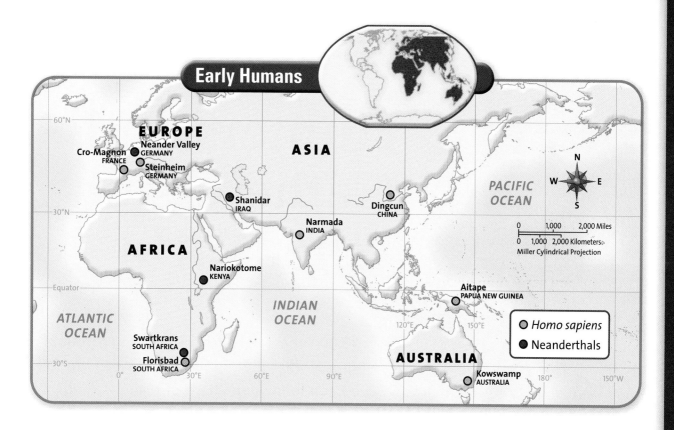

Early Humans

EUROPE
Cro-Magnon FRANCE
Neander Valley GERMANY
Steinheim GERMANY
Shanidar IRAQ
ASIA
Dingcun CHINA
Narmada INDIA
PACIFIC OCEAN
AFRICA
Nariokotome KENYA
INDIAN OCEAN
Aitape PAPUA NEW GUINEA
ATLANTIC OCEAN
Swartkrans SOUTH AFRICA
Florisbad SOUTH AFRICA
AUSTRALIA
Kowswamp AUSTRALIA

0   1,000   2,000 Miles
0   1,000   2,000 Kilometers
Miller Cylindrical Projection

○ Homo sapiens
● Neanderthals

Most maps and globes do not show every parallel and meridian. Sometimes you must estimate the number of degrees. Base your estimate on how close a place is to the lines that are labeled.

▶ PRACTICE THE SKILL

This map shows where early humans lived. Study the map, and answer the following questions based on what you have just learned about longitude and latitude.

1 On which continent does the equator cross 30°E?

2 Which line of longitude is closest to Dingcun?

3 What place is located near 30°S, 150°E?

4 Between which two lines of latitude shown on the map is Nariokotome located?

▶ APPLY WHAT YOU LEARNED

Using the map, make up five more questions about latitude and longitude. Write them on a sheet of paper. Then exchange papers with a classmate, and answer each other's questions.

 Practice your map and globe skills with the **GeoSkills CD-ROM**.

Map and Globe Skills

Time

15,000 YEARS AGO

10,000 YEARS AGO

12,000 years ago
Humans adapt to most
parts of Earth

11,000 years ago
Large Ice Age animals
begin to decrease

Hunters and Gatherers of the World

WHAT TO KNOW
Why did humans around
the world develop different
ways of life?

✓ Identify the locations
where early people were
living during the later
years of the last Ice Age.

✓ Describe the ways in
which these people
adapted to a variety of
environments.

VOCABULARY
nomad p. 31
society p. 31
role p. 31
culture p. 31

PLACES
Sahara
Nelson's Bay Cave
Abu Hureyra
Japan
China
Australia
Mexico
Monte Verde
Chile
Peru
Brazil

**MAIN IDEA
AND DETAILS**

**California
Standards**
HSS 6.1, 6.1.1, 6.1.2, 6.1.3

YOU ARE THERE

It's 12,000 years ago. You're crawling through tall grass with other hunters. Since early morning, you have been following a herd of bison. Taking care not to be seen or heard, you move closer.

Suddenly, one of the hunters shouts a signal, and everyone chases the bison. You help drive the animals toward a swamp, where the land slows down the herd.

You and your people have great respect for the bison. Your group's survival depends on their meat for food, hides for clothing and shelter, and bones for tools.

Around the World

As the Ice Age ended about 12,000 years ago, climatic changes altered environments around the world. Temperatures began to rise and glaciers melted. Oceans rose and covered the old coastlines as well as land bridges. Grasslands grew in some places, and forests rose up in others. Large Ice Age animals gradually disappeared, while smaller animals flourished.

By this time, human communities had populated the major regions of the world. Most people had no settled home. These **nomads** followed the migrations of animals and the seasons of plants. Some set up camps, returning to the same places every year. Others began to live in more permanent camps in places where food was available through most of the year.

As different groups of humans adapted to a variety of environments, each group developed a different society. A **society** is a group of people living and working under a set of rules and traditions. Each person in a society has a **role**, or responsibility.

❱ Stone carving of a bison, found in France

To express how much environments have affected humans and their societies, scientist Jared Diamond wrote,

> ❝History followed different courses for different peoples because of differences among peoples' environments . . .❞*

As humans around the world interacted, or had contact, with their local environments, they developed more complex **cultures**, or ways of life shared by members of a group.

READING CHECK ⟳ **MAIN IDEA AND DETAILS**
What changes occurred in Earth's environments about 12,000 years ago?

*Jared Diamond, *Guns, Germs, and Steel*. W. W. Norton & Company, 1999.

❱ All around the world, different groups of humans adapted to their local environment to survive. Over time, each group began to develop its own way of life.

Africa

As Earth's climate changed, deserts in northern Africa became more livable. The **Sahara**, today a huge desert, received enough rain for grasses and other plants to grow. Early Africans began to migrate across these regions. Some stayed and adapted to life there, learning ways to find water, food, and shelter.

Others roamed the African savannas in search of food. These grassy plains were rich in wild game, while nearby woodlands provided seasonal plants.

Still others moved toward the rivers, lakes, and coasts, where fishing became important. These people set up permanent camps along the Nile River in northern Africa, where they found plenty of water, wild plants, and game. Using twine nets and bone hooks, fishers caught an abundance of fish from the Nile River.

By 15,000 years ago, people had set up a camp at **Nelson's Bay Cave**, on the coast of southern Africa. Hunters there killed antelope, wild pigs, and seabirds. Fishers used nets and hooks to catch fish.

At about the same time, a new weapon improved the skills of hunters in Africa— the bow and arrow. Archaeologists have found many artifacts of stone arrow points in different parts of the continent.

The development of the bow and arrow was important. It allowed people to hunt with more accuracy. It also let them kill prey from a distance, providing greater safety for the hunter.

READING CHECK **MAIN IDEA AND DETAILS**
What details support the idea that the Nile River area was a good place to live?

Cultural Heritage

The San Culture

Some early cultures have survived to the present day. One such group is the San, of the Kalahari Desert, in southern Africa. Many members of the San culture have kept a traditional way of life that dates back to prehistoric times. Others have chosen to live a more modern way of life.

Many of the San are hunters and gatherers. The women and children gather nuts and plants. The men use bows and arrows to hunt antelope and other game. They also trap small animals, using thin rope.

We may never know exactly how early people lived. However, understanding people such as the San can help us get a better idea of life in the prehistoric past.

Toolmaking in Europe

ANALYSIS SKILL **Analyze Drawings**

The males of hunter-gatherer societies made tools and weapons.

❶ Flint is chipped into pieces.

❷ A piece of flint is shaped.

❸ The shaped flint is attached to a wooden shaft or antler.

◆ What weapons or tools might the hunters and gatherers have made?

Europe

Europe's landscape changed dramatically from plains to forests. In the past, early Europeans had hunted on wide, open plains. Now they hunted for game in thick forests and fished on shorelines. As part of adapting to this environment, they learned to make tools that could do special jobs.

People living along the Baltic Sea came up with tools for catching fish. They used fishing spears, harpoons, nets, and traps and made their spear tips from stone, bone, or antlers.

People living near forests developed tools for making things out of wood. Along waterways, they used these tools for making canoes. By 12,000 years ago, people were crossing the open waters of the Mediterranean Sea.

Early Europeans improved their skills at hunting and gathering. Like other early people, they began to use bows and arrows for hunting. They found new kinds of plants to eat and better ways to gather and store these plants. Food became so plentiful that populations increased.

As populations grew, early Europeans began to move less often. Some made camps along rivers, lakes, and seacoasts where sea life could be found. Others built shelters of wood and animal skins. Archaeologists have found the remains of simple huts with fireplaces in what is now France. The end of the last Ice Age not only changed Europe's climate, but it also allowed people to develop new cultures.

READING CHECK **⚙MAIN IDEA AND DETAILS**
What fishing tools did people living along the Baltic Sea develop?

Asia and the Pacific

By 14,000 years ago, people lived along the eastern coast of the Mediterranean Sea. In this part of southwestern Asia, they spent their summers in the hills, where it was cooler. In winter, they moved into rock shelters and caves near lakes.

As temperatures warmed, people moved to higher ground where the soil was better for wild plants. With grains and nuts in good supply, they began to stay longer in the same places.

One of the world's first settlements grew along the Euphrates River, in what is now Syria. **Abu Hureyra** (AH•boo hoo•RAY•ruh) was located where wild plants and animals were plentiful. Each year, hunters killed migrating gazelles and stored the meat. With reliable food supplies, Abu Hureyra supported more than 300 people. They lived in shelters with reed roofs built partly underground.

In eastern Asia, populations of people grew in what are now **Japan** and **China**. People living in heavily forested areas used bamboo and wood to make tools. About 12,000 years ago, people made the first known clay pots in what is now Japan. They used these containers for carrying water and storing food.

People also lived in the thick forests of southeastern Asia. They used bamboo and stone to make tools. Sharpened bamboo proved to be a good tool and weapon.

Early Asians of southeastern Asia likely settled the southwestern Pacific islands. They may have done this when ocean levels were low during the last Ice Age. When the oceans rose again, the southwestern Pacific, including what is now **Australia**, was cut off from the rest of the world. The early Pacific islanders settled mainly on the ocean coasts or near rivers and lakes.

READING CHECK Ⓞ**MAIN IDEA AND DETAILS**
What were the first clay pots used for?

❯ Where there was a steady food supply, early people in what is now Japan built settlements. Some early Japanese settlers built villages near the sea, where they could catch fish easily.

FAST FACT

Clovis points were carved so that they detached from a spear once they struck an animal. That way, the spears could be reused.

▶ As the large Ice Age animals gradually died out, the Clovis people of North America began hunting smaller game.

North America

As different groups of early people spread throughout North America, they found a variety of environments. They learned to adapt to environments that ranged from deserts to rain forests.

The Clovis people were one of the first early cultures in North America. They skillfully made spear points called Clovis points, which they mounted on wooden shafts. The name *Clovis* comes from the town of Clovis, New Mexico, where the points were first found. Archaeologists have found Clovis points all over North America and in South America.

When they could, Clovis hunters used their spears to kill large Ice Age animals. These animals, such as mammoths and large bison, would provide meat for weeks as well as materials for tools, clothing, and tents. Smaller game and wild plants were also part of their diet.

About 11,000 years ago, the number of large Ice Age animals began to decrease. As people adapted to this change, the Clovis culture began to die out. People turned to hunting smaller animals, such as deer and small bison, using smaller spear points and tools.

People in the desertlike areas of North America camped in rock shelters and caves. They hunted desert animals, such as rabbits, and gathered wild plants.

In the forests of eastern North America, people learned to make use of their land's resources. From trees, they got nuts and sap for food, branches for clubs and wooden spears, and bark for shelters.

In what is now **Mexico**, some people lived in large camps when food was plentiful. To survive, they learned to divide into smaller groups when food was scarce.

READING CHECK ⚪ **MAIN IDEA AND DETAILS**
What are some ways in which people living in eastern North America used trees?

South America

In time, people migrated from North America to South America. Some migrated to the cold ocean coasts at the southern tip of South America. Others adapted to life high up in the Andes Mountains. Still others moved into the dense rain forests surrounding the Amazon River.

One important archaeological site in South America is **Monte Verde**. It lies in a small river valley in what is now southern **Chile**. The early people there lived in wood-frame houses covered with animal skins. Each house had a fireplace for cooking. The people ate many different kinds of plants, including wild potatoes. They also hunted small animals as well as camel species and mastodons that are now extinct.

Archaeological dating for Monte Verde shows that people lived there about 12,500 years ago. This date suggests that the Americas may have been settled earlier than 12,000 years ago.

Along the coastal waters of what is now **Peru**, early people caught seafood year-round. Using baskets, people could catch thousands of anchovies. They also relied on plant foods, which grew well in the moisture provided by coastal fogs.

In time, fishing settlements began to grow at the mouths of the coastal rivers near the Pacific Ocean. Farther inland, people were living in the highlands of the Andes.

In what is today **Brazil**, archaeologists found evidence of an early settlement

GEOGRAPHY

Andes Mountains

The Andes mountain range stretches more than 4,500 miles. It is one of the largest and highest ranges in the world. The mountain region has different environments, such as rain forests, deserts, and fertile plains. The early people who came to the Andes region found a variety of plants and animals. Later, they discovered that crops grew well there. These people became successful at growing corn, beans, and squash. Today, the ruins of these early cultures are still being discovered in the Andes.

ANDES MOUNTAINS

SOUTH AMERICA

ATLANTIC OCEAN

PACIFIC OCEAN

N W E S

0   500   1,000 Miles
0   500   1,000 Kilometers

inside a cave. Located in the rain forest, the cave provided shelter for early people who depended mostly on plants for food for their survival. These early people found Brazil nuts and palm seeds in the hot, humid rain forest environment.

READING CHECK ○ **MAIN IDEA AND DETAILS**
What kinds of environments did early people adapt to in South America?

Summary

Groups of hunters and gatherers around the world found ways to survive in a wide range of environments. Among these environments were deserts, grasslands, forests, coastlines, and rain forests. As early people learned to adapt to their local environments, they developed ways of life that were different from one another. Even by 10,000 years ago, unique cultures existed around the world.

REVIEW

1. Why did humans around the world develop different ways of life?

2. Use the term **culture** to describe how early people adapted to different environments.

3. What advantages did the bow and arrow give to hunters?

CRITICAL THINKING

4. **ANALYSIS SKILL** Why do you think early people did not migrate to Antarctica?

5. **ANALYSIS SKILL** What individual parts would a hunter need to make a bow and arrow?

6. **Write Questions** Write three questions about early humans. The questions should ask for information about how they adapted to their environments. Questions might focus on food, tools, clothing, or shelter.

7. **Focus Skill** **MAIN IDEA AND DETAILS**
On a separate sheet of paper, copy and complete the graphic organizer below.

Main Idea

One of the world's first settlements developed at Abu Hureyra in southwestern Asia.

Details

Studying Early People

Imagine digging through layers of rocks and sand to find out about people and places of the past. That is what archaeologists do to help us learn about what happened before the invention of writing. To find out about this "prehistory," as it is called, archaeologists must look for evidence, or proof, other than written words. They must search for clues to piece together the puzzle of life in the distant past.

Archaeologists study artifacts to gather evidence. For example, they can find out how old the artifacts are. This helps them identify the early people who made the objects. With that information, they can also figure out what the objects were used for.

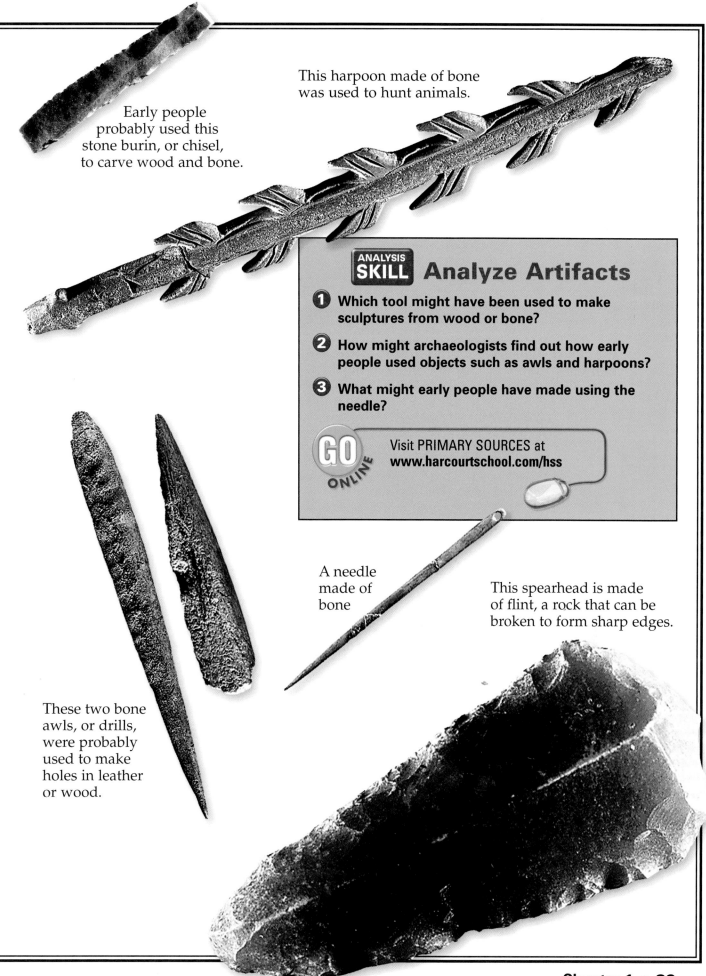

Early people probably used this stone burin, or chisel, to carve wood and bone.

This harpoon made of bone was used to hunt animals.

ANALYSIS SKILL Analyze Artifacts

1. Which tool might have been used to make sculptures from wood or bone?

2. How might archaeologists find out how early people used objects such as awls and harpoons?

3. What might early people have made using the needle?

GO ONLINE Visit PRIMARY SOURCES at www.harcourtschool.com/hss

A needle made of bone

This spearhead is made of flint, a rock that can be broken to form sharp edges.

These two bone awls, or drills, were probably used to make holes in leather or wood.

200,000 years ago
Early modern humans first appear in tropical Africa

Reading Social Studies

The **main idea** is the most important idea in a passage.
Details give information that supports the main idea.

Focus Skill

Main Idea and Details

Complete this graphic organizer to show that you can identify the main idea and supporting details of how early people adapted to their environments. A copy of this graphic organizer appears on page 10 of the Homework and Practice Book.

The World's Early People

Main Idea

Early humans adapted to a variety of environments.

Details

Early humans built temporary shelters out of dried mud and tree branches.		

California Writing Prompts

Write a Persuasive Speech Imagine that you are the leader of a group of hunters and gatherers living in Siberia. You want to migrate across a land bridge to find a new home. Write a speech that you will give to persuade the rest of your group that this is a good idea.

Write a Research Report Write a research report about how early humans adapted to their environments. Before you begin, list five questions that you want your report to answer and three sources that you will use in your research.

50,000 years ago
Early humans improve language

12,000 years ago
Last Ice Age ends
People live on most parts of Earth

11,000 years ago
Large Ice Age animals begin to die out

Use Vocabulary

Identify the term that correctly matches each definition.

	prehistory, p. 15
	archaeology, p. 15
	technology, p. 23
	adapt, p. 24
	nomad, p. 31

1. change to fit new surroundings
2. ways to make and do things
3. a person who has no settled home
4. the period before people began to write
5. the study of things that earlier people left behind

Use the Time Line

 Use the summary time line above to answer these questions.

6. When did early humans improve language?
7. What happened 12,000 years ago?

Apply Skills

Use Latitude and Longitude

 Examine the map on page 29 and answer these questions.

8. Near which two lines of latitude did early humans live in Africa?
9. Near which line of longitude is the Cro-Magnon, France, site located?

Recall Facts

Answer these questions.

10. Which early hominid was first to develop stone tools?
11. What is the Paleolithic era?
12. How did early hunters and gatherers adapt to the environment of the desert-like areas in North America?

Write the letter of the best choice.

13. Which early hominids first mastered the use of fire?
    A australopithecines
    B *Homo erectus*
    C *Homo habilis*
    D *Homo sapiens*

14. Which of the following happened after the last Ice Age ended?
    A Small animals died out.
    B Ocean levels dropped.
    C New forests appeared.
    D The climate grew colder.

Think Critically

15. **ANALYSIS SKILL** What conclusions can you draw about early hominids from the artifacts shown in this chapter?
16. **ANALYSIS SKILL** How do you think the use of fire affected early humans' ability to migrate and adapt to different environments?

Study Skills

USE A WORD WEB TO LEARN VOCABULARY

Using a word web can help you learn new words and see how they are related.

➤ A word web is a way of taking notes about words and their meanings.

➤ The word at the center of a web relates to all the words around it.

➤ Words connected to each other are closely related.

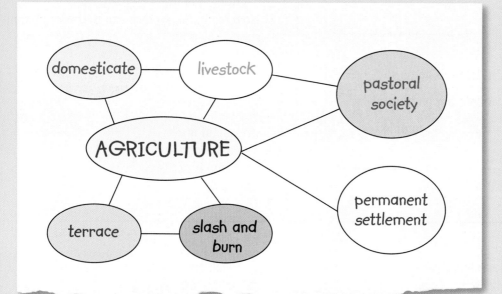

Apply As You Read

As you read each lesson in this chapter, notice how vocabulary words and other terms are used to explain main ideas. For each lesson, make a word web that shows how the terms are related.

California History-Social Science Standards, Grade 6

6.1 Students describe what is known through archaeological studies of the early physical and cultural development of humankind from the Paleolithic era to the agricultural revolution.

Early Farmers and City Dwellers

A present-day woman in Peru carries her harvest much like her ancestors once did.

THE STONE AGE NEWS

by Fiona Macdonald

Early people found that they could not always depend on hunting and gathering for food. For a steady supply of food, some people began to produce their own food by growing crops and raising animals. Farming settlements started to develop in what is often called the Middle East—the regions of southwestern Asia and northeastern Africa. Find out more about early farmers by reading this fictional newspaper about life in ancient times.

NEW-FANGLED FARMING

illustrated by Sharif Tarabay

THIS SPECIAL REPORT, first printed in 8400 B.C., broke the hottest news story of recent times. In it, our Middle East reporter describes a new way of gathering food that was developed there—called farming.

I'D HEARD a rumor that some people in Syria were experimenting with a new way of producing food, and that instead of following the herds like the rest of us, they were living in one place; I just had to go and investigate this strange behavior.

When I arrived, one of the women offered to show me around. She took me to an area where hundreds of tall plants were growing in clusters. I recognized them as wheat, rye, and barley, but I'd never seen so many growing this close together before. Usually, you find just one or two small clumps at a time. I asked my guide to tell me how these big clusters of plants had come about.

Apparently, some years ago, the climate in this region became extremely dry. Reliable sources of water were harder and harder to find, so people couldn't roam as widely as they once had. Instead, they were forced to remain close to rivers.

Because they could no longer go far in search of food, they started to build up a store of grains and nuts to last them through the winter months. Then one spring, they noticed how grains that had been dropped on the ground had sprouted.

As an experiment, they tried spilling more seeds, this time on land they had cleared by gathering wild grain the previous year. It took several attempts, but at last they managed to grow their own plants. Now they scatter grain each spring.

When the seed heads become ripe, they are cut off using curved flint-bladed knives. The grain is then separated from the husks and spread out to dry in the sun, before being stored in baskets.

I was astounded by all that I had seen. The more I thought about it, the more this "farming" idea made sense. It could change everything—just

REAPING THE BENEFITS: Harvesting a field of grain is hard but rewarding work.

think, we could settle in one place and grow our own food plants, as the people here do. Then we wouldn't have to spend all those long fall days scouring the land for enough wild food to last through the winter. And whenever animals are scarce and the hunting is poor, there will still be a supply of food at home.

Stone Age people can be set in their ways, but you have to move with the times. And I, for one, hope that this newfangled farming catches on!

GRANNY'S KITCHEN

illustrated by
Emily Hare and Mike White

THEY SAY THAT experience is the best teacher! So why not learn some handy hints from Granny, our food expert, who has been feeding a hungry family for many a year.

IT'S THE SAME every fall—piles of food all ripening at once and not enough time to eat them. But there are ways to make food last longer. Try some of these:

• Drying is a good way to make sure you have a stock of fruits and vegetables for the winter.

Cut them into small pieces and put them on flat stones or wooden platters in a clean, airy place. Make sure the pieces don't touch one another—they dry much more quickly if the air can flow all around them. If the weather's bad, leave them to dry near a fire.

• You can dry fish and meat, too. Cut the flesh into thin strips. Most people leave them to dry outside, but I prefer to hang them over a fire, since the strips dry more quickly and the smoke seems to give them a pleasant taste, too.

• When all your food has dried, store it on some grass mats or in baskets raised above the ground. Try to keep everything very dry.

• And do remember to put aside some grains, such as wheat, barley, and maize, to see you through the winter. It's so important to have a properly balanced diet. Store them in baskets beside your stock of dried foods. Eat well this winter!

THE FINISHING TOUCHES

illustrated by Sue Shields

EVERYONE CAN GET fed up with wearing old clothes. If you're in one of those moods, here's how to jazz up your image without sewing a thing.

• Jewelry, colorful face paint, and a really good hairstyle will make all the difference in your appearance. If you want a change, wear bright bead necklaces to liven up your clothing. And if your tunic's gotten baggy, try using an old belt that's been newly decorated with shells.

• Plant seeds, animal teeth, various seashells, and even fish scales can make interesting necklaces. Drill a hole in each of the pieces and then thread them onto strings. The strings must be strong, so use either twisted plant fibers or strips of tough hide.

• Most men are happy to let their hair and beards grow as nature intended, but women prefer to create new styles. Nowadays, the fashion is for shoulder-length hair with bangs. Many women with this style braid their hair to keep it off their face when they're working and cooking.

Response Corner

1. How did farming change the lives of the people of the Stone Age?

2. Compare and contrast the preparation of food in ancient times and today.

10,000 years ago
People adapt plants and animals for their use

8,000 years ago
Farming develops in many places around the world

Producing Food

WHAT TO KNOW
How did changes in the world's climate at the end of the last Ice Age affect the way people got their food?

✔ Describe the first crops people grew and the first animals they kept.

✔ Describe how farming and keeping animals changed the way people lived.

✔ Identify ways that people changed the environment.

VOCABULARY
drought p. 49
domesticate p. 50
livestock p. 51
agriculture p. 51
slash-and-burn farming p. 52
surplus p. 52

PLACES
Abu Hureyra
Jericho

MAIN IDEA AND DETAILS

California Standards
HSS 6.1, 6.1.3

YOU ARE THERE It is 9,500 years ago. Your herd of goats has wandered about and fed on grass all day. Now the animals are huddled together, ready to settle down for the night. You'll rest, too, but you'll remain watchful. There is always the chance that a goat might stray from the herd or a predator might try to attack the herd.

The night is peaceful, but you know that you can never let down your guard. Your village of **Abu Hureyra** needs goats for meat and milk and for skins to make clothing. It pleases you to know that even though you're still young, you have an important job to do.

Adapting to Change

Before 10,000 years ago, all humans were hunters and gatherers. Then, the end of the last Ice Age brought about climate changes that affected environments around the world. To survive, some people learned to adapt, or modify, their physical environment.

In many places, warmer temperatures allowed people, animals, and plants to spread farther north and south from the equator. People began to see animals and plants they had never seen before. This meant additional food sources, and where food was plentiful, populations grew.

While some animals flourished, others did not. It is still a mystery why many large Ice Age animals became extinct. Perhaps warmer temperatures, loss of habitat, or overhunting killed off the huge mammals. Whatever the reason, their disappearance meant the loss of an important source of meat for some people.

For a time, the climate of southwestern Asia and other places grew drier, causing long periods with little or no rain. These **droughts** caused food shortages in those areas.

Different groups of people around the world faced challenges in feeding themselves. With growing populations, animal extinctions, or droughts, people found a variety of new ways to survive. Some people became better at storing food, and others developed new weapons for hunting smaller prey.

In southwestern Asia, gatherers, who were usually women, tried planting the seeds of wild grasses. Already familiar with the life cycles of plants, they successfully planted and grew rye, barley, and a wheat called einkorn (YN•kawrn). They became the world's first farmers.

READING CHECK Ⓞ**MAIN IDEA AND DETAILS**
What challenges did people face as Earth's climate changed after the last Ice Age?

The Animals that helped people in the Ice age became extinct. The people needed water, food, clothes,8 shelter.

FAST FACT

Herds drink from the Euphrates River near Abu Hureyra (below), where people first learned to grow crops such as einkorn (above). The actual site of Abu Hureyra has been under water in Lake Assad since the Tabqa Dam was put into operation in 1973. To learn about Abu Hureyra, archaeologists had to collect materials quickly from the site before it was flooded.

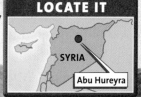

LOCATE IT

SYRIA

Abu Hureyra

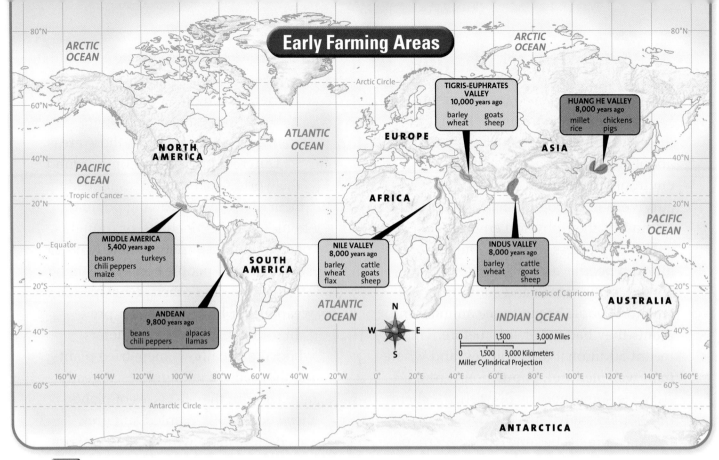

Early Farming Areas

TIGRIS-EUPHRATES VALLEY
10,000 years ago
barley   goats
wheat   sheep

HUANG HE VALLEY
8,000 years ago
millet   chickens
rice   pigs

MIDDLE AMERICA
5,400 years ago
beans   turkeys
chili peppers
maize

NILE VALLEY
8,000 years ago
barley   cattle
wheat   goats
flax   sheep

INDUS VALLEY
8,000 years ago
barley   cattle
wheat   goats
sheep

ANDEAN
9,800 years ago
beans   alpacas
chili peppers   llamas

0   1,500   3,000 Miles
0   1,500   3,000 Kilometers
Miller Cylindrical Projection

ANALYSIS SKILL Analyze Maps

◈ **Regions** Which early farming areas developed at the same time?

◈ **Regions** Which early farming areas had similar plants and animals?

Agricultural Revolution

About 10,000 years ago, some people in southwestern Asia became the first to **domesticate** plants and animals. Facing food shortages, they learned to adapt plants and to tame animals for their own uses. People at Abu Hureyra and **Jericho** were among the first to practice the domestication of wild plants and animals.

These early people in southwestern Asia learned to plant seeds from wild plants so that new plants would grow. They carefully chose the seeds to plant, which made it possible for them to grow better and better crops each season.

Before this time, people had tamed wild dogs to help them in hunting. Now, the people of southwestern Asia began to capture wild sheep and goats and keep them in pens. By doing this, they could be sure of their meat supplies during droughts. Over time, these penned animals became tame, and people could herd them in pastures. Soon, **livestock**, or domesticated animals that provide resources, became the main source of meat for many people.

By 8,000 years ago, people in northern Africa, southern Asia, eastern Asia, and the Andes region of South America had changed from hunters and gatherers to food producers without having learned about farming from others. From these regions, the knowledge of farming and herding spread around the world.

Before **agriculture**, or the knowledge of raising plants and animals, most people lived their lives as nomads. Some people settled where water, wild plants, and wild animals were plentiful. However, those who learned about agriculture and began to farm built longer-lasting shelters in permanent settlements.

Along the Euphrates River, Abu Hureyra began in this way. Hunters and gatherers found wild grasses and herds of migrating gazelles in the area, so they returned to the area each year for these food supplies. In time, they built a permanent settlement and began farming.

At first, the people of Abu Hureyra lived in pits dug into the ground and covered with reeds. Later, they built houses of mud bricks. Each house had several rooms and provided living space for an entire family. Narrow pathways separated the houses and offered routes to nearby farm fields.

Because agriculture completely changed most people's lives, its beginnings are often referred to as the agricultural revolution. Agriculture allowed people to produce larger food supplies in one place, so more and more people began to live together in permanent settlements. Soon people in permanent settlements began to work together, to organize, and to develop rules for their community.

READING CHECK ⚲**MAIN IDEA AND DETAILS**
In which regions around the world did farming develop independently? *The regions are abu hureyra, and other settlements across the world.*

▶ **By adapting the physical environment to their needs, people were able to domesticate plants and animals and to live in permanent settlements, such as Abu Hureyra.**

▶ Loaded with newly harvested crops, two donkeys are led down a street to a market in what is today Babylon, Iraq. The people of this region have practiced farming for 10,000 years.

Farming as a Way of Life

Agriculture brought a steady source of food, yet it was often more work than hunting and gathering. Land had to be cleared, and seeds had to be planted and cared for. Livestock also needed care.

People developed new roles in early agricultural societies. Men cleared the land, protected crops and herds, and hunted. Women and children planted, cared for, and harvested the crops and prepared and stored food.

Farmers searched for fertile soil in which to plant crops. In southwestern Asia and in other places, they often planted crops in river valleys. Farmers in areas of thick forests used **slash-and-burn farming** to prepare the soil for planting. This farming method required them to clear the trees and brush from the land, burn the trees and mix the ashes with the soil to fertilize it, and plant their crops.

In each farming settlement, a group of related families owned the land, passing on the ownership of the land to the next generation. The people of farming settlements worshipped their ancestors because people believed that the spirits of their dead ancestors guarded the land.

When they could, farmers grew enough crops to give them a **surplus**, or extra supply, of seeds. They could use the surplus to plant during the next season. They could also use surplus grain as food in seasons when plants were not plentiful.

Often, people would lend surplus food to other settlements, sometimes developing friendships among communities. Some people presented surplus food as gifts to their dead ancestors to show respect to them.

In time, people began to exchange their surplus food for goods not found in their local areas. They exchanged surplus food for other foods, home-building materials, clothing, or tools. In this way, surplus food helped people develop trade. Over time, the growth of trade would lead to more advanced societies.

READING CHECK Ŏ **MAIN IDEA AND DETAILS**
In what ways did people use surplus food?

They people Used the surplus as ~~energ~~ as the crop + the next year.

Summary

After the last Ice Age, people developed agriculture. By growing crops and keeping livestock, people created surplus food. With extra food, groups of people could stay in one place and support more people. They could also share food with other groups. They could even trade for goods not found near their settlements. This trade was an important step toward building larger, more advanced societies.

Growth of World Population

YEARS AGO	POPULATION
12,000	👤
10,000	👤
6,000	👤👤👤👤👤👤👤👤👤👤👤👤👤👤👤👤👤

👤 = 5,000,000 People

ANALYSIS SKILL **Analyze Graphs** The population of the world grew dramatically because of the introduction of agriculture. With this growth, containers (below) for storing food and water became more important.
◆ What was the world's population 6,000 years ago?

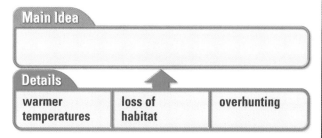

REVIEW

1. 💡 How did changes in the world's climate at the end of the last Ice Age affect the way people got their food?

2. Use the term **slash-and-burn farming** to describe how early farmers in forested areas changed their environment.

3. How did early people domesticate animals?

4. What were some of the first crops that early farmers raised?

CRITICAL THINKING

5. **ANALYSIS SKILL** What might have happened to the discovery of agriculture if the last Ice Age ended 1,000 years later than it did?

6. **Make It Relevant** How is modern farming similar to and different from early farming?

7. 🖌 **Make Sequence Cards** Make a set of sequence cards about how climate change led to early farming. Write a card for each important event. Exchange cards with a classmate, and put each other's cards in the correct order.

8. **Focus Skill** **MAIN IDEA AND DETAILS**
On a separate sheet of paper, copy and complete the graphic organizer below.

Main Idea

Details		
warmer temperatures	loss of habitat	overhunting

Read Parallel Time Lines

▶ WHY IT MATTERS

Just as maps help you understand *where* something happened, time lines help you understand *when* something happened. Time lines show events in the order, or sequence, in which they happened. A **parallel time line** is made up of two or more time lines. Each time line covers the same period of time, but for a different person or place.

▶ WHAT YOU NEED TO KNOW

The development of agriculture was a key event in the history of many early cultures. The parallel time line on the following page helps you compare when different cultures developed agriculture.

Time lines usually show specific dates for events. However, no one knows exactly when some events happened long ago. Therefore, time line dates for prehistoric events are often approximate, or not exact. Approximate dates are often shown after the Latin word *circa* or after its abbreviation, *c.* The word *circa* means "about."

When you look closely at the parallel time line on the following page, you can see that each time line covers the same period of time. Each begins at 8000 B.C.

▶ A farmer in Bolivia harvests barley, a crop that was first grown in southwestern Asia about 10,000 years ago.

and ends at A.D. 2000. Each is divided into periods of 2,000 years.

B.C. stands for "Before Christ." A.D. stands for *anno Domini*, a Latin phrase meaning "in the year of the Lord." The number that follows the abbreviation A.D. tells how many years have passed since the year in which, according to what some people believe, Jesus Christ was born.

In the case of B.C. dates, the bigger the number, the longer ago it was that an event took place. For example, something that happened in 2000 B.C. took place 500 years before something that happened in 1500 B.C. Remember that B.C. always comes after a date and A.D. always comes before a date.

You will find that some time lines are labeled B.C.E. and C.E. instead of B.C. and A.D. The abbreviation B.C.E. stands for "before the Common Era," and C.E. stands for "Common Era." These abbreviations refer to the same years as B.C. and A.D.

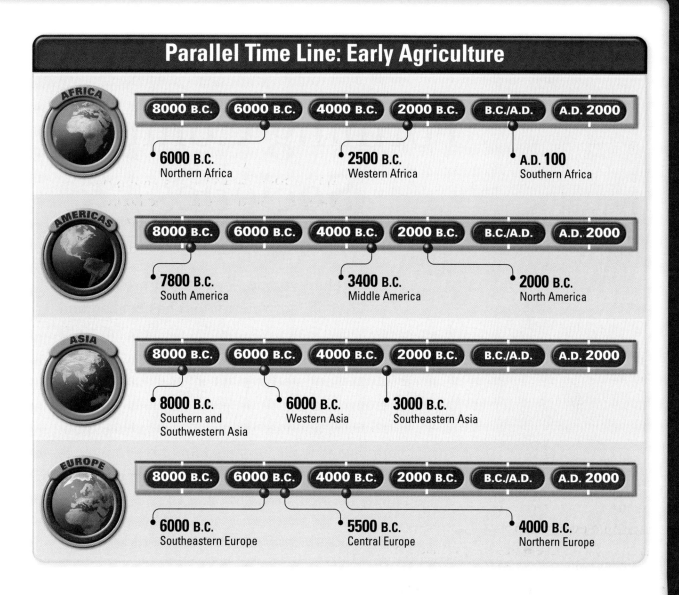

Parallel Time Line: Early Agriculture

AFRICA

8000 B.C. | 6000 B.C. | 4000 B.C. | 2000 B.C. | B.C./A.D. | A.D. 2000

6000 B.C.
Northern Africa

2500 B.C.
Western Africa

A.D. 100
Southern Africa

AMERICAS

8000 B.C. | 6000 B.C. | 4000 B.C. | 2000 B.C. | B.C./A.D. | A.D. 2000

7800 B.C.
South America

3400 B.C.
Middle America

2000 B.C.
North America

ASIA

8000 B.C. | 6000 B.C. | 4000 B.C. | 2000 B.C. | B.C./A.D. | A.D. 2000

8000 B.C.
Southern and
Southwestern Asia

6000 B.C.
Western Asia

3000 B.C.
Southeastern Asia

EUROPE

8000 B.C. | 6000 B.C. | 4000 B.C. | 2000 B.C. | B.C./A.D. | A.D. 2000

6000 B.C.
Southeastern Europe

5500 B.C.
Central Europe

4000 B.C.
Northern Europe

❱ PRACTICE THE SKILL

ANALYSIS SKILL Now use what you have learned about parallel time lines to answer the following questions.

① When did agriculture begin in Africa?

② Which part of Africa developed agriculture first?

③ Where else in the world did agriculture develop at about the same time as in northern Africa?

④ Where did people first develop agriculture?

❱ APPLY WHAT YOU LEARNED

ANALYSIS SKILL Think about other developments of early people, such as new tools for hunting or farming. Use encyclopedias, reliable Internet sources, and information you have read in this chapter to construct a parallel time line of early people's developments. Make a time line for each continent you include on your parallel time line, and make sure that each time line covers the same span of time. Write three questions for a classmate to answer by using your parallel time line.

Chart and Graph Skills

Time

| 7000 B.C. | 5000 B.C. | 3000 B.C. |

6000 B.C.
New ways of farming develop

5000 B.C.
Farmers in southern Asia grow cotton

Forming Complex Societies

WHAT TO KNOW
Why did early people begin to live together in villages?

✔ Explain how living in villages changed the way people related to one another.

✔ Describe inventions that helped people of this time lead better lives.

VOCABULARY
subsist p. 57
terrace p. 58
plow p. 59
irrigation p. 59
barter p. 60
pastoral society p. 61

PLACES
Abu Hureyra
Jericho
Jarmo
Çatal Hüyük
Mehrgarh

MAIN IDEA AND DETAILS

California Standards
HSS 6.1, 6.1.3, 6.2, 6.2.1, 6.2.2

YOU ARE THERE

Be careful—you don't want to drop the pot that you're holding. Your mother has shaped and dried some round clay pots, and for the first time, she is going to let you decorate one.

It is 5500 B.C., and you live in a village near a river in central Europe. You and your friends usually help with work in the fields and learn to tend the animals. Safe inside your village walls, you also find time to play. For now, however, you must focus on the pot in your hands as you apply the first stroke of paint.

❱ Making pots required technology and skill. The clay had to be mixed, shaped, and baked before it could be decorated.

▶ The ruins of Jarmo, in present-day Iraq, show one of the world's earliest farming villages. People settled there 9,000 years ago, herding goats and growing wheat and barley.

Farming Villages

The earliest farming settlements were small, consisting of only a few families. Most people in these communities lived from one harvest to the next, and hunger was a constant threat. Bad weather, such as drought, storms, or extreme cold or heat, affected them seriously. It killed crops and livestock, making life difficult.

When they could, farming communities grew surplus food to carry them through harsh times. In some places, water was plentiful, the soil was good, and the climate was mild. There, early farming communities were highly successful. Farmers raised many kinds of crops, including grains, root vegetables, and plants they could use as medicines. They learned to use some plants as new sources of materials for making clothing and for building shelters. They also kept many kinds of animals, from oxen and camels to dogs and guinea pigs.

Some farming communities not only just **subsisted**, or survived, but also produced enough surplus food for more and more people. These settlements grew into villages with up to several hundred people.

By 7000 B.C., farming villages had spread across southwestern Asia, and the early settlements of **Abu Hureyra** and **Jericho** grew into farming villages. The nearby village of **Jarmo** had more than 25 houses.

Dozens of farming villages grew up in what is now Turkey. Some of them, such as **Çatal Hüyük** (chah•TAHL hoo•YOOK), were rebuilt many times because the baked clay bricks of the houses crumbled over time. Çatal Hüyük, also written Çatalhöyük or Çatalhüyük, was an advanced community. Its people decorated their homes with paintings and carvings of women, bulls, and other images.

READING CHECK ♂MAIN IDEA AND DETAILS
Near what resources did highly successful farming communities develop?

Farming Communities Spread

By 6000 B.C., agriculture had spread to Europe—first to what is now Greece and later across southeastern Europe. People in these areas grew wheat, barley, and other grains and kept cattle, sheep, and pigs. They built homes using wood, straw, or other materials they found nearby.

By 5500 B.C., people of the Bandkeramik (BAHND•keh•rah•mik) culture had established farming communities across much of Europe. The name *Bandkeramik* comes from their pottery, which they carved with lines.

Farming communities spread in Asia at about the same time. People grew grains and other crops and herded cattle, water buffalo, and other animals in what are now India and Pakistan.

By 5000 B.C., many communities in Asia had mastered agriculture. In villages such as **Mehrgarh** (MAIR•gar), west of the Indus River, people grew cotton to weave into cloth. They used the cloth to fashion into clothing and sell for trade.

In what is today northern China, the Yangshao (yahng•SHOH) farming culture had developed by 4800 B.C. The Yangshao people built most of their villages on terraces overlooking river valleys and their fields. They formed the **terraces** by cutting steps of flat land into the sides of hills and mountains. This made more flat land available for farming and protected the village from destructive floods.

Archaeologists have found few artifacts from early farming along the Nile River in northern Africa because, over thousands of years, Nile floods buried most artifacts. Experts believe that farming flourished along the Nile River by at least 5000 B.C.

READING CHECK ⚡**MAIN IDEA AND DETAILS**
What two advantages did terraces provide for the Yangshao people?

Changes in Technology

The earliest farming tools were simple—early farmers used sticks to dig up roots and to make holes to plant seeds. Later, they developed the hoe, and farmers used the hoe's wooden or stone blade to break up and turn over soil for planting. They also used it to dig out rocks and tree roots.

People in southwestern Asia developed the **plow** around 6000 B.C. This tool could cut, lift, and turn over soil. Farmers sharpened one end of a large forked branch and used the sharpened end to dig rows in the soil. Farmers could then place seeds or young plants in these rows.

In time, farmers replaced the stick plow with one that had a wooden or stone blade. This plow could cut through the ground faster than the stick plow. Later, farmers used strong animals, such as cattle, to pull plows. Plows allowed fewer people to plant larger crops.

Farmers used plows to prepare land that they had not been able to farm before. In Europe, the soil was too hard and rocky to dig by hand with just a stick. With plows, such soil became usable for growing crops.

Early farmers also discovered **irrigation**, or ways to move water to land. These farmers had depended on rain to water their crops, but the crops failed if rains did not come. To solve their problem, the farmers dug ditches from rivers to their fields to bring water to their crops when there was no rain. Farmers in southwestern Asia discovered irrigation in about 6000 B.C., and later so did others around the world.

READING CHECK ☼ **MAIN IDEA AND DETAILS**
What benefits did the development of the plow bring?

A Closer LOOK

Early Farming Village

The raising of plants and animals caused the first farming communities to develop in southwestern Asia.

1. Oxen and other animals pulled wooden plows. The sharp ends of the plows loosened the soil so that seeds could be planted.
2. Early farmers dug irrigation ditches.
3. Early farmers harvested wheat, barley, and other crops that could feed large populations.
4. Farmworkers stored the harvested crops in permanent buildings.

❖ How do you think farming led to the development of new kinds of tools?

Economic and Social Change

Successful farming villages produced more than enough food for their people. Some farming villages also had surpluses of valuable resources, such as stones for toolmaking. Others had surpluses of goods, such as art objects or pottery. With these economic surpluses, trade began to grow.

Before the development of money, people would **barter** for the things they wanted. By trading with each other, they could gain these items. The practice of bartering began as far back as 30,000 years ago.

When farming communities spread, villagers began to use their local resources to barter for things they did not have. A village with extra food but few clay pots might trade with a village that had many clay pots but little food.

The people of Çatal Hüyük developed a trading center for obsidian, a volcanic glass, found nearby. Archaeologists have found tools made from obsidian throughout the region. In Jarmo, archaeologists have discovered obsidian, seashells, and other valuable materials brought there by traders.

As trade between villages grew, so did a need for leadership. Members of the most important family group within a village often became community leaders. These leaders controlled trade.

Leaders also had other responsibilities such as resolving conflicts. People within a village might have had disagreements. Neighboring villages might have argued over who owned land or a resource. Sometimes a strong leader united several settlements with a common culture. As the number of people under a leader grew, so did the leader's power.

➤ Early people found many uses for obsidian (below). Skilled hands (left) chipped and shaped pieces of obsidian into tools, weapons, or art objects (right).

▶ Cave painters from an early pastoral society in northern Africa left behind a scene of their lives there.

Some early people did not settle down to village life. In **pastoral societies**, people continued to live as nomads with herds of animals. They raised goats, sheep, horses, and cattle, which provided milk, hides, and bones for tools. As needed, they moved on to new pastures with their herds.

Sometimes pastoral people came across farming villages where they traded their surplus meat and hides for grains and other supplies. In places such as northern and eastern Africa, groups of pastoral people continued to live this way for thousands of years.

READING CHECK Ŏ**MAIN IDEA AND DETAILS**
What resources did pastoral people get from their animals?

Summary

Changes in agriculture that began before 7000 B.C. caused dramatic changes in societies. Surplus food allowed farming settlements to grow into villages. Surpluses of food and other resources led to trade. With trade, people developed more complex societies and economies.

REVIEW

1. Why did early people begin to live together in villages?

2. What is a **pastoral society**? How do people in a pastoral society live?

3. How did living in villages change people's way of life?

CRITICAL THINKING

4. **ANALYSIS SKILL** In what ways would irrigation require cooperation among people in a farming settlement?

5. **ANALYSIS SKILL** How do archaeologists know that the village of Jarmo traded with other villages?

6. **Draw a Picture** Draw a picture of an early farming village and its surroundings. Include the shelters that people lived in as well as their fields or pastures. Add captions to explain how the villagers changed their environment.

7. **Focus Skill** **MAIN IDEA AND DETAILS**
On a separate sheet of paper, copy and complete the graphic organizer below.

Main Idea

Details		
Abu Hureyra	Jericho	Jarmo

Use Relief and Elevation Maps

> ## WHY IT MATTERS

To find the heights of physical features in a region, you would look at an **elevation map**. It shows the elevation of the land in relation to sea level. To get an idea of the physical features of a region, you would look at a relief map. A **relief map** shows differences in the height or depth of hills, valleys, and other physical features. It can help you picture the different lands that early people adapted to.

> ## WHAT YOU NEED TO KNOW

On an elevation map (Map B), the land is measured from sea level. The elevation of land at sea level is 0 feet. Find sea level on

Drawing A in the Reading Contour Lines diagram. The lines that circle the hill are **contour lines**. They connect all points of equal elevation. On Drawing A, the 100-foot contour line connects all points that are 100 feet above sea level.

On a relief map (Map A), shading is often used. Heavy shading shows steep rises and drops in the land. Light shading is used where the land rises or falls gently. No shading shows land that is mainly flat.

The red and green lines on Drawings A and B show how sharply the land rises and falls. Drawing B shows the hill from above. On the steeper side of the hill, the contour lines are closer together. On the gently sloping side, the lines are farther apart.

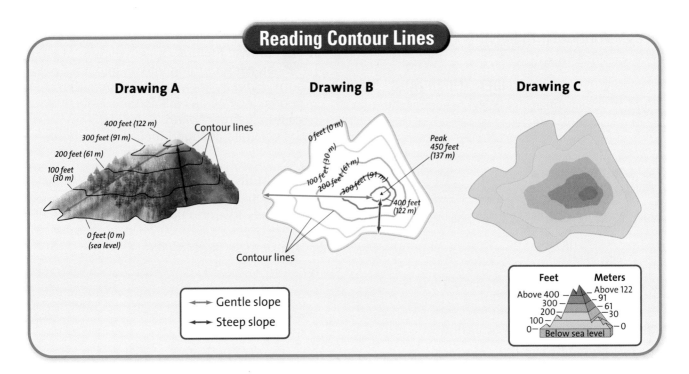

Reading Contour Lines

Drawing A

400 feet (122 m)
300 feet (91 m)
200 feet (61 m)
100 feet (30 m)
Contour lines
0 feet (0 m) (sea level)

Drawing B

0 feet (0 m)
100 feet (30 m)
200 feet (61 m)
200 feet (91 m)
400 feet (122 m)
Peak 450 feet (137 m)
Contour lines

Drawing C

⟷ Gentle slope
⟷ Steep slope

Feet		Meters
Above 400		Above 122
300		91
200		61
100		30
0		0
	Below sea level	

Map A: Relief Map of Eastern China

Map B: Elevation Map of Eastern China

On Drawing C, the color between contour lines shows elevation. The land shown in green is between sea level and 100 feet. Drawing C, however, does not show exact elevations. Instead, the key, or legend, shows the range of elevations that each color stands for.

▶ PRACTICE THE SKILL

ANALYSIS SKILL Use the maps above to answer the following questions.

1 How can you tell that Lanzhou has a higher elevation than Chongqing?

2 Which city has a lower elevation, Changchun or Harbin?

3 How would you describe most of the land in eastern China?

▶ APPLY WHAT YOU LEARNED

ANALYSIS SKILL Write a paragraph describing the elevations that you would cross on a journey from Chongqing to Lanzhou.

Practice your map and globe skills with the **GeoSkills CD-ROM**.

LOYALTY

"What is the quality to look out for as a warrant for the stability . . . of friendship? It is loyalty."*

—Cicero, *On Friendship*, 43 B.C.

In ancient days, hunters and gatherers lived together in small groups made up of several related families. For the most part, all the people in the group had equal rights. Early people cooperated with and were loyal to their family members. After all, they were dependent on one another for their survival. Being a good citizen and being a good family member were the same.

This changed as people began to settle in farming communities. Instead of living as family units, unrelated people lived in the same village. People became loyal not only to family but also to friends and neighbors.

*Marcus Tullius Cicero. *Letters of Marcus Tullius Cicero: With His Treatises on Friendship and Old Age.* Evelyn S. Shuckburgh, trans. P.F. Collier and Son, 1909.

❯ The people of the early town of Çatal Hüyük (left) were loyal to their families, friends, and neighbors. The ruins of Çatal Hüyük can be seen below.

▶ People can show their loyalty to their community by looking out for the safety of others.

At this time, division of labor began. A few people became community leaders. Others became traders, craftworkers, farmers, or even servants within the community. Instead of living as equals, people began to live within social classes and divisions.

These new ways of life brought about the need for good citizens. People had to obey their community's laws rather than just their family's traditions. They became loyal to both their community and their leaders. They defended their community and built its economy. They also paid taxes to support their government. In these ways, they became more like citizens of countries today.

▶ Communicating and working together with neighbors are ways people can make their community a better place to live.

Think About It!

Make It Relevant How do citizens show loyalty to their country or community today?

Lesson 3

7000 B.C.
The earliest towns form

3500 B.C.
Cities develop

3100 B.C.
First civilizations emerge

Building Communities

WHAT TO KNOW
How did early cities begin?

✔ Explain the conditions that helped make towns successful.

✔ Describe the social and economic changes that resulted from the growth of cities.

VOCABULARY
division of labor p. 69
merchant p. 69
social class p. 69
government p. 69
urban p. 70
taxation p. 70
civilization p. 70

PLACES
Jericho
Syrian Desert
Çatal Hüyük
Eridu
Kish
Ur
Uruk
Mesopotamia

MAIN IDEA AND DETAILS

California Standards
HSS 6.2, 6.2.1, 6.2.2

YOU ARE THERE
It's a dark night in 7000 B.C., with clouds covering the moon. The chilly wind makes you shiver. You wish you were home, curled up and asleep. However, it's your turn to stay up in the watchtower.

Suddenly you hear something moving at the bottom of the wall that surrounds your town of **Jericho**. Could it be a thief who wants to rob the storehouse of grain?

Then you hear a BAAAHH sound. It's not a person at all—it's a sheep! It must have gotten out of its pen and wandered off. You'll tell someone in the morning where to look for it. Until then, you'll struggle to stay alert.

▶ The ancient ruins of Jericho (below) attract thousands of visitors each year. Archaeologists found this clay statue with shells for eyes (right) at Jericho.

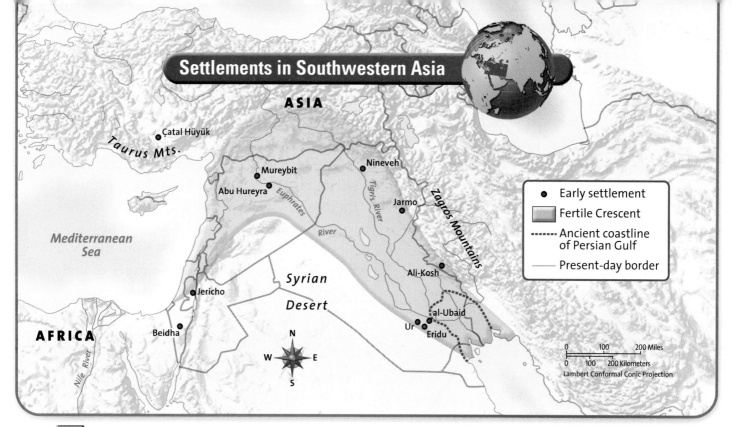

Settlements in Southwestern Asia

- • Early settlement
- ▨ Fertile Crescent
- ┈ Ancient coastline of Persian Gulf
- — Present-day border

0   100   200 Miles
0   100   200 Kilometers
Lambert Conformal Conic Projection

ANALYSIS SKILL **Analyze Maps** Some of the earliest settlements developed in a region in southwestern Asia called the Fertile Crescent.

❖ **Location** Near what natural feature did early people often build settlements?

Early Towns

Success at farming or trading allowed many early villages to grow into towns. These communities could support up to a few thousand people. The ruins of some of the earliest towns offer us a fascinating look at how they developed.

In about 7000 B.C., the village of Jericho grew into one of the earliest-known towns. Plentiful water made it an ideal place to live. Crops grew well in the fertile soil. Farmers grew wheat and barley and raised sheep and goats and produced enough to have surplus crops and goods.

By about 6500 B.C., Jericho had grown into an important trading town with between 2,000 and 3,000 people. It provided water and a place to rest for traders and nomadic herders crossing the **Syrian Desert**. As it grew in size, Jericho's beehive-shaped huts covered almost 10 acres.

To defend Jericho from enemies and wild animals, the people who lived there built a large stone wall around the town. Then they dug a wide ditch around the outside of the wall. Watchtowers along the wall allowed guards to see approaching danger.

Little is known about daily life in Jericho. Archaeologists believe that the people treated the dead with great respect. They buried the dead carefully, sometimes under the homes in which they had lived. The remains of shrines and artifacts, such as sculptures of ancestors, show that religious beliefs were important.

In about 6000 B.C., the people of Jericho abandoned their settlement. Experts do not know why they deserted the area. Since then, two other places named Jericho have been built near the original site.

READING CHECK ⏺ **MAIN IDEA AND DETAILS** What allowed many early villages to grow into towns?

Çatal Hüyük

The early town of **Çatal Hüyük** was like Jericho in many ways. It was near a good supply of water, and it was in an area with good soil for crops. Çatal Hüyük was also near important trade routes, which helped its people exchange goods with people far away. By 6500 B.C., the town's control of the obsidian trade had made it a success.

In Çatal Hüyük, the people also had special practices for burying their dead. Archaeologists have found sculptures, jewelry, and weapons in graves. Like the people of Jericho, the people of Çatal Hüyük built many shrines.

Even though Çatal Hüyük and Jericho were alike in these ways, they were also different. The people of Çatal Hüyük lived in small houses rather than the beehive-shaped huts of Jericho. Their houses had separate rooms for cooking, sleeping, and other activities, including worshipping. The people of Çatal Hüyük are believed to have made the first-known linen in the world. They wove the fiber of a plant called flax into cloth for making clothes.

The people of Çatal Hüyük did not surround their town with a wall to protect themselves. Instead, the walls of the houses formed the defenses of the town. The houses could be entered only from the roof. When danger struck, people simply pulled up their ladders and remained safe inside.

Not long after the towns of Jericho and Çatal Hüyük developed, other towns began to form rapidly all around the world. As trade between towns grew, people exchanged more resources, goods, and ideas. These exchanges changed their lives in many ways.

READING CHECK ⏰**MAIN IDEA AND DETAILS**
What artifacts have archaeologists found in graves at Çatal Hüyük?

Labor, Leaders, and Laws

With larger numbers of people living together in towns, important social and political changes took place. Societies became more complex, and new kinds of leadership developed.

Improved agricultural techniques allowed more people to work in jobs other than as farmers. A **division of labor** developed as people began to work according to their abilities. Some people grew crops while others made tools or clothing. Still others were **merchants**, people who sold goods they had bought from traders.

Division of labor greatly changed society. Because the work of groups of people had different levels of responsibility, society became divided into **social classes**. The highest social class was usually made up of rulers, priests, and other important leaders and their families.

Important family members ruled in towns, just as in villages. The leaders of towns began to pass on their positions to chosen family members, keeping power within each leader's family.

The leaders of towns had to control more people, larger food surpluses, and wider trade than did village leaders. With more responsibilities, their power grew.

The leaders of towns created many unwritten laws that townspeople had to live by. This kind of leadership was the beginning of **government**, an organized system of leaders and laws.

READING CHECK ⏾ **MAIN IDEA AND DETAILS**
What social divisions developed among people of early towns?

A Closer Look

Çatal Hüyük

The town of Çatal Hüyük formed a complex society with division of labor and a religion.

1. Craftworkers included weavers, potters, and those who worked with obsidian.
2. Because Çatal Hüyük controlled the obsidian trade, traders brought goods from far away.
3. Homes held shrines decorated with art.
4. Vultures played an important role in religion. Images of them have been found on murals.

❔ What benefits did building flat roofs provide to the people of Çatal Hüyük?

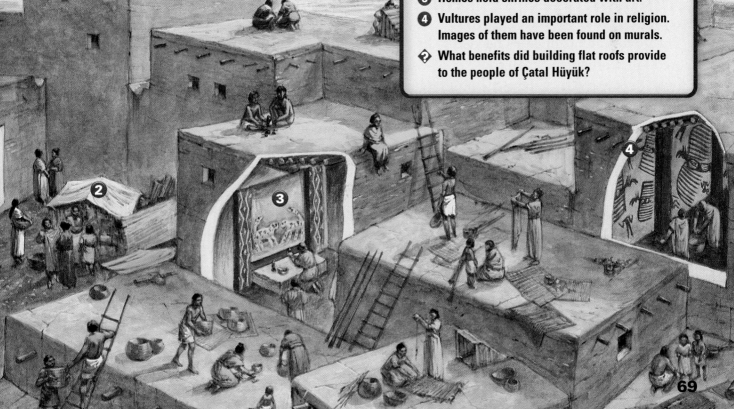

▶ Specialized workers, such as the artists who created these objects more than 5,000 years ago, appeared in more complex societies.

Cities and Civilizations

Around 3500 B.C., some towns in southwestern Asia developed into cities. Life in these **urban** areas was different from life in towns. Early cities often had 5,000 people or more. Also, people in cities lived closer together than did people in towns.

The governments of cities needed to be more highly organized than those of towns. City leaders had to organize the building of longer walls for defense. They had to maintain water supplies and nearby irrigation systems. The leaders also supervised the construction of the temples, palaces, and other buildings.

In cities, people learned to do even more specialized jobs. Some still worked as merchants, craftworkers, and traders, and most cities had a marketplace where goods could be exchanged. Other people began to work for the city government as officials who helped manage the city.

The management of cities led to **taxation**, or a system in which people support the government. Many people paid their taxes by working on government projects while others paid their taxes with crops. The city used these to pay city officials and to trade for other goods and materials.

The world's first cities, including **Eridu** (AIR•ih•doo), **Kish**, **Ur**, and **Uruk** (OO•rook), developed where farming first began in southwestern Asia. This area was part of a region once called **Mesopotamia**.

In about 3100 B.C., cities in Mesopotamia as well as those in Egypt gave rise to the world's first **civilizations**. Soon other civilizations also developed in other parts of the world.

Early civilizations shared some common features. Compared to cities, they covered larger areas, had better-organized societies and economies, and constructed larger buildings and temples. A central government usually controlled a civilization.

People living in civilizations made advances in science, mathematics, and transportation. Most of them developed some form of writing, keeping records of events, trade, and taxes. People also began to follow religions supported and controlled by their governments.

READING CHECK ⏀**MAIN IDEA AND DETAILS**
What were some of the responsibilities of government in early civilizations?

Summary

Improvements in agriculture allowed some farming villages to grow into towns, then cities, and eventually civilizations. These changes happened over thousands of years. Social and economic changes took place at each step. As civilizations developed, technology and communication advanced rapidly.

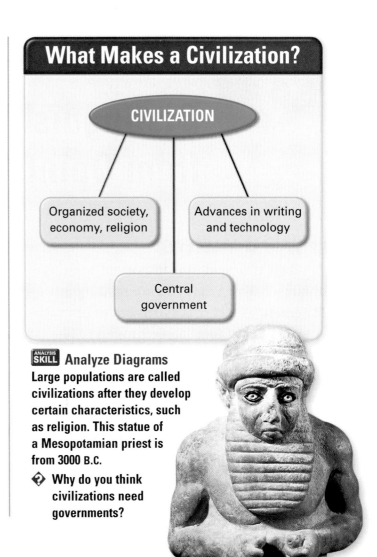

What Makes a Civilization?

CIVILIZATION

Organized society, economy, religion

Advances in writing and technology

Central government

ANALYSIS SKILL Analyze Diagrams
Large populations are called civilizations after they develop certain characteristics, such as religion. This statue of a Mesopotamian priest is from 3000 B.C.

❖ Why do you think civilizations need governments?

REVIEW

1. 💡 How did early cities begin?
2. Use the term **urban** to describe what life was like in early cities.
3. Where did the earliest cities develop?
4. How were early cities different from early towns?
5. Why did a system of taxation come about in early cities?

CRITICAL THINKING

6. **ANALYSIS SKILL Make It Relevant** Do you think taxation is still an important part of government? Why or why not?
7. **ANALYSIS SKILL** What caused social classes to develop?

8. **✏ Make a Poster** Work with a group of classmates to make a poster about early cities. Draw a circle in the center of the poster. In it, write the word *City*. Draw eight to ten branches coming off the circle. Each branch should describe one of the features of the first cities.

9. **Focus Skill MAIN IDEA AND DETAILS**
On a separate sheet of paper, copy and complete the graphic organizer below.

Main Idea

A town's leader had areas of responsibility that were greater than those of a village's leader.

Details

Distinguish Fact from Opinion

▶ WHY IT MATTERS

When you read, it is important to think about whether what you are reading is a statement of fact or a statement of opinion. A statement of **fact** can be proved to be true. An **opinion** is a statement that cannot be proved. It expresses only the belief, attitude, or viewpoint of the person making it.

The following statement is a fact: "The people of Çatal Hüyük lived in small houses, rather than the beehive-shaped huts of Jericho." You can check this information in an encyclopedia or other resources.

The following statement is an opinion: "The small houses of Çatal Hüyük were much better than the beehive-shaped houses of Jericho." This statement expresses a belief that cannot be proved, even though you may agree with it. Being able to distinguish fact from opinion can help you decide what to believe when you read.

▶ This painting of a deer hunt, from the 6000s B.C., was found at Çatal Hüyük.

❯ Many artifacts found at Çatal Hüyük—such as this clay seal stamp, flint dagger, animal figurine, and necklace made from limestone beads and deer teeth—are more than 8,000 years old.

❯ WHAT YOU NEED TO KNOW

The following can help you identify whether statements are facts or opinions.

1 Ask yourself whether the statement can be proved to be true. Have you personally observed or experienced the events described in the statement? Can the statement be checked in a reliable, up-to-date reference source?

2 Certain words may be clues that a statement is an opinion. Words that express feelings or judgments, such as *best*, *worst*, *good*, *bad*, *wonderful*, or *terrible*, are clues that an opinion is being expressed.

3 Although you may agree with an opinion, that does not make it a fact. If it cannot be proved to be true, it is an opinion.

❯ PRACTICE THE SKILL

ANALYSIS SKILL Read the statements in the next column, and decide whether each is a statement of fact or of opinion.

1 Success at farming or trading allowed many early villages to grow into towns.

2 In about 6000 B.C., the people of Jericho abandoned their settlement.

3 Jericho was a better place to live in than Çatal Hüyük.

4 The people of Çatal Hüyük made the first known linen.

5 Craftworkers in early cities made very poor tools.

❯ APPLY WHAT YOU LEARNED

ANALYSIS SKILL Reread the section of the lesson titled Çatal Hüyük on page 68. Write six statements about the information in the section—three that state facts and three that are your own opinions. Trade papers with a classmate. See whether you can identify which of your partner's statements are facts and which are opinions.

• **8000** B.C.
People in southwestern
Asia begin to domesticate
plants and animals

7000 B.C.
Jericho becomes
one of the first
farming villages

Reading Social Studies

The **main idea** is the most important idea in a passage.
Details give information that supports the main idea.

(Focus Skill) Main Idea and Details

Complete this graphic organizer to show that you can identify
the main idea and supporting details of how farming and keeping animals changed the way early people lived. A copy of this
graphic organizer appears on page 22 of the Homework and
Practice Book.

Early Farmers

Main Idea

Details

| People could now live in permanent settlements. | People had enough surplus to trade with others. | Livestock became a main source of meat. |

California Writing Prompts

Write an Expository Paragraph Write a
paragraph that explains why laws were created
in early towns and cities. Use details from the
chapter to support your explanation.

Write a Narrative Write a short narrative set
in ancient Çatal Hüyük. Create characters and a
plot that are realistic in this setting. Use details
from the chapter to help you write your narrative.

6000 B.C.
People develop
the plow and discover
irrigation

3500 B.C.
Some towns
in southwestern
Asia develop
into cities

Use Vocabulary

Identify the term that correctly matches each definition.

1. adapt or tame for human use

2. survive

3. of or like a city

4. extra supply

5. a person who sells goods bought from traders

domesticate, p. 50

surplus, p. 52

subsist, p. 57

merchant, p. 69

urban, p. 70

Use the Time Line

ANALYSIS SKILL **Use the summary time line above to answer these questions.**

6. Which developed first, cities or irrigation?

7. About how long after people began to domesticate plants did people develop the plow?

Apply Skills

Read Parallel Time Lines

ANALYSIS SKILL **Study the parallel time line on page 55 and answer this question.**

8. How long after farming began in southwestern Asia did farming begin in South America?

Recall Facts

Answer these questions.

9. What changes after the Ice Age led humans to begin farming?

10. What were two animals that early farmers in southwestern Asia kept?

11. How did the Yangshao people change their land to make it better for farming?

Write the letter of the best choice.

12. What kinds of crops did the first farmers grow?
   A fruits
   B grains
   C nuts
   D vegetables

13. Which of the following is true about the people of Abu Hureyra and Jericho?
   A They were fierce soldiers.
   B They had a written language.
   C They learned to build dams.
   D They domesticated plants and animals.

Think Critically

14. **ANALYSIS SKILL** What sequence of events led to the domestication of plants and animals?

15. **ANALYSIS SKILL** How did agriculture change the ways in which people made clothing?

Lascaux Cave

GET READY

Lascaux, France, is the site of one of the world's most amazing and best-preserved examples of the art of early humans. The cave paintings at Lascaux were found in 1940 and are believed to be between 15,000 and 17,000 years old. They were found not by archaeologists but by four boys playing in the woods with their dog.

To protect the paintings, the caves were closed to the public in 1963. Today, visitors can see Lascaux II, an exact reconstruction of the caves and the paintings.

WHAT TO SEE

Four boys with a garden hoe, a rope, and a lantern made one of the most important archaeological discoveries of the twentieth century.

The Dordogne River winds its way among forested hills near Lascaux, in central France, as it did when the cave paintings were created long ago.

LOCATE IT

FRANCE

Lascaux Cave

Visitors of all ages can walk through the replica of the cave (left) and see lifelike images of horses and bulls (top).

To protect the original cave paintings (below) from the 300,000 or more visitors who come each year, a team of artists (above), made a reconstruction of the cave, called Lascaux II. It is now the fourth most visited tourist site in France.

A VIRTUAL TOUR

GO ONLINE

Visit VIRTUAL TOURS at
www.harcourtschool.com/hss

Unit 1 Review

 THE BIG IDEA

Environment Early people adapted to their environment to survive.

Summary

Early Humankind

Archaeologists and other scientists use artifacts and fossils to learn about early humans. They know that the first humans were hunters and gatherers who migrated from Africa to other continents. Most experts think that humans migrated in search of food. They also think that land bridges may have allowed humans to reach other of the world's continents.

Humans adapted to varied environments, from deserts to rain forests. They used whatever plants, animals, and other resources they could find for food, shelter, and tools.

After the last Ice Age, the climate became warmer and drier. Humans found new food sources as environmental changes affected old sources. They learned to grow grains and, later, other crops. They domesticated animals, such as goats and sheep, for food.

Agriculture produced food surpluses. Surpluses allowed people to live in larger groups and freed some people to do work besides getting food. Villages grew into towns and then cities—complex societies with governments and public works paid for by taxation.

Main Ideas and Vocabulary

Read the summary above. Then answer the questions that follow.

1. What are artifacts?
   A objects made by people
   B plants that can be eaten
   C remains of ancient animals
   D scientists who study early humans

2. Where did the first humans live?
   A in Asia
   B in Africa
   C in Europe
   D in the Americas

3. What does the word agriculture mean?
   A systems for bringing water to crops
   B living in a permanent settlement
   C raising plants and animals
   D a period with little or no rain

4. Which of the following were among the first animals to be domesticated?
   A cows
   B pigs
   C horses
   D goats

Recall Facts

Answer these questions.

5. Besides farming, what was another way in which people changed how they got food after the last Ice Age?

6. What were two early tools that helped ancient people grow more food with less work?

7. Why was the innovation of irrigation so important?

8. What caused pastoral people to move from one place to another in ancient times?

9. What were some ways that early farming communities used their food surpluses?

10. What were the houses like in which people lived in Jericho?

11. What plant did the people of Çatal Hüyük grow to make a new source of cloth?

Write the letter of the best choice.

12. Where were the earliest-known farms?
    A in Africa
    B in South America
    C in southwestern Asia
    D in northeastern Siberia

13. What material did the early farmers of Abu Hureyra use to build their shelters?
    A stone
    B mud
    C wood
    D animal hides

14. Which plant did early farmers in Asia grow to weave into cloth?
    A wheat
    B rice
    C cotton
    D maize

15. Which of the following was a direct effect of the division of labor in towns?
    A food surpluses
    B taxation
    C social classes
    D war

Think Critically

16. Describe one important event in prehistory that scientists are unsure about. Explain what kind of evidence could help scientists learn more about this event.

17. How do civilizations differ from cities?

Apply Skills

Use Relief and Elevation Maps

ANALYSIS SKILL Use the elevation map on this page to answer the following questions.

18. What is the highest point in Turkey? What is its elevation?

19. Which parts of Turkey have the lowest elevation?

20. What is the elevation range around Istanbul?

21. Which city is on higher land, Istanbul or Kayseri?

22. Why do you think the lowest points of Turkey are located where they are?

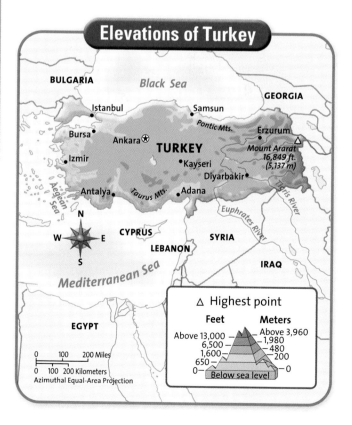

Elevations of Turkey

Read More

■ *The Secrets of Lascaux Cave* by Richie Chevat.

■ *Discovering the Iceman* by Jeffrey Nelson.

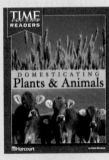

■ *Domesticating Plants and Animals* by Robin Warshaw.

Show What You Know

Unit Writing Activity

Write a Summary Write a one- or two-page summary of how human life changed from the end of the last Ice Age to the building of the first cities.

Unit Project

Make a Research Notebook Create a research notebook about how early humans adapted to their environments. Scientists often create research notebooks as they study their subjects. Like a scientist, fill your notebook with ideas, information, or questions you develop about a subject. Illustrate your notebook with maps and drawings about the subject you are researching.

GO ONLINE Visit ACTIVITIES at **www.harcourtschool.com/hss**

Mesopotamia, Egypt, and Kush

START WITH THE STANDARDS

California History-Social Science Standards

6.2 Students analyze the geographic, political, economic, religious, and social structures of the early civilizations of Mesopotamia, Egypt, and Kush.

The Big Idea

INNOVATIONS

Early cultures often borrowed ideas from other cultures but also developed ideas of their own.

What to Know

✓ What agricultural techniques developed in early civilizations?

✓ How did cities come to be?

✓ What was the relationship between religion and the social and political order in Mesopotamia and Egypt?

✓ What political, commercial, and cultural relationships did Egypt and Kush have?

Show What You Know

★ Unit 2 Test

✎ Writing: A Narrative

 Unit Project: A "Patterns of Civilization" Display

Time

6000 B.C.   **4000 B.C.**

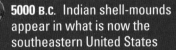

At the Same Time   **5000 B.C.** Indian shell-mounds appear in what is now the southeastern United States

Mesopotamia, Egypt, and Kush

1650 B.C. The Kushites gain their independence from Egypt, p. 176

1552 B.C. Egypt's New Kingdom begins, p. 159

730 B.C. The Kushite dynasty begins its rule of Egypt, p. 179

2000 B.C.

B.C./A.D.

2000 B.C. Farming villages are common in Middle America

2000 B.C. Agriculture begins in the Middle West region of what is now the United States

1150 B.C. Olmec artisans begin making large stone head sculptures in what is now Mexico

Narmer

3000s B.C.

- Ruler of Upper Egypt who conquered Lower Egypt and united the two kingdoms
- Established the First dynasty

Sargon

Reigned 2350 B.C. – 2295 B.C.

- Created the world's first empire
- Established trade with many lands

People

3000 B.C.

2200 B.C.

3000s B.C. • Narmer

Reigned 2350 B.C. – 2295 B.C. • Sargon

Akhenaton and Nefertiti

Reigned 1364 B.C. – 1347 B.C.

- Abandoned worship of Amon and all other gods for one single god—Aton
- Nefertiti might have been from Mesopotamia

Ramses II

Reigned 1289 B.C. – 1224 B.C.

- Built magnificent temples all over Egypt
- Signed peace treaty after many years of war with the Hittite Empire

Hammurabi

Reigned
1790 B.C. – 1750 B.C.

- Best known for the Code of Hammurabi
- United most of Mesopotamia into the Babylonian Empire

Hatshepsut

1504 B.C. – 1458 B.C.

- One of the only women to become pharaoh in Egypt
- One of the strongest pharaohs of Dynasty 18

1400 B.C.   **600 B.C.**

 Reigned 1790 B.C. – 1750 B.C. • Hammurabi

1504 B.C. – 1458 B.C. • Hatshepsut

 Reigned 1364 B.C. – 1347 B.C. • Akhenaton and Nefertiti

Reigned 1289 B.C. – 1224 B.C. • Ramses II

Reigned 780 B.C. – 760 B.C. • Alara

Reigned 747 B.C. – 716 B.C. • Piye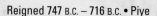

Alara

Reigned
780 B.C. – 760 B.C.

- Powerful Nubian chieftain who started a new dynasty of Kushite kings
- Began the kingdom of Napata

Piye

Reigned
747 B.C. – 716 B.C.

- Conquered Lower Egypt
- Brought all of Egypt under Kushite control

EUROPE

Mediterranea

ATLANTIC
OCEAN

AFRICA

At The Same Time

The Olmec civilization
in Mexico, about
1100 B.C.

NORTH
AMERICA

ATLANTIC
OCEAN

SOUTH
AMERICA

Mesopotamia

Egypt

Nubia

● City or settlement

◇ Copper

⬭ Gold

▱ Granite

◁ Iron

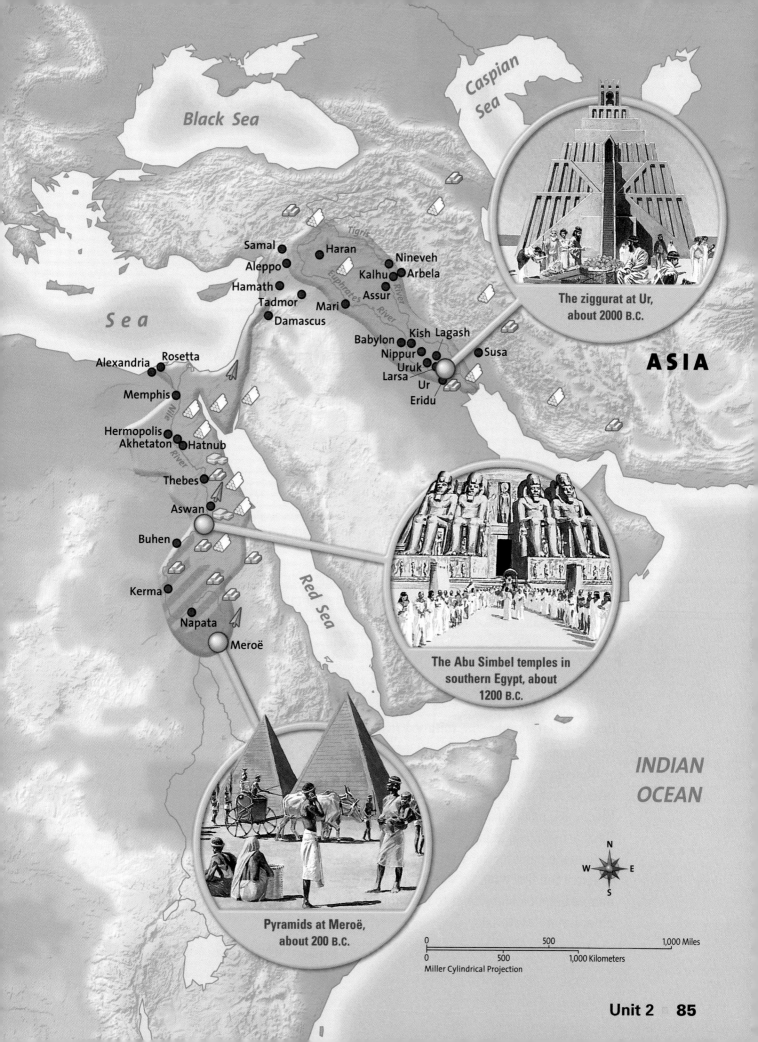

Black Sea

Caspian Sea

Samal
Aleppo
Hamath
Tadmor
Damascus

Haran
Mari

Tigris
Euphrates River
River

Nineveh
Kalhu
Assur
Arbela

Sea

Babylon
Nippur
Uruk
Larsa
Eridu
Kish Lagash
Ur

Susa

The ziggurat at Ur, about 2000 B.C.

ASIA

Alexandria
Rosetta
Memphis

Hermopolis
Akhetaton
Hatnub

Nile River

Thebes
Aswan

Buhen

Kerma

Napata
Meroë

Red Sea

The Abu Simbel temples in southern Egypt, about 1200 B.C.

INDIAN OCEAN

Pyramids at Meroë, about 200 B.C.

N
W   E
S

0   500   1,000 Miles

0   500   1,000 Kilometers

Miller Cylindrical Projection

Unit 2   85

Reading Social Studies

 **Focus Skill**

Summarize

When you **summarize**, you tell a shortened version of what you have read.

Why It Matters

Summarizing can help you understand and remember the most important information in a passage.

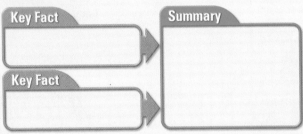

Key Fact → Summary

Key Fact →

✓ A summary includes only the important facts and details from what you have read.

✓ Always use your own words when you summarize.

✓ A summary of a paragraph may be a single sentence. A summary of a longer passage may be several sentences.

Practice the Skill

Read the paragraphs that follow. Write your own summary for the second paragraph.

Facts

Studying the art of ancient times helps us imagine what life was like when the artwork was made. During the last Ice Age, cave art was the main form of art. Most cave paintings feature animals such as bison, horses, and woolly mammoths.

Summary

Cave art showing animals was the main form of art during the last Ice Age.

To make paint for cave art, early people mixed powdered rock with animal fat. Much of the first cave art was monochromatic, or all one color. As time passed, early people began adding color to their paintings by using different kinds of rocks and other natural materials.

Summarize **Read the paragraphs, and answer the questions.**

Sumerian Sculpture

The artwork of ancient Sumer can tell us a lot about that civilization, from what kind of clothing people wore to how they defined beauty. One of the earliest known Sumerian sculptures was carved from marble. It dates to between 3500 B.C. and 3000 B.C. The sculpture is of the head of a woman with large eyes and eyebrows, balanced features, and a calm expression. Art historians think the sculpture is of a goddess. They think this because to the Sumerians, a goddess was the ideal of beauty. Historians also say that the artist placed colored material of some kind in the eyes and added hair made of gold or copper. These parts of the sculpture did not survive, but the methods were common at the time.

Another important Sumerian work of art is a group of marble statues that was found in a temple. Made in about 2500 B.C., these figures also have large eyes and calm expressions on their faces. However, these figures still have the colors in their eyes. Since they are full-length statues, they show the long skirts that both men and women of Sumer wore.

Art historians draw conclusions about the meanings of the statues by studying Sumerian culture. From information they have found through research, they believe that the two tallest marble statues, which have especially large eyes, represent a god and a goddess.

Summarize

1. **Which facts from the first paragraph should be included in a summary of the whole article?**

2. **What is one detail that would *not* be included in a summary? Why?**

3. **Summarize this article. How does your summary compare with those of your classmates?**

Study Skills

ORGANIZE INFORMATION

Graphic organizers can help you understand information presented in what you read.

- ❯ Tables, charts, and webs are graphic organizers that can show how main ideas and important details are connected to each other.

- ❯ Graphic organizers can help you classify and categorize information.

- ❯ Graphic organizers can also help you understand the relationship between the subject of the chapter and the information in each of the chapter's lessons.

Geographic	Political	Economic	Religious	Social
Tigris and Euphrates Rivers	monarchy	surplus	polytheism	writing

Apply As You Read

Make a graphic organizer for Chapter 3, using the table above as a guide. As you read this chapter, fill in each column of the table with important information from each lesson.

California History-Social Science Standards, Grade 6

6.2 Students analyze the geographic, political, economic, religious, and social structures of the early civilizations of Mesopotamia, Egypt, and Kush.

Civilizations in Mesopotamia

Ruins of a Mesopotamian religious building

GILGAMESH THE KING

RETOLD AND ILLUSTRATED BY LUDMILA ZEMAN

Sumer was one of the world's first civilizations. The people of Sumer believed in many gods. They also believed that their kings were part god and part human. The following story is about Gilgamesh, a real king who ruled over the ancient Sumerian city-state of Uruk. Over years, many legends formed about Gilgamesh and all that he supposedly did. These legends were passed on as oral tradition for many centuries. The story of Gilgamesh is one of the oldest in the world.

Long ago in the land of Mesopotamia, a king by the name of Gilgamesh was sent by the Sun God to rule over the city of Uruk.

Gilgamesh was part god and part man. He looked human, but he did not know what it was to be human. He had power and wealth but he was not happy. He had everything except friends. He was always alone. Because of this he grew bitter and cruel.

One day, he decided to show how strong and powerful he was and make the people remember him forever.

So it was that Gilgamesh ordered a great wall to be built around the city. He ordered the men to leave their jobs and families to work on it. He made the women bring food. Children were kept away so no one would stop to play with them. At first, the people helped willingly. Their king must have good reason for wanting the wall. Was an enemy planning to attack the city?

But as the wall got higher and higher, the people grew restless. How high did it have to be? It went up higher than any wall in the world, but Gilgamesh pushed on day and night. Men fainted from work and hunger. Food grew scarce. The people cried out for mercy, begging Gilgamesh to stop but he would not listen. In despair, they prayed to the Sun God for help.

The Sun God heard their prayers and ordered the creation of another man as strong as Gilgamesh. His name was Enkidu. He was made from the clay of the earth. Since Gilgamesh had learned nothing from living with people, Enkidu was sent to live with the animals of the forest. As he got to know the animals, he learned to care for them. But he did not know human kindness for he had never seen another person.

The first man Enkidu saw he did not like. It was a hunter chasing animals through the forest, trying to kill them. Why would anyone want to do that? Enkidu wondered. He rushed to help his friends. He threw the hunter from his chariot and rescued the wounded animals. The hunter ran back to Uruk to warn Gilgamesh about the new danger in the forest. He called Enkidu "the strongest man in the world."

Gilgamesh was furious. "There is no one as strong as I am," he said. "Bring this creature to me so I can prove it. I will destroy him in front of all the people of Uruk."

 Gilgamesh prepared to fight Enkidu to the death of one of them. Gilgamesh was certain that it would be Enkidu who met defeat. However, all those who listen to or read the complete legend are in for a surprise. Here's a hint—history tells us that Gilgamesh did not die. In fact, he became a well-liked leader. How do you think the legend ends?

Response Corner

1 How do you think both Gilgamesh and Enkidu change as the legend continues?

2 Write an ending to the legend. Then find out how the legend really ends. Compare your ending to the legend's ending.

5000 B.C.
Ubaid culture begins in southern Mesopotamia

4000 B.C.
Farming spreads throughout southern Mesopotamia

3500 B.C.
Cities develop in Sumer

WHAT TO KNOW
How did the world's major river systems support the development of early civilizations?

✓ Locate the major river systems where the earliest civilizations developed.

✓ Describe the physical settings that supported permanent settlements and early civilizations.

VOCABULARY
tributary p. 96
plateau p. 96
alluvial plain p. 96
silt p. 96

PLACES
Sumer
Mesopotamia
Eridu
Uruk
Kish
Ur

SUMMARIZE

California Standards
HSS 6.2, 6.2.1, 6.2.2

The Land Between Two Rivers

YOU ARE THERE

It is 4000 B.C. With a herd of goats, you and your family round a bend in the path. Then, in the early light of dawn, you see houses in the distance.

Smoke from cooking fires rises lazily in the warm air as women prepare their morning meals. Nearby, fields of grain blow gently in the breeze. Men are checking their tools for the day's work and children run here and there, playing a game.

This is the village you and your family have been seeking. When you reach the nearest house, your father gives the hand signal for "peace" to the people of the village. Will your family be welcome to settle here? In friendship, your father offers some goats to the people.

FAST FACT

At 1,700 miles in length, the Euphrates River is the longest river in southwestern Asia. Because of the region's hot, dry climate, the Euphrates River loses a large amount of water through evaporation and irrigation. Only flat-bottomed boats can travel the shallow waters of the Euphrates River.

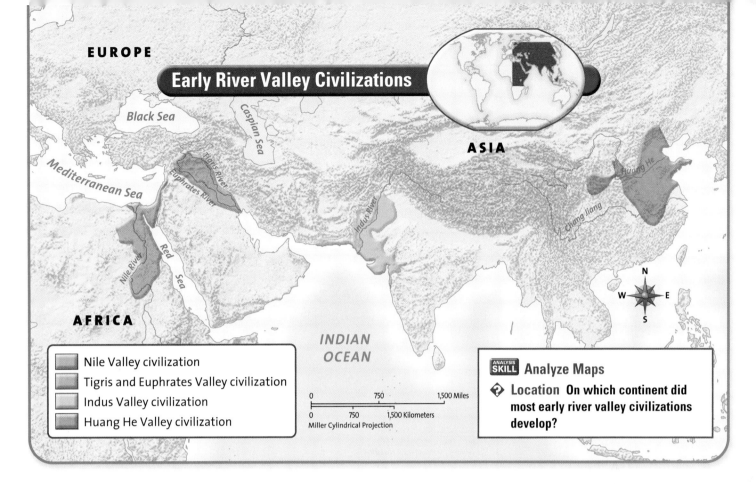

Early River Valley Civilizations

EUROPE

Black Sea

Caspian Sea

ASIA

Mediterranean Sea

Tigris River

Euphrates River

Indus River

Huang He

Chang Jiang

Nile River

Red Sea

AFRICA

INDIAN OCEAN

N
W E
S

- Nile Valley civilization
- Tigris and Euphrates Valley civilization
- Indus Valley civilization
- Huang He Valley civilization

0   750   1,500 Miles
0   750   1,500 Kilometers
Miller Cylindrical Projection

ANALYSIS SKILL Analyze Maps

? **Location** On which continent did most early river valley civilizations develop?

Importance of Major River Systems

The world's major river systems formed valleys that held a special attraction for many early people. The physical settings of these river valleys supported permanent settlements and, in time, early civilizations.

In these valleys, people found plenty of water for drinking, cooking, and bathing. Fishers speared, hooked, and netted fish from the rivers and farmers raised crops and grazed their livestock on the wide, fertile plains. With so many resources, these river valleys provided people with a good place to build permanent settlements.

Soon, these early farmers learned to grow surpluses of crops. To do this, they had to develop new agricultural techniques. With food surpluses, some people could do activities besides farming. This allowed people to create more-advanced cultures, leading to early civilizations.

The earliest civilizations developed in the valleys of four major river systems—the Tigris and Euphrates (yoo•FRAY•teez) Rivers in southwestern Asia, the Nile River in northern Africa, and the Indus River in southern Asia. Later, one formed along the Huang He (HWAHNG HUH) of eastern Asia.

READING CHECK **SUMMARIZE**
How did major river systems support permanent settlements? The tigers ephrates

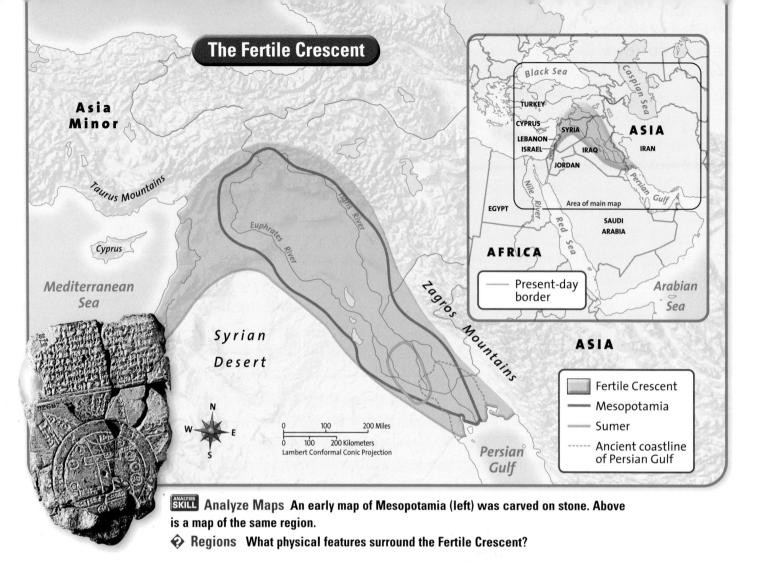

The Fertile Crescent

Asia Minor

Taurus Mountains

Cyprus

Mediterranean Sea

Euphrates River

Tigris River

Syrian Desert

Zagros Mountains

Persian Gulf

ASIA

N
W   E
S

0   100   200 Miles
0   100   200 Kilometers
Lambert Conformal Conic Projection

Black Sea

TURKEY

CYPRUS

LEBANON
ISRAEL

SYRIA

IRAQ

JORDAN

Nile River

EGYPT

AFRICA

Red Sea

Caspian Sea

IRAN

Persian Gulf

Area of main map

SAUDI ARABIA

Arabian Sea

ASIA

—— Present-day border

Fertile Crescent
—— Mesopotamia
—— Sumer
----- Ancient coastline of Persian Gulf

ANALYSIS SKILL **Analyze Maps** An early map of Mesopotamia (left) was carved on stone. Above is a map of the same region.

❓ **Regions** What physical features surround the Fertile Crescent?

The Tigris and Euphrates

One of the world's first civilizations formed in the valley between the Tigris and Euphrates Rivers. This civilization arose in a land that came to be known as **Sumer** (SOO•mer).

The land of Sumer lay in the southern part of a region called the Fertile Crescent. On a map, the Fertile Crescent appears to be shaped like a crescent moon. *Fertile* refers to the rich soil found there.

From the Taurus Mountains, the Tigris and Euphrates Rivers flow southeast across the Fertile Crescent. Many **tributaries**, or rivers that flow into larger rivers, join the Tigris. Eventually, the Tigris and Euphrates Rivers join and flow into the Persian Gulf.

Long ago, the land between the Tigris and Euphrates Rivers was known as **Mesopotamia**, meaning "the land between the rivers." Northern Mesopotamia sat on the high, flat land of a **plateau**. Southern Mesopotamia lay on the low, flat land of an **alluvial plain**, a plain formed from fine soil left behind by streams or rivers.

In the spring, the Tigris and Euphrates Rivers often overflowed their banks. As the floodwaters drained, they deposited soil and tiny rocks on the land to form a new layer of **silt**. It was on this fertile soil in southern Mesopotamia that the people of Sumer built their civilization.

READING CHECK 🌀**SUMMARIZE**

What made the land of southern Mesopotamia good for farming? The alluvial plain

The Need for Irrigation

The annual flooding of the Tigris and Euphrates Rivers enriched the soil, but it could not be counted on to water the farmers' crops. When the unpredictable floods came, floodwaters often rushed over the land, destroying crops and livestock as well as sweeping away villages.

While northern Mesopotamia received enough rainfall for farmers to grow crops, southern Mesopotamia did not. People in this hot, dry climate had to deal with frequent droughts. During these times, the heat of the sun baked the clay soil.

Imagine how frustrated the people of southern Mesopotamia must have been. They had plenty of river water near them but no way to use it to farm the dried-out land. They were at the mercy of the hot sun and unpredictable floods and rainfall.

In time, someone realized that irrigation would help solve this problem. So, people in southern Mesopotamia dug canals to carry water from the rivers to the land. They also stored water in areas of low land called basins to supply them with water in times of drought. To protect their lands from floods, they put up dikes, or walls of dirt, along riverbanks. They also built dams to help control the flow of water.

The development of these agricultural techniques changed the lives of the people in southern Mesopotamia. It allowed them to take up farming as a way of life and provided them with ways to produce surpluses of crops. With more than enough food, these early people developed new, more complex cultures.

READING CHECK ⭕ **SUMMARIZE**

How did the people learn to deal with droughts and floods? Through conserving water and using in irrigation

❯ Even today, farmers along the Euphrates River use irrigation to water their fields.

Ubaid Culture

TIME 5000 B.C.–4000 B.C.

PLACE Southern Mesopotamia

The first known settlements in southern Mesopotamia formed in about 5000 B.C. This culture is known today as the Ubaid (oo•BY•ud) culture.

▶ **Ubaid pottery**

For the most part, the people of the Ubaid culture lived simply, raising just enough crops to survive. They used stone hoes to work their fields and clay sickles to harvest their wheat and barley crops. The Ubaid people lived close to their fields in huts made of reeds and mud. They worshipped their gods in small, one-room temples. By about 4500 B.C., this ancient culture had spread across much of the Fertile Crescent.

Over time, the way of life of the Ubaid people began to change. The people built more-advanced irrigation systems and produced surpluses of crops.

The simple life gave way to one that required rules and organization. Leaders were needed, and one person in each community served as village chief. The Ubaid people began living in larger homes and building larger temples to honor their many gods.

At about this time, the Ubaid people began creating painted pottery. Boats carried the pottery and other trade goods to villages throughout the region.

In about 4000 B.C., a new more-advanced culture developed from the Ubaid culture. Still, the Ubaid culture formed the foundation for the civilization that eventually developed in southern Mesopotamia.

READING CHECK ☼**SUMMARIZE**

How did life change for the people of the Ubaid culture? *The buit more complex systems*

Cultural Heritage

Marsh Arabs

Today the Madan, or Marsh Arabs, live near the lakes and marshes of southern Iraq. The Marsh Arabs have something in common with the Ubaid people. They depend on many of the same natural resources that the ancient people once did. The wetlands on which the Marsh Arabs live have shaped their way of life. The Marsh Arabs fish, herd water buffalo, and collect reeds for making mats. These mats are used to make canoes, roofs for their mud-brick houses, and pillars to support their homes. The Marsh Arabs dry fish for food and for export to other areas where fish are less plentiful. They also depend on water buffalo for meat and milk production as part of their livelihood.

From City to Civilization

After the Ubaid culture, the people known as the Sumerians developed many new ideas in southern Mesopotamia. These ideas led to complex cultures in the region.

By 4000 B.C., farming villages had spread in southern Mesopotamia. Using agricultural techniques to produce food surpluses, some villages emerged as the first cities. The cities of **Eridu**, **Uruk**, **Kish**, and **Ur** had developed by 3500 B.C. Soon, the Sumerians formed one of the world's first civilizations in Sumer.

READING CHECK ᐧDRAW CONCLUSIONS
What was necessary for the development of the first cities? *leɡers & goverment*

Summary

Like some other major river systems, the Tigris and Euphrates Rivers gave rise to an early civilization. Between these rivers in southern Mesopotamia, the Sumerians developed new ideas for more complex cultures there. This led to one of the world's first civilizations in Sumer.

REVIEW

1. How did the world's major river systems support the development of early civilizations?

2. Use the terms **alluvial plain** and **silt** to tell how agriculture developed in Mesopotamia.

3. What role did the Ubaid people play in the development of Mesopotamian civilization?

CRITICAL THINKING

4. **ANALYSIS SKILL** Do you think that a civilization would have developed in the Tigris and Euphrates Valley if irrigation had not been developed there? Explain.

5. From what you have read, how do you think villagers probably reacted when their villages were washed away?

6. **Do Research** Using maps and reference books, locate and describe the four major river systems discussed in this lesson. For each river, write down its source, its length, the body of water it empties into, and the present-day countries it flows through.

7. **Focus Skill** **SUMMARIZE**
On a separate sheet of paper, copy and complete the graphic organizer below.

Key Fact		Summary
	→	New agricultural techniques allowed people to develop early civilizations.
Key Fact		
	→	

Read a Land Use and Products Map

❯ WHY IT MATTERS

Like the early Mesopotamians, the people who live in southwestern Asia today depend on their land and natural resources to survive. How do they use the land? What kinds of natural resources does the region have? What kinds of products do southwestern Asians make with those resources? To find the answers, you might use a map that shows how land is used and where products are made.

❯ WHAT YOU NEED TO KNOW

The map on the next page is a land use and products map of present-day southwestern Asia. This is the same area that was once home to some of the world's earliest towns and cities.

Colors on the map show **land use**, or what is done with most of the land in a particular place or region. Study the map key to learn which color stands for each kind of land use.

The picture symbols on the map show some of the products made in southwestern Asia today. Study the map key to learn which symbol stands for each product. The map cannot show exactly how all land in southwestern Asia is used or every product made there. Instead, the map shows the main uses of the land and the major products of the region.

❯ A man herds his flock of sheep in northern Iraq.

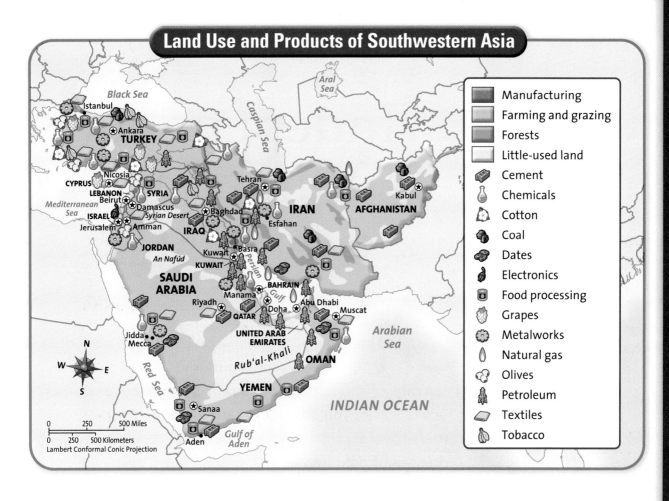

Land Use and Products of Southwestern Asia

Manufacturing
Farming and grazing
Forests
Little-used land
Cement
Chemicals
Cotton
Coal
Dates
Electronics
Food processing
Grapes
Metalworks
Natural gas
Olives
Petroleum
Textiles
Tobacco

0   250   500 Miles
0   250   500 Kilometers
Lambert Conformal Conic Projection

> **PRACTICE THE SKILL**

ANALYSIS SKILL Look at the map and the map key to answer these questions.

1. What are two crops that farmers grow in southwestern Asia?

2. What kinds of products are manufactured in southwestern Asia?

3. Where is most of the little-used land in southwestern Asia? Why do you think it is little used?

4. Where is most of the petroleum found in southwestern Asia?

5. Which land uses and products shown in the map key might be the same on a land use and products map of early Mesopotamia?

> **APPLY WHAT YOU LEARNED**

ANALYSIS SKILL Do research at the library or on the Internet to find a land use and products map for the United States. Compare the resources found in southwestern Asia to the ones found in the United States. How do you think life is different in these two parts of the world, based on the resources and land uses in each?

Practice your map and globe skills with the **GeoSkills CD-ROM**.

Time

| 6000 B.C. | 3000 B.C. | B.C./A.D. |

3000 B.C.
City-states flourish in Sumer

2000 B.C.
The city-state of Ur is abandoned

Independent Sumerian City-States

WHAT TO KNOW
What were the world's first city-states like?

✓ Explain the relationship among city-states.

✓ Understand the religious beliefs of people in city-states.

VOCABULARY
city-state p. 103
monarchy p. 104
authority p. 104
polytheism p. 104
caravan p. 105
architecture p. 106

PEOPLE
Leonard Woolley

PLACES
Ur
Mesopotamia
Kish
Uruk
Eridu
Sumer

SUMMARIZE

California Standards
HSS 6.2, 6.2.1, 6.2.2, 6.2.3

YOU ARE THERE
The year is 1933, and you're hard at work on an archaeological dig in Iraq. Uncovering the remains of the ancient Sumerian city of **Ur** is exciting work. So far, you and your team have found what seem to be royal tombs. You have identified beautiful head-dresses of gold and jewels, golden cups, and even bones of people who once lived there. You wonder what the people's lives were like, what they thought about, how they dressed, and what they ate. You know that the artifacts you are finding may help answer these questions.

▶ This photo, taken in 1933, shows the excavation of the city of Ur.

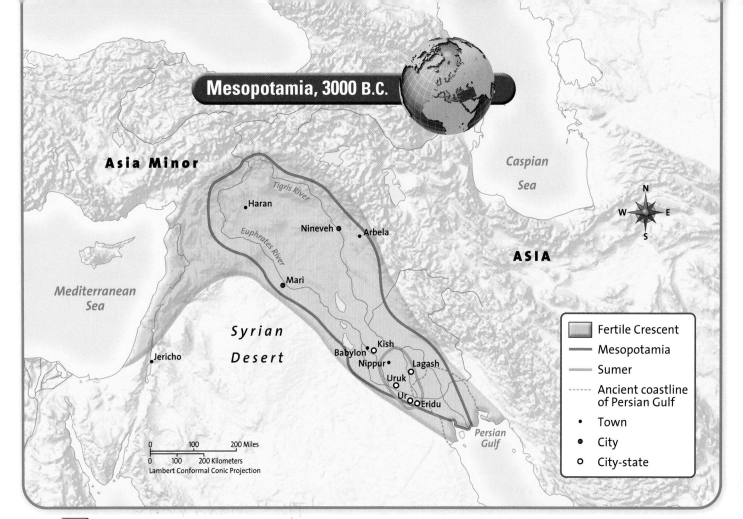

Mesopotamia, 3000 B.C.

Asia Minor

Tigris River

Haran

Nineveh   Arbela

Euphrates River

Mari

Mediterranean
Sea

Syrian
Desert

Jericho

Kish
Babylon   Nippur   Lagash
Uruk
Ur   Eridu

Persian
Gulf

Caspian
Sea

ASIA

N
W   E
S

Legend:
Fertile Crescent
Mesopotamia
Sumer
Ancient coastline of Persian Gulf
• Town
• City
○ City-state

0   100   200 Miles
0   100   200 Kilometers
Lambert Conformal Conic Projection

ANALYSIS SKILL **Analyze Maps** Sumerian city-states were located within the larger region of Mesopotamia. Mesopotamia is part of the Fertile Crescent.

❖ **What physical features made Sumer a good place to settle?**

[handwritten: buidings, arts & crafts& language and writing]

The Emergence of Cities

In southern **Mesopotamia**, Sumerian cities such as Ur, **Kish**, **Uruk**, and **Eridu** proved to be very successful. Economic surpluses allowed these and other cities to emerge as centers of culture and power. By 3000 B.C., about 12 cities in **Sumer** had developed into the world's first city-states.

In ancient times, a city-state included a walled city and the land around it, such as farmland. Each also had its own government. Inside clearly marked borders, most early city-states covered several square miles and had populations of about 5,000 people. Over time, some city-states grew to more than 1,500 square miles, with populations of as many as 60,000 people.

Although each Sumerian city-state was independent, the people shared a common culture. They followed similar religious practices, spoke the Sumerian language, and developed a writing system. They also created buildings, art, and crafts that were unique to Sumerian society.

The Sumerians and earlier people of the region made achievements in technology as well. Many advances, such as irrigation, helped them produce economic surpluses.

All this led to the development of an early civilization in Sumer. Over time, this civilization would spread throughout Mesopotamia.

READING CHECK ⏻ **SUMMARIZE**
What were the main features of a Sumerian city-state? *[handwritten: a writing system]*

Government and Religion

The first political, or government, structure of each city-state was made up of a small group of leaders and a chief leader chosen by the group. Together, they made laws, decided what work had to be done, and dealt with disputes over land or water rights. While some disputes were settled peacefully, others led to war.

When faced with war, the different leaders who ruled a city-state could not always agree about what to do. It became clear that a single leader was needed. This led the Sumerians to form the world's first **monarchy**, or governing system ruled by a king or a queen. In Sumerian city-states, the rulers were always kings.

When a king died, his son became the new king. This change made Sumerian monarchies more stable than previous kinds of government.

From a walled palace, the king governed firmly. He had complete **authority**, or power, over religion, the economy, and everyday life. The king appointed officials to carry out his orders, often concerning economic surpluses and building projects.

Below the king, priests were the most important people in society. Sumerians practiced **polytheism**, the belief in many gods. They believed that each natural event had its own god and that one god protected each different city-state. A temple was built in the center of the city-state to worship that god. At temples, the priests held ceremonies to please the gods, especially those connected to agriculture. This religious structure was central to life.

READING CHECK ☼ **SUMMARIZE**
What new governing system came to be used in Sumer? The monarchy.

A Commercial Society

The cities of Sumer buzzed with activity. Their economic structures were based on economic surpluses. The ability to create surpluses led to new kinds of jobs, to the production of new goods, and to trade.

Surpluses of crops enabled some Sumerians to perform work other than farming. In each city, some people became craftworkers, metalworkers, and builders.

Finding raw materials for these workers was not always easy—neither metals nor trees could be found in Sumer. To get raw materials, the city-states exported agricultural surpluses such as grains and dates. In exchange, Sumerians imported metals, wood, and other resources.

Sumerians depended on long-distance trade. Groups of traders traveled together on long journeys. These **caravans** carried trade goods by donkeys throughout the Fertile Crescent and beyond. Later, traders used sailboats to carry goods on waterways to distant places. By 2300 B.C., Sumerian trade extended from Egypt and the eastern Mediterranean to perhaps as far as the Indus Valley in what is now Pakistan.

The Sumerians needed a way to keep track of what they traded. They began to use clay tokens to record trade. Later, they recorded such information on clay tablets.

READING CHECK **CAUSE AND EFFECT**
Why were the Sumerians able to perform work other than farming?

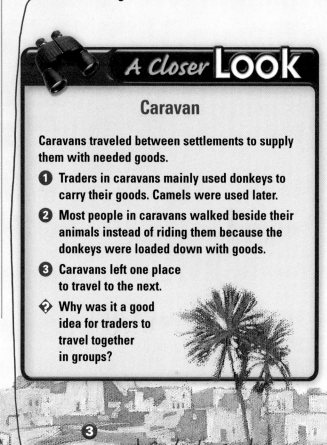

A Closer LOOK

Caravan

Caravans traveled between settlements to supply them with needed goods.

1 Traders in caravans mainly used donkeys to carry their goods. Camels were used later.

2 Most people in caravans walked beside their animals instead of riding them because the donkeys were loaded down with goods.

3 Caravans left one place to travel to the next.

? Why was it a good idea for traders to travel together in groups?

> They traded and used new materials and used in their needs

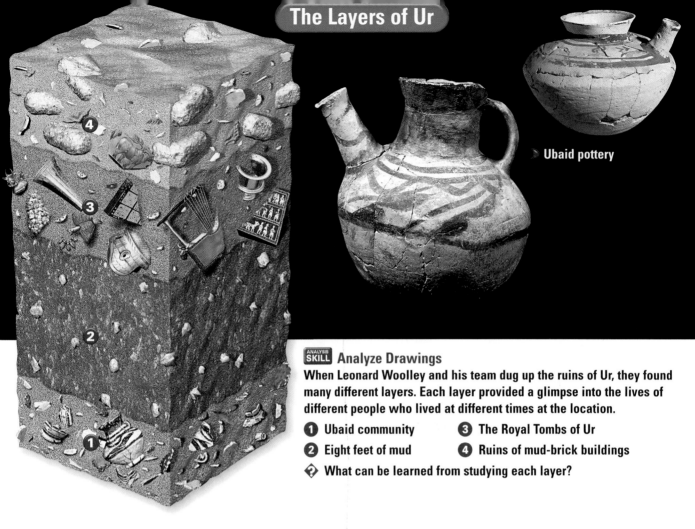

▷ Ubaid pottery

ANALYSIS SKILL **Analyze Drawings**

When Leonard Woolley and his team dug up the ruins of Ur, they found many different layers. Each layer provided a glimpse into the lives of different people who lived at different times at the location.

1 Ubaid community   **3** The Royal Tombs of Ur

2 Eight feet of mud   **4** Ruins of mud-brick buildings

◆ What can be learned from studying each layer?

Discoveries at Ur

⏱ **TIME** 5000 B.C. to 2000 B.C.

🌐 **PLACE** Ur

Long ago, the city of Ur lay close to the Euphrates River, but the river has changed its course many times through the years. Today, the land where the city once stood is now 12 miles from the Euphrates, and its once fertile fields are part of a desert. Even so, the ruins of Ur offer clues to life in the area from about 5000 B.C. to 2000 B.C.

Beginning in the 1920s, a British archaeologist named **Leonard Woolley** led an excavation at Ur. He and his team uncovered many different layers in the ruins. Each layer held artifacts from a different period of Ur's history.

In the deepest layer, archaeologists found the remains of an Ubaid village. Above that layer was 8 feet of mud, evidence that a flood destroyed Ur soon after it was built.

After the flood, the Sumerians rebuilt Ur. In the ruins of the rebuilt city, Woolley and his team found the Royal Cemetery of Ur, which held tombs from the 2500s B.C.

The tombs at Ur reveal a highly developed society. Artifacts from the tombs showed the skill of Sumerian craftworkers and the existence of long-distance trade. Tombs of royalty and high priests contained valuable items made of precious metals and stones. Tombs of other Sumerians often held such items as jewelry and weapons.

Discoveries at Ur included a large temple that was dedicated to the Sumerian moon god, Nanna. The temple's **architecture**, or building style, followed that of temple ruins found at the sites of other city-states.

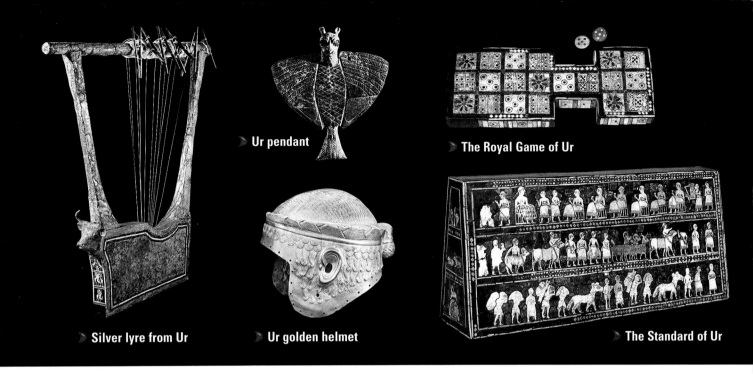

> **Silver lyre from Ur**

> **Ur pendant**

> **Ur golden helmet**

> **The Royal Game of Ur**

> **The Standard of Ur**

The rest of the city consisted of small mud-brick houses built along narrow alleys.

The highest layer of ruins dates from about 2000 B.C. At that time, the Euphrates changed course and Ur was abandoned.

READING CHECK 🔄 **SUMMARIZE**

What do the tombs at Ur reveal about the city's culture? Their life and social class and arts

Summary

Some Sumerian cities grew into city-states, which led to an early civilization in Mesopotamia. The Sumerians had an advanced government, economy, and society. The discoveries at Ur show much about how the Sumerians lived.

REVIEW

1. 💡 What were the world's first city-states like?

2. Write a sentence that includes the terms **city-state** and **monarchy**.

3. When and why was Ur abandoned?

4. What tools did the Sumerians use to keep track of trade, and how do you think they used them?

CRITICAL THINKING

5. **ANALYSIS SKILL** What clues do you think led archaeologists to conclude that a terrible flood had destroyed Ur?

6. How might archaeologists have known which tombs at Ur were those of royalty or priests and which tombs were not?

7. ✏️ **Write an Explanation** Using the information about Ur in this lesson, write an essay that explains the importance of religion in Sumerian city-states. Tell how archaeological discoveries at Ur support your explanation.

8. ⭐Focus Skill **SUMMARIZE**
On a separate sheet of paper, copy and complete the graphic organizer below.

Key Fact	Summary
Sumerian priests were just below the king.	
The tombs of priests held valuable items.	

Time

6000 B.C. ———————— 3000 B.C. ———————— B.C./A.D.

3100 B.C.
Sumerians develop
a system of writing

2500 B.C.
Mesopotamian farmers
use bronze-tipped plows

WHAT TO KNOW
What were the
achievements of people
in Mesopotamia?

✓ Explain how the
Mesopotamians were
able to achieve all
they did.

✓ Describe the
development of
Sumerian writing.

VOCABULARY
innovation p. 109
almanac p. 109
ziggurat p. 111
cuneiform p. 112
scribe p. 112

PLACES
Mesopotamia
Ur
Kish
Uruk

SUMMARIZE

 California
Standards
HSS 6.2, 6.2.2, 6.2.3, 6.2.9

Mesopotamian Achievements

YOU ARE THERE Times are changing in **Mesopotamia** in
2500 B.C. You've just loaded newly harvested
wheat into your wheeled cart. You hitch your oxen to
the cart and head for the place where surplus grain is
stored. There, workers load your grain into baskets and
weigh it, allowing you to learn exactly how much grain
your farm has produced.

Afterward, you visit the metalworkers' neighborhood
to trade some grain for new products. They have sturdy
plows, smooth cups, and beautiful ornaments, all made
of bronze. Everything looks as though it'll last forever!

▶ This close-up of the
Standard of Ur shows a
wheeled chariot carrying
a Sumerian soldier.

FAST FACT

The Sumerians developed an agricultural technique called shade planting. They planted crops in the shade of tall trees to protect them from the sun and wind. Today, farmers still use shade planting to grow crops. In this photograph, farmers in what is now Baghdad, Iraq, harvest parsley grown using shade planting.

Agricultural Techniques

The people of Mesopotamia, especially the Sumerians, are remembered for their many **innovations**, or new ways of doing things. For example, early farmers developed new agricultural techniques, such as irrigation, leading to economic surpluses.

At first, the Mesopotamians used only simple technology for farming. Early tools, such as sickles and hoes, were made of clay and copper. In time, metalworkers started mixing copper with tin to produce bronze, which is much stronger than copper alone. By 2500 B.C., many farmers were using bronze tools such as bronze-tipped plows. With stronger plows, farmers could turn soil more easily, which led to larger fields that produced larger crops.

Next, farmers found a way to plow and plant at the same time by attaching a funnel filled with seeds to the plow.

↪ *It is copper hoes.*

As the plow moved along each row, the seeds were released from the funnel. This agricultural technique allowed fewer farmers to plant more crops.

The Sumerians even wrote advice for farmers. In Mesopotamia, archaeologists have found **almanacs** written on clay tablets. These writings included information that described the best way to plant, to irrigate land, and to care for crops. One ancient Sumerian almanac contained these instructions:

> 66 When you are about to cultivate your field, take care to open the irrigation works [so that] their water does not rise too high [in it]. 99 *

READING CHECK ♻SUMMARIZE

What agricultural techniques helped the Mesopotamians produce economic surpluses?

*Samuel Noah Kramer. *History Begins at Sumer.* The University of Pennsylvania Press, 1981.

Measurements

Growing city-states needed larger farms to feed all the people. Because of this, land became more important than ever to the early Sumerians. City officials wanted to know how much land each farmer used so that they could keep accurate records. Farmers, too, wanted to know how much land they had so that they could clearly mark the boundaries of their farms. These needs led the Sumerians to develop standard measurements of land.

One measure of land area was an *iku*, also known as the *ikum*, meaning "the field." An *iku* equaled about 37,600 square feet. The idea of the present-day acre, which equals 43,560 square feet, comes from the *iku*.

Sumerians also developed standard units of measurements for weight and volume, including the quart. They used these units to measure crop harvests and to conduct trade. Farmers no longer had to guess how much wheat or barley they were exchanging for a plow or other product.

Measurements required a carefully planned number system. The Sumerians based their number system on the number 60. Our division of time into hours, minutes, and seconds came from this system.

The Sumerians even found a way to measure time. By about 2100 B.C., the Sumerians counted off days in a year, using a 360-day calendar.

READING CHECK ☼SUMMARIZE
What advances in measurements did the Sumerians develop?

60 minutes

Building

Because southern Mesopotamia had few trees, people used the resource they had plenty of for building—mud. The Sumerians formed bricks out of mud, let them dry, and then used them to build everything from houses to large temples.

Most Sumerians lived in simple flat-roofed, mud-brick houses. Groups of houses were built close together, all facing an open court. Their thick walls kept them cool in summer and warm in winter.

Kings and other people of high rank lived in larger houses of two or more stories. Artists made beautiful clay-tile designs to decorate the walls of the houses.

The largest and tallest building in every city-state was the **ziggurat** (ZIH•guh•rat). This temple developed from the simple, one-room temples of the Ubaid culture.

In describing the city of **Ur**, archaeologist Leonard Woolley wrote,

> 66 **The outstanding feature of the city [Ur] was the Ziggurat. . . an artificial mountain** 99*

*C. Leonard Woolley. *The Sumerians*. W.W. Norton & Company, 1965.

Ziggurats grew as the wealth and power of cities grew. Builders constructed the mud-brick ziggurat in layers. Some temples stood as high as seven-story buildings. At the top of each ziggurat stood a shrine for the city's special god. Palaces for kings and houses for priests often stood inside a wall that surrounded the ziggurat.

Over time, the Sumerians began building smaller buildings along the outside wall of the ziggurat. Some were shops, others were workshops, and still others were homes. Many city-states also placed parks near their ziggurat. Soon the ziggurat and the area around it became the busy center of the city. Today, wind-eroded ruins are all that is left of these ancient buildings.

READING CHECK **SUMMARIZE**
How do ziggurats show that religion was important to the Sumerians? The social ziggurat

A Closer Look

Ziggurat

Analyze Illustrations Some historians believe that ziggurats were built to represent mountains. Others think that ziggurats were built as bridges between the heavens and Earth. These mud-brick structures towered over Sumerian cities. To build such a structure required teamwork and skills.

1. Builders constructed a ziggurat in layers, each one smaller than the one below it.
2. At the top of a ziggurat stood a shrine to a god.
3. Trees and bushes may have covered the ziggurat.
4. Smaller buildings stood along the outside wall of the ziggurat.
- Why do you think ziggurats were built in layers?

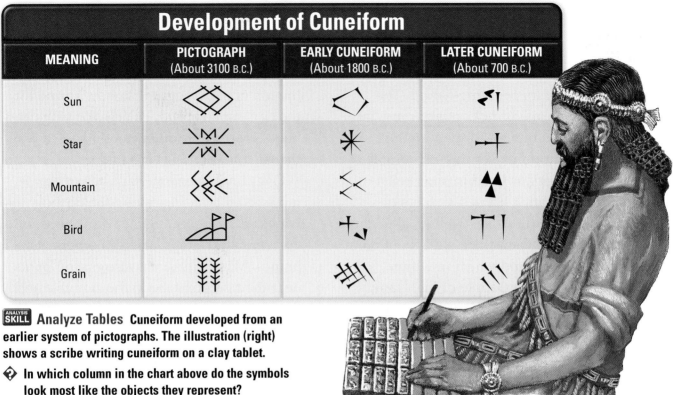

Development of Cuneiform

MEANING	PICTOGRAPH (About 3100 B.C.)	EARLY CUNEIFORM (About 1800 B.C.)	LATER CUNEIFORM (About 700 B.C.)
Sun			
Star			
Mountain			
Bird			
Grain			

ANALYSIS SKILL **Analyze Tables** Cuneiform developed from an earlier system of pictographs. The illustration (right) shows a scribe writing cuneiform on a clay tablet.

❖ In which column in the chart above do the symbols look most like the objects they represent?

Transportation

Archaeologists found the world's oldest wheels in Mesopotamia, dating to about 3500 B.C. The Sumerians were the first to attach wheels to carts. They built two-wheeled and four-wheeled carts and chariots pulled by oxen or donkeys.

For long journeys over land, traders in Mesopotamia led caravans of donkeys. Following the same paths over and over again, they established trade routes.

For water travel, the Mesopotamians built various kinds of boats. Their earliest boat was shaped like a basket and built from reeds and covered by animal skins. A mast and sail were in the center of the boat, making it perhaps the world's first sailboat. People also built canoe-shaped boats that they guided with poles.

READING CHECK DRAW CONCLUSIONS
How did new forms of transportation change people's lives?

Writing and Literature

The Sumerians made the first known written records. The earliest known writing was found on a clay tablet in **Kish** that dates to about 3500 B.C. On the tablet are picture symbols that recorded trade.

Hundreds of clay tablets found at the city of **Uruk** provide evidence that by 3100 B.C., the Sumerians had developed a writing system. This system was based on **cuneiform** (kyoo•NEE•uh•fawrm), or wedge-shaped symbols. Each of the 700 symbols stood for a different syllable and was based on a spoken sound.

At that time, few people knew how to write. Because of this, **scribes**, or people who recorded things for others, became important. Scribes used sharpened reeds to write in cuneiform on soft clay.

Writing made developments of the Sumerian government, economy, and society possible. With writing, scribes

▶ This statue (right) is of the ancient Sumerian king Gilgamesh, who was known as the Lion Spirit. The artwork (far right) shows Gilgamesh crossing the Water of Death in search of answers.

recorded boundary lines, wars, lists of kings, and gifts to temples. They also kept records of trade and food supplies.

Later, scribes recorded literature, writing down songs and stories. The most famous tale is the *Epic of Gilgamesh*, a story about legendary King Gilgamesh.

READING CHECK ☼ **SUMMARIZE**
How did writing help make the development of civilization possible?

Summary

People in Mesopotamia, especially the Sumerians, made many achievements. They created innovations in agriculture, measurements, building, and transportation. They were perhaps the first to use the wheel, the sailboat, and writing. These innovations helped the people of Mesopotamia build an early civilization.

REVIEW

1. 💡 What were the achievements of people in Mesopotamia?

2. Use the terms **scribe** and **cuneiform** in a sentence to describe how writing affected Sumerian society.

3. Why was it important for the Sumerians to have food surpluses each year?

CRITICAL THINKING

4. 📊 **SKILL** How did importing metals affect life in Sumer?

5. Which of the Sumerian innovations do you think was the most important? Why?

6. ✏️ **Make a List** Using the information in this lesson, make a list of the information that scribes recorded.

7. ⭐ (Focus Skill) **SUMMARIZE**
On a separate sheet of paper, copy and complete the graphic organizer below.

Key Fact	Summary
The Mesopotamians made many innovations.	
The Mesopotamians developed a civilization.	

2300s B.C.
A Sumerian city-state ruler creates
laws to protect the poor

2000 B.C.
The oldest-known record
of laws is made

Daily Life in Sumer

WHAT TO KNOW
What was daily life like in
a Sumerian city-state?

✓ Describe the role of
government and religion
in Sumerian daily life.

✓ Discuss the role of trade
in Sumerian city-states.

✓ Describe the social
order and roles of the
Sumerian people.

VOCABULARY
deity p. 118

PEOPLE
Urukagina
Ur-Nammu

PLACES
Sumer
Lagash
Ur

SUMMARIZE

California
Standards
HSS 6.2, 6.2.2, 6.2.3

YOU ARE THERE

It's 2300 B.C. You've been learning metalworking
from your father. You began by watching him
carefully melt copper and tin together to make bronze.
Then he showed you how to hammer the hot bronze
into different shapes. You've practiced using his tools so
much that they now seem like parts of your own hands.
Finally, your father says that the bronze cups you've
made are good enough to sell or trade.

At last, this is the day you've been waiting for! You're
going to the marketplace to sell your very own cups. You
wonder how many you'll sell and how much silver you'll
get for them.

▶ Ancient Sumerian figurines

Sumerian Metalworking

ANALYSIS SKILL **Analyze Illustrations**

Sumerian metalworkers discovered how to make bronze from tin and copper.

1 Workers bring tin ore and copper ore from mines.

2 Workers separate the metals from the ore.

3 Tin and copper are melted in furnaces to make bronze.

4 Metalworkers hammer the bronze into shape.

◈ How does the illustration above show the idea of the division of labor?

Life in a City-State

Picture an ancient Sumerian city. Imagine the glistening ziggurat that stood in the center of the city. All around the ziggurat were temples and other buildings. The Sumerian cities were centers for trade, government, and religion, and the area around the ziggurat was where much of this happened.

Without agriculture, Sumerian city-states could not have survived or grown. People in the cities relied on the work of farmers, herders, and fishers, who lived in small villages or towns near the cities. Each day, they brought meat, fish, grain, and fruit to city markets. They produced more than enough food for themselves and the growing populations in the cities.

City dwellers often lived in different parts of the city, depending on the kind of work they did. For example, craftworkers set up shop in a part of the city with others who did similar work. Their small shops lined the narrow streets, and often craftworkers and their families lived above or behind their shops. They passed their skills down from generation to generation. Some hardly ever left their part of the city.

READING CHECK ☼**SUMMARIZE**

Why were many Sumerians able to do work other than farming?

Government and Law

The ruler's palace and the homes of important people were built close to the ziggurat. From the palace, officials governed the city's day-to-day activities. Besides controlling surpluses of food and collecting taxes, the officials settled disputes and took part in making new laws. They also oversaw the building of temples and monuments.

For the most part, everyone in **Sumer** had certain rights under the law. However, to pay for wars fought against other city-states, officials sometimes took away people's rights to their property. The officials claimed people's land, cattle, and boats and made people pay taxes on everything, including burials.

In the 2300s B.C., **Urukagina** (oo•roo•kah•GEE•na), the ruler of the city-state of **Lagash**, made some changes. He created laws to prevent government leaders or the wealthy from taking advantage of the poor.

About 300 years later, **Ur-Nammu**, the ruler of **Ur**, made changes related to that city-state's laws. All of the laws were written in the form of *if-then* statements. Ur-Nammu ordered his seven laws carved onto a stone monument for all to see. This informed the people of Ur of both the laws and the punishment for breaking the laws. Today Ur-Nammu's monument still exists. It is the oldest-known record of ancient laws.

READING CHECK **MAIN IDEA AND DETAILS**
How did the government officials pay for wars?

❯ Sumerians could find almost everything they needed in the marketplace. Food, cloth, pottery, and bronze tools were in great demand.

Specialization and Trade

As more people began living permanently in one place, they developed new ways of working together to make their lives easier. In Sumerian cities, this change happened, in part, by increased specialization in the division of labor. When people specialized, they learned all of the information and skills necessary to do one job well. Then, people traded their services or the goods that they made with others.

A few people studied to become priests, government officials, doctors, and scribes. Managers and government officials supervised the work of others. They oversaw irrigation, building projects, and the storage and distribution of food. They also were responsible for schools and tax collection.

Most officials were specially trained as scribes. Scribes kept records, wrote letters for others, and wrote down stories and songs. Because scribes controlled information, they became very powerful.

Sumerian craftworkers used natural resources to make everyday objects and luxury goods. Jewelers used lapis lazuli (LAP•uhs LA•zuh•lee), a highly prized blue stone, to fashion necklaces. Carpenters built ships out of wood brought from other places. These ships then carried goods up and down the Tigris and Euphrates Rivers. Still others trained as weavers, potters, stonemasons, leatherworkers, bricklayers, and metalworkers.

Merchants bought and sold goods to make a living. Sumerian merchants traded within the Fertile Crescent and even as far away as the Mediterranean Sea. The Sumerians traded what they had in surplus—wheat, barley, and metal tools. In return, they got resources they wanted, including wood, salt, precious stones, and raw copper and tin.

READING CHECK ☉**SUMMARIZE**
How did Sumerians meet their daily wants?

Pleasing the Gods

Sumerians did not know what caused events in nature. They could not predict dust storms, swarms of insects, or floods. However, they fully understood that when these forces of nature hit, they might lose their crops, their homes, or even their lives.

Sumerians worshipped gods, or **deities**, that they believed could control nature. In the hopes of avoiding natural disasters, they offered gifts of animals, fruits, and grain to the deities. They hoped their gifts would persuade the deities to protect them.

The Sumerians believed in thousands of gods. The most important were the air god, Enlil, and the water god, Enki, who was also the god of wisdom.

READING CHECK ☼**SUMMARIZE**
Why did the Sumerians offer gifts to deities?

Social Structure

Over time, ancient Sumerian society became divided into social classes, or groups with different levels of importance. The highest social class in Sumer was made up of the king and his family, nobles, priests, and military leaders.

Most Sumerians were members of the middle class, which included merchants, scribes, craftworkers, and farmers. Sumerians were not locked into a certain class for their entire life. Instead, successful people could rise to a higher class.

Slaves were at the bottom of Sumerian society. Often, enemies in battle became slaves. Also, Sumerians who owed money could sell themselves into slavery. After working off their debt, they could buy back their freedom.

Sumerian Social Structure

ANALYSIS SKILL **Analyze Illustrations**
This diagram uses a ziggurat to show the social order of classes in Sumerian society.

❶ The king and his family, nobles, priests, and military leaders

❷ Merchants, scribes, craftworkers, and farmers

❸ Slaves

◈ Which Sumerians were in the middle of the social order?

Children IN HISTORY

Sumerian Children

Children in ancient Sumer enjoyed swimming in rivers and playing games. In the ruins of Sumer, archaeologists have even found a board game that they call the Royal Game of Ur.

Life for Sumerian children was not all fun and games. Before the age of ten, boys were usually sent to work with their fathers. Girls stayed home to help their mothers. In this way, they learned their adult roles.

Boys from wealthy families attended school to learn reading, writing, and math. Few girls from wealthy families attended school.

Sumerian women had more rights and freedoms than women in many other ancient civilizations. In addition to running their households, Sumerian women could own property, run businesses, divorce cruel husbands, and train to be priestesses or scribes.

READING CHECK ✓ **SUMMARIZE**

How could Sumerians change their social class?

Summary

The Sumerian cities were centers for trade, religion, and government. City life was supported by the food farmers provided and by the work done by government officials. Sumerians worshipped many gods that represented nature. Over time, social classes developed in Sumerian society.

REVIEW

1. What was daily life like in a Sumerian city-state?

2. Use the term **deity** in a paragraph to describe Sumerian religious beliefs.

3. What role did merchants play in the Sumerian economy?

CRITICAL THINKING

4. **ANALYSIS SKILL** Why do you think city life contributed to new social roles?

5. **Make It Relevant** How are the roles of children in the present-day United States similar to and different from those in Sumerian society?

6. **Make a Chart** Make a chart to show the Sumerian social classes. Then use your chart to explain to a classmate the relationship between Sumerian religion and its society and government.

7. (Focus Skill) **SUMMARIZE**
On a separate sheet of paper, copy and complete the graphic organizer below.

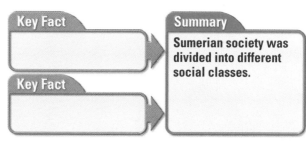

Key Fact		Summary
	➤	Sumerian society was divided into different social classes.
Key Fact		
	➤	

Lesson 5

Time

6000 B.C.	3000 B.C.	B.C./A.D.

2350 B.C.
Sargon rules
Mesopotamia

1790 B.C.
Hammurabi rules the
Babylonian Empire

609 B.C.
The Assyrian
Empire falls

WHAT TO KNOW
How did the first empires
develop in Mesopotamia?

✓ Describe how the first
empires developed.

✓ Explain the significance
of the Code of
Hammurabi.

✓ Describe the
accomplishments
of the first empires.

VOCABULARY
conquer p. 121
empire p. 121
emperor p. 121
standing army p. 121
tribute p. 121
Code of Hammurabi p. 122

PEOPLE
Hammurabi
Sargon
Nebuchadnezzar

PLACES
Kish
Mesopotamia
Akkad
Babylon

 SUMMARIZE

 California
Standards
HSS 6.2, 6.2.2, 6.2.4

The First Empires

YOU ARE THERE It is 1775 B.C. You hurry toward the center of the
city, following a rapidly growing crowd. A new
stone marker, or stela, is being put in place. Like everyone else, you want to see what the stela shows.

As you push your way to the front of the crowd, you
can see a carving at the top of the stela. It shows the
noble king, **Hammurabi**, standing before the sun god,
Shamash. The rest of the stela is covered with words
describing laws. Some are new, but you recognize others from the old tablets that you've read in school.
Hammurabi has given his people
an organized code of laws!

The Akkadian Empire

The Sumerian city-states wanted the wealth that came from controlling land and water. Because of this, they were often at war with one another.

Eventually, an enemy army did come to **conquer** the Sumerians. The leader of the army that attacked the Sumerian city-states was **Sargon** (SAR•gahn).

Sargon was not a Sumerian, but he had served in the army of the Sumerian king of **Kish**. Around 2350 B.C., Sargon rebelled against the king and defeated him. Then, Sargon marched his army across **Mesopotamia**, conquering one Sumerian city-state at a time. In doing so, he created the world's first **empire**, bringing vast lands and varied peoples under his control.

Sargon set up his capital at the city of **Akkad** (A•kad), in central Mesopotamia. For 55 years, Sargon ruled as **emperor** of what became known as the Akkadian (uh•KAY•dee•uhn) Empire. Akkad became the most splendid city in all of Mesopotamia.

Sargon used force and an organized government to maintain control over his empire. He was one of the first rulers to keep a **standing army**, a permanent army of paid soldiers. Sargon chose officials who he knew would remain faithful and appointed loyal nobles as governors to control conquered cities.

Each governor provided Sargon with tribute collected from the conquered people. **Tribute** is a required payment from one ruler to a more powerful ruler. This tribute brought much wealth under Sargon's control.

The Akkadian Empire lasted for more than 200 years after Sargon's death. In about 2300 B.C., the empire stretched from what is now Iran to the Mediterranean Sea. It eventually fell, and Sumer's city-states once again became independent.

READING CHECK ⟳ SUMMARIZE

How did Sargon maintain control over his empire?

Through Dictation

❯ Sargon (left) leads his army into battle. Through conquest, he brought new lands and people under his control.

Equal Justice

In addition to putting together a code of laws, Hammurabi introduced the idea of equal justice, or fair treatment, under the laws. His equal justice, however, was limited to equality within each social class. Under the Code of Hammurabi, members of the ruling class were favored over people of other classes. The punishments they received were often lighter than those received by other people. At that time, this was considered fair and just. Today, the United States Constitution provides for equal treatment for all people without regard for a person's position in our society.

▶ Emperor Hammurabi in prayer

Hammurabi and the Babylonian Empire

TIME 1790 B.C.

PLACE Mesopotamia

Between 1790 B.C. and 1750 B.C., Hammurabi (ha•muh•RAH•bee), the king of the city-state of **Babylon**, conquered and united most of Mesopotamia under his rule. In this way, he formed a large empire that became known as the Babylonian Empire.

As emperor, Hammurabi both encouraged trade and oversaw agriculture, irrigation, and building projects. In addition, he changed the tax system so that all people in the empire paid a fair share.

Hammurabi is perhaps best remembered for organizing the laws of his land. Each city-state had long had its own laws. Hammurabi collected all these laws, sorted them, and came up with one collection of laws known as the **Code of Hammurabi**.

The Code of Hammurabi consisted of 282 laws. They covered such matters as

family relationships, taxes, land and business deals, trade, loans, debts, wages, and crime.

Hammurabi changed the old laws that were unfair and made clear those that were confusing. He had the code carved into stone and placed in a public place for everyone to see. To Hammurabi, the code represented a way to rule

> **66** so that the strong should not harm the weak. **99***

Some of the laws followed the idea of "an eye for an eye." These laws called for punishments that matched the crimes that had been committed. For example, a person who broke someone's arm in a fight would be punished by having his or her arm broken. Hammurabi's code lasted over the years, but his empire did not. By about 1600 B.C., the Babylonian Empire had fallen.

READING CHECK ☼ **SUMMARIZE**

How did Hammurabi organize the laws of Babylon?

To have a equal country

*Hammurabi. *The Letters and Inscriptions of Hammurabi, King of Babylon.* L.W. King, ed., trans. AMS Press, 1976.

Kassite and Assyrian Rule

After the fall of the Babylonian Empire, several different groups invaded and ruled Mesopotamia. In the 1600s B.C., the Hittites, armed with war chariots and iron weapons, captured and looted Babylon.

The Hittites soon returned to their homeland, and their neighbors, the Kassites, moved in and conquered Babylon. They ruled the city for more than 500 years. The Kassites adopted Babylonian laws, religion, and literature, which helped Babylonian culture live on.

In time, the Assyrian Empire gained control of the region. The Assyrians had a great desire to control the trade routes in southwestern Asia. Their mastery over powerful new weapons helped them meet this goal. From the Hittites, they had learned how to make and use iron weapons and war chariots. The Assyrian army introduced the battering ram, a heavy wooden beam used to break down walls. They were also among the first to use the lance, a spear attached to a long handle.

One by one, the Assyrians conquered their neighbors. By the 700s B.C., the Assyrians ruled the largest empire in the world. They controlled all of Mesopotamia, as well as lands in present-day Turkey, Egypt, and the Persian Gulf.

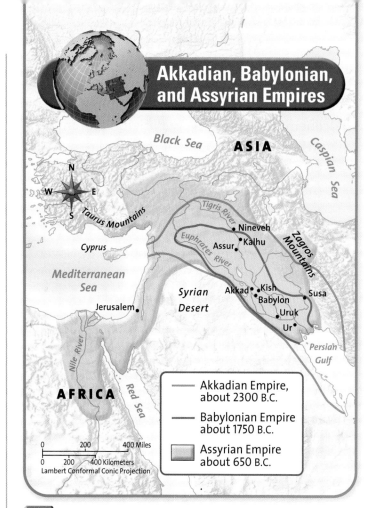

Akkadian, Babylonian, and Assyrian Empires

Akkadian Empire, about 2300 B.C.

Babylonian Empire about 1750 B.C.

Assyrian Empire about 650 B.C.

ANALYSIS SKILL Analyze Maps At its peak, the Assyrian Empire stretched more than 1,500 miles.

❖ **Regions** What geographic feature may have stopped the Assyrians from expanding southward?

The Assyrians were great innovators. Assyrian kings united their huge empire by building the world's first system of paved roads and developing a postal system. The Assyrians were the first to make locks that opened with keys.

▶ Under the rule of Nebuchadnezzar, Babylon reached its greatest glory.

They also invented the magnifying glass and built the first libraries.

In 609 B.C., the Assyrian Empire fell to its enemies, and the New Babylonian Empire rose in its place. One of this empire's best-known rulers was **Nebuchadnezzar** (neb•uh•kuhd•NEZ•er). He is believed to have built the terraced garden known as the Hanging Gardens of Babylon. This garden is remembered as one of the Seven Wonders of the Ancient World.

READING CHECK MAIN IDEA AND DETAILS
What helped the Assyrians gain control of trade?

They had new ways of making stronger weapons

❯ Skilled chariot drivers and archers helped the Assyrians win and keep their empire.

Summary

Competition for resources gave rise to early empires in Mesopotamia. Sargon built the region's first empire, the Akkadian Empire. The Babylonian Empire grew under Hammurabi, who is remembered for his code of laws. Over time, the Kassites and the Assyrians also built empires in the region.

REVIEW

1. How did the first empires develop in Mesopotamia?

2. Use the terms **conquer** and **empire** to describe an **emperor**.

3. What were the major accomplishments of the Assyrian Empire?

CRITICAL THINKING

4. **ANALYSIS SKILL** Why do you think early empires needed a standing army?

5. **Make It Relevant** Hammurabi had laws written down and made open to the public, just as many governments do today. How is this practice important to maintaining equality and justice?

6. **Write a Classroom Code** With a group of classmates, come up with a code of classroom rules. First, make a list of rules with your group. Then, pick the five most important rules, and display them in your classroom.

7. **Focus Skill** SUMMARIZE
On a separate sheet of paper, copy and complete this graphic organizer.

Key Fact		Summary
	❯	Mesopotamia was the home of many early empires.
Key Fact		
	❯	

Hammurabi

"[The gods] called by name me, Hammurabi, the exalted prince, . . . to bring about the rule of righteousness in the land."*

Biography

Trustworthiness
Respect
Responsibility
Fairness
Caring
Patriotism

Much of what we know about Hammurabi was written by the leader himself. The words above are part of Hammurabi's introduction to his famous Code of Laws. Perhaps the best-known principle of the code is the one called "an eye for an eye." This principle means that anyone causing injury to another person would be punished with the same injury.

▶ Hammurabi's laws are carved on the base of this stela, or stone marker.

Hammurabi wrote that he was a religious man who had helped make the Babylonian Empire wealthy. He also told of his success as a warrior. However, the strongest theme in Hammurabi's writings is fairness. Hammurabi called himself "the shepherd of the oppressed and of the slaves." He said that he had "brought about the well-being of the oppressed" and mentioned that he had spared the lives of people who lived in the lands he conquered. These statements show Hammurabi's belief that all people—even the defeated and the powerless—deserve protection and justice.

Hammurabi knew that it would not be right to do everything that he had the power to do. He could have let the poor starve, denied rights to the powerless, and killed conquered people. Instead, his actions were guided by fairness.

*Hammurabi. *The Letters and Inscriptions of Hammurabi, King of Babylon, about B.C. 2200.* AMS Press, 1976.

Why Character Counts

❓ **How did Hammurabi show fairness in how he ruled?**

Bio Brief

1790 B.C.	1750 B.C.
Reign began	Reign ended

1790 B.C.
Hammurabi becomes king of Babylonian Empire

1750 B.C.
Hammurabi's rule ends with his death

GO ONLINE
Interactive Multimedia Biographies
Visit **MULTIMEDIA BIOGRAPHIES** at
www.harcourtschool.com/hss

Compare Tables

▶ WHY IT MATTERS

Using a table is a good way to **classify**, or group, items of information. When information is shown in a table, you can easily find and compare specific facts, such as figures and dates.

▶ WHAT YOU NEED TO KNOW

When you read about early empires, you learned many names, dates, and other facts. You learned when empires were founded, who their founders were, what the names of their capital cities were, and when the empires ended. This kind of information can be shown in a table to make it easier to find and compare facts about the empires.

The tables on the next page classify information about early empires. The same information is shown in both tables, but each table classifies the information in a different way. Table A lists the empires in alphabetical order. In Table B, the empires are listed according to the order in which they were founded.

▶ This wall relief shows the Assyrians laying siege to an Egyptian town.

Table A: Early Empires		
EMPIRE	**APPROXIMATE DATES OF EMPIRE**	**ACHIEVEMENTS**
Akkadian Empire	2350 B.C. – 2190 B.C.	World's first known empire
Assyrian Empire	934 B.C. – 609 B.C.	First civilization to build paved roads and libraries; developed postal system, locks, and the magnifying glass
Babylonian Empire	1830 B.C. – 1595 B.C.	Advancements in mathematics, law, and astronomy; Code of Hammurabi
New Babylonian Empire	626 B.C. – 539 B.C.	Hanging Gardens of Babylon; Tower of Babel; Gate of Ishtar

Table B: Early Empires		
APPROXIMATE DATES OF EMPIRE	**EMPIRE**	**ACHIEVEMENTS**
2350 B.C. – 2190 B.C.	Akkadian Empire	World's first known empire
1830 B.C. – 1595 B.C.	Babylonian Empire	Advancements in mathematics, law, and astronomy; Code of Hammurabi
934 B.C. – 609 B.C.	Assyrian Empire	First civilization to build paved roads and libraries; developed postal system, locks, and the magnifying glass
626 B.C. – 539 B.C.	New Babylonian Empire	Hanging Gardens of Babylon; Tower of Babel; Gate of Ishtar

▶ PRACTICE THE SKILL

ANALYSIS SKILL Use Tables A and B to answer these questions.

1. Which empire was the earliest empire? Which table did you use to find this information? Why?
2. Which empires were founded after the Babylonian Empire ended?
3. Which empire developed a postal system?
4. What are the advantages and disadvantages of using each table? Explain your answer.

▶ APPLY WHAT YOU LEARNED

Make a table that compares the early civilizations that you have learned about in this chapter. Use the Internet or other sources to find out more about these civilizations. Compare your finished table with that of a classmate.

▶ Assyrian servants bring food to a king's feast.

Chart and Graph Skills

5000 B.C.
Ubaid culture
begins in southern
Mesopotamia

Reading Social Studies
When you **summarize**, you tell a shortened version of what you have read.

Focus Skill: Summarize

Complete this graphic organizer to show that you can summarize the achievements of the Mesopotamians. A copy of this graphic organizer appears on page 34 of the Homework and Practice Book.

Mesopotamian Achievements

Key Fact
Improved irrigation and farming tools

Key Fact
Developed a writing system

Summary

California Writing Prompts

Write a Narrative Imagine that you are a reporter in ancient Sumer. A Sumerian has built the first wheeled cart. Compose a narrative story announcing this innovation. Invent details such as who built the cart and how that person expects the invention to affect people's lives.

Write a Persuasive Advertisement Imagine that you are a Mesopotamian trader. Choose one or more goods that you trade, and write a persuasive advertisement for your business. Provide details that describe the quality of your goods to help persuade people to buy them.

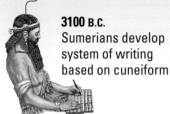

3000 B.C.

3100 B.C.
Sumerians develop system of writing based on cuneiform

1500 B.C.

1790 B.C.
Hammurabi rules the Babylonian Empire and establishes laws

B.C./A.D.

700s B.C.
Assyrians rule the largest empire in the world

Use Vocabulary

Use each term in a sentence or two to explain both what the term means and how that meaning relates to the civilizations described in this chapter.

1. **plateau** (p. 96)

2. **caravan** (p. 105)

3. **innovation** (p. 109)

4. **deity** (p. 118)

5. **empire** (p. 121)

Use the Time Line

 Use the summary time line above to answer these questions.

6. About how many years passed between the beginning of Ubaid culture and the development of Sumerian writing?

7. What happened in 1790 B.C.?

Apply Skills

Read a Land Use and Products Map

 Study the land use and products map on page 101 and answer this question.

8. What products do you think the countries of southwestern Asia sell to countries in other parts of the world?

Recall Facts

Answer these questions.

9. What achievements in technology helped people in Mesopotamia produce economic surpluses?

10. In which four major river systems did the earliest civilizations develop?

11. How did the Sumerians try to please their gods?

Write the letter of the best choice.

12. In ancient Sumer, who were part of the highest social class with the king?
    A nobles, priests, and military leaders
    B scribes and farmers
    C soldiers, merchants, and craftworkers
    D traders and slaves

13. Who ruled the world's first empire?
    A Akkad
    B Hammurabi
    C Kish
    D Sargon

Think Critically

14. **ANALYSIS SKILL** What factors do you think caused Hammurabi to put together a code of laws?

15. **ANALYSIS SKILL** How do you think the work of archaeologist Leonard Woolley changed people's interpretation of the history of southwestern Asia?

Study Skills

USE VISUALS

Visuals can help you understand and remember the information you read and may give you additional information.

➤ **Photographs, illustrations, maps, diagrams, graphs, and charts are all visuals. Many visuals have titles, captions, or labels that help readers understand what is shown.**

➤ **Visuals often show information in a different way than it appears in the text. They may also add new information that is not in the text.**

✓	**What kind of visual is used?**
	a photograph of pyramids
✓	**What does the visual show?**
	a scene in Egypt
✓	**What does the visual tell you about the subject?**
	It tells me what the pyramids look like.
	How does the visual help you better understand the subject of what you are reading?

Apply As You Read

As you read this chapter, look closely at the visuals and their captions. Answer the questions in the checklist to understand how a visual helps you as you read.

California History-Social Science Standards, Grade 6

6.2 Students analyze the geographic, political, economic, religious, and social structures of the early civilizations of Mesopotamia, Egypt, and Kush.

Egyptian Civilization

The pyramids at Giza, in present-day Egypt

THE SHIPWRECKED SAILOR:
AN EGYPTIAN TALE WITH HIEROGLYPHS

written and illustrated by Tamara Bower

The early Egyptians lived along the Nile River in northern Africa more than 5,000 years ago. One way that we know about these early people is through their writing. Unlike most people today, the ancient Egyptians used picture symbols to record their thoughts. Over time, archaeologists have been able to translate many of the ancient stories of the Egyptians. Here is an excerpt from one of them. This ancient story was written in picture writing about 4,000 years ago. The sentence highlighted below is shown on the next page as it would have been written using picture symbols.

I was sailing the Red Sea on a great ship, 120 cubits long and 40 cubits wide, bound for the gold mines of Nubia. There were 120 of the best and bravest sailors of Egypt. There wasn't a fool among them. Their hearts were fiercer than lions. The arm of each one was stronger than the next, and the heart of each one was braver. They laughed at the thought of a storm!

cubit an ancient measurement

ma 'ka	ib-sen	er	maw
fiercer	their hearts	than	lions

But suddenly, a great wind arose, and a mighty wave dashed against our ship, breaking the mast. I grabbed hold of a piece of wood, and none too soon! The ship sank, and of those in it, I was the only one to survive.

I floated until the surf cast me on an island shore. I crawled beneath some trees and fell asleep.

When I awoke, I found myself in paradise. All around me were good things to eat: ripe figs, grapes, vegetables, grain, and an abundance of fish and wildfowl. I ate until I was full.

The sailor's paradise does not last long. Soon he comes face to face with a giant serpent. Fortunately, they become friends. When it is time for the sailor to return home, the serpent presents him with gifts for the pharaoh.

Response Corner

❶ Why do you think the storyteller describes in great detail the sailors that did not survive?

❷ Draw a picture of the island and the shipwrecked sailor. Be creative, and include as many of the story's details as you can.

Time

6000 B.C.　　　3000 B.C.　　　B.C./A.D.

4000 B.C.
Farming villages exist
all along the Nile River

About 3100 B.C.
Upper Egypt and Lower
Egypt form by this time

The Nile Valley

WHAT TO KNOW
How did the Nile River
support early civilization in
ancient Egypt?

✓ Describe the location
and geography of the
Nile River.

✓ Explain how geography
affected the political,
economic, and religious
structures of the early
civilization of Egypt.

VOCABULARY
delta p. 135
cataract p. 135
arid p. 135
predict p. 137
afterlife p. 137

PLACES
Egypt
Lower Egypt
Upper Egypt
Nubia

Focus
Skill **SUMMARIZE**

**California
Standards**
HSS 6.2, 6.2.1, 6.2.2, 6.2.6

YOU ARE THERE It's late October in **Egypt** in 3500 B.C. For
months, the Nile River has been flowing over
its banks, as it does every year. Now the water level is
falling, and the land can be seen again. "After such good
flooding, there will be a plentiful harvest," your mother
says. Your father says that it's time to start planting and
asks you to get the plow and seeds. You attach the plow
to the animals and fill your sack with seeds. Your father
guides the cows so
that the plow digs
long, straight furrows
in the soft, rich soil.
You drop the seeds
into the furrows.
Another year of
farming has begun.

❱ For thousands of years, people have farmed the fertile land along the Nile
River (below). Ancient Egyptian wall paintings show farm scenes (above).

The Land of the Nile

The Nile River is the world's longest river. From east-central Africa, the Nile flows north for 4,160 miles until it empties into the Mediterranean Sea.

The ancient land once called **Lower Egypt** lies at the Nile's mouth at the Mediterranean Sea and is made up mainly of the Nile Delta. A **delta** is a triangular piece of rich land formed from soil deposited at the mouth of some rivers.

The higher land to the south was known as **Upper Egypt**. There, the narrow and fertile Nile Valley follows the Nile River for more than 600 miles. Even farther south, the Nile runs between desert cliffs in a series of six **cataracts**, or waterfalls.

The Nile River cuts across the **arid**, or dry, desert known as the Sahara. Only on the fertile lands by the Nile could early Egyptians grow crops of wheat and barley.

Heavy rains fall in the mountains at the Nile's source far to the south. This rainfall caused the river to overflow its banks. The yearly flooding deposited silt along each bank, making the soil fertile.

This physical setting supported permanent settlement. By 4000 B.C., farming villages lined the Nile River from the delta to the first cataract. To the ancient Egyptians, the Nile was "the giver of life."

READING CHECK ☼SUMMARIZE
What are the major features of the Nile River?

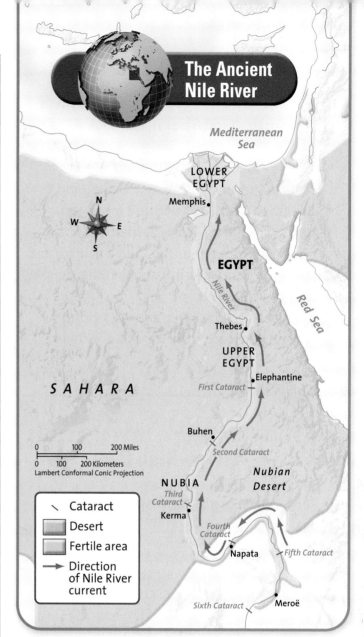

The Ancient Nile River

ANALYSIS SKILL **Analyze Maps** The Nile River flows from higher land in the south to lower land in the north.

❖ **Place** Why do you think the land in northern Egypt was called Lower Egypt?

Controlling the River

To the ancient Egyptians, the Nile was "the giver of life," but it also took life away. In some years, the rains were not heavy enough to make the Nile overflow its banks. The land baked in the sun, and the crops dried up. Without a harvest, many Egyptians starved. In other years, too much rain fell at the Nile's source, and the river flooded wildly, drowning people and destroying crops.

Over time, the Egyptians developed agricultural techniques that gave them some control of the Nile. At first, they built simple irrigation ditches to bring water to their fields. Later, they built dams and dikes to control the yearly flooding. They also learned to store water in ponds or pools for use during times when the river was low.

As the Egyptians learned to benefit more and more from the Nile, the populations of settlements along its shores increased. Irrigation became so important to the food supply in these growing communities that it was supervised by government officials. Eventually, the government began to have complete control over all farming and irrigation.

The authority of early Egyptian leaders was based on their ability to provide water for crops. Over time, they built more complex irrigation systems. In good years, large harvests produced surplus food so the rulers stored it to feed people in times of drought. They also used surplus food to feed the laborers on public works projects.

READING CHECK ⏳**SUMMARIZE**

How did ancient Egyptians control the flooding waters of the Nile?

GEOGRAPHY

Aswan High Dam

In 1970, Egypt completed the Aswan High Dam, one of the world's largest embankment dams. Embankment dams are constructed of earth and rock.

The Aswan High Dam holds back floodwater during rainy seasons and releases water during times of drought. It also generates huge amounts of electricity. Because of the dam, the Nile no longer overflows its banks to deposit rich soil. Farmers now depend on fertilizers to enrich their land. Also, the lack of new deposits of silt has caused land along the Nile to erode.

The lake formed by the dam would have covered ancient temples and settlements. So, in the 1960s, an international team of workers cut apart the temples and moved them to higher ground, where they were reassembled.

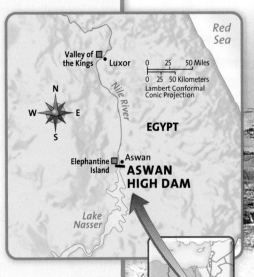

Red Sea

Valley of the Kings ■• Luxor

0 25 50 Miles
0 25 50 Kilometers
Lambert Conformal Conic Projection

N W E S

EGYPT

Elephantine Island ■• Aswan
ASWAN HIGH DAM

Lake Nasser

▶ **Visitors to the Aswan High Dam can view Lake Nasser, the artificial lake created by the dam.**

❯ These ancient paintings show a queen holding the hand of the goddess of life, Isis (left), the sky-god Horus (above), and Osiris, god of the next world (right).

A Source of Religion

Even though the Egyptians learned to control the Nile with irrigation systems, they could not always **predict**, or tell in advance, what each year's flooding would be like. They nervously wondered if the Nile's water would be too low or too high. The Egyptians also could not predict exactly when the floods would come. In some years, the floods arrived early, but in others the floods arrived late.

The flooding of the Nile influenced the early Egyptians' religious beliefs. To find order in the world around them, the Egyptians created stories to explain events in nature. In these stories, gods or goddesses controlled a specific part of nature. From these stories, the Egyptians developed beliefs in many gods and goddesses. In this way, like the Sumerians, the early Egyptians formed a polytheistic religion.

One of the Egyptians' most important gods was the sun god, Ra (RAH), also pronounced Re (RAY). Early Egyptians noticed that the sun's position is predictable. Every day, the Egyptians saw the sun rise, move across the sky, and set. They believed that the sun was a god who was born each day and died each night. This cycle led the Egyptians to believe that their own lives would continue in an **afterlife**, or a life after death. Belief in the afterlife became an important part of early Egyptian culture.

Another important god was Hapi, god of the flood. The Egyptians held many festivals to honor Hapi, hoping he would reward them with good harvests. Other important gods included Horus, the sky god, and Osiris, the god of the next world.

Each Egyptian city had one or more special gods or goddesses. As a city gained strength, its god became more important. For example, when the city of Thebes grew powerful, belief in the city's god, Amon, spread. The Egyptians combined Amon and Ra, considering Amon-Ra their most powerful god.

READING CHECK ⊙ SUMMARIZE
How did the unpredictability of the Nile's floods affect early Egyptians' religious beliefs?

Toward Civilization

By 3100 B.C., the early Egyptians were developing an advanced civilization in towns along the Nile. They built temples as places to worship their gods and stone tombs to hold the bodies of rulers who had died. Early writing appears on these temples and tombs. The Egyptians made pottery on which they painted scenes from their lives. They mined copper for tool-making and gold for decorative art.

Farming along the Nile made all these advances possible. In the fertile soils of the Nile Delta and the Nile Valley, farmers grew surplus crops of wheat and barley. They used donkeys to carry grain to storehouses in towns, where scribes recorded it and rulers distributed it. The Egyptians ground the wheat into flour for making bread, the main part of their diet.

Having a surplus of grain allowed farmers in some towns to use the surplus grain for trade. The Sinai Peninsula was a crossroads for the early Egyptians and traders from southwestern Asia.

Trade also took place on the Nile River. The Nile served as a highway connecting Egyptian settlements. To use this "highway," the Egyptians became expert ship-builders. At first, the Egyptians built their boats from bundles of reeds. Later, they made large sailing ships out of wood from what is now Lebanon.

Sails did more than just increase traveling speed. They also made it possible for ships to sail upstream against the river's current. This meant that nearly all the Nile,

ANALYSIS SKILL **Analyze Time Lines** **The early Egyptians made many advances in technology to improve their ways of farming.**

❖ **How are the events that are shown related to one another?**

Early Egypt

6000 B.C.　　　　**4500 B.C.**　　　　**3000 B.C.**

6000 B.C.
Early people begin farming on the Nile Delta

3350 B.C.
The invention of sail improves travel on the Nile

3100 B.C.
Egypt is made up of two kingdoms— Upper Egypt and Lower Egypt

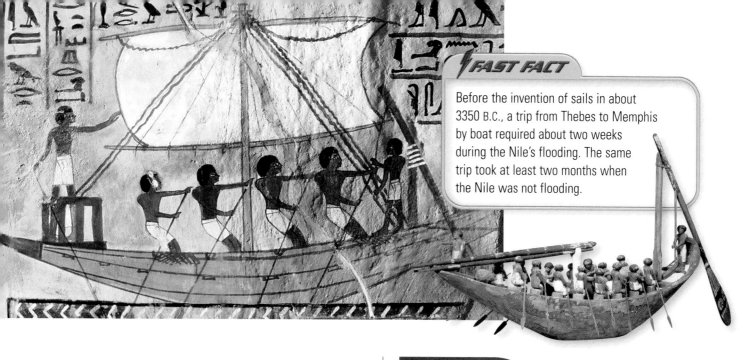

FAST FACT

Before the invention of sails in about 3350 B.C., a trip from Thebes to Memphis by boat required about two weeks during the Nile's flooding. The same trip took at least two months when the Nile was not flooding.

except for the cataracts in **Nubia**, could be used for travel and trade.

Trade and travel along the Nile made it possible for some towns to grow into cities. Then some of these trade centers emerged as separate cultures and powers. By 3100 B.C., Egypt consisted of two kingdoms—Upper Egypt and Lower Egypt.

READING CHECK **CAUSE AND EFFECT**
How did trade along the Nile support the growth of Egypt?

Summary

The physical setting of the Nile River supported permanent settlements and an early civilization in ancient Egypt. The Egyptians developed agricultural techniques, such as irrigation, along the Nile River. It was these techniques that permitted the Egyptians to grow surplus food. Over time, Egyptian trade in surpluses allowed the growth of cities.

REVIEW

1. How did the Nile River support early civilization in ancient Egypt?

2. Describe ancient Egypt's major river, using the words **delta** and **cataract**.

3. How did Egypt's location make it an ideal center for trade?

4. What agricultural items were some Egyptian towns able to trade?

CRITICAL THINKING

5. Why do you think the Egyptians believed in gods and goddesses?

6. **ANALYSIS SKILL** What were some of the most important advances in Egypt that allowed the early farming villages along the Nile to grow into an advanced civilization?

7. **Write a Narrative** The ancient Egyptians told stories to explain events in nature. Think of an event in nature, and write a story to explain it.

8. **Focus Skill** **SUMMARIZE**
On a separate sheet of paper, copy and complete the graphic organizer below.

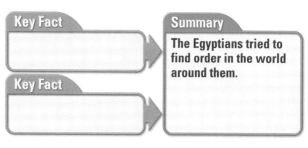

Key Fact		Summary
	→	The Egyptians tried to find order in the world around them.
Key Fact	→	

Compare Map Projections

❱ WHY IT MATTERS

Egyptian cartographers, or mapmakers, drew maps of ancient Egypt. Since then, cartographers have found different ways to show the round Earth on a flat map. These different views are called **projections**.

To draw maps, cartographers must change Earth's shape by splitting or stretching it. Because of this, every map projection has **distortions**, or parts that are not accurate. Some map projections distort the shape or the size of the area shown. One way that cartographers classify map projections is by the features that are distorted the least. By learning about these distortions, you will understand how different map projections can best be used.

❱ WHAT YOU NEED TO KNOW

Maps A and B show the same area. Map A shows an equal area on either side of the prime meridian and on either side of the equator. This is an **equal-area projection**. The sizes of regions are correct in relation to one another, but the shapes are distorted.

Map B is a **conformal projection**. It shows directions correctly but distorts the sizes of places. On a conformal projection, the lines of longitude are all an equal distance apart. On a globe, the lines get closer together near the poles. On a conformal projection, the lines of latitude get farther apart near the poles. On a globe, they are an equal distance apart.

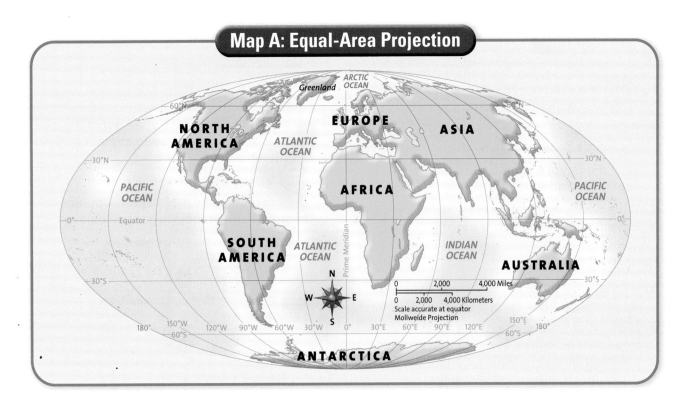

Map A: Equal-Area Projection

Map B: Conformal Projection

ARCTIC OCEAN

Greenland

ARCTIC OCEAN

NORTH AMERICA

ATLANTIC OCEAN

EUROPE

ASIA

AFRICA

PACIFIC OCEAN

SOUTH AMERICA

PACIFIC OCEAN

INDIAN OCEAN

AUSTRALIA

ATLANTIC OCEAN

0   2,000   4,000 Miles
0   2,000   4,000 Kilometers
Scale accurate at equator
Mercator Projection

ANTARCTICA

Prime Meridian

Equator

N W E S

Map and Globe Skills

▶ PRACTICE THE SKILL

Use the maps to answer the following questions.

1 Africa is really much larger than Greenland. Which projection shows Greenland's size more accurately?

2 The greatest east-west distance in Africa is about the same as the greatest north-south distance. Which projection shows Africa's shape more accurately, Map A or Map B?

▶ APPLY WHAT YOU LEARNED

Write a paragraph about the advantages and disadvantages of using an equal-area projection map and a conformal projection map.

Practice your map and globe skills with the **GeoSkills CD-ROM**.

Time

6000 B.C.	3000 B.C.	B.C./A.D.

About 3100 B.C.
King Narmer unites
Upper and Lower Egypt

About 3100 B.C.
Egyptians invent
hieroglyphs

About 2566 B.C.
The Great Pyramid
is completed

WHAT TO KNOW
How was ancient Egypt's religion related to its society and its government?

✓ Explain ancient Egypt's political structure.

✓ Describe the earliest uses of Egyptian writing.

✓ Describe early Egyptian architecture.

VOCABULARY
diplomacy p. 143
nation-state p. 143
dynasty p. 143
vizier p. 143
hieroglyph p. 144
papyrus p. 144
pyramid p. 145
mummy p. 146

PEOPLE
Narmer
Zoser
Khufu
Khafre

PLACES
Giza
Upper Egypt
Lower Egypt
Memphis

SUMMARIZE

California
Standards
HSS 6.2, 6.2.3, 6.2.5, 6.2.9

The Old Kingdom

YOU ARE THERE You're visiting the Egyptian city of **Giza** in 2510 B.C. Gazing out into the desert, you stare in awe at the gigantic rock carving rising from the sands. It has the body of a lion and the head of a man.

For years, you have heard of this wonder—the great monument called the Sphinx. Work on this project was begun before you were born. Even now, long lines of workers are hauling huge blocks of stone on a series of rollers to the construction site. Nearby stand three huge tombs of Egyptian kings.

You pass along a street of artisans. The air rings with the sound of chisels striking stone. Many sculptures are needed to prepare the tombs of kings for a royal afterlife.

▶ The Great Sphinx of Egypt still stands after being carved more than 4,000 years ago.

The Crowns of Early Egypt

Upper

Lower

Unified

ANALYSIS SKILL **Analyze Illustrations** The double crown of unified Egypt was formed by placing the crown of Upper Egypt inside the crown of Lower Egypt.

❓ Why do you think the crowns of Upper and Lower Egypt were combined?

Egypt Unites

Between 3500 B.C. and 3100 B.C., **Upper Egypt** grew in wealth and power. The kingdom traded goods and conducted **diplomacy**, or relations between countries, with **Lower Egypt**. However, the Upper Egyptians wanted to control all Egypt.

About 3100 B.C., King **Narmer** of Upper Egypt, who some experts believe was the legendary King Menes (MEE•neez), had conquered Lower Egypt. He united the Two Lands and built the city of **Memphis** as the new capital.

Egypt's union established the world's first **nation-state**, a region with a united people and a single government. King Narmer's rule marks Egypt's first dynasty, or Dynasty 1. A **dynasty** is a series of rulers from the same family. About 31 dynasties ruled Egypt over more than 3,000 years. Historians divide Egypt's dynasties into three periods: the Old Kingdom, the Middle Kingdom, and the New Kingdom.

The Egyptians considered the kings of the Old Kingdom to be living gods, acting as the connection between the gods and the people of Egypt. The people believed that kings could never be wrong and were able to control the Nile's flooding and the food supply. These beliefs not only helped unify the Egyptian people but also allowed the kings to maintain their authority.

The king owned all the land and so controlled both the economy and government. The **vizier** (vuh•ZIR), or chief adviser, carried out the king's orders. Other officials collected taxes, planned building projects, and made sure the laws were obeyed.

Members of the royal family held the highest public offices. Beginning in Dynasty 5, many helped the king rule by acting as nomarchs, or governors, who ruled administrative areas called nomes. Ancient Egypt was divided into 42 nomes.

READING CHECK ⊙**SUMMARIZE**
How did the belief that the kings were living gods help the kings maintain their authority?

Egyptian Hieroglyphs

HIEROGLYPH	ENGLISH WORD	HIEROGLYPH	ENGLISH WORD
	Female		Male
	Life		Live
	Water		Mouth
	See		Eyes
	You		Peace

Analyze Tables The ancient Egyptians used many different hieroglyphs for their written records. Above are just a few, along with their meanings.

◆ Which symbols do you think most clearly show what they mean?

Written Forms of Language

About 3100 B.C., the Egyptians developed a writing system that used **hieroglyphs** (HY•ruh•glifs), or picture symbols. The Egyptians may have borrowed the idea of writing from the Sumerians.

Early Egyptian hieroglyphic writing had more than 700 symbols. Each glyph represented a sound, an object, or an idea.

At first, the Egyptians used hieroglyphs mostly for religious purposes. In fact, *hieroglyphic* means "holy carving." Scribes carved hieroglyphs on the stone walls of temples, tombs, and palaces. Later, scribes began to record government information, such as royal ceremonies, tax collecting, and even the depth of the Nile.

To keep more and more records, the Egyptians invented a paperlike material called **papyrus** (puh•PY•ruhs). To make papyrus, the Egyptians pressed together strips from the stalk of the papyrus plant, a reed that grows in marshy areas. Scribes wrote on papyrus with tools made from reeds sharpened to a point. Soot—the fine, black powder from smoke—was mixed with water to serve as ink.

For the Egyptians, a "book" was a scroll, a roll of papyrus sheets joined end to end. Some scrolls were more than 100 feet long.

READING CHECK ☼SUMMARIZE
For what purpose were hieroglyphs first used?

Building the Pyramids

The Old Kingdom is known as the Age of Pyramids. During this 500-year period, the Egyptians developed the technology to build the largest stone structures in the world—the **pyramids**. These structures served as tombs for Egyptian rulers.

In the 2600s B.C., King **Zoser** of Dynasty 3 became the first king to be buried in a stone pyramid. This was the famous Step Pyramid at Saqqara (suh•KAR•uh), named for its steplike sides.

No one knows exactly why Egyptian kings began building pyramids, but these structures symbolize many ideas. For example, the pyramid shape is identified with the sun god, Ra.

The best known of Egypt's pyramids is the Great Pyramid at Giza. It was built for King **Khufu** of Dynasty 4 and completed about 2566 B.C. Originally 480 feet high, it is made up of more than 2.3 million stone blocks. Each block averages about 2.5 tons! King Khufu's son, King **Khafre**, ordered the building of one of the other two pyramids at Giza as well as the Sphinx.

The pyramids help us understand the relationship between religion and the social and political order in early Egyptian society. As godlike rulers, the kings were able to use huge amounts of Egypt's resources and the whole society to build pyramids. Farmers may have worked on pyramids during periods of Nile flooding. It is likely that female workers were responsible for feeding and clothing the pyramid builders.

READING CHECK   ⚙SUMMARIZE

How do the pyramids show the relationships between religion and society in Egypt?

A Closer Look

The Pyramids at Giza

Analyze Diagrams The illustration shows what the area of Giza might have looked like at the time of the Old Kingdom.

❶ Sparkling pyramids made of stone and covered with white limestone tower over the city.

❷ The Sphinx, half man and half lion, seems to crouch in the distance.

❸ The nearby workers' village itself bustled with the activity of craftworkers and others who lived there.

◆ Why do you think a workers' village was built near the pyramids?

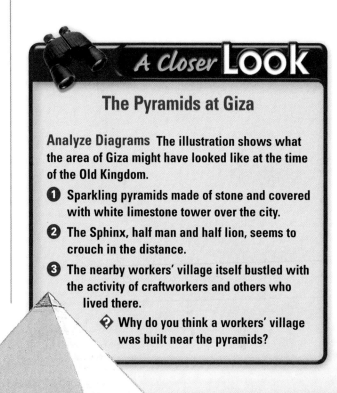

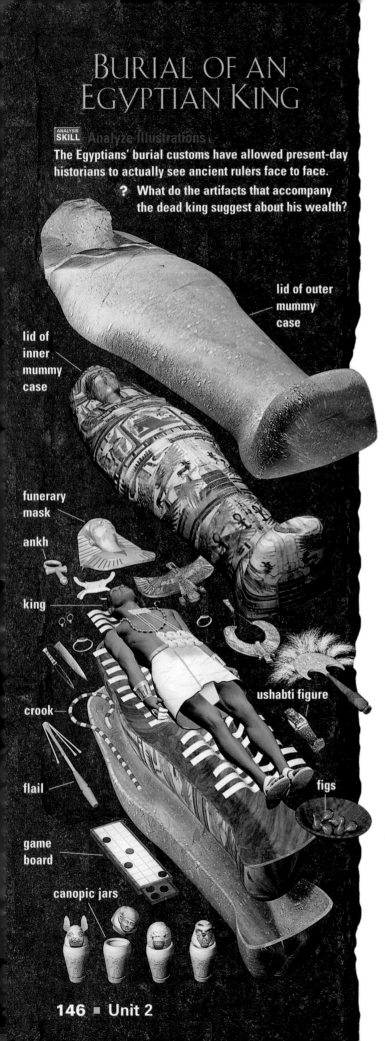

BURIAL OF AN EGYPTIAN KING

ANALYSIS SKILL Analyze Illustrations

The Egyptians' burial customs have allowed present-day historians to actually see ancient rulers face to face.

? What do the artifacts that accompany the dead king suggest about his wealth?

lid of outer mummy case

lid of inner mummy case

funerary mask

ankh

king

crook

flail

ushabti figure

figs

game board

canopic jars

Preparing for the Afterlife

One of the Egyptians' strongest religious beliefs was that there was an afterlife. Believing that the dead would need their bodies in the afterlife, the Egyptians developed ways to preserve bodies. By 2500 B.C., Egyptian priests had invented new techniques for making a **mummy**, or preserved body. They began by removing all the body organs except the heart. They placed these organs in special jars. The heart remained in the body because the Egyptians believed that the heart was the home of the soul.

The body was then dried using a salt called natron, and the body was wrapped in linen bandages. Then the royal mummies were placed in their tombs. Everything a royal person might need in the afterlife, such as clothing, jewelry, furniture, and even games, was placed in the tomb.

Later, during the time of the New Kingdom, priests placed a collection of writings, known as the *Book of the Dead*, in the tombs. It was not until after the discovery of the Rosetta Stone in A.D. 1799 that scholars could decipher hieroglyphs and read Egyptian writings such as the *Book of the Dead*.

One of the most important writings in the *Book of the Dead* explains the "weighing of the heart." The Egyptians believed that the soul of a dead person appeared before the god Osiris and a group of judges. The judges placed the dead person's heart on one side of a scale and a feather, the symbol of truth, on the other side. If the two balanced, the soul earned life forever. The judges would say, "I have judged the heart of [the dead person], and his soul stands as a witness for him. His deeds are

PRIMARY SOURCES

The Rosetta Stone

ANALYSIS SKILL **Analyze Artifacts**

Discovered in A.D. 1799, the Rosetta Stone helped scientists decode hieroglyphs. Carved in the stone's surface were three kinds of writing. In A.D. 1822, Jean-Francois Champollion decoded the hieroglyphs, using the other forms of writing as a guide.

1 This Egyptian writing uses hieroglyphs.

2 This Egyptian writing, called demotic writing, was the cursive form used when writing on papyrus.

3 This writing is ancient Greek, the language of the rulers of Egypt at the time of the carving of the stone.

◈ Why do you think decoding hieroglyphs was important?

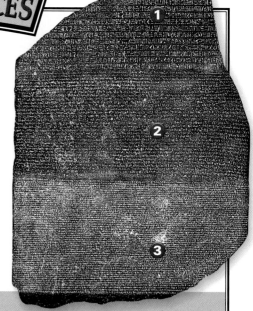

righteous in the great balance, and no sin has been found in him."* Heavy souls, the Egyptians believed, would be eaten by a monster that was part crocodile, part lion, and part hippopotamus.

READING CHECK ⏾**SUMMARIZE**
Why did the Egyptians want to preserve bodies?

*E.A. Wallis Budge. *The Book of the Dead: The Papyrus of Ani in the British Museum.* Dover Publications, 1967.

Summary

The belief that Egyptian kings were living gods helped them maintain their authority. The kings ordered pyramids built as their burial places. The Egyptians came to believe that all people could enter the afterlife.

REVIEW

1. How was ancient Egypt's religion related to its society and its government?

2. Use the term **papyrus** in a sentence about Egyptian **hieroglyphs**.

3. What was the role of the vizier in the Egyptian nation-state?

4. How did the Egyptians use their pyramids?

CRITICAL THINKING

5. **ANALYSIS SKILL** Why do you think the Egyptians developed hieroglyphs at about the same time the Mesopotamians developed their writing system?

6. **Make It Relevant** What is the relationship between religion and government in the United States today?

7. **Create Hieroglyphs** On a sheet of paper, draw your own hieroglyphs. Write the English word for the idea, sound, or object shown by each hieroglyph. On the same sheet of paper, write a sentence using your hieroglyphs.

8. (Focus Skill) **SUMMARIZE**
On a separate sheet of paper, copy and complete the graphic organizer below.

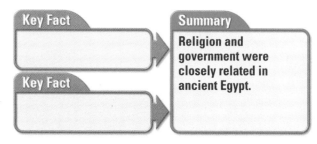

Key Fact	Summary
	Religion and government were closely related in ancient Egypt.
Key Fact	

Points of View

Why Were the Pyramids Built?

The mysteries of the Egyptian pyramids include several unanswered questions. Why were the pyramids built? Why would kings undertake such long and costly projects? Why would people work for so many years to build such huge structures? Experts in Egyptian history have different ideas about why the pyramids were built. Here are some points of view on the subject.

▶ This illustration shows workers who helped build the pyramids.

In Their Own Words

Herodotus, a Greek historian, who visited Egypt and the pyramids in about 450 B.C.

❝These chambers, King Cheops [Khufu] made as burial chambers for himself. . . .❞

— from *The History* by Herodotus. David Grene, trans. University of Chicago Press, 1987.

HERODOTUS

Allen Winston, a writer who specializes in ancient Egypt

❝While the pyramids built in Egypt seem to be all funerary [for burial] in nature, to regard them as merely tombs is an oversimplification. It involved a complex [group] of buildings because it was the dead pharaoh's palace of the afterlife. . . .❞

— from the essay "The Pyramids of Ancient Egypt" by Allen Winston at *http://www.touregypt.net/featurestories/pyramids.htm*

ALLEN WINSTON

Miroslav Verner, professor at Charles University in Prague, Czech Republic, and former director of the Czech Institute of Egyptology

❝The architectural and religious development that . . . led to the royal tomb in the form of a pyramid was . . . part of the process of shaping and strengthening the oldest strongly centralized Egyptian state. In this context, the pyramid becomes more than just a royal tomb; it becomes a symbol of the ruler's historical and state-building role. . . .❞

— from *The Pyramids: The Mystery, Culture, and Science of Egypt's Great Monuments* by Miroslav Verner. Grove Press, 2001.

It's Your Turn

ANALYSIS SKILL Analyze Points of View Work with a classmate to summarize each point of view. Then discuss how all three views could be correct.

Make It Relevant What do you think people in the future might think about monuments found in the United States today?

Lesson 3

Time

6000 B.C.   3000 B.C.   B.C./A.D.

2040 B.C.
The Middle
Kingdom begins

1991 B.C.
Amenemhet
becomes king

1640 B.C.
The Hyksos conquer
Lower Egypt

The Middle Kingdom

YOU ARE THERE

The year is 1900 B.C., and you are proud to be an Egyptian. **Egypt** is united again under powerful leaders. They have defeated Egypt's enemies and built fortresses along the borders to guarantee that Egypt will never be threatened again.

Valuable goods flow into Egypt's cities from other lands. Old irrigation systems have been repaired, and new ones are being built. New temples and pyramids rise from the sands just as precious crops rise from the Nile's fertile banks.

▶ This wall painting (below) describes in hieroglyphs and pictures the first ruler of the Middle Kingdom, King Amenemhet. Above is an Egyptian craftworker.

WHAT TO KNOW

How did Egypt change during and after the Middle Kingdom?

✓ Describe the major achievements of the Middle Kingdom.

✓ Describe Egyptian trade in the eastern Mediterranean and the Nile Valley.

VOCABULARY

civil war p. 151
famine p. 151
cost-benefit analysis p. 152

PEOPLE

Neferti
Amenemhet

PLACES

Egypt
Nubia
Syria
Crete

 SUMMARIZE

 California Standards
HSS 6.2, 6.2.3, 6.2.5, 6.2.6

Reuniting the Kingdom

At the end of the Old Kingdom, in about 2181 B.C., Egypt fell into **civil war**, or war between two groups in the same place. At about the same time, a long drought set in. Farmland dried up and crops failed. **Famines**, or food shortages, plagued the war-torn country. No longer united by one king, Egyptian nobles fought one another for power. A scribe named **Neferti** described these troubled times:

> **❝One can cross the water [Nile] on foot. . . . The land is in sickness. . . . One will take up weapons of warfare . . . a son as an enemy, a brother as a foe. ❞***

Egypt reunited in about 2040 B.C. That year marks the beginning of the Middle Kingdom, a time of stability and growth that lasted until about 1786 B.C.

The rule of Dynasty 12 is considered the high point of this period. The dynasty started in about 1991 B.C., when a vizier named **Amenemhet** (AH•muhn•em•het) from Lower Egypt became king. He and those who ruled after him conquered all of northern **Nubia**. They set up a chain of forts to protect the region. Along their northeastern border, the Egyptians built the Walls of the Prince, a series of forts, to protect the Nile Delta.

The rulers of Dynasty 12 undertook massive building projects. To help secure water for food crops, they built more irrigation canals. To honor the dead, they built temples and pyramids. They also built an elaborate temple now known as Labyrinth that was said to have had 3,000 rooms connected by a maze of hallways.

*Neferti from *The Protocol of Neferyt (The Prophecy of Neferti)* translated by Hans Goedicken. Johns Hopkins University Press, 1977.

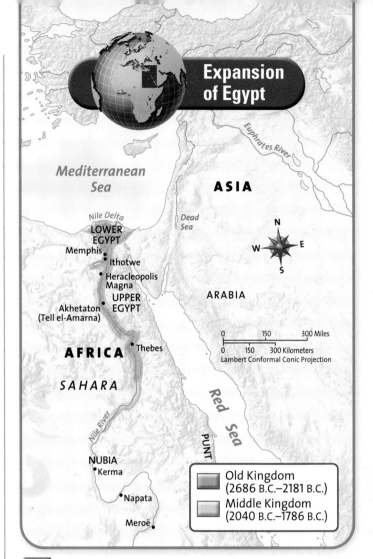

Expansion of Egypt

ANALYSIS SKILL **Analyze Maps** This map shows the borders of Egypt during the Old Kingdom and the Middle Kingdom.

❖ **Human–Environment Interactions** How may improved ways of agriculture have affected the growth of Egypt?

The Middle Kingdom was also a time of advances in art and literature. Egyptian artists revived the wall-painting style of the Old Kingdom and began crafting the finest jewelry ever made in Egypt. Writers of the time produced Egypt's earliest literature.

Middle Kingdom literature included not only religious writings but also writings about everyday life. For example, Middle Kingdom writers provided guidelines for living in society.

READING CHECK ⟳**SUMMARIZE**
What achievements were made during the Middle Kingdom?

Trade

Trade with other regions increased during the Middle Kingdom. Caravans and ships carried goods between Egypt and parts of southwestern Asia, eastern Africa, and the eastern Mediterranean region.

Egypt had plenty of resources of its own to trade, especially grains. It also was rich in valuable minerals and semiprecious stones. However, Egypt lacked some important resources, such as wood for building and copper for metalworking.

Caravans brought silver from **Syria** and copper and turquoise from the Sinai Peninsula. Ships sailing from what is now Lebanon brought cedar and pinewood. Gold, ebony, ivory, and incense came to Egypt through trade with southern Nubia.

Whether by land or by sea, trade could be difficult and dangerous. Caravans moved slowly along desert routes, traveling only about 10 miles a day. Overland traders often faced robbers and sandstorms on their long journeys. Trade by sea was faster, but pirates were a danger. Sea traders also had to brave strong winds and rough waves during the winter months.

Although difficult and risky, trade brought much wealth to those who could overcome its dangers. Even in ancient times, a trader needed to do a **cost-benefit analysis** to decide whether to carry out trade. In this kind of study, a person tries to determine whether the economic benefit of doing something makes it worth the risk.

READING CHECK ⧂ **SUMMARIZE**
Why did Egypt trade with other regions?

Egyptian Trade

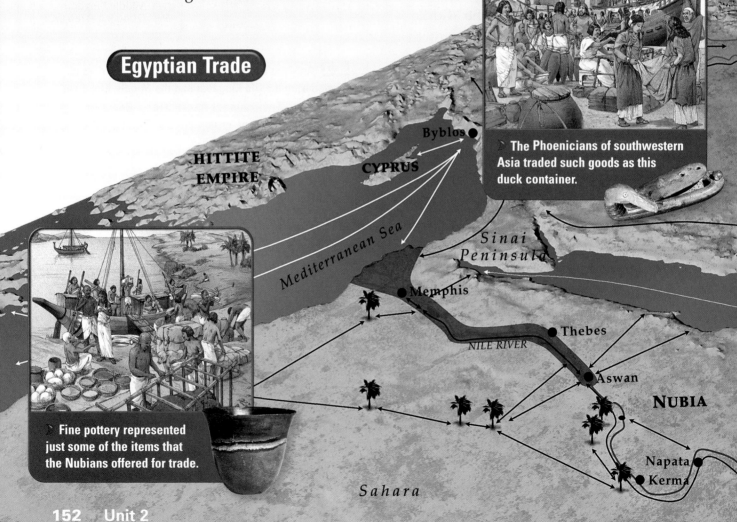

▷ The Phoenicians of southwestern Asia traded such goods as this duck container.

▷ Fine pottery represented just some of the items that the Nubians offered for trade.

HITTITE EMPIRE

CYPRUS

Byblos

Mediterranean Sea

Sinai Peninsula

Memphis

NILE RIVER

Thebes

Aswan

NUBIA

Napata

Kerma

Sahara

A Time of Invasion

After Dynasty 12, Egypt faced attacks from invaders. At first, Egypt remained united, but the government was weak. As many as 70 kings ruled during Dynasty 13.

Also at this time, large groups of people from southwestern Asia crossed into Egypt by way of the Sinai Peninsula. Over time, these people settled in the area around the northeastern Nile Delta. The Egyptians called the people the Hyksos (HIK•sohs), meaning "rulers of foreign lands." The Hyksos brought about the end of the Middle Kingdom and tore Egypt apart.

The Hyksos had superior military technology. They fought from horse-drawn chariots, wore body armor, and used a stronger kind of bow. Without armor, the Egyptian foot soldiers were no match for the Hyksos. In about 1640 B.C., the Hyksos conquered Lower Egypt.

Hyksos kings ruled Lower Egypt for about 100 years and established Dynasty 15. Egyptian rulers remained in power only in Upper Egypt.

The time of the Hyksos brought important cultural exchanges in Egypt. Besides superior weapons, the Hyksos introduced horses, upright looms, and new musical instruments—the lyre and the lute.

▷ Vases like this were traded by people living in Mesopotamia.

Babylon

Arabian Desert

Analyze Illustrations This physical map shows the part of Earth where the continents of Africa, Europe, and Asia meet. The water on the far left part of the map is the Mediterranean Sea. Flowing into the Mediterranean is the winding Nile River. Long ago, the ancient Egyptians used both water and land routes to trade with other peoples.

❓ Why do you think Egyptian traders used both water and land routes?

YEMEN

Red Sea

SHEBA

	MIDDLE KINGDOM OF EGYPT
🌴	OASIS
●	CITY
→	LAND TRADE ROUTE
⇒	WATER TRADE ROUTE

PUNT

N E S W

● Meroë

▶ In this Egyptian painting, an enemy, possibly the Hyksos, attacks from atop a horse-drawn war chariot. The painting was originally part of an ancient chest. The painting clearly shows the advantages of using chariots in war.

In turn, the Hyksos learned hieroglyphs and began to worship Egyptian gods.

Under the Hyksos, Egypt changed in other important ways. The Hyksos greatly expanded trade routes as far as **Crete**, now a Greek island.

In the mid-1500s B.C., Egyptian rulers in the south declared war on the Hyksos kings. The Egyptians regained power and drove the Hyksos into southwestern Asia.

READING CHECK ⏺**SUMMARIZE**
How were the Hyksos able to conquer Lower Egypt?

Summary

In 2040 B.C., strong leaders reunited Egypt, beginning the Middle Kingdom. Dynasty 12 kings, who ruled for much of the Middle Kingdom, oversaw the expansion of land and trade as well as the construction of many building projects. During the Middle Kingdom, artists and writers produced Egypt's finest jewelry and earliest literature. In time, Egypt fell to the Hyksos, ending the Middle Kingdom.

REVIEW

1. 💡 How did Egypt change during and after the Middle Kingdom?

2. Use the term **civil war** to describe life in ancient Egypt before the Middle Kingdom.

3. What area did the ancient Egyptians conquer during the Middle Kingdom?

4. What other regions did Egypt trade with during the Middle Kingdom?

CRITICAL THINKING

5. 🟦**SKILL** **Make It Relevant** In what ways might you perform a cost-benefit analysis in your daily life?

6. 🟦**SKILL** What do you think the Egyptians might have learned from the Hyksos that later would have helped them drive the Hyksos out of Egypt?

7. 🖌 **Make a Table** Make a table that compares the achievements of the different Egyptian dynasties that you have learned about in this lesson. Use library or Internet resources to learn more about them.

8. (Focus Skill) **SUMMARIZE**
On a separate sheet of paper, copy and complete the graphic organizer below.

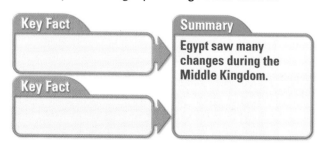

Key Fact		Summary
	→	Egypt saw many changes during the Middle Kingdom.
Key Fact		
	→	

Hatshepsut

"Her majesty grew beyond everything...."[*]

Hatshepsut is considered one of the greatest rulers in the history of Egypt. Many men ruled in ancient Egypt, but Hatshepsut was one of the very few women to gain the title of pharaoh.

Born in about 1504 B.C. to King Thutmose I and Queen Ahmose, Hatshepsut learned how to read and write hieroglyphs from a royal scribe. When Hatshepsut's husband, King Thutmose II, died unexpectedly in about 1479 B.C., the next person in line to be pharaoh was Hatshepsut's stepson, Thutmose III. Thutmose III, however, was considered too young to serve as ruler, so Hatshepsut ruled for a while as the boy's regent, or acting ruler. Eventually, Hatshepsut took the title of pharaoh herself.

Being pharaoh was a responsibility Hatshepsut took very seriously. In addition to expanding Egypt's borders, Hatshepsut sent expeditions to other countries. This brought much trade to Egypt. Hatshepsut also restored many old temples, where statues were built in her likeness. Some of the pieces in these temples show Hatshepsut wearing the traditional royal robes of pharaohs. Some of the statues and sphinxes even show Hatshepsut with a beard, which was a standard feature of male pharaohs before her rule. Historians have suggested that she may have posed as a man during her reign.

Hatshepsut ruled for a longer time than any other female pharaoh. During her years in power, she maintained peace and stability in Egypt. Her life following her rule remains a mystery.

*Ancient Records of Egypt. Edited and translated by James Henry Breasted, Russel & Russel, 1962.

Biography

Trustworthiness

Respect

Responsibility

Fairness

Caring

Patriotism

Why Character Counts

? How did Hatshepsut show her responsibility as a pharaoh?

Bio Brief

1504 B.C.				1455 B.C.
Born				Died

1479 B.C.
Thutmose II dies, Hatshepsut becomes regent

1473 B.C.
Hatshepsut claims the title of pharaoh

1458 B.C.
Hatshepsut disappears and Thutmose III reclaims the title of pharaoh

GO ONLINE
Interactive Multimedia Biographies
Visit **MULTIMEDIA BIOGRAPHIES** at
www.harcourtschool.com/hss

Critical Thinking Skills

Distinguish Importance of Information

▶ WHY IT MATTERS

You cannot always remember everything you read. However, there are ways to determine what you really need to know from your reading. Learning how to distinguish important information from less important information will help you organize your studying.

▶ WHAT YOU NEED TO KNOW

One way to analyze the importance of information is to identify relevant from irrelevant information. **Relevant** information is directly related to the subject you are reading. **Irrelevant** information is unrelated to the subject.

You also need to be able to tell essential information from incidental information. **Essential** information is needed to understand a subject fully. **Incidental** information does not affect your knowledge of a subject.

Finally, you need to know the difference between verifiable and unverifiable information. **Verifiable** information can be proved while **unverifiable** information cannot be proved.

To determine the importance of information, ask yourself the questions shown in the flow chart below. If you can answer yes to any or all these questions, then you know to remember the information.

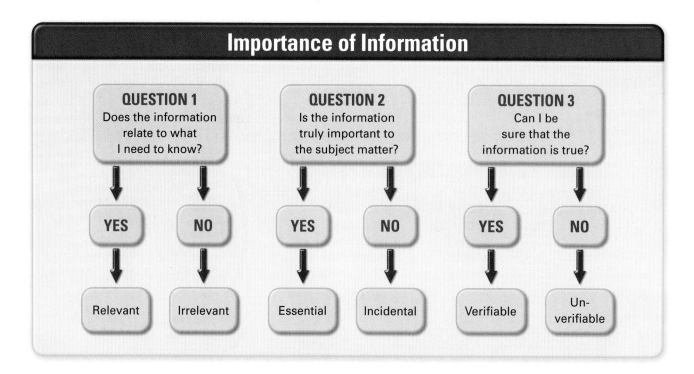

Importance of Information

QUESTION 1	QUESTION 2	QUESTION 3
Does the information relate to what I need to know?	Is the information truly important to the subject matter?	Can I be sure that the information is true?
YES ↓ / NO ↓	YES ↓ / NO ↓	YES ↓ / NO ↓
Relevant / Irrelevant	Essential / Incidental	Verifiable / Un-verifiable

▶ This painted, etched tablet (above) shows Egyptian officials under the command of Senwosret (right).

▶ PRACTICE THE SKILL

ANALYSIS SKILL The passage below describes an important time in the life of Senwosret I, the son of Amenemhet I. Read the passage carefully. Then determine which information is the most important for you to remember.

Senwosret was away from home on duty in the Egyptian army. He was a brave soldier, never showing fear or retreating. He was also very handsome. One day, while preparing for a long journey, he was summoned. A messenger had come to share with Senwosret news from home: his father had been killed. Senwosret was filled with grief and rushed home to claim the land that was rightfully his.

① The sentence "Senwosret was away from home on duty in the Egyptian army" is a relevant piece of information. Which sentence is irrelevant? Why?

② Which of the following sentences contains the most essential piece of information?

  A "A messenger had come to share with Senwosret news from home: his father had been killed."

  B "He was a brave soldier, never showing fear or retreating."

▶ APPLY WHAT YOU LEARNED

ANALYSIS SKILL Use information in encyclopedias or other sources to determine what information about Senwosret I in the passage is verifiable or unverifiable.

Lesson 4

Time

| 6000 B.C. | 3000 B.C. | B.C./A.D. |

1552 B.C.
The New Kingdom begins

1364 B.C.
Amenhotep IV becomes pharaoh

1280 B.C.
Ramses II becomes pharaoh

The New Kingdom

YOU ARE THERE It's the year 1360 B.C., and a new king has recently come to the throne. He is different from the kings of the past. He and his wife don't believe in the ancient Egyptian gods. They say there's only one god, the Aton, and they've commanded the people to stop worshipping the other gods.

People are in an uproar! You hear some say that the king just wants to take power from the priests who serve the other gods. One thing is certain—this king and his wife are bringing change to the land. You wonder if this change will be good or bad for Egypt.

The ruins of the ancient temple of Karnak remain an amazing sight for visitors to Luxor, Egypt.

WHAT TO KNOW
What achievements did the ancient Egyptians make during the New Kingdom?

✓ Explain how religion and government changed during the New Kingdom.

✓ Describe the structure of ancient Egyptian society.

✓ State the importance of Queen Hatshepsut and Ramses the Great.

✓ Identify the features of Egyptian art and architecture.

VOCABULARY
pharaoh p. 159
reign p. 159
rural p. 161

PEOPLE
Hatshepsut
Thutmose III
Amenhotep IV
Nefertiti
Akhenaton
Tutankhamen
Ramses the Great

PLACES
Nubia
Akhetaten

SUMMARIZE

California Standards
HSS 6.2, 6.2.3, 6.2.5, 6.2.7, 6.2.8

158 ▪ Unit 2

Children IN HISTORY

Egyptian Children

In ancient Egypt, children were considered to be gifts of the gods. In Egyptian art, children are usually shown with their parents or playing games. Archaeologists digging in Egypt have found the remains of toy animals carved out of ivory or wood, toy boats, clay dolls, spinning tops, and balls made of leather skins filled with dry papyrus stalks or rags. Egyptians of all ages loved board games. Zenet, played on a 30-square board, was the most popular. Egyptian children also enjoyed wrestling, leapfrog, tug-of-war, and a game similar to hockey.

Make It Relevant How were ancient Egyptian games and toys similar to and different from those of today?

Kings of the Great House

The New Kingdom began in 1552 B.C. with the rule of Dynasty 18. During this time, Egyptian kings took the title of **pharaoh** (FAIR•oh), meaning "great house." In earlier times, the word referred to the king's magnificent palace. Now it referred to the kings themselves. The power of the pharaohs was based in large part on gold. The Egyptians believed that the flesh of their gods was made of gold.

Egypt's first full-time army began during the New Kingdom. Under Dynasty 18, Egypt sent troops as far north as the Euphrates River. Egypt also conquered parts of **Nubia**, a land rich in gold. The pharaohs placed part of Nubia—also called Kush—under the rule of an Egyptian official.

Queen **Hatshepsut** (hat•SHEP•soot) was one of the few women to rule Egypt as pharaoh. Under her **reign**, or time of rule,

Hatshepsut sent armies into Nubia and southwestern Asia. She demanded that the conquered lands pay tribute to Egypt in exchange for protection. She also sent a trading expedition south across the Red Sea. It returned with animal skins, myrrh (MUR) trees, ebony, and gold.

Hatshepsut's stepson, **Thutmose III**, followed her as pharaoh. Under his rule, the Egyptian Empire reached its greatest size. By 1450 B.C., Egypt controlled lands from the fourth cataract in Nubia all the way north to the Euphrates River in southwestern Asia.

The early years of the New Kingdom were a time of splendor. The Egyptians of this period built huge temples to the gods, larger than any before them. The temple of Amon-Ra at Karnak was the largest in all Egypt.

READING CHECK ☼SUMMARIZE
How did the pharaohs of the New Kingdom change Egypt?

A Time of Change

In 1364 B.C., **Amenhotep IV** became pharaoh. He and his wife, **Nefertiti** (neh•fer•TEE•tee), brought change to Egypt. They abandoned the worship of Amon and the other Egyptian gods. They favored a single god, the Aton, god of the sun.

Amenhotep was so devoted to the Aton that he changed his own name to **Akhenaton** (ahk•NAH•tuhn), meaning "servant of the Aton," and had the names of the other gods removed from temples and tombs. When he moved Egypt's religious capital to a new city, **Akhetaten**, he built large religious temples to the Aton.

After Akhenaton's death, the throne passed to a nine-year-old boy named Tutankhaton. Under pressure from his advisers, he restored the old Egyptian gods

and changed his name to **Tutankhamen** (too•tang•KAH•muhn), or "living image of Amon." At the age of 18, Tutankhamen died. He was buried in a solid-gold coffin in a tomb packed with treasure.

In about 1289 B.C., Ramses II, also known as **Ramses the Great**, came to power. During his 65-year-rule, Ramses II defended Egypt and made the kingdom prosperous. Early in his reign, he fought the Hittites. Later, he focused on building magnificent temples all over Egypt.

By about 1215 B.C., Egypt was slipping into decline. It was losing land to the Sea Peoples, invaders from Asia Minor and lands near the Mediterranean Sea. Even so, Egypt managed to stay united through the end of Dynasty 20 in about 1075 B.C.

READING CHECK ● SUMMARIZE
What was the significance of Ramses the Great to Egypt's history?

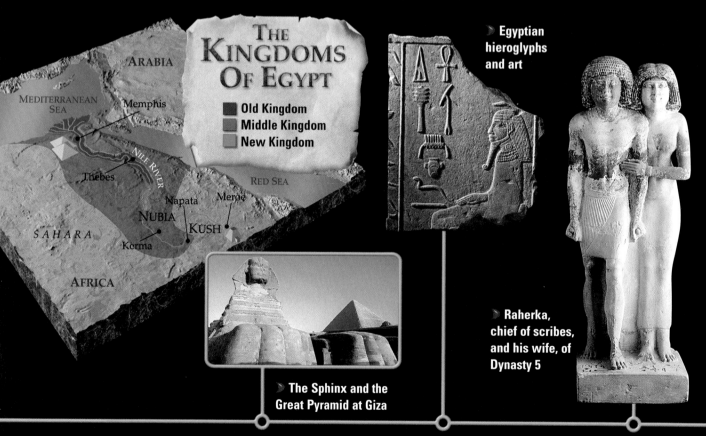

> Egyptian hieroglyphs and art

THE KINGDOMS OF EGYPT

■ Old Kingdom
■ Middle Kingdom
■ New Kingdom

ARABIA
MEDITERRANEAN SEA
Memphis
NILE RIVER
Thebes
RED SEA
Napata Meroë
NUBIA KUSH
SAHARA
Korma
AFRICA

> Raherka, chief of scribes, and his wife, of Dynasty 5

> The Sphinx and the Great Pyramid at Giza

THE OLD KINGDOM
2686 B.C.–2181 B.C.

Egyptian Society

Historians have compared the structure of ancient Egyptian society to that of a pyramid. At the top was the pharaoh. Then came royal family members, priests, and nobles. Below them were craftworkers, scribes, and merchants. Egypt's largest class came next. It included farmers and unskilled workers. At the pyramid's bottom were the slaves.

Most of Egypt's slaves had been captured in war. Unlike slaves in some societies, those in Egypt could own personal items and hold government jobs. They were also able to earn their freedom.

Most Egyptians lived in villages in rural, or country, areas. Only about 5 percent of Egyptians lived in cities.

Like in most ancient societies, men and women had very different roles in Egyptian society. Most government officials and craftworkers were men. For the most part, Egyptian women raised the children and ran households. In Egypt, women were highly respected and had more rights than women in some other ancient societies. For example, Egyptian women could own property and businesses.

Education started at an early age in Egypt. Usually, only the children of the nobles learned mathematics, literature, and writing. Most boys learned their fathers' trades. Girls learned household skills and weaving from their mothers by the age of 12.

READING CHECK MAIN IDEA AND DETAILS **Which groups of people were just below the pharaoh on the Egyptian social pyramid?**

> **Hedgehog figurine**

> **Abu Simbel, a religious site in southern Egypt**

> **Granite statue of Ramses II, Dynasty 19**

> **Chest plate in shape of scarab, or Egyptian beetle**

> **Queen Nefertiti, Dynasty 18**

THE MIDDLE KINGDOM
2040 B.C.–1786 B.C.

THE NEW KINGDOM
1552 B.C.–1069 B.C.

Egyptian Art and Architecture

Most of the monumental architecture that remains from ancient Egypt, such as pyramids, temples, and government buildings, was built of stone. However, the main material for other buildings was mud brick. The bricks were made by filling rectangular molds with mud and leaving them in the sun to dry.

Most people lived in small houses that were two or three stories high. The first floor might be a shop or business, while the upper floors provided living spaces. Some houses were built around open courtyards where people cooked, played, and relaxed. Most houses also had special areas for worshipping a favored god. In the summer, people often slept on the roof to stay cool.

▶ **New Kingdom medicine jar**

Over time, Egypt's rulers stopped building pyramids, which became too expensive to construct. Pharaohs, their families, and wealthy nobles were buried instead in tombs cut into rock walls.

Major temples, such as those at Luxor and Karnak, took a number of centuries to build. Some temple complexes even included a sacred lake. Most Egyptian temples followed a similar design. A long path lined with statues of sphinxes led up to the temple gate, which opened into a courtyard. In turn, the courtyard led to a large hall that represented the "swamp of creation." The hall was lined with stone columns crafted to look like papyrus reeds, lotus plants, or palm trees. An altar stood at the very rear of the temple.

Most Egyptian art was very formal. In sculptures and paintings, pharaohs and other important people were often shown conducting religious ceremonies or alongside gods.

⚡ **FAST FACT**

These two giant statues, known as the Colossi of Memnon, are all that remains of the Temple of Amenhotep III that once stood at Luxor.

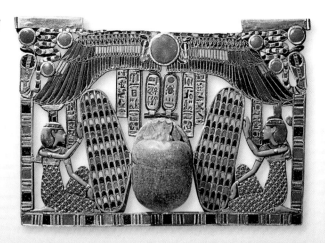

▶ This painted metal was valued for both its beauty and its religious significance.

The ancient Egyptians loved music. Many tomb paintings and other artworks show scenes of people dancing and playing instruments such as lutes and harps.

Literature was also important. Scribes continued to record popular stories on papyrus scrolls. *The Tale of the Shipwrecked Sailor* tells the adventures of a sailor who is lost in the Red Sea, rescued, and then returned to Egypt.

READING CHECK DRAW CONCLUSIONS
Why do you think that most Egyptian buildings were made of mud bricks?

Summary

Pharaohs of the New Kingdom of Egypt enlarged Egypt's territory, expanded trade, and started massive building projects. Egyptian society was divided into different social classes. Most people worked as farmers and lived in rural areas. The New Kingdom was also a time of achievement in architecture, art, and literature.

LOCATE IT

EGYPT

Luxor

REVIEW

1. 💡 What achievements did the ancient Egyptians make during the New Kingdom?

2. Use the words **pharaoh** and **reign** in a paragraph explaining the role of Egypt's leader.

3. Why was the reign of Queen Hatshepsut significant?

CRITICAL THINKING

4. **ANALYSIS SKILL** What do you think led Akhenaton to try to make changes in Egyptian religion?

5. Why do you think that Akhenaton's changes to religion failed to last?

6. 🖌 **Make a Table** Make a table that describes the geography, government, economy, religion, and society of Egypt's New Kingdom. In your table, write at least one statement for each category. Include a title for your table.

7. **Focus Skill** **SUMMARIZE**
On a separate sheet of paper, copy and complete the graphic organizer below.

Key Fact	Summary
Akhenaton favored a single god.	
Akhenaton moved Egypt's capital.	

Treasures of Tutankhamen

Tutankhamen ruled Egypt for only nine years and died at the age of 18. The "boy king" was buried in a solid-gold coffin, and his tomb was filled with gold and jewelry. The tomb of Tutankhamen lay hidden in Egypt's Valley of the Kings for more than 3,300 years. In November 1922, Howard Carter, an expert in the study of ancient Egypt, discovered it. Today the golden coffin still contains the young pharaoh's remains, hidden from view inside two outer coffins. The Egyptian Museum in Cairo displays many of Tutankhamen's treasures to show Egypt's great wealth during the height of its civilization.

❯ Tutankhamen's golden mask

Golden hieroglyphs

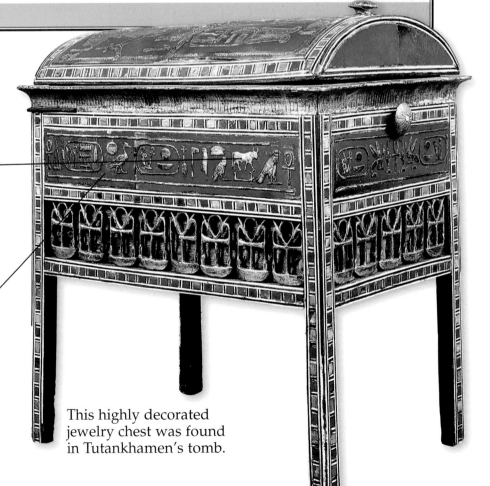

This highly decorated jewelry chest was found in Tutankhamen's tomb.

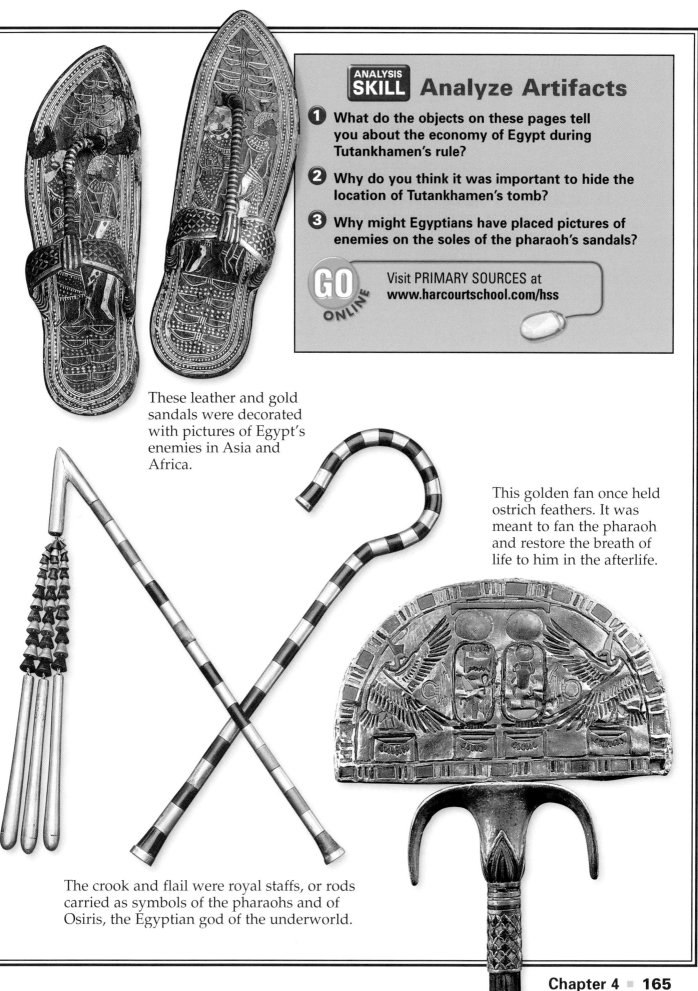

ANALYSIS
SKILL Analyze Artifacts

1 What do the objects on these pages tell you about the economy of Egypt during Tutankhamen's rule?

2 Why do you think it was important to hide the location of Tutankhamen's tomb?

3 Why might Egyptians have placed pictures of enemies on the soles of the pharaoh's sandals?

GO Visit PRIMARY SOURCES at
ONLINE www.harcourtschool.com/hss

These leather and gold sandals were decorated with pictures of Egypt's enemies in Asia and Africa.

This golden fan once held ostrich feathers. It was meant to fan the pharaoh and restore the breath of life to him in the afterlife.

The crook and flail were royal staffs, or rods carried as symbols of the pharaohs and of Osiris, the Egyptian god of the underworld.

Time

5000 B.C.

3750 B.C.

4000 B.C.
Farming villages
line the Nile River

3100 B.C.
Upper and Lower
Egypt are united

Reading Social Studies

When you **summarize**, you tell a shortened version of
what you have read.

Summarize

Complete this graphic organizer to show that you can summarize how geography affected the Egyptian civilization. A copy of
this graphic organizer appears on page 46 of the Homework and
Practice Book.

Early Egyptian Civilization

Key Fact

Egypt's political
structure was affected
by geography.

Key Fact

The economic structure
of early Egypt was
affected by geography.

Summary

California Writing Prompts

Write a Narrative Imagine that you are a tour
guide at the Great Pyramid. Write a narrative
script for what you will tell tourists. Tell when,
why, and how the Great Pyramid was built.

Write an Expository Paragraph Write an
expository paragraph that describes the Nile
Valley in 4000 B.C. Describe the area's geography,
climate, and settlements.

2500 B.C. **1250 B.C.** **B.C./A.D.**

2566 B.C.
The Great
Pyramid at Giza
is completed

1552 B.C.
The New
Kingdom begins

1280 B.C.
Ramses II
becomes
pharaoh

Use Vocabulary

Use one of the terms in the box to complete each sentence.

delta, p. 135

cataract, p. 135

papyrus, p. 144

civil war, p. 151

reign, p. 159

1. The Egyptians kept records on _____ .

2. A _____ is a triangular piece of rich land formed from soil deposited at the mouth of some rivers.

3. A _____ can be found in a place where the Nile River runs between desert cliffs.

4. A _____ is a time of rule.

5. A _____ is a war between two groups in the same place.

Use the Time Line

 Use the summary time line above to answer these questions.

6. When were Upper and Lower Egypt united?

7. What happened in 1552 B.C.?

Apply Skills

Compare Map Projections

 Look again at the maps on pages 140 and 141 and answer this question.

8. Which map should you use if you want to compare the sizes of the United States and Africa? Explain your answer.

Recall Facts

Answer these questions.

9. What was Egyptian hieroglyphic writing mostly used for at first?

10. During the Middle Kingdom, what other regions did Egypt trade with?

11. What was often shown in ancient Egyptian paintings and sculptures?

Write the letter of the best choice.

12. Into what body of water does the Nile River empty?
    A the Red Sea
    B the Tigris River
    C the Indian Ocean
    D the Mediterranean Sea

13. Why is Hatshepsut important in Egypt's history?
    A She oversaw the building of the Great Pyramid.
    B She was the goddess of farming.
    C She was one of only a few women pharaohs.
    D She was the first non-Egyptian to rule Egypt.

Think Critically

14. Why are the pyramids an example of a link between religion and society in ancient Egypt?

15. What were the costs and benefits of long-distance trade in ancient Egypt?

Study Skills

USE AN ANTICIPATION GUIDE

An anticipation guide can help you anticipate, or predict, what you will learn as you read.

➤ **Look at the lesson and section titles. These are clues that tell what you will read about.**

➤ **Preview the Reading Check questions. Use what you know about the subject of each lesson to predict the answers to the questions.**

➤ **Read the lesson to find out whether your predictions were correct.**

Lesson 1: The Land Called Nubia

Reading Check	Prediction	Correct?
What is the Nile River like in the land once known as Nubia?	It is probably a lot like the Nile in Lower Egypt, prone to flooding.	No, it is not like the Nile in Lower Egypt. It has high cliffs that cause rapids and waterfalls.
Reading Check	Prediction	Correct?

Apply As You Read

Make an anticipation guide for each lesson in this chapter, using the above guide as a model. Before you read this chapter, add to the anticipation guide the Reading Check questions for each lesson. Then make a prediction about the answer to each question. As you read each lesson, go back and see if your predictions were correct.

California History-Social Science Standards, Grade 6

6.2 Students analyze the geographic, political, economic, religious, and social structures of the early civilizations of Mesopotamia, Egypt, and Kush.

Nubia and Kush

▶ Ancient Kushite pyramids of Meroë, in present-day Sudan

MODERN RHYMES ABOUT ANCIENT TIMES

ANCIENT AFRICA

WRITTEN BY SUSAN ALTMAN AND SUSAN LECHNER
ILLUSTRATED BY DONNA PERRONE

As neighbors, the people of Egypt and Nubia interacted from the earliest of times. They traded, battled, and even exchanged ideas. Much more is known about Egypt than about Nubia. However, over the years, historians have pieced together the story of Egypt's neighbor in Africa. The poems that follow describe the land of Nubia and the kingdoms that formed there.

NUBIA

To the south of Egypt's cloudless skies, the sun-scorched land of Nubia lay,
Ancient traders traveled its paths, their camels passing along the way.
The Nubian women were known for their grace, their elegant beauty, and pride.
Egyptian pharaohs would often choose a Nubian queen for a bride.

South of Egypt's cloudless skies stretched Nubia's sun-scorched land.
The kingdoms of Axum, Kerma, and Kush arose from its desert sand.
Though little is known of Nubia's ways, its mysteries beckon us still.
Historical treasure, a time beyond measure, its promises yet to fulfill.

KERMA

In a kingdom called Kerma,
The folks were well known
For making fine pots
That glittered and shone.

The merchants all gathered
In Kerma to trade.
And craftsmen would offer
The things they had made.

The kingdom of Kerma
Was something to see,
This realm south of Egypt—
2000 B.C.

KUSH

It's mentioned in the Bible—
This great and ancient land.
A kingdom known to all as Kush—
Famous, rich, and grand.

One thousand years Kush lasted,
Then all was swept away
By a kingdom known as Axum,
Which then began its sway.

MEROE
CAPITAL OF KUSH

This fabled ancient city
Was famous, rich, and pretty,
The capital and hub of mighty Kush.
It processed its iron ore
For use in peace and war,
Giving African technology a push.

This fabled ancient city,
In Africa, so pretty,
Changed life across the land for all to see.
Iron weapons, tools, and rings,
And many other things,
Now had a solid-iron guarantee.

This fabled ancient city
Was famous, rich, and pretty,
With pyramids and palaces aglow.
A meeting point for caravans
Traveling desert sands
To Meroe, a city on the go.

Response Corner

1 From reading these poems, what additional information do you want to find out about these places?

2 Write two sentences describing each place featured in the poems.

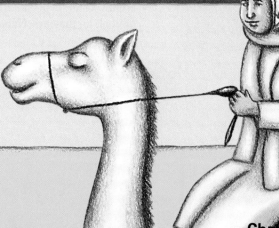

Time

6000 B.C.   3000 B.C.   B.C./A.D.

About 2000 B.C.
Egypt annexes northern Nubia;
Kush civilization begins

1650 B.C.
Nubians gain freedom
from Egypt

WHAT TO KNOW

What was the relationship between the civilizations of Kush and Egypt?

✓ Locate and describe the physical settings of Nubia and Kush.

✓ Describe the relations between the cultures, governments, and economies of Kush and Egypt.

VOCABULARY

commercial p. 173
raw material p. 174
import p. 175
export p. 175
annex p. 175
independence p. 176

PLACES

Nubia
Egypt
Khartoum
Kush
Kerma

SUMMARIZE

California
Standards
HSS 6.2, 6.2.1, 6.2.8

The Land Called Nubia

YOU ARE THERE

The year is 2000 B.C., and you live in the land of **Nubia**, south of **Egypt**. Your father is a Nubian trader, and your mother makes woven cloth. Today, an Egyptian has come to trade with your father. Boasting about the glory of Egypt, the Egyptian describes amazing buildings, statues, clothing, foods, and decorations. Only when the Egyptian leaves does your father speak out. He says bitterly, "The stone for his fine buildings comes from Nubia, and so does the gold for Egyptian statues. And where do the leopard skins, ostrich eggs, feathers, ivory, ebony, and spices they use come from? Nubia, of course!"

▶ This painted Nubian sculpture (right) is made of bronze. Cataracts made traveling on the Nile River difficult for the early Nubians (below).

Cataracts Pose Dangers

The ancient land known as Nubia stretched along the Nile River from the southern border of Egypt to the city of **Khartoum** (kar•TOOM) in Sudan. It was in ancient Nubia that in about 2000 B.C. the Kush civilization began to develop.

Because Egypt and Nubia were neighboring lands, the people of each place adopted some of the ideas and customs of the other. Over time, the two came to have political, cultural, and commercial relationships. Something that is **commercial** relates to large-scale buying and selling.

The geography of the two lands could not have been more different. In the land once known as Nubia, high cliffs rise straight up along the banks of the Nile. In contrast, wide plains lie on both sides of the river as it flows north through Egypt.

As the Nile travels through what was Nubia, its course is not as smooth as it is downstream in Egypt. In the south, large granite boulders block portions of the river, causing rapids and waterfalls. These groups of rocks form the six large areas of cataracts found along the southern, or upper, part of the Nile.

The cataracts made travel on the upper Nile difficult. To travel the cataracts, sailors waited for high waters or pulled their boats over and around them.

Egypt and what was Nubia do have one important feature in common. The intense heat of the sun dries out both regions. Rain

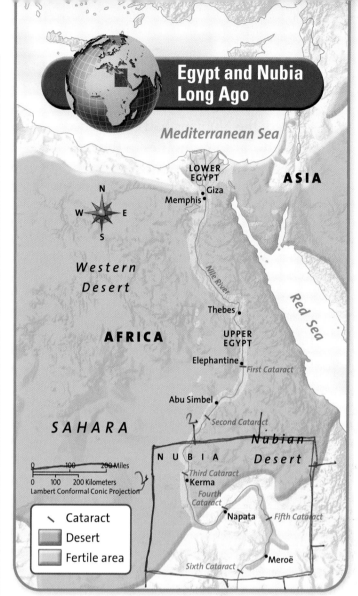

Egypt and Nubia Long Ago

Mediterranean Sea

ASIA

LOWER EGYPT

Giza

Memphis

Western Desert

AFRICA

Thebes

UPPER EGYPT

Elephantine

First Cataract

Abu Simbel

Second Cataract

SAHARA

Nubian Desert

NUBIA

Third Cataract

Kerma

Fourth Cataract

Napata

Fifth Cataract

Sixth Cataract

Meroë

Red Sea

Nile River

0   100   200 Miles
0   100   200 Kilometers
Lambert Conformal Conic Projection

\ Cataract
■ Desert
■ Fertile area

ANALYSIS SKILL Analyze Maps

◆ **Location** How would you describe the location of Abu Simbel in relation to the Nile's cataracts?

almost never falls, so the Nile is the main source of water. Like the Egyptians, most Nubians lived alongside the Nile.

READING CHECK ⟲ **SUMMARIZE**
What is the Nile River like in the land once known as Nubia?

A Wealth of Resources

Long before the Kush civilization formed, the Nubians had established agricultural communities in the region. This had occurred at the same time that the Egyptian civilization was beginning to develop, in about 3500 B.C.

While most Egyptians of the time worked as farmers, many Nubians chose to be cattle herders. In fact, cattle owners were often the richest and most powerful people in all of Nubia. These herders were pastoral nomads who moved their herds from place to place with the seasons. Only a small number of Nubians were farmers who stayed on the same land year after year.

Within Nubia's rocky land were many resources, including copper and gold. In some areas, cliffs of granite and other kinds of rock useful for construction rose high above the land.

The Nubians realized that their land held valuable **raw materials**, or natural resources that can be formed into useful products. Raw materials such as gold could be turned into beautiful jewelry while iron could be crafted into tools as well as weapons.

Like the Egyptians and other peoples, the Nubians used clay to craft pottery. This product was especially valuable to settled people such as the Nubian farmers. Nubian pottery could be used to store grain, to hold water, to cook in, and to keep supplies. In contrast, Nubian cattle herders rarely used pottery because it could get broken on long trips.

The Nubians made pottery as early as 6000 B.C. Eventually, their pottery became of fine quality, and the Nubians began to offer their pottery as valued trade items.

READING CHECK ⟳ **SUMMARIZE**
What were some of the natural resources of ancient Nubia?

A Closer LOOK

Life in a Kushite City

Ancient Kushite cities were busy places. They served not only as centers of trade but also as manufacturing centers.

1 **Center of Trade.** Traders from both northern and southern Africa traveled to Kushite cities to exchange goods.

2 **Manufacturing Center.** Kushite cities became well known for products produced there. These included iron tools, woven cloth, and pottery containers.

3 **Thriving City.** Thousands of people lived and worked in Kushite cities. Many others visited the cities to buy products made there.

◈ How do you think visitors to a Kushite city affected that city?

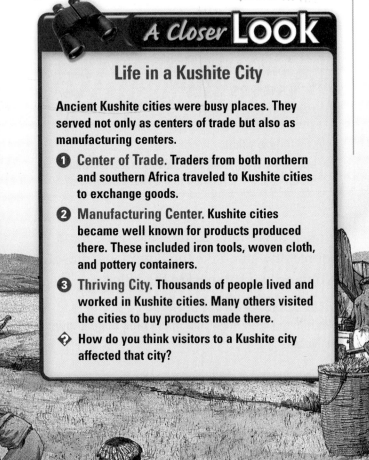

Nubian Trade

Nubia's location between northern Africa and southern Africa made it an ideal trading center. The Nubians served as go-betweens for traders. From the south, Nubians **imported**—or brought in—items such as leopard skins, ostrich eggs, feathers, ivory, ebony, spices, and gold. They then **exported**—or sent out—these same items to the north. The items were in great demand by the Egyptians and the early peoples of southwestern Asia.

▶ Nubians bring tribute to the Egyptians.

The Egyptians particularly valued Nubian gold, which the Nubians not only mined but also purified. The Egyptians used it lavishly to construct statues and decorations.

As Nubian trade flourished, so did the Nubian economy. The control of the gold trade served to make Nubia rich—and its neighbors jealous.

At first, Egypt and Nubia traded peacefully for raw materials. Then, at some point, the Egyptians realized that they could gain greater wealth if they controlled Nubia's trade routes.

By 2600 B.C., Egyptian monarchs had claimed all the trade routes in northern Nubia. The Egyptians also began looting Nubia's rich natural resources. They cut and hauled away blocks of stone, such as granite, which they used for statues and buildings. They also mined Nubian copper and gold.

In about 2000 B.C., the Egyptian king began to **annex**, or add on, the land of northern Nubia. First, he conquered the region. Then, he ordered mud-brick forts built near the second cataract to protect the newly annexed land. By annexing northern Nubia, the Egyptians gained Nubian resources and Nubian soldiers.

READING CHECK ⓢ **SUMMARIZE**
What made Nubia's location ideal for trade?

CITIZENSHIP

Democratic Values

The right to govern is an important part of freedom.

Throughout history, groups of people have sought the freedom to govern themselves. The Nubians were just one group of people who strived for freedom. In about 2000 B.C., the Egyptians conquered northern Nubia. The Egyptian pharaoh forced the Nubians there to adopt Egyptian customs, pay tribute, and follow Egyptian laws. By about 1650 B.C., some Nubians had regained their freedom and reunited with Kush.

Make It Relevant Where in the present-day world are people today working to gain the freedom to govern themselves?

❯ Nubian archers fought for independence.

Freedom and Reconquest

 **TIME** 2000 B.C.

PLACE Kerma

Egyptian control of Nubia did not last long. At the same time, a powerful kingdom arose in southern Nubia and began to drive the Egyptians out of Nubian lands.

The ancient Egyptians called the new kingdom **Kush**. Historians today call it the kingdom of Kerma for its capital, located near the third cataract, where the modern town of **Kerma**, Sudan, is today. The kingdom of Kush represents the early beginnings of the Kush civilization.

By 1650 B.C., the Kushites had regained their **independence**, or freedom, from Egypt. Free from Egyptian rule, Kerma became a major center for both river and overland trade. Goods such as gold, salt, spices, elephant tusks, and rhinoceros horns moved through Kerma to markets in Egypt and across the Red Sea to Asia. This trade brought great wealth to Kerma.

During Kerma's days of prosperity, Kushite kings gained power as well as wealth. Over time, they gained control of much of northern Nubia.

The same period was not as good for the Egyptians, especially since the Hyksos controlled northern Egypt. To keep the Egyptians from invading his kingdom, the Kushite king decided to become an ally, or supporter, of the Hyksos.

Kushite kings had no way of knowing that the Egyptians would soon regain their land. The victorious Egyptians forced the Hyksos out of Egypt and into southwestern Asia. Then the Egyptians turned south and destroyed Kush's capital city of Kerma.

Following their military successes, the Egyptians claimed control of much of Nubia. This time, Egypt's control of Nubia stretched past the Nile's fourth cataract. As a demonstration of strength, the Egyptians built cities and temples all over Nubia.

Egypt's rule over Nubia lasted for about 550 years. During that time, the Egyptian pharaoh created a special position called the King's Son of Kush. This person was responsible for the day-to-day governing of Nubian lands and for collecting taxes.

Under Egyptian rule, the Kushites were encouraged to become much like the Egyptians. Many Kushites adopted Egyptian religious beliefs, writing, customs, and ways of dressing.

READING CHECK ŎSUMMARIZE
Why did the Kushite king become an ally of the Hyksos?

Summary

The land of Nubia was rich in natural resources. The early Nubians built a strong economy based on trade. Egypt claimed the trade routes in northern Nubia and later annexed the land. The Kush civilization began when the Nubians began to drive the Egyptians out of Nubia. Later, the Egyptians again captured Nubian land.

REVIEW

1. What was the relationship between the civilizations of Kush and Egypt?

2. Use the terms **raw material**, **annex**, and **independence** to tell more about the relationship between Egypt and Kush.

3. Why did the Egyptians become interested in the land of Nubia?

CRITICAL THINKING

4. How would you describe the relative location of the Kush civilization's land in Nubia on the continent of Africa?

5. **ANALYSIS SKILL** What is one fact and one opinion that might appear in a book about Kush?

6. **Draw a Map** Draw a map of Kush and Egypt. Then, using the information in this lesson, add labels and arrows to the map to show the goods that Kush and Egypt traded.

7. **Focus Skill** SUMMARIZE
On a separate sheet of paper, copy and complete the graphic organizer below.

Key Fact	Summary
Egyptians valued Nubian gold.	
Key Fact	
Egyptians wanted control of Nubian trade routes.	

❯ Agriculture is an important part of the life of people living in the present-day village of Kerma in Sudan, Africa.

Lesson 2

Time

6000 B.C. 3000 B.C. B.C./A.D.

780 B.C.
The Kushites rebuild the
kingdom of Kush in Napata

730 B.C.
The Kushite dynasty
begins its rule of Egypt

270 B.C.
The kingdom of Kush
at Meroë thrives

WHAT TO KNOW
How did Kush's
relationship with Egypt
change over time?

✓ Analyze how the people
of Kush went from being
controlled by Egypt to
conquering Egypt.

✓ Examine how the
Kushites developed their
own written language.

VOCABULARY
trade network p. 181
decipher p. 181

PEOPLE
Alara
Kashta
Piye
Shabaka
Taharqa
Amani-Shakete

PLACES
Napata
Meroë

 SUMMARIZE

 California
Standards
HSS 6.2, 6.2.8, 6.2.9

New Kingdoms of Kush

YOU ARE THERE It is 700 B.C., and you are proud to be a Kushite
living in a beautiful and busy city. New temples
and palaces rise toward the sky. Groups of small pyramids dot the land. Everywhere you walk, traders are
busy exchanging goods. Visitors from Egypt buy grains,
cotton, and cattle. Those from farther south in Africa
buy products made of iron. In exchange, Kushite traders accept exotic animals, glassware, and statues of
Egyptian gods.

❯ These pyramids are reminders of the early civilizations
that developed in ancient Nubia.

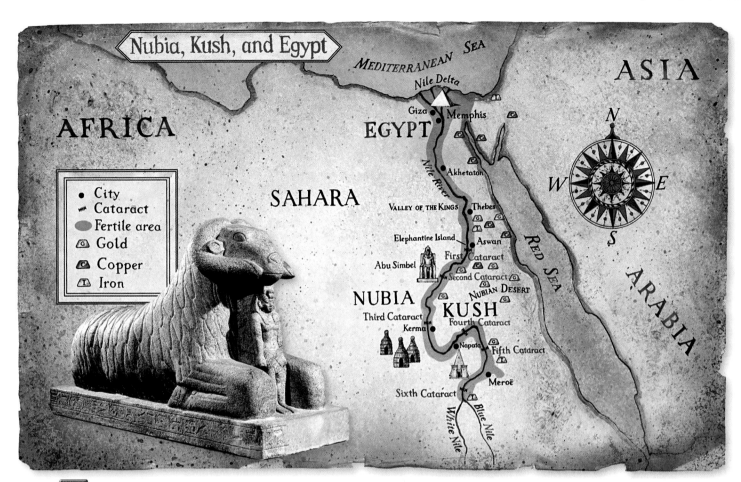

Nubia, Kush, and Egypt

MEDITERRANEAN SEA

ASIA

AFRICA

SAHARA

EGYPT

Nile Delta

Giza • Memphis

Akhetaton

VALLEY OF THE KINGS • Thebes

Elephantine Island • Aswan

Abu Simbel • First Cataract

Second Cataract

NUBIA

NUBIAN DESERT

Third Cataract

KUSH

Kerma • Fourth Cataract

Napata • Fifth Cataract

Meroë

Sixth Cataract

White Nile   Blue Nile

RED SEA

ARABIA

N
W   E
S

• City
〰 Cataract
⬭ Fertile area
⬚ Gold
⬚ Copper
⬚ Iron

ANALYSIS SKILL Analyze Maps The ancient Nubians built their largest cities along the Nile between the third and sixth cataracts. Above left is statue of a Kushite pharaoh.

◈ Place What are the names of these three cities, and which was farthest south?

Kush Conquers Egypt

TIME 780 B.C.

PLACE Napata

By 800 B.C., the kingdom of Kush had begun to regain its strength. The Kushites built a new capital city called **Napata** (NA•puh•tuh) farther south on the Nile, where they were free of Egypt's rule.

In 780 B.C., a Nubian chieftain named **Alara** started a new dynasty of Kushite kings. This began what some historians call the time of the kingdom of Napata.

King **Kashta** followed his brother Alara as Kush's leader. Kashta kept a careful watch on the weakened Egypt. In about 750 B.C., Kush captured Upper Egypt.

Later, Kashta's son **Piye** (PEE•yeh), or Piankhi (PYANG•kee), conquered Lower Egypt. Piye's conquest brought all of Egypt under Kushite control.

After Piye's death, his brother **Shabaka** (SHA•bah•kah) claimed the Egyptian pharaoh's throne. He and the Kushite pharaohs who followed him ruled as Egypt's Dynasty 25, or the Kushite dynasty.

Perhaps the most successful of all the Dynasty 25 pharaohs was **Taharqa** (tuh•HAR•kuh). Pharaoh Taharqa is remembered for the temples he ordered built.

The Kushite pharaohs ruled Egypt from about 730 B.C. to 671 B.C. and helped restore Egypt to its former glory. They rebuilt temples that had been destroyed and built new ones.

READING CHECK ⏀SUMMARIZE

How was Dynasty 25 different from earlier Egyptian dynasties?

▶ The Kushites built this temple (above) in the first century A.D., during the Meroitic period. The Kushite statue (left) is from around 700 B.C.

A New Beginning

 **TIME** 591 B.C.

PLACE Meroë

The Kushites' rule over Egypt came to an end when the Assyrians invaded Egypt. Kushite and Egyptian soldiers could not compete with the large Assyrian army. When the Assyrians destroyed the combined Kushite and Egyptian armies, Taharqa and his Kushite army retreated to Napata.

King Taharqa died in Napata. Soon after, the Assyrian rulers of Egypt robbed and plundered Napata. The Assyrian attack on Egypt proved to be a major setback for the Kushites. However, the Kushites learned new techniques about iron-making from the Assyrians. Kushite skill in iron-making would help them build a new kingdom.

In 591 B.C., Kushite leaders moved their capital south to **Meroë** (MAIR•oh•ee), near the sixth cataract of the Nile River. There, farther from Egypt, the Kushites once again rebuilt the kingdom of Kush, also known as the kingdom of Meroë.

At Meroë, the Kush civilization lived on and made many advances. This time of achievement, which lasted from 270 B.C. to A.D. 350, is known as the Meroitic period.

During the Meroitic period, Kush included most of Nubia as well as regions far south of Khartoum. Across the kingdom, the Kushites built temples to their own gods as well as palaces and pyramids for their rulers. They also created new customs of their own. As in earlier times, the Kushites became known for trade.

READING CHECK CAUSE AND EFFECT
What event caused the Kushites to lose control of Egypt?

The City of Meroë

One of Meroë's greatest advantages was its location. The city was not only on the Nile River but also at the meeting point of several overland trade routes.

In Meroë, Kushite merchants revived their **trade network**, or group of buyers and sellers. Using caravans of camels, traders from southwestern Asia and from other parts of Africa traveled to Meroë. Along with gold, cattle, cotton, and wheat, the Kushites began to offer iron products to their trade partners.

The need to keep trade records led the people of Meroë to create the first Nubian written language. Before this time, the Nubian language was only spoken, and any written communication used Egyptian hieroglyphs. The new Meroitic alphabet had 23 symbols, which stood for sounds in the Nubian language. Today, the sounds of the symbols are known, but no one has been able to **decipher** (dee•SY•fur), or figure out the meaning of, the language.

Because of its success at trade, the city of Meroë grew. Soon, new palaces, temples, pyramids, and ironworking shops arose. With just one look at the city, a visitor could tell that the people of Meroë were wealthy.

Trade brought the Kushites much wealth, but its rulers gave Meroë its strength. Just as the pharaohs of Dynasty 25 had claimed to be sons of the god Amon, so, too, did the leaders of Meroë.

In some ways, the rulers of Meroë were very different from Egyptian rulers. In Meroë, women played an important role in governing. In fact, many historians believe that the right to rule was passed on through the queen, not the king. Women could also be rulers themselves, and many were. These powerful queens are even known to have led troops into battle. For example, **Amani-Shakete** (uh•MAN•uh shuh•KAY•tay) led her army against the mighty Roman army.

READING CHECK ⚙SUMMARIZE
How did trade affect the kingdom of Meroë?

Cultural Heritage

The Queens of Kush

Queens played an important role in Kushite society. While men usually were the rulers of Kush, the Kushites traced their family lines through their mothers. Because of this, the queen mother in the Kushite monarchy held a position of great respect and influence. When a king died, the queen mother and the leaders of the kingdom chose the next ruler from among the members of the royal family. If the chosen ruler was too young to govern, the queen mother ruled for him. Ruling queens in Kush were known as Kandakes (kahn•dah•KAYZ). Some queens ruled together with their husbands. Queen Shanakdakhete, one of the most powerful rulers of Meroë, ordered the building of many temples and palaces.

▶ **Mask of a Kushite queen**

The Fall of Meroë

During the 200s B.C., Greek rulers in Egypt had ordered ports built on the Red Sea. Traders began to use sea routes rather than the land routes that passed through the once-busy city of Meroë. No longer a center of trade, Meroë lost much of its power, importance, and wealth.

Also, soldiers from the African kingdom of Axum, in what is now Ethiopia, began making raids on Kushite towns. By about A.D. 350, the people of Axum had defeated the Kushites. The king of Axum wrote, "I burned their villages, both those with walls of stone and those of straw."* By the end of the fourth century A.D., the Kush civilization had fallen.

READING CHECK CAUSE AND EFFECT
What caused Meroë to lose much of its power, importance, and wealth?

King Ezana, from *The Deutsche Aksum-Expedition* written by Enno Littmann, Reimer, 1913.

Summary

The Kushites built a new capital called Napata, near the fourth cataract. In time, the Kushites were able to take over Egypt. Kushite rule over Egypt did not last long. The Kushites founded a new capital at Meroë. From there, the kingdom of Kush grew, gaining fame as a trade center. When traders began to use sea routes, Meroë lost much of its power, importance, and wealth.

⚡ FAST FACT

The word *obelisk* comes from the Greek word *obelos*, which means "spit," or "skewer." These monuments reminded the Greeks of a *spit*, a cooking utensil for roasting meat.

REVIEW

1. 💡 How did Kush's relationship with Egypt change over time?

2. Write a sentence that describes what is known about the Nubian alphabet. Use the word **decipher**.

3. What led the people of Meroë to create the first Nubian written language?

CRITICAL THINKING

4. **ANALYSIS SKILL** During the fall of Meroë, why do you think sea trade became more important than overland trade?

5. **ANALYSIS SKILL** Why do you think the Kushites kept building their capital cities farther and farther from Egypt?

6. 🖌 **Design an Obelisk** The Kushites and the Egyptians often placed obelisks at the entrances to their temples. The sides of the obelisks had hieroglyphs or designs. Design and draw your own obelisk.

7. **Focus Skill** SUMMARIZE
On a separate sheet of paper, copy and complete the graphic organizer below.

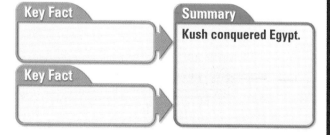

Key Fact	Summary
	Kush conquered Egypt.
Key Fact	

182 ■ Unit 2

Piye

*"He... decided then and there to invade Egypt, so that he might restore order to that land."**

Biography

Trustworthiness
Respect
Responsibility
Fairness
Caring
Patriotism

Piye, also known as Piankhi, was a strong Nubian ruler who wanted to conquer all of Egypt. He inherited his throne from his father, King Kashta. King Kashta had extended the rule of the kingdom of Kush as far north as Thebes, but Piye wanted to spread his rule farther.

Piye wanted to conquer Lower Egypt. He marched his army there to challenge the four kings who ruled the surrounding area. Piye did not believe he was invading Thebes. Instead, he thought he was bringing peace to an unsettled country at his northern border.

Why Character Counts

How did Piye demonstrate fairness in the way he ruled Egypt?

▶ Piye's cartouche, or emblem, uses symbols to represent sounds in his name.

To fulfill his goal of conquering all of Egypt, Piye was determined to capture Memphis, the ancient capital of Egypt. Memphis was well protected by walls. However, Piye's army used the masts of boats in the river to climb over the walls and capture the city.

After the capture of Memphis, most other rulers also submitted to Piye. He became the first Kushite king to rule both Kush and all of Egypt. Piye is known as a ruler who did not wish to fight with his enemies. Instead, he preferred making treaties and alliances with them.

*Robert Steven Bianchi. *The Nubians: People of the Ancient Nile.* Millbrook Press, 1994.

Bio Brief

747 B.C.		716 B.C.
Reign began		Reign ended
	730 B.C. Piye conquers Lower Egypt	716 B.C. Piye dies

GO ONLINE

Interactive Multimedia Biographies
Visit MULTIMEDIA BIOGRAPHIES at
www.harcourtschool.com/hss

183

Solve a Problem

▶ WHY IT MATTERS

Think about what you read about the Kushites. They faced different problems at different times. First, the Egyptians conquered their lands and took away their independence. Later, after the Kushites had gained control of Egypt, the Assyrians invaded Egypt and destroyed the Kushite and Egyptian armies. Each time a new problem arose, Kushite leaders had to find a solution.

No matter where or when people live, they all face problems from time to time. Knowing how to solve problems is an important skill for a Kushite king of the past or a student today.

▶ WHAT YOU NEED TO KNOW

Here are five steps that you can use to help solve a problem.

Step 1 Identify the problem.

Step 2 Think of possible solutions. Come up with at least two that you think might work.

Step 3 Look at the facts of the situation, and think about how each of your ideas might work. After comparing the possible solutions, rule out those that are not good choices.

Step 4 Choose the best solution, and plan a way to carry it out.

Step 5 Try your solution, and think about how well it solves the problem.

▶ Under the control of Egypt, the Kushites took on many of the ways of the Egyptians.

❯ Conquered princes declare loyalty to the Kushite king Piye.

❯ PRACTICE THE SKILL

1. Think of a problem the Kushite kings faced when the Assyrians invaded Egypt. What are two possible solutions to the problem?

2. Which of the solutions is the better choice? Why?

3. How would you carry out the solution?

4. What solution did the Kushites choose?

5. How well do you think the solution would solve the problem?

❯ APPLY WHAT YOU LEARNED

Identify a problem in your community or school. Use the steps on page 184 to write a plan for solving the problem. In your plan, explain why you think that the solution you chose is the best one.

Participation Skills

2000 B.C.
Kushite civilization
begins at Kerma

1650 B.C.
Nubia gains
freedom
from Egypt

Reading Social Studies

When you **summarize**, you tell a shortened version of
what you have read.

Focus Skill Summarize

Complete this graphic organizer to show that you can summarize
Kushite rule of Egypt. A copy of this graphic organizer appears
on page 55 of the Homework and Practice Book.

Kushite Rule of Egypt

Key Fact	Summary
In 750 B.C., a Kushite king conquered Upper Egypt.	
Key Fact	
Later, his son Piye conquered Lower Egypt.	

California Writing Prompts

Write a Persuasive Letter Imagine that you
are a teenager in Nubia. Your father is a herder,
and he wants you to follow in his footsteps.
However, you want to become a trader. Write a
letter to your father in which you try to persuade
him to agree with your plan to become a trader.

Write a Narrative Write a short narrative
about sailors on the Upper Nile. Describe the
setting. Make sure that your plot is one that
these sailors could really encounter. Include
dialogue and a clear beginning, middle, and
ending.

1000 B.C.

730 B.C.
King Piye of
Kush captures
Lower Egypt

500 B.C.

270 B.C.
Kush civilization
is centered at
Meroë

B.C./A.D.

Use Vocabulary

Identify the term that correctly matches each definition.

annex, p. 175

decipher, p. 181

commercial, p. 173

import, p. 175

independence, p. 176

1. to add on

2. to figure out the meaning of

3. having to do with large-scale buying and selling

4. to bring in from another country or region

5. freedom

Use the Time Line

 Use the summary time line above to answer these questions.

6. When did Nubia gain freedom from Egypt?

7. When did Meroë become the center of Kush civilization?

Apply Skills

Solve a Problem

8. Kushite civilization lost power and wealth when traders began to use sea routes rather than land routes. What could the Kushites have done to try to solve this problem? Explain why you think your solution might have worked.

Recall Facts

Answer these questions.

9. What raw materials did Egypt get from Nubia?

10. Why did the Nubians create a written language?

11. What achievements did the Kushites make during the Meroitic period?

Write the letter of the best choice.

12. What contributed most to Nubia's wealth?
   A farming
   B herding
   C trading
   D building

13. How were the rulers of Meroë different from Egyptian rulers?
   A They were not interested in trading with other countries.
   B Women played a more important role in governing.
   C They were elected by the people.
   D They did not build pyramids.

Think Critically

14. **ANALYSIS SKILL** How did the Nubian civilization's political relationship with Egypt change over time?

15. **ANALYSIS SKILL** What caused the Kushite civilization to come to an end?

Chapter 5 ■ 187

Field Trip

The Nile Valley

GET READY

The whole length of the Nile seems to have well-known, ancient, and beautiful places to see. From the city of Cairo and the pyramids at Giza in northern Egypt to the temples and pyramids of Meroë in central Sudan, people from all over the world visit places along the Nile every year.

Much has changed in Egypt and Sudan since ancient times. Voyages south once made by sail or caravan can now be made by motorboat or airplane. Yet reminders of the past survive. The importance of the Nile civilizations to world heritage has not been forgotten.

WHAT TO SEE

Egypt's thriving agriculture, such as that along the Nile Delta, is only possible through intensive irrigation.

LOCATE IT

Nile River

EGYPT

SUDAN

Standing near the head of the Nile Delta, Cairo, the Egyptian capital and the largest city in Africa, is home to more than 10 million people. It features skyscrapers, subways, ancient ruins, mosques, and medieval fortresses.

The famous pyramids at Giza are not in the middle of a desert. In fact, the Giza plateau is situated alongside the Nile River.

The ruins at Luxor are a very popular tourist destination. Located near the ancient Egyptian capital of Thebes, these ruins contain many symbols of the former power of the pharaohs.

Feluccas (above and left), narrow and swift Egyptian boats, once carried goods such as ivory and gold. Today they often carry tourists.

Farther south are the pyramids of Meroë. Once the burial places of royalty, they are now one of Sudan's most popular tourist attractions.

A VIRTUAL TOUR

GO ONLINE

Visit VIRTUAL TOURS at
www.harcourtschool.com/hss

Unit 2

Review

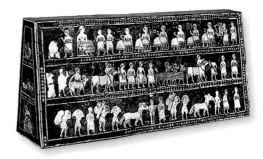

THE BIG IDEA

Innovations Early cultures often borrowed ideas from other cultures but also developed ideas of their own.

Summary

Mesopotamia, Egypt, and Kush

The Sumerians built one of the world's first civilizations in Mesopotamia, the area between the Tigris and Euphrates Rivers. They used the wheel, the plow, irrigation, and other advanced farming techniques. They also created a writing system and a system of standard measurements. These innovations allowed the Sumerians to build large city-states ruled by kings.

Later, the Babylonians and Assyrians built civilizations in the same region. In time, these peoples each built a large empire.

The Egyptians developed a civilization in the fertile Nile River valley. Farming and trade helped the Egyptians create a powerful empire. The ideas that the Egyptians had about religion, art, and architecture allowed them to create a complex culture.

The Kushite civilization grew along the upper Nile in a region called Nubia. Trade made the Kushites rich, and their use of iron weapons made them powerful. The Kushites even conquered Egypt. They also developed an alphabet.

Main Ideas and Vocabulary

Read the summary above. Then answer the questions that follow.

1. What does the word empire mean?
   A an army
   B a ruler who has complete power
   C lands and peoples ruled by one power
   D the products that the people in a region produce

2. What does the word architecture mean?
   A farming methods
   B building style
   C laws and justice
   D government

3. Which civilization arose in a region called Nubia?
   A Babylonian
   B Egyptian
   C Kushite
   D Assyrian

4. What kind of writing system did the Kushites use?
   A an alphabet
   B cuneiform
   C pyramids
   D picture writing

Answer these questions.

5. Why did the location of major river systems attract the first civilizations?

6. What agricultural techniques did the people of southern Mesopotamia use to farm the dried-out land?

7. What allowed some Sumerian farming villages to emerge as the first cities?

8. What did ancient Egyptians use as a writing material?

9. Where was Nubia?

Write the letter of the best choice.

10. Where is the Fertile Crescent?
  A in southwestern Asia
  B at the mouth of the Nile River
  C along the Nile River valley
  D along the shore of the Mediterranean Sea

11. Which civilization is known for forming the world's first monarchy?
  A Assyrian
  B Egyptian
  C Kushite
  D Sumerian

12. Which of the following best describes the upper Nile River in ancient times?
  A It was broad, and the current was slow.
  B It had many rapids and waterfalls.
  C It flowed through low-lying marshes.
  D It was narrow and dried up during droughts.

13. Which period of Egyptian history is also known as the Age of Pyramids?
  A Dynasty 5
  B the Old Kingdom
  C the Middle Kingdom
  D the New Kingdom

14. During which Egyptian dynasty did Kushite pharaohs rule Egypt?
  A Dynasty 5
  B Dynasty 12
  C Dynasty 18
  D Dynasty 25

Think Critically

15. How might you compare and contrast the Sumerian and Egyptian civilizations? Tell two ways in which they were similar and two ways in which they differed.

16. Put these civilizations in time order from earliest to latest—Assyrian, Babylonian, Sumerian.

Apply Skills

Read a Land Use and Products Map

ANALYSIS SKILL Use the map on this page to answer the following questions.

17. What products are found near Alexandria?

18. For what is most of the land along the Nile used?

19. What products come from Egypt's oasis areas?

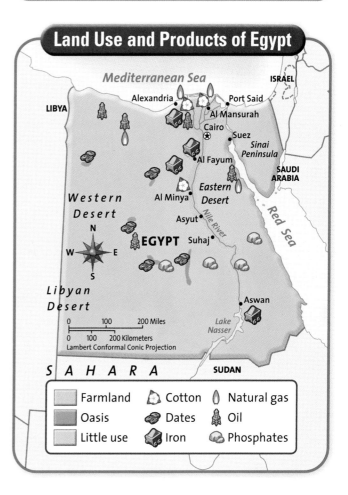

Land Use and Products of Egypt

Read More

■ *Life in Ancient Egypt* by Scott Cameron.

■ *Meroë and the Kingdom of Kush* by Karen Odom.

■ *Sumerian Achievements* by Karen Odom.

Show What You Know

Unit Writing Activity

Write a Narrative Imagine that you are an ancient Egyptian official planning a pharaoh's pyramid. Write a story about your experiences. Be sure to tell what treasures you will place in the tombs. How do you hide the entrance to protect those treasures against robbers?

Unit Project

Develop a Patterns of Civilization Display Gather information you learned about the main features of the earliest civilizations. Then make a display that shows the patterns of development that these civilizations had in common. Do some research and develop your own opinion about why the world's first civilizations often followed many of the same patterns.

GO ONLINE

Visit ACTIVITIES at **www.harcourtschool.com/hss**

The Ancient Hebrews

Unit
3

START WITH THE STANDARDS

California History-Social Science Standards

6.3 Students analyze the geographic, political, economic, religious, and social structures of the Ancient Hebrews.

The Big Idea

BELIEFS AND CUSTOMS

Beliefs and customs played an important role in the development of the culture of the ancient Hebrews.

What to Know

✓ Where did the ancient Hebrews settle, and to where did they later migrate?

✓ What is the significance of Judaism as the first monotheistic religion?

✓ What are the sources of the ethical teachings and central beliefs of Judaism?

✓ How did individuals affect the development of the Jewish religion?

Show What You Know

★ Unit 3 Test

✎ Writing: Expository Paragraph

🖌 Unit Project: A History Book

Time

The Ancient
Hebrews

1900s B.C. Abraham
and his family move
to Canaan, p. 205

1225 B.C. Moses
receives the
Ten Commandments,
p. 208

2400 B.C.   **1600 B.C.**

At the
Same Time

2000 B.C.
Agricultural
societies develop
in the Americas

1150 B.C.
The Olmec civilization
of what is now Mexico
begins building temples

The Ancient Hebrews

928 B.C. The kingdom of Israel splits into two parts, Israel and Judah, p. 221

722 B.C. The Assyrians conquer Israel, p. 222

515 B.C. The Jewish people finish rebuilding the Temple, p. 237

167 B.C. The revolt of the Maccabees happens, p. 245

800 B.C.

B.C./A.D.

 1000 B.C. The Adena culture develops in the Ohio Valley in North America

 400 B.C. The Olmec civilization ends

Abraham

1900s B.C.
- Founder of Judaism
- According to the Bible, he followed God's orders to move to Canaan

Moses

1200s B.C.
- Convinced the pharaoh to free Israelites from slavery in Egypt
- According to the Bible, he received the Ten Commandments from God

People

2000 B.C.   **1500 B.C.**   **1000 B.C.**

1900s B.C. • Abraham

1200s B.C. • Moses

1100s B.C. • Deborah

1100s B.C. • Ruth

1025 B.C. – 967 B.C. • David

Reigned 967 B.C. – 931 B.C. • Solomon

David

1025 B.C. – 967 B.C.
- According to the Bible, he was a strong king of the Israelites who defeated the Philistines
- Established Jerusalem as the new capital of the kingdom of Israel

Solomon

Reigned 967 B.C. – 931 B.C.
- According to the Bible, he built the Temple in Jerusalem to worship God and to hold the Ark of the Covenant
- Made Israel's economy very strong

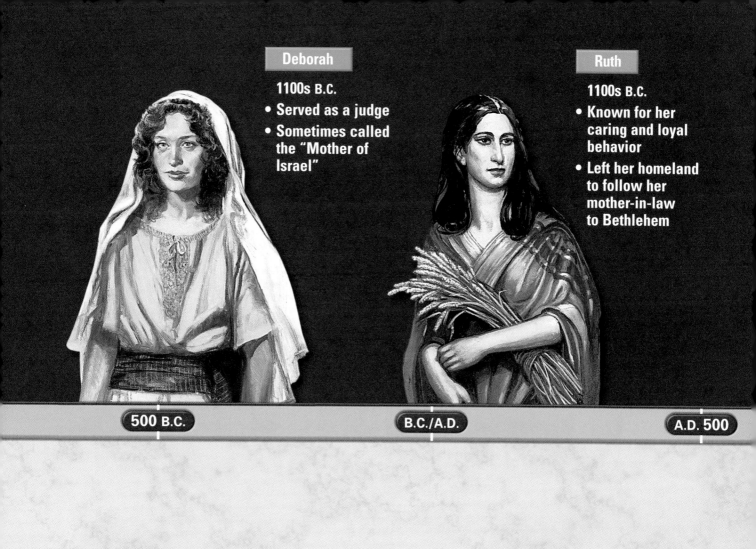

Deborah

1100s B.C.
- Served as a judge
- Sometimes called the "Mother of Israel"

Ruth

1100s B.C.
- Known for her caring and loyal behavior
- Left her homeland to follow her mother-in-law to Bethlehem

500 B.C.   B.C./A.D.   A.D. 500

400s B.C. • Ezra

15 B.C. — A.D. 85 • Yohanan ben Zaccai

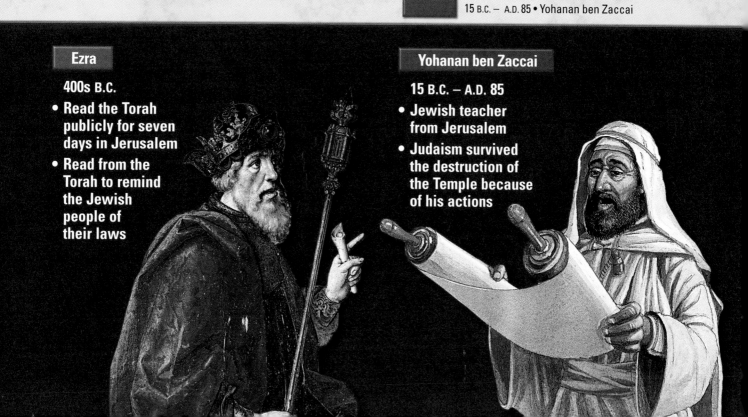

Ezra

400s B.C.
- Read the Torah publicly for seven days in Jerusalem
- Read from the Torah to remind the Jewish people of their laws

Yohanan ben Zaccai

15 B.C. — A.D. 85
- Jewish teacher from Jerusalem
- Judaism survived the destruction of the Temple because of his actions

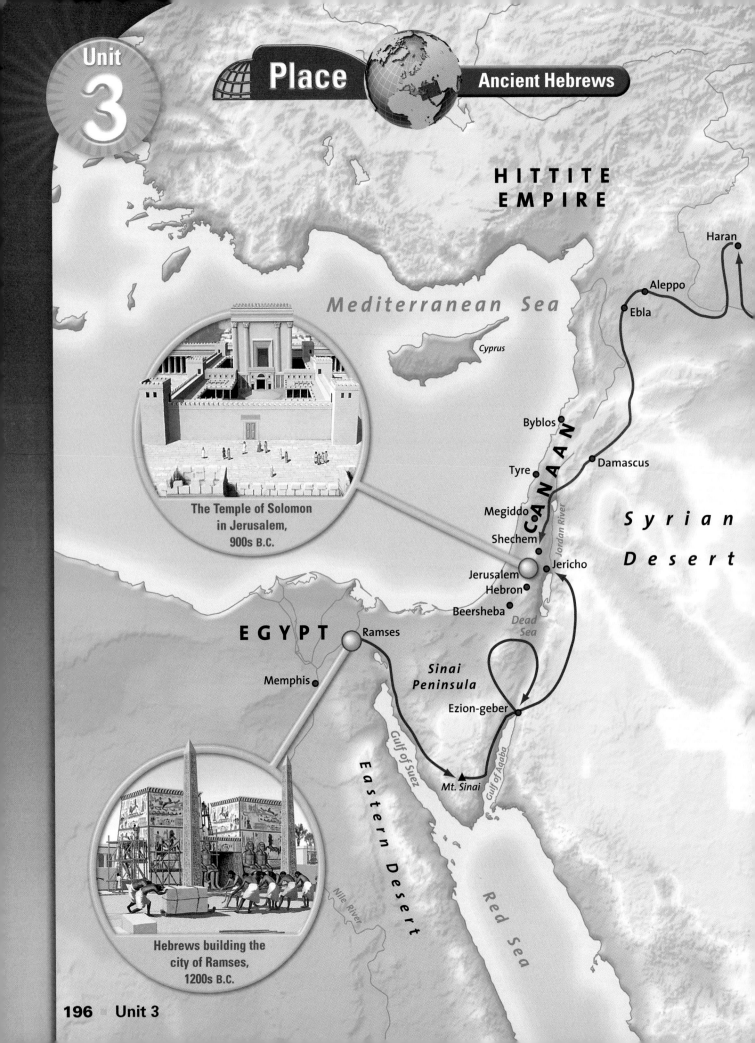

HITTITE EMPIRE

Mediterranean Sea

Cyprus

Haran

Aleppo

Ebla

CANAAN

Byblos

Damascus

Tyre

Megiddo

Jordan River

Shechem

Jerusalem

Jericho

Hebron

SYRIAN DESERT

Beersheba

Dead Sea

The Temple of Solomon
in Jerusalem,
900s B.C.

EGYPT

Ramses

Memphis

Sinai
Peninsula

Ezion-geber

Gulf of Suez

Eastern Desert

Mt. Sinai

Gulf of Aqaba

Nile River

Red Sea

Hebrews building the
city of Ramses,
1200s B.C.

Caspian Sea

ASSYRIA

Nineveh

Zagros Mountains

Tigris River

Euphrates River

AKKAD

Babylon

Nippur

SUMER

Ur

The city of Nineveh, about 700 B.C.

Arabian Peninsula

N
W   E
S

At The Same Time

Adena Indian village, Ohio Valley, about 900 B.C.

NORTH AMERICA

PACIFIC OCEAN

SOUTH AMERICA

→ Possible route of Abraham, 1900s B.C.
→ Possible route of Moses, 1200s B.C.

0   50   100 Miles
0   50   100 Kilometers
Lambert Conformal Conic Projection

Reading Social Studies

Generalize

(Focus Skill)

When you **generalize**, you make a statement that summarizes a group of facts and shows how they are related.

Why It Matters

Generalizing can help you summarize and remember what you read.

Facts

Generalization

✓ A generalization is always based on facts.

✓ To generalize, ask yourself, "What general statement do most or all the facts support?"

✓ A generalization tells what is true most of the time.

Practice the Skill

Read the paragraphs that follow. Then make a generalization for the second paragraph.

Facts

In Mesopotamia, the first civilization developed between two rivers—the Tigris and the Euphrates. Early Egyptian civilizations grew up along the banks of the Nile River. However, not every early civilization was dependent on a river. Early Hebrew civilizations began near the Jordan River but were not closely tied to it. (Most early civilizations developed along rivers.)

Generalization

The Nile Valley had fertile land, which made farming an important way of life. Wealthy landowners controlled the land, and farmers rented it to grow their crops. Many people made a living by farming. Because farmers were able to grow as much food as was needed, other people were able to become craftworkers.

Generalize Read the paragraphs, and answer the questions.

Building Blocks of Civilization

The ancient civilizations of Sumer and Egypt were advanced in many ways. They developed new political systems, new mathematical systems and calendars, the first written languages, and technologies such as wheeled vehicles. They were able to meet many kinds of challenges that came their way. As a result, these civilizations survived for long periods of time. Many other groups in nearby areas also made outstanding advancements.

The Assyrians were skilled engineers who used their technology to develop weapons. Both their military and their society in general were organized for efficiency. The Assyrian military included foot soldiers, expert archers, troops on horseback, and charioteers. Together, these units made up a fierce and successful army.

The Chaldeans, of Mesopotamia, used their understanding of the phases of the moon to develop an accurate calendar. Their knowledge of the stars was recognized throughout the region.

The Phoenicians lived on the eastern shore of the Mediterranean. They advanced the art of shipbuilding and the science of navigation. The Phoenicians were among the best sailors of the ancient world. Their achievements enabled them to set up long-distance trade networks.

▶ A stone carving of a Phoenician ship

Generalize

1. **What generalization can you make about the Assyrians?**

2. **What generalization can you make about the Chaldeans?**

3. **What generalization can you make about the Phoenicians?**

Study Skills

USE OUTLINES

Making an outline is a good way to record main ideas and supporting details.

▶ Topics in an outline are identified with Roman numerals.

▶ Main ideas about each topic are identified with capital letters.

▶ Details that support each main idea are identified with numbers.

Origins of Judaism

I. The Hebrew People
   A. Abraham
      1. Founder of Judaism
      2. From Mesopotamia
      3. Journey to Canaan
   B. The Israelites
      1.
      2.

Apply As You Read

As you read this chapter, notice the topics, main ideas, and details. Use that information to complete an outline of the chapter.

California History-Social Science Standards, Grade 6

6.3 Students analyze the geographic, political, economic, religious, and social structures of the Ancient Hebrews.

Origins of Judaism

▶ Judaean Desert in present-day Israel

The Tower of Babel

retold by Geraldine McCaughrean
illustrated by Peter Siu

The ancient Hebrews were the ancestors of the Jewish people. The Hebrew Bible, or holy book of the Jewish people, tells about the history of the ancient Hebrews, their belief in God, and a set of laws for living. It also contains many stories related to the world long ago, including this one.

In the early days of the world, all the people on Earth were of one wandering tribe—tent-dwellers in search of somewhere to build in brick and stone. The place they chose was a great plain in a land called Shinar.

But not content to build a house, or a street of houses, or a city of streets, they said, "Let's build a tower—the highest the world has ever seen. Let's build it so high that its roof bangs against Heaven and people can see it from half a world away! We shall be famous forever!"

They could do it, too, because they all spoke the same language and could cooperate, plan, send messages from bottom to top of the tower and, above all, *think in the same words.* Their great fault was pride: the wish to be on a level with God, without first measuring up to Him in goodness.

They built, and as they built God watched with mounting anger. Between each baked brick was a mortar of slime, and a slimier layer of arrogance. "Soon we'll be equal with God!" they crowed, from on top of their monumental chimney pot. "We'll be up among the angels!"

So God pulled a brick from the base of the tower and breathed on it: *huh.*

And they said . . . let us build us a city and a tower, whose top may reach unto heaven; and let us make us a name . . .

GENESIS 11:4

Down it came, with the slowness of a falling tree, and shattered along the ground in a mile-long cloud of dust. All the builders who clung to its sides were hurled to the four quarters of the Shinar Plain and far beyond. And when they got to their feet and began the long walk back, they found their mouths full of dust. Calling out to their comrades, they heard their words come out as gibberish: words and accents and alphabets had all been jarred by the fall into a confusion of sound, a babble.

And that is how the tower gained its name, how Language broke into a thousand different languages, and how men were parted from each other forever by the difference.

Response Corner

1. What problems do you think pride creates in the world today?

2. This story offers an explanation for why people speak different languages. Why do you think so many languages are spoken throughout the world today?

Time

2500 B.C.		1250 B.C.		B.C./A.D.

About 2000 B.C.
Abraham is born
in Mesopotamia

About 1225 B.C.
The Israelites make
their Exodus from Egypt

WHAT TO KNOW
Why was the development
of Judaism by the ancient
Hebrews important?

✔ Explain the significance
of Abraham and Moses
in Jewish history.

✔ Describe the Exodus,
and explain why it is
important in Jewish
history.

VOCABULARY
Judaism p. 205
monotheism p. 205
Torah p. 205
covenant p. 205
plague p. 207
Exodus p. 207
Ten Commandments p. 208

PEOPLE
Abraham
Isaac
Jacob
Joseph
Moses

PLACES
Mesopotamia
Canaan
Egypt
Mount Sinai

 GENERALIZE

 California
Standards
HSS 6.3, 6.3.1, 6.3.2, 6.3.3, 6.3.4

Beginnings of the Hebrew People

YOU ARE THERE It is not long after 2000 B.C.
You live in a pastoral family
south of **Mesopotamia**. Your
family's herd of sheep has thinned
the grass in this area. "It's time to
move on," your father has said.

As your family and its herd move to the north, you
pass another family of herders traveling to the south.

Your father asks the family's leader, Abram, about
available grasses farther north. Abram reassures your
father but also tells him that he is taking his family
south to the land of **Canaan** (KAY•nuhn).

LOCATE IT

ISRAEL

Aravah
Valley

❯ The ancient Hebrews left behind this clay vessel
(above) more than 3,000 years ago in the land once
known as Canaan (below).

Abraham

The ancient Hebrews are the early ancestors of the Jewish people. Long ago, the ancient Hebrews founded new ideas in religion, which became the origins of **Judaism**, the religion of the Jewish people.

Judaism was the first religion based on **monotheism** (MAH•nuh•thee•ih•zuhm), the concept of one God, who set down moral laws for humanity. These laws provide people with rules for living good lives.

The ancient Hebrews are described in the **Torah**—the oldest religious writings of the Jewish people. The Torah is part of the Hebrew Bible, or Tanakh (tah•NAHK). The Old Testament of the Christian Bible contains the same text as the Hebrew Bible.

Many people use the Hebrew Bible or the Old Testament as a source of information about the ancient Hebrews. Scholars use other ancient writings and archaeological findings to add to our knowledge.

The account of the Hebrews begins with **Abraham.** Some historians think Abraham —known as Abram in his early life—was born in Mesopotamia in about 2000 B.C.

Mesopotamians believed in many gods, but Abram believed in one God. According to the Hebrew Bible, God spoke to Abram, telling him to leave Mesopotamia and settle with his family in Canaan.

After traveling across the desert, Abram and his family reached Canaan. There, the Bible says, Abram heard God say, "I will assign this land to your offspring."*

*Genesis 12:7, *JPS Hebrew-English Tanakh.* The Jewish Publication Society, 1999.

> This nineteenth-century painting shows Abraham leading his family through the desert to Canaan.

The Bible says that God made a **covenant** with Abram. In this special agreement, God promised that Canaan would always belong to Abram and his descendants. For his part of the covenant, Abram agreed to worship God alone. Later, all Hebrews came to hold this belief.

The Bible tells that God told Abram to change his name to Abraham, which means "father of many" in Hebrew. Through one of his sons, **Isaac**, Abraham became known as the father of the Jewish people.

READING CHECK 🌀 GENERALIZE
What was Abraham's main religious belief?

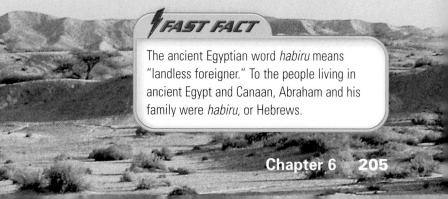

⚡FAST FACT

The ancient Egyptian word *habiru* means "landless foreigner." To the people living in ancient Egypt and Canaan, Abraham and his family were *habiru*, or Hebrews.

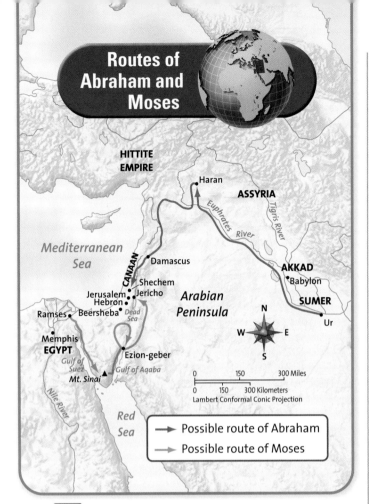

Routes of Abraham and Moses

HITTITE EMPIRE

Haran

ASSYRIA

Euphrates River

Tigris River

Mediterranean Sea

Damascus

CANAAN

Shechem

Jerusalem Jericho

Hebron

Beersheba Dead Sea

Ramses

AKKAD

Babylon

Arabian Peninsula

SUMER

Ur

N W E S

Memphis

EGYPT

Gulf of Suez

Mt. Sinai

Ezion-geber

Gulf of Aqaba

0   150   300 Miles

0   150   300 Kilometers

Lambert Conformal Conic Projection

Nile River

Red Sea

→ Possible route of Abraham

→ Possible route of Moses

ANALYSIS SKILL Analyze Maps Historians believe that Abraham and Moses followed the routes shown on this map.

❓ **Movement** In what area did both routes end?

The Israelites

Abraham's son Isaac had a son named **Jacob**. Jacob, who became known as Israel, had 12 sons.

The Hebrew Bible states that Jacob loved his son **Joseph** more than his other sons.

The other sons became jealous when Jacob gave Joseph a beautiful multicolored robe.

Joseph had a dream that one day his brothers would bow down to him. In anger, the brothers sold Joseph to traders on their way to **Egypt**. They let their father think that a wild animal had killed Joseph.

Joseph lived for many years in Egypt. Although the Egyptians worshipped many gods, Joseph continued to follow Abraham's religion, worshipping God only.

Because Joseph was a gifted thinker, the pharaoh made him a trusted adviser. In time, Joseph's authority grew to be second only to that of the pharaoh.

At about this time, famine struck Canaan. Joseph's brothers could not find food there. They traveled to Egypt to buy food, not knowing that Joseph was there. The brothers soon reunited.

Later, Jacob's entire family moved to Egypt. Each of Jacob's sons headed a separate tribe, or group, of decendants of Israel. The Israelites continued to live in Egypt for many years.

In time, life in Egypt changed for the Israelites. The pharaoh of later times feared that the Israelites might gain power in Egypt. As a result, the pharaoh enslaved the Israelites.

READING CHECK **CAUSE AND EFFECT**
Why did the Israelites move to Egypt?

▶ In this painting, Joseph's brothers beg for food.

THE TEN COMMANDMENTS

According to the Bible, God spoke to Moses, and these were His words*:

1. I the Lord am your God who brought you out of the land of Egypt, the house of bondage: You shall have no other gods besides Me.

2. You shall not make for yourself a sculptured image [idol]. . . .

3. You shall not swear falsely by the name of the Lord your God. . . .

4. Remember the sabbath day and keep it holy.

5. Honor your father and your mother. . . .

6. You shall not murder.

7. You shall not commit adultery.

8. You shall not steal.

9. You shall not bear false witness against your neighbor.

10. You shall not covet your neighbor's house . . . or anything that is your neighbor's.

*Exodus 20: 2–14, JPS Hebrew-English Tanakh. The Jewish Publication Society, 1999.

Moses and the Exodus

TIME About 1300 B.C.

PLACE Ancient Egypt

The Bible explains that the Israelites were slaves at the time **Moses** was born. Even so, the pharaoh worried that the Israelites might overthrow the Egyptians. To prevent this, the pharaoh ordered that every Israelite baby boy be drowned in the Nile River. One such baby was Moses.

Moses' mother set him afloat in a basket on the Nile, hoping that someone would save him. The pharaoh's daughter rescued Moses and raised him as an Egyptian. However, early on, Moses learned that he was an Israelite.

The Bible tells that God told Moses to demand freedom for the Israelites. Moses did as God said, but the pharaoh refused.

To change the pharaoh's mind, God sent ten **plagues** (PLAYGZ), or disasters, to Egypt. The first nine plagues included the turning of the Nile waters into blood, swarms of insects, and hail. Even so, the pharaoh would not free the Israelites.

The tenth plague persuaded the pharaoh to set the Israelites free. In one night, the Bible says, God killed the firstborn son of every Egyptian, including the pharaoh's.

The Israelites' mass departure from Egypt to escape slavery is known as the **Exodus**. Experts believe this event may have taken place in 1225 B.C. This event is described in the second book of the Bible, which is called Exodus.

After departing Egypt, the Israelites traveled on the Sinai Peninsula along the Red Sea. They wandered for 40 years, facing shortages of water and food.

Passover

Every spring, Jewish people around the world celebrate Passover, a holy day that honors the Exodus. The name *Passover* comes from the tenth plague. According to the Bible, God allowed the tenth plague to pass over the houses of the Israelites, so it would not affect them. God passed over their houses, sparing their children. After this plague, the pharaoh freed the Israelites.

Jewish families hold a special ceremony called the *Seder*. During this service, families read about the Exodus, express sorrow for the plagues God sent to the Egyptians, and eat certain foods. Jews observe Passover for eight days in memory of the Exodus when their ancestors escaped from Egyptian slavery.

The Bible says that God spoke to the Israelites at **Mount Sinai** along their route. There, God renewed his covenant with the Israelites. God also presented Moses with two stone tablets carved with a set of laws called the **Ten Commandments**.

The Ten Commandments differed from earlier laws, which described crimes and punishments for those crimes. The Ten Commandments gave rules for responsible behavior and for worshipping God properly. They became an important part of Judaism.

READING CHECK ⚙ **GENERALIZE**
Why were the Ten Commandments important to the Israelites?

Summary

Abraham and Moses are important to the history of the ancient Hebrews and to the origins of Judaism. Abraham founded Judaism, the first monotheistic religion. Moses led the Israelites out of slavery in Egypt and received the Ten Commandments from God.

REVIEW

1. 💡 Why was the development of Judaism by the ancient Hebrews important?

2. Use the term **Exodus** in a sentence.

3. How did the Ten Commandments differ from earlier laws?

CRITICAL THINKING

4. **ANALYSIS SKILL** Why was the Exodus a turning point in the history of the Israelites?

5. **ANALYSIS SKILL** **Make It Relevant** Why do people today remember and celebrate events of the past?

6. 🖌 **Make a Diagram** Using the information in this lesson, make a diagram that shows the sequence of major events in the life of Moses. Write a brief description of each event.

7. **Focus Skill** **GENERALIZE**
On a separate sheet of paper, copy and complete the graphic organizer below.

Facts		

Generalization
The actions of the ancient Hebrews are still remembered today.

Moses

Biography

Trustworthiness
Respect
Responsibility
Fairness
Caring
Patriotism

*"Have no fear! Stand by... for the Egyptians whom you see today you will never see again."**

According to the Hebrew Bible, these were the words that Moses spoke to the Israelites as he led them out of Egypt in the 1200s B.C. Moses was one of the most important leaders in Jewish history. According to the Hebrew Bible, God selected Moses to free the Hebrews from slavery in Egypt. Moses then led the Hebrews through the desert to the Promised Land, Canaan.

In the Hebrew Bible, writings tell about Moses protecting and speaking up for others. Moses bravely tells the pharaoh to release the Hebrews from slavery. He even pleads the Hebrews' case before God. After leaving Egypt and traveling for several years, the Hebrews forget their covenant with God and begin worshipping idols. Moses begs God not to punish them, saying, "Let not Your anger, O Lord, blaze forth against Your people. . . ."*

▶ According to the Bible, Moses was found as a baby near the bank of the Nile.

Moses was important to the Jewish people because he received the Ten Commandments from God. The Ten Commandments, which became the basis for the laws of Judaism, tell people how to worship God and how to behave responsibly.

*Moses. Exodus 14:13, 32:11. *JPS Hebrew-English Tanakh: The Traditional Hebrew Text and the New JPS Translation,* Second Edition, The Jewish Publication Society, 1999.

Why Character Counts

❓ How did Moses' actions make him a responsible leader?

Bio Brief

1300 B.C. ——————————————— 1200 B.C.

About 1225 B.C. ●
Moses leads the
Hebrews out of
Egypt to Canaan

FREEDOM AND THE RULE OF LAW

"Let my people go."*

— from the Bible, Exodus 5:1

When the early Israelites moved from Canaan to Egypt, they remained free people. They could own land in Egypt and become successful. Over time, the number of Israelites in Egypt increased. Some even rose to positions of power in the Egyptian government. However, the Israelites' freedom was not guaranteed. In ancient Egypt, a person's freedom was based on the pharaoh's decision. A pharaoh might enslave people who were not strong enough to defend themselves.

According to the Bible, that is exactly what happened. It tells that one pharaoh worried about the large number of Israelites

⚡ FAST FACT

Many Egyptian laws were passed down from generation to generation. However, pharaohs had complete authority to change old laws or to make new laws.

*Moses. Exodus 5:1, *JPS Hebrew-English Tanakh: The Traditional Hebrew Text and the New JPS Translation,* Second Edition. Jewish Publication Society, 1999.

Moses defended his people and worked toward their freedom.

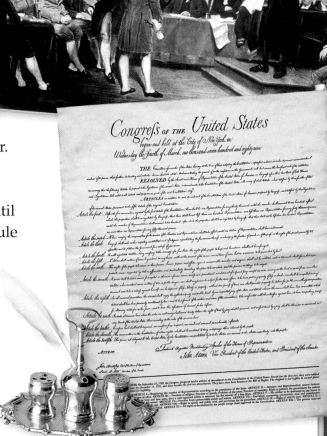

living in Egypt. He feared that they might try to overthrow him. The Bible says that the pharaoh enslaved the Israelites to prevent this from happening. He made life difficult for them with harsh labor.

In the United States and other present-day democracies, this would not happen. Slavery was legal in some parts of the United States until it was outlawed in 1865. Today, however, the rule of law prevents leaders from taking away a people's freedom. The rule of law is a basic principle of democracy. It says that all citizens of a nation, including leaders, must act according to the law. No leader can take away freedoms that are guaranteed by written laws, such as those in the United States Constitution.

After the United States Constitution was signed (top), delegates voted for it to become law. The Bill of Rights (above) in the Constitution guarantees important rights and freedoms to the American people. The people below are exercising their right to freedom of assembly.

Think About It!

Make It Relevant Why is it important for a country to have laws to protect the freedom of its citizens?

Lesson 2

Time

2500 B.C.	1250 B.C.	B.C./A.D.

About 1020 B.C.
Saul becomes the first king of a united Israel

About 1000 B.C.
David becomes king of Israel

928 B.C.
King Solomon dies

The Kingdom of Israel

YOU ARE THERE

It is about 1200 B.C. Imagine you are living in the world described by the Hebrew Bible. You live with your family in a small farming village in **Canaan**.

You've heard about the Israelites who recently arrived in the region. Your uncle says that the Israelites spent years traveling through the desert after leaving Egypt.

Although this was the home of their ancestors long ago, the Israelites have returned to a very different place. Many different people now live here. The Philistines (FIH•luh•steenz) and the Phoenicians (fih•NEE•shuhnz) control the coast. Other Canaanites have settled on the farmland.

LOCATE IT

ISRAEL

Judean Desert

▶ Patches of desert flowers bloom in the land once known as Canaan.

WHAT TO KNOW
How did Israel become a kingdom, and what changes did this bring for the Israelites?

✔ Explain how the achievements of Saul, David, and Solomon led to the growth of the kingdom of Israel and the Jewish religion.

✔ Describe what everyday life was like for the ancient Israelites after their return to Canaan.

VOCABULARY
territory p. 214
proverb p. 216

PEOPLE
Samuel
Saul
David
Solomon
Deborah

PLACES
Canaan
Egypt
Mesopotamia
Jerusalem
Phoenicia

 GENERALIZE

 California Standards
HSS 6.3, 6.3.3, 6.3.4

212 ■ Unit 3

➤ The first panel of this illustration shows Samuel giving his blessings to Saul as the new king of the Israelites. The second panel shows offerings being made in honor of Saul.

The Israelites Get a King

TIME About 1020 B.C.
PLACE Southern Canaan

The Hebrew Bible says that the Israelites reached Canaan 40 years after the Exodus. They settled in villages in the hills there. Unfortunately, enemies—including the Philistines—surrounded them on all sides, and neighboring kingdoms often attacked.

In Canaan, the Israelites lived as 12 independent tribes, each with its own leader. In times of war, an Israelite with strong military skills, called a judge, would rise to power to lead the people. A judge's leadership was temporary—it lasted only for the length of a conflict.

Without unity, the Israelites had trouble fighting off their attackers. The Bible says, "In those days there was no king in Israel; everyone did as he pleased."* To survive, the Israelites decided that they needed to unite under a single king.

According to the Bible, the Israelites went to **Samuel**, a respected tribal judge. They asked Samuel to "appoint a king for us, to govern us like all other nations."** Samuel reminded the Israelites that God should be their only leader. He said that they would suffer for choosing a king.

Samuel reluctantly selected **Saul**, from an Israelite tribe, to serve as the first ruler of the kingdom of Israel. Historians believe that this took place in about 1020 B.C.

READING CHECK ⓖGENERALIZE
Why did the Israelites decide they needed a king?

*Judges 21:25 and ** 1 Samuel 8:4, *JPS Hebrew-English Tanakh*. The Jewish Publication Society, 1999.

213

David

According to the Bible, David was special even as a boy. Young David was a shepherd as well as a musician. Once King Saul invited David to play the harp for him. The Bible credits David with writing many of the Psalms.

The Bible also tells about David and Goliath. The Philistines had a mighty warrior named Goliath. Goliath challenged the Israelites to send one soldier to fight him. After no Israelite soldier would accept the challenge, young David volunteered. David quickly made a slingshot, and with just one stone, he brought down Goliath. David had defended his people.

Make It Relevant What other ways can conflicts be settled?

Saul and David

Except for the Philistines, King Saul defeated many of the Israelites' enemies. By conquering new **territories**, or regions, Saul expanded his kingdom.

According to the Bible, Saul did not follow God's commands. As a result, God rejected him, and Saul soon died in war. By 1000 B.C., **David**, of the tribe of Judah, had become the new king.

King David proved to be the strong ruler that the Israelites wanted. David expanded the kingdom, even defeating the Philistines. In time, the kingdom of Israel stretched from **Egypt** to **Mesopotamia**.

David named the newly conquered city of **Jerusalem** as the new capital of the kingdom of Israel. Jerusalem was a good choice for a capital city. It lay between the lands of David's tribe, Judah, and the lands of the other tribes. Jerusalem did not belong to any single Israelite tribe.

Under David, Jerusalem grew as the center of government and religious life in Israel. David's government continued after his death. King David's descendants ruled for another 400 years.

READING CHECK 🔾 **GENERALIZE**
Why was Jerusalem a good choice for a capital city?

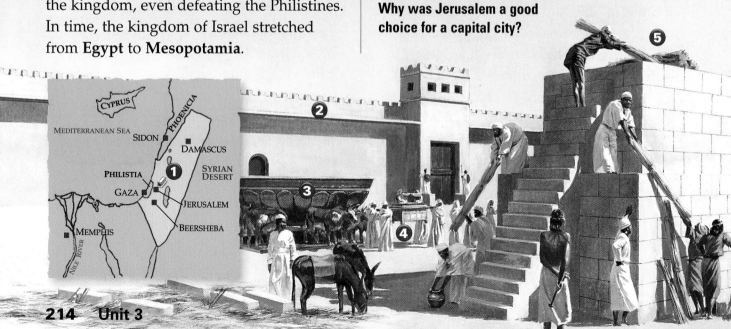

The Kingdom of Solomon

David died in about 967 B.C., after ruling for 40 years. His son **Solomon** became the next king of Israel.

As king, Solomon began planning a temple in Jerusalem. He wanted the temple to be a place to worship God and to keep the Ark of the Covenant—the box that held the two stone tablets on which the Ten Commandments were carved.

According to the Bible, Solomon quickly put his plan into action. He directed workers to construct a building of limestone and to line the inside walls with cedarwood. Solomon placed the Ark, covered with gold and colored glass, in a special room in the temple.

Called "the Temple" from then on, it was not Solomon's only building project. Solomon also directed the building of forts, grain storehouses, and water systems. To pay for his projects, Solomon placed heavy taxes on the Israelites and drafted thousands of them to work as builders. It was standard practice at the time for rulers to require people to work on building projects.

To organize the kingdom, Solomon divided the kingdom into 12 tax districts, which were similar to states. Each district had its own governor and public services. The Torah was the law of the land.

Israel's economy performed well under Solomon. Trade agreements with **Phoenicia** and Egypt helped the economy grow. With Phoenicia, Israel traded food for wood for Solomon's building projects.

To protect trade routes and the kingdom, Solomon created a large army, equipped with horses and chariots. He also formed alliances with Israel's neighbors. These actions by Solomon led to peace in the region during his rule.

READING CHECK ⟳**GENERALIZE**
What does Israel's trade with Phoenicia and Egypt say about its relations with them?

A Closer **LOOK**

Solomon's Temple

Solomon's Temple in Jerusalem became the center of worship and unity for the Israelites.

1. The Temple was at the kingdom's center.
2. Walls surrounded the Temple.
3. A huge bowl held water for use in religious ceremonies.
4. Processions of people displayed the Ark.
5. Priests burned offerings, or a gift as part of worship, on an altar.
6. The Temple was a place for keeping the Ark and for holding religious services.

The Proverbs *of* Solomon

The Proverbs of Solomon, or Book of Proverbs, from the Hebrew Bible is a collection of moral and religious advice and sayings. The Proverbs were used to educate Hebrew children to become responsible adults. Below are a few examples of sayings from the Book of Proverbs.*

"A kindly man benefits himself;
   A cruel man makes trouble for himself."
(Proverbs 11:17)

"The way of a fool is right in his own eyes;
   But the wise man accepts advice."
(Proverbs 12:15)

"Truthful speech abides forever,
   A lying tongue for but a moment."
(Proverbs 12:19)

* JPS Hebrew-English Tanakh. The Jewish Publication Society, 1999.

Life in Ancient Israel

With war no longer a constant worry, the Israelites turned their attention to everyday life. These peaceful times allowed for the growth of religion. Religious beliefs and laws continued to guide everyday life.

The Israelities found all kinds of work in the kingdom. Many men were farmers, while others worked as metalworkers, carpenters, or weavers. Some became government officials or soldiers.

Women ran the households and raised the children. Mothers and daughters cooked, cleaned, collected water, and made clothing for their families. Some women had jobs outside the home, such as working for wealthy Israelites. A few women, such as **Deborah**, who acted as a judge and an adviser, rose to positions of power.

King Solomon contributed much to the success of the kingdom. Solomon was known far and wide for his wisdom. Other rulers traveled to Jerusalem with gifts for Solomon to seek his advice. The Hebrew Bible says,

> **66 God endowed Solomon with wisdom . . . in great measure, with understanding as vast as the sands on the seashore. 99** *

Solomon was particularly known for his **proverbs**, short sayings that express a truth about life. Similar proverbs appear in other cultures as well. Solomon is also said to be the author of two books, Proverbs and the Song of Songs. These books are part of the Bible.

* 1 Kings 5:9, JPS Hebrew-English Tanakh. The Jewish Publication Society, 1999.

Selected Hebrew Letters

LETTER	ה	ד	ג	ב	א
NAME OF LETTER	He	Dalet	Gimel	Bet	Alef
ENGLISH SOUND	H	D	G	B	Silent

ANALYSIS SKILL **Analyze Tables** This table shows that Hebrew letters stand for certain sounds, just as English letters do. Unlike English, Hebrew writing (right) is read from right to left.

◆ In what other ways are these letters different?

According to the Hebrew Bible, not everyone in ancient Israel was happy. Samuel had warned that the Israelites would suffer for having a king. The Israelites faced high taxes, drafted labor, and a king who seemed not to care about them. By the time Solomon died in 928 B.C., the kingdom was coming apart.

READING CHECK **GENERALIZE**
How did the kingdom of Israel allow for the growth of Judaism?

Summary

The Israelites settled in Canaan. Attacks by unfriendly neighbors convinced them that they needed a king. Saul served as the first king. King David, the second king, expanded the kingdom. David's son Solomon brought wealth and stability. He built a temple in Jerusalem. For the most part, life in the kingdom was peaceful.

REVIEW

1. How did Israel become a kingdom, and what changes did this bring for the Israelites?

2. Write a sentence about King Solomon, using the term **proverb**.

3. What were some of the jobs that ancient Israelites held?

4. Why did King Solomon build a temple in Jerusalem?

CRITICAL THINKING

5. **ANALYSIS SKILL** How do you think David's decision to make Jerusalem the capital of the kingdom of Israel might have helped unify the Israelites?

6. **ANALYSIS SKILL** How might a leader's ability to carry out building projects be used to measure economic performance?

7. **Make a Time Line** Make a time line of the kings who ruled the kingdom of Israel between 1020 B.C. and 928 B.C. Be sure to label your time line.

8. **Focus Skill** **GENERALIZE**
On a separate sheet of paper, copy and complete the graphic organizer below.

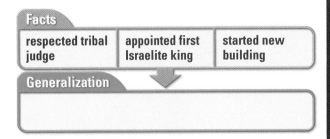

Facts		
respected tribal judge	appointed first Israelite king	started new building

Generalization

Make an Economic Choice

▶ WHY IT MATTERS

When King Solomon decided it was time to carry out God's request to build the Temple, he made an economic choice about how to use his resources.

Every economic choice requires a **trade-off**—the giving up of one thing to get another. When Solomon used his resources to build a temple, he gave up the ability to use them to build ships. What is given up because of an economic choice is called the **opportunity cost** of the choice. Building the Temple may have cost Solomon the opportunity to strengthen Israel's military.

Making economic choices is not reserved for kings and other leaders. Whether you know it or not, you make economic choices nearly every day.

▶ WHAT YOU NEED TO KNOW

You often make choices about your **personal finances**, or individual money matters. For example, you can decide to spend money that you have earned washing cars, or you can deposit it in a savings account at a bank. One choice will give you something you want now. The other choice will mean giving up what you want now to save your money and earn interest. **Interest** is the extra money a bank pays you to let it use your funds until you need them.

You can use these steps to make wise economic choices.

Step 1 Identify your goal and the resources you have to meet it.

Step 2 Identify your alternatives.

▶ This illustration of workers building the Temple shows some of the human and natural resources that Solomon chose to use on the project.

❯ Every day, people make economic choices. This girl is choosing to spend money on groceries instead of buying something else.

Step 3 Discuss the advantages and disadvantages of each alternative.

Step 4 Choose and identify the opportunity cost of your choice.

❯ PRACTICE THE SKILL

Imagine that you are an adviser to King Solomon. The king has to choose whether to use resources for great buildings or for making ships. Use the steps to help the king make his choice. Write a paragraph to advise the king about what to do.

❯ APPLY WHAT YOU LEARNED

Write a journal entry titled "The Best Economic Choice I Ever Made." What choice did you make? What was the trade-off? What was the opportunity cost? Why do you think that you made the right economic choice?

Time

2500 B.C. — 1250 B.C. — B.C./A.D.

928 B.C.
The kingdom of Israel splits into two

722 B.C.
The Assyrians conquer Israel

701 B.C.
Judah survives the Assyrian attack

WHAT TO KNOW
What people and events played an important part in changes in Israel?

✔ Explain why the kingdom of Israel ended.

✔ Describe the changes that the fall of Israel brought for the Israelites and their culture.

PEOPLE
Rehoboam
Sargon II
Hezekiah

PLACES
Shechem
Israel
Samaria
Jerusalem
Judah
Mesopotamia
Assyria

GENERALIZE

California Standards
HSS 6.3, 6.3.2, 6.3.4

Changes for Israel

YOU ARE THERE
The year is 928 B.C. Imagine you are living in the world described by the Hebrew Bible. The Israelites have gathered in the town of **Shechem**. King Solomon has just died. His son **Rehoboam** (ree•uh•BOH•uhm) is about to become king. Some Israelites fear that Rehoboam will be like his father. They don't want to pay high taxes and be drafted to work.

The crowd in Shechem is restless. Finally, someone shouts to Rehoboam, "Your father made our yoke heavy. Now lighten the harsh labor and the heavy yoke which your father laid on us, and we will serve you."* How will Rehoboam answer? Will the Israelites be happy with his reply?

*1 Kings 12:4, JPS Hebrew-English Tanakh. The Jewish Publication Society, 1999.

▶ Rehoboam becomes king of Israel.

Israel and Judah

⏱ **TIME** 928 B.C.

🌐 **PLACE** Kingdom of Israel

The northern Israelite tribes in the kingdom of Israel disliked Solomon. They believed that he had given special treatment to his own tribe, Judah. They wondered why the members of the tribe of Judah did not have to pay taxes or work on building projects.

When Solomon died and Rehoboam became king, the northern tribes wanted him to end taxes and drafted labor. After thinking about their request, Rehoboam told the tribes that he would not agree to their demands. In fact, he promised them harsher treatment than before.

Hearing this, the northern tribes rebelled, causing the kingdom of Israel to split into two parts in 928 B.C. The northern tribes formed their own kingdom, keeping the name **Israel**. The city of **Samaria** became Israel's capital.

Only the southern tribes of Judah and Benjamin remained loyal to Rehoboam. Their kingdom, whose capital was **Jerusalem**, became known as **Judah**. The word *Jew* comes from the name Judah.

For the next 200 years, the two kingdoms remained politically divided and sometimes even fought against each other. Yet they remained united by the same basic religious beliefs. However, Jerusalem and the Temple remained holy places to the kingdom of Judah, and Israel built its own holy places in Samaria.

In other ways, the two kingdoms were very different. Judah was small but strong,

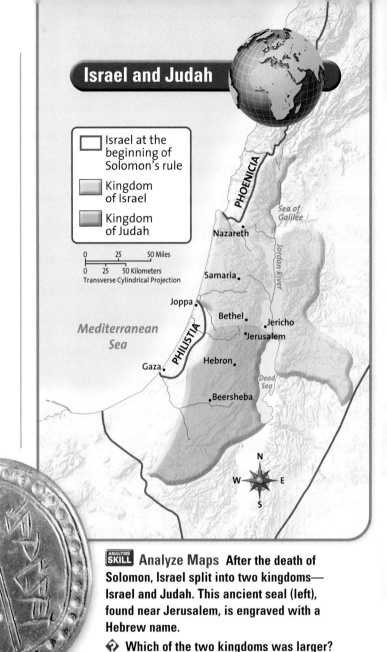

Israel and Judah

- ☐ Israel at the beginning of Solomon's rule
- ☐ Kingdom of Israel
- ☐ Kingdom of Judah

0   25   50 Miles
0   25   50 Kilometers
Transverse Cylindrical Projection

PHOENICIA
Sea of Galilee
Nazareth
Jordan River
Samaria
Joppa
Bethel
Jericho
Jerusalem
Mediterranean Sea
PHILISTIA
Hebron
Gaza
Dead Sea
Beersheba
N W E S

ANALYSIS SKILL **Analyze Maps** After the death of Solomon, Israel split into two kingdoms—Israel and Judah. This ancient seal (left), found near Jerusalem, is engraved with a Hebrew name.

❖ **Which of the two kingdoms was larger?**

and its kings came from only one family, the House of David. This helped keep Judah's government stable. Israel had more people than Judah, and it faced more problems. The ten tribes of Israel often fought over who would lead the kingdom. Also, many Israelites were poor. According to the Bible, faced with hard lives, some Israelites began to turn away from God.

READING CHECK ⟲ **GENERALIZE**
What problems did Israel face after it split from Judah?

▶ The fortress city of Lachish fell to the Assyrians, as did all of Israel.

Israel Falls to the Assyrians

Not far from Israel lay the growing Assyrian Empire. The Assyrians were fierce warriors from northern **Mesopotamia** who expanded their empire by conquering other peoples. By 730 B.C., they had reached Israel's borders.

In 722 B.C., **Assyria** conquered the weak and disorganized kingdom of Israel. The Assyrian king, **Sargon II,** boasted about his capture of Israel's capital, Samaria. He claimed, "I led away 27,290 of its inhabitants as captives. . . . I have rebuilt the city better than it had been before and settled it with people which I brought from the lands of my conquests."*

The Assyrians had a two-step plan for controlling territories they conquered. First, they forced many of the conquered people to leave their land. Second, they brought Assyrians into the conquered area. In this way, they tried to remove any connections that the conquered people had to their land.

The Assyrians followed this plan when they conquered Israel. Many Israelites had to leave their land, especially Israelite leaders and wealthy Israelites. In this way, the Assyrians made sure that the remaining Israelites did not have the resources or the leadership to rebel.

▶ Sargon II, Assyrian warrior king

*Barnavi, Elie and Miriam Eliav-Feldon. *A Historical Atlas of the Jewish People from the Time of the Patriarchs to the Present.* Knopf, 1992.

Large numbers of Assyrians settled in Samaria and the surrounding areas. There they mixed with the Israelites who were allowed to stay. The new population became known as Samaritans.

The Israelites who were forced to move lost contact with those who remained in Israel and Judah. Many of these "ten lost tribes of Israel" continued to practice Judaism in their new lands.

The Assyrians did not stop with the conquest of Israel. Next, they prepared to conquer Judah.

READING CHECK ⚙ **GENERALIZE**
How did the Assyrians control the conquered population of Israel?

Judah Remains Independent

Just as David had faced Goliath in the story told in the Bible, the people of Judah stood up to the mighty Assyrian army. They fought back as the Assyrians swept into their land.

In 701 B.C., **Hezekiah** (hez•uh•KY•uh), the king of Judah, protected Jerusalem from an Assyrian invasion. The Assyrian army had completely surrounded the walled city. The people could not leave their city without being captured or killed.

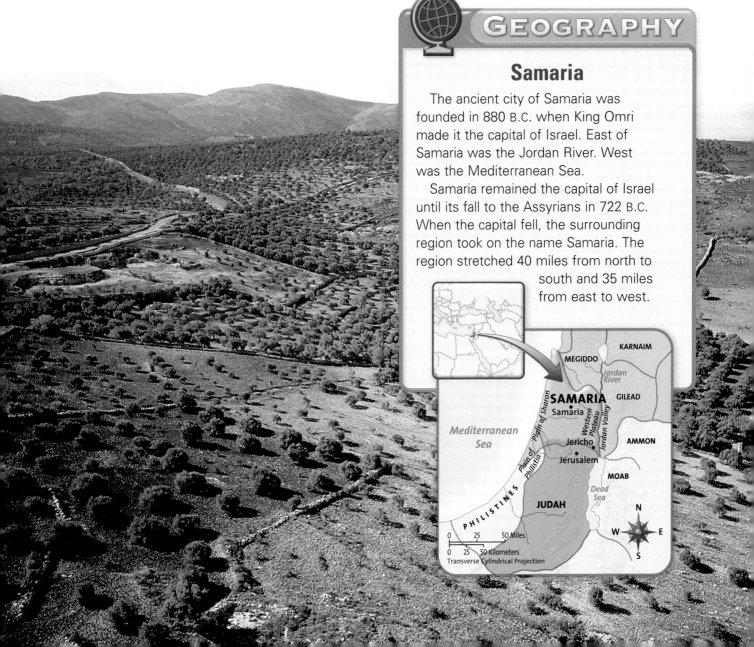

GEOGRAPHY

Samaria

The ancient city of Samaria was founded in 880 B.C. when King Omri made it the capital of Israel. East of Samaria was the Jordan River. West was the Mediterranean Sea.

Samaria remained the capital of Israel until its fall to the Assyrians in 722 B.C. When the capital fell, the surrounding region took on the name Samaria. The region stretched 40 miles from north to south and 35 miles from east to west.

KARNAIM
MEGIDDO
Jordan River
SAMARIA GILEAD
Samaria
Western Plateau
Plain of Sharon
Mediterranean Sea
Jericho
Jordan Valley
AMMON
Jerusalem
MOAB
Dead Sea
PHILISTINES
Plain of Philistia
JUDAH

0   25   50 Miles
0   25   50 Kilometers
Transverse Cylindrical Projection

N W E S

▶ Hezekiah (above) ordered the tunnel at the Pool of Siloam (right) built.

They had no way to get the resources they needed. Hezekiah ordered a tunnel built so that water from a nearby spring could flow into Jerusalem. With a supply of water, the people of Judah outlasted their attackers.

Judah remained independent for almost 100 years after the Assyrian attack. Then the Judaeans once again faced danger.

READING CHECK 🔵 **GENERALIZE**
How did Hezekiah save the people of Judah from the Assyrian invasion?

Summary

In 928 B.C., the kingdom of Israel split into two parts, Israel and Judah. The two existed side by side for 200 years. In 722 B.C., the Assyrian Empire conquered Israel. The Assyrians sent away many of the Israelites, who became known as the ten lost tribes of Israel. Judah fought off the Assyrians. Judaism survived, and Jerusalem remained the center of Jewish religious life.

REVIEW

1. 💡 What people and events played an important part in changes in Israel?

2. What effect did the Assyrian conquest have on the kingdom of Israel?

3. Why did the kingdom of Israel split into two kingdoms?

CRITICAL THINKING

4. **ANALYSIS SKILL** Why was Judah able to stand up to the Assyrians while Israel was not?

5. **ANALYSIS SKILL** How did the kingdom of Judah contribute to the survival of Judaism?

6. **Make It Relevant** Why might it be important for each person of a country to pay his or her fair share of taxes?

7. 🖌️ **Make Flash Cards** Write the name of a person, an event, or a place discussed in this lesson on the front of a card. On the back, write a description. Use your cards to quiz yourself or a classmate.

8. **Focus Skill** **GENERALIZE**
On a separate sheet of paper, copy and complete the graphic organizer below.

Facts	

⬇

Generalization
Sometimes culture can unite people that are politically divided.

Deborah

"The Lord's people won my victory over the warriors."

Biography

Trustworthiness
Respect
Responsibility
Fairness

Caring

Patriotism

Deborah sang these words about the Israelites after they won a victory against their enemies. Deborah was a judge long ago. She inspired the Israelites to stand up to their enemies because she cared about their survival.

▶ Deborah is shown on this page from the A.D. 1400s.

What we know about Deborah comes from the Hebrew Bible. Deborah lived in the kingdom of Israel after the Exodus. At that time, the tribes of Israel were scattered in villages throughout the land and the people were ruled by judges. Deborah was one of the most respected judges.

One day, according to the Hebrew Bible, Deborah told Barak, a warrior, that God had commanded him to lead his tribe against Sisera. Sisera was the army commander for King Jabin, a leader whose people mistreated the Israelites. Barak looked to Deborah for courage. He told her, "If you will go with me, I will go. . . ."* Deborah agreed. She went with Barak and ten thousand soldiers to the battlefield.

On the day of the battle, the Israelites faced Sisera's nine hundred iron chariots and won. Deborah became a hero to her people. Her song in the Hebrew Bible calls her "Deborah … O mother, in Israel!"*

*Deborah. Judges 5:13, 4:8, 5:7. *JPS Hebrew-English Tanakh: The Traditional Hebrew Text and the New JPS Translation,* Second Edition, The Jewish Publication Society, 1999.

Why Character Counts

❔ **How did Deborah show caring toward her people?**

Bio Brief

1200 B.C. — 1100 B.C.

1100s B.C. ●
Deborah and Barak lead their tribe to victory against Sisera and the army of King Jabin

GO ONLINE

Interactive Multimedia Biographies
Visit MULTIMEDIA BIOGRAPHIES at
www.harcourtschool.com/hss

Make a Thoughtful Decision

▶ WHY IT MATTERS

The ancient Hebrews faced many difficult decisions. Abraham had to decide whether to break away from the religious ideas of the Mesopotamians. Abraham's decision to worship one God rather than many gods changed the world forever. Later, the Israelites had to decide whether to join together under a single king.

Today, as in the past, people have to make many decisions throughout their lives. All decisions have consequences. A consequence is what happens because of an action. Some decisions may be short-lived while others, like Abraham's, are long-lasting. A decision can have positive consequences, negative consequences, or both.

▶ WHAT YOU NEED TO KNOW

You can use these steps to make a thoughtful decision.

Step 1 Identify a goal, and make a list of choices that might help you reach your goal.

Step 2 Gather the information you will need to make a good decision.

Step 3 Think about the possible consequences of each choice.

Step 4 Decide which choice will have the best consequences.

Step 5 Put your decision into action. Make sure to follow through, so that you will have the best chance to succeed.

▶ **King Rehoboam consulted with his advisers to help him make decisions.** *Bible Historiale.* Guiart des Moulins.

Matrix of Time and Place

CENTRAL ISSUES AND PROBLEMS	PEOPLE AND EVENTS	TIME AND PLACE	DECISIONS/SOLUTIONS

> **PRACTICE THE SKILL**

Long ago, the northern tribes of the kingdom of Israel had to decide what action to take when Rehoboam became king. According to the Bible, they had the choice of remaining loyal to King Rehoboam or joining Jeroboam, another leader, in starting a new state. Pick one of the following people. Describe how that person may have followed the steps for making a thoughtful decision. What decision do you think your person would have made?

1 A member of Rehoboam's tribe of Judah

2 A member of the small tribe of Benjamin in the south, near the land of Judah

3 A member of the tribe of Ephraim in the north (The city of Shechem is in Ephraim's territory. Jeroboam wants to make Shechem his capital when he becomes king of the new state.)

> **APPLY WHAT YOU LEARNED**

ANALYSIS SKILL Think about the similar issues and problems faced by the Mesopotamians, Egyptians, Nubians, and ancient Hebrews. Use the table above to put people and events from each culture in a matrix of time and place to help explain their common issues and problems. List the decisions that people made to try to solve the problems.

1900s B.C.
Abraham leads
his family to
Canaan

Reading Social Studies

When you **generalize,** you make a statement that summarizes
a group of facts and shows how they are related.

Make a Generalization

Complete this graphic organizer to make a generalization about
the development of the ancient Hebrews' religion. A copy of
this graphic organizer appears on page 66 of the Homework and
Practice Book.

Origins of Judaism

Facts

Judaism is based on monotheism.	The Ten Commandments became an important part.	The Israelites formed a kingdom.	King Solomon built a temple in Jerusalem.

Generalization

California Writing Prompts

Write an Expository Paragraph Imagine that
you are an Egyptian newspaper reporter. Write an
expository paragraph in the form of a newspaper
article. Write about the significance of the Exodus
and the events that led up to it.

Write a Persuasive Speech Think about
why David chose Jerusalem to be the capital
of the kingdom of Israel. Write a speech to the
Israelites persuading them that Jerusalem was a
good choice.

1000 B.C.
David is king
of Israel

722 B.C.
The Assyrians
conquer Israel

Use Vocabulary

Use each term in a sentence or
two to explain both what the
term means and how that meaning
relates to the ancient Hebrews.

1. **monotheism** (p. 205)

2. **covenant** (p. 205)

3. **Exodus** (p. 207)

4. **territory** (p. 214)

5. **prophet** (p. 222)

Use the Time Line

ANALYSIS SKILL Use the summary time line above to answer these questions.

6. How long after David became king did the Assyrians conquer Israel?

7. What happened in 722 B.C.?

Apply Skills

Make a Thoughtful Decision

8. After the Hebrews returned to Canaan, they were constantly attacked by hostile neighbors. They decided to appoint a king to unite them. If it had been your decision, what would you have done? Explain the steps that led to your decision.

Recall Facts

Answer these questions.

9. How did Abraham's religion differ from the religions of other peoples in Mesopotamia?

10. How were the Proverbs important to ancient Hebrews?

11. How did the people of Jerusalem survive attacks from the Assyrians?

Write the letter of the best choice.

12. Which of the following was an important event during King David's rule?
    A The Israelites conquered Egypt.
    B David made Jerusalem the capital.
    C David built a temple.
    D The kingdom split into two parts.

13. What was the Ark of the Covenant?
    A the box that held Solomon's proverbs
    B the Israelites' place to worship God
    C the box that held the Ten Commandments
    D the place where God spoke to Abraham

Think Critically

14. **ANALYSIS SKILL** What might have happened to Judaism if the Egyptian pharaoh had not freed the Israelites?

15. **ANALYSIS SKILL** What are the origins of Judaism, and how did Abraham and Moses help develop Judaism?

Study Skills

PREVIEW AND QUESTION

Previewing a lesson to identify main ideas can help you concentrate on the most important information. Asking yourself questions about these ideas can also help.

- ❯ **Preview a lesson by reading the lesson titles and the section titles. Then look at the pictures and other visuals and read their captions. Try to identify the main ideas of the lesson.**

- ❯ **Think of questions you have about the main ideas.**

- ❯ **Read the lesson to find the answers to your questions. Then recite, or say, the answers aloud. Finally, review what you have read.**

Changes for the Jewish People

Preview	Questions	Read	Recite	Review
Lesson 1 Judaism changed under Babylonian and Persian rule.	How did Judaism change under the Babylonian captivity? How did the Persians affect the Jewish people? Why did the Jewish people migrate?	✓	✓	✓
Lesson 2				

Apply As You Read

Use a table similar to the one above to preview and question ideas as you study each lesson in this chapter. First, identify the main ideas of each lesson. Next, write down questions about the main ideas. Then, read the lesson. Finally, recite the answers and review what you have read to be sure you understand the lesson.

California History-Social Science Standards, Grade 6

6.3 Students analyze the geographic, political, economic, religious, and social structures of the Ancient Hebrews.

Changes for the Jewish People

▶ Jerusalem's Western Wall

Masada:
The Last Fortress

by Gloria D. Miklowitz   illustrated by Barbara Kiwak

The kingdom of Judah, founded by the Israelites, did not remain free for long. Enemy after enemy took control of the land. In time, Judah fell under the control of the Roman Empire. About 1,000 Jews escaped to a mountain fort called Masada. The following story begins with the Jews learning that the Roman army is about to attack them. It is told from the point of view of a 17-year-old boy.

My father's confidence was contagious. Almost before he had finished speaking, a spirit of comradeship and hope pervaded the crowd. Even I felt a difference. All the tightness of a few moments before was gone, and in its place was strength. My body felt tireless, eager to be doing what must be done; my mind did not question the future. It knew! We would win. I was sure of it. I would question no longer. My heart said Eleazar was right, but when I thought ahead, my courage faltered. Action was the only answer now. In doing, there would be no time for thought. And once done, no going back.

Before this spirit of hope could wither, Eleazar issued orders. Even he seemed caught up in the excitement. The twitch in his face was gone. A small smile pulled at his lips. His eyes sparkled with the reflections of his fast-moving mind. His voice gained strength and warmth as thoughts and orders tumbled forth.

"We must make sure our water supply is adequate. After the Romans come, it will be increasingly difficult to bring the water up without being observed and fired upon. Berenice?" Eleazar called. My mother raised her hand in the crowd. "You will take as many women and children as you need to the cisterns and bring back enough water to replenish our storage tanks here...."

cisterns tanks for storing water

contagious easily spread

pervaded extended throughout

faltered gave way

"John," my father next ordered. "Organize all fighting men into units of ten and meet me as soon as possible." John frowned, but his fair skin colored suddenly, and though his thick, dark brows nearly joined, I realized they masked his true reaction. John wasn't at all displeased. Though he shifted his tall frame from foot to foot in what might appear to be awkward embarrassment, he was already signaling, with a nod of the head or a raised finger, who was to join him when Eleazar finished.

"Check the lookout towers, Simon. See that each man knows his watch and where to report any unusual movement below. Then, back to me!"

I tried to swallow my disappointment. Was I, a man of seventeen, to be a messenger boy? Was this all the responsibility I would be given? I listened hard for more orders, but one by one the important tasks of leadership were given to others, and soon I found I could not look my father in the face.

And so it went. Women were called upon to tend our small fields, to organize stores of food, to prepare strips of linen as bandages, to keep the small children busy while the preparations for defense occupied their brothers and fathers. Many of the older people would spend their time in prayer, for no matter how well prepared we might be, the final outcome of our actions would be the will of God.

"And now," my father said, smiling at our people, "one thing further. Despite these preparations, some things will not change. We will continue to observe the Sabbath, and the holidays as well—within reason. Rabbi Hillel will see to that. The children will continue to attend school, because without knowledge, man is no better than an animal." The children groaned in disappointment, and their elders laughed. "As always, the sick, the poor, and the elderly will be properly cared for. And we will help each other in whatever ways we can."

Response Corner

1. Why was Simon disappointed at the job his father assigned to him?

2. Why do you think it was so important to Eleazar that some things remain the same even though his people would be going through war?

586 B.C.
Babylonians destroy
Jerusalem and the Temple

538 B.C.
The Jewish people
return to Judah

515 B.C.
A second Temple is
completed in Jerusalem

WHAT TO KNOW

How did Judaism change
under Babylonian and
Persian rule?

✓ Describe the location of
Jewish people in lands
outside Judah.

✓ Discuss the treatment
of the Jewish people by
the Babylonians and the
Persians.

✓ Explain how Judaism
developed despite the
scattering of Jews to
other lands.

VOCABULARY

exile p. 235
prophet p. 236
synagogue p. 236
rabbi p. 236
Diaspora p. 237
canonize p. 238
theocracy p. 238

PEOPLE

Jeremiah
Cyrus
Ezra

PLACES

Judah
Babylon
Jerusalem

 GENERALIZE

 California
Standards
HSS 6.3, 6.3.2, 6.3.4, 6.3.5

Defeat and New Beginnings

YOU ARE THERE

The year is 597 B.C., and the Assyrian Empire
has fallen. The land you stand on in **Judah** is
now part of the New Babylonian Empire.

Everyone living in Judah must pay taxes to the
Babylonians. The people of Judah do not like this forced
taxation at all. You've just heard that the king of Judah
himself has refused to pay taxes to the Babylonians.

Now, the Babylonians are on their way to punish
the citizens of Judah. In a few days, the people will
face the most powerful force they have ever seen—the
Babylonian army.

LOCATE IT

NEW
BABYLONIAN
EMPIRE

Jerusalem

The Babylonian Captivity

TIME 597 B.C.

PLACE Kingdom of Judah

In 597 B.C., the Babylonians conquered the land of Judah. To help keep it part of their empire, they forced Judah's king to move to their capital city, **Babylon**. They sent 10,000 other people from Judah there as well.

The Babylonians appointed a new king to rule Judah from **Jerusalem**. Even though the king was from Judah, the Babylonians believed that he was loyal to them. The king of Judah proved them wrong when he and other citizens rebelled against the Babylonians.

In 586 B.C., the Babylonians conquered Judah a second time. The Babylonians were so angry about the rebellion that they destroyed Jerusalem. The Bible says that the Babylonians "tore down the walls of Jerusalem on every side."* They also burned the Temple to the ground.

*2 Kings 25:10. *The JPS Hebrew-English Tanakh.* The Jewish Publication Society, 1999.

▶ **A Babylonian tax receipt, written in cuneiform**

This time, the Babylonians sent nearly every citizen of Judah to live in Babylon, an action that resulted in what was known as the Babylonian Captivity. It is also known as the Babylonian Exile because most citizens were **exiled**, or forced to leave their homeland.

READING CHECK ⭘ **GENERALIZE**

How did the Babylonians keep control of Judah?

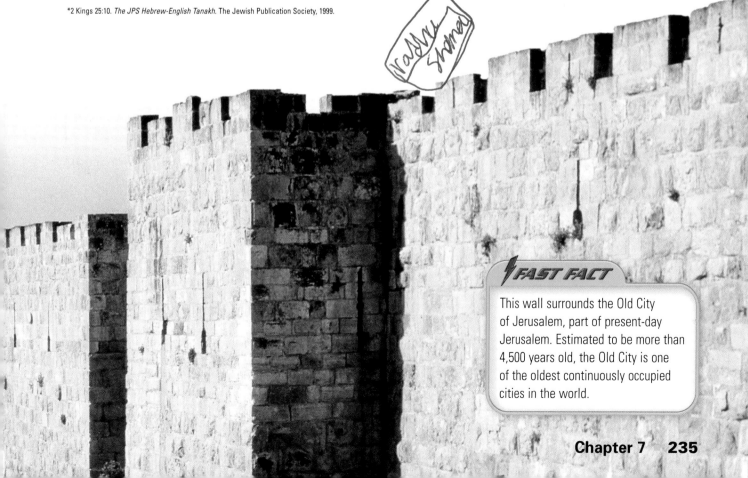

⚡**FAST FACT**

This wall surrounds the Old City of Jerusalem, part of present-day Jerusalem. Estimated to be more than 4,500 years old, the Old City is one of the oldest continuously occupied cities in the world.

Judaism Changes

The prophet **Jeremiah** introduced new ideas to the exiles. **Prophets** are people who are believed to receive messages from God. Jeremiah taught that God could be worshipped not just in the Temple but everywhere. He said that God could hear the exiles' prayers no matter where they were. Jeremiah also said that one day the exiles would return to Judah.

Life under the Babylonians differed from life under the Assyrians. When the Assyrians conquered Israel, they sent the Israelites to live all over the empire. The Israelites adopted Assyrian ways of life and lost their own culture. In contrast, the Babylonians kept the exiles from Judah together in one community in Babylon. Because of this, the exiles were able to continue following their cultural and religious traditions.

Since the exiled people of Judah, now called Jews, no longer had the Temple, they began to create community centers for prayer and study. Later, the Greeks gave the Jewish community center the name **synagogue** (SIH•nuh•gahg), meaning "assembly." Today, Jewish places of worship are still called synagogues.

Jewish leadership also changed in exile. In Judah, priests had led worship in the Temple. In exile, teachers called **rabbis** led the synagogues. Rabbis around the world still teach the history and laws of Judaism.

The Jewish experience of exile changed Judaism. In turn, by changing the practices of Judaism, the Jewish people were able to keep their faith and their culture alive.

READING CHECK **MAIN IDEA AND DETAILS**
What new ideas did Jeremiah bring to the exiled people from Judah?

A Closer LOOK

Community Center

As a place of learning and worship, the synagogue was the center of Jewish community life. Outside the synagogue, Jewish communities bustled with activity.

❶ Farmers grew vegetables in gardens.

❷ Farmers used oxen to plow their fields.

❸ Wells provided fresh water and a meeting place.

❹ Women baked bread in clay ovens.

❺ Vendors sold food and other goods.

❻ Rabbis taught the Jewish faith and traditions.

✛ How were the Jews reminded daily of their faith?

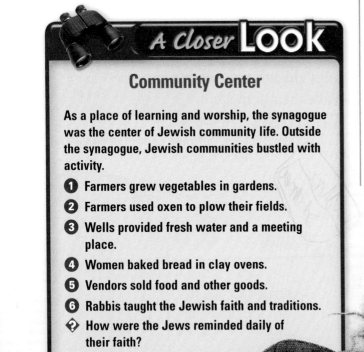

The Jewish Diaspora

Some of the Jews in exile began to feel at home in Babylon, but others longed to return to Jerusalem. One prophet reminded the Jews that God had promised the Jews the land of Canaan.

The Jews did not have to wait long. In about 538 B.C., the Persian Empire conquered Babylon. Their leader, **Cyrus**, believed that as long as conquered people accepted his rule, he would respect their religious beliefs. Cyrus allowed the Jews to reclaim Judah and to rebuild the Temple.

In 515 B.C., the Jews finished building a second Temple, but not all Jews moved back to Judah. The Babylonian Exile had begun the Jewish **Diaspora**, the scattering of Jews outside their homeland. Since this time, Jews have settled all over the world. Sometimes, they moved to new places by choice while at other times, governments or wars forced them to move.

Other cultures in the world have experienced diasporas as well. One of the largest diasporas came about because of the African slave trade. Millions of Africans were forced from their homelands between about the A.D. 700s and the A.D. 1800s.

READING CHECK ⚙ **GENERALIZE**
How did the Babylonian Exile affect the Jewish people?

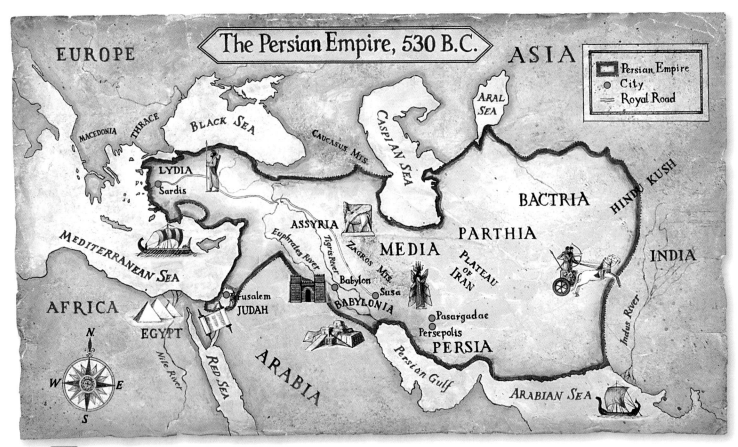

The Persian Empire, 530 B.C.

EUROPE   ASIA

Persian Empire
City
Royal Road

MACEDONIA
THRACE
BLACK SEA
CAUCASUS MTS.
CASPIAN SEA
ARAL SEA
LYDIA
Sardis
BACTRIA
HINDU KUSH
ASSYRIA
PARTHIA
Euphrates River
Tigris River
ZAGROS MTS.
MEDIA
PLATEAU OF IRAN
INDIA
MEDITERRANEAN SEA
Babylon
Susa
BABYLONIA
Indus River
AFRICA
Jerusalem
JUDAH
Pasargadae
Persepolis
PERSIA
EGYPT
Nile River
RED SEA
ARABIA
Persian Gulf
ARABIAN SEA

ANALYSIS SKILL Analyze Maps This map shows the Persian Empire under Cyrus the Great.
❓ What feature formed the empire's western border?

Ezra and the Torah

 **TIME** 450 B.C.

PLACE Jerusalem

Jewish cultural life in Judah suffered during the Babylonian Exile. However, as exiles returned to Judah, the Jewish community grew stronger there.

A scribe named **Ezra** helped restore Judaism in Jerusalem. In about 450 B.C., Ezra led a number of Jews back to Jerusalem from Babylon. Later, Ezra gave a series of public readings from the Torah. The Torah, or "the Law" in Hebrew, contains Jewish law, including the Ten Commandments. Ezra read the Torah for seven days straight.

These readings inspired many Jews to renew their faith. According to the Bible, the Jews signed a pledge on the last day of the reading, in which they promised to

❝ . . . follow the Teaching of God, given through Moses the servant of God, and to observe carefully all the commandments of the Lord our Lord . . . . ❞ *

Ezra also wrote the Torah's laws on a scroll, creating one of the first written documents of Judaism. Later, the Torah was **canonized** (KA•nuh•nyzd), or made an official part of, the teachings of Judaism. This made law central to Judaism.

The Torah became the law of Judah, which was, at that time, a **theocracy** (thee•AH•kruh•see), or a state ruled by religious law. The law applied to everyone, even rulers. The idea that everyone was equal under the law is important in many countries in the world today, including the United States.

*Nehemiah 10:30. *JPS Hebrew-English Tanakh.* The Jewish Publication Society, 1999.

Many of the Torah's laws describe how to practice Judaism. Some tell how to celebrate Jewish traditions and holidays. Other laws tell how to behave and treat people fairly while still others guide daily life. For example, the Torah explains when to plant crops and how to punish criminals. Rulers and rabbis worked together to enforce the law of the Torah in Judah.

READING CHECK ⚫ **GENERALIZE**
How did Ezra help restore Judaism in Jerusalem?

Summary

In 586 B.C., the Babylonians destroyed Jerusalem and the Temple. They sent many Jews into exile in Babylon. The Jewish people kept their faith by changing the practices of Judaism. When the Persian Empire conquered Babylon, King Cyrus allowed Jews to return to Judah and to rebuild the Temple. Many Jews, however, remained outside Judah, forming the Jewish Diaspora.

▶ This painting shows Jewish people of the diaspora celebrating a wedding in Morocco, a part of northwestern Africa.

REVIEW

1. How did Judaism change under Babylonian and Persian rule?

2. Write a paragraph that explains the terms **exile** and **diaspora**.

3. What happened in 538 B.C. that made it possible for the Jews to return to Judah from exile?

CRITICAL THINKING

4. Why do you think so many Jews chose to stay in Babylon after Cyrus let them return to Judah?

5. **ANALYSIS SKILL** How did Cyrus's views on religion help Judaism survive?

6. Make It Relevant How do you think the Diaspora affects Jews today?

7. Make a Chart Make a chart that shows the changes in Judaism under the Babylonians and the Persians. Your chart should have two columns. Label the first column *Babylonians* and the second column *Persians*. List at least two changes in each column.

8. **Focus Skill GENERALIZE**
On a separate sheet of paper, copy and complete the graphic organizer below.

Facts

⬇

Generalization

The Jewish people have faced many changes over their long history.

Use a Cultural Map

▶ WHY IT MATTERS

A cultural map shows the locations of people who share a certain way of life. The map can be based on language, religion, or any other part of culture. Often a cultural map uses color or symbols to show places where most of the people share a cultural trait. Studying cultural maps can help you learn more about present-day people and people of the past, such as the ancient Hebrews.

▶ WHAT YOU NEED TO KNOW

The cultural map on page 241 shows the languages spoken by people of southwestern Asia today. By reading the map, you can see which languages are spoken in different regions of southwestern Asia. To understand the map, you need to use the map legend. The different colors in the map legend stand for the languages spoken in the regions shown on the map.

▶ Jewish people gather at the Western Wall in Jerusalem to recite prayers in Hebrew.

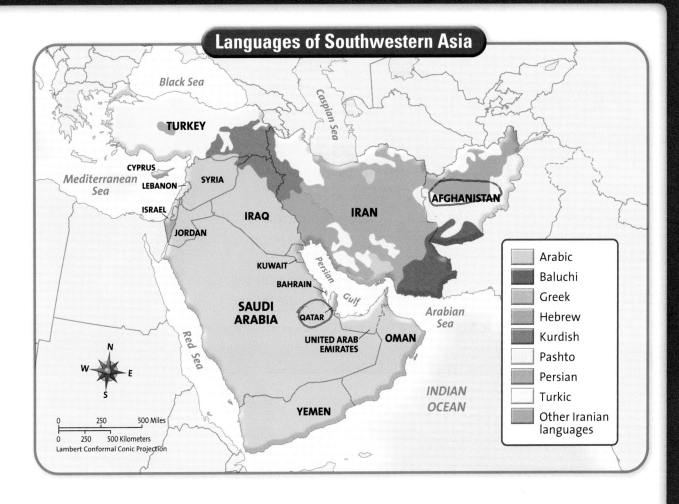

Languages of Southwestern Asia

Black Sea

Caspian Sea

TURKEY

CYPRUS

Mediterranean Sea

LEBANON

SYRIA

ISRAEL

AFGHANISTAN

IRAQ

IRAN

JORDAN

KUWAIT

BAHRAIN

Persian Gulf

SAUDI ARABIA

QATAR

Arabian Sea

UNITED ARAB EMIRATES

OMAN

Red Sea

INDIAN OCEAN

YEMEN

N
W E
S

0   250   500 Miles

0   250   500 Kilometers

Lambert Conformal Conic Projection

	Arabic
	Baluchi
	Greek
	Hebrew
	Kurdish
	Pashto
	Persian
	Turkic
	Other Iranian languages

This cultural map also shows national boundaries for countries in this region. Having both countries and languages on the same map allows you to compare the two kinds of information.

▶ PRACTICE THE SKILL

ANALYSIS SKILL Use the cultural map above to answer these questions.

① In which country do people speak Hebrew?

② What languages do people speak in Iran? Which language do you think is spoken by the most people?

③ In which countries is Kurdish spoken?

④ What language do most people speak in Turkey?

▶ APPLY WHAT YOU LEARNED

ANALYSIS SKILL Make your own cultural map, showing the official languages of South America. Use an encyclopedia, atlas, or almanac to gather information about the official languages of each country in South America. Be sure to label each country, and use different colors to indicate the countries' official languages.

Practice your map and globe skills with the **GeoSkills CD-ROM**.

Map and Globe Skills

Jewish Religious Artifacts

Religion has been a uniting force for the Jewish people throughout their history. The artifacts you see on these pages were created in different centuries in different countries by Jewish people sharing a common faith. That faith continues to be a source of inspiration and identity for Jewish people today.

▶ **A rabbi holds a Torah scroll, which is stored in an ark.**

The Torah is read or sung during religious services. Each Torah scroll is written by hand using special ink.

A mezuzah is sometimes placed at entrances in Jewish homes to symbolize faith.

Children and adults spin tops called dreidels (DRAY•duhlz) during the Hanukkah holiday.

ANALYSIS SKILL Analyze Artifacts

1 What does the look of these religious objects suggest about Jewish people's reverence for their faith?

2 What does the dreidel, a religious toy, suggest about the role of religion in the lives of young Jewish people?

3 Why might sacred objects such as the Torah scroll have to be made by hand?

GO ONLINE Visit PRIMARY SOURCES at www.harcourtschool.com/hss

Noisemakers are used in cheerful Purim holiday celebrations.

Some Jewish people wear amulets for good luck.

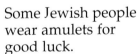

The menorah is used in Hanukkah celebrations. It has been a symbol of Israel since ancient times.

Lesson 2

167 B.C.
The Revolt of the
Maccabees begins

A.D. 70
The Romans destroy the
Temple in Jerusalem

A.D. 132
Bar Kokhba leads a fight
against the Romans

WHAT TO KNOW
How did Judaism develop
from the 300s B.C. through the
A.D. 100s?

✓ Explain the significance
of Ruth, Naomi, and
Rabbi Yohanan ben
Zaccai to Judaism.

✓ Explain how Judaism
survived after the
Romans destroyed the
Temple in A.D. 70.

✓ Identify the sources of
teachings in Judaism.

VOCABULARY
Christianity p. 247
Islam p. 247

PEOPLE
Judah Maccabee
Yohanan ben Zaccai
Simon Bar Kokhba
Hillel
Ruth
Naomi
Jesus
Muhammad
Ishmael

PLACES
Jerusalem
Judaea

GENERALIZE

California
Standards
HSS 6.3, 6.3.2, 6.3.3, 6.3.5

Continuing Traditions

You can hardly believe what is happening in
Jerusalem in 167 B.C. The Greeks have ruled
Judaea for more than 30 years. Their king has built a
fort in the center of Jerusalem, and his soldiers have
killed many Judaeans. Taxes are so high that Judaeans
struggle to survive.

Worst of all, the Greek rulers outlawed Judaism.
They even stole money that belonged to the Temple.
Now the Temple has an altar to a Greek god in what
was Judaism's most sacred place!

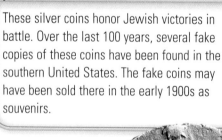

FAST FACT

These silver coins honor Jewish victories in
battle. Over the last 100 years, several fake
copies of these coins have been found in the
southern United States. The fake coins may
have been sold there in the early 1900s as
souvenirs.

▶ This illustration from a French book published in the A.D. 1300s shows the fighting between the Jews and Greeks during the revolt of the Maccabees.

The Maccabees

In 332 B.C., the Judaeans faced another conqueror—the Macedonian emperor Alexander the Great. Because he loved Greek culture, Alexander brought many Greek customs to his conquered lands, including Judah, then called Judaea.

At first, the Jewish people were allowed to practice their religion freely. This freedom ended in 200 B.C., when a Greek ruler outlawed Judaism and forced all Judaeans to worship Greek gods.

In 167 B.C., a man named Judah, the son of a Jewish priest, led a revolt. During the revolt, Judah became known as **Judah Maccabee** (MAK•uh•bee). Today, the event is remembered as the Revolt of the Maccabees.

Judah Maccabee proved to be a strong leader. He recruited thousands of Jews to fight, and they recaptured Jerusalem and all of Judaea. They restored Jewish worship in the Temple.

In 63 B.C., the Roman Empire took control of Judaea, choosing Jewish kings who were loyal to Rome. Roman officials mistreated the Jews, causing the Jewish people to rebel. In A.D. 70, the Romans laid siege to Jerusalem, leaving it and the Temple in ruins.

After the destruction of the Second Temple, Rabbi **Yohanan ben Zaccai** (yoh•HAN•uhn ben ZAK•ay•eye), also written Johanan ben Zakkai, founded a Jewish school in Yavneh west of Jerusalem. Soon the school grew into a center for Jewish life. Synagogues, too, continued to gain importance as places of prayer and study. Both of these events helped Judaism survive.

In A.D. 132, the Jewish people tried again to overthrow the Romans. **Simon Bar Kokhba** (BAR KAWK•bah) was the leader of the revolt. The Romans brutally crushed the revolt and sent nearly all the Jews of Jerusalem into exile from their homeland. The Jewish people would not rule Judaea again for 1,800 years.

READING CHECK ☼GENERALIZE
How did Judaism survive after the Temple was destroyed in A.D. 70?

▶ Many artists have been inspired by the writings of Judaism. These three paintings illustrate the story of Ruth from the Ketuvim.

The Writings of Judaism

The Hebrew Bible is both history and literature. It tells the stories of the Jewish people to about 300 B.C. The Hebrew Bible has three parts. First is the Torah, or "the Law," including the Ten Commandments. Next is the Nevi'im (neh•vee•EEM), or "the Prophets." The third part is the Ketuvim (keh•too•VEEM), or "the Writings."

Genesis, the first book of the Torah, describes how God created the universe. One of the best-known accounts in Genesis is about Noah and the flood. God orders Noah to build an ark, a large boat, and take aboard two of every living creature. Noah and the others on the ark survive the flood to renew life on Earth.

In places, the Torah may be difficult to understand. Because of this, scholars and rabbis have tried to help Jews understand it. Some scholars created writings called the Commentaries to explain questions that come up about Jewish law. Others, such as Rabbi **Hillel**, devoted their lives to studying and teaching the Torah. In the first century B.C., Hillel founded a school to share his ideas with others.

The Nevi'im includes the words of prophets, such as Jeremiah and Ezekiel, who spoke to the Jewish people as representatives of God. It also tells about Israelite kings, including David and Solomon.

The Ketuvim contains several kinds of written works, including poems, proverbs, and other writings. One of the most popular writings is about friendship and loyalty. The book of **Ruth** tells of a young woman who married into a Jewish family. When her husband died, Ruth stayed to care for her mother-in-law, **Naomi**, instead of returning to her own family. Ruth told Naomi, "Your people shall be my people, and your God my God."*

READING CHECK ☼GENERALIZE
What are the Commentaries?

*Ruth 1:16. JPS Hebrew-English Tanakh. The Jewish Publication Society, 1999.

Jewish Traditions and Influence

The Jewish people observe many holy days and traditions. Two of the most important Jewish holy days are Rosh Hashanah (RAHSH huh•SHAH•nuh) and Yom Kippur (YOHM kih•PUR). Rosh Hashanah is the first day of the Jewish New Year, the beginning of the High Holy Days. The last day of the High Holy Days is Yom Kippur.

Rosh Hashanah is known as the Day of Judgment. Jews believe that on this day, God judges them. They examine their actions during the past year and think about any sins they have committed.

Yom Kippur is the Day of Atonement. On Yom Kippur, Jews express regret for their sins and ask God to forgive them.

Throughout the year, the Jewish people celebrate a number of other holy days. As you have learned, Passover is an important Jewish holy day that marks the Israelites' escape from Egypt.

Judaism influenced two of the world's largest religions, Christianity and Islam (is•LAHM). According to tradition, Abraham is an important figure to Judaism, Christianity, and Islam. Judaism also has other connections to Christianity and Islam.

Jesus, on whom **Christianity** was founded, was Jewish. He taught many of the ideas of Judaism, such as belief in God, the Ten Commandments, and love of God and of your neighbor. In addition, Jesus taught new religious ideas like love your enemies.

Muslims, who practice the religion of **Islam**, say that Abraham, an early prophet and the father of the Jewish people, received messages from God. They also say that **Muhammad** (moh•HA•muhd) was God's final prophet. Muhammad said that he was a descendant of Abraham's son **Ishmael**.

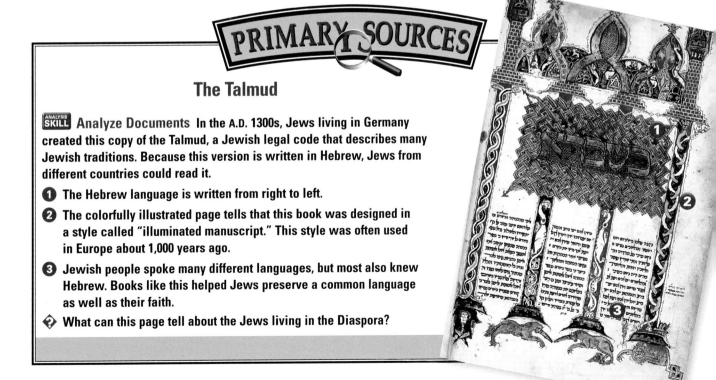

PRIMARY SOURCES

The Talmud

ANALYSIS SKILL **Analyze Documents** In the A.D. 1300s, Jews living in Germany created this copy of the Talmud, a Jewish legal code that describes many Jewish traditions. Because this version is written in Hebrew, Jews from different countries could read it.

❶ The Hebrew language is written from right to left.

❷ The colorfully illustrated page tells that this book was designed in a style called "illuminated manuscript." This style was often used in Europe about 1,000 years ago.

❸ Jewish people spoke many different languages, but most also knew Hebrew. Books like this helped Jews preserve a common language as well as their faith.

◆ What can this page tell about the Jews living in the Diaspora?

▶ This group of Ethiopian Jews celebrates Passover in Jerusalem.

Judaism, Christianity, and Islam have many differences, but they have a very important similarity. All three focus on the belief in one God who sets down moral laws for their followers.

READING CHECK 👁️ **GENERALIZE**

How did Judaism influence Christianity and Islam?

Summary

After many years under Greek rule, the Jews regained control of Judaea. The Roman Empire took control of Judaea in 63 B.C. The Romans destroyed the Second Temple in A.D. 70 and later exiled nearly all the Jews. Judaism, however, survived under the leadership of rabbis. It influenced two other world religions, Christianity and Islam.

REVIEW

1. 💡 How did Judaism develop from the 300s B.C. through the A.D. 100s?

2. Write a paragraph explaining how Judaism influenced **Christianity** and **Islam**.

3. How did the Jewish people respond to Greek and Roman rule?

4. How is the account of Ruth and Naomi important?

CRITICAL THINKING

5. **ANALYSIS SKILL** Why do you think the Romans destroyed the Temple in A.D. 70?

6. Why do you think the Hebrew Bible is considered both history and literature?

7. ✏️ **Write a List** Make a list of the traditions and holy days of Judaism. Then tell how each is related to Judaism or the history of the Jewish people.

8. (Focus Skill) **GENERALIZE**
On a separate sheet of paper, copy and complete the graphic organizer below.

Facts		

Generalization

Judaism influenced Christianity and Islam.

Yohanan ben Zaccai

Biography

Trustworthiness

Respect

Responsibility

Fairness

Caring

Patriotism

*"Make me a coffin, and I will sleep in it."**

Rabbi Yohanan ben Zaccai's unusual request of his friends was part of his plan to help preserve Judaism.

It was A.D. 68, and the Roman army had surrounded Jerusalem. A group of Jews called the Zealots controlled the city. They refused to compromise with the Romans.

Yohanan ben Zaccai wanted to talk to the Romans, but he had to get past the Zealots. He had an idea of how to get past them. Jerusalem buried its dead outside the city walls, so Yohanan ben Zaccai had his friends carry him out of the city in a coffin. The Zealots never suspected that a living man was inside.

When he reached the Romans, Yohanan ben Zaccai asked them to let him set up a center of Jewish study in the town of Yavneh. The Romans agreed.

Yohanan ben Zaccai's actions helped Judaism survive Rome's attack two years later, when the Romans stormed Jerusalem and burned the Temple. Because of Yohanan ben Zaccai, there was still a place where learned men could study ideas from the Bible about how Jews must live. These men became Rabbis—the new leaders of the Jewish people. Judaism survived the destruction of the Temple in part because of the actions of Yohanan ben Zaccai.

*New Edition of the Babylonian Talmud. 2nd Edition. Michael Levi Rodkinson, ed. and trans., Isaac Mayer Wise, ed., and Godfrey Taubenhaus, ed. Talmud Society, 1918.

Why Character Counts

> How did Yohanan ben Zaccai take responsibility for protecting Judaism?

Bio Brief

15 B.C.		A.D. 85
Born		Died

A.D. 68
Yohanan ben Zaccai escapes from Jerusalem to make a deal with the Romans

A.D. 68–70
Yohanan ben Zaccai establishes Jewish study in Yavneh

A.D. 70–85
Yohanan ben Zaccai begins building Yavneh as the center of Judaism

GO ONLINE
Interactive Multimedia Biographies
Visit MULTIMEDIA BIOGRAPHIES at
www.harcourtschool.com/hss

Time

600 B.C.   400 B.C.

586 B.C.
The Babylonians destroy the First Temple in Jerusalem

515 B.C.
The Second Temple is built in Jerusalem

Reading Social Studies

When you **generalize**, you make a statement that summarizes a group of facts and shows how they are related.

 (Focus Skill) **Generalize**

Complete this graphic organizer to make a generalization about how changes affected the Jewish people. A copy of this graphic organizer appears on page 74 of the Homework and Practice Book.

Changes for the Jewish People

Facts

Babylonians destroyed Jerusalem.	Judaism survived and changed.	Romans conquered Judaea.	Judaism survived under rabbi leadership.

Generalization

 ## California Writing Prompts

Write an Interpretation Much of Jewish law was based on rabbis' interpretations of the Torah. Choose one of the Ten Commandments. Then write a paragraph describing what you think it means and how it applies to life today.

Write a Research Report Choose one of the people you read about in this chapter. Write five questions that you would like answered about that person. Then do research and write a report that answers your questions.

167 B.C.
The revolt of the Maccabees begins

63 B.C.
Judaea becomes part of Roman Empire

A.D. 70
The Romans destroy the Second Temple in Jerusalem

Use Vocabulary

For each pair of terms below, write a sentence or two that shows how the two terms are related.

1. **Diaspora** (p. 237), **exile** (p. 235)

2. **rabbi** (p. 236), **synagogue** (p. 236)

3. **canonize** (p. 238), **theocracy** (p. 238)

Use the Time Line

 Use the summary time line above to answer these questions.

4. How many years passed between the destruction of the First Temple in Jerusalem and the completion of the Second Temple?

5. What happened in A.D. 70?

Apply Skills

Use a Cultural Map

 Use the cultural map on page 241 to answer this question.

6. In which country do most people speak Hebrew today?

Recall Facts

Answer these questions.

7. What new idea did Jeremiah introduce to the Judaeans, and how did it change the practice of their religion?

8. What two major religions were influenced by Judaism?

Write the letter of the best choice.

9. Which event marked the beginning of the Jewish Diaspora?
   A the building of the Second Temple
   B the Babylonian Exile
   C the Revolt of the Maccabees
   D the writing of the Torah

10. What kind of government did Judah have during the time of Ezra?
    A a democracy
    B a theocracy
    C an oligarchy
    D a dictatorship

Think Critically

11. **ANALYSIS SKILL** Other than the Tanakh and the Talmud, what sources do you think historians use in order to learn about the history of the ancient Hebrews? How do you think these sources differ in point of view?

12. **ANALYSIS SKILL** In what ways did movement and change affect the ancient Hebrews?

Field Trip

Jerusalem

GET READY

Jerusalem has been ruled by Egyptian pharaohs, Jewish kings, Babylonian and Persian emperors, Greek kings, Roman and Byzantine emperors, Muslim caliphs, European princes, Turkish sultans, and British and Israeli Prime Ministers. Layer upon layer of history is visible on the city's streets and among its numerous historical sites.

Today, the city of Jerusalem is the capital of Israel. Known in Hebrew as Yerushalayim and in Arabic as Al-Quds, it is considered holy by the Jewish, Christian, and Islamic religions. Because of the unique history of the city, it attracts tourists as well as religious pilgrims from all over the world every year.

LOCATE IT

WHAT TO SEE

The Western Wall (above) is holy to the Jewish people and is the last remnant of the Temple that was destroyed by the Romans in A.D. 70. Christian tradition holds that the Church of the Holy Sepulchre (below) is built on the site where Jesus was buried.

Orthodox Jews greet one another in Jerusalem (above). The Hurva Arch (background) stands at the site of a synagogue that was destroyed in 1948.

The Dome of the Rock is one of Islam's holiest sites. It is built upon the Temple Mount, the holiest site of Judaism.

In Jerusalem, people from all different cultures gather to trade at marketplaces. At this marketplace, people buy and trade for food, clothing, and other products.

A VIRTUAL TOUR

GO ONLINE

Visit VIRTUAL TOURS at www.harcourtschool.com/hss

Review

THE BIG IDEA

Beliefs and Customs Beliefs and customs played an important role in the development of the culture of the ancient Hebrews.

Summary

The Ancient Hebrews

Abram, later called Abraham, lived in Mesopotamia in the 1900s B.C. The Mesopotamians believed in many gods. According to the Bible, God told Abraham to move his family to Canaan. Abraham promised to worship only God.

When famine struck Canaan, Abraham's descendants moved to Egypt. They prospered there for 400 years. Then the pharaoh enslaved them, but Moses won the Hebrews' freedom. Moses also received the Ten Commandments from God.

The Hebrews appointed a king, made Jerusalem their capital, and built a Temple. In 928 B.C., the kingdom split into two states, Israel and Judah. The Assyrian Empire conquered Israel in 722 B.C. In 586 B.C., the Babylonians destroyed the First Temple and drove the Jews into exile.

When the Persians conquered Babylon, the Jews were able to return to Jerusalem and build the Second Temple. The Torah became Jewish law. Later, Judaism influenced Christianity and Islam.

Main Ideas and Vocabulary

Read the summary above. Then answer the questions that follow.

1. Why did Abraham move to Canaan?
   A because God told him to, according to the Bible
   B because there was a famine
   C because conquerors forced him to move
   D because Cyrus allowed him to return there

2. What foreign power first conquered Judah?
   A the Assyrian Empire
   B the Roman Empire
   C the Persian Empire
   D the Babylonian Empire

3. What does the word exile mean?
   A forced work without pay
   B a place that has been conquered
   C forced from one's homeland
   D a place where no people live

4. What is the Jewish escape from slavery in Egypt to freedom in the Promised Land called?
   A the Diaspora
   B the Exodus
   C Yom Kippur
   D Hanukkah

Answer these questions.

5. How did the Hebrews' belief in monotheism separate them from other peoples of the time?

6. In the covenant between Abraham and God, what did God promise Abraham?

7. What did Moses accomplish?

8. What was the role of judges in the ancient Hebrew civilization?

9. Why did the Israelites want a king?

10. Who built the First Temple in Jerusalem?

Write the letter of the best choice.

11. Where did Moses grow up?
    A in Canaan
    B in Babylon
    C in Egypt
    D in Mesopotamia

12. What quality was King Solomon known for?
    A wisdom
    B military skills
    C peacemaking
    D conquest

13. Who allowed the Jews to reclaim Judah and build the Second Temple?
    A the Assyrians
    B the Babylonians
    C the Persians
    D the Egyptians

14. Which Jewish leader freed Jerusalem from Greek rule?
    A Judah Maccabee
    B Yohanan ben Zaccai
    C King Hezekiah
    D King David

15. What was the first written document of Judaism?
    A the Torah
    B the Nevi'im
    C the Ketuvim
    D the Commentaries

16. What is one idea or principle in Jewish law that is also important in United States law today?

17. Explain how the destruction of the First Temple affected Judaism.

18. How did the Jewish religion continue even though the Jewish people were dispersed?

Use a Cultural Map

ANALYSIS SKILL Use the cultural map on this page to answer the following questions.

19. What four cultures are represented by the quarters of the Old City?

20. What important site is shown in the Jewish Quarter? Why do you think this site is important to the Jewish culture?

21. In which quarter is the Church of the Holy Sepulchre located?

22. Which two quarters border the Western Wall?

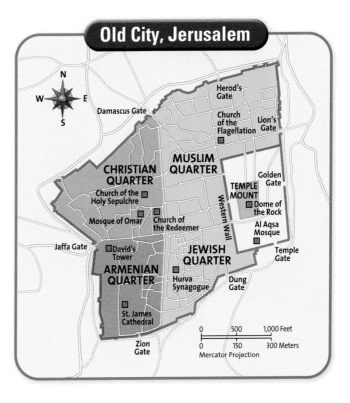

Old City, Jerusalem

Read More

■ *Archaeologists at Work* by Sandy Damashek.

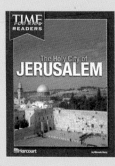

■ *The Holy City of Jerusalem* by Miranda Barry.

■ *The Jewish Diaspora* by Sima Bernstein Kern.

Show What You Know

Unit Writing Activity

Write an Expository Paragraph
Write an expository paragraph explaining how Judaism influenced the moral and ethical traditions of Western civilization.

Unit Project

Publish a History Book Compile information on the ancient Hebrews and the development of Judaism to make a history book. Make a list of important topics in the unit, and write an informative entry about each one. Illustrate the entries with maps, time lines, drawings, and charts.

GO ONLINE

Visit ACTIVITIES at
www.harcourtschool.com/hss

The Ancient Greeks

 **START WITH THE STANDARDS**

California History-Social Science Standards

6.4 Students analyze the geographic, political, economic, religious, and social structures of the early civilizations of Ancient Greece.

The Big Idea

GOVERNMENT AND LEADERSHIP

The ancient Greeks made many contributions in areas of government and leadership.

What to Know

✓ What are the key differences between direct democracy and representative democracy?

✓ How were Athens and Sparta alike? How were they different?

✓ How did Alexander the Great spread Greek culture?

✓ What are some enduring contributions of the ancient Greeks?

Show What You Know

★ Unit 4 Test

✎ Writing: A Summary

🖌 Unit Project: A Museum Exhibit

Time

At the Same Time

1900 B.C. The
Andean civilization
develops in what
is now Peru

1000 B.C. The
wheel is used
throughout
southwestern Asia

The Ancient Greeks

750 B.C. Greek city-states begin to form, p. 289

500s B.C. Democracy begins in Athens, p. 300

460 B.C. The Peloponnesian War begins, p. 335

325 B.C. Alexander's empire stretches from Greece to India, p. 346

700 B.C.

B.C./A.D.

600 B.C. The Mayan civilization begins

200 B.C. The city of Teotihuacán is founded in what is now central Mexico

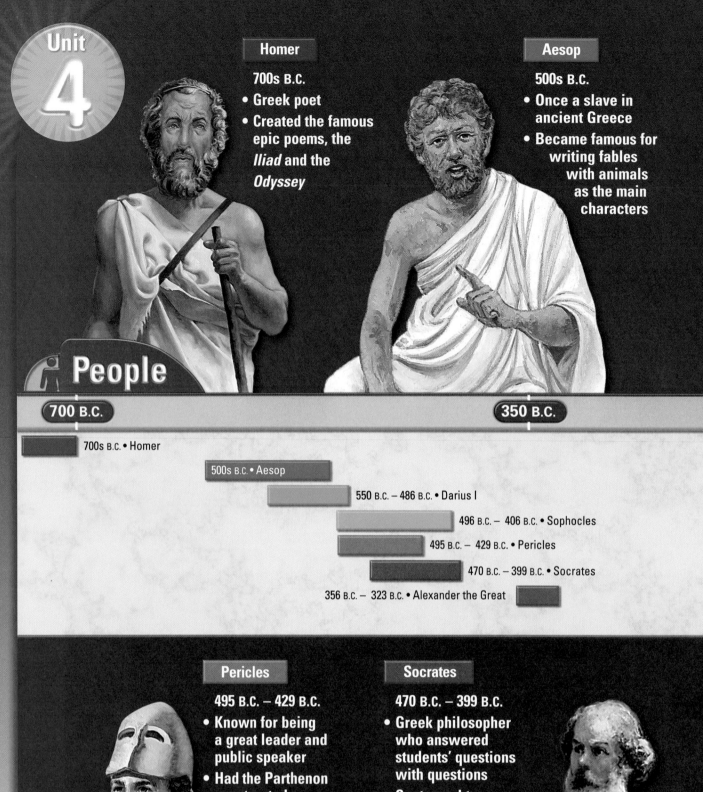

Homer

700s B.C.
- Greek poet
- Created the famous epic poems, the *Iliad* and the *Odyssey*

Aesop

500s B.C.
- Once a slave in ancient Greece
- Became famous for writing fables with animals as the main characters

People

700 B.C.   350 B.C.

700s B.C. • Homer

500s B.C. • Aesop

550 B.C. – 486 B.C. • Darius I

496 B.C. – 406 B.C. • Sophocles

495 B.C. – 429 B.C. • Pericles

470 B.C. – 399 B.C. • Socrates

356 B.C. – 323 B.C. • Alexander the Great

Pericles

495 B.C. – 429 B.C.
- Known for being a great leader and public speaker
- Had the Parthenon constructed

Socrates

470 B.C. – 399 B.C.
- Greek philosopher who answered students' questions with questions
- Sentenced to end his own life because of his beliefs

Darius I

550 B.C. – 486 B.C.

- Persian king who wanted to conquer the Greeks, expanding his empire to the west
- His soldiers were defeated by the Greeks at Marathon

Sophocles

496 B.C. – 406 B.C.

- Well-known Greek playwright
- The first play that Sophocles presented in the Athens theater competition took the top prize in 468 B.C.

B.C./A.D. — A.D.350

A.D. 370 – A.D. 415 • Hypatia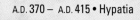

Alexander the Great

356 B.C. – 323 B.C.

- Conquered many lands as leader of Macedonia
- Fair ruler of a multicultural empire

Hypatia

A.D. 370 – A.D. 415

- Head of a school of philosophy
- Became one of the first women to be head of a school

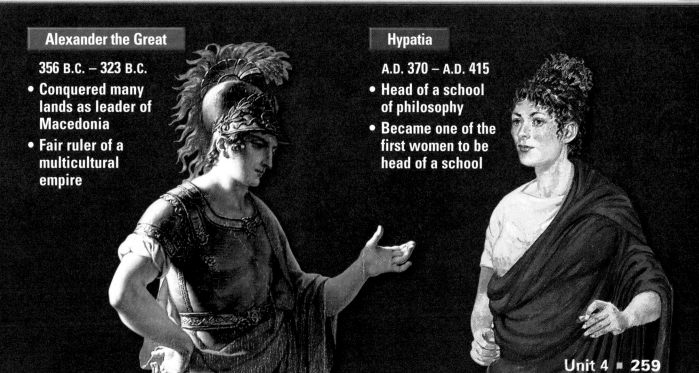

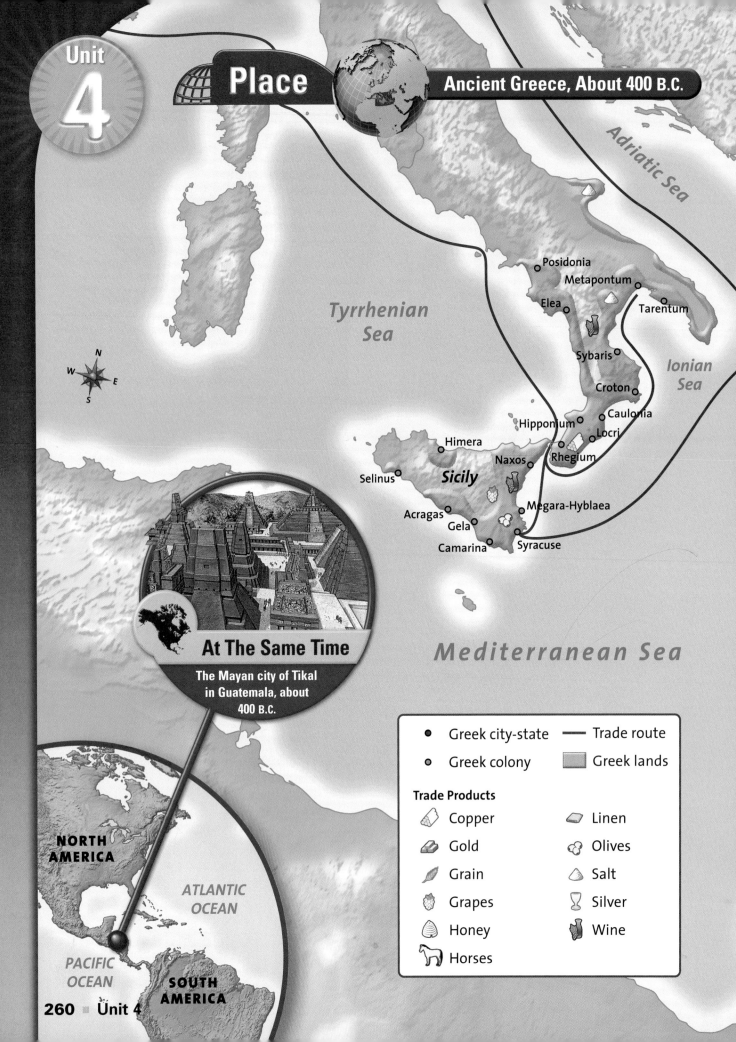

Place

Ancient Greece, About 400 B.C.

Adriatic Sea

Tyrrhenian Sea

N
W   E
S

Posidonia
Metapontum
Elea
Tarentum

Sybaris

Croton

Ionian Sea

Caulonia
Hipponium
Locri

Himera

Naxos
Rhegium

Selinus

Sicily

Megara-Hyblaea

Acragas

Gela

Camarina

Syracuse

Mediterranean Sea

At The Same Time

The Mayan city of Tikal in Guatemala, about 400 B.C.

NORTH AMERICA

ATLANTIC OCEAN

PACIFIC OCEAN

SOUTH AMERICA

● Greek city-state	— Trade route	
○ Greek colony	▭ Greek lands	

Trade Products

Copper	Linen
Gold	Olives
Grain	Salt
Grapes	Silver
Honey	Wine
Horses	

Black Sea

EUROPE

Asia Minor

GREECE

Aegean Sea

Crete

Cyprus

AFRICA

A training camp in Sparta, about 400 B.C.

The Parthenon in Athens, about 400 B.C.

The palace at Knossos, 1900s B.C.

Neapolis
Thasos
Potidaea
Torone
Mende
Abudus
Corcyra
Elatea
Chalcis
Eretria
Megara
Zacynthus
Olympia
Argos
Corinth
Athens
Sparta
Melos
Knossos
Itanos

Byzantium
Chalcedon
Aenus
Sestus
Lampsacus
Abydus
Assus
Mytilene
Phocaea
Erythra
Teos
Ephesus
Samos
Priene
Miletus
Halicarnassus
Cos
Cnidus
Ialysus
Lindus

Cyrene
Apollonia
Tauchira
Barca
Naucratis

Nile River

0   50   100 Miles
0   50   100 Kilometers
Lambert Conformal Conic Projection

Reading Social Studies

 Cause and Effect

A **cause** is an event or action that makes something else happen.
An **effect** is what happens as a result of that event or action.

Why It Matters

Understanding causes and effects can help you see why events and actions happen.

```
Cause              ▶    Effect
[          ]            [          ]
```

✓ Words and phrases such as *because*, *since*, *so*, and *as a result* are clues to cause and effect.

✓ A cause can have more than one effect, and an effect can have more than one cause.

Practice the Skill

Read the paragraphs that follow. Identify the cause and the effect in the second paragraph.

Cause
Effect

According to the Bible, God spoke to Abraham and told him to leave his country. Abraham followed God's advice and left southern Mesopotamia. He and his family traveled toward Canaan.

A famine came to the land where Abraham's people, the Israelites, had settled. Many Israelites left Canaan because of the famine. They found jobs and food in Egypt. However, after many years, the rulers of Egypt began to treat the Israelites harshly.

Apply What You Learned

Find Cause and Effect Read the paragraphs, and answer the questions.

Digging Up a Palace

Much of what we know about the beginnings of Greek civilization is the result of the work of Arthur Evans. Evans was an English archaeologist and adventurer. He went to the island of Crete in 1894 to study and translate the writing found on small stone seals. The seals were used in ancient times much like a signature is used today—to show who wrote or owned something.

Because of political events, Evans ended up studying much more than just seals. The Turkish government, which ruled Crete at the time, had forbidden excavation of ancient sites on the island. However, when Crete won its independence, the new government allowed Evans to buy land that included the site of the ancient city of Knossos. Starting in 1899, he and his workers dug up a huge palace. It was the first important evidence of the earliest Greek civilization.

Evans compared art and artifacts found in the palace to what he knew of Greek myths. One myth was the story of Minos, the legendary king of Crete. From evidence he found in the palace, Evans concluded that Minos had been a real person and that Knossos had been his palace. For this reason, Evans named these early Greeks the Minoans.

Since neither Evans nor anyone else has been able to translate the Minoan writings, the palace remains the best evidence we have of Minoan culture. Evans restored the palace, and visitors today can get an idea of what it looked like in ancient times.

Find Cause and Effect

➤ The palace at Knossos

1. What caused Evans to do more work than study seals on Crete?

2. Why did Evans call the civilization he uncovered the Minoan culture?

3. What has been one effect of experts not being able to translate Minoan writings?

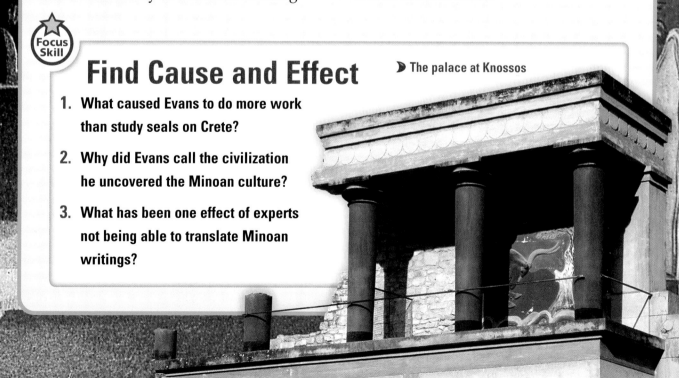

Study Skills

TAKE NOTES

When you take notes, you write down the important ideas and details that you read or hear in class. Some people take notes by using a two-column table.

▶ **Draw a line down your paper to form two columns.**

▶ **In the right-hand column, write notes as you read your textbook or listen to your teacher.**

▶ **Later, reread the right-hand column, and write questions based on your notes in the left-hand column.**

▶ **Fold back the right-hand column and use the left-hand column as a study guide.**

The Early Greeks

Questions	Class Notes
Lesson 1: Mountains and Seas • What makes Greece a peninsula? • Why was sea trade easier than land trade in ancient Greece?	• Greece is a peninsula; water on 3 sides. • Inland travel and trade was difficult; mountains. Sea trade easier because of coasts/good ports
Lesson 2 • _____	• _____

Apply As You Read

As you read this chapter, take notes in a two-column table.

California History-Social Science Standards, Grade 6

6.4 Students analyze the geographic, political, economic, religious, and social structures of the early civilizations of Ancient Greece.

The Early Greeks

▶ Ancient Greek ruins at Corinth

Tales from the Odyssey

written by Mary Pope Osborne
illustrated by David Scott Meier

Like many people today, the ancient Greeks enjoyed a good story. The Greek poet Homer, who lived about 2,800 years ago, created long story-poems based on old stories that had been retold through the centuries. Two of his poems, the *Iliad* and the *Odyssey*, kept the memory of an ancient Greek civilization alive. The *Iliad* is a story about a great war. The *Odyssey* follows the hero Odysseus on his ten-year journey home from that war. Read now a retelling of a part of the *Odyssey*.

Prologue

In the early morning of time, there existed a mysterious world called Mount Olympus. Hidden behind a veil of clouds, this world was never swept by winds, nor washed by rains. Those who lived on Mount Olympus never grew old; they never died. They were not humans. They were the mighty gods and goddesses of ancient Greece.

The Olympian gods and goddesses had great power over the lives of the humans who lived on earth below. Their anger once caused a man named Odysseus to wander the seas for many long years, trying to find his way home.

The Call to War

Long ago on the island of Ithaca in ancient Greece, there lived a man named Odysseus. Though he was king of the island, Odysseus lived a simple life. He enjoyed tending his fields and orchards and working with his hands as a craftsman and carpenter. More than anything, he enjoyed the company of his family—his aged mother and father; his loving wife, Penelope; and their small son, Telemachus.

One day as Odysseus was plowing his fields, he gazed for a long time at Penelope and Telemachus. The baby was sleeping in his mother's arms under a nearby tree. Odysseus imagined that someday he would teach his son to farm the land and care for the orchards. He would teach him to sail a ship around the Greek islands.

As Odysseus dreamed of his son's future, a servant ran from the palace. "A messenger from King Agamemnon has arrived!" the servant shouted.

Dread crept over Odysseus. He knew why the messenger had come. Agamemnon, the ruler of all the Greek islands, was calling for the kings and princes of Greece to wage war against the faraway city of Troy. A Trojan prince had kidnapped a Greek queen named Helen, taking her from her husband.

"Odysseus of Ithaca!" the messenger shouted. "I bring orders for you to join King Agamemnon in the fight against Troy!"

Odysseus glared at the man, trying desperately to think of some way to avoid leaving his family. Though he was a brave warrior and leader of men, his love for his family overshadowed all else. He loathed the thought of having to leave his home.

"Odysseus!" the messenger shouted. "Remember it was you yourself who first called for our countrymen to swear to defend the marriage of Helen!"

Odysseus remembered this well. Helen was the most beautiful woman in all the world. When she was old enough to wed, all the princes and kings of Greece had wanted to marry her. Fearing that the men's jealousies would bring their nation to ruin, Odysseus had urged them all to swear to defend Helen's marriage always, no matter who she chose for her husband.

"In the name of Agamemnon, I command you to set sail at once!" the man shouted.

Ignoring the messenger, Odysseus began to behave in a strange way.

loathed hated

Instead of yoking two oxen together to pull his plow, he yoked an ox to a small donkey. Instead of casting seeds into the furrows of his fields, he cast salt. He hoped the messenger would think he had gone mad.

But the messenger suspected Odysseus was only pretending. To test him, the messenger snatched Telemachus from Penelope's arms and placed the baby in front of Odysseus' plow.

Penelope screamed.

Odysseus quickly turned his plow so he would not harm the boy. And in that moment, he knew he had sealed his fate. He had proved his sanity. He would now have to leave his family and answer the call to war.

yoking attaching

furrow deep grooves made by a plow

Response Corner

1 Why did Odysseus want the messenger to think he had gone mad?

2 Write a persuasive message to King Agamemnon, telling him why Odysseus should or should not have to fight in the war.

CRETE

Mountains and Seas

WHAT TO KNOW

How did geography influence the development of early civilizations in Greece?

✓ Describe the geography of Greece.

✓ Analyze how the ancient Greeks adapted to the land and sea.

✓ Discuss the importance of trade to the ancient Greeks.

VOCABULARY

peninsula p. 271
isthmus p. 271
harbor p. 273

PLACES

Greece
Balkan Peninsula
Asia Minor
Crete

 CAUSE AND EFFECT

 California Standards
HSS 6.4, 6.4.1

YOU ARE THERE

The year is 1000 B.C., in the land that will some-day be part of the country of **Greece**. You're helping your father herd your family's goats by guiding them along a rocky path in the mountains.

It's midday—the sun is shining brightly, and the air is hot and dry. Your father signals you to stop and join him. You sit under an olive tree for a meal of cheese made from goat's milk and crusty barley bread baked by your mother.

You enjoy the stillness and quiet of the noon break. The sky is a cloudless blue. Far below the rocky moun-tainside, the sea stretches into the distance. You wonder how far it goes and what lands are on its distant shores.

❯ A scenic view of the Mediterranean Sea from ruins on mainland Greece

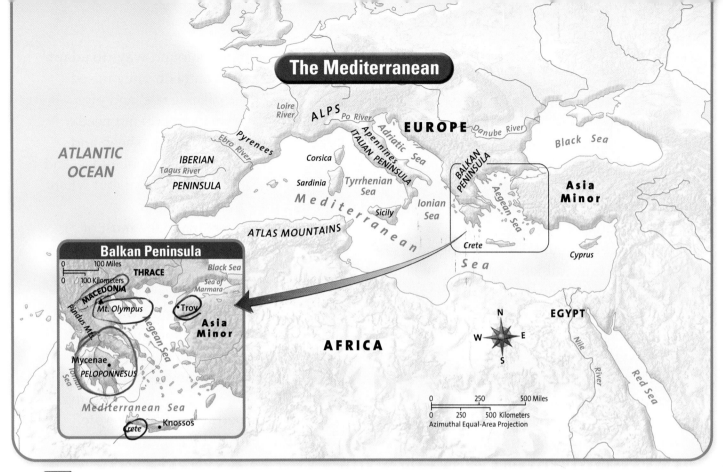

The Mediterranean

ATLANTIC OCEAN

EUROPE

Loire River
ALPS
Po River
Apennines
ITALIAN PENINSULA
Adriatic Sea
Danube River
Black Sea

Pyrenees
Ebro River
IBERIAN PENINSULA
Tagus River

Corsica
Sardinia
Tyrrhenian Sea
Sicily
Ionian Sea

BALKAN PENINSULA
Aegean Sea
Asia Minor

Mediterranean

Crete
Cyprus

ATLAS MOUNTAINS

Sea

N
W E
S

EGYPT

AFRICA

Nile River
Red Sea

Balkan Peninsula

0   100 Miles
0   100 Kilometers

THRACE
Black Sea
Sea of Marmara
MACEDONIA
Pindus Mts.
Mt. Olympus
Troy
Asia Minor
Aegean Sea
Mycenae
PELOPONNESUS
Ionian Sea
Mediterranean Sea
Crete
Knossos

0   250   500 Miles
0   250   500 Kilometers
Azimuthal Equal-Area Projection

ANALYSIS SKILL Analyze Maps

❖ **Regions** Which seas border on the Balkan Peninsula?

The Land of Greece

Present-day Greece is located in southeastern Europe on the **Balkan Peninsula**. A **peninsula** is a stretch of land that is almost completely surrounded by water. Greece's southernmost tip reaches into the Mediterranean Sea. To the west lie the Ionian Sea and the Italian Peninsula while to the east is the Aegean Sea.

The Balkan Peninsula curves south and east toward a part of Asia called **Asia Minor**, or "Little Asia." Today, Asia Minor is part of the country of Turkey.

The Ionian and Aegean Seas almost separate the southern part of Greece from the rest of the mainland. Only a small strip of land called an **isthmus** (IS•muhs) connects them. The southern part of Greece is called the Peloponnesus (peh•luh•puh•NEE•suhs).

Mountains cover nearly three-fourths of mainland Greece. The heavily forested Pindus Mountains run north and south through the center of Greece. Between the mountains lie narrow valleys and small plains. Because the region is so mountainous, much of the soil is thin and rocky.

The jagged coastline of Greece is cut by many inlets and is surrounded by as many as 2,000 islands. These islands are also part of present-day Greece. The largest of the islands is **Crete**, located southeast of the Peloponnesus, in the Mediterranean. The early people of Greece also settled on these small islands, as well as along the coasts of northern Africa, Asia Minor, and what are now parts of Spain and Italy.

READING CHECK ⭕ **CAUSE AND EFFECT**
What causes much of the soil on mainland Greece to be thin and rocky?

Life Among Mountains

The ancient Greeks settled in the narrow valleys among the mountains. As a result, the mountains separated settlements, and each community developed on its own. For many centuries, the mountains kept the people of Greece from uniting under one government.

The rugged mountains made inland travel and trade difficult. To travel by land from one community to another, people had to hike through the mountains on dirt paths. The rivers of Greece were of no use for travel because they often dried up.

The mountainous land also affected agriculture. Only about 20 percent of the land is good for agriculture. Greece's soil, for the most part, is poor and rocky, and its climate is dry. There is little flat land available for farming or raising large animals, such as cattle and horses.

The ancient Greeks found ways to adapt to their rocky environment. They raised animals, such as sheep, goats, and pigs, which are fairly small and do not need large areas for grazing. From sheep and goats, the Greeks obtained wool, hides, and cheese. They ate very little meat, but when they did, they preferred pork.

The early farmers made the most of the region's dry climate and poor soil by planting crops well-suited to the area, such as barley, wheat, olives, and grapes. They ground the barley and the wheat into flour for baking breads and cakes, which they sweetened with honey. They ate olives and crushed them to make olive oil for cooking, for lamp fuel, for use in bathing, and for use in perfumes. They also ate grapes and pressed them to make wine.

READING CHECK ☼ **CAUSE AND EFFECT**
How did the mountains affect inland travel and trade in ancient Greece?

❯ Olive groves still flourish in the dry, rocky soil of present-day Greece.

▶ Built in 444 B.C., the Temple of Poseidon overlooks Cape Sounion on the Aegean Sea.

Life by the Seas

The seas surrounding Greece provided an abundance of fish and an easier way to travel than hiking across mountains. For these reasons, the ancient Greeks started most of their settlements near the coast.

The Greeks developed into a seafaring culture of fishers, sailors, and traders. Greece has many fine natural **harbors**, or sheltered places with deep water close to shore. The ancient Greeks sailed close to the shoreline, from one harbor to another.

Through sea travel, people in coastal settlements had contact with one another. Over time, some people migrated from one coastal village to another, and others moved from the mainland to the surrounding islands. In the process, the early Greeks exchanged ideas and religious beliefs.

The early fishers knew well the sea's fearful power. Sailing was dangerous, especially in winter, when the winds were strong and the waters rough.

According to the ancient Greeks, the god Poseidon (puh•SY•duhn) ruled the seas and watched over sailors and their boats. The ancient Greeks believed that Poseidon expressed his moods through the sea. A terrible storm rocking the sea was a sign that Poseidon was angry.

Despite the dangers of the sea, the Greeks depended on it for food and transportation. Sea travel also connected the Greeks with other cultures around the Mediterranean, resulting in an exchange of ideas and goods across great distances.

READING CHECK ♻ **CAUSE AND EFFECT**
Why did the ancient Greeks start most of their settlements near the coasts?

Exchange and Trade

The success of early Greek farmers made exchange and trade possible. Their discovery that olives, grapes, and grain could be grown in the dry climate and rocky soil of Greece was a powerful one. Not only could they produce a steady food supply, they could provide a surplus. The abundance of food supported a growing population in Greek lands.

In time, farmers improved their tools and techniques. Not everyone was busy working in the fields or helping herd goats, sheep, and pigs. Some people began to specialize in new jobs. Craftworkers fashioned tools, containers, clothing, and decorative objects from natural resources such as wood, clay, bone, wool, stone, and metal. Weavers, metalworkers, and potters did not grow their own food. Instead, they exchanged their goods with farmers for food.

Olives and grapes could also be made into such valuable products as olive oil and wine. Both products required new storage jars. Potters devoted much of their time to making storage jars from clay.

To get the goods and resources they lacked or desired, the ancient Greeks began to trade with other groups of people in the Mediterranean. For example, Greek farmers could grow barley and wheat, but they had less success growing wheat, which made tastier bread. Over time, this led the ancient Greeks to import wheat from other places.

In exchange, the early Greeks exported their own goods. These goods included wine, olive oil, pottery, and wood.

GEOGRAPHY

The Cyclades

The Cyclades (SIH•kluh•deez) are a group of about 200 islands located southeast of mainland Greece. The islands spread over about 1,000 square miles in the Aegean Sea. Winters are mild and the summers cool. The weather and the beautiful coast make the Cyclades a popular tourist destination. These islands were once the home of the Cycladic people, who flourished from about 3000 B.C. to 2000 B.C. Most Cycladic people made their living as fishers, farmers, traders, or craftworkers.

> ❱ A view of Koufonissi Island, in the Cyclades

GREECE

CYCLADES ISLANDS

N
W · E
S

Ándros
Gyaros
Tínos
Kéa
Síros
Mikonos
Kíthnos
Rhenea
Delos
Serifos
Páros
Donousa
Sifnos
Náxos
Keros
Kimolos
Antíparos
Iraklia
Amorgos
Mílos
Sikinos
Shinousa
Folegandros
Íos
Thíra
Anafi

0   25   50 Miles
0   25   50 Kilometers

Trade resulted in an exchange of ideas, too. The sharing of ideas between cultures was an important means of technological and cultural change. For instance, using a process they learned from civilizations in southwestern Asia, the people of early Greece mixed copper and tin to make bronze. They then made weapons, tools, and bowls from their new metal.

READING CHECK ⚙ **CAUSE AND EFFECT**
What led the early Greeks to trade with people in other parts of the Mediterranean region?

Summary

The geography of Greece affected the lives of its early people. Mountains separated settlements and made inland travel difficult. Early farmers learned to grow crops suited to the rocky soil and dry climate. Settlements along the seas developed into seafaring cultures. Through trade, the early people of Greece exchanged goods and ideas with other cultures in the Mediterranean.

REVIEW

1. 💡 How did geography influence the development of early civilizations in Greece?

2. Use the words **isthmus** and **harbor** to describe Greece's geography.

3. How did the early Greek farmers adapt to the land?

4. What effect did trade have on the early Greeks?

CRITICAL THINKING

5. **ANALYSIS SKILL** How might life have been different for the early Greek farmers if better farmland had been available?

6. **Make It Relevant** Do you think the people in Greece today are as affected by Greece's mountains as the Greek people of long ago? Explain.

7. ✏ **Write a Paragraph** Describe how sea travel affected the way of life of the ancient Greeks.

8. (Focus Skill) **CAUSE AND EFFECT**
On a separate sheet of paper, copy and complete the graphic organizer below.

Cause		Effect
Mountains separate early settlements.	▶	

Cause		Effect
The seas have an abundance of fish.	▶	

Read a Population Map

❯ WHY IT MATTERS

Most population maps show which areas of the world are most crowded with people and which areas are the least crowded. They can show this information for the past or for the present day. A population map of ancient Greece in 1000 B.C. could show you how little populated the region was at that time. Later, when Greek civilization became more complex, cities were founded and the population increased. Reading population maps will help you make connections between population and geography, history, and government.

❯ WHAT YOU NEED TO KNOW

Look at the map legend for the map titled World Population. The map legend tells you that the colors on the map stand for different population densities. **Population density** is the number of people who live in 1 square mile or 1 square kilometer of land. A square mile is a square area of land 1 mile long on each side. A square kilometer is a square area of land 1 kilometer long on each side.

The white areas of the map are places where no people live permanently. The tan areas are the least crowded. The population is sparse, which means that people live far from one another. The red areas on the map are the most crowded. The population in these areas is dense, which means that the people live close together. The other colors stand for other levels of population density.

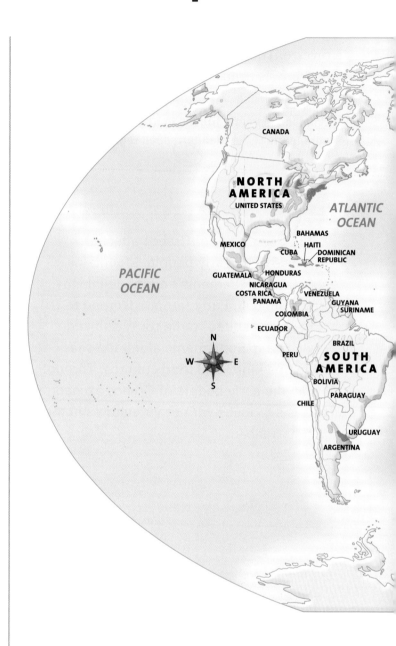

❯ PRACTICE THE SKILL

ANALYSIS SKILL Use the population map to answer the following questions.

❶ Which continent has the highest population density?

❷ On which continent does no one live permanently?

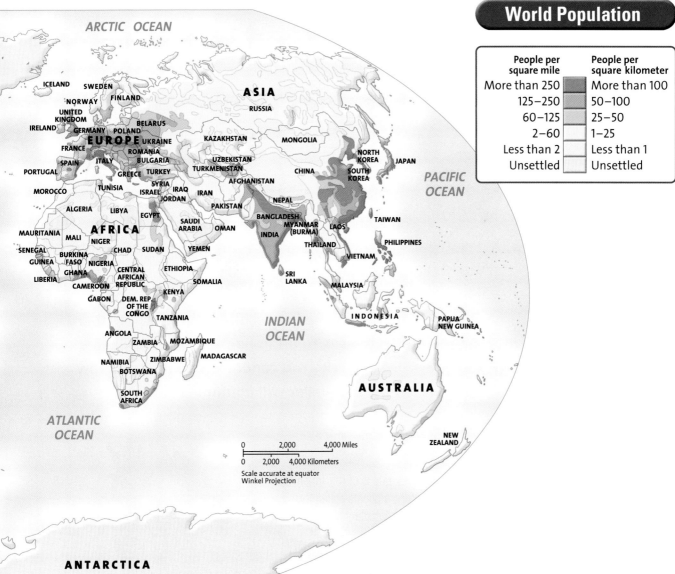

World Population

People per square mile	People per square kilometer
More than 250	More than 100
125–250	50–100
60–125	25–50
2–60	1–25
Less than 2	Less than 1
Unsettled	Unsettled

ARCTIC OCEAN

ICELAND
SWEDEN
NORWAY FINLAND
UNITED KINGDOM
IRELAND
GERMANY POLAND
BELARUS
EUROPE UKRAINE
FRANCE
ROMANIA
SPAIN ITALY
BULGARIA
PORTUGAL GREECE TURKEY
MOROCCO TUNISIA
SYRIA IRAQ
ISRAEL JORDAN
ALGERIA LIBYA EGYPT
MAURITANIA AFRICA
SENEGAL MALI NIGER
GUINEA BURKINA FASO CHAD SUDAN
GHANA NIGERIA
LIBERIA CAMEROON CENTRAL AFRICAN REPUBLIC ETHIOPIA
GABON DEM. REP. OF THE CONGO KENYA
TANZANIA
ANGOLA
ZAMBIA MOZAMBIQUE
NAMIBIA ZIMBABWE MADAGASCAR
BOTSWANA
SOUTH AFRICA

ASIA
RUSSIA
KAZAKHSTAN
MONGOLIA
UZBEKISTAN
TURKMENISTAN
AFGHANISTAN CHINA
NORTH KOREA
JAPAN
SOUTH KOREA
PACIFIC OCEAN
IRAN
PAKISTAN NEPAL
BANGLADESH
INDIA MYANMAR (BURMA) LAOS TAIWAN
THAILAND
VIETNAM PHILIPPINES
SRI LANKA
MALAYSIA
SAUDI ARABIA OMAN
YEMEN
SOMALIA
INDONESIA
PAPUA NEW GUINEA

INDIAN OCEAN

AUSTRALIA

ATLANTIC OCEAN

NEW ZEALAND

```
0        2,000      4,000 Miles
0   2,000   4,000 Kilometers
Scale accurate at equator
Winkel Projection
```

ANTARCTICA

3 What is the population density of most of Australia?

4 Which country has a higher population density—Greece or Italy?

5 Why do you think areas with a high population density are often located along the coast?

► APPLY WHAT YOU LEARNED

ANALYSIS SKILL With a partner, prepare a list of five questions you might ask to see how well other classmates know how to use population maps. Exchange lists with other partner pairs, and answer their questions.

Practice your map and globe skills with the **GeoSkills CD-ROM**.

Time

2000 B.C.   1000 B.C.   B.C./A.D.

2000 B.C.
Minoans begin to build palaces on Crete

1450 B.C.
Mycenaeans invade Crete

1100 B.C.
The Greek Dark Age begins

WHAT TO KNOW

How did people in the earliest civilizations of ancient Greece live?

✓ Describe the achievements of the Minoans and Mycenaeans.

✓ Describe the importance of Homer.

✓ Explain the importance of Greek mythology to the everyday life of the ancient Greeks.

VOCABULARY

peasant p. 281
cultural borrowing p. 281
bard p. 282
legend p. 282
epic p. 282
myth p. 283
mythology p. 283

PEOPLE

Homer

PLACES

Crete
Mycenae
Troy

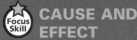

CAUSE AND EFFECT

California Standards
HSS 6.4, 6.4.4

Early Civilization in Greece

YOU ARE THERE

It is 1000 B.C. The fire crackles on the hearth. You stare into the flames and listen as a storyteller tells of heroes who fought in a war long ago. The storyteller describes how the conflict began. Helen, the beautiful wife of a Greek king, ran away with a prince from another land. Greek ships filled with warriors then set sail across the sea to bring her home. As you listen, the hours pass quickly. You cannot wait until tomorrow night, when the storyteller will continue his tale.

FAST FACT

One famous Greek tale is of the Trojan Horse. In the story, a people called the Trojans accepted a wooden horse as a gift, not knowing it was filled with enemy soldiers. They were fooled by the disguise and attacked by surprise. Today, a Trojan horse can mean a harmful computer program disguised as a useful program.

▶ The palace at Knossos served as the city's center for economic, government, and religious activity.

The Minoans

 TIME 2000 B.C.

 **PLACE** Crete

One of the earliest civilizations in Greece developed on the island of **Crete**. This was the Minoan (muh•NOH•uhn) civilization, named after the legendary king of Crete, King Minos (MY•nuhs).

Crete is a long, narrow island with rugged mountains and flat plains. It lies about 60 miles southeast of Greece's mainland. The Greek poet **Homer** described Crete as "handsome country, fertile, thronged [crowded] with people. . . ."* Olive trees filled ancient Crete, and the climate, like today, was mild, never too hot or too cold. The Minoans lived on this pleasant island in small farming and fishing villages.

In about 2000 B.C., the Minoans began building cities. In each city, the Minoans built a large and richly decorated palace. Inside, the palaces seemed like mazes, with many rooms and winding passages.

The palace was at the heart of Minoan social life and served as the center for government and religion. It was also a place where food could be stored and distributed. Beyond the palace were houses, small villages, and farms.

The largest Minoan palace was built in the city of Knossos (kuh•NAH•suhs). Constructed in 1700 B.C., the palace covered more than three acres and was at least three stories high.

READING CHECK ☼**CAUSE AND EFFECT**
What made Crete a pleasant place for Minoans to live?

*Homer, *The Odyssey*. Robert Fagles, trans. Viking, 1996.

▶ Dating to the 1200s B.C., this painting shows a fleet of Minoan ships entering a port.

Minoan Life

Beautiful paintings found on the ruins of palace walls tell much about the Minoans. They show that the Minoans enjoyed dancing, music, and sports. In many of the paintings, both women and men wear gold jewelry and have long, flowing hair.

The wall paintings also show the importance of the sea to Minoan life. The Minoans were expert sailors and sea traders, and their trading partners included the early Greeks, as well as the Mesopotamians and Egyptians. Minoan trading ships carried olive oil, wine, wool, and pottery from Crete to other places and returned with copper, tin, and gold.

▶ An early Minoan vase

The Minoans developed a system of writing that helped them record their trading activities. Some of their writing, on clay tablets, has survived to this day, but no one has been able to translate it.

By about 1100 B.C., the Minoan culture had come to an end. The Minoans had suffered through a terrible fire, a volcanic eruption, and an earthquake. They may have also been overrun by the warlike Mycenaeans (my•suh•NEE•uhnz) from mainland Greece. The Minoan culture declined as the Mycenaean culture flourished. Historians believe that one of these events, or a combination of them, led to the end of Minoan civilization.

READING CHECK ☼ **CAUSE AND EFFECT**
What events do historians believe led to the end of Minoan civilization?

The Mycenaeans

TIME 1600 B.C.

PLACE Mainland Greece

The Mycenaean civilization was named after the city of **Mycenae** (my•SEE•nee), located on the Peloponnesus. Experts believe that the Mycenaeans were a war-like people. The Mycenaeans were mostly **peasants**, or poor farmers, who were ruled by warrior kings. They spoke an early form of the Greek language. For this reason, they are considered to be the first Greeks.

The Mycenaeans learned many Minoan customs and made them part of their own culture. The process by which a culture takes ideas from other cultures is called **cultural borrowing**. For example, the Mycenaeans learned how to sail from the Minoans and became a great seafaring culture. They adapted the Minoan writing system to their own language. They also borrowed Minoan art and pottery styles, adjusting them to suit Mycenaean tastes.

In about 1450 B.C., the Mycenaeans invaded Crete. Mycenae would control Crete and much of the Peloponnesus until about 1100 B.C. During this time, the Mycenaeans continued spreading their culture throughout the region.

In about 1100 B.C., Mycenaean control weakened. Some historians believe that invasions by a Greek-speaking people from the north called the Dorians may have weakened the Mycenaeans. Others argue that fighting within their own culture caused the decline of Mycenaean culture.

READING CHECK Ở CAUSE AND EFFECT

Why are the Mycenaeans considered the first Greeks?

ANALYSIS SKILL Analyze Maps After invading Crete, the Mycenaeans gained control of Minoan trading routes in the region.

❖ How did the location of Crete help the Mycenaeans trade with other cultures?

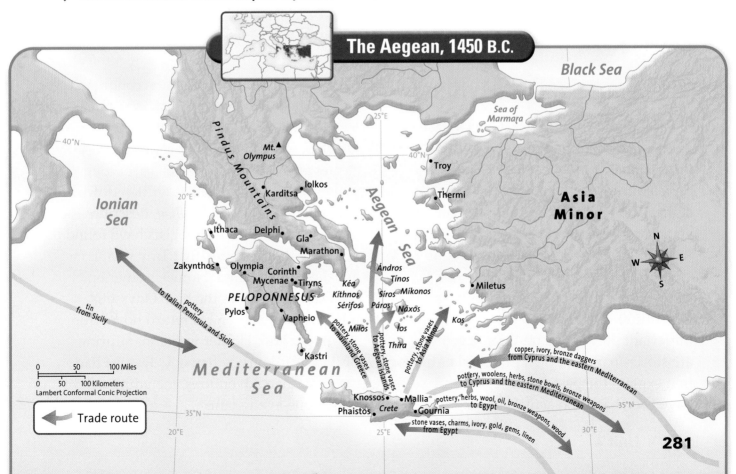

The Aegean, 1450 B.C.

Black Sea

Sea of Marmara

Pindus Mountains

Mt. Olympus

Troy

Thermi

Asia Minor

Ionian Sea

40°N

20°E

25°E

40°N

Iolkos

Karditsa

Aegean Sea

Ithaca

Delphi

Gla

Marathon

Zakynthos

Olympia

Corinth

Mycenae

Tiryns

PELOPONNESUS

Kéa

Kíthnos

Sérifos

Ándros

Tínos

Síros

Mikonos

Páros

Miletus

Pylos

Vapheio

Milos

Náxos

Íos

Kos

Thira

pottery to Italian Peninsula and Sicily

tin from Sicily

pottery, stone vases to mainland Greece

pottery, stone vases to Aegean Islands

pottery, stone vases to Asia Minor

Kastri

Mediterranean Sea

copper, ivory, bronze daggers from Cyprus and the eastern Mediterranean

pottery, woolens, herbs, stone bowls, bronze weapons to Cyprus and the eastern Mediterranean

Knossos

Mallia

pottery, herbs, wool, oil, bronze weapons to Egypt

Phaistos

Crete

Gournia

stone vases, charms, ivory, gold, gems, linen from Egypt

0   50   100 Miles

0   50   100 Kilometers

Lambert Conformal Conic Projection

← Trade route

35°N

20°E

25°E

35°N

30°E

LEGENDS AND MYTHS

Across centuries, the Greeks passed down stories of heroes, gods, and goddesses by word of mouth.

❯ The forest god Pan and his flute (left), and Pegasus, the flying horse (right).

❯ The hero Achilles fighting in the Trojan War

❯ In a scene from the *Odyssey*, Odysseus sails home.

Legends and Myths

Early in their history, the Greeks developed a great tradition of storytelling. Professional storytellers called **bards** traveled from town to town, telling stories and singing songs about Greek gods, goddesses, and heroes. These stories were entertaining, but they also taught Greek ideals, values, and beliefs.

Legends telling of human events and the adventures of heroes and heroines are an important part of this tradition. **Legends** are stories handed down from earlier times that explain the past. Some legends may have been based on actual events.

In 1200 B.C., the Mycenaeans conquered a city called **Troy** in the Trojan War. Greek legends tell of this event. In the 700s B.C., a Greek bard named Homer collected these stories and composed two **epics**, or long poems, that would later be written down.

Homer's first epic, the *Iliad*, describes the attacks on Troy. Archaeologists have found evidence that suggests that Troy was in fact attacked and burned. Homer's other epic, the *Odyssey*, follows the hero Odysseus (oh•DIH•see•uhs) on his return home from the Trojan War. Homer wrote that during his ten-year journey home, Odysseus had many strange adventures, including a fight with a one-eyed giant.

GODS AND GODDESSES

The Greeks worshipped many gods and goddesses. Religion and everyday life were closely connected in ancient Greece.

▶ Hera, queen of the Greek gods

▶ The sea god Poseidon sitting with Apollo, the god of music and poetry, and Artemis, the goddess of the hunt

▶ Zeus, the most powerful Greek god

▶ Athena, goddess of wisdom

The Greeks told many stories about how the actions of gods and goddesses affected the lives of people. These stories are called **myths**. Greek **mythology** includes all such stories and was passed down from generation to generation.

Myths were an important part of the everyday practice of Greek religion. They offered an explanation of how things in nature or how human events came to be. They also described the personalities and roles of the many gods and goddesses that the Greeks believed in.

Each Greek god and goddess possessed a special power or controlled a specific part of human life. For example, Zeus was the god of thunder and lightning. Hera was the goddess of marriage and childbirth. Together, from their home atop Mount Olympus in northern Greece, they ruled as king and queen over all the Greek gods.

One famous myth tells how Athena, the goddess of wisdom, competed with Poseidon, the god of the sea, to win over the people of Athens, a Greek city. Poseidon threw a spear into the ground, giving rise to a spring. However, Athena won the contest by giving the people of Athens the olive tree.

READING CHECK **SUMMARIZE**
How was Greek mythology important to the everyday life of the ancient Greeks?

The Greek Dark Age

By the 1100s B.C., ancient Greece had entered into an uncertain time that some historians call the Dark Age. The Greeks abandoned their palaces and cities. Trade between the Greeks and others stopped.

Poverty set in and the Greeks returned to a simpler way of life, living as farmers and herders. In search of a better life, some people left mainland Greece for Greek islands.

Many of the cultural achievements made by the Minoans and Mycenaeans were lost in this time. Writing all but disappeared, as did decorative pottery, luxury goods, and bronze metalwork. Interestingly, toward the end of the Dark Age, a new, stronger metal was introduced—iron.

Through legends and myths, the traditions and beliefs of the early Greeks survived. By about 750 B.C., the Dark Age was coming to an end. The ancient Greeks were about to enter a more fortunate time.

READING CHECK **SUMMARIZE**
What was the Greek Dark Age?

Summary

The Minoans and the Mycenaeans developed two of Greece's earliest civilizations. The Minoans built cities around great palaces. Considered the first Greeks, the Mycenaean culture borrowed from the Minoan culture.

By the 1100s B.C., these civilizations had disappeared. Legends and myths kept the traditions and beliefs of Greece's early civilizations alive.

▶ Decorative pottery reappeared by 750 B.C.

REVIEW

1. How did people in the earliest civilizations of ancient Greece live?

2. Use the terms **bard**, **legend**, and **myth** in a paragraph about the ancient Greeks.

3. What ideas did the Mycenaeans borrow from the Minoans?

CRITICAL THINKING

4. **ANALYSIS SKILL** How might control of trading routes by the Minoans suggest they had a strong economy?

5. **ANALYSIS SKILL** Why might Homer's work be important to historians of Greek culture?

6. **Make It Relevant** What might cause a culture today to decline or disappear?

7. **Write a Myth** Try your hand at writing your own Greek myth. In the myth, explain how a natural event came to be. Be sure to include the adventures of a hero or heroine as well.

8. **Focus Skill** **CAUSE AND EFFECT**
On a separate sheet of paper, copy and complete the graphic organizer below.

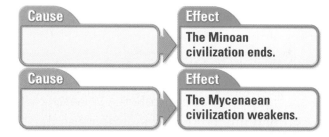

Cause		Effect
	▶	The Minoan civilization ends.
Cause		Effect
	▶	The Mycenaean civilization weakens.

Homer

*"The Muse inspired the bard to sing the famous deeds of fighting heroes—the song whose fame had reached the skies those days. . . ."**

In the quote above from the *Odyssey*, Homer tells of a bard who sings about the famous deeds of the Greek hero Odysseus.

Historians know very little about Homer. He probably grew up in Ionia in Asia Minor sometime between the years 800 B.C. and

❯ Homer recites to a group of people in Greece.

700 B.C. Tradition says that Homer was blind and that he recited from memory the 28,000 verses of his epic poems. During the Greek Dark Age, Greeks had forgotten how to write. A tradition of storytelling took the place of writing.

Storytelling helped keep the early Greek past alive. Stories were passed from person to person. Each story-teller may have added some details to the narrative. During long winter nights in the Greek Dark Age, it might have been common for people to settle in around a story-teller to hear a tale.

Some historians now believe that Homer may have been only one of several authors of the *Iliad* and the *Odyssey*. Even so, he was probably one of the greatest of these storytellers. After his death, the two epic poems were written down. The stories helped define the Greek identity.

*Homer. *The Odyssey*. Robert Fagles, trans. Bernard Knox, ed. Viking, 1996.

Trustworthiness
Respect
Responsibility
Fairness
Caring
Patriotism

Why Character Counts

❓ How did Homer's care for the early Greek past help define the Greek identity?

Bio Brief

800 B.C.   700 B.C.

700s B.C. ●
Homer collects stories and composes the *Iliad* and the *Odyssey*

GO ONLINE
Interactive Multimedia Biographies
Visit MULTIMEDIA BIOGRAPHIES at
www.harcourtschool.com/hss

Critical Thinking Skills

Compare Primary and Secondary Sources

❯ WHY IT MATTERS

Learning about history is like trying to solve a mystery. To know what happened years ago, you have to find and piece together clues, or evidence.

The evidence people use to learn about history comes from two kinds of sources—primary sources and secondary sources. By studying and comparing these kinds of sources, you can find evidence of what actually happened in different periods of history.

❯ WHAT YOU NEED TO KNOW

Primary sources are records made by people who saw or took part in a past event. These people may have recorded information or told their stories in journals, letters, official documents, speeches, or poems. Primary sources also include artifacts such as paintings, coins, jewelry, pottery, and tools. By providing information about the time in which they were created, primary sources give people of today a direct link to past events.

❯ This Minoan wall painting was created in ancient times.

▶ This painting of an ancient Minoan ship was created by a present-day artist.

Critical Thinking Skills

Secondary sources provide information about events by people who were not eyewitnesses. Secondary sources are not direct links to an event. A magazine article, a newspaper story, or an encyclopedia entry written by someone who researched an event, but was not at the event, is a secondary source.

Some sources can be either primary or secondary, depending on how the event is reported. A newspaper article that contains the exact words of a person who witnessed the event would be a primary source. Oral histories, works of art, and online resources can be either primary or secondary sources.

▶ **PRACTICE THE SKILL**

ANALYSIS SKILL Look at the paintings on these pages to answer these questions.

1 Which painting is a primary source? Which is a secondary source? Explain your answers.

2 What conclusions can you draw about Minoan culture from each painting?

3 Which source do you think provides more credible, or believable, information about the Minoans—the primary source or the secondary source? Why?

▶ **APPLY WHAT YOU LEARNED**

ANALYSIS SKILL Find examples of primary and secondary sources in this chapter. Explain to a classmate what makes each source primary or secondary.

Chapter 8 ■ **287**

750 B.C.
Greek city-states
begin to form

725 B.C.
Hoplite warfare
is invented

700s B.C.
The Greek alphabet
is developed

WHAT TO KNOW
How did the governments of Greek city-states change over time?

✓ Explain the relationship between Greece's geography and the development of Greek city-states.

✓ Trace the development of early forms of democracy and citizenship.

VOCABULARY
polis p. 289
acropolis p. 289
agora p. 289
oligarchy p. 290
tyrant p. 290
democracy p. 290
commerce p. 291
colony p. 291

PEOPLE
Homer
Hesiod

PLACES
Sparta
Athens
Delphi
Olympia

CAUSE AND EFFECT

California Standards
HSS 6.4, 6.4.1, 6.4.2, 6.4.4

Greek City-States

YOU ARE THERE

Today is the day you've been waiting for—the Olympic Games are about to begin! You're excited to be in the crowd of spectators. Everyone is in a festive mood, ready to cheer for the athletes who will compete in today's events.

Here they come! Young athletes from the many Greek city-states parade by, strong and proud, looking like heroes already.

The best athletes will be crowned with victory wreaths of olive leaves. Long after the Olympics end, the winners will still be celebrated. Statues will be built in their honor.

The Rise of City-States

By 750 B.C., settlements in what is today Greece had grown into city-states, such as **Sparta, Athens**, Argos, and Corinth. In Greece, a city-state was called a **polis** (PAH•luhs). Each polis connected a city and the farms, towns, and villages around it. The English word *politics* comes from the Greek word *polis*.

In a polis, all free people were citizens, unless they or their parents were foreigners. The Greek philosopher Aristotle later proposed the idea that it was natural for a group of people to live in a polis. Aristotle wrote,

> **❝Man is by nature . . . intended to live in a polis❞***

Most Greek city-states had fewer than 5,000 people, but some, such as Corinth, had as many as 10,000 people. Athens may have been the only city-state to have more than 20,000 people.

The Greek city-states developed in similar ways. Most of them started at the base of a large hill on which a fort known as an **acropolis** (uh•KRAH•puh•luhs) was built. During enemy attacks, people from the countryside moved to this protected place for safety. Later, the acropolis became a center of religion in many city-states.

Outside the acropolis were houses, temples, and an open-air market called an **agora** (A•guh•ruh). The agora was the political center of a city-state. There people traded and discussed the news of the day.

Greek city-states were separated by natural barriers, such as the mountains and the seas. This caused the city-states to develop independently and kept them from uniting under one government.

READING CHECK ⟳ **CAUSE AND EFFECT**
How did geography affect the development of Greek city-states?

*Aristotle. *The Politics*. Ernest Barker, trans. Oxford University Press, 1946.

▶ The agora was an open-air market and gathering place surrounded by public buildings, temples, and shops.

New Ways of Governing

By 750 B.C., small groups of aristocrats, or the wealthy ruling class, had begun to rule most Greek city-states. They replaced the kings, who had ruled in the Dark Age. This form of government is an **oligarchy** (AH•luh•gar•kee), or rule by a few.

The oligarchies ruled over almost every part of society. Each one controlled the army, the economy, and the religion of the city-state it ruled. It also decided laws and the punishments for breaking those laws.

Before long, oligarchies faced problems. Poor people wanted new leaders who could provide them with a better life. Also, sharing power within an oligarchy was difficult. Ambitious aristocrats struggled to become the sole ruler of their city-state.

In the 600s B.C., individual aristocrats claimed the right to rule in many of the city-states. These rulers were known as tyrants. To the ancient Greeks, a **tyrant** was someone who took control of a government by force and ruled alone.

Many tyrants had the support of the people. At first, most tyrants ruled well and improved the lives of people within their city-states. Later, some tyrants began to rule harshly. The word *tyrant* came to mean "a cruel ruler," just as it does today.

By 500 B.C., the people of many Greek city-states had overthrown unpopular tyrants. In a few city-states, such as Athens, tyranny transitioned, or changed, into early forms of **democracy**, or rule by the people.

Early democracies in ancient Greece were not perfect. For example, only free males over 18 years of age could vote in Athens. However, these democracies laid the foundation for future democracies.

READING CHECK ☉ **CAUSE AND EFFECT**
What caused some tyrannies to transition, or change, into early democratic forms of government?

CITIZENSHIP

Democratic Values

The invention of the idea of citizenship helped early forms of democracy develop in ancient Greece.

Before 750 B.C., kings and the aristocracy ruled the ancient Greeks, but as city-states grew, this changed. Free people were no longer subjects—they were citizens. Male citizens were eligible to participate in governing because they had ties to a place, their city-state. This paved the way for democratic forms of government.

In time, male citizens helped make laws, voted for leaders, and served on juries. In other words, they worked together to make decisions for their city-state.

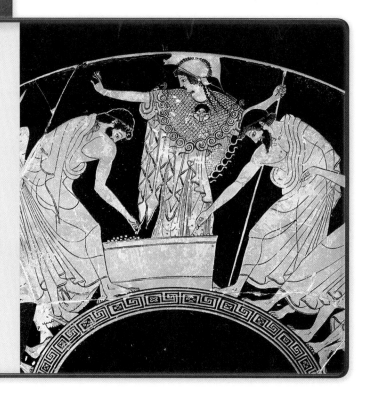

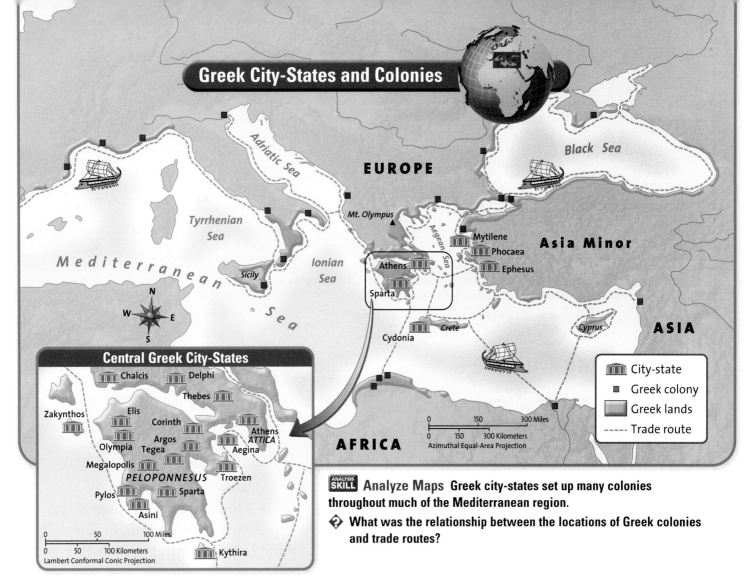

Greek City-States and Colonies

Adriatic Sea

Tyrrhenian Sea

EUROPE

Mt. Olympus ▲

Black Sea

Asia Minor

Mytilene
Phocaea
Ephesus

Aegean Sea

Athens

Sparta

Ionian Sea

Sicily

Mediterranean Sea

N
W E
S

ASIA

Cyprus

Crete
Cydonia

AFRICA

0   150   300 Miles
0   150   300 Kilometers
Azimuthal Equal-Area Projection

Legend:
- 🏛 City-state
- ■ Greek colony
- ▨ Greek lands
- --- Trade route

Central Greek City-States

Chalcis   Delphi

Thebes

Zakynthos
          Elis
          Corinth
Argos   Athens
Olympia   Tegea   ATTICA
                   Aegina
Megalopolis
     PELOPONNESUS   Troezen
Pylos   Sparta
     Asini

0   50   100 Miles
0   50   100 Kilometers
Lambert Conformal Conic Projection

Kythira

ANALYSIS SKILL **Analyze Maps** Greek city-states set up many colonies throughout much of the Mediterranean region.

❓ What was the relationship between the locations of Greek colonies and trade routes?

Commerce and Colonies

By about 700 B.C., the Greeks had become part of growing **commerce**, or large-scale trade. This trade brought much-wanted goods and resources to the city-states.

Trade among the Greek city-states involved the exchange of grain, wine, olive oil, wood, pottery, and metalworks, such as iron weapons and tools.

The use of iron greatly affected the Greeks. Much harder than bronze tools, iron tools helped Greek farmers produce more food. As a result,

▶ An Athenian coin

the population grew, leading to more competition over farmland. In search of land and resources, such as iron ore, people in these city-states looked beyond the Aegean.

People in Greek city-states started new settlements all along the coastlines of the Mediterranean and Black Seas. Each of these **colonies** became an independent city-state but remained tied to the homeland through religion and trade. By 500 B.C., the Greeks had founded colonies in southern Europe, northern Africa, and Asia Minor.

READING CHECK **MAIN IDEA AND DETAILS** What led Greek city-states to set up colonies?

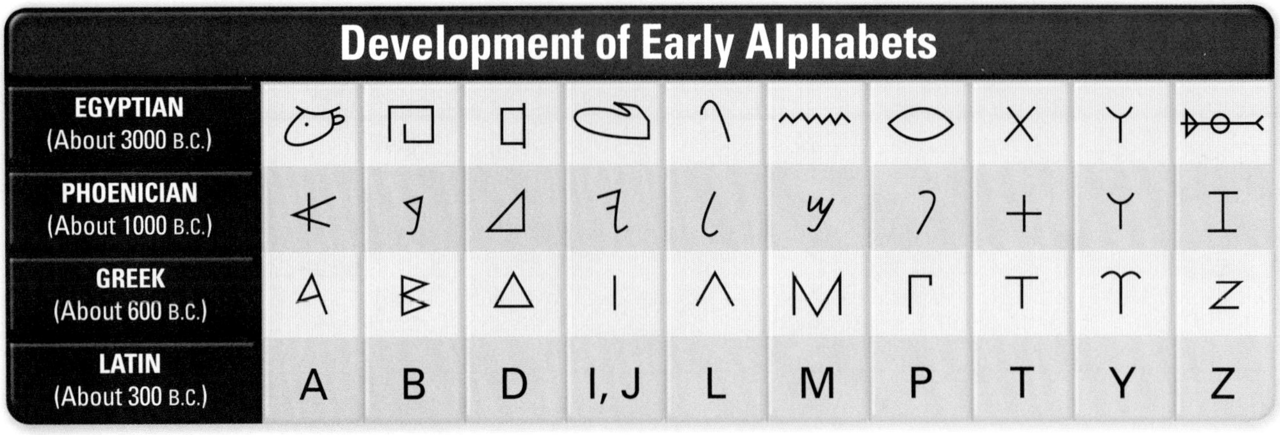

Development of Early Alphabets

EGYPTIAN (About 3000 B.C.)	𓃾	⌐	▯	◠	⌐	∿∿	◯	✕	Υ	⊢○⊣
PHOENICIAN (About 1000 B.C.)	⪢	𝈬	◁	⅂	(	𝈸	�	+	Υ	𝈿
GREEK (About 600 B.C.)	Α	Β	△	Ι	Λ	Μ	Γ	Τ	Υ	Ζ
LATIN (About 300 B.C.)	A	B	D	I, J	L	M	P	T	Y	Z

ANALYSIS SKILL **Analyze Tables** Early alphabets developed over centuries. The Greeks borrowed letters from the Phoenicians to develop their own alphabet.

◈ Which Greek letters look most like letters you would use today?

Greek Culture

Greeks identified with their own city-state. They also felt a strong connection, or cultural identity, with all other Greeks. Besides having a common language, this connection came from having a shared culture, including shared history, writing, religion, and athletics.

In the 700s B.C., the Greeks developed their own alphabet. Having a common writing system helped bring the city-states closer together. They called the first letter of their alphabet *alpha* and the second letter *beta*. The word *alphabet* comes from the names of those letters.

The Greeks based their alphabet on the Phoenician alphabet. The Phoenicians were traders who developed a writing system to keep track of their trade. Their writing system used symbols to stand for single sounds. This made Phoenician writing different from the writing of the Egyptians, who used symbols to stand for ideas.

Like the Phoenicians, the Greeks used writing to keep records of business and trade. Writing also made it possible for the Greeks to record codes of law, government business, and taxes.

The Greeks began writing down their history and beliefs, too. The legends and myths that they had kept alive through storytelling could now be written down, shared, and preserved for future generations. The Greeks recorded **Homer's** epics, the *Iliad* and the *Odyssey*.

▶ Athletes from many nations still compete in the Olympics.

Homer's poems connected the Greeks to the distant past and a shared cultural heritage. From the heroes of the Trojan War, the Greeks learned their strong codes of honor and courage.

Much of what later Greeks learned about religion came from the works of Homer and **Hesiod** (HEE•see•uhd). Their works taught the Greeks about the gods, including the gods' names, their special skills, their appearance, and how to honor them. The religion the Greeks shared also set them apart, in their minds, from other peoples who lived along the Mediterranean.

The ancient Greeks believed that Zeus and their other gods controlled daily events in the world. They often went to an oracle, a divine place where they could ask the gods for advice. The most famous oracle was located at **Delphi**. There, a temple for Apollo, the god of light and music, sat at the foot of Mount Parnassus. People from city-states far and wide traveled to the oracle at Delphi for advice from Apollo.

To honor the god Zeus, the Greeks competed at athletic festivals. Beginning in about 776 B.C., the Greeks held a large athletic festival every four years in **Olympia**. As a result, this became known as the Olympic Games.

Athletes from all the city-states came to compete in the games. The events included wrestling, long jumping, discus and javelin throwing, boxing, and running. The winners of the events were crowned with wreaths of olive leaves. When the winners returned to their city-states, they were treated as heroes.

The Olympic Games were a uniting force for the Greek city-states for almost 1,200 years. Even when city-states were at war with each other, they laid down their weapons to compete in the games!

READING CHECK Ŏ **CAUSE AND EFFECT**
How did Homer's work help connect Greeks to one another?

The First Olympic Games

In about 776 B.C., athletes from many Greek city-states met in the valley of Olympia near the city-state of Elis (EE•luhs). The athletes competed in a single event—a footrace. The games brought the city-states together in peaceful competition.

The spirit of the early Olympic Games is still alive today. In 2004, the Olympics were even held in Athens, Greece!

A New Kind of Warfare

Even though they had a common culture, the Greek city-states were rivals. They often fought over land and resources. To defend this territory, city-states kept large armies. Between 725 B.C. and 650 B.C., the Greeks developed a new, highly organized kind of warfare to defend their lands.

All the adult male citizens of a city-state served at least some time in the army. A man's wealth and status determined his rank. The wealthiest men served as leaders. Those who could afford to own a horse served in the cavalry. The army's next rank consisted of foot soldiers called hoplites. In the lowest rank were the poorest men, who served as archers and stone throwers.

The army was made up mostly of the hoplites. They were outfitted with at least 70 pounds of bronze body armor, including a helmet and a chest piece. Hoplites carried a long spear in their right hands and a round shield in their left hands. They had to be strong enough to fight under the weight of heavy armor and wealthy enough to pay for it.

The hoplite soldiers fought in a rectangular formation. They marched in rows, sometimes hundreds of soldiers long and eight or more deep. The warriors fought shoulder to shoulder, with their shields nearly touching. Each hoplite counted on the soldiers next to him for protection. Archers, chariots, and cavalry backed up the hoplites.

Hoplite Warfare

Pike or spear point

Brass helmet

Shield

Shin guards

❯ Hoplites marched row upon row into battle. They were the best-trained fighting force in the Mediterranean region.

Hoplite formation

Hoplite soldiers decorated their shields with bronze plates (left, center) and wore helmets (right).

Hoplite foot soldiers marched forward like a thick, moving wall. In warfare, one army's wall of hoplites pushed against the other army's wall in a brutal style of fighting. Even so, it was an important fighting method for several hundred years.

READING CHECK **MAIN IDEA AND DETAILS**
Why did Greek city-states often fight among themselves?

Summary

Mountains separated the independent Greek city-states. City-states were active in commerce and developed new forms of warfare and government, including democracy. Across the city-states, the Greeks shared a strong cultural connection with one another.

REVIEW

1. How did the governments of Greek city-states change over time?

2. Write a paragraph that describes how the **acropolis** and the **agora** were important in a **polis**.

3. What cultural features did the ancient Greeks share?

4. How did trade develop among Greek city-states and within the wider Mediterranean region?

CRITICAL THINKING

5. **ANALYSIS SKILL** How did the development of writing affect Greek culture?

6. **ANALYSIS SKILL** **Make It Relevant** How is citizenship in the present-day United States different from and similar to citizenship in ancient Greece?

7. **Make a Diorama** Make a diorama of a part of a Greek city-state. Show the relationship of the city to the outlying farms and to the sea. Present your diorama to the class.

8. **Focus Skill** **CAUSE AND EFFECT**
On a separate sheet of paper, copy and complete the graphic organizer below.

Cause	Effect
The Greeks use iron tools.	

Cause	Effect
The Greeks develop an alphabet.	

Lesson 4

Time

2000 B.C.   1000 B.C.   B.C./A.D.

620 B.C.
Athens creates its
first code of written laws

594 B.C.
Solon leads Athens

539 B.C.
Cyrus II founds
the Persian Empire

WHAT TO KNOW
How were Sparta and
Athens alike, and how
were they different?

✔ Describe daily life in
Sparta and Athens.

✔ Describe the
governments of
Sparta and Athens.

✔ Explain the organization
of the Persian Empire.

VOCABULARY
helot p. 297
assembly p. 297
reform p. 299
majority rule p. 300
fable p. 301
league p. 303

PEOPLE
Draco
Solon
Aesop
Cyrus II
Darius I

PLACES
Sparta
Athens
Mesopotamia

CAUSE AND
EFFECT

California
Standards
HSS 6.4, 6.4.2, 6.4.4, 6.4.5, 6.4.6

Sparta and Athens

YOU ARE THERE

It is 600 B.C. The hot sun blasts down on you
and sweat pours down your face. Your throat is
dry, but you stand tall. You would never complain. As a
Spartan, you must learn to go without food and water
when necessary. It's all part of a Spartan education.

You're at a Spartan camp, where all day you practice
military drills on the training ground. Later, you will eat
a simple dinner, your only meal of the day.

Many more years of training lie ahead of you. Then,
one day, you'll be ready for an important role in Spartan
life. Sparta is the mightiest of the Greek city-states, and
all the hardships you are going through are worth it.
You are proud to be a Spartan!

▶ From age 7 to age 30, Spartan males lived in training camps where
they learned to be good soldiers.

Sparta's Government

TIME 600s B.C.
PLACE Sparta

The city-state of **Sparta** was located on a fertile plain on the Peloponnesus. Sparta's inland location separated it from the sea and other city-states. Even so, during the 600s B.C., Sparta became the most powerful city-state on the Peloponnesus.

The Spartans, descendants of the Dorians, proudly conquered their neighbors. The Spartan government then forced the conquered people to be **helots** (HEH•luhts), slavelike workers owned by the Spartan city-state.

In time, the helot population of Sparta became huge. Sparta may have had four or more helots for every citizen. Outnumbered, the Spartans constantly feared that the helots would rebel. To stay prepared to fight against the helots and Sparta's enemies, the Spartans lived a military life.

The Spartans developed an unusual form of government. In times of war, two kings ruled, each from a different royal family. These kings shared authority to decide issues related to war. In times of peace, an oligarchy made up of 30 elders over the age of 60 ruled Sparta. They proposed new laws to an **assembly**, a lawmaking group.

The assembly was made up of adult male citizens of Sparta. It mainly approved

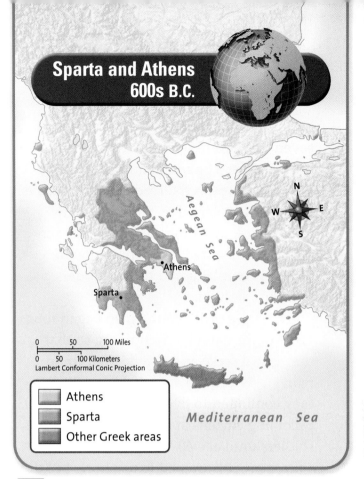

Sparta and Athens 600s B.C.

- Athens
- Sparta
- Other Greek areas

Aegean Sea

Athens

Sparta

0   50   100 Miles
0   50   100 Kilometers
Lambert Conformal Conic Projection

Mediterranean Sea

ANALYSIS SKILL **Analyze Maps** This map shows the land controlled by the two rival city-states.

❖ **Regions** Which city-state controlled lands bordering the Aegean Sea?

laws proposed by the elders and elected five wealthy landowners, called ephors (EH•ferz), to handle day-to-day governing. Although the assembly was important, the elders and the ephors held the real power in Sparta.

READING CHECK ⓧ **CAUSE AND EFFECT**
Why did the Spartans protect themselves with a military way of life?

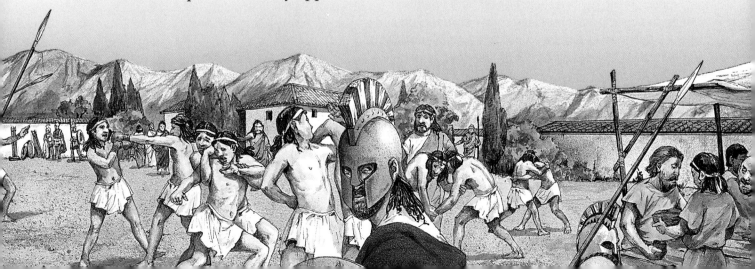

Life in Sparta

From an early age, Spartans learned to be strong and disciplined. At the age of seven, boys were sent to live in training camps to get a Spartan education. At the training camps, boys lived and ate together in barracks. Every day, they practiced gymnastics, wrestling, and military exercises. They learned to accept hardship without complaint and to obey orders without question.

At the age of 18, young men began four years of formal military training so that they could serve as soldiers. Men could marry between the ages of 20 and 30, but they continued to live in the barracks until becoming citizens at age 30. Men served as soldiers until age 60.

Spartan girls trained to be strong but did not serve in the military. Like boys, they exercised outdoors daily. However, raising children would be their main role.

Spartan women had more freedom than did women in other Greek city-states. They were highly respected and moved freely around the city. Since the men were often away on military duty, the women managed household and family matters.

Spartan leaders feared that new ideas would bring unwanted changes to their society. Because of this, citizens were rarely allowed to travel beyond Sparta and trade with outsiders was discouraged.

Spartans followed a strict way of life. They dressed and lived plainly and ate simple meals. Today, the word *spartan* is used to refer to something that is simple, strict, and highly disciplined.

Spartans had a strong sense of honor. They were trained never to give up in battle. They believed there was no greater act than to die defending their city-state.

READING CHECK ☼ **CAUSE AND EFFECT**
Why were Spartan citizens rarely allowed to travel outside Sparta?

Children IN HISTORY

Spartan Children

To Spartans, the purpose of education was to develop a responsible, well-trained army of citizens, loyal to the city-state of Sparta. Children were taught to live a life of self-denial, discipline, and simple ways. Girls and boys were both taught to read and write. However, the main concentration was on physical education, which included running, gymnastics, boxing, and wrestling.

Spartan children did not have much time for fun and games. When they did have time, they enjoyed playing with dolls, hobbyhorses, kites, and toy horse-drawn carts. Children also enjoyed playing board games and ball games. Although life was hard for these children, they were proud to be Spartans. They would go through anything to become a citizen of Sparta.

Make It Relevant **What do you think is the purpose of an education today?**

> In ancient Athens, the area inside and around the agora bustled with activity.

New Ideas in Athens

TIME 600s B.C.
PLACE Athens

Athens was very different from Sparta. Located on an excellent harbor off the Aegean Sea, Athens was at a crossroads of the ancient world—between Asia Minor, Africa, and Europe. This location allowed Athens to have many trading partners, and many Athenians grew wealthy from trade.

In 683 B.C., an oligarchy replaced the monarchy of Athens. Even under the oligarchy, the Athenians continued to live without written laws. Finally, in 620 B.C., a lawmaker named **Draco** wrote the first recorded laws for Athens, but these laws were very harsh.

In about 600 B.C., the ruling oligarchy faced a crisis. The farmers who supplied Athens with food fell into debt. Many had to sell themselves into slavery to survive. Anger and distrust spread among the poor people of Athens.

In 594 B.C., a leader named **Solon** was given the authority to deal with the debt crisis. Solon was a respected leader, known for his fair handling of government and business matters. Solon set out to end the crisis by making **reforms**, or changes. First, he canceled all debts. Then, he freed all Athenians who had sold themselves into slavery. He also replaced many of Draco's harsh laws with fairer laws. Solon wrote,

> 66 [Lawfulness] makes all things well ordered and fitted and often puts chains on the unjust. 99*

READING CHECK ⟳ CAUSE AND EFFECT
Why did Athens's poor people grow angry?

*Solon. "Eunomia," Oswyn Murray, trans., in Freeman, Charles. *Egypt, Greece, and Rome: Civilizations of the Ancient Mediterranean.* Oxford University Press, 1996.

Toward Democracy

After dealing with the immediate crisis of debt reform, Solon made reforms that allowed more citizens to participate in government. In this way, he laid the foundation on which Athenian democracy would be built.

Solon set up a system that based political rights on wealth and not on birth. He divided male citizens into four classes according to their agricultural wealth. This wealth included ownership of land, grain, and olive oil. Citizens with the most wealth were in the highest class. The greater a man's wealth, the higher the government position he could hold.

Men without property made up the lowest class and could only attend the assembly and serve on juries. However, citizens could rise to a higher class by acquiring more wealth.

Under Solon, all male citizens were allowed to attend the assembly in Athens. The assembly passed laws, elected leaders, and helped decide court cases. Decisions were made by **majority rule**. Every member had one vote, and the idea that received the most votes passed.

Solon has also been credited with establishing a council to support the assembly. The sole purpose of the council was to decide which topics the assembly would discuss. The council consisted of 400 citizens who served one-year terms. Every year, council members were selected in a random drawing.

For his times, Solon's reforms were remarkable. Never before had so many citizens been able to meaningfully take part in government.

READING CHECK SUMMARIZE
What is the significance, or importance, of Solon's reforms to the idea of citizenship?

▶ In this painting, Solon upholds his laws against the objections of the Athenians.

The Ant AND The Grasshopper

from *Aesop's Fables**

In a field one summer's day a Grasshopper was hopping about, chirping and singing to its heart's content. An Ant passed by, bearing along with great toil an ear of corn he was taking to the nest.

"Why not come and chat with me," said the Grasshopper, "instead of toiling and moiling in that way?"

"I am helping to lay up food for the winter," said the Ant, "and recommend you to do the same."

"Why bother about winter?" said the Grasshopper; "we have got plenty of food at present." But the Ant went on its way and continued its toil. When the winter came the Grasshopper had no food and found itself dying of hunger, while it saw the ants distributing every day corn and grain from the stores they had collected in the summer. Then the Grasshopper knew:

"It is best to prepare for the days of necessity."

*Aesop's Fables from Folk-Lore and Fable. The Collier Press. New York, 1909.

Life in Athens

In Athens, education was just as important to producing good citizens as it was in Sparta. Young Athenians learned about good behavior from the **fables** of **Aesop** (EE•sahp), a legendary storyteller. These stories used animals to teach moral lessons, such as "Honesty is the best policy."

From the age of 7 to about 14, all but the poorest of Athenian boys passed the day in school. They studied arithmetic, reading, writing, physical education, as well as the arts—painting, poetry, and music. After the age of 14, boys from wealthy families could continue their studies with a private tutor. Most boys began learning their father's trade, studying to become bronze workers, blacksmiths, carpenters, and potters.

Athenian girls studied reading, writing, arithmetic, and music at home. Because women were in charge of Greek home life, girls also learned skills such as spinning, weaving, sewing, cooking, and childcare. Wealthy women ran large households, overseeing servants and slaves. Poorer women often worked alongside men on farms and in family-run businesses.

About one third of the people in Athens were slaves. Many were educated, and some even became doctors and teachers. Others cleaned, cooked, farmed, and mined for silver. Neither slaves nor women could participate in the Athenian assembly, vote, or serve on juries.

READING CHECK **COMPARE AND CONTRAST**
How was an Athenian education different for boys and girls?

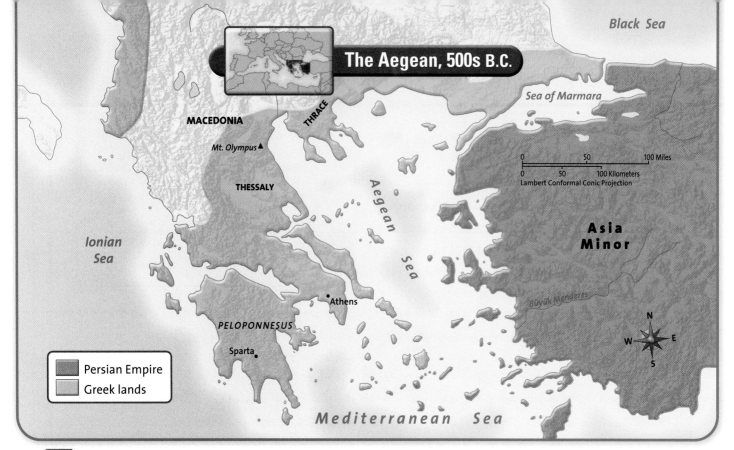

The Aegean, 500s B.C.

Black Sea

Sea of Marmara

MACEDONIA

THRACE

Mt. Olympus ▲

THESSALY

Aegean Sea

Ionian Sea

Asia Minor

Büyük Menderes

Athens

PELOPONNESUS

Sparta

N
W E
S

Persian Empire
Greek lands

0   50   100 Miles
0   50   100 Kilometers
Lambert Conformal Conic Projection

Mediterranean Sea

 **Analyze Maps** The Persian Empire gained control of Greek colonies in Asia Minor.

◆ Which bodies of water separated Greek lands from the Persian Empire?

Concerns About Persia

TIME 539 B.C.

PLACE Persia

In the 500s B.C., the Greek city-states faced a serious threat from the east. This threat came from the Persian Empire.

The Persians ruled from **Mesopotamia** in what is today Iraq. In 539 B.C., the Persian king **Cyrus II**, known as "Cyrus the Great," founded the Persian Empire by conquest. Cyrus led his army to conquer much of Asia Minor and the entire Babylonian Empire.

The emperors who followed Cyrus expanded the empire even more. Cambyses (kam•BY•seez) added all of Egypt. **Darius I** (duh•RY•us) made the Persian Empire the largest empire in history up to that time.

To rule over such a huge empire, Darius I developed a well-organized system of government. He divided the government into 20 small regions. Each had a governor who reported to the emperor.

To maintain control, the Persians built a road more than 1,500 miles long that linked the Persian kings to distant areas of the empire. Persian couriers carried mail and orders from the king across the empire and returned with news of the land.

When the Persians conquered Asia Minor, they gained control of several Greek colonies. Not satisfied, the Persians wanted to control all the Greek city-states and their trade routes.

The Greeks feared the Persians, whose empire was a threat to Greek culture. They did not want to be ruled by others. The city-states had to make a decision. Alone, each city-state could not hope to defend itself against Persia's army. Together, however, they might be strong enough.

The Persians even worried Sparta, the most powerful city-state on the Peloponnesus. In the 500s B.C., Sparta created a **league**, or a group of allies, called the Peloponnesian League, which included many other city-states. Initially, the league's goal was to protect its members against the growing power of Athens and its allies. Under Sparta's leadership, the Peloponnesian League became a major fighting force that would help defend against the Persians.

READING CHECK Ŏ **CAUSE AND EFFECT**
What made the Greek city-states fear the Persian Empire?

Summary

Sparta was ruled both by an oligarchy and two kings. Spartans led a strict military life. Athens gave rise to early democratic forms of government. Athenians were educated to be well-rounded citizens. Many city-states joined Sparta in the Peloponnesian League for better defense.

❯ Persian couriers, or messengers, carried messages across their large empire.

REVIEW

1. How were Sparta and Athens alike, and how were they different?

2. Write a paragraph about the life of a Spartan citizen, using the terms **assembly** and **helot**.

3. Why did Sparta create the Peloponnesian League?

4. How did Darius I organize the Persian government?

CRITICAL THINKING

5. **Make It Relevant** How might people in the present-day United States react to basing the rights of citizens on wealth? Why?

6. **ANALYSIS SKILL** Why do you think Athens and Sparta developed such different ways of life?

7. **Write a Letter** Suppose you live in ancient Athens or Sparta. Write a letter describing a typical day in your life.

8. **Focus Skill** **CAUSE AND EFFECT**
On a separate sheet of paper, copy and complete the graphic organizer below.

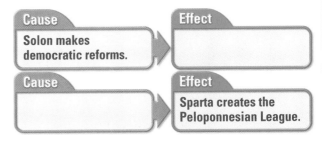

Cause		Effect
Solon makes democratic reforms.	➤	
Cause		Effect
	➤	Sparta creates the Peloponnesian League.

How Strong Was Athenian Democracy?

Today, many people believe that democracy is the best form of government. Some people praise the government of ancient Athens as a model of democracy. Others say that the Athenian democracy was flawed or full of weaknesses. They believe that most people in ancient Athens had few rights or none at all.

The good and the bad sides of Athenian democracy have long been debated—even in ancient Athens! Here are some points of view about ancient Athenian democracy.

In Their Own Words

Pericles, an Athenian leader and general

❝ [Our] administration favors the many instead of the few; this is why it is called a democracy. . . . If we look to the laws, they afford equal justice to all. . . . ❞

— from *The Landmark Thucydides: A Comprehensive Guide to the Peloponnesian War.* Robert B. Strassler, ed. Free Press, 1996

Solon, an Athenian leader and poet

" For I granted the people an adequate amount of power and sufficient prestige [level of respect]—not more nor less.... I stood protecting rich and poor with my stout shield, and saw that neither side prevailed unjustly. "

— from *Greek Lives: A Selection of Nine Greek Lives* by Plutarch. Philip A. Stadter, ed. Oxford University Press, 1998.

SOLON

Plato, a Greek philosopher

" Liberty overmasters [overpowers] democracy—the truth being that excessive increase of anything often causes a reaction in the opposite direction; and this is the case ... above all in forms of government. "

— from *The Republic* by Plato. Benjamin Jowett, trans. The Modern Library, 1941.

PLATO

C. W. BLACKWELL

Christopher W. Blackwell, a historian

" Democracy in Athens was not limited to giving citizens the right to vote.... In a very real sense, the people governed themselves, debating and voting individually on issues great and small, from matters of war and peace to the proper qualifications for ferry-boat captains.... "

— from "Athenian Democracy: A Brief Overview" by Christopher W. Blackwell. *Demos: Classical Athenian Democracy.* The Stoa, 2003.

It's Your Turn

ANALYSIS SKILL **Analyze Points of View** With a classmate, determine which viewpoints support the idea that democracy was strong in ancient Athens and which viewpoints indicate it might have had weaknesses. Discuss how you came to your conclusions.

Make It Relevant How is democracy in the United States different from that in ancient Athens? How is it the same?

Time

2000 B.C.

1500 B.C.

2000 B.C.
The Minoans build
palaces on Crete

1450 B.C.
The Mycenaeans
invade Crete

Reading Social Studies

A **cause** is an event or action that makes something else happen.
An **effect** is what happens as a result of that event or action.

Focus Skill **Cause and Effect**

Complete this graphic organizer to show that you understand
how the geography of Greece affected Greek civilization.
A copy of this graphic organizer appears on page 86 of the
Homework and Practice Book.

Greece's Geography

Cause

Mountains cover most
of mainland Greece.

Effect

California Writing Prompts

Write a Persuasive Editorial Decide whether
you would prefer to live in ancient Sparta or in
ancient Athens. Write a newspaper editorial
about why the city-state you chose is a better
place to live. Try to persuade people from the
other place to come and live in your city-state.

Write a Response to Literature Read
one of Aesop's fables, or recall one that you
might already know, such as "The Hare and the
Tortoise." Write an interpretation of the fable.
Explain what lesson the fable teaches and what
it means to today's readers.

750 B.C.
Greek city-states
begin to form

700s B.C.
The Greek alphabet
is created

500s B.C.
Democracy
begins in Athens

Use Vocabulary

Identify the term that correctly matches each definition.

peninsula, p. 271

epic, p. 282

polis, p. 289

democracy, p. 290

league, p. 303

1. a city-state

2. a group of allies

3. rule by the people

4. a piece of land that is almost completely surrounded by water

5. a long poem

Use the Time Line

 ANALYSIS SKILL **Use the summary time line above to answer these questions.**

6. At what time in history were the Mycenaeans a threat to the Minoans on Crete?

7. What happened in the 500s B.C.?

Apply Skills

ANALYSIS SKILL **Compare Primary and Secondary Sources**

8. Look through the chapter and determine which pictures show primary sources and which show secondary sources. What conclusions can you draw from these sources about the early Greek people?

Recall Facts

Answer these questions.

9. What are three crops that grew well in Greece's soil?

10. What events do the *Iliad* and the *Odyssey* tell about?

11. What form of government replaced the kings of early Greek city-states?

Write the letter of the best choice.

12. Which of the following goods were traded among the Greek city-states?
    A salt, gold, and ivory
    B grain, wood, and metalworks
    C horses and wheeled carts
    D granite, silver, and sculptures

13. Which of the following people helped lay the foundation for Athenian democracy?
    A Homer
    B Hesiod
    C Solon
    D Draco

Think Critically

14. **ANALYSIS SKILL** Describe three forms of government that existed in ancient Greece and the order in which they developed.

15. **ANALYSIS SKILL** What effects did the Persian Empire have on the Greek city-states?

Study Skills

MAKE A K-W-L CHART

A K-W-L chart can help you focus on what you already know about a topic and what you want to learn about it.

▶ In the K column of the chart, list what you already know about a topic.

▶ In the W column, list what you want to find out about the topic.

▶ After reading, in the L column, list what you learned about the topic.

The Golden Age		
what I <u>KNOW</u>	what I <u>WANT</u> to Know	what I <u>LEARNED</u>
• Sparta and Athens were two important city-states in ancient Greece.	• How did Sparta and Athens change during the Golden Age?	_____ _____ _____ _____

Apply As You Read

Complete your own K-W-L chart, using the one above as a model.

California History-Social Science Standards, Grade 6

6.4 Students analyze the geographic, political, economic, religious, and social structures of the early civilizations of Ancient Greece.

CHAPTER

The Golden Age

9

Ruins of the Acropolis in present-day Athens, Greece

• ALL IN A DAY'S WORK •

ATHLETES
AND
ACTORS

AND OTHER JOBS FOR ANCIENT GREEKS

written by Anita Ganeri

Long ago, the ancient Greeks built large independent city-states. Citizens as well as rulers of these city-states had different ways of life and laws. Two of the most powerful city-states were Sparta and Athens. Sparta was known for its soldiers and military strength. Athens was known for its form of government, which today we call democracy. No matter which city-state they lived in, ancient Greeks had different roles in their societies. Read now about some of the jobs they performed.

Welcome to Ancient Greece! You've gone back in time almost 2,500 years and arrived in Athens during its "Golden Age." At this time, Greece is divided into lots of city-states, each with its own rulers and laws. Athens is the greatest of these, with Sparta close behind. Take a stroll through the city and see how the people spend their days. A merchant is loading his wares on to his ship in the port. A teacher scolds a lazy pupil. In the the theater, the actors are busy rehearsing for tonight's performance. Will you find the job for you?

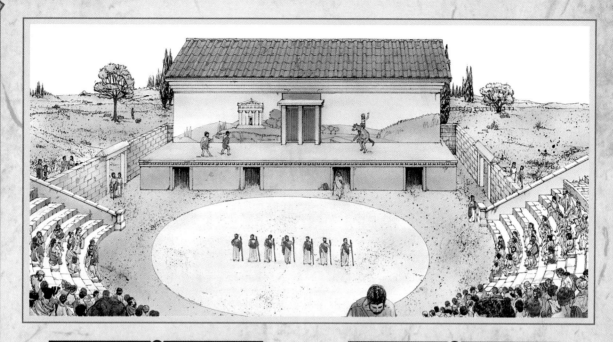

· TEACHER ·

The ancient Greeks were very keen on education and being a teacher was a good job to have. There were three types of school. You might run a general school, where you taught the three Rs—reading, writing, and arithmetic.

GREECE

NEEDS YOU!
- POLITICIANS • HOPLITES •
- SPARTANS • ATHLETES •
- MERCHANTS • TEACHERS •
- SCIENTISTS • DOCTORS •
- ORACLES • ACTORS •
- ARCHITECTS • FARMERS •
AND MANY MORE JOBS AVAILABLE
APPLY AT THE AGORA

You might run a music school, teaching singing, poetry, and playing the lyre. Or you might run a sports school, training boys to run, wrestle, and use weapons. It depended on what you were good at.

Your pupils were boys from wealthy homes. Poor families couldn't afford the fees. They started school at seven years old, and left at 18 to start their military training.

· ACTOR ·

The stage is set, the audience quiet. The play is about to begin. . . .

The ancient Greeks loved going to the theater. The most popular plays were tragedies: the gloomier, the better. Open-air theaters sprung up all over Greece. The audience sat in a circle. The best seats were in the front row. These were reserved for important officials and visitors.

If you liked dressing up, had a strong voice, and didn't get stage-fright, you might have become an actor. You needed a good memory for learning lines, and lots of energy—some plays lasted all day. And you had to be a man. If you were really good, you might be cast in a starring role. If not, you could still be part of the chorus. A wealthy Greek paid for the play and gave you your wages. Top actors were in demand.

· ARCHITECT ·

Being an architect was a very good job. The Greeks liked their buildings grand and graceful. You were kept hard at work designing theaters, temples, schools, and public buildings, some of which still stand today. You were paid by the state or by a rich citizen who wanted to make his mark. Many architects started out as masons or carpenters and worked their way up from there.

It helped to have friends in high places. When Pericles ruled Athens, he hired a leading architect, called Ictinus, to design a magnificent temple on the Acropolis hill, dedicated to Athena and called the Parthenon. It took ten years to complete, from 447–438 B.C. The temple was built of huge slabs of marble, dragged up the hill by ox-cart. They were hauled into place with ropes and pulleys, and fixed with metal pegs. The outside was decorated with colorful painted statues and carvings.

· FARMER ·

Being a farmer wasn't an easy life. The soil was poor and stony, and it didn't rain for months on end. Most farms were small. On them, farmers grew food for their families and a bit extra to sell at market. If the harvest was bad, you could borrow money to help you get by. But if you couldn't pay off your debt, your land was confiscated and you might have to sell yourself and your family into slavery. Many ordinary Greeks worked as farmers in winter, and sailors in summer.

Other farms were much bigger. They were owned by wealthy Greeks who lived in the city, and were run by bailiffs, or managers. Most of the hardest work was done by slaves.

Response Corner

1 Since boys were the only ones who went to school, what kind of education do you think girls received?

2 Work with a partner to decide which job you think you would enjoy most. Come up with three reasons, and present your ideas to the class.

490 B.C.
The Greeks defeat the
Persians at Marathon

480 B.C.
The Persian army
captures Athens

461 B.C.
Pericles becomes
a leader in Athens

Lesson 1

WHAT TO KNOW
What people and events
helped the city-state of
Athens rise to power?

✓ Analyze the roles of
Athens and Sparta
in the wars with the
Persian Empire.

✓ Identify the
differences between
direct democracy
and representative
democracy.

VOCABULARY
direct democracy p. 318
veto p. 318
representative democracy
   p. 318

PEOPLE
Darius I
Xerxes
Cleisthenes
Pericles

PLACES
Marathon
Persia
Asia Minor
Sardis
Thermopylae
Salamis

CAUSE AND EFFECT

California
Standards
HSS 6.4, 6.4.2, 6.4.3, 6.4.5, 6.4.6

A Time of Glory in Athens

YOU ARE THERE It's 490 B.C., and everyone in Athens is
nervous! Just north of the city-state, on the
plain of **Marathon**, Greek soldiers are fighting to hold
back an army of invaders from Persia. People say that
if the Persians win, they will make the Greeks their
slaves. Democracy will end, and so will freedom!

You climb up to the Acropolis of Athens, hoping to
see the action from the city's highest point. Shading
your eyes, you look out across the plain far below. You
can't see the armies, but still, you worry. Will the Greek
army be able to stop the mighty Persians before they
reach Athens?

LOCATE IT

GREECE

Athens

▶ Overlooking present-day Athens, the Acropolis
once provided defense for the city.

The Persian Wars

TIME 490s B.C.

PLACE Mainland Greece

For centuries, the Greek city-states fought each other over land and trade. Then, in the 400s B.C., the Greek people united to face a common enemy—**Persia**. Persia had built an enormous empire that stretched from what is now India in the east to Egypt in the west. It had also gained control over the Greek cities along the coast of **Asia Minor**.

In about 499 B.C., the people of Greek city-states in Asia Minor rebelled against Persia. During the uprising, they burned **Sardis**, the western capital of the Persian Empire. Athens sent a small fleet of ships to help the rebelling Greeks, but the Persians crushed the rebellion.

These events angered **Darius I**, the leader of the Persian Empire. For some time, Darius had wanted to expand his empire by conquering the Greek city-states. He was not willing to give up his dream of victory over the Greeks.

In 492 B.C., Darius sent a huge army across land and sea to conquer the Greeks. His forces were stopped short when a storm wrecked the Persian fleet. Even so, the Persian Wars had begun.

Two years later, Darius attacked again, with his forces landing safely near the plain of Marathon, just 26 miles north of Athens. Darius's soldiers outnumbered the Greek troops two to one. With reason to worry, the Athenians sent word to Sparta to send help.

Fearing that the Spartans would arrive too late, the Athenian general took a chance. The general ordered the hoplites to line up facing the invaders as usual, but he packed the wings, or the far ends of the line, tightly with soldiers.

As the Athenian general had predicted, the Persians attacked the middle of the line and pushed forward. The Greek wings then moved in to surround the Persians. In this way, the much smaller Greek force trapped the mighty Persians and defeated them.

READING CHECK ☼**CAUSE AND EFFECT**
What caused the Greek city-states to unite?

FAST FACT

A Greek legend tells about a messenger running all the way from Marathon to Athens to report the Greek victory over the Persians. After completing the 26-mile run to Athens, the messenger died while proclaiming victory. In his honor, the Greeks added a 26-mile race called a marathon to the Olympic Games.

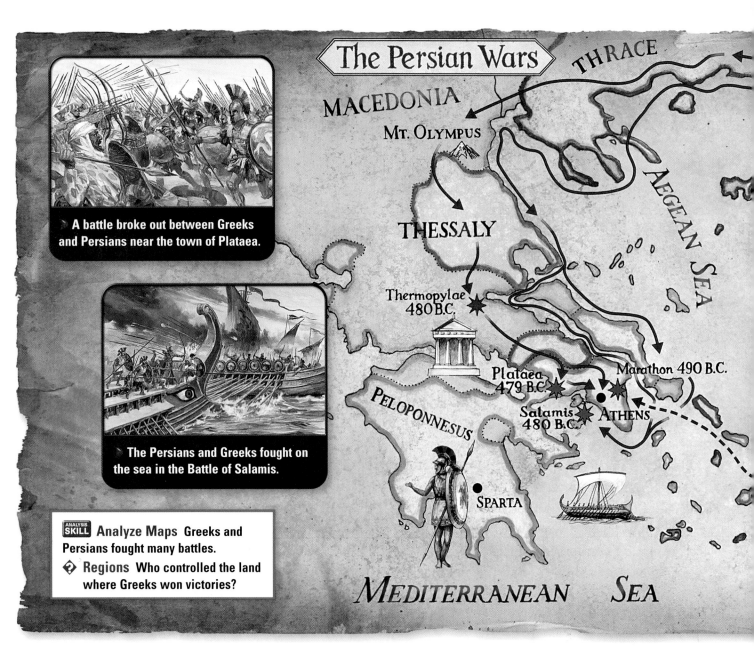

The Persian Wars

THRACE

MACEDONIA

MT. OLYMPUS

THESSALY

AEGEAN SEA

Thermopylae
480 B.C.

Plataea
479 B.C.

Marathon 490 B.C.

PELOPONNESUS

Salamis
480 B.C.

ATHENS

SPARTA

MEDITERRANEAN SEA

> A battle broke out between Greeks and Persians near the town of Plataea.

> The Persians and Greeks fought on the sea in the Battle of Salamis.

ANALYSIS SKILL Analyze Maps Greeks and Persians fought many battles.

✦ **Regions** Who controlled the land where Greeks won victories?

Greek Victories

Persian emperor **Xerxes** (ZERK•seez), Darius's son, came close to conquering the Greeks. In 480 B.C., Xerxes led an expedition of about 200,000 soldiers and more than 600 ships to conquer Greek territory.

The Greeks prepared for the Persians' return. At sea, Athens's navy had 200 ships, while on land, Sparta led the Peloponnesian League's army. Even so, the Persians greatly outnumbered the Greeks.

A small Greek force fought Xerxes' army at a mountain pass called **Thermopylae** (ther•MAHP•uh•lee). The Greeks defended

the pass until their last soldier fell. In the end, the Persians broke through, captured Athens, and set the city on fire.

Meanwhile, the Athenian navy withdrew to a narrow strait between the Greek coastline and the island of **Salamis** (SA•luh•muhs). The Battle of Salamis was about to begin.

The Persian ships that sailed into the strait far outnumbered the Greek ships. Fortunately for the Greeks, the Persian ships were too large to turn quickly in the narrow strait. The lighter, faster Greek ships rammed into the Persian ships and sank them. By the battle's end, the Greeks

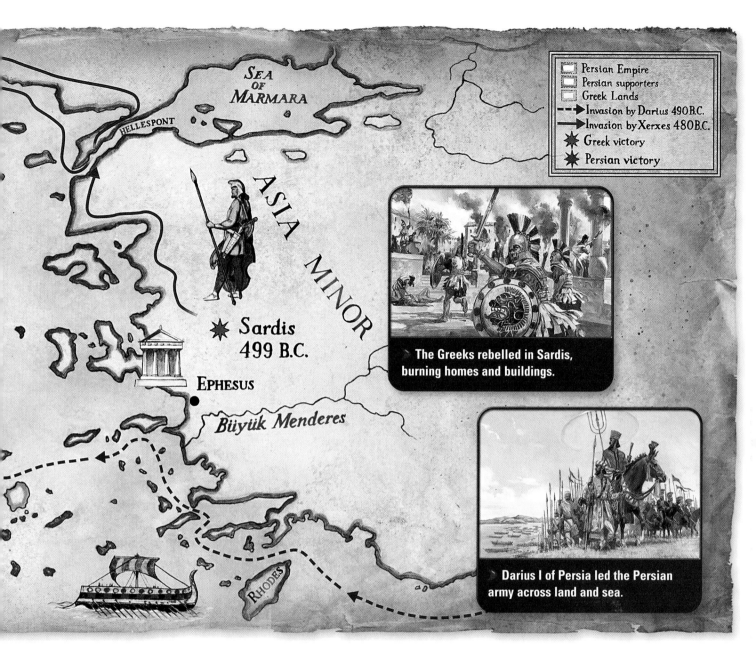

SEA OF MARMARA

HELLESPONT

ASIA MINOR

★ Sardis
499 B.C.

EPHESUS

Büyük Menderes

RHODES

Persian Empire
Persian supporters
Greek Lands
- - -➤ Invasion by Darius 490 B.C.
———➤ Invasion by Xerxes 480 B.C.
✶ Greek victory
★ Persian victory

The Greeks rebelled in Sardis, burning homes and buildings.

Darius I of Persia led the Persian army across land and sea.

had destroyed about 200 ships. Defeated, Xerxes returned to Asia Minor with his army and his remaining ships.

On land, the Spartans led the Greek army to victory in the Battle of Plataea (pluh•TEE•uh). Although an official peace agreement would not be made for another 30 years, the Persian threat to mainland Greece had been quieted.

After the Persian Wars began, Athens and about 150 city-states formed a new alliance called the Delian (DEE•lee•uhn) League. They vowed to fight the Persians and free the Greek lands still under Persian rule. The league's members also agreed to pay tribute to Athens in the form of money or ships. In return, Athens promised to protect the city-states with its powerful navy.

The Delian League won many victories. In 467 B.C., at the battle of the Eurymedon (yoo•RIH•muh•dahn) River, the league freed several Greek city-states, pushing the Persians away from the Aegean.

Together, Athens and Sparta had played their roles to win the Persian Wars. However, the victory set the stage for conflict between the two city-states.

READING CHECK **COMPARE AND CONTRAST**
How were the roles of Athens and Sparta in the Persian Wars alike and different?

Democracy in Athens

Earlier, in about 508 B.C., a leader named **Cleisthenes** (KLYS•thuh•neez) made reforms that helped Athens form an early democracy. Now, citizens—not a king, a tyrant, or an oligarchy—could make decisions about their government.

Cleisthenes' reforms created an Athenian democracy that was a **direct democracy**. This gave every Athenian who was a free male over 18 years of age an equal vote in the assembly. Women and slaves were not allowed to vote. A council proposed laws to the assembly, which would accept or veto them by majority rule. To **veto** something means to reject it. In this way, many Athenian citizens began to make decisions directly about their government.

In contrast, a **representative democracy** is a democracy in which citizens elect other people to make decisions for them. The government of the United States is a representative democracy.

Direct and representative democracies have other key differences, too. All citizens living in small communities, such as a city-state, could take part in a direct democracy. Today, populations of most democracies are too large to do this, so a representative democracy is more practical. Also, in a direct democracy, citizens all met in one place. This is not possible for the citizens of today's democracies.

In 461 B.C., a new leader named **Pericles** (PAIR•uh•kleez) made more democratic reforms. He believed that all citizens, rich and poor, should be able to serve equally in government. Pericles explained, "No one . . . is barred [refused] because of poverty or humble origins."*

Pericles' reforms laid a foundation for future democracies. Many Americans, such as Cesar Chavez, have worked to see that all citizens are treated equally. In the 1960s, Chavez worked for equal rights and justice for poor farmworkers, most of whom were Mexican American. He formed a group that would become the United Farm Workers of America. This group used nonviolent actions to get higher wages and better working conditions for farmworkers.

READING CHECK COMPARE AND CONTRAST
What are the key differences between a direct democracy and a representative democracy?

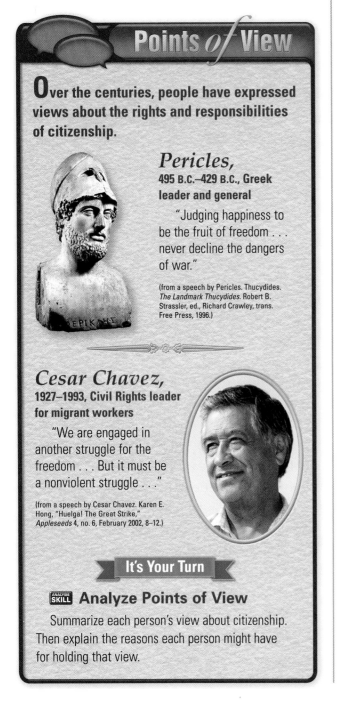

Points of View

Over the centuries, people have expressed views about the rights and responsibilities of citizenship.

Pericles,
495 B.C.–429 B.C., Greek leader and general

"Judging happiness to be the fruit of freedom . . . never decline the dangers of war."

(from a speech by Pericles. Thucydides. *The Landmark Thucydides.* Robert B. Strassler, ed., Richard Crawley, trans. Free Press, 1996.)

Cesar Chavez,
1927–1993, Civil Rights leader for migrant workers

"We are engaged in another struggle for the freedom . . . But it must be a nonviolent struggle . . ."

(from a speech by Cesar Chavez. Karen E. Hong, "Huelga! The Great Strike," *Appleseeds* 4, no. 6, February 2002, 8–12.)

It's Your Turn

ANALYSIS SKILL Analyze Points of View

Summarize each person's view about citizenship. Then explain the reasons each person might have for holding that view.

*Thucydides. *The Landmark Thucydides.* Robert B. Strassler, ed., Richard Crawley, trans. Free Press, 1996.

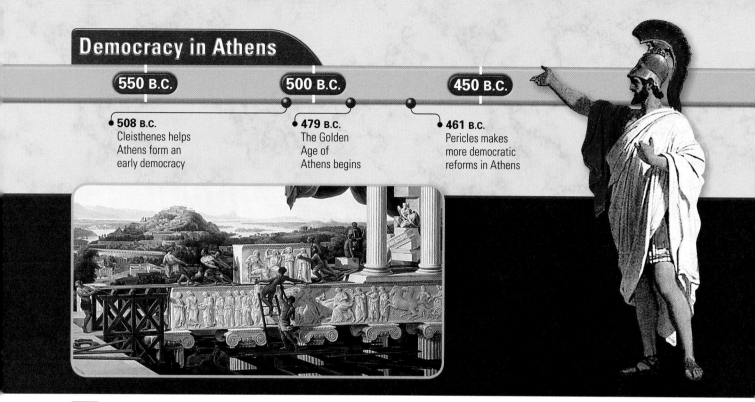

Democracy in Athens

550 B.C.   **500 B.C.**   **450 B.C.**

508 B.C.
Cleisthenes helps
Athens form an
early democracy

479 B.C.
The Golden
Age of
Athens begins

461 B.C.
Pericles makes
more democratic
reforms in Athens

ANALYSIS SKILL Analyze Time Lines Democracy in Athens developed over time.

❖ When did an early democracy begin in Athens?

The Golden Age

With the Persian Wars behind them, the Athenians began rebuilding their city-state. They felt a sense of great pride because they had defeated the strong Persian army. Also, Athens continued to receive tribute from members of the Delian League. This tribute gave Athens the money it needed to rebuild. In addition, Athens had strong leadership, especially that of Pericles.

All this gave rise to a time of great cultural achievement in Athens. This period, now known as the Golden Age of Athens, lasted from 479 B.C. to 431 B.C.

Pericles' goal was to make Athens an example to all of Greece. Pericles wanted to rebuild Athens as the model for respected political, economic, and social structures. He also set out to make Athens a center for art and learning. He hired the best architects and artists that the Greek world had to offer.

Architects designed new government buildings, schools, temples, and theaters. Hundreds of builders made the designs a reality. They used gleaming white marble dug from a nearby mountain. Artists decorated the buildings with murals. Soon, Athenian officials dedicated new buildings to the public in a celebration of Athenian democracy and culture.

Throughout Athens, the Athenians built many open-air theaters out of stone and wood. One theater held more than 17,000 people. Athenians loved plays, and often every seat was filled for a performance. Athenian playwrights were considered the best in Greece.

Every spring, a theater contest in Athens honored the Greek god Dionysus, the god of wine. On the day of the festival, each playwright produced four plays, one after the other. The top prize was awarded, in democratic fashion, by the decision of ten judges according to majority rule.

▶ In this painting (far right), a teacher in ancient Greece instructs his students on the subject of astronomy. Notice that the students draw the solar system on the ground. Usually, students wrote on wax tablets using a stylus (right).

While the great architects, artists, and playwrights contributed to the Golden Age of Athens, so did others. Greeks advanced art, poetry, education, philosophy, science, mathematics, and medicine. Today, more than 2,000 years later, people are still influenced by these contributions.

READING CHECK MAIN IDEA AND DETAILS
What contributed to the rise of the Golden Age of Athens?

Summary

Greek city-states united to fight the Persian Empire in the Persian Wars. Greek victories led to a time of growth and wealth for Athens and its early democracy. This began a period of cultural achievement called the Golden Age of Athens. These enduring contributions continue to influence people.

REVIEW

1. 💡 What people and events helped the city-state of Athens rise to power?

2. Use the term **direct democracy** in a sentence about Athenian democracy.

3. How did the Greek forces win the battle against the Persians at Marathon?

CRITICAL THINKING

4. **ANALYSIS SKILL** What parts of Athens's democracy might be considered unfair today?

5. What problems might occur when a country changes from one form of government to another?

6. **ANALYSIS SKILL** **Make It Relevant** How do you think early Greek democracy affects American democracy today?

7. ✏️ **Conduct an Interview** Imagine that you are a newspaper reporter. Write three interview questions about early democracy, and use them to interview two classmates. Write their responses in the form of a newspaper article.

8. **Focus Skill** **CAUSE AND EFFECT**
On a separate sheet of paper, copy and complete the graphic organizer below.

Cause	Effect
	The Persians attack the Greek city-states.

Cause	Effect
The Persians attack the Greek city-states.	

Pericles

Biography

Trustworthiness

Respect

Responsibility

Fairness

Caring

Patriotism

"Our constitution does not copy the laws of neighboring states; we are rather a pattern to others than imitators ourselves."

Pericles believed that citizens should participate in and take an interest in the democratic process. Under his leadership, the assembly became the central power of the city-state of Athens. All free-born male citizens had the right—and the responsibility —to serve in the assembly.

Pericles began his political career at an early age. Coming from a well-known, aristocratic family, he received a classical Greek education. Pericles studied politics, debate, public speaking, and ethics, or the study of right and wrong.

▶ Pericles gives a Funeral Oration to honor Greeks who had died in the Peloponnesian War.

Pericles led Athens for 40 years. Under his leadership, Athens grew to be a great city-state. He had many new buildings constructed, including the Parthenon, a temple of the city-state's patron goddess, Athena. Theaters, baths, and other buildings were built and opened to the public. Pericles also hired artists to tell Athens's history in paintings, statues, plays, and poetry. This period, with its flowering of culture and building, is known as the Golden Age of Athens. Some have also called it the Age of Pericles.

*Pericles. *The Landmark Thucydides: A Comprehensive Guide to the Peloponnesian War.* Robert B. Strassler, ed., Richard Crawley, trans. Free Press, 1996.

Why Character Counts

❖ How do Pericles' words express his love of the city-state of Athens?

Bio Brief

495 B.C.		429 B.C.
Born		Died

461 B.C.
Pericles becomes a leader in Athens

447 B.C.
Construction on the Parthenon begins

431 B.C.
Pericles delivers the Funeral Oration

Interactive Multimedia Biographies
Visit **MULTIMEDIA BIOGRAPHIES** at
www.harcourtschool.com/hss

Read a Circle Graph

▶ WHY IT MATTERS

Suppose you wanted to show in a simple, clear way how the population of Greece was divided during the time of Pericles. You could make a circle graph. A **circle graph** shows information on a circle that is divided into parts. Circle graphs are often called pie charts, because they look like pies with different-sized slices. The larger a slice is, the greater the percent it stands for.

▶ WHAT YOU NEED TO KNOW

The circle graph on the next page shows the population of Athens in about 430 B.C. The graph's parts are the various groups of people that made up the city-state's population.

The slices of every circle graph add up to 100 percent. The size of each slice represents part of the whole 100 percent. For example, a slice that takes up exactly half of the graph stands for 50 percent. It is not always easy to know exactly what percent a slice shows just by looking at it, so slices are often labeled with their percents.

One of the most useful features of circle graphs is their ability to show information at a glance. For example, just by glancing at the Population of Athens graph, you can tell that the families of male citizens made up about one-third of the population.

▶ A group of colorfully dressed Athenian citizens enjoy a day at the theater.

▶ PRACTICE THE SKILL

Study the circle graph to answer the following questions.

1 Which group made up the largest part of the population of Athens?

2 Which group made up the smallest part of the population?

3 What percent of the population did male citizens make up?

4 Together, what percent of the population was made up of male citizens and their families?

▶ APPLY WHAT YOU LEARNED

With a partner, think of other kinds of information that could be shown on a circle graph. Choose one kind of information, and locate figures for it on reliable Internet sites or in other sources. Then make your own circle graph. Next, write questions that could be answered by looking at your circle graph. Ask other students to take your circle graph quiz while you and your partner take theirs.

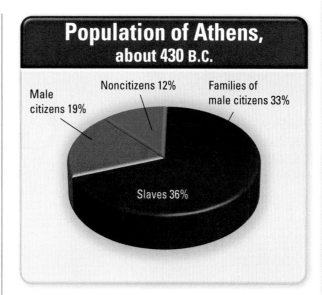

Population of Athens,
about 430 B.C.

Male citizens 19%

Noncitizens 12%

Families of male citizens 33%

Slaves 36%

Time

| 2000 B.C. | 1000 B.C. | B.C./A.D. |

438 B.C.
The Parthenon
is completed

399 B.C.
The Athenian court
sentences Socrates

335 B.C.
Aristotle opens the
Lyceum in Athens

Greek Gifts

WHAT TO KNOW
What enduring
contributions to the arts
and sciences did the
ancient Greeks make?

✓ Describe how Greek
mythology affected the
arts and sciences of the
ancient Greeks.

✓ Explain what ideas and
beliefs shaped cultural
achievements in Athens.

VOCABULARY
tragedy p. 327
comedy p. 327

PEOPLE
Socrates
Hesiod
Homer
Sophocles
Aristophanes
Pythagoras
Hippocrates
Democritus
Herodotus
Thucydides
Plato
Aristotle

PLACES
Athens

CAUSE AND EFFECT

**California
Standards**
HSS 6.4, 6.4.4, 6.4.8

YOU ARE THERE
It's 445 B.C. All around you, **Athens** bustles
with activity. Many new buildings are under
construction. In one area, stonemasons are busy shaping columns. Across from them, workers haul in more
marble for the new temple being built on the Acropolis.
You duck into a promenade, an open, porchlike building,
to get out of their way.

There you see the famous teacher **Socrates**
(SAH•kruh•teez) speaking with his students. You have
heard that he always answers a student's question with
another question. People say that Socrates does this
to help his students discover the answers on their
own. You move closer to hear what he is saying.

LOCATE IT

GREECE

Athens

Art and Architecture

The history of ancient Greece is filled with Greek figures, or important people, who made enduring contributions in the arts and sciences. In architecture, for example, Pericles directed architects and builders to create many beautiful structures. People use these same designs for modern buildings.

In the center of the Acropolis of Athens, Pericles oversaw the building of a magnificent temple, the Parthenon, which honored the goddess Athena. Completed in 438 B.C., the Parthenon took 9 years to build and required more than 22,000 tons of white marble. Its architecture expresses balance and simplicity, qualities valued by the Greeks. Many modern buildings, such as the United States Supreme Court Building in Washington, D.C., use

> Once brightly painted and adorned with jewelry, this statue stood inside the Acropolis of Athens.

designs based on the architecture of Greek temples.

Statues of Greek gods and of people decorated Greek buildings, both inside and outside. Never before had statues been created to look so lifelike.

Greek painters took the same care to portray people and scenes realistically. Artists decorated buildings with murals, or wall paintings, showing lifelike scenes from Athens's history and from Greek myths.

Paintings on ancient vases provide evidence of the skill of Greek artists. Using black or red paint, artists decorated the vases with scenes from Greek mythology and from their own daily life. By carefully observing these vases, we can see how people dressed, how they wore their hair, and even what they ate.

READING CHECK ○ CAUSE AND EFFECT
What effect did Greek mythology have on art and architecture?

> Even today, the ruins of the Parthenon in Athens reveal one of the finest examples of classical Greek architecture.

Literature and Theater

Ancient Greek writers left a treasure chest of literature, which included new styles of writing. They created the foundation for literature in many later Western cultures. Even today, Greek literature permeates our literature and language.

In the 700s B.C., one of the earliest Greek epic poets, **Hesiod**, wrote down the myths and legends that had long been told in Greek mythology. In other poems, Hesiod described the difficulties of everyday life in ancient Greece. His poems have provided modern historians with useful information about early Greek culture.

Homer's *Iliad* and *Odyssey* became the later Roman culture's first literature. The main themes of the *Odyssey*—adventure and returning home—continue to be used in literature as well as in movies.

The stories of *Aesop's Fables* still teach moral lessons to children and adults alike. Among Aesop's best-known fables are "The Shepherd Boy and the Wolf" and "The Hare and the Tortoise."

Many words in the English language come from Greek literature. For example, we call a book of maps an atlas, after the Greek god Atlas. Atlas was said to carry on his shoulders the columns that separated the heavens and the earth. Another example is the saying *Achilles' heel*, which is sometimes used to describe a person's weak spot. It comes from the myth about Achilles (uh•KIH•leez), a Greek hero of the Trojan War.

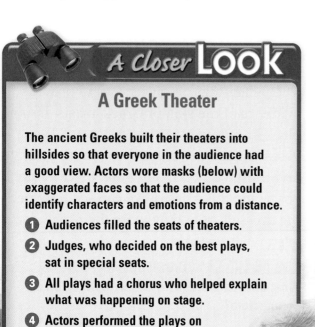

A Closer Look

A Greek Theater

The ancient Greeks built their theaters into hillsides so that everyone in the audience had a good view. Actors wore masks (below) with exaggerated faces so that the audience could identify characters and emotions from a distance.

1. Audiences filled the seats of theaters.
2. Judges, who decided on the best plays, sat in special seats.
3. All plays had a chorus who helped explain what was happening on stage.
4. Actors performed the plays on a stage.
5. Background scenery made the play appear more realistic.
6. To represent Greek gods appearing from the sky, stage workers used a crane to lower actors who played the roles of gods to the stage.

❓ How does Greek theater show the importance of Greek mythology?

Through theater, plays became an important part of Greek literature. Even the word *theater* comes from a Greek word that means "a place to see." During the Golden Age, Athens was known throughout Greece for its fine theaters and skilled playwrights.

One of the most famous playwrights was **Sophocles** (SAH•fuh•kleez), whose works are still performed today. Sophocles' plays are **tragedies**, serious plays in which the main characters come to an unhappy end. In Sophocles' tragedies, heroes always struggle to do the right thing. In one play, a young woman named Antigone (an•TIH•guh•nee) faces a terrible choice. If she chooses to do the right thing, she will break an unfair law. The punishment for breaking the law is death. Antigone chooses to do the right thing and accepts the consequences.

By contrast, Greek comedies always end happily for the main characters. A **comedy** is a humorous play, and Greek comedies often poke fun at people and ideas. **Aristophanes** (ar•uh•STAH•fuh•neez)

was the master of Greek comedies. In his comedies, he used humor to make serious statements about political and social life.

Greek theater was different from theater today. First, a trip to the theater in ancient times was an all-day outdoor event. Also, only men could appear on stage, so men had to play women's roles. Since the cast often included only a few people, the actors took on many different parts. This fact made costumes important. All actors wore masks designed to represent different characters and emotions.

Theater in the Golden Age was a place for both popular entertainment and ideas. Plays dealt with issues ranging from political and religious conflicts to problems of everyday life. Since every generation faces issues such as these, Greek plays continue to influence our literature.

READING CHECK **MAIN IDEA AND DETAILS**
How does the Greek literature of Homer influence our literature and movies today?

▶ Pythagoras was a mathematician, philosopher, and early astronomer. This woodblock print from A.D. 1492 shows Pythagoras performing experiments with sound.

▶ Hippocrates paved the way for modern medicine. The Greek god Hermes' winged staff is a symbol of the medical profession.

▶ Democritus, a Greek scientist and philosopher, was one of the first scientists to come up with an atomic theory. The diagram shows the structure of an atom.

Science, Mathematics, and History

Even before the Golden Age of Athens, the Greeks had begun questioning old ways of thinking. Their ideas led to the dawn of rational, or logical, thought in science, mathematics, history, and philosophy.

Some ancient Greek thinkers doubted that gods and goddesses caused events in nature, as many other Greeks believed. Instead, these thinkers sought to understand the world by studying it carefully.

Ancient Greek scientists worked in much the same way that modern scientists do. They used scientific methods to develop theories. This led to new discoveries that changed the way people saw the world.

About 600 B.C., the Greek mathematician **Pythagoras** (puh•THA•guh•ruhs) believed that everything in the universe could be understood by using numbers. Today, Pythagoras is best remembered for his theorem, or formula, that expresses the relationship among the lengths of the sides of a right triangle. This formula is called the Pythagorean theorem.

Hippocrates (hih•PAH•kruh•teez), a Greek doctor, changed the way people thought about medicine. Many people believed that illnesses were punishments from the gods. Hippocrates knew that illnesses had natural causes. He carefully studied his patients and their illnesses to find and treat the causes. In modern medicine, most doctors use this method.

Hippocrates' name is associated with the Hippocratic oath, a pledge of duties and responsible actions made by doctors. Today, doctors still promise to follow these rules when they graduate from medical school.

▶ Herodotus was one of the earliest geographers and Greece's first historian. This book is one of nine that he wrote about the Persian Wars.

▶ Thucydides was a Greek historian. His detailed writings give us a glimpse of life in ancient Greece.

▶ Socrates was one of the great Greek philosophers. People learn about his ideas from the writings of his student Plato.

The Golden Age scientist **Democritus** (dih•MAH•kruh•tuhs) explained that all matter is made up of building blocks called atoms. He believed that people could understand nature by learning about the movement of atoms. His ideas eventually led to such branches of science as chemistry.

Other Greek figures contributed to the importance of historical records. **Herodotus** (hih•RAH•duh•tuhs) was Greece's first historian. His books about the Persian Wars included not only facts but also differing views about the wars and their causes. Herodotus' method of collecting data and drawing conclusions from it has influenced historical writing over the centuries.

The Greek historian **Thucydides** (thoo•SIH•duh•deez) wrote about another war. During his lifetime, the rivalry between Athens and Sparta led to a period of war. Thucydides witnessed the war from beginning to end and wrote about the war as it unfolded. His writings also have provided modern historians with valuable information about Greek political, economic, and social structures.

Thucydides served as a general in the Athenian army. Athenian leaders exiled Thucydides from Athens after he accepted the blame for losing a battle. Thucydides spent several years in lands allied with Sparta. This experience helped him write about the war from the points of view of both the Athenians and the Spartans.

Thucydides is credited with creating a method in which historians write about historical events without including their personal opinions. He wanted "the accuracy of the report being always tried by the most severe and detailed tests possible."*

READING CHECK SUMMARIZE
What contributions did Herodotus and Thucydides make to the recording of history?

*Thucydides. *The Landmark Thucydides*. Robert B. Strassler, ed., Richard Crawley, trans. Free Press, 1996.

▶ This painting is called *The School of Athens*. It was painted in about A.D. 1510 by the Italian artist Raphael. The two figures in the center represent Aristotle and Plato.

Philosophy and Teaching

During and after the Golden Age, many thinkers and teachers called Athens home. They often disagreed with each other, but these philosophers, or "lovers of wisdom," were united in a search for knowledge and truth. Three ancient Greek philosophers laid the foundation for many ideas of later Western civilizations.

Socrates was one of the city-state's most brilliant philosophers and teachers. His teachings focused on morals, knowing right from wrong. Socrates taught by asking his students questions. This required them to think for themselves. His way of teaching, called the Socratic method, continues to be a model for debating ideas.

Many people disliked Socrates because he openly criticized the leaders of Athens's democracy. Socrates felt that the leaders were morally weak. Such criticism would have been fine in Pericles' day, but it angered the leaders of Athens. Socrates hoped that his criticisms would convince the Athenians to change their government.

The Athenian leaders arrested Socrates and put him on trial. In 399 B.C., an Athenian court found him guilty of teaching dangerous ideas. The court ordered Socrates to end his own life by drinking poison. Socrates' friends and family wanted him to leave the city to escape punishment, but Socrates refused. Believing that all citizens should obey the law, he drank the poison.

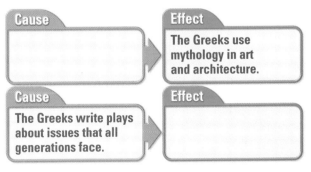

This artwork shows Aristotle teaching astronomy to Persian students. The writing shown is Persian.

The philosopher **Plato** (PLAY•toh) was one of Socrates' most gifted students. After his teacher's death, Plato started a new school called the Academy in Athens. There, he taught philosophy, law, and science. Plato's writings on politics, justice, religion, and education are still read today.

One of Plato's students in the Academy was **Aristotle** (AR•uh•stah•tuhl). In his quest for knowledge, Aristotle collected, organized, and classified information, a method important to modern science. He studied astronomy, law, and economics and was a pioneer in zoology—the study of animals—and in botany—the study of plants. In 335 B.C., Aristotle opened his own school, called the Lyceum (ly•SEE•uhm).

READING CHECK ☉**CAUSE AND EFFECT**
Why did Athenian leaders dislike Socrates?

Summary

The ancient Greeks made many lasting contributions. Greek literature, including mythology, poetry, and plays, continues to influence our literature and language today. The Greeks also challenged the ideas of their times in science, history, medicine, mathematics, and philosophy.

REVIEW

1. What enduring contributions to the arts and sciences did the ancient Greeks make?

2. Explain how a **tragedy** and a **comedy** are alike and how they are different.

3. Which ancient Greek philosophers laid the foundation for many ideas of later Western civilizations?

CRITICAL THINKING

4. **ANALYSIS SKILL** Do you think Socrates was right to criticize Athenian leaders? Why or why not?

5. How did the ancient Greek thinkers challenge the religious beliefs held by most Greeks?

6. **Make It Relevant** Do you think it is better for news to be reported without personal opinion?

7. **Make a Table** Create a matrix of time and place table that shows the enduring contributions of Greek figures from this lesson. Then, in a group, research one contribution further. Make a poster that presents your findings.

8. (Focus Skill) **CAUSE AND EFFECT**
On a separate sheet of paper, copy and complete the graphic organizer below.

Cause	Effect
	The Greeks use mythology in art and architecture.
The Greeks write plays about issues that all generations face.	

Greek Architecture

The ancient Greeks built magnificent stone temples and public buildings. They invented new forms of architecture with high roofs supported by strong columns. Sculptures often decorated both the inside and outside of temples. There were three main forms of Greek architecture—Doric, Ionic, and Corinthian. Later, builders in Europe and around the world borrowed ideas from Greek architecture. Many buildings in Washington, D.C., including the White House, the United States Capitol, and the Supreme Court, are based on Greek designs.

Capital, or top, of
a Doric column

Capital of an
Ionic column

Capital of a
Corinthian column

A Doric temple built by
the ancient Greeks

In Greek architecture, pediments are triangle shapes containing sculptures found on the sides of temple roofs. Shown here is part of a pediment with a sculpture of a three-headed creature with a snake's tail.

A tool used by Phidias, a famous Greek sculptor

These caryatids (kar•ee•A•tuhdz), or columns in the shape of human figures, support the roof of an ancient Greek temple in Athens.

ANALYSIS SKILL Analyze Artifacts

1. What can you tell about the role of religion in Greek society from the temples that Greeks built to their gods?

2. How do you think Phidias's tool was used?

3. Why do you think architects chose to borrow from the architecture of the ancient Greeks for the most important buildings of the United States government?

GO ONLINE

Visit PRIMARY SOURCES at
www.harcourtschool.com/hss

Time

2000 B.C. 1000 B.C. B.C./A.D.

431 B.C.
The Peloponnesian
War resumes

404 B.C.
Athens surrenders
to Sparta

403 B.C.
Athenians set about
restoring democracy

Times of Conflict

💡 **WHAT TO KNOW**
How did the rivalry
between Sparta and Athens
lead to the Peloponnesian
War?

✓ Identify events
that caused the
Peloponnesian War.

✓ Compare and contrast
the roles of Athens
and Sparta during the
Peloponnesian War.

✓ Explain how the
government of Athens
changed as a result of
the Peloponnesian War.

VOCABULARY
demagogue p. 336
dictatorship p. 337
mercenary p. 339

PEOPLE
Pericles

PLACES
Athens
Sparta
Thebes
Corinth
Argos

 **CAUSE AND
EFFECT**

 California
Standards
HSS 6.4, 6.4.2, 6.4.6

**YOU
ARE
THERE**
It's 431 B.C., and disaster has struck **Athens**!
The city-state of **Sparta** has invaded Attica,
the area surrounding Athens. In the marketplace, you
see people from the countryside streaming into Athens.
They are seeking protection within the city walls.

Everyone is talking about war. Some speak confi-
dently of the Athenians' ability to conquer their enemies. Others worry that the Spartans are too smart and
too fierce to be defeated in battle. They say that the
Spartans will try to cut off Athens's food supply. By
taking the port, where the city's grain shipments arrive,
the Spartans could starve the people of Athens.

▶ This wall relief shows an ancient
Greek battle.

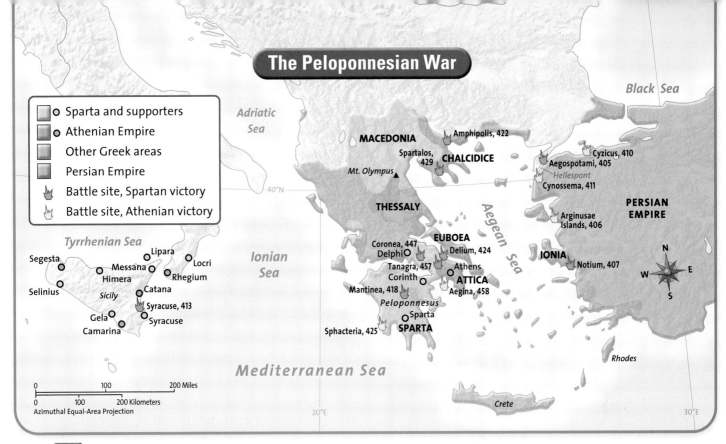

The Peloponnesian War

Sparta and supporters
Athenian Empire
Other Greek areas
Persian Empire
Battle site, Spartan victory
Battle site, Athenian victory

ANALYSIS SKILL **Analyze Maps** The Spartans and Athenians battled for many years through most of Greece and part of the Persian Empire.

❖ **Regions** Who controlled the land where Sparta won most of its battles?

The Peloponnesian War Begins

In the 400s B.C., Athens and Sparta were the most powerful of all the Greek city-states. Still, neither city-state was satisfied. The leaders of Athens wanted even greater power over the other city-states. The leaders of Sparta feared that Athens would become stronger than their own city-state. This rivalry led to a long series of battles known as the Peloponnesian War.

Athens placed the city-states of the Delian League under an Athenian Empire. Its treasury overflowed with tribute collected from the members. **Pericles** used much of this wealth to strengthen the city's defense walls. The Long Walls, as they were known, connected the city of Athens to the port of Piraeus (py•REE•uhs). The walls protected the movement of grain and goods from the port to the city.

Pericles also invested money in Athens's navy. The Athenian fleet was already the largest in the entire region. Having such a powerful navy allowed Athens to pressure more city-states to come under its rule.

These actions alarmed the Spartans. In 460 B.C., the tension between Sparta and Athens exploded into war. For the next 15 years, both sides celebrated victories and suffered defeats.

Finally, in about 445 B.C., both sides grew tired of fighting. Athens and Sparta signed a peace treaty called the Thirty Years' Peace. Unfortunately, the treaty neither resolved the bad feelings between Athens and Sparta, nor did it last for 30 years.

READING CHECK ⟳**CAUSE AND EFFECT**
What was the effect of Athens's desire for more power?

Renewed Fighting

In 431 B.C., only 14 years after Sparta and Athens had agreed on the Thirty Years' Peace, war broke out between them again. This time, the fighting lasted for 27 years and had even more devastating results. The Golden Age of Athens was at an end.

The Spartan army launched an attack on Attica. People from the countryside poured into Athens, seeking protection inside its walls. Although it was crowded in Athens, the people felt safe and could get food. Meanwhile, as the Spartan army destroyed the homes and crops they had abandoned, the Athenian navy attacked Sparta's allies.

The historian Thucydides wrote about an event that weakened Athens. A plague spread in the overcrowded city and killed many Athenians, including Pericles.

After Pericles' death, Athens went through a series of leaders. Some of them were **demagogues** (DEH•muh•gahgz), or weak leaders who were popular because they told the people what they wanted to hear, even though it was not true.

All the while, Sparta built up its navy with help from the Persians. In 405 B.C., the Spartans surprised the Athenian fleet near the Hellespont and destroyed it. Ruined, Athens surrendered to Sparta in 404 B.C.

READING CHECK ☼**CAUSE AND EFFECT**
What events helped cause Athens's defeat in the Peloponnesian War?

A Closer Look

Peloponnesian Sea Battle

During the Peloponnesian War, a sea battle broke out between Athens and Sparta near the Hellespont, a strait connecting the Aegean Sea and the Sea of Marmara. Sailors and soldiers rowed triremes (TRY•reemz), or warships, which carried about 200 people each.

1 About 170 rowers powered each trireme.

2 The masts were removed before fighting began.

3 A battering ram stuck out from each trireme.

4 Spartan ships rammed Athenian ships.

5 Soldiers fought on the decks of ships.

❖ Why do you think the masts were removed?

The Thirty Tyrants

TIME 404 B.C.

PLACE Athens

As the winners of the war, the Spartans decided the terms of peace. They broke up the Athenian Empire and limited the Athenian navy to 12 ships. They also ordered Athens to take apart the Long Walls and close the port of Piraeus. Athens had to give up all claims to lands outside the city-state. Most important, Sparta took control of the Athenian government.

The Spartans replaced the democracy of Athens with a **dictatorship**, or government with absolute power. This dictatorship was made up of an oligarchy ruled by 30 pro-Spartan aristocrats. Because of the cruel way they ruled, the members of this oligarchy became known as the Thirty Tyrants. They threw the former city-state's leaders into prison, ordered many other Athenians killed, and forced thousands more into exile.

The Thirty Tyrants completely ignored the democratic laws of Athens and took away many of the rights of citizens. The requirements for Athenian citizenship changed as well. Many people even had their citizenship revoked, or taken away. Only 3,000 of the richest citizens of Athens, known as the Three Thousand, still had the right to a trial. The people of Athens had long thought of this right as a symbol of true citizenship. The loss of all these rights angered the Athenians.

The Thirty Tyrants did not stop there with their antidemocratic reforms. They replaced the Athenian council with their own council. The members of this council filled the government jobs that had once been held by citizens of Athens. The Thirty Tyrants also formed their own police force. They assigned members of this force to guard the city-state, especially its port.

READING CHECK **SUMMARIZE**

What change did the Spartans make to Athens's form of government?

Athens Regains Independence

Other Greek city-states supported Athens by taking in exiled citizens. In **Thebes**, an exiled Athenian general formed an army in an effort to win back his city-state. The Thebans helped the general and other exiles recapture the port of Piraeus. The leader of the Thirty Tyrants died in this battle. Worried, the other tyrants requested help from Sparta.

By this time, changes had taken place in Sparta and across other Greek lands. People had seen the cruelty of the Thirty Tyrants, and they began to feel sorry for the defeated Athenians. Agreeing that the rule of the Thirty Tyrants had been a terrible failure, Sparta and the other city-states refused to help the tyrants.

After the Spartans refused to help the Thirty Tyrants, the Three Thousand regained control of Athens. They threw out all the laws that the Thirty Tyrants had passed. In 403 B.C., the Athenians set about restoring democracy to their city-state.

Uneasy times followed the rule of the Thirty Tyrants. People felt little confidence in their government and wanted stronger leaders. Philosophers Plato and Aristotle both wrote about these times, trying to decide what was best for Athens.

Eventually, a new Athenian council gained authority to govern the city-state. The council granted citizenship using Pericles' system. Even so, Athenian democracy never fully recovered.

READING CHECK **SUMMARIZE**
What changes in governing did Athens experience after the Three Thousand regained control of the city-state?

❯ These ruins in present-day Greece are of the Temple of Apollo in what was once the city-state of Corinth.

Competition Among City-States

Like Athens, even Sparta, the winner of the Peloponnesian War, suffered from years of fighting. To rebuild its strength, Sparta tried to gain control of trade in the region by conquering city-states in Asia Minor under Persian control.

To counter Sparta's ambitions, the city-states of **Corinth**, Athens, and **Argos** formed the Corinthian Alliance in 375 B.C. Both sides hired **mercenaries**, or soldiers willing to fight for anyone who pays them. In the end, Sparta defeated the alliance, but the war slowed Sparta's conquests.

Soon after, Athens and 70 other city-states allied with the city-state of Thebes to defeat Sparta. The democracy of Thebes had made it a strong power on mainland Greece. In 371 B.C., the alliance succeeded in defeating Sparta. Afterward, the Thebans broke up Sparta's Peloponnesian League and formed a new league that did not include Sparta. They also freed all of Sparta's helots and allowed them to form their own city-state, called Messene.

Many city-states resented the strength of the Thebans. Athens and its allies attacked Thebes but lost. Even so, the death of the Theban leader in the battle caused Thebes to lose power over Greece.

❱ Divers (center) excavate the remains of the *Kyrenia*, a Greek trading ship that sank in the Mediterranean about 2,300 years ago. A replica, the *Kyrenia II* (top), sailed from Cyprus to Athens for the 2004 Summer Olympics. Divers label finds (below right) and recover artifacts such as pottery (below left).

By 355 B.C., competition for power and wealth among the Greek city-states had led to conflicts. No single city-state had the power to control the region. All this made Greece become unstable.

READING CHECK **SUMMARIZE**
After the Peloponnesian War, why did Athens, Corinth, and Argos form the Corinthian Alliance?

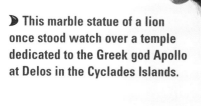

▶ This marble statue of a lion once stood watch over a temple dedicated to the Greek god Apollo at Delos in the Cyclades Islands.

Summary

During Athens's Golden Age, Sparta and Athens were the two most powerful Greek city-states. Their rivalry led to the Peloponnesian War, which ended the Golden Age of Athens. Sparta's victory in the war marked the beginning of a period of conflict and competition among the city-states. This caused the Greek city-states to become unstable.

REVIEW

1. How did the rivalry between Sparta and Athens lead to the Peloponnesian War?

2. Use the word **demagogue** in a paragraph about one of the reasons for Athens's defeat in the Peloponnesian War.

3. What event caused the Golden Age of Athens to come to an end?

CRITICAL THINKING

4. How did shifts in power cause Athens's democracy to change to an oligarchy and then back to a democracy again?

5. **ANALYSIS SKILL** Why do you think the war between Athens and Sparta was named the Peloponnesian War? Whose point of view is represented by this name?

6. **Write a Newspaper Article** At the end of the rule of the Thirty Tyrants, Athenians set about restoring democracy to their city-state. Write a newspaper article that describes this event. Include a headline for your article.

7. **Focus Skill** **CAUSE AND EFFECT**
On a separate sheet of paper, copy and complete the graphic organizer below.

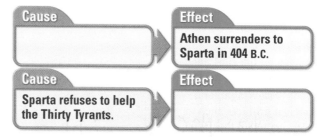

Cause		Effect
	→	Athen surrenders to Sparta in 404 B.C.
Sparta refuses to help the Thirty Tyrants.	→	

340 ▪ Unit 4

Socrates

Trustworthiness

Respect

Responsibility

Fairness

Caring

Patriotism

"The only good is knowledge and the only evil is ignorance." *

Socrates believed that philosophy, the study of knowledge, was the most important study of all. He was interested in finding out the truth about important things such as virtue. He believed in being fair and open-minded.

Socrates lived during a time of great change. He saw the Athenian Empire at its height and also lived through the city-state's defeat by Sparta. He himself fought in many battles and was even honored for his bravery. In one instance, he helped a wounded friend, saving his life.

> Socrates instructing two students

As a teacher, Socrates taught by asking questions. He also raised questions about the people in power. The leaders of Athens eventually put Socrates on trial for questioning their authority. In the end, they found him guilty and condemned him to die by drinking poison. Many of Socrates' friends wanted to help him escape, but he refused. He thought it would not be fair to try to avoid the court's verdict.

Socrates wrote no books and kept no written records of his life and ideas, but other people did. What is known about Socrates comes from the writings of others, such as his student Plato.

Why Character Counts

❓ How did Socrates show fairness in his life?

*Socrates. *The Lives and Opinions of Eminent Philosophers.* Diogenes Laertius, author, Charles Duke Yonge, trans. Bell and Sons Ltd., 1915.

Bio Brief

470 B.C.		399 B.C.
Born		Died

431 B.C.
The Peloponnesian
War resumes

404 B.C.
Athens surrenders
to Sparta

399 B.C.
Socrates is condemned
to die by drinking poison

 Interactive Multimedia Biographies
Visit **MULTIMEDIA BIOGRAPHIES** at
www.harcourtschool.com/hss

Participation Skills

Resolve Conflicts

▶ WHY IT MATTERS

Disagreements, or **conflicts**, were common among the ancient Greek city-states. Sometimes the conflicts became so heated that they led to war. At other times people found peaceful ways to resolve their differences.

Like long ago, many conflicts today can be settled without fighting. When people disagree, there are many ways to settle differences and avoid fighting. Each side could walk away and let anger or other strong feelings fade. Each side could also explain its ideas and try to get the other side to agree.

Often, the best way to resolve a conflict is to compromise. In a **compromise**, each person gives up some of what he or she wants. Sometimes this is the fairest way to resolve a conflict.

▶ WHAT YOU NEED TO KNOW

Here are some steps that can help you resolve conflicts through compromise.

Step 1 **Say clearly and politely what you want. Then listen to the other side's views.**

Step 2 **Decide which of the things you want are most important to you.**

▶ This picture shows a battle in the Peloponnesian War.

▶ This painting (above) shows a time of peace in Athens. The Greek goddess Athena (right) was believed to help people resolve conflicts.

Step 3 **Let each side make a plan for a possible compromise.**

Step 4 **Talk about any differences in the two plans.**

Step 5 **Continue talking until both sides agree on a plan. If anyone becomes angry or upset, take a break.**

Step 6 **To prevent future conflicts, make sure that the compromise will work for a long time.**

▶ PRACTICE THE SKILL

The citizens of different ancient Greek city-states often fought with one another over alliances, trade, and power. Review the content of this chapter. What issues led to conflicts between neighboring city-states in ancient Greece? With a classmate, role-play a discussion in which the two of you represent city-state leaders on different sides of one of those issues. Try to resolve the conflict.

Follow the steps to work out a plan that will settle the conflict. After you have reached a compromise, write a paragraph explaining it. Tell whether you think the compromise is or is not fair, and list any ideas you may have for improving it.

▶ APPLY WHAT YOU LEARNED

Identify a current issue about which two countries of the world disagree. Use newspapers or the Internet to research the most important points for each side. Then write a report that tells about the conflict and suggests a way to reach a compromise.

Participation Skills

Time

2000 B.C.   1000 B.C.   B.C./A.D.

338 B.C.
King Philip II defeats the Greeks
at the Battle of Chaeronea

336 B.C.
Alexander becomes
king of Macedonia

323 B.C.
Alexander
the Great dies

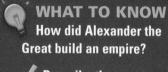

WHAT TO KNOW
How did Alexander the
Great build an empire?

✓ Describe the events
that led to the rise of
Alexander the Great's
empire.

✓ Explain how Greek
culture spread during
and after Alexander's
rule.

VOCABULARY
Hellenistic Age p. 347
multicultural p. 348

PEOPLE
Philip II
Alexander the Great
Euclid
Eratosthenes
Hypatia
Archimedes
Aristarchus

PLACES
Alexandria
Macedonia
Sparta
Egypt
Babylon
Athens

**CAUSE AND
EFFECT**

**California
Standards**
HSS 6.4, 6.4.7, 6.4.8

Alexander Builds an Empire

YOU ARE THERE Lucky you! Your parents have sent you to study
in the city of **Alexandria**, Egypt, in 300 B.C.
Before school, you explore the harbor, where ships
unload goods from all over the Mediterranean. Then you
visit Alexandria's lively marketplace. Ships bring goods
here from as far away as India. You see many fascinating
items to buy at the marketplace.

At the famous Museum school where you study,
scholars ask you questions that seem impossible to
answer. How far away are the sun and the moon? How
big and wide is Earth? Then they show you how to use
mathematics to answer such questions. Alexandria is
an amazing city.

▶ The lighthouse
in Alexandria

PHAROS

▶ Using this sword, King Philip's son, Alexander, cuts the Gordian knot. Legends claimed that the knot could only be undone by the future conqueror of Asia.

The End of Greek Independence

After the Peloponnesian War, the Greek city-states continued to fight among themselves. Meanwhile, in **Macedonia**, an area north of the Greek city-states on the Balkan Peninsula, a strong new king came to the throne. **Philip II** had brought his own people together under his rule. He wanted to do the same thing for the Greek lands.

Philip had a great love for and knowledge of Greek culture. As a boy, he had received a Greek education. Philip used what he knew about the Greeks to beat them in battle.

In 338 B.C., Philip's army fought Greek soldiers at the Battle of Chaeronea (kayr•uh•NEE•uh). The king's 18-year-old son, Alexander, led part of the attack. The Macedonians were victorious, and King Philip claimed the Greek city-states.

After conquering the Greeks, King Philip set out to unite them. He wanted to put an end to the constant fighting among city-states. To do this, Philip formed the League of Corinth, which he controlled. Members of the league had to promise to support him and to agree not to fight any other member. All the major Greek city-states joined except **Sparta**.

With the Greeks united and supporting him, Philip prepared for his next conquest —the Persian Empire. He wanted to free all Greek cities under Persian control. King Philip was killed before he could complete his plan. His son Alexander, then 20 years old, rose to the throne in 336 B.C.

READING CHECK ⟳ **CAUSE AND EFFECT**

How did Philip of Macedonia end the independence of the Greek city-states?

He conquered

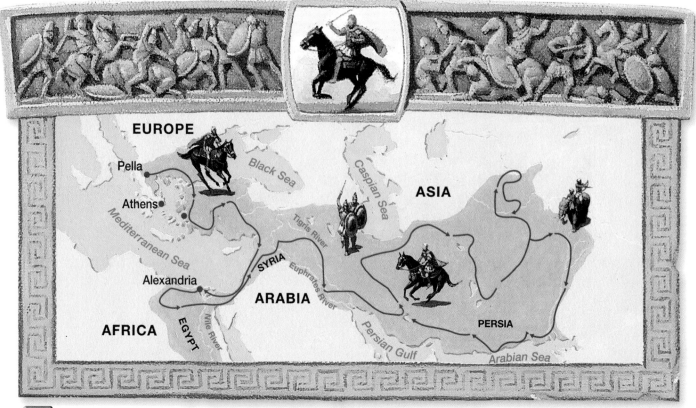

ANALYSIS SKILL **Analyze Maps** Alexander and his army conquered many lands.

Regions What city in Egypt did Alexander establish?

Alexander's Conquests

Years before, Philip had hired the Greek philosopher Aristotle to teach his son Alexander. From Aristotle, Alexander learned Greek philosophy and science. From his father, he learned how to rule and how to wage war. Legends say that Alexander slept with both a dagger and a copy of Homer's *Iliad* under his pillow.

As king, Alexander wanted to complete his father's plan to rule Persia—and then to rule the entire world. The world known to Alexander was eastern Europe, northern Africa, and western Asia. In 334 B.C., he led a well-trained army of about 40,000 Greek and Macedonian soldiers into Asia Minor.

Alexander and his army blazed through Asia Minor, across **Egypt**, and into Mesopotamia. In 330 B.C., they took over the Persian Empire and then marched east into India. There they defeated an Indian army that had more than 200 war elephants.

Alexander's conquests made him the ruler of a huge empire made up of many different peoples and unique cultures. Across his new empire, Alexander introduced the Greek language and spread Greek culture. To rule many different peoples, Alexander adopted some of their customs and allowed them some degree of self-rule. This practice made people more willing to accept him as their new king.

By 325 B.C., Alexander had completed one of the most successful military campaigns in history. His empire stretched eastward from Greece all the way to the Indus Valley in ancient India. The leader would soon be known to the world as **Alexander the Great**.

READING CHECK **COMPARE AND CONTRAST**
How was Alexander's plan similar to his father's plan? He conquered the known world

The End of an Empire

Alexander wanted to conquer more of India. However, his soldiers refused to go on. They had followed Alexander for more than 11,000 miles and had fought for eight years. Disappointed, Alexander turned around and began the long march home.

By the time he had reached **Babylon** in 323 B.C., Alexander was planning new conquests. In the same year, however, he fell ill with a fever. Alexander died a few days later, shortly before his thirty-third birthday.

A legend says that before Alexander died, he was asked to name a successor. Alexander answered that the rule of the empire should go "to the strongest!"*

*Richard Covington, "Mighty Macedonian," *Smithsonian*, November 2004.

No one leader proved strong enough to hold Alexander's empire together. After his death, his generals fought each other for control. This conflict caused the empire to split into separate kingdoms. The three largest of these—Macedonia, Syria, and Egypt—often fought with one another.

Even though his empire had ended, Alexander's influence lived on for nearly 300 years after his death. Greek culture spread eastward and into Egypt. For this reason, this period of time is called the **Hellenistic Age**, or Greeklike Age. Like the Golden Age, the Hellenistic Age was a time of great cultural achievements.

READING CHECK **CAUSE AND EFFECT**
What caused Alexander to stop conquering more of India?

The soliders refused to move on, because they were tired

❯ Alexander the Great's army defeated Indian warriors on elephants.

▶ Hypatia wrote books on mathematics and astronomy. She also invented tools for measuring the properties of water.

▶ Eratosthenes invented new methods in mathematics, drew a world map, and logged hundreds of stars.

▶ Euclid summarized all the mathematical knowledge of his time in the thirteen books of the *Elements*.

Alexandria: A Center of Learning

During his rule, Alexander founded new cities, using the model of Greek city-states. Many of these cities, and older ones as well, he named Alexandria, after himself.

Over time, the city of Alexandria, Egypt, stood out from all the rest. Because of a location along the Mediterranean Sea, it became the center of trade with Asia in goods as well as ideas. Alexandria grew into a **multicultural** city, or a city with many cultures. Egyptians, Greeks, Arabs, and Jews met in the city and exchanged ideas and, in doing so, created new ones.

Soon, this Egyptian city replaced **Athens** as the center of culture and learning. The library there became the largest in the world. It held more than 700,000 scrolls—rolled-up sheets of papyrus with writing on them. Connected to the library was a place of learning known as the Museum, where scholars researched, wrote, and exchanged ideas.

In Alexandria, scholars made enduring contributions in many fields. Doctors there built on the ideas of Hippocrates and made discoveries of their own. For example, they learned that the brain is the center of the human body's nervous system.

Alexandria was also home to scientists who used mathematics to help them understand the world. The Greek mathematician **Euclid** (YOO•kluhd) did work in geometry, the study of points, lines, angles, surfaces, and solids. He is sometimes called the Father of Geometry. The astronomer **Eratosthenes** (air•uh•TAHS•thuh•neez) used mathematics, including geometry, to estimate—quite closely—Earth's diameter and circumference.

Years later, in A.D. 400, the Egyptian mathematician and philosopher **Hypatia** (hy•PAY•shuh) headed a school of philosophy in Alexandria. She developed many theories in mathematics and invented tools for measuring the properties of water.

READING CHECK SUMMARIZE
What enduring contributions did Euclid and Hypatia make to learning?

The Hellenistic Age

Hellenistic culture also flourished outside of Alexandria, Egypt. The kings who ruled after Alexander did more than just fight to control territory. They also introduced Greek culture to all parts of the former empire. This spread of culture had an effect on architecture, politics, law, literature, philosophy, religion, and art.

In cities all over the former empire, rulers began large building projects. These cities became exciting places in which to live. Many Greek people moved to cities to become merchants, doctors, scribes, athletes, and actors. The leaders of the cities also gave money to support scholars and artists who made contributions to learning and the arts.

Archimedes (ar•kuh•MEE•deez), a scholar from Syracuse (SIR•uh•kyoos), on the island of Sicily, used mathematics to invent many machines, including water pumps. He also explained how pulleys and levers work. He is reported to have said, "Give me a lever long enough and a place to stand, and I will move the world."*

The astronomer **Aristarchus** (ar•uh•STAR•kuhs) of Samos (SAY•mahs), an island in the Aegean Sea, used mathematics to discover that Earth rotates and moves in a path around the sun. He also tried to calculate the size of the sun and the moon.

The work of many scholars was collected in the library in Alexandria. Texts from many different cultures could be found there. Over time, many of these works were translated into Greek so that they could be shared with Greek scholars. The translations helped spread ideas in religion, astronomy, science, and medicine.

*Bartlett, John. *Familiar Quotations*. Emily Morison Beck, ed. Little, Brown and Company, 1980.

❯ During the Hellenistic Age, Greek culture influenced the architecture of this tomb (left) in Petra, Jordan, and the artistic style of this sculpture (below).

▶ The Greek scholar Archimedes was a mathematician, a physicist, and an inventor. In this painting from the A.D. 1800s, Archimedes uses a pulley to move a ship.

By 146 B.C., another group of people, the Romans, had grown strong enough to gain control of the Mediterranean world. However, the knowledge that the Greeks had gained was not forgotten. The Romans borrowed from the religion, art, architecture, philosophy, literature, and language of the Greeks to build their own civilization in the region.

READING CHECK ☼ CAUSE AND EFFECT
What caused the spread of Greek culture in the Hellenistic Age? *The architecture engineering*

Summary

The Greek city-states fell to Philip II, the king of Macedonia. His son Alexander went on to build the largest empire the world had known. Through his conquests, Alexander spread Greek culture. When he died, his empire broke up, but Greek culture lived on throughout parts of Europe, Asia, and Africa.

REVIEW

1. How did Alexander the Great build an empire?

2. Write a description of a **multicultural** society.

3. How did the location of Alexandria, Egypt, help the city become a center of learning?

4. In what year did Alexander become the king of Macedonia?

CRITICAL THINKING

5. How was Alexander able to rule an empire made up of different peoples and different cultures?

6. **ANALYSIS SKILL** Why do you think Alexander built new cities modeled on the Greek city-states throughout his empire?

7. **Plan a Center of Learning** Alexander the Great founded the city of Alexandria, Egypt, which became a center of learning. Make a plan for a center of learning. Be sure to include places that are important for learning.

8. **Focus Skill** CAUSE AND EFFECT
On a separate sheet of paper, copy and complete the graphic organizer below.

Cause	Effect
	King Philip fights against the Persian Empire.

Cause	Effect
No strong leader replaces Alexander.	

Hypatia

"And among those great men was a great woman, Hypatia, mathematician and astronomer, the last light of the library [at Alexandria]. . ."

Biography

Trustworthiness
Respect
Responsibility
Fairness
Caring
Patriotism

Hypatia was a philosopher, mathematician, scientist, author, and teacher. She lived in Alexandria at a time when the city was an important center of learning. She was an important part of this learning center, respecting the differences of others while teaching the community.

Hypatia's father, Theon, was a philosopher and mathematician. He was Hypatia's first teacher. Later, Hypatia helped her father write books that made advanced math easier to understand. These books influenced how math was taught for centuries.

Hypatia continued to study on her own and became a respected teacher. She was well liked by many people in the city, but the rulers of the city were suspicious of her.

One of those rulers was Cyril, the leader of the Christian Church in Alexandria. He opposed Hypatia because she was not a Christian. However, Hypatia was a friend and teacher to people of many beliefs, including Christians. Still, Cyril saw her as an enemy of the church. According to some sources, he led a mob that ended up killing her.

▶ The library at Alexandria

*Carl Sagan. Cosmos. Random House, 2002.

Why Character Counts

❓ How did Hypatia show respect for people who held different beliefs?

Bio Brief

A.D. 370		A.D. 415
Born		Died
A.D. 370 Hypatia is born in Alexandria	**A.D. 400** Hypatia becomes head of a school of philosophy	**A.D. 415** Hypatia is murdered by a mob

GO ONLINE
Interactive Multimedia Biographies
Visit **MULTIMEDIA BIOGRAPHIES** at
www.harcourtschool.com/hss

Read a Time Zone Map

☽ WHY IT MATTERS

Because the sun does not rise at the same time all over the world, the time is not the same everywhere. Instead, the world is divided into time zones. These **time zones** are regions of Earth within which the same time is used. During the time of Alexander, time zones had not been created yet. People in one part of Alexander's empire did not need to know what time it was in other parts.

Today, many people communicate with each other over long distances. Being familiar with time zones helps people plan the best time to communicate.

☽ WHAT YOU NEED TO KNOW

Time zones are divided by meridians, or lines of longitude. The prime meridian, or the line at 0° longitude, is the starting point for all time zones. The prime merid-

ian passes through Greenwich, England. The Greenwich meridian was chosen as the prime meridian for the world in 1884.

The world has 24 standard time zones. Half of them lie to the east of Greenwich and half lie to the west. Each time zone covers 15 degrees of longitude. For every 15 degrees east, an hour is added to the time in Greenwich. For every 15 degrees west, an hour is subtracted.

All time zones to the east of the prime meridian are ahead of Greenwich time. Time zones to the west are behind. The **international date line** is the meridian where the eastern and western time zones meet. Since the date line is 12 time zones from the prime meridian, when it is noon in Greenwich, it is midnight at the international date line, and the date changes.

The time zone map on the next page shows all 24 time zones. It tells what time

☽ **A radio-controlled clock from the United States**

☽ **Antique iron clock from Europe**

☽ **Ancient Athenian water clock**

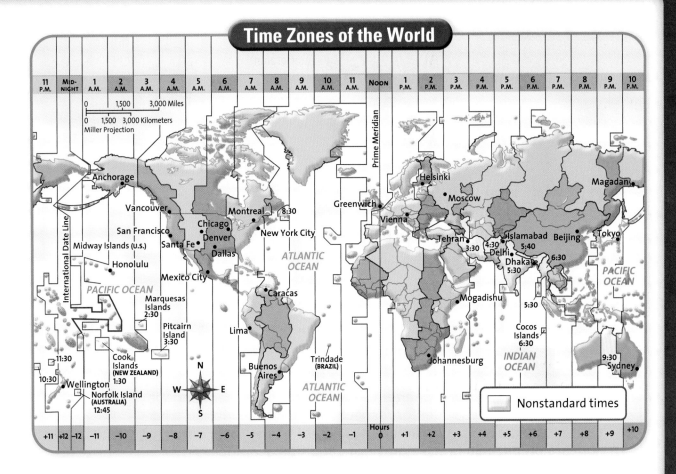

Time Zones of the World

it is in each zone when it is noon at the prime meridian. In each zone, the time is one hour ahead of the time in the zone just to the west and one hour behind the time in the zone just to the east. As you go east from Greenwich, the time in each zone you come to is one hour later than in the last.

Notice that some of the boundaries on the map zigzag. These zigzags occur when a city or region falls directly on a time zone boundary. These cities will often choose to be part of one time zone or another to avoid confusion. The map also shows some places that do not use the standard time zones. Those places are shown as having nonstandard times.

▶ PRACTICE THE SKILL

Study the maps, and answer the following questions.

1. If it is noon in Greenwich, what time is it in Beijing, China?

2. If it is noon in Greenwich, what time is it in Anchorage, Alaska?

3. How many time zones cover the area that was once Alexander's empire?

▶ APPLY WHAT YOU LEARNED

Write five word problems about time zones. Exchange papers with a partner and solve each other's problems.

 Practice your map and globe skills with the **GeoSkills CD-ROM**.

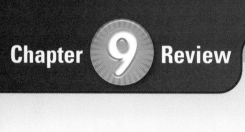

Chapter 9 Review

Time

500 B.C.

492 B.C.
The Persian
Wars begin

450 B.C.

461 B.C.
Pericles
makes
democratic
reforms
in Athens

Reading Social Studies

A **cause** is an event or action that makes something happen.
An **effect** is what happens as a result of that event or action.

 Focus Skill ## Cause and Effect

Complete this graphic organizer to show that you understand why
Athens became the model for respected political, economic, and
social structures for all of Greece. A copy of this graphic organizer
appears on page 98 of the Homework and Practice Book.

The Golden Age

Cause		Effect
	→	Athens experiences many cultural achievements.

 # California Writing Prompts

Write a Ballad A ballad is a narrative poem
or song. Write a ballad about a person you read
about in this chapter. Tell about the person's
achievements, and also include your feelings
about the person.

Write a Persuasive Speech When Alexander
hoped to expand his empire into present-day
India, his soldiers refused to follow him. Write a
speech that Alexander could have used to try to
persuade the soldiers to fight on.

| 400 B.C. | 350 B.C. | 300 B.C. |

338 B.C.
Philip of Macedonia
conquers the Greeks

334 B.C.
Alexander sets
out on path
of conquest

Use Vocabulary

Use each term in a sentence or two to explain both what the term means and how that meaning relates to the Golden Age of Greece or the time of Alexander.

1. **direct democracy** (p. 318)

2. **tragedy** (p. 327)

3. **demagogue** (p. 336)

4. **Hellenistic Age** (p. 347)

5. **multicultural** (p. 348)

Use the Time Line

 Use the summary time line above to answer these questions.

6. When did Philip of Macedonia conquer the Greeks?

7. What happened in 334 B.C.?

8. What happened first, the Persian Wars or Philip's conquest of the Greeks?

Apply Skills

 Read a Time Zone Map

9. Use the maps on pages 346 and 353 to figure out how many of the world's present-day time zones Alexander's empire covered when it was at its height.

Recall Facts

Answer these questions.

10. How do the ideas of Hippocrates continue to influence doctors today?

11. What are two things that Alexander the Great did to make conquered peoples more willing to accept his rule?

Write the letter of the best choice.

12. In what class would the Pythagorean theorem be used?
    A art
    B literature
    C math
    D music

13. Outside of Athens, where was the most important center of Greek culture in Alexander's time?
    A in Egypt
    B in Italy
    C in Sparta
    D in Babylon

Think Critically

14. Write three questions about Alexander the Great that could be answered by doing research.

15. **Make It Relevant** Alexandria was a multicultural city. What cultures are represented in your community? How is your community similar to Alexandria? In what ways is it different?

Field Trip

ATHENS, GREECE

GET READY

History did not stand still in Athens after the time of the city-states and Alexander the Great. The city came under the rule of the Roman Empire and remained a center of culture and education for many years. As time passed, the city was ruled by various empires and European powers until Greece became an independent kingdom in 1832.

Today, Athens is the capital of the democratic nation of Greece. About 12 million tourists come to Greece each year, and many of them visit Athens to see its historical landmarks.

Athens is the hub of Greece's highway and rail transportation network and the center of the country's industry. Its port at Piraeus, once the base of the mighty Athenian fleet, is now a busy trade port.

WHAT TO SEE

Tourists admire the ruins of the Temple of the Olympian Zeus. The Acropolis can be seen in the background.

LOCATE IT

GREECE

Athens

This Greek shopkeeper is busy making sandals for sale. Life in modern Athens bustles among its ancient ruins.

Visitors explore the ruins of the Theater of Dionysus (above). Some of the world's most well-known comedies and tragedies were performed there. Athens's shops and cafes (right) squeeze together beneath the walls of the Acropolis (below).

Many ancient tombs can be found at the Kerameikos (ker•uh•MY•kohs) Cemetery (above). Greek dancers in folk costume (bottom) celebrate their nation's more than 3,000-year history.

A VIRTUAL TOUR

GO ONLINE   Visit VIRTUAL TOURS at www.harcourtschool.com/hss

Unit 4 Review

THE BIG IDEA

Government and Leadership The ancient Greeks made many contributions in areas of government and leadership.

Summary

The Ancient Greeks

The mountains of Greece made land travel difficult, so city-states developed independently of one another. The different city-states, including Sparta and Athens, had different forms of government. Athens created an early form of democracy.

The ancient Greeks traveled by sea to trade among themselves and with other peoples. Seeking farmland and iron ore, the Greek people began to set up colonies beyond the Aegean Sea.

The city-states joined forces to defend themselves against a Persian invasion. Later, however, Athens and Sparta became enemies in a series of wars that weakened Greek civilization.

Through trade and, later, through Alexander's conquests, Greek ideas spread widely. The ideas of democracy that began in Athens eventually spread to other parts of the world. The influences of Greek art and architecture can still be seen in some modern styles. Greek plays are still performed, and the epic poems of Homer are widely read. The Greeks also made lasting contributions to philosophy and science.

Main Ideas and Vocabulary

Read the summary above. Then answer the questions that follow.

1. What does the word democracy mean?
   A a group of allies
   B rule by the people
   C a group that makes laws
   D rule by force

2. What are colonies?
   A ovens for melting iron
   B large fighting ships powered by rowers
   C conquered peoples who are forced into slavery
   D settlements away from the settlers' homeland

3. What unified the Greek city-states for a time?
   A a long drought
   B the Trojan War
   C invasions by Persia
   D the development of democracy

4. What was Homer?
   A a poet
   B a doctor
   C a ruler
   D a scientist

Recall Facts

Answer these questions.

5. What was the significance of Greek mythology to the everyday life of the ancient Greeks?

6. How would you describe life in ancient Sparta?

7. In Athenian democracy, who was allowed to vote?

8. What important contribution did Socrates make to philosophy and education?

9. In what region did Alexander begin his conquests?

Write the letter of the best choice.

10. Where did the Minoan people live?
    A on the Greek mainland
    B on the island of Crete
    C in the city of Troy
    D in the city-state of Sparta

11. Who helped bring an end to the rule of oligarchies in ancient Greece?
    A traders from Asia Minor
    B poor people who wanted a better life
    C soldiers who wanted military rule
    D aristocrats who no longer wanted to rule

12. How were the fables of Aesop important to early Greeks?
    A They recorded history from the earliest times.
    B They provided laws for early city-states.
    C They taught young people the Greek alphabet.
    D They taught young people good behavior.

13. Who founded the Persian Empire?
    A Cyrus II
    B Darius I
    C Cambyses
    D Xerxes

14. Who was Greece's first historian?
    A Aristotle
    B Herodotus
    C Plato
    D Sophocles

Think Critically

15. **Make It Relevant** How do the Olympic Games today serve as a uniting force for nations all over the world?

16. 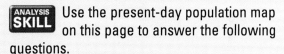 What are the differences between direct democracy and representative democracy? What caused later democracies to become representative democracies rather than direct democracies?

Apply Skills

Read a Population Map

ANALYSIS SKILL Use the present-day population map on this page to answer the following questions.

17. What is the population density around Greece's capital?

18. What is the population density around Sparta?

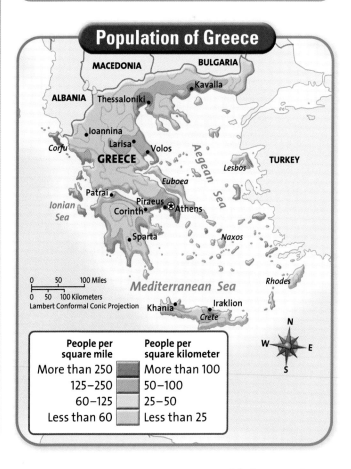

Population of Greece

People per square mile		People per square kilometer	
More than 250		More than 100	
125–250		50–100	
60–125		25–50	
Less than 60		Less than 25	

Unit 4 Activities

Read More

■ *Athens and Sparta: Rival Ancient Greek City-States* by Richie Chevat.

■ *Seven Wonders of the Ancient World* by Sarah Kinney.

■ *Ideas of the Ancient Greeks* by Jeffrey Nelson.

Show What You Know

Unit Writing Activity

Write a Summary Summarize the development of democracy in Athens. Include details about how the new government was run and who could take part. Name the leaders who helped create democracy in Athens.

Unit Project

Make a Museum Exhibit Create a museum exhibit related to your study of the ancient Greeks. Include maps, models of buildings, artifacts, drawings, and journal entries. Also write paragraphs to provide information about the items in your exhibit.

GO ONLINE Visit ACTIVITIES at www.harcourtschool.com/hss

Early Civilizations of India and China

Unit 5

START WITH THE STANDARDS

California History-Social Science Standards

6.5 Students analyze the geographic, political, economic, religious, and social structures of the early civilizations of India.

6.6 Students analyze the geographic, political, economic, religious, and social structures of the early civilizations of China.

The Big Idea

CULTURE

The people of ancient India and China had many new ideas about society, religion, and government.

What to Know

- ✓ How did the physical settings of ancient India and China support the rise of civilization?
- ✓ How did the ideas of Hinduism affect Asia?
- ✓ How did the ideas of the Buddha change Asia?
- ✓ What were the achievements of the emperor Ashoka?

Show What You Know

★ Unit 5 Test

✎ Writing: A Comparison–Contrast Essay

🖌 Unit Project: An Illustrated Map

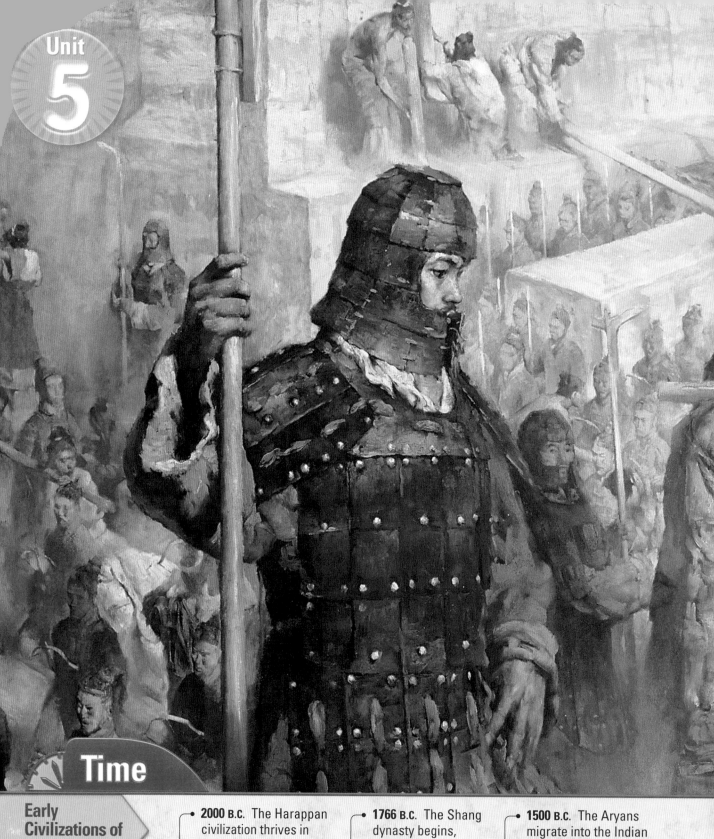

Time

Early
Civilizations of
India and China

2000 B.C. The Harappan
civilization thrives in
the Indus Valley, p. 377

1766 B.C. The Shang
dynasty begins,
p. 423

1500 B.C. The Aryans
migrate into the Indian
subcontinent, p. 385

2000 B.C.

1500 B.C.

1000 B.C.

At the
Same Time

1500 B.C. The Olmec
civilization begins in
what is now Mexico

Early Civilizations of India and China

320 B.C. Chandragupta Maurya forms the Maurya Empire in India, p. 397

221 B.C. Shi Huangdi founds the Qin dynasty, p. 433

202 B.C. The Han dynasty begins in China, p. 443

A.D. 320 The Gupta Empire begins, p. 400

500 B.C.

B.C./A.D.

A.D. 500

 200 B.C. The Moche civilization begins in what is now Peru

100 B.C. The Anasazi civilization begins in what is now the southwestern United States

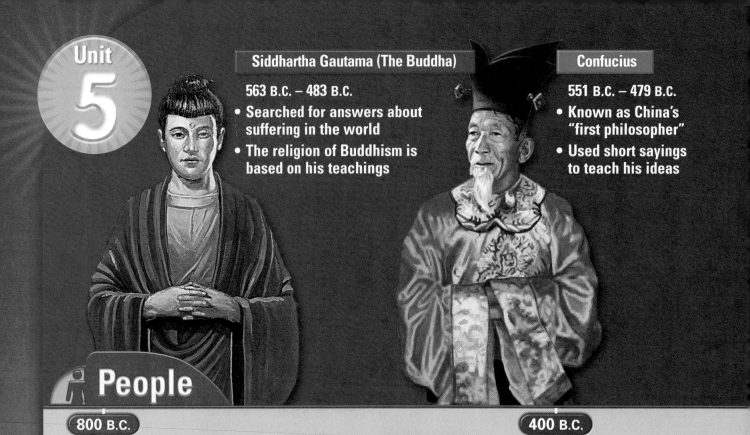

Siddhartha Gautama (The Buddha)

563 B.C. – 483 B.C.
- Searched for answers about suffering in the world
- The religion of Buddhism is based on his teachings

Confucius

551 B.C. – 479 B.C.
- Known as China's "first philosopher"
- Used short sayings to teach his ideas

People

800 B.C.	400 B.C.

563 B.C. – 483 B.C. • Siddhartha Gautama (The Buddha)

551 B.C. – 479 B.C. • Confucius

Reigned 273 B.C. – 232 B.C. • Ashoka

259 B.C. – 210 B.C. • Shi Huangdi

Wu Di

Reigned
141 B.C. – 86 B.C.
- Set up China's civil service
- Brought peace to the empire

Ban Zhao

A.D. 45 – A.D. 115
- *Wrote Instruction for Chinese Women and Girls* and worked as an imperial historian for the Han dynasty
- Taught leading women in the Chinese court

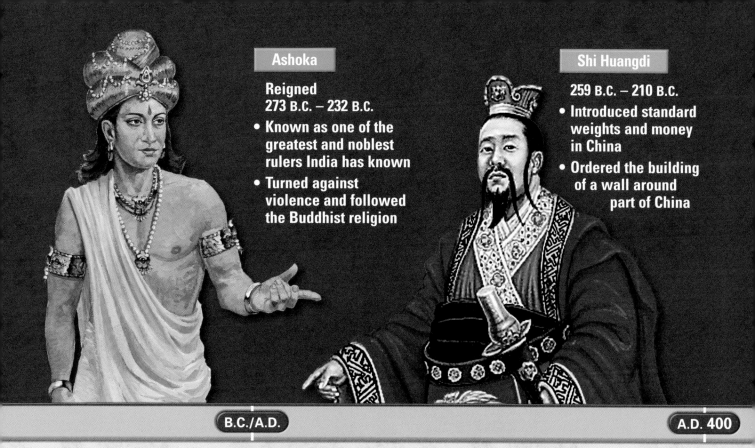

Ashoka

Reigned
273 B.C. – 232 B.C.

• Known as one of the greatest and noblest rulers India has known

• Turned against violence and followed the Buddhist religion

Shi Huangdi

259 B.C. – 210 B.C.

• Introduced standard weights and money in China

• Ordered the building of a wall around part of China

B.C./A.D.   A.D. 400

Reigned 141 B.C. – 86 B.C. • Wu Di

A.D. 45 – A.D. 115 • Ban Zhao

Reigned A.D. 375 – A.D. 415 • Chandragupta II

A.D. 400 – A.D. 455 • Kalidasa

Chandragupta II

Reigned
A.D. 375 – A.D. 415

• Added lands to the Maurya Empire in India

• Contributed to the arts

Kalidasa

A.D. 400 – A.D. 455

• Popular writer in ancient India

• Lived during the Golden Age

363

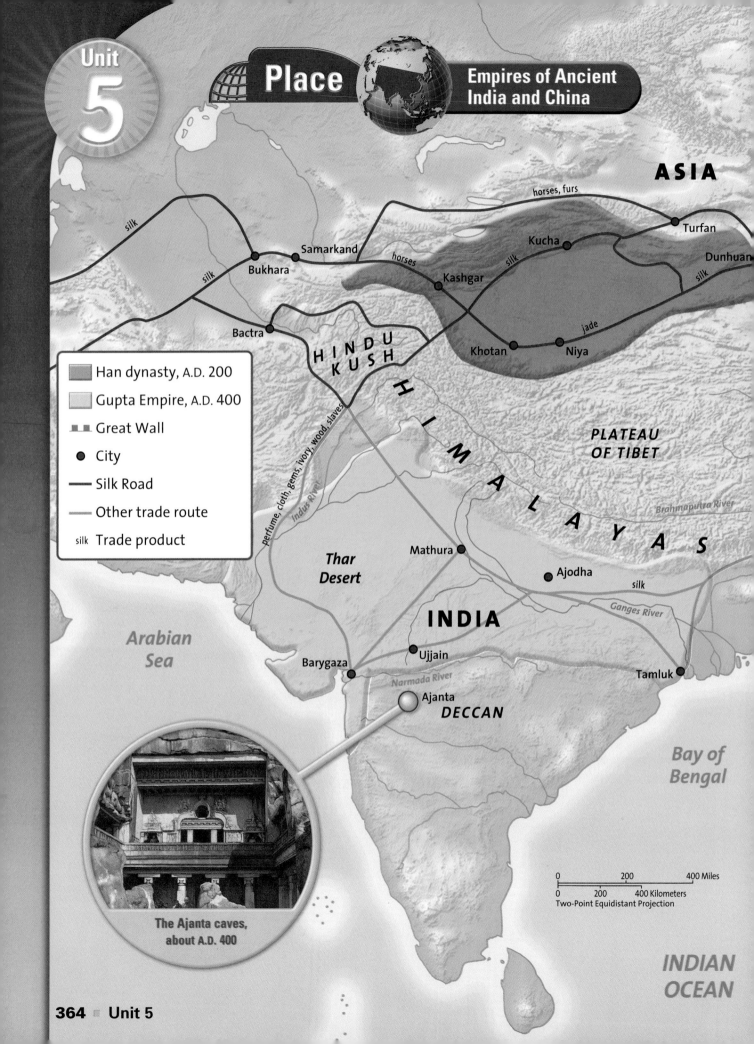

Place — Empires of Ancient India and China

ASIA

horses, furs

silk

Turfan

Kucha

Dunhuan

silk

Samarkand

horses

Bukhara

silk

Kashgar

silk

Bactra

jade

Khotan

Niya

HINDU KUSH

H I M A L A Y A S

PLATEAU OF TIBET

Brahmaputra River

perfume, cloth, gems, ivory, wood, slaves

Indus River

Thar Desert

Mathura

Ajodha

silk

INDIA

Ganges River

Arabian Sea

Barygaza

Ujjain

Narmada River

Ajanta

DECCAN

Tamluk

Bay of Bengal

The Ajanta caves, about A.D. 400

0   200   400 Miles
0   200   400 Kilometers
Two-Point Equidistant Projection

INDIAN OCEAN

Legend:
- Han dynasty, A.D. 200
- Gupta Empire, A.D. 400
- Great Wall
- City
- Silk Road
- Other trade route
- silk Trade product

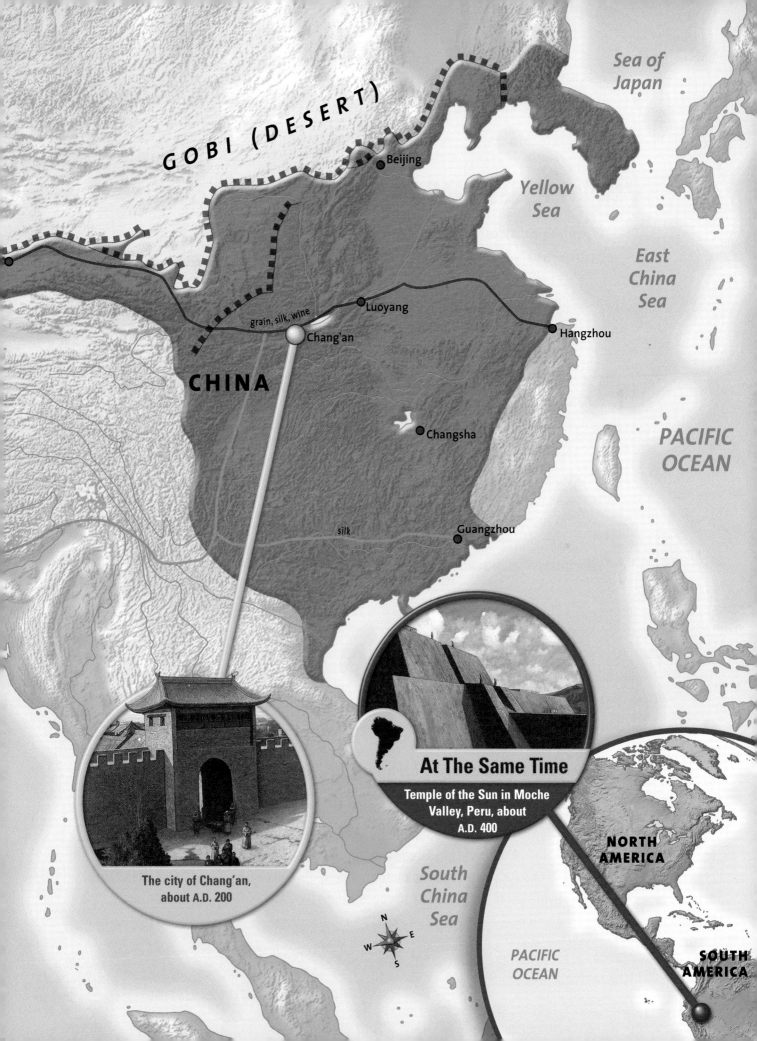

GOBI (DESERT)

Sea of Japan

Beijing

Yellow Sea

East China Sea

grain, silk, wine

Luoyang

Chang'an

Hangzhou

CHINA

Changsha

PACIFIC OCEAN

silk

Guangzhou

The city of Chang'an, about A.D. 200

At The Same Time

Temple of the Sun in Moche Valley, Peru, about A.D. 400

NORTH AMERICA

South China Sea

N
W   E
S

PACIFIC OCEAN

SOUTH AMERICA

Reading Social Studies

Focus Skill Compare and Contrast

When you **compare**, you tell how two or more things are alike. When you **contrast**, you tell how two or more things are different.

Why It Matters

Comparing and contrasting can help you understand how people, places, events, and ideas are similar and how they are different.

Topic 1 — Similar — Topic 2

✓ *Like, alike, both, also, same,* and *similar* are words that compare.
✓ *But, instead, however, differ,* and *different* are words that contrast.

Practice the Skill

Read the paragraphs that follow. Compare and contrast the civilizations of India and China with those of Greece and Mesopotamia. One example has been done for you.

Similar
Different

Ancient civilizations thrived in India and China as well as in Greece. However, the ancient civilizations of India and China had different forms of government and religion than those found in ancient Greece.

Rivers played important roles in the development of India and China and of Greece. However, some of the rivers in Greece dry up during part of the year. This makes them useless at times for watering crops and traveling. Because China and India have rainy climates, rivers there are usually full year-round.

Apply What You Learned

Compare and Contrast Read the paragraphs, and answer the questions.

Development of Chinese and Hindi

Ancient China and India were two civilizations whose contributions to the world are still seen today. In each, language was an important development. The Chinese language developed in about 1200 B.C. and is the national language of China today. Hindi, the national language of India, developed in about A.D. 9.

Both Hindi and Chinese are said to be musical languages because they sound beautiful when spoken. They both are studied widely and spoken throughout the world. More people today speak Chinese than any other language in the world. Hindi is the third-most-spoken language, after English.

People from different regions of both China and India speak in various dialects, or different forms, of their languages.

As a result, a person from one part of China might not be able to understand someone from another part. This is also true of India. Still, a person who speaks one dialect of a language will have an easier time learning another dialect of that same language than will someone who knows nothing about the language.

Chinese writing began as pictures drawn to represent things. As time passed, the pictures came to represent meanings. There are more than 6,000 Chinese symbols, all of which represent meanings, not sounds. However, Hindi is written with the Devanagari alphabet, which uses 49 letters that stand for sounds.

Compare and Contrast

1. **How does the language of India compare to the language of China? Make at least two comparisons.**

2. **How are the Hindi and Chinese languages different?**

3. **How are Hindi and Chinese viewed in the world?**

Study Skills

CONNECT IDEAS

You can use a web to show how different ideas and information are connected.

▶ **List important chapter themes in the ovals in the web's center.**

▶ **Next, add ovals showing the chapter's main ideas that support each theme.**

▶ **Then add circles showing the important facts and details that support each main idea.**

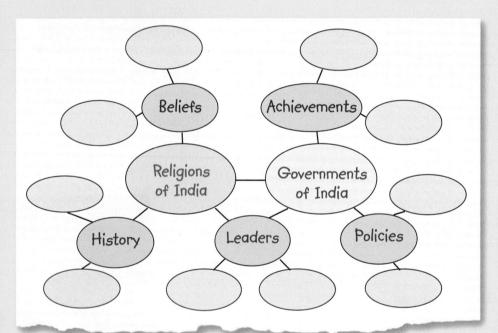

Apply As You Read

Make your own web graphic organizer. As you read this chapter, complete the web by filling in the facts and details that support each main idea. This will help you understand how important ideas in the chapter are related.

California History-Social Science Standards, Grade 6

6.5 Students analyze the geographic, political, economic, religious, and social structures of the early civilizations of India.

Ancient India

▷ The Ajanta caves in India were built as a shrine to the Buddha.

THE RAJAH'S RICE

adapted by David Barry
illustrated by Donna Perrone

Long ago in India, princes, or rajahs, ruled over large cities and their surrounding territories. The following is a folktale from that time. A folktale is a story that often teaches a lesson about right and wrong. In this folktale, a rajah refuses to share rice with the people when they are hungry. Find out how a village girl outsmarts the rajah with a clever plan to feed the people.

Once upon a time a long time ago, a girl named Chandra lived in a small village in India. Chandra loved elephants. She also loved numbers. So of course she loved all numbers to do with elephants: two tusks to polish on each elephant, eighteen toenails to clean, a hundred scrubs on a side at each bath. Chandra had many chances to think about elephant numbers because she had a special job: She was the bather of the Rajah's elephants.

Chandra liked other numbers, too. As she walked past rice paddies, muddy after the harvest, she counted the snowy egrets that flew above her.

She passed through the marketplace at the edge of the village and stopped to help the spice peddler count change.

When she joined her friends where they stood watching the Rajah's elephants parade through the town square, she remembered every elephant number she knew. Then she started thinking about rice.

It was rent collection day, and bags bulging with rice hung from the sides of the elephants.

No wonder the people looked sad. The Rajah had taken so much rice for himself that the whole village would be hungry.

But this was the way it had always been. For thousands of years, the villagers had farmed the Rajah's land. For thousands of years, he had come with his elephants to take most of the rice harvest.

The whole thing made Chandra angry, but what could she do?

On the elephants' next bath day, Chandra packed up her equipment and walked over the fields to the palace. She was about to enter the gates when the guard stopped her.

"You cannot come in this morning, Elephant Bather. The elephants have taken sick."

Chandra peered through the bamboo gate into the elephant yard. There she could see her elephants lying on the ground as still as felled trees. No amount of calling, singing, or cooing made them so much as raise their heads.

Over the days that followed Chandra sat watch over her precious elephants. She was not allowed inside, so she waited at the gate, watching medical men from all across the land come to cure the elephants.

The first doctor sat on cushions in the courtyard and feasted: he ate eight meat pastries, ten chickpea dumplings, and twelve sand lobsters served on banana leaves at each meal. While he ate, the elephants got sicker.

Another doctor spent all day and most of the night in the elephant yard chanting and burning incense. The elephants got even sicker.

Seven more doctors came and went, but the elephants got still sicker.

One morning, the Rajah returned from a walk in the gardens to find Chandra at the gate, staring in at the elephants. "What are you doing here, Elephant Bather?" he asked.

"I worry about the elephants," she said. "I love them all and know them well. Maybe I can help them."

The Rajah thought for a moment. "Go ahead and try," he said. "I need those elephants. Without them, I will not be able to carry the rice to market on market day. If you can save them, you may choose your own reward."

The guard opened the gates, and Chandra and the Rajah walked in silence to the elephant yard. Chandra approached Misha, the Rajah's favorite elephant. She studied his feet: the nails, the pads, the cuticles. She studied his tusks and the eight molars deep inside his mouth. She studied the lips, the tongue and the throat. She looked deep into his eyes.

When Chandra got to the first ear, she discovered a painful-looking infection inside the ear canal. The other ear was the same. So were the ears of the other elephants. Chandra cleaned their ears, sang the elephants a soothing song, and went home.

At dawn the next day, when Chandra returned, the elephants were walking unsteadily around their yard. They greeted her with joyful trumpeting.

The Rajah was overjoyed. He declared a festival day and invited everyone in the land to the palace.

The Rajah led Chandra to the ceremony room. Piled on a long table, next to the Rajah's chessboard, was a glittering array of gold necklaces, brilliant sapphires and rubies, diamond brooches, bags of gold rupees, and other treasures.

The guests began to arrive, and soon the ceremony room was crowded with villagers.

"Name your reward, Elephant Bather," said the Rajah.

Chandra looked at the beautiful jewels on the table before her. She thought about her elephants and the hundreds of sacks of rice they carried away from the village each year. And then she noticed the chessboard.

"The villagers are hungry, Rajah," she began. "All I ask for is rice. If Your Majesty pleases, place two grains of rice on the first square of this chessboard. Place four grains on the second square, eight on the next, and so on, doubling each pile of rice till the last square."

The villagers shook their heads sadly at Chandra's choice.

The Rajah was secretly delighted. A few piles of rice would certainly be far cheaper than his precious jewelry. "Honor her request," he boomed to his servants.

Two servants brought out a small bowl of rice and carefully placed two grains of rice on the first square of the board. They placed four grains on the second square. Then eight on the third square, sixteen on the fourth square, thirty-two on the fifth square, sixty-four on the sixth square, 128 on the seventh

square, and finally 256 grains of rice on the eighth square at the end of the row.

Several servants snickered at Chandra's foolishness, for although the 256 grains filled the eighth square completely, they amounted to only a single teaspoon of rice.

At the first square of the second row, the servants stood awkwardly, not knowing how to count out the rice. The next number was 512, but that was too high to count quickly, and besides, it was too many grains of rice to fit on one square of the chessboard.

Chandra started to explain, "Since you had one teaspoon of rice at the end of the first row, why not just put two teaspoons—"

But the Rajah cut in. "Just keep doubling the rice," he ordered. "You don't need to count every grain."

So the servants put two teaspoons of rice into a bowl for the first square of the second row. For the second square, they put four teaspoons of rice in the bowl. Then eight teaspoons of rice for the third square, and so continued, doubling the number of teaspoons each square.

The eighth square on the second row needed 256 teaspoons of rice, which by itself filled another bowl.

On the third row, the servants started to count by teaspoons again, but the Rajah cut in. Showing off his knowledge of mathematics, he said, "If the sixteenth square takes one bowl of rice, then the seventeenth square takes two bowls of rice. You don't need to count by teaspoons anymore."

So the servants counted by bowls. Two bowlfuls for the first square, then four, then eight, then sixteen, and so on. The rice for the last square of the third row completely filled a large wheelbarrow.

Chandra's neighbors smiled at her. "Very nice," one of them said. "This would feed my family for a whole year."

As the servants worked through the fourth row, wheelbarrow by wheelbarrow, the Rajah paced back and forth, his eyes wide in amazement. His servants gathered around him. "Shall we bring rice from your royal storehouses?" they asked.

"Of course," was the reply. "A Rajah never breaks a promise." The servants took the elephants and headed out to the first storehouse to get more rice.

By late afternoon, the Rajah had collapsed onto his couch. As his attendants fanned him with palm fronds, the servants started on the fifth row of the chessboard, and soon they were emptying entire storehouses into the courtyard.

Within several squares, rice poured from the windows of the palace and into the gardens beyond. By the middle of the fifth row, all of the Rajah's storehouses were empty.

He had run out of rice.

The Rajah struggled to his feet and ordered the rice to be loaded onto the elephants and taken to the village. Then he approached Chandra.

"Elephant Bather," he said to her, "I am out of rice and cannot fill the chessboard. Tell me what I can give you to be released from my vow."

"You can give the people of the village the land they farm, and take only as much rice as you need for yourself," answered Chandra.

The Rajah gazed at the mountains of rice that filled his palace and gardens, then out beyond the gardens to the fields the villagers farmed, stretching as far as he could see. Then he looked back at Chandra, the elephant bather.

"It is done," he said.

That night the Rajah arrived in the village as Chandra and the other villagers prepared a celebration feast.

"Would you be so kind as to join me for a short walk, Chandra?" he asked. "I have a question for you."

As they strolled toward the village square, the Rajah spoke. "I am a very rich man, and it took all of the rice I owned to fill little more than one-half of the chessboard. How much rice would it have taken to fill the whole board?" he asked.

"If you had kept doubling the rice to the last square of the chessboard, all of India would be knee deep in rice," said Chandra, and smiled.

Response Corner

1. In the beginning, why was the Rajah secretly delighted with what Chandra chose as her reward?

2. Imagine that you live in the same province as this Rajah. Write a letter to Chandra, telling her how you feel about the deal she made with him.

Lesson 1

2500 B.C.
Harappan civilization develops
in the Indus River valley

Around 1750 B.C.
Harappan civilization
mysteriously declines

WHAT TO KNOW
How did the physical setting of the Indus River valley make it possible for a civilization to form there?

✓ Describe the location and features of the Indus River valley.

✓ Explain how the Indus River supported the growth of India's early civilization and city-states.

VOCABULARY
subcontinent p. 375
monsoon p. 376
citadel p. 377
granary p. 377

PLACES
Pakistan
India
Bangladesh
Deccan
Harappa
Lothal
Mohenjo-Daro

COMPARE AND CONTRAST

California
Standards
HSS 6.5, 6.5.1

Indus Valley Civilization

YOU ARE THERE

The rains were late in coming this year in 2500 B.C., leaving the land dry for too long. Your family's crops began to die. Then suddenly, the rains came. Ever since then, it has rained on and on, day and night.

It's been raining now for many months, and still more water pours down from the clouds. The Indus River is so full, it's about to overflow its banks and rush over your family's fields.

You help move your family's animals away from the river. You can't afford to lose any of them to the raging water. Why, you wonder, does this dangerous rainy season come every year? Why has your family chosen to live so close to a river?

❯ The Indus River winds its way through what is today the country of Pakistan.

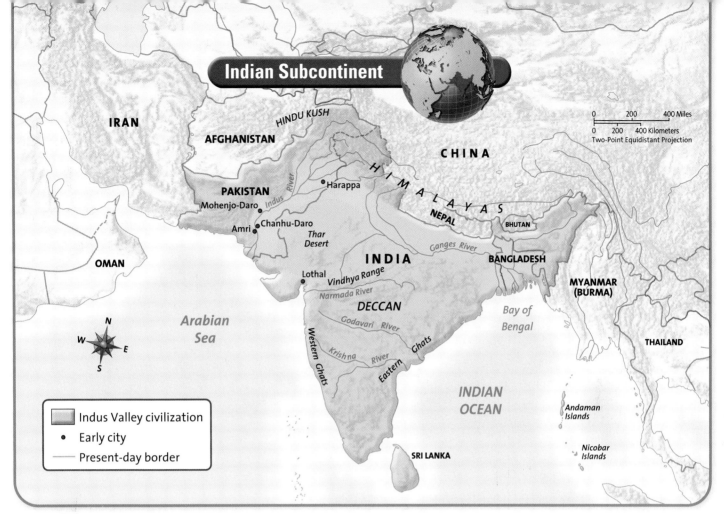

Indian Subcontinent

ANALYSIS SKILL Analyze Maps

❖ **Regions** In which present-day countries was the Indus Valley civilization located?

The Indian Subcontinent

The present-day countries of **Pakistan**, **India**, and **Bangladesh** make up what was ancient India, on the Indian subcontinent. A **subcontinent** is a large area of land separated from the rest of a continent by geographic features. The Himalayas (hih•muh•LAY•uhz), the tallest mountains in the world, separate the Indian subcontinent from the rest of Asia.

The Indian subcontinent can be divided into two regions—the northern plains and the **Deccan** (DEH•kuhn). In the north is the flat, low land of the northern plains with its fertile soil. To the south lies the high, hilly land of the plateau known as the Deccan.

The two great rivers of the Indian subcontinent, the Indus River and the Ganges (GAN•jeez) River, lie in the northern plains region. Both rivers have their source in the snowy peaks of the Himalayas.

The Indus and Ganges have carved wide river plains. The Indus River valley includes the Punjab Plain. The Ganges River valley includes the Ganges Plain.

The Indus River valley offers the best conditions for agriculture on the Indian subcontinent. Its fertile plains are ideal for growing crops and raising animals, leading southern Asia's first civilization to form there.

READING CHECK ♻ **COMPARE AND CONTRAST** How do the northern plains and the Deccan differ?

▶ People today still use traditional farming methods along the Indus River valley.
Embankments have been built along the Indus River, but this does not prevent all flooding.

Importance of Floods

Agriculture began in ancient India in the Indus River valley around 4000 B.C. Each year for thousands of years, the Indus River flooded, leaving silt along its banks. Early farmers grew such crops as rice, peas, and barley in this fertile soil and raised livestock, including sheep, goats, and cattle.

The Indus River and other rivers often flood during the summer **monsoon**, or seasonal wind. This wind from the Indian Ocean blows moist air over the Indian subcontinent, bringing heavy rains. In the winter, the winds reverse direction. The winter wind brings little rain, because it comes from dry inland areas of Asia.

When the summer monsoon arrived, the rains it brought could last for months. All over the Indian subcontinent, heavy rains caused rivers to flow over their banks and flood the surrounding lands.

Flooding brought advantages and disadvantages to ancient India. The rushing waters could ruin crops, drown livestock and people, and destroy villages. Yet these floods deposited fresh silt on the land, making the soil more fertile for crops.

The early farmers of the Indus River valley made good use of the yearly floods by planting cotton and sesame seeds just before the monsoon began. By the time the rain stopped and the Indus River shrank to its normal level, the crops were ready to be harvested. Often, the ground stayed moist enough to grow winter crops, such as barley and wheat.

READING CHECK ○COMPARE AND CONTRAST
Why was flooding both bad and good in ancient India?

Well-Planned Cities

TIME 2500 B.C.

PLACE Indus River valley

The people of the Indus River valley built their farming villages on the tops of large mounds made from mud and stones. They took this action to keep the villages above the flood level of the Indus River.

Over time, some farming villages in the Indus River valley grew into cities, and the most powerful cities became city-states. By 2500 B.C., these city-states had developed an early civilization, covering parts of what are today Pakistan and western India.

Three of the largest and most important cities were **Harappa** (huh•RA•puh), **Lothal**, and **Mohenjo-Daro** (moh•HEN•joh DAR•oh). Harappa is a town in Pakistan where archaeologists found the first evidence of the civilization. As a result, the Indus River valley civilization is often called the Harappan civilization.

Harappa, Lothal, and Mohenjo-Daro were well-planned cities, with many common features. Each city had streets laid out in a grid. The grid divided the city into blocks of brick buildings. Each city also had a **citadel**, a fortlike structure. Inside the walls were government buildings, palaces, religious buildings, and **granaries**, or places for storing grain.

In addition, the people of these cities used the same script, or writing system, although it has not been deciphered. They also used the same units for measuring length and weight. These similarities have led some scholars to suggest that the cities were united under a central government.

READING CHECK SUMMARIZE
How do we know that Harappan cities were well planned?

▶ Archaeologists have uncovered many parts of the ancient city of Harappa, including this drainpipe.

FAST FACT

The ancient city of Harappa is believed to have been rebuilt at least six times due to flooding.

Harappan Trade

Much about the social and political life of the early Indus River valley people remains a mystery. Historians do know that trade was important to Harappan cities.

Harappan workers in craft workshops produced many useful and decorative items. Weavers made cloth from the cotton plant. Potters shaped clay into figurines, perhaps for use in religious ceremonies, and pots. Metalworkers made silver and gold jewelry and copper and bronze tools.

Traders carried these Harappan products to faraway places and returned with timber, grain, and metals. They marked their goods with stone seals engraved with writing and drawings of animals. Harappan stone seals have been found in central Asia, Mesopotamia, and along the Persian Gulf.

READING CHECK **SUMMARIZE**
What did the Harappans trade?

Mohenjo-Daro

Mohenjo-Daro is probably the best known Indus city. In its time, the city was a model of thoughtful planning. The fact that Mohenjo-Daro was so carefully planned shows that it must have had a strong government.

Archaeologists believe that more than 35,000 people lived in Mohenjo-Daro. Most people lived in small huts in surrounding villages. Inside the city walls, wealthy families lived in brick houses, some of which were two or three stories high.

Nearly every city home in Mohenjo-Daro had separate rooms for cooking, sleeping, and bathing. People bathed by emptying jugs of fresh water over themselves. The water drained into brick pipes that carried the water to other pipes under the streets.

Mohenjo-Daro's citadel was the center of the city's economic, political, and religious

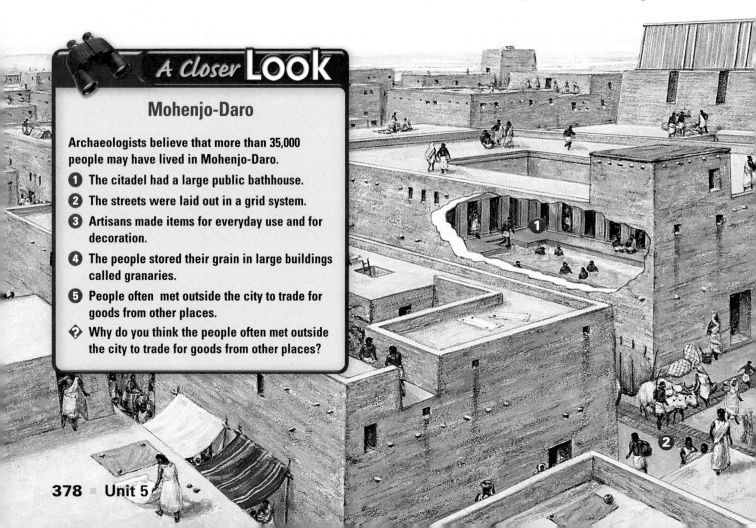

A Closer LOOK

Mohenjo-Daro

Archaeologists believe that more than 35,000 people may have lived in Mohenjo-Daro.

1. The citadel had a large public bathhouse.
2. The streets were laid out in a grid system.
3. Artisans made items for everyday use and for decoration.
4. The people stored their grain in large buildings called granaries.
5. People often met outside the city to trade for goods from other places.

❖ Why do you think the people often met outside the city to trade for goods from other places?

life. It stood above the city on a brick platform near the Indus River.

Mohenjo-Daro and the Harappan civilization declined sometime after 1750 B.C. Archaeologists have found evidence that invaders, floods, or earthquakes may have driven people from the city.

READING CHECK ☼COMPARE AND CONTRAST
How did homes in Mohenjo-Daro differ?

Summary

The ancient peoples of the Indian subcontinent lived with drought, rain, and floods. In the Indus River valley, the Harappan people found fertile soil and traded as far away as Mesopotamia. The three largest cities were Harappa, Lothal, and Mohenjo-Daro. Thousands of people lived in these city-states before the Harappan civilization ended.

REVIEW

1. 💡 How did the physical setting of the Indus River valley make it possible for a civilization to form there?

2. Explain the function of a **citadel**.

3. In which region is the Indus River located, the northern plains or the Deccan?

4. How do we know that Harappan products were traded to places as far away as Mesopotamia?

CRITICAL THINKING

5. Why do you think Harappan civilization developed in northern India instead of in the Deccan?

6. **ANALYSIS SKILL** What are three questions you have about life in Mohenjo-Daro? Write them down, and share them with your classmates. Discuss possible answers or ways to find answers.

7. 🖌 **Make a Map** Imagine a single raindrop falling onto the Himalayas. Then imagine it making its way to the Indus River and being carried all the way to the Arabian Sea. Using the map on page 375 as a reference, make a map of the major routes that the raindrop might take.

8. **Focus Skill** **COMPARE AND CONTRAST**
On a separate sheet of paper, copy and complete the graphic organizer below.

Harappa

Mohenjo-Daro

Similar
Streets laid out in a grid

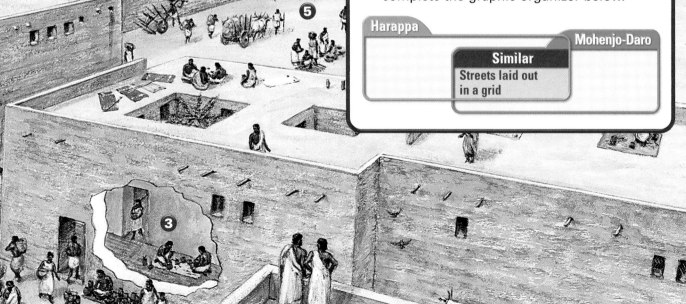

Follow a Flowchart

❱ WHY IT MATTERS

Often it is easier to understand a process, such as how something is made, if it is shown on a flowchart. A **flowchart** is a graphic organizer that shows the sequence, or order, of the steps in a process. Flowcharts can help you understand how or why something happens. Flowcharts can also help show cause-and-effect relationships clearly.

❱ WHAT YOU NEED TO KNOW

You have just read about the Indus Valley civilization. The flowchart on page 381 shows how the Harappan people made clay bricks for building. Like most flowcharts, it is made up of boxes containing text. Arrows connect related boxes to show the steps in the process. Flowcharts can be arranged in a line or in a circle, or they can branch out like a tree. The arrangement of the chart depends on the information it contains.

Follow these steps to read the flowchart on page 381.

Step 1 Read the title of the flowchart. It tells you the subject of the chart or the process that is explained.

Step 2 Identify the steps. Brief descriptions of the steps in a process usually appear in boxes or ovals.

Step 3 Follow the arrows between the steps. They show how the steps are related in time. Most flowcharts "flow" from left to right or from top to bottom.

Step 4 Look for "if-then" situations. A step may be followed by more than one possible next step. Two or more arrows leading to the possible next steps show the choices.

❱ Thousands of clay bricks were used to build the city of Mohenjo-Daro.

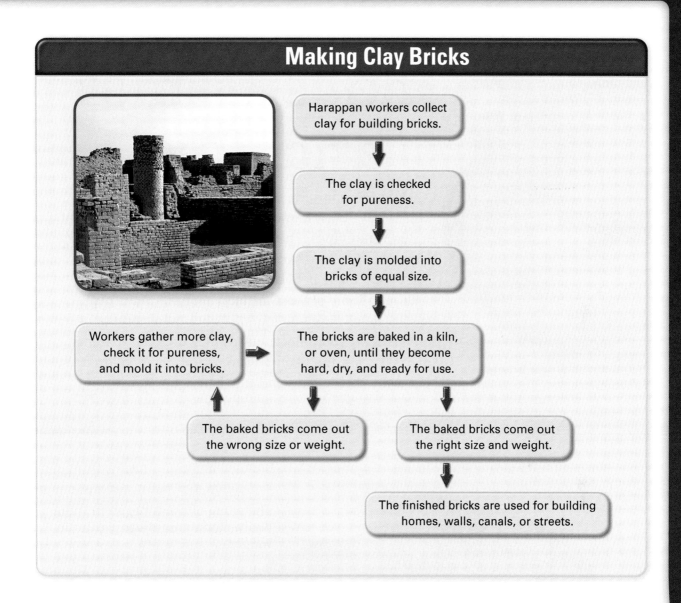

Making Clay Bricks

Harappan workers collect clay for building bricks.

↓

The clay is checked for pureness.

↓

The clay is molded into bricks of equal size.

↓

The bricks are baked in a kiln, or oven, until they become hard, dry, and ready for use.

Workers gather more clay, check it for pureness, and mold it into bricks. →

↓

The baked bricks come out the wrong size or weight.

↓

The baked bricks come out the right size and weight.

↓

The finished bricks are used for building homes, walls, canals, or streets.

> ## PRACTICE THE SKILL

ANALYSIS SKILL Now use the flowchart above to answer the following questions.

1 What process does this flow chart show?

2 What happens if the bricks are not the right size or weight?

3 What do the Harappans do with the bricks after they are baked?

4 Which event comes first, collecting clay or building houses?

> ## APPLY WHAT YOU LEARNED

ANALYSIS SKILL Using the library and reliable Internet sources, make a cause-and-effect flowchart that shows why and how something happened. Your subject should be about ancient India. For example, you might explain how Buddhism was founded and how it became a popular religion. Or you might show how the Gupta Empire rose to power.

Chart and Graph Skills

Indus Games and Toys

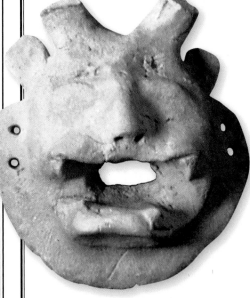

Models, marbles, masks, and other recreational objects have been found in the sands around the ancient Indus Valley cities. The artifacts you see on these pages were found in Harappa, Mohenjo-Daro, and Lothal. They were made between 3000 B.C. and 2000 B.C. Although some of these artifacts are 5,000 years old, similar items might be found in your own closet or on the living room floor. Just as they do today, parents of 5,000 years ago likely had to remind their children to put away their games and toys before bedtime!

▶ This mask may have been used for storytelling.

The game of chess began in India. Boards today are much lighter in weight.

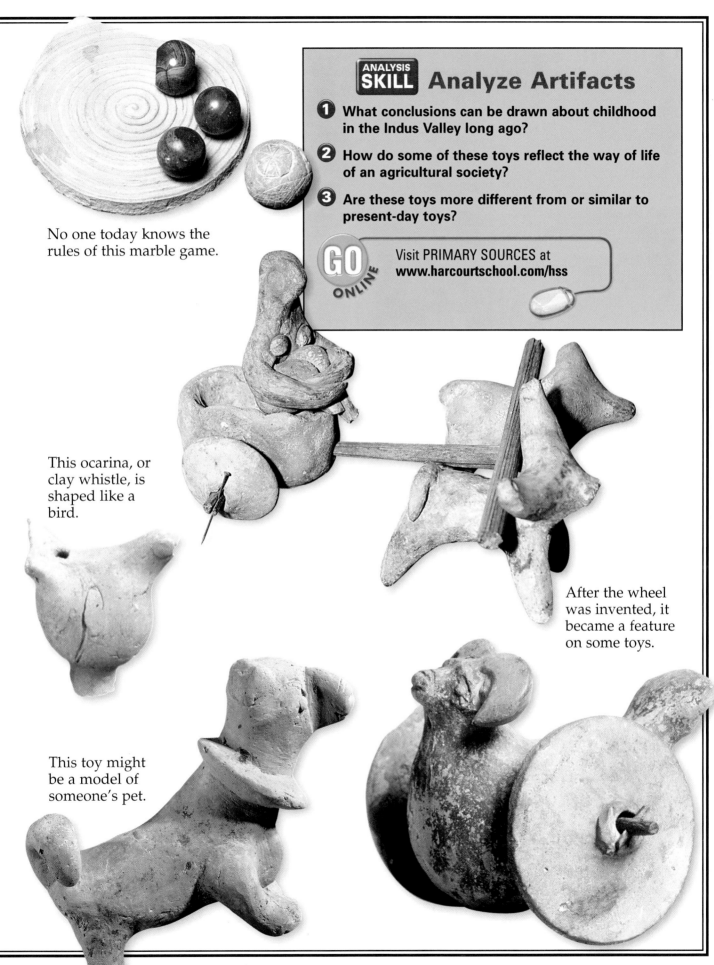

No one today knows the rules of this marble game.

ANALYSIS SKILL **Analyze Artifacts**

① What conclusions can be drawn about childhood in the Indus Valley long ago?

② How do some of these toys reflect the way of life of an agricultural society?

③ Are these toys more different from or similar to present-day toys?

GO ONLINE Visit PRIMARY SOURCES at www.harcourtschool.com/hss

This ocarina, or clay whistle, is shaped like a bird.

After the wheel was invented, it became a feature on some toys.

This toy might be a model of someone's pet.

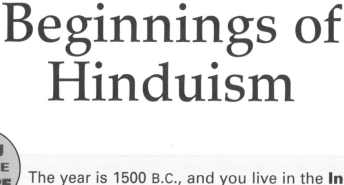
Time

3000 B.C.   1500 B.C.   B.C./A.D.

1500 B.C.
Aryan people begin
a migration into India

1000 B.C.
The caste system is in
place in India

WHAT TO KNOW
How did Hinduism affect
India's society?

✓ Discuss the importance
  of the Aryan migrations.

✓ Outline the features
  of the caste system.

VOCABULARY
Aryan p. 385
Sanskrit p. 386
Vedas p. 386
caste p. 387
Hinduism p. 388
reincarnation p. 389
dharma p. 389
karma p. 389

PLACES
Indus River valley
Mesopotamia
Persia
Hindu Kush
Pakistan

**COMPARE AND
CONTRAST**

**California
Standards**
HSS 6.5, 6.5.2, 6.5.3, 6.5.4, 6.5.7

Beginnings of Hinduism

YOU ARE THERE
The year is 1500 B.C., and you live in the **Indus
River valley**. You and your older brother are
walking home after helping your father in the fields.

Coming toward you on the road are men arriving from
the west. You've never seen these people before. They
are riding on horses and in chariots. You are excited to
see new people but also a little afraid.

Your brother grabs your hand, and you both run
home. You ask your brother who these strangers are and
why they are coming here. He says he's heard that they
are from a land far away, but he doesn't know why they
have come or if they will stay.

The Aryan Migrations

About 1500 B.C., after the Harappan civilization collapsed, people known as **Aryans** (AIR•ee•uhnz) began waves of migrations to the Indian subcontinent. Originally from the dry plains near the Black and Caspian Seas, the Aryans brought their influence to the Punjab and Ganges Plains.

It is still unknown just who the Aryans were. Their name simply meant "noble," but experts believe they were both herders and warriors. The reason they left their homeland is also unknown. Perhaps overpopulation drove them to look for new lands on which to live and raise their herds of goats and sheep.

From the north, the Aryans moved south into **Mesopotamia**. They traveled across **Persia** with their horses and chariots and continued east. After crossing a range of mountains known as the **Hindu Kush**, the Aryans began settling on the Punjab Plain, which today is part of **Pakistan**.

At first, the Aryans kept their traditional way of life. They continued to keep herds and live in family tribes, which were ruled by warrior chiefs. In time, their life began to change, and they became farmers, growing barley and wheat. Also, the organization of their tribes changed. Geography and place became more important than family ties.

By the time the Aryan migrations ended, a new civilization had developed across the Punjab and Ganges Plains. However, not everyone believes that the Aryans migrated into India. Some experts believe that the Aryan culture developed directly from the Harappan culture while others claim that the Aryans invaded the region. In any case, some elements of this Indian civilization that resulted were a blend of both Aryan culture and ancient Indian culture. Other elements were completely Aryan.

READING CHECK ⟳ **COMPARE AND CONTRAST**
How had life in ancient India changed by the time the Aryan migrations ended?

❯ The Aryans may have migrated to the Indian subcontinent from near the border between Europe and Asia (below). Possible routes are shown at the right.

ASIA

Black Sea

Caspian Sea

Plateau of Iran

AFGHANISTAN

IRAN

INDIA

Persian Gulf

INDIAN OCEAN

Influences on Indian Culture

Many traces of Aryan culture can still be found in India today. For example, the Aryans brought their language, **Sanskrit** (SAN•skrit), to ancient India. Many Indian languages of today have their roots in Sanskrit. These include Hindi, the most commonly spoken language in India.

The Aryans also influenced Indian culture through Sanskrit literature known as the **Vedas** (VAY•duhz). The word *Veda* means "knowledge" in Sanskrit. The Vedas formed the foundation of the Aryan religion. They are some of the oldest religious texts in the world.

Compiled between 1500 B.C. and 800 B.C., the Vedas are based on oral traditions that had been passed down for hundreds of years. There are four Vedas. Each is made up of hymns, tales, lessons, and even battle songs.

A story called the *Mahabharata* (mah•huh•BAH•ruh•tuh) was written soon after the Vedas. More than 200,000 lines long, it is the longest epic poem ever written. The best-known part of the *Mahabharata* is the *Bhagavad Gita* (BAH•guh•vahd GEE•tuh). The *Bhagavad Gita* describes a discussion between Krishna and Arjuna about the importance of following established duties.

A later addition to the Vedas are the *Brahmanas*, or "priestly books," which describe important practices. In one practice, the priests, or Brahmans (BRAH•muhnz), burned offerings of food or plants to honor the deities. The Vedas are the earliest textual source for the religion that became Hinduism.

> **Indian god Vishnu**

READING CHECK SUMMARIZE
How did the Vedas affect India?

A Selection From The Bhagavad Gita

The Bhagavad Gita, *or Song of the Lord, is part of the larger ancient Indian poem called the* Mahabharata. *In this selection, the Hindu deity Vishnu speaks to Arjuna, a character in the poem:*

*Bhagavad Gita: A New Translation. Stephen Mitchell, trans., ed. Harmony Books, 2000.

"There is no doubt that you will know me
   in my total being when you persist
In discipline and rely on me,
   and when your thoughts cling to me. Listen.

Without holding back anything, I shall teach you
   wisdom, and explain how it can be attained,
Knowing which, there is nothing left to be
   known.

One out of thousands
   may strive for success.
And even of these only a few
   may know me as I really am."*

Ancient Indian Epic Poem

ANALYSIS SKILL **Analyze Documents**

In this illustrated page from the *Mahabharata*, the Padavas battle their cousins, the Kauravas, for control of ancient India.

1. This page from the *Mahabharata* was created in the A.D. 1500s.
2. This is Sanskrit, the language in which the poem was written.
3. The Padavas and Kauravas fought on war chariots.
◆ In what ways is the page like a storybook page today?

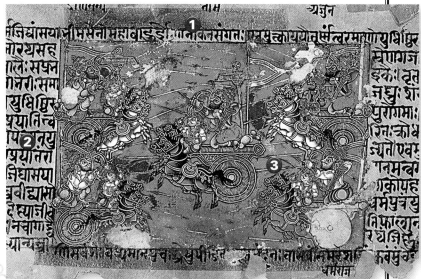

India's Classes

The Aryans who first settled in India lived in tribes. A warrior-chief called a *raja*, or *rajah*, a ruling council, and a chief priest governed each tribe. The people were divided into two classes—nobles and commoners. In time, a third social class came about that was made up of the descendants of the ancient people of India.

By 1000 B.C., Indian society came to include four main classes. The Indians believed that society worked the way a human body does. Different groups of people made up the different parts of society's body. The head was the highest class, the Brahmans. They were the priests and scholars. The arms were the Kshatriyas (KSHAH•tree•uhz), who were the rulers and warriors. The body and legs were the Vaisyas (VYSH•yuhz), who were the farmers, traders, and merchants. Last came the feet, the Sudras (SOO•druhz). They were the servants and laborers.

In Indian society, castes existed within these four classes. A **caste**, or *jati*, is a group of people in a particular social class. The caste a person belonged to determined how he or she could live. People from different castes had little contact with one another. Also, a person could not change from the caste into which he or she was born.

The people at the very bottom of the social order, outside and beneath the caste system, were called untouchables. These people were regarded as unclean and did the most undesirable work in order to survive. They were forbidden to have contact with anyone but other untouchables. They could not even let their shadows touch the shadows of members of the upper castes.

Discrimination against people because of their caste is illegal in present-day India. Yet some of the features of the old caste system still exist.

READING CHECK ♻ COMPARE AND CONTRAST
How did the Indians compare their society to the human body?

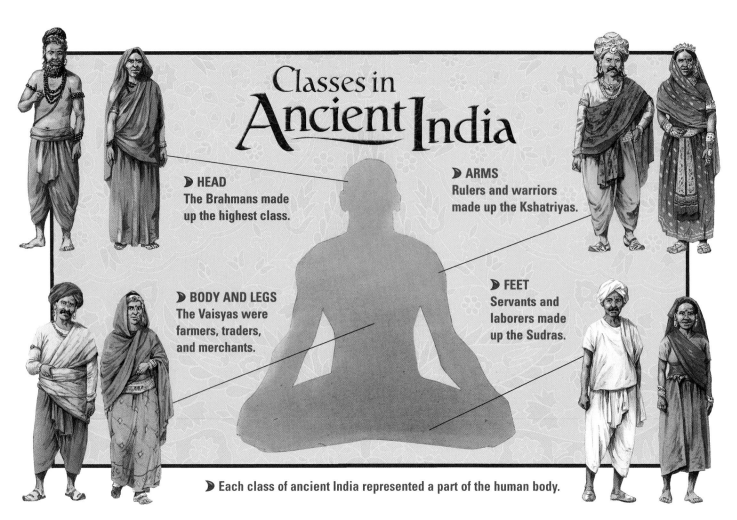

Classes in Ancient India

▶ **HEAD**
The Brahmans made up the highest class.

▶ **ARMS**
Rulers and warriors made up the Kshatriyas.

▶ **BODY AND LEGS**
The Vaisyas were farmers, traders, and merchants.

▶ **FEET**
Servants and laborers made up the Sudras.

▶ Each class of ancient India represented a part of the human body.

Ideas of Hinduism

Hinduism evolved, or developed, from the Aryans' religious beliefs and those of the ancient people of India. Hindus believe in many deities. The most important Hindu deities are Brahma the Creator, Vishnu the Preserver, and Shiva the Destroyer.

The Upanishads (oo•PAH•nih•shahdz) are the most ancient Hindu literature. Hindus based these spiritual writings on the teachings of the Vedas.

In Hinduism, what people do and how they act toward other living things is important. One of the basic beliefs of Hinduism is that both people and animals have a soul, or *atman*, that is reborn into

▶ The city of Varanasi and the Ganges River are sacred to the Hindus.

other beings after death. This rebirth is called **reincarnation**.

Hindus believe that people have a position in a caste system. **Dharma**, or religious duty, and **karma**, or actions, determine the caste into which a person will be reborn. Those who follow their dharma and have good karma will be rewarded, advancing to a higher caste in their next life. Those who do not follow their religious duty and have bad karma will be reincarnated into a lower position. In Hinduism, only those who have achieved spiritual purity, or *moksha*, can escape this cycle of death and rebirth.

READING CHECK **SUMMARIZE**
What are the basic beliefs of Hinduism?

Summary

The Aryan migrations changed the way people lived in ancient India. Aryan customs and religion spread throughout the Indian subcontinent. Social classes developed into a strict caste system. The ancient language, Sanskrit, is the basis of many languages of the people of India. Aryan religious practices, based on the Vedas, developed into Hinduism.

REVIEW

1. How did Hinduism affect India's society?

2. **Dharma** and **karma** sound similar, but they mean very different things. Write a short description for each.

3. How would you describe the structure of ancient India's caste system?

4. Why was the Indus River valley a good place for the Aryans to settle?

CRITICAL THINKING

5. **ANALYSIS SKILL** For thousands of years, the caste system played a role in the organization of India's society. Do you think this system is a good way to organize a society? Why or why not?

6. **ANALYSIS SKILL** Study the map on page 385. Why do you think the Aryans chose the routes they did as they migrated from their homeland?

7. **Write a Narrative** Picture a farmer living in ancient India. Describe the arrival of the Aryans in the Indus River valley from the point of view of the ancient farmer. Tell about some of the new ideas the Aryans are introducing to Indian culture. Also, describe how the migration of the Aryan people has affected the farmer's life.

8. **Focus Skill** **COMPARE AND CONTRAST** On a separate sheet of paper, copy and complete the graphic organizer below.

Hindus | Similar: Caste system | Aryans

Lesson

Time

3000 B.C.   1500 B.C.   B.C./A.D.

599 B.C.
Vardhamana Mahavira is born

563 B.C.
Buddha is born

483 B.C.
Buddha dies

WHAT TO KNOW
How did Buddhism develop and spread?

✓ Describe the life and moral teachings of the Buddha.

✓ Compare and contrast Buddhism and other Indian religious traditions.

✓ Explain how Buddhism spread throughout India, Ceylon, and central Asia.

VOCABULARY
Buddhism p. 391
meditate p. 391
enlightenment p. 392
nirvana p. 392
monk p. 394

PEOPLE
Buddha
Vardhamana Mahavira
Mohandas Gandhi
Dr. Martin Luther King, Jr.

PLACES
India

COMPARE AND CONTRAST

California Standards
HSS 6.5, 6.5.5

The Beginning of Buddhism

YOU ARE THERE

The year is 530 B.C. You live in a village in the northeastern part of **India**. You're walking through the village with your mother when you see a stranger sitting in the shade of a tree. He seems to be concentrating on something very important. Your mother says that he's a prince named Siddhartha Gautama (sih•DAR•tuh GOW•tuh•muh), who has been wandering around the countryside. You wonder why the prince would be living this kind of life and what he could be thinking about.

▶ Sculpted head of the Buddha

❯ Siddhartha Gautama fled his palace, leaving his life as a prince behind to share his beliefs with the world.

The Birth of Buddhism

By the 600s B.C., reincarnation had become a very important idea in Hinduism. Many Hindus believed that, after death, a person's soul could return to the world in a different form—human, animal, or even plant. This happened again and again in a cycle of birth, death, and rebirth. Many Hindus, especially those with difficult lives, wanted to escape this cycle.

In the 500s B.C., a young Indian prince named Siddhartha Gautama introduced new ideas about reincarnation. He believed that if people were good and pure, they could rid their lives of suffering and break the cycle of reincarnation. His ideas became the foundation of a new religion called **Buddhism** (BOO•dih•zuhm).

Siddhartha was born in about 563 B.C. to a royal family in northern India. His father

ordered that he be raised entirely inside the royal palace, away from the rest of the world. As a young man, Siddhartha lived the rich life of a prince, but he eventually found this life to be unfulfilling.

At age 29, Siddhartha ventured out of the palace. He saw for the first time the realities of human life, including sickness, old age, poverty, and death. He abandoned his royal life and set out to find why such miseries exist.

After years of searching, Siddhartha sat under the shade of a tree and meditated on the idea of suffering. To **meditate** is to concentrate so deeply that the mind becomes clear and calm. Once Siddhartha had found the answers he sought, he became the **Buddha**, or the "Enlightened One."

READING CHECK ♂ COMPARE AND CONTRAST
How did Siddhartha Gautama's life change after he ventured out of the royal palace?

THE LIFE OF THE BUDDHA

▷ Siddhartha cuts off his hair during his wandering.

▷ The Buddha is born Siddhartha, a prince.

563 B.C.

▷ Siddhartha becomes the Buddha.

Teachings of Buddhism

After his **enlightenment**, or complete understanding of truth, the Buddha wandered across the land, teaching his ideas to the people he met. By the time he died in 483 B.C., his ideas were becoming more and more popular.

The Buddha's teachings centered on Four Noble Truths. The first noble truth says that suffering is part of human life. The second states that wanting things is the root of all suffering. The third says that the way out of suffering is to become wise enough to not want things. The fourth is a guide to proper living called the Eightfold Path.

The Eightfold Path is often symbolized by a wheel with eight spokes. Each spoke on the wheel represents a step toward achieving *nirvana*. According to Buddhism, **nirvana** is the highest state of the human

mind, free from the ignorance and desires that lead to human suffering.

The eight steps on the path to nirvana include right thought, right speech, right understanding, right action, right livelihood, right effort, right mindfulness, and right concentration. Buddhists follow this path to move toward enlightenment and live in harmony with others.

To stay on the path to enlightenment, Buddhism encourages people to live in the Middle Way. One way to do this is to live in moderation by avoiding extreme behavior. For example, one should eat neither too much nor too little. Practicing meditation is also very important to the Middle Way.

The Buddha's teachings differ from Hinduism in many ways. For example, Buddhism does not focus on the worship of many gods or even one god. From the beginning, Buddhism was open to

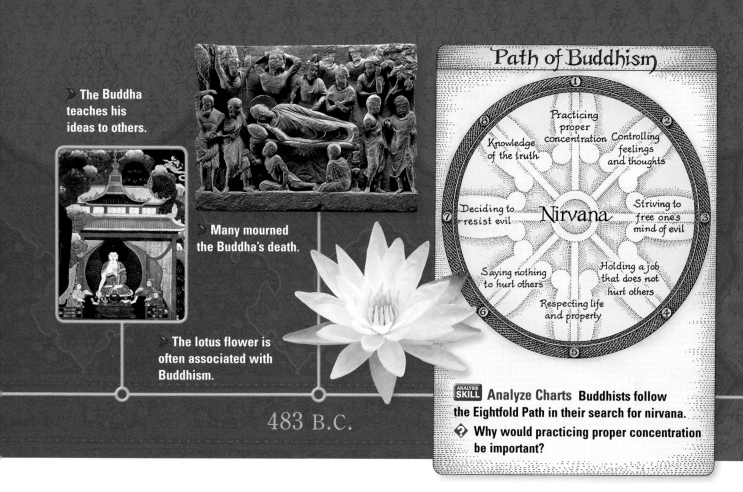

> The Buddha teaches his ideas to others.

> Many mourned the Buddha's death.

> The lotus flower is often associated with Buddhism.

483 B.C.

Path of Buddhism

Practicing proper concentration

Controlling feelings and thoughts

Knowledge of the truth

Deciding to resist evil

Nirvana

Striving to free one's mind of evil

Saying nothing to hurt others

Holding a job that does not hurt others

Respecting life and property

ANALYSIS SKILL **Analyze Charts** Buddhists follow the Eightfold Path in their search for nirvana.

❓ Why would practicing proper concentration be important?

people of all castes and had neither priests nor a special holy language. Instead, the Buddha's teachings used the everyday language of the people.

Buddhism also accepted many Hindu ideas. Both Buddhists and Hindus believe in reincarnation. Another belief held by both is *ahimsa*, which means "nonviolence" in Sanskrit. Both Buddhists and Hindus believe that it is wrong to harm people and animals. The idea of *ahimsa* contributed to the belief in peaceful ideas and to the growth of vegetarianism in India.

Another religion with ideas similar to Buddhism came into being in India during the 500s B.C. This religion was called Jainism (JY•nih•zuhm). It was begun by **Vardhamana Mahavira** (var•duh•MAH•nuh mah•hah•VEE•ruh), who was born in 599 B.C. Like the Buddha, he gave up all he owned to live a religious life. He spent 12 years seeking

enlightenment. Then he became a teacher of religion.

Mahavira believed that the best way to bring about change was through peaceful action. Like Hindus and Buddhists, Jainists believe in reincarnation and *ahimsa*. They believe in trying to reach freedom from reincarnation, as Hindus and Buddhists do, and they follow a path of three "jewels"—right faith, right knowledge, right conduct—that is similar to the Buddhist Eightfold Path.

Jainism's emphasis on peaceful action has influenced many Indian leaders. Later, these ideas guided **Mohandas Gandhi**, who used nonviolence to help free India from British rule. Gandhi's actions later inspired the American leader **Dr. Martin Luther King, Jr.**, to use nonviolence in the struggle for civil rights.

READING CHECK MAIN IDEAS AND DETAILS
What are the main ideas of Buddhism?

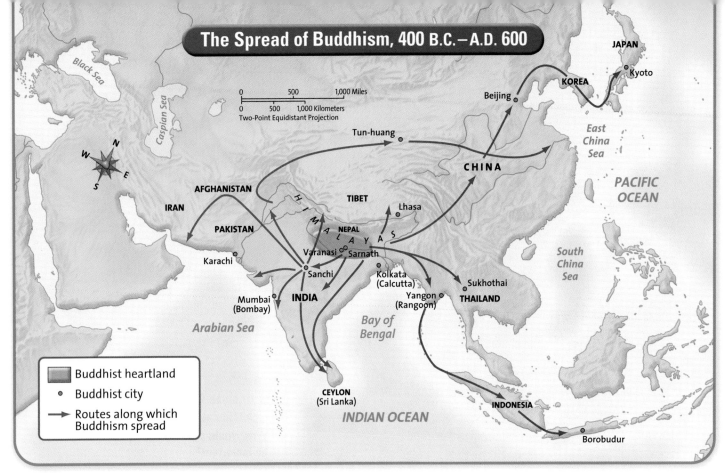

The Spread of Buddhism, 400 B.C.–A.D. 600

Legend:
- Buddhist heartland
- Buddhist city
- Routes along which Buddhism spread

ANALYSIS SKILL Analyze Maps

◆ **Movement** Which regions did Buddhism spread across to reach Japan?

The Growth of Buddhism

The Buddha lived a long life, spreading his teachings throughout northern India. Some of his followers became monks. A **monk** is a man who devotes his life to practicing and teaching religious beliefs.

Buddhist monks closely follow the Four Noble Truths, the Eightfold Path, and the Middle Way. They also meditate for many hours every day. The Buddha's wandering monks kept his teachings alive after he died. Later, they built monasteries, settled down, and taught Buddhism to others.

For a long time, the Buddha's message was passed down only through the spoken word. The first written versions of the Buddha's teachings began to appear between 200 B.C. and 100 B.C. It was not until about 200 years later that the poet Ashvaghosa wrote the *Buddha Charita*, or *Life of the Buddha*.

Over time, Buddhism split into several groups, or "schools," each with its own view of the Buddha's teachings. Of the schools of Buddhism that exist today, the Theravada school is most like early Buddhism. There are also the Pure Land, the Zen, and the Tantra schools of Buddhism that emerged in the first century A.D. These three schools make up what is called Mahayana Buddhism. Mahayana Buddhism teaches social concern and compassion for others.

For a time, Buddhism was popular among the people of India. However, as time passed, Hinduism regained popularity by emphasizing local gods. By about A.D. 1200, a Muslim empire ruled over India, and Buddhism was in decline there.

Leaders throughout history have had different ideas about the use of violence and non-violence to bring about change.

Mohandas Gandhi, an
Indian independence movement leader

"Non-violence...does not mean meek submission to the will of the evil-doer, but it means the putting of one's whole soul against the will of the tyrant."

—from the journal *Young India,* August 2, 1920

Patrick Henry,
American patriot

"Unfortunately, nothing will preserve [liberty] but downright force. Whenever you give up that force, you are inevitably ruined."

—from a speech given on June 5, 1788. *The Debates in the Several State Conventions on the Adoption of the Federal Constitution.* Edited by Jonathan Elliot. Public Journals of Congress, 1836.

It's Your Turn

ANALYSIS SKILL **Analyze Points of View** What is each person's point of view? How might the circumstances in which they lived have affected their points of view?

Outside India, Buddhism had remained popular. Traders, travelers, monks, and others spread Buddhism to the ancient lands of Ceylon (now called Sri Lanka), China, Korea, central Asia, and Japan.

READING CHECK SUMMARIZE
How did Buddhism spread?

Summary

In the 500s B.C., Siddhartha Gautama founded Buddhism in India. Buddhism offered an end to suffering for those who lived the Middle Way and followed the Four Noble Truths and the Eightfold Path.

REVIEW

1. How did Buddhism develop and spread?

2. Use the terms **meditate** and **nirvana** in a paragraph about how Siddhartha Gautama became the Buddha.

3. What are the Four Noble Truths?

4. How are the beliefs of Buddhists, Hindus, and Jainists similar?

CRITICAL THINKING

5. **ANALYSIS SKILL** **Make It Relevant** Do you think nonviolence is an important part of today's society? Explain.

6. **ANALYSIS SKILL** Why do you think so many people responded to the Buddha's ideas for ending human suffering?

7. **Illustrate Scenes** Look at the map on p. 394. Illustrate scenes that could appear on the map to help describe the spread of Buddhism. For example, you might show the enlightenment of the Buddha or monks spreading the word of Buddhism.

8. **Focus Skill** **COMPARE AND CONTRAST**
On a separate sheet of paper, copy and complete the graphic organizer below.

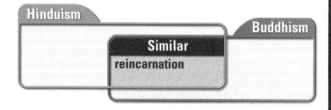

Hinduism | Similar | Buddhism
reincarnation

Lesson

Time

| 3000 B.C. | 1500 B.C. | B.C./A.D. |

327 B.C.
Alexander the Great
invades India

320 B.C.
Chandragupta Maurya
founds the Maurya Empire

A.D. 320
Chandragupta I founds
the Gupta Empire

WHAT TO KNOW
How did the rise of empires change India?

✓ Describe the growth of the Maurya and Gupta empires.

✓ Compare how Ashoka changed government and religion in ancient India.

✓ Describe the cultural achievements of India's Golden Age.

VOCABULARY
turning point p. 399
missionary p. 399
aesthetic p. 400
metallurgy p. 401
Hindu-Arabic numeral p. 401

PEOPLE
Ashoka
Chandragupta Maurya
Chandragupta I
Samudragupta
Chandragupta II
Kalidasa

PLACES
India
Afghanistan
Bangladesh
Pakistan

COMPARE AND CONTRAST

California
Standards

HSS 6.5, 6.5.5, 6.5.6, 6.5.7

Empires of India

YOU ARE THERE
It is the 260s B.C. You've been providing water to soldiers fighting at the side of Emperor **Ashoka** in the long and fierce battle for Kalinga. Now victory has come, but at a great cost. The bodies of the dead cover the ground for as far as the eye can see. The time has come, Ashoka tells everyone, for all this to change.

Ashoka has long known the teachings of the Buddha, but until now, he knew only the words, not their meaning. This battle, he says, has helped him understand the Buddha's wisdom. Ashoka declares that, instead of fighting, he will end people's suffering by showing kindness to all living things. You hope that he will do what he says and make **India** a better place to live.

FAST FACT

According to tradition, the city of Sarnath is where the Buddha first began teaching his followers.

The Struggle for United Rule

For many years, ancient India was a land divided into many city-states and kingdoms, each ruled by its own leader. Some kings tried to expand their territory by conquering neighboring kingdoms. In the 500s B.C., this was especially true of the city-states in the Ganges River valley, where kings fought one another. Controlling this area meant controlling trade and the wealth that trade brings.

No one ruler, however, had yet attempted to unite all the lands of ancient India. Most of ancient India was on a large peninsula. Inside the peninsula, mountain ranges and great distances made it difficult for a single ruler to unite ancient India.

These challenges did not stop invaders from northwestern lands from trying to conquer India. In 518 B.C., King Darius (duh•RY•uhs) of the Persian Empire led his armies from present-day Iran into India in search of new territory and plunder. For almost 200 years, the Persians claimed lands in the Indus River valley and the western Punjab. Then, in about 327 B.C., Alexander the Great, having just conquered the Persians, led Greek troops into India. In the end, both Darius and Alexander failed to conquer all of India.

After Alexander's death in 323 B.C., some of his generals tried to control parts of India, but they were soon driven out. One of the Indian rulers who helped defeat the Greeks was **Chandragupta Maurya** (chuhn•druh•GUP•tuh MOWR•yuh). He continued fighting, defeating other kings and taking their lands. In about 320 B.C., he founded the Maurya Empire and united under his rule the lands he had conquered.

READING CHECK ⚫ COMPARE AND CONTRAST
How was ancient India ruled before and after the founding of the Maurya Empire?

➤ Ashoka had this building constructed as a spiritual monument to the Buddha. Its ruins are still visited by many people today.

LOCATE IT

Sarnath

INDIA

Arabian Sea

Bay of Bengal

The Maurya Empire

Chandragupta Maurya formed a well organized empire. He ordered land cleared and swamps drained to gain more farmland. He had workers improve the empire's roads. To do these things, Chandragupta supported his empire with taxes. Collecting taxes provided funds for powerful armies to win Chandragupta's battles.

The ruling class of Chandragupta's empire lived well, but the common people suffered. Chandragupta was a cruel ruler, taking as his guide a text called the *Arthashastra* (ar•thuh•SHAH•struh), or the *Science of Material Gain*. Written in the 300s B.C. by one of Chandragupta's top advisers, this book said that rulers should use punishment to get what they wanted. "Whoever imposes punishment as deserved," it declared, "becomes respectable."* Chandragupta followed these ideas strictly during his rule.

Chandragupta's way of governing helped him expand his empire across most of northern India. It also made his overworked and overtaxed people hate him.

Knowing how unpopular he was, Chandragupta feared that an enemy might try to kill him. He slept in a different room every night and had servants taste his food for poison. His methods succeeded, and he lived to turn over his empire to his son, Bindusara, in 297 B.C.

Bindusara ruled in the same cruel manner as his father until about 273 B.C. His son, Ashoka, also written as Asoka, however, was one of the greatest rulers of ancient India.

READING CHECK **CAUSE AND EFFECT**
Why did the people of the Maurya Empire hate Chandragupta?

*Kautilya. *Arthashastra*. R. Shamasastry, trans. Bangalore Government Press, 1915.

> This entrance to an ancient Buddhist worship center was built during the time of the Maurya Empire.

Democratic Values

Working for the common good was important to Ashoka's leadership.

Ashoka ruled for the good of all people. He tried to let people know of his teachings and work by having his edicts, or commands, carved into rock and stone pillars. These edicts suggested Buddhist ideas as a code to live by. They also urged people to accept those of other cultures. The following part of an edict shows how Ashoka believed in his "principles of [the] right life": "There is no better work than promoting the welfare of all the people, and whatever efforts I am making is to repay the debt I owe to all beings to assure their happiness in this life and to attain heaven in the next."*

Analyze the Value Why do you think it was important that Ashoka share his beliefs in written edicts?

*Ashoka, from the *Sixth Rock Edict of Ashoka*. Ven Shravast Dhammika's, trans. 1993

▶ **Lion sculptures from one of Ashoka's pillars**

The Reign of Ashoka

Emperor Ashoka was a fierce warrior. He led his armies into many battles, adding both people and land to his empire. He not only united almost all of India but extended the Maurya Empire into what are today **Afghanistan**, **Bangladesh**, and **Pakistan**.

As a young ruler, Ashoka was cruel and violent like the other Maurya emperors. "Any power superior in might to another should launch into war,"* he believed.

After he conquered the kingdom of Kalinga in 261 B.C., Ashoka experienced a sudden **turning point**, or change, in his life. The sight of the many thousands who lay dead filled Ashoka with regret. Because of this event, he began to reject violence and became a peace-loving Buddhist.

After his change, Emperor Ashoka made many political and moral achievements. He became a fair and kind ruler. He established Buddhism as the state religion. He built Buddhist temples and sent out missionaries. A **missionary** is a person who takes his or her religious ideas to other parts of the world. As a result, Ashoka helped spread Buddhism in India, Ceylon (now called Sri Lanka), and central Asia.

Ashoka had edicts, or commands, based on Buddhist rules for living carved into stone pillars. He renounced violence as a national policy. Kindness to animals, obedience to parents, fair treatment of servants, and helping others were considered very important.

Ashoka had the pillars posted across his empire and sent government officials to help explain the edicts to his people. In turn, his officials reported to him on the feelings and thoughts of his people. Some of these pillars still stand today, reminding people of the philosopher-king Ashoka.

READING CHECK ⚙ **COMPARE AND CONTRAST**
How did Ashoka change after conquering Kalinga?

*Kautilya. *Arthashastra*, from *A New History of India* by Stanley Wolpert. Oxford University Press, 1997.

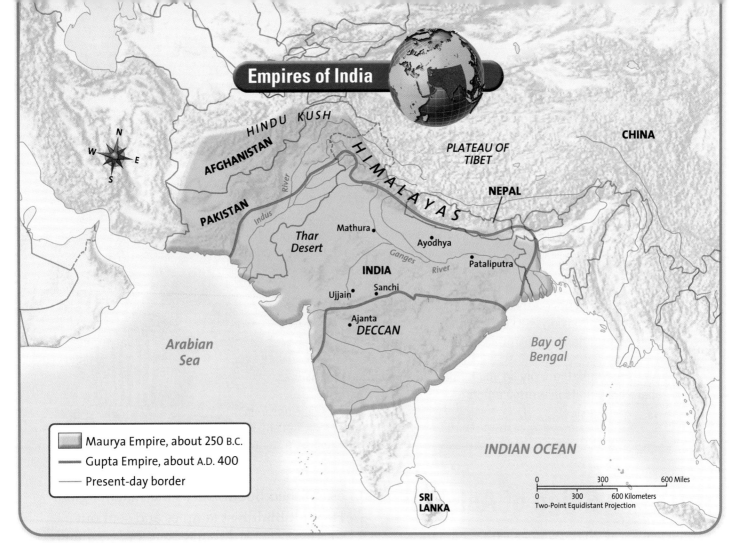

Empires of India

Maurya Empire, about 250 B.C.
Gupta Empire, about A.D. 400
Present-day border

ANALYSIS SKILL Analyze Maps

♦ **Regions** What part of the Indian subcontinent was ruled by neither the Maurya Empire nor the Gupta Empire?

India's Golden Age

TIME A.D. 320–A.D. 535
PLACE Gupta Empire

Soon after Ashoka died in 232 B.C., the Maurya Empire began to fall apart. For the next 550 years, ancient India was once again a land of small kingdoms.

In about A.D. 320, a new empire called the Gupta Empire began to rise. Under its early rulers—**Chandragupta I**, **Samudragupta** (sa•MU•druh GUP•tuh), and **Chandragupta II**—the empire included central and northern India. Chandragupta I and Chandragupta II were not related to Chandragupta of the Maurya Empire.

The period of the Gupta Empire has become known as India's Golden Age. It was a time of peace, wealth, and great cultural achievement.

During India's Golden Age, the number of followers of Hinduism, Buddhism, and Jainism grew. Chandragupta II encouraged traditions that were **aesthetic**, or related to beauty. He supported artists and writers so they would not have to worry about earning a living.

The best-known writer of the Golden Age was a poet and playwright named **Kalidasa** (kah•lih•DAH•suh). He wrote of love, war, and kings. Three of his plays and two of his poems have survived.

Others wrote down the folktales that were part of ancient India's oral tradition. One collection of these folktales is called the *Panchatantra* (puhn•chah•TAHN•trah). In it are some of the oldest known stories and fables in the world, including "Sinbad the Sailor" and "Jack the Giant-Killer."

During the Golden Age, artists were also busy. Many worked on wall paintings called frescoes. Some of the most famous frescoes are in the Ajanta Caves, an ancient temple in central India. This beautiful work tells the story of the Buddha's life.

Indian metalworkers came up with new ideas in **metallurgy**, the science and technology of metals. They developed the earliest-known techniques for producing the metal zinc. Unlike other metals used during ancient times, zinc is the most difficult metal to smelt. Few other ancient cultures learned to produce zinc.

READING CHECK ⟳ **COMPARE AND CONTRAST**
How was India different after the Maurya Empire from how it was during the empire?

Indian Intellectual Achievements

Achievements made during India's Golden Age were not only in the arts. Many intellectual advances were made in mathematics and medicine.

Indian mathematicians were the first to use a base-ten number system. This is the system in use today, based on nine numerals and a zero. The numbers 1, 2, 3, 4, 5, 6, 7, 8, 9, and 0 are known as **Hindu-Arabic numerals**. They are called this because Arab traders helped spread their use in other parts of the world.

Indian doctors made great advances in medicine, helping people live healthier, longer lives. They developed ways of setting broken bones so that people could recover more fully. They also developed inoculations by giving someone a mild case of a disease which prevented him or her from getting a serious case of that disease.

ANALYSIS SKILL Analyze Time Lines **The Golden Age was a time of great achievement.**
❖ **Why do you think so many advances took place at about the same time?**

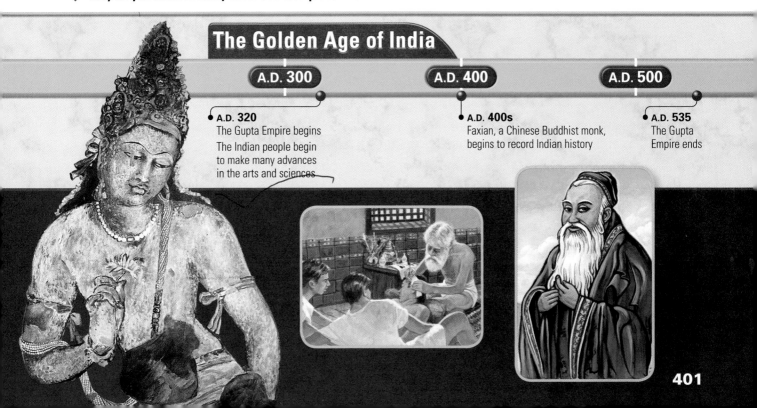

The Golden Age of India

A.D. 300   A.D. 400   A.D. 500

A.D. 320
The Gupta Empire begins
The Indian people begin to make many advances in the arts and sciences

A.D. 400s
Faxian, a Chinese Buddhist monk, begins to record Indian history

A.D. 535
The Gupta Empire ends

Development of Hindu-Arabic Numerals		
HINDU	EARLY ARABIC (WESTERN)	PRESENT-DAY HINDU-ARABIC
o	0	0
१	I	1
२	2	2
३	3	3
४	ع	4
५	Y	5
६	6	6
७	1	7
८	8	8
९	9	9
१०	I0	10

SKILL Analyze Tables

❖ Which Hindu and early Arabic numerals are the most like the Hindu-Arabic numerals we use?

Doctors also helped women give birth more easily and safely. Doctors today have built on many of the ideas of the Golden Age of India.

In addition to spices, cotton cloth, carpets, and jewelry from the Gupta Empire, Arab traders carried news of Indian achievements to places all along the Mediterranean Sea. Indian ideas reached places as far away as Europe and Africa.

Around A.D. 455, the Gupta Empire began to be threatened by invaders known as the Huns. Slowly, these invaders carved away at the empire. By A.D. 535, the Gupta Empire was disappearing, ending India's Golden Age.

READING CHECK MAIN IDEA AND DETAILS
What were two specific achievements made during India's Golden Age?

Summary

In about 320 B.C., Chandragupta Maurya united much of ancient India, creating the Maurya Empire. Ashoka, known for his kindness, spread Buddhism throughout ancient India. In about A.D. 320, the Gupta Empire arose, and India's Golden Age began. The Guptas made achievements in art, literature, mathematics, and medicine.

REVIEW

1. How did the rise of empires change ancient India?

2. Have you had a **turning point** in your life? Explain.

3. How did Chandragupta Maurya increase the size of the Maurya Empire?

4. What were some of the Gupta Empire's major exports?

CRITICAL THINKING

5. Why do you think the time of the Gupta Empire is called India's Golden Age?

6. **SKILL** How did Ashoka's Buddhist beliefs change the way he ruled his empire?

7. **Write a Paragraph** Write a paragraph describing the Indian achievement that you think was the most important. Give reasons to support your choice.

8. **COMPARE AND CONTRAST** On a separate sheet of paper, copy and complete the graphic organizer below.

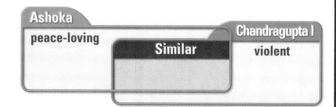

Ashoka — peace-loving | Similar | Chandragupta I — violent

Ashoka

"There is no better work than promoting the welfare of all the people."*

These words were spoken by Ashoka, one of the great leaders of the ancient world. However, Ashoka was not always the kind and peaceful ruler that people remember today.

In about 320 B.C., Ashoka's grandfather, Chandragupta I, united much of northern India into the Maurya Empire. Chandragupta's son, Bindusara, became the next emperor and ruled with a hand as firm and cruel as his father's.

▶ Stone relief from Ashoka's Great Stupa at Sanchi

Ashoka ruled in much the same way at first. He was especially cruel in war. He led his armies into battles in which more than 100,000 people died. Then, after the bloody Battle of Kalinga, Ashoka had a change of heart. He realized the suffering his actions had caused and became a devout Buddhist. He gave up military conquest for what he called "conquest by dharma," meaning "by right life."

Ashoka also launched helpful projects, including building hospitals, digging wells, and providing medicine to his people. Ashoka passed laws to prevent cruelty to people and animals and appointed special officials to relieve suffering. He sent the special officials to different parts of the empire to teach people and to work to ease the suffering he saw.

*Ashoka. *The Edicts of Ashoka*. Narayanrao Appurao Nikam and Richard Peter. University of Chicago Press, 1966.

Biography

Trustworthiness
Respect
Responsibility
Fairness
Caring
Patriotism

Why Character Counts

❓ **How did Ashoka's actions later in his life show caring?**

Bio Brief

273 B.C.	232 B.C.
Reign began	Reign ended

About 273 B.C.
Ashoka takes the throne, and rules strictly

About 261 B.C.
Ashoka becomes a Buddist and turns away from violence

About 250 B.C.
Ashoka sends Buddhist missionaries to other parts of Asia

GO ONLINE

Interactive Multimedia Biographies
Visit MULTIMEDIA BIOGRAPHIES at
www.harcourtschool.com/hss

403

Act as a Responsible Citizen

▶ WHY IT MATTERS

Governments depend on citizens to act responsibly. One way to act responsibly is to keep informed about what is happening in your nation and your community. By keeping informed about current events, citizens prepare themselves to participate in their nation's and their community's government. Then, when the nation faces problems, the citizens can work together to solve those problems.

▶ WHAT YOU NEED TO KNOW

Fortunately for the people he ruled, Ashoka was unlike the other Mauryan rulers. He acted responsibly by being a fair ruler rather than a cruel one. In a democracy such as the United States, all citizens have the opportunity to act responsibly. Here are some steps that you can follow to act as a responsible citizen:

Step 1 Keep informed about problems and concerns in your nation and your community.

Step 2 Think about ways to solve these problems.

Step 3 Decide how to bring about change in ways that would be good for the entire nation or community.

Step 4 Think about how you can help, either alone or with other citizens.

▶ Buddhism inspired Ashoka (left) to rule responsibly. Ashoka and other Mauryan rulers built large Buddhist shrines, called *stupas*, like the one below.

▶ These Japanese-American family members help better their community by cleaning up a park.

▶ PRACTICE THE SKILL

Reread the information about Ashoka in Lesson 4 and in the Biography in this chapter. Then answer the questions.

1 What was life like under the Mauryan rulers before Ashoka?

2 How did Ashoka change life for his people?

3 In what ways did Ashoka act responsibly for his empire?

▶ APPLY WHAT YOU LEARNED

Work with a classmate to identify a problem in your community. Think about how citizens might solve the problem by acting responsibly. Present your ideas to the class.

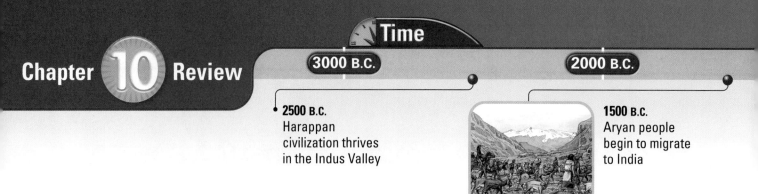

Chapter **10** Review

Time

3000 B.C.　　　　2000 B.C.

2500 B.C.
Harappan
civilization thrives
in the Indus Valley

1500 B.C.
Aryan people
begin to migrate
to India

Reading Social Studies

When you **compare**, you tell how two or more things are alike.
When you **contrast**, you tell how two or more things are different.

Focus Skill Compare and Contrast

Complete this graphic organizer to compare and contrast information about ancient India. A copy of this graphic organizer appears on page 110 of the Homework and Practice Book.

Religions of Ancient India

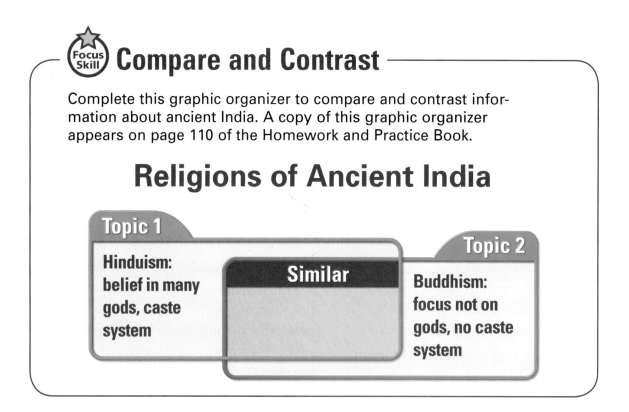

Topic 1

Hinduism:
belief in many
gods, caste
system

Similar

Topic 2

Buddhism:
focus not on
gods, no caste
system

 California Writing Prompts

Write a Research Report Choose a leader from ancient India who you would like to learn more about. Pose questions you would like answered to guide you as you do your research.

Write a Travel Narrative Imagine that you are a traveler in India during its Golden Age. Write a travel narrative about the sights you see and the people you meet.

563 B.C.
The Buddha
is born

261 B.C.
Ashoka
becomes
a Buddhist

A.D. 320
The Golden Age
of India begins

Use Vocabulary

Identify the term that correctly matches each definition.

subcontinent, p. 375

monsoon, p. 376

caste, p. 387

monk, p. 394

turning point, p. 399

1. a seasonal wind

2. an important change

3. a man who devotes his life to studying and teaching religious beliefs

4. a large area of land separated from the rest of a continent by geographic features

5. a group of people in a particular social class

Use the Time Line

 Use the summary time line above to answer these questions.

6. How long after the Buddha was born did Ashoka become a Buddhist?

7. When did the Golden Age of India begin?

Apply Skills

Follow a Flowchart

8. Review pages 380 and 381. Make a flowchart showing how you make something, such as your favorite meal or a craft project.

Recall Facts

Answer these questions.

9. What ancient language gave rise to many languages now spoken in India, and what people spoke this ancient language?

10. What invention of Indian mathematicians does much of the world use today?

11. What advances in medicine did Indian doctors make in ancient India?

Write the letter of the best choice.

12. In the Indian caste system, which group made up the highest class?
    A priests and scholars
    B rulers and warriors
    C farmers, traders, and merchants
    D servants and laborers

13. What happened to Ashoka after he conquered the kingdom of Kalinga?
    A He conquered kingdoms in China.
    B He gave up his rule of India.
    C He rejected violence and became a Buddhist.
    D He started the caste system.

Think Critically

14. **ANALYSIS SKILL** How are Hinduism and Buddhism alike? How are they different?

15. **ANALYSIS SKILL** How did Chandragupta II contribute to India's cultural achievements during the Golden Age?

Study Skills

SKIM AND SCAN

Skimming and scanning are two ways to learn from what you read.

▶ To skim, quickly read the lesson titles and the section titles. Look at the pictures, and read the captions. Use this information to figure out the main topics.

▶ To scan, look quickly through the text for specific details, such as key words or facts.

Skim	Scan
Lesson: The Landscape of China	**Key Words and Facts:**
Main Idea: Geography helped shape early Chinese culture.	• Huang He, Chang Jiang, loess, valleys, floods, "China's Sorrow"
Titles: Mighty Rivers; Mountains, Plateaus, Deserts, and Plains; A World Apart	• This lesson tells how geography affected the people of ancient China.
Visuals: Map showing the geographic features of China	• _____ • _____

Apply As You Read

Before you read each section of a lesson, skim the text to find the topic or main idea of the section. Then, look for key words and facts. If you have any questions about a topic, scan the text to find the answers. Finally, read the entire lesson more slowly and carefully for a more complete understanding.

California History-Social Science Standards, Grade 6

6.6 Students analyze the geographic, political, economic, religious, and social structures of the early civilizations of China.

Ancient China

The Great Wall of China

THE EMPEROR'S SILENT ARMY

TERRACOTTA WARRIORS OF ANCIENT CHINA   BY JANE O'CONNOR

Civilization in China began many thousands of years ago. As early as 100 B.C., the people of China had a written record of their history. Over the years, however, some parts of China's history were lost. Artifacts and other clues about ancient China lay buried, waiting to be rediscovered. In 1974, three farmers made one such discovery. Read on to learn about what they found and how important this discovery is to experts studying China's history today.

It's just an ordinary day in early spring, or so three farmers think as they trudge across a field in northern China. They are looking for a good place to dig a well. There has been a drought, and they must find water or risk losing their crops later in the year.

The farmers choose a spot near a grove of persimmon trees. Down they dig, five feet, ten feet. Still no water. They decide to keep on digging a little deeper. All of a sudden, one of the farmers feels his shovel strike against something hard. Is it a rock? It's difficult to see at the bottom of the dark hole, so the farmer kneels down for a closer look. No, it isn't a rock. It seems to be clay, and not raw clay but clay that has been baked and made into something. But what?

Now, more carefully, the men dig around the something. Perhaps it is a pot or a vase. However, what slowly reveals itself is the pottery head of a man who stares back at them, open-eyed and amazingly real looking. The farmers have never seen anything like it before. But they do remember stories that some of the old people in their village have told, stories of a "pottery man" found many years ago not far from where they are now. The villagers had been scared that the pottery man would bring bad luck so they broke it to bits, which were then reburied and forgotten.

The three well-diggers are not so superstitious. They report their discovery to a local official. Soon a group of archaeologists arrives to search the area more closely. Maybe they will find pieces of a clay body to go with the clay head.

In fact, they find much more. ▶

The entrance to the tomb (above) in Shaanxi Province, China

During the weeks and months that follow, the archaeologists dig out more pottery men, which now are called by a more dignified term—terracotta figurines. The figurines are soldiers. That much is clear. But they come from a time long ago, when Chinese warriors wore knee-length robes, armor made from small iron "fish scales," and elaborate topknot hairdos. All of the soldiers are life-size or a little bigger and weigh as much as four hundred pounds.

They stand at attention as if waiting for the command to charge into battle. The only thing missing is their weapons. And those are found too—hundreds of real bronze swords, daggers, and battle-axes as well as thousands of scattered arrowheads—all so perfectly made that, after cleaning, their ancient tips are still sharp enough to split a hair!

Today, after nearly thirty years of work, terracotta soldiers are still being uncovered and restored. What the well-diggers stumbled upon, purely by accident, has turned out to be

among the largest and most incredible archaeological discoveries of modern times. Along with the Great Pyramids in Egypt, the buried army is now considered one of the true wonders of the ancient world. Spread out over several acres near the city of Xian, the soldiers number not in the tens or hundreds but in the thousands! Probably 7,500 total. Until 1974, nobody knew that right below the people of northern China an enormous underground army had been standing guard, silently and watchfully, for more than 2,200 years. Who put them there?

One man.

Known as the fierce tiger of Qin, the divine Son of Heaven, he was the first emperor of China.

In the tomb, the terracotta soldiers stand in neat rows (left). All of the soldiers were once brightly painted like the soldier at the far left.

1 How do you think archaeologists knew that the terracotta statues represented soldiers from long ago?

2 Do you think artifacts are an important tool in learning about cultures of the past? Why?

Lesson 1

The Landscape of China

WHAT TO KNOW

How did geography help shape early Chinese culture?

- ✓ Explain the role of rivers in the development of early Chinese cultures.
- ✓ Describe how geographic features helped shape life in ancient China.
- ✓ Identify how legends can provide information about life in ancient China.

VOCABULARY

loess p. 415
steppe p. 416
terrace farming p. 416
dialect p. 417
heritage p. 417

PEOPLE

Yu the Great
Shen Nong
Huang Di
Xilingshi

PLACES

Huang He Valley
Chang Jiang Valley

COMPARE AND CONTRAST

California Standards
HSS 6.6, 6.6.1, 6.6.2

YOU ARE THERE

The Huang He has flooded again. Everyone calls this river "China's Sorrow" because of all the trouble and sadness it has caused. You thought you were lucky because no one in your family has drowned. However, so much water has flooded the fields that your family's crops are lost and your family could starve.

You remember the story that your grandmother liked to tell about an ancient hero who conquered the floods. His name was **Yu the Great**, and he lived long ago, before your grandfather's grandfather was born. For 13 years, Yu the Great dug canals that routed flood-waters away from farmers' fields and into the sea.

Digging such big canals must have been hard work. Still, it couldn't have been harder than trying to live with all this water!

FAST FACT

In 1887, the Huang He flooded an area of more than 50,000 square miles. This was the worst flood in the recorded history of the river.

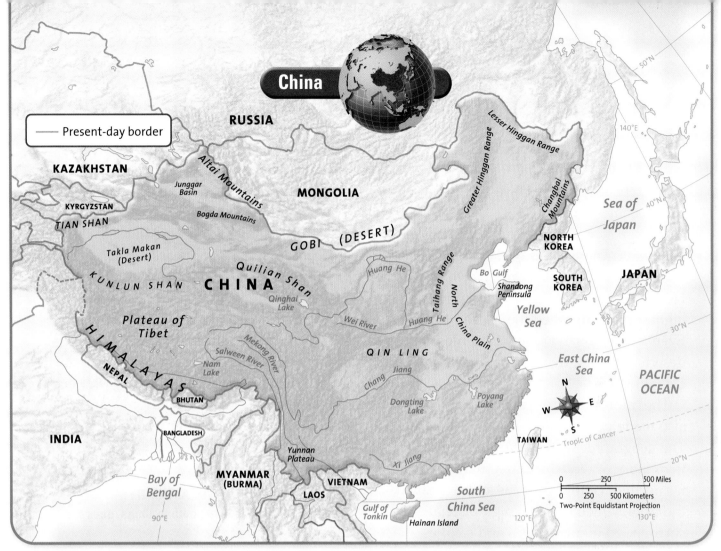

China

Present-day border

RUSSIA
KAZAKHSTAN
Junggar Basin
Altai Mountains
KYRGYZSTAN
Bogda Mountains
TIAN SHAN
MONGOLIA
GOBI (DESERT)
Takla Makan (Desert)
KUNLUN SHAN
Quilian Shan
CHINA
Qinghai Lake
Plateau of Tibet
HIMALAYAS
Salween River
Mekong River
Nam Lake
NEPAL
Wei River
Huang He
QIN LING
Chang Jiang
Dongting Lake
Poyang Lake
BHUTAN
INDIA
BANGLADESH
Yunnan Plateau
Xi Jiang
Bay of Bengal
MYANMAR (BURMA)
VIETNAM
LAOS
Gulf of Tonkin
South China Sea
Hainan Island
Lesser Hinggan Range
Greater Hinggan Range
Changbai Mountains
Huang He
NORTH KOREA
Bo Gulf
Shandong Peninsula
Taihang Range
North China Plain
SOUTH KOREA
Sea of Japan
JAPAN
Yellow Sea
East China Sea
PACIFIC OCEAN
TAIWAN
Tropic of Cancer
50°N
140°E
40°N
30°N
20°N
90°E
120°E
130°E

0   250   500 Miles
0   250   500 Kilometers
Two-Point Equidistant Projection

ANALYSIS SKILL Analyze Maps China's geographic features shaped its early civilizations.

◈ **Regions** Where do you think early civilizations developed in China?

Mighty Rivers

China's rivers helped shape the early civilizations that developed there. This is especially true of the Huang He (HWAHNG HUH) in the north and the Chang Jiang (CHAHNG JYAHNG) in the south.

From the high plateaus of western China, the snow-fed waters of the Huang He flow eastward for about 2,900 miles. As the river crosses China's northern deserts, it cuts through deposits of yellow silt called **loess** (LES). This yellow silt colors the water and gives the Huang He, or "Yellow River," its name. Farther downstream, the Huang He drops the loess along its banks before emptying into the Yellow Sea.

The Chang Jiang, or "Long River," is also known as the Yangtze (YANG•SEH). This river flows about 3,430 miles from the highlands of Tibet to the East China Sea.

Both the Huang He and the Chang Jiang have carved valleys that open to large fertile plains. The Huang He flows through the North China Plain, where China's first farmers lived in the **Huang He Valley** near the Yellow Sea. The soil there is fertile from the loess deposited by the Huang He.

Both rivers can cause terrible floods that destroy homes and drown people. The Huang He's floods can be so bad that the ancient Chinese called it "China's Sorrow."

READING CHECK ✪ **COMPARE AND CONTRAST**
How are the Huang He and the Chang Jiang similar?

Mountains, Plateaus, Deserts, and Plains

To understand the landscape of China, imagine stairs with three steps. If you move across China from west to east, each step becomes lower.

The top step, the highest, would be western China. There stand the Himalayas, the highest mountains on Earth. North of the Himalayas is the world's largest and highest plateau, called the Plateau of Tibet. Even farther north are more tall mountains, deserts, and dry, treeless grasslands called **steppes**.

The middle step, or central China, is also made up of mountains and plateaus. The geographic features are lower here than those of western China. Across the far north of central China is a desert called the Gobi, which sits on a high plateau surrounded by mountains and steppes.

The bottom step, or eastern China, has China's lowest land. The wide valleys and fertile plains of the Huang He and Chang Jiang are located here. A long coastline along the Pacific Ocean makes up almost the entire eastern border of this region.

Eastern China has a varied climate, with the northern part having cold, dry winters and warm, rainy summers. Although the growing season is short, early farmers grew plentiful crops in the Huang He Valley's fertile soil. The warmer, rainier climate of the southern part provides a longer growing season. For centuries, farmers have grown rice in the **Chang Jiang Valley**.

Some Chinese farmers grew rice using **terrace farming**. They dug terraces on the slopes of hills and mountains. Along each terrace's edge, a small wall held in water. Rice was planted in the water-filled terrace.

READING CHECK **MAIN IDEA AND DETAILS**
If you travel from north to south in China, does the climate get wetter or drier?

▶ China is home to a variety of climates and geographic features. The snow-capped Himalayas—the highest mountain range on Earth—help form China's southern border.

▶ A camel caravan follows an ancient desert route in the Takla Makan.

▶ A traveler leads his horse across China's rocky, barren steppes.

A World Apart

In ancient times, the geographic features of China isolated the country from the rest of the world. Natural barriers, such as mountains, deserts, rivers, and seas, made travel to and from China challenging.

The Himalayas in the west and the Gobi in the north were two important geographic barriers. They made the spread of ideas and goods between the ancient Chinese and others outside the region difficult.

The early Chinese were so isolated that they came to believe that China was the world's only civilization. They called the world *Tian Xia* (TYEN SYAH), which means "All Under Heaven." They believed that China was the center of All Under Heaven.

Many geographic features also separated the people living within ancient China. Rivers, deserts, mountains, and great distances made the governing, or rule, of large areas of China difficult. These features also allowed people living in different parts of China to develop their own cultures. The people of each region even had their own **dialect** (DY•uh•lekt), or way of speaking, just like people in China today.

In time, the people of ancient China came to share a common **heritage**, or set of ideas passed down from one generation to another. China's ancient heritage includes legends, or stories passed down from earlier generations.

Many of these legends explain the origins of the land and people of China. One well-known legend tells that the universe began as an egg. Pan Gu, the creator, slept inside the egg until the egg cracked. Then Pan Gu climbed out. He pushed up the top half of the eggshell, and it formed the sky. The bottom half became Earth.

READING CHECK **CAUSE AND EFFECT**
How did geography shape the way that the ancient Chinese understood their place in the world?

▷ In the Chang Jiang Valley, farmers grow rice in water-filled terraces.

▷ Two women walk across a bridge in one of China's rain forests.

Legendary Rulers

Many legends tell of ancient rulers and how they contributed to the Chinese way of life. One such ruler was **Shen Nong**. According to legend, Shen Nong brought agriculture to the people of China. He also studied different herbs to find out which were poisonous and which could be used as medicine. In this way, he is said to have invented traditional Chinese medicine, which is practiced today in China and other parts of the world.

Chinese legends tell of a great ruler known as **Huang Di**, or the "Yellow Emperor." These stories tell that Huang Di ordered the invention of Chinese writing and that he himself created carts, bows and arrows, and houses. They also tell how **Xilingshi** (SEE•LING•SHIR), Huang Di's wife, invented silk cloth.

▶ **Shen Nong**

The story of Yu the Great and the Great Flood may be the most famous Chinese legend of all. This legend tells of a time when terrible floods covered much of China. To save China, Yu the Great dug deep canals that led the floodwaters into the sea. For 13 years, Yu worked to control the floods. When his work was done, farmers could once again plant their crops. People in China still say, "If it were not for Yu the Great, we would all be fishes."

According to other legends, Yu's son became king after Yu's death. His reign is said to have begun the Xia (SHEE•AH) dynasty, which may have ruled parts of China from about 2200 B.C. to about 1766 B.C.

Although historians once believed that the Xia dynasty was pure legend, recent archaeological findings suggest that it probably did exist. This does not mean

▶ According to legend, Yu the Great saved the ancient Chinese people by working to remove the floodwaters covering farmers' lands.

that all of the stories about the dynasty are true, but it is a reminder that legends may contain some truth.

Most of what is told in the legends of ancient China may never have really happened. Even so, these legends give us valuable information about the people of ancient China. They tell us not only how these people lived but also what they believed and what they valued.

READING CHECK **SUMMARIZE**
What can legends tell us about the ancient Chinese?

Summary

China's land and rivers shaped the development of ancient Chinese culture. The Huang He and Chang Jiang gave rise to fertile farmlands and, at times, destructive floods. Geographic features separated the people of ancient China from one another and from other civilizations. In time, the people of China came to share a heritage that includes many legends about the origins of Chinese culture.

REVIEW

1. How did geography help shape early Chinese culture?

2. Write a sentence about China's geography, using the term **steppe**.

3. Why did China's earliest farmers live in the Huang He Valley?

CRITICAL THINKING

4. **ANALYSIS SKILL** What new information might change how historians interpret the Xia dynasty?

5. **Make It Relevant** China's earliest civilizations started near rivers. Where does your community's water come from, and how do you use it in your daily life?

6. **Make a Map** Using maps in this textbook, make a physical map of China that shows the geographic features that helped shape early civilization in China. Be sure to label both land and water features.

7. **Focus Skill** **COMPARE AND CONTRAST** On a separate sheet of paper, copy and complete the graphic organizer below.

Topic 1		Topic 2
Huang He	Similar	Chang Jiang

Read a Climograph

▶ WHY IT MATTERS

The ancient Chinese learned about their climates by recording the amount of rainfall throughout the year. Today people can learn about the climate of a place by studying a **climograph**. This graph shows the average monthly temperature and precipitation of a place.

▶ WHAT YOU NEED TO KNOW

A climograph is both a line graph and a bar graph. The months of the year are shown along the bottom. Along the left-hand side is a temperature scale. Along the right-hand side is a precipitation scale.

Temperatures are shown as a line graph. A dot is placed to show the average temperature for each month. These dots are connected with a line. By studying the line, you can see which months are hotter and which are colder.

Precipitation is shown as a bar graph. A bar is drawn up to the average amount of precipitation for each month. The heights of the bars tell you which months are drier and which months have more rain or snow.

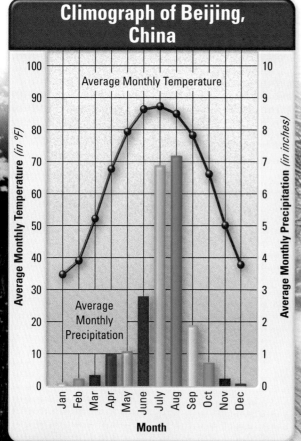

Climograph of Beijing, China

Average Monthly Temperature (in °F) / Average Monthly Precipitation (in inches)

Average Monthly Temperature

Average Monthly Precipitation

Month: Jan Feb Mar Apr May June July Aug Sep Oct Nov Dec

▶ A snowy day in Beijing, China

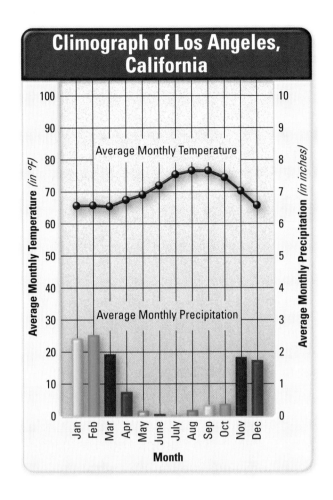

Climograph of Los Angeles, California

Average Monthly Temperature *(in °F)*

Average Monthly Precipitation *(in inches)*

Average Monthly Temperature

Average Monthly Precipitation

Month

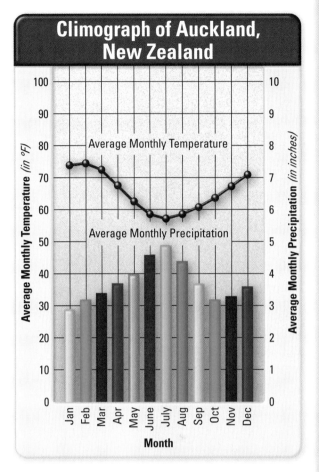

Climograph of Auckland, New Zealand

Average Monthly Temperature *(in °F)*

Average Monthly Precipitation *(in inches)*

Average Monthly Temperature

Average Monthly Precipitation

Month

◗ PRACTICE THE SKILL

The climographs on these pages show weather averages for Beijing, China; Los Angeles, California; and Auckland, New Zealand. Use the climographs to answer these questions.

1 Which are the wettest and driest months in Beijing? in Los Angeles? in Auckland?

2 Which are the hottest and coldest months in Beijing? in Los Angeles? in Auckland?

3 Which city has the highest and lowest average monthly temperatures?

4 In what months do you think China's Huang He River might flood?

◗ APPLY WHAT YOU LEARNED

For the next week, collect information about the weather for the area where you live. Each day, write down the average temperature and precipitation. Try checking the news for this information. Have a family member help. When you have finished collecting information, create your own climograph. Share your graph with classmates to see how your graph compares with their graphs.

Time

3000 B.C.		1500 B.C.		B.C./A.D.

About 1766 B.C.
The Shang control the
Huang He Valley

Around 1122 B.C.
The Zhou dynasty
begins

Around 403 B.C.
The Warring States
Period begins

WHAT TO KNOW
What lasting contributions
did the Shang dynasty and
Zhou dynasty make to China?

✓ Describe the rise of the
Shang dynasty.

✓ Explain how China's
society and government
changed during the Zhou
dynasty.

✓ Describe the basic
teachings of Daoism and
Confucianism.

VOCABULARY
character p. 424
oracle bone p. 424
diviner p. 424
Mandate of Heaven p. 425
virtue p. 425
feudalism p. 425
filial piety p. 427
Confucianism p. 427

PEOPLE
Tang the Successful
Wu
Confucius

PLACES
Huang He Valley
Wei River Valley

**COMPARE AND
CONTRAST**

California
Standards
HSS 6.6, 6.6.1, 6.6.3, 6.6.4

Early Chinese Civilization

YOU ARE THERE

The year is 1766 B.C. Today you are very busy.
Your job is to take care of your family's silkworms. Silkworms don't like noise or strong smells,
but they love to eat mulberry leaves.

After quietly feeding the silkworms, you start to collect
their soft fuzzy cocoons. Once you've gathered enough,
you take them to your mother. She drops them into
boiling water, and they unwind into delicate strands
as thin as hair.

Your mother will need six strands to spin a single
thread. Then she will weave silk cloth from the thread.
Silk is precious and can get a high price.

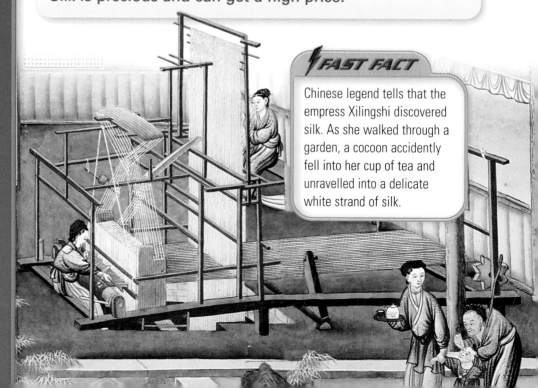

⚡ FAST FACT

Chinese legend tells that the
empress Xilingshi discovered
silk. As she walked through a
garden, a cocoon accidently
fell into her cup of tea and
unravelled into a delicate
white strand of silk.

The Shang Dynasty

TIME 2000 B.C.

PLACE Huang He Valley

In about 2000 B.C., there were hundreds of farming settlements in eastern China near the Huang He and the Chang Jiang. Over time, some settlements grew into villages and a few into powerful kingdoms.

By 1766 B.C., a leader called **Tang the Successful** had brought more than 1,800 villages in the **Huang He Valley** under his rule. This began the Shang dynasty, which ruled more than 600 years.

The origins of Chinese civilization can be traced to the Huang He Valley during the Shang dynasty. Shang society invented a writing system, worked with bronze, had social classes, and lived under a monarchy.

The Shang began their rule by force. Unlike their enemies, the Shang armies used new technologies, including war chariots and bronze-tipped spears. This may have helped the Shang conquer the kingdoms of the Huang He Valley.

During the Shang dynasty, most people lived in farming villages. Farmers grew grain, kept chickens and pigs, and raised silkworms for silk cloth. Metalworkers made bronze tools and weapons as well as beautiful containers that were used in ceremonies to honor ancestors.

Little evidence exists of Shang buildings. Built mostly of wood and mud, these crumbled away long ago. Even so, building foundations of pounded earth show that some Shang cities were large. Some were surrounded by high walls. One Shang city found near the present-day city of Zengzhou (JUHNG•JOH) was protected by walls 6 feet wide and 30 feet high.

While few Shang buildings remain, many Shang artifacts still exist. Archaeologists

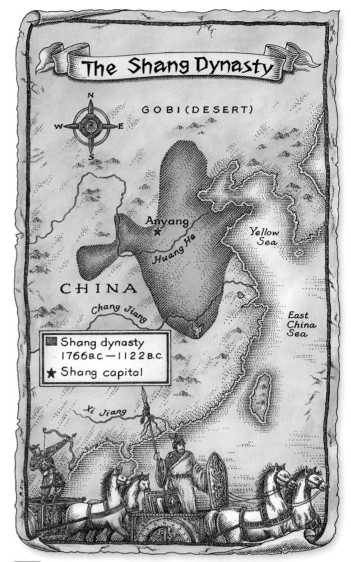

ANALYSIS SKILL **Analyze Maps** The Shang dynasty controlled lands in much of central eastern Asia.

◈ **Regions** Why do you think other groups may have wanted the land controlled by the Shang?

have discovered marble and jade figurines, silk fabrics, and bronze containers buried inside the tombs of wealthy Shang. The Shang made their bronze containers by melting bronze and pouring the liquid metal into molds, an advanced way of working with metal. Their skill in working with bronze also helped the Shang make strong weapons and farming tools.

READING CHECK ☿ **COMPARE AND CONTRAST** What made the Shang armies more powerful than their enemies?

Early Writing and Oracle Bones

One of the most important Shang advances was the invention of a writing system. The Shang writing system consisted of **characters**, or symbols, that represented whole words. Like Egyptian hieroglyphs, many Shang characters were pictures of the things that they named. Present-day Chinese writing has strong roots in Shang characters.

The earliest evidence of Chinese writing is found on animal bones and turtle shells called **oracle bones**. The Shang used these in ceremonies to find out about the future.

Shang kings would visit a **diviner**, a person they believed could help them to speak to the gods and ancestors. The diviner answered questions by touching a bone or shell with a hot metal stick. This caused the bone or shell to crack. The Shang king "read" the cracks to find out the answer to his question. Then, a scribe carved the question and its answer into the oracle bone.

READING CHECK MAIN IDEA AND DETAILS
Why did the Shang kings use oracle bones?

Chinese Writing

WRITING FROM SHANG PERIOD	ENGLISH WORD	PRESENT-DAY CHINESE WRITING
⊙	Sun	日
🌙	Moon	月
Ⴤ	Tree	木
𝇇	Rain	雨

ANALYSIS SKILL **Analyze Tables** This table compares Shang writing to present-day Chinese characters.
❖ **What similarities can you see between the Shang characters and those of the present?**

The Zhou Dynasty

The Zhou (JOH) dynasty was China's longest-ruling dynasty. The dynasty began in 1122 B.C. and ended in 256 B.C. Under the Zhou and the dynasties that followed, China became powerful.

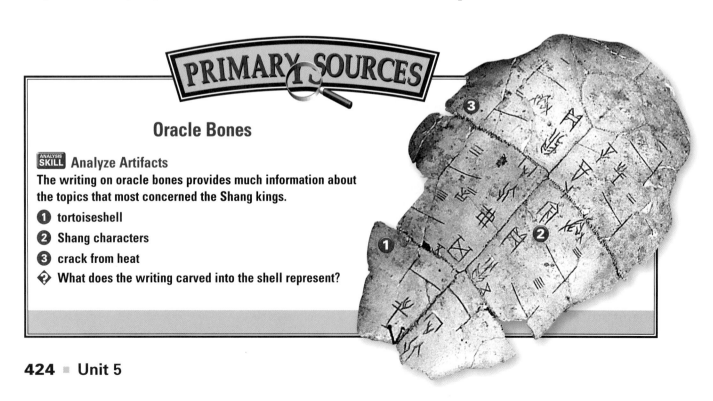

PRIMARY SOURCES

Oracle Bones

ANALYSIS SKILL **Analyze Artifacts**
The writing on oracle bones provides much information about the topics that most concerned the Shang kings.
❶ tortoiseshell
❷ Shang characters
❸ crack from heat
❖ What does the writing carved into the shell represent?

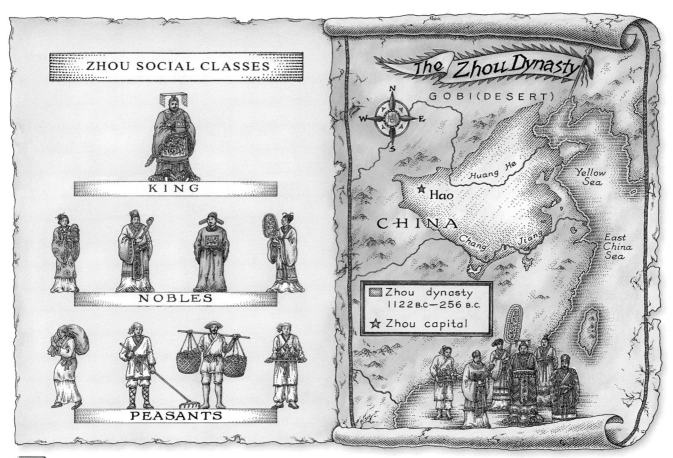

ZHOU SOCIAL CLASSES

KING

NOBLES

PEASANTS

The Zhou Dynasty

GOBI (DESERT)

Huang He

Yellow Sea

★ Hao

CHINA

Chang Jiang

East China Sea

Zhou dynasty
1122 B.C.—256 B.C.

★ Zhou capital

ANALYSIS SKILL **Analyze Maps** The Zhou society was made up of three classes.
❖ What major rivers flowed through the land of the Zhou?

Most historians believe that the Zhou culture began in the **Wei River Valley**, west of the Shang kingdom. In time, the Zhou moved east until they finally met the Shang.

The Zhou worshiped a god they called Tian (TYEN), or "Heaven." In about 1122 B.C., the Zhou ruler, King **Wu**, won victory over the Shang. This conquest led to the beginning of the Zhou dynasty. According to the Zhou, the god Tian allowed King Wu to conquer the Shang kingdom. Tian did this, the Zhou said, because the Shang kings were cruel.

The Zhou believed that Tian gave certain people an order, known as the **Mandate of Heaven**, to rule over China. Zhou kings thought that they would be able to keep the mandate as long as they continued to show **virtue**, or good qualities.

During Zhou rule, the kings set up a social structure with three classes—the king and his family, noble families, and peasant families. Families of each class were expected to show their virtues by offering services to the other classes.

The nobles got their land from the king. In return, they gave the king military support and other services. This political system of exchanging land for loyalty is known as **feudalism**.

The peasants worked the nobles' land and paid them for its use with goods and services. The lives of peasants were full of hardships. Not only did the peasants farm, they also served in Zhou armies. In return, the nobles protected the peasants from the enemies of the Zhou people.

READING CHECK **SUMMARIZE**
What was the social structure of the Zhou?

Decline of the Zhou

In time, the power of the Zhou kings weakened. By 800 B.C., warlike nomads from the north and the west had begun invading Zhou lands. In about 771 B.C., the enemies attacked the Zhou capital of Hao (HOW). They killed the Zhou king and took control of the whole Wei River Valley. Because of this, the Zhou moved their capital city east to the North China Plain.

After the move, the Zhou dynasty was weakened even more by a threat from within. Over time, the power of local nobles had grown. Many nobles began ruling their own lands, claiming independence. Some even called themselves kings.

Those kings fought the Zhou and one another for control over China. During the last two hundred years of the dynasty, the fighting grew worse. For this reason, this time—beginning in 403 B.C.—is sometimes called the Warring Kingdoms Period or the Warring States Period.

The decline of the Zhou dynasty was also a time of cultural growth. The Zhou introduced the use of cavalry, iron tools and weapons, plows pulled by animals, and money in the form of coins.

As the Zhou declined, rulers came up with new forms of government as a way to restore law and order. As early as the 600s B.C., the kingdom of Chu (JOO) had replaced feudalism with a new kind of government. The Chu kings divided their kingdom into counties. They selected people to run the counties based on their skill.

In 535 B.C., the king of Zheng (JUHNG), a kingdom in the North China Plain, decided that virtue alone was not enough to keep order. Instead, he ordered that written laws be created to make sure people could tell right from wrong. These were the first written laws in China.

READING CHECK **MAIN IDEA AND DETAILS**
How did the Zheng king try to maintain order in his kingdom?

▶ Archaeologists carefully excavate a carriage dating to the Zhou dynasty.

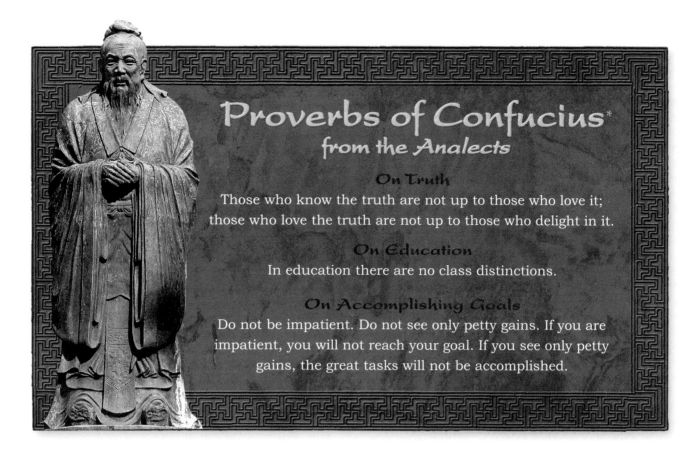

Proverbs of Confucius*
from the Analects

On Truth
Those who know the truth are not up to those who love it;
those who love the truth are not up to those who delight in it.

On Education
In education there are no class distinctions.

On Accomplishing Goals
Do not be impatient. Do not see only petty gains. If you are
impatient, you will not reach your goal. If you see only petty
gains, the great tasks will not be accomplished.

The Ideas of Confucius

One of China's greatest teachers and thinkers lived during the Zhou dynasty. He was called Kong Fuzi, or **Confucius** (kuhn•FYOO•shuhs), meaning "Great Master Kong." Confucius was very concerned by the fighting, the problems of government, and the loss of traditional values of his times. He spent his life thinking about how to return goodness and order to China.

Confucius used short sayings to teach his ideas. These were easy to understand and remember. His goal was to have people live and work well together. His sayings often told of the importance of good behavior, kindness, tradition, respect for elders, and education.

Confucius also taught that the family was a model for government and society. In Chinese culture, children were expected to treat their parents with honor and respect, called **filial piety**. Confucius thought that

people should use filial piety as a model for showing honor and respect for their rulers.

In return, Confucius said that rulers should show others the same love that parents show to their children. He did not think that written laws and punishment could bring social order. Instead, he drew on the old Zhou ideas of showing virtue and leading by example.

Confucius taught that every person had to do specific duties to bring goodness to society. He thought of these duties in terms of five relationships—parent to child, ruler to subject, older brother to younger brother, husband to wife, and friend to friend.

For Confucius, a good society was not an equal society. For example, as a wife, a woman's duty was to obey and follow her husband.

For the most part, Confucius's ideas were ignored during his life. After his death, however, his ideas spread across eastern Asia and came to be called **Confucianism**.

*Confucius. *The Analects of Confucius.* Simon Leys, trans. Norton, 1997.

► This bronze disk (above) is one symbol of Chinese philosophy. Laozi (statue at right) started Daoism.

Another philosophy, that of Daoism (DOW•ih•zuhm), also spelled Taoism, grew up alongside Confucianism. Daoists, like Confucianists, opposed violence. In addition to following human laws, they believed that people should follow the laws of the universe. They did this by living in peace with one another and with nature.

READING CHECK SUMMARIZE
How did events in China influence Confucius?

Summary

China's early dynasties made many contributions to Chinese culture. The Shang dynasty used new technologies to conquer its neighbors and developed China's first writing system. Under the Zhou dynasty, rulers introduced feudalism. Trouble and violence in the Zhou dynasty gave rise to new forms of government and thought, including Confucianism and Daoism.

REVIEW

1. What lasting contributions did the Shang dynasty and the Zhou dynasty make to China?

2. How are **virtue** and the **Mandate of Heaven** related?

3. How does the political system of feudalism work?

CRITICAL THINKING

4. **ANALYSIS SKILL** Which of the basic teachings of Confucianism do you think would have best helped the Chinese people restore order?

5. **Make It Relevant** Are proverbs still a good way to pass along knowledge? Explain.

6. **Write a Paragraph** Imagine that you are an archaeologist who has just found a collection of oracle bones. Write a paragraph that tells why the bones should be studied.

7. **Focus Skill** **COMPARE AND CONTRAST**
On a separate sheet of paper, copy and complete the graphic organizer below.

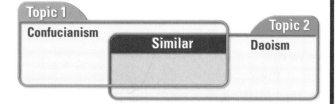

Topic 1
Confucianism

Similar

Topic 2
Daoism

Confucius

*"What you do not wish for yourself, do not do to others."**

Biography

Trustworthiness
Respect
Responsibility
Fairness
Caring
Patriotism

Confucius was born during the second half of the Zhou dynasty. By the age of 15, he was a gifted student. By the age of 30, Confucius had become a well-known teacher, wanting to make education available to all men.

Confucius developed his ideas as he looked at the world around him. He grew unhappy with the moral values of his society. Confucius saw people committing crimes. He became disturbed when he saw the rich become richer while the poor became poorer.

Confucius believed strongly in the idea of respect. He taught that respect for oneself and for other people are the keys to a virtuous life and an orderly society. That is why he created his Golden Rule: "What you do not wish for yourself, do not do to others."*

Confucius believed that the goal of every person should be to gain *jen*, or humanity. Living by the Golden Rule and respecting and obeying family members would help a person gain *jen*. Confucius also believed that people and their rulers should respect each other just as they should respect the members of their families.

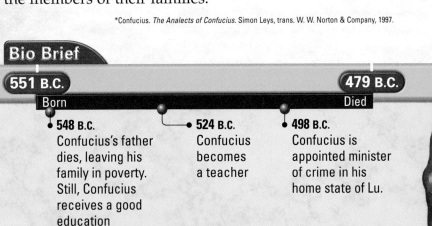

▶ Confucius with a group of students

*Confucius. *The Analects of Confucius.* Simon Leys, trans. W. W. Norton & Company, 1997.

Why Character Counts

❓ **What role did respect play in the teachings of Confucius?**

Bio Brief

551 B.C.		479 B.C.
Born		Died

548 B.C.
Confucius's father dies, leaving his family in poverty. Still, Confucius receives a good education

524 B.C.
Confucius becomes a teacher

498 B.C.
Confucius is appointed minister of crime in his home state of Lu.

Interactive Multimedia Biographies
Visit **MULTIMEDIA BIOGRAPHIES** at
www.harcourtschool.com/hss

The Best Way to Govern

Between 600 B.C. and 200 B.C., four of China's most important thinkers wrote about government. One of these was Confucius. Laozi, another important thinker, was the founder of the philosophy known as Daoism. Sunzi wrote *The Art of War* and is believed to have lived in the 300s B.C. Hanfeizi helped create the philosophy of Legalism. These philosophers had different ideas about the world. They also had different views about government and how rulers should act. Here are some of their thoughts about government and rulers.

In Their Own Words

Confucius, the author of *Lunyu,* or *The Analects*

❝...When the ruler is correct himself, all the people will follow his government. What the ruler does is what the people follow. How should they follow what he does not do?❞

— from *Book of Rites: An Encyclopedia of Ancient Ceremonial Usages, Religious Creeds, and Social Institutions.* Vol. I. James Legge, trans., Ch'u Chai and Winberg Chai, eds. University Books, 1967.

CONFUCIUS

430

LAOZI

Laozi, the founder of Daoism

"The best rulers are scarcely known by their subjects;
The next best are loved and praised;
The next are feared;
The next despised:
They have no faith in their people,
And their people become unfaithful to them.
When the best rulers achieve their purpose
Their subjects claim the achievement as their own. "

— from *Dao De Jing* by Lao-tzu. Penguin Books, 1963.

Sunzi, the author of *The Art of War*

"The consummate [best] leader cultivates the moral law,
and strictly adheres to method and discipline; thus it is in his
power to control success. "

— from *The Art of War*, by Sun-tzu. James Clavell, ed. Delacorte Press, 1983.

SUNZI

HANFEIZI

Hanfeizi, the author of *Han Fei Zi*

"That being so, rewards should not be other than great
and certain, thus making the people regard them as profitable;
punishments should not be other than severe and definite, thus
making the people fear them; and laws should not be other
than uniform and steadfast, thus making the people compre-
hend [understand] them. "

— from *The Complete Works of Han Fei Zi: A Classic of Chinese Political Science*.
Vol II. W. K. Liao, ed., trans. Arthur Probsthian, 1959.

It's Your Turn

ANALYSIS SKILL **Analyze Points of View** Work with a partner
to describe the kind of government each philosopher
would want to see. Then choose the philosopher you
agree with the most, and give reasons for your choice.

Make It Relevant What do you think is the best way to
govern a nation in today's world?

Lesson 3

Time

3000 B.C.   1500 B.C.   B.C./A.D.

256 B.C.
The Zhou dynasty
collapses

221 B.C.
The Qin dynasty
unites China

210 B.C.
Shi Huangdi, China's
first emperor, dies

WHAT TO KNOW
What did Shi Huangdi do
to unite northern China?

✔ Describe Shi Huangdi's
policies and rule.

✔ Explain the lasting
influences of the Qin
dynasty and Shi Huangdi.

VOCABULARY
Legalism p. 433
bureaucracy p. 434
province p. 434
standardization p. 435

PEOPLE
Shi Huangdi
Li Si

PLACES
Wei River Valley

 COMPARE AND
CONTRAST

 California
Standards
HSS 6.6, 6.6.5

Uniting China

YOU ARE THERE

The year is 210 B.C. For months, your father has
been living with soldiers. Not real ones—these
soldiers are statues made of clay.

Your father is a master sculptor in the service of the
emperor **Shi Huangdi**, ruler of all China. Every day,
your father molds and shapes clay into soldiers. When
he finishes one, he takes it to a huge cave guarded by
the emperor's soldiers—real ones!

Today, you traveled with your father to deliver the
statue to the cave. Inside, you saw thousands and
thousands of soldiers like the one your father sculpted
for the emperor!

The First Chinese Empire

⏱ **TIME** 256 B.C.

🌐 **PLACE** Wei River Valley

Qin (CHIN) began as a small state in the western region of the **Wei River Valley**. During the Warring States Period, the kingdom grew as Qin generals conquered other states. The unbeatable Qin army rode horses into battle and fought with iron weapons. When the Zhou dynasty finally fell in 256 B.C., Qin became northern China's most powerful state.

In 246 B.C., a 13-year-old boy took the Qin throne. With the help of a powerful Qin government official named **Li Si** (LEE SUH), the boy grew to become a successful king. By 221 B.C., the Qin kingdom controlled all of the northern states. The Warring States Period was over—the Qin king now ruled over China's first empire.

After founding the Qin Empire, the king named himself Qin Shi Huangdi (CHIN SHIR HWAHNG•DEE), or the "First Emperor of China."

ANALYSIS SKILL **Analyze Maps** Shi Huangdi (left) conquered several warring kingdoms in northern China and founded the Qin dynasty.

❓ **Regions** Why do you think the Qin built a capital near the Huang He?

Shi Huangdi expected his dynasty to rule for generations, but that was not to be. The Qin dynasty lasted only 15 years, until 206 B.C., just four years after his death. Yet in this short time, Shi Huangdi unified northern China and made changes that had a lasting influence on China. Even the name *China* comes from the name *Qin*.

Shi Huangdi did not rule by showing respect, as Confucius had taught. Shi Huangdi relied on fear to rule. His way of governing, called **Legalism**, gave absolute power to one ruler, who governed under strict laws. Legalism allowed Shi Huangdi to create an efficient government, but it was cruel. The government strictly enforced its laws. Those who did not obey faced severe punishments. Shi Huangdi ruled harshly and killed those who opposed him.

READING CHECK 🔍 **COMPARE AND CONTRAST**
How did Shi Huangdi's philosophy of governing differ from that of Confucius?

more monch by the well

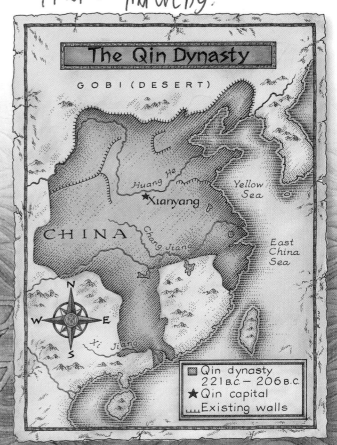

The Qin Dynasty

GOBI (DESERT)

Huang He

Yellow Sea

★ Xianyang

CHINA

Chang Jiang

East China Sea

N W E S

Xi Jiang

■ Qin dynasty 221 B.C. – 206 B.C.
★ Qin capital
⌐⌐ Existing walls

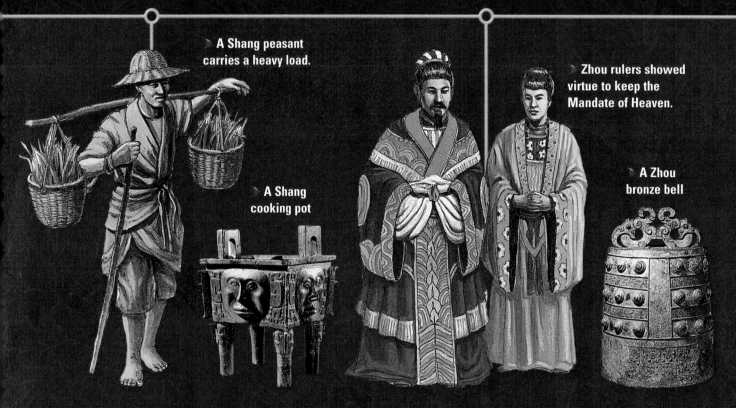

SHANG DYNASTY
AND FEUDALISM
1766 B.C.–1122 B.C.

ZHOU DYNASTY
AND THE MANDATE OF HEAVEN
1122 B.C.–256 B.C.

▶ A Shang peasant
carries a heavy load.

▶ A Shang
cooking pot

▶ Zhou rulers showed
virtue to keep the
Mandate of Heaven.

▶ A Zhou
bronze bell

Building a Bureaucracy

Legalism needed a strong government to control the people and the economy. To keep this control, Shi Huangdi built both a strong army and a bureaucracy (byu•RAH•kruh•see). A **bureaucracy** is a large group of appointed officials.

The old feudal system, which depended on noble families, had to be broken apart before Legalism could replace it. Feudal lords ruled their land and collected taxes. Shi Huangdi wanted his own officials to control the land and taxes. He also did not trust the nobles, so he ordered land to be taken away from them. Then he gave some of the land to the peasants. The peasants' taxes went straight to his government instead of first passing through the hands of feudal lords.

To prevent the nobles from turning against him, Shi Huangdi forced them all to move to the Qin capital city of **Xianyang** (SHYEN•YANG). There, officials watched the nobles to make sure they did not rise up against the emperor.

To further protect against rebellion, Shi Huangdi made it against the law for people who were not in his army to have weapons. Any weapons that did not belong to the army were collected and melted.

In place of feudal lands, Shi Huangdi divided the empire into many **provinces**, or administrative regions. He further divided each province into districts. Shi Huangdi then picked officials to manage the provinces and districts. He also sent out people to report back on the officials. This system of dividing large areas and the management of those areas among officials was important for China's later dynasties.

READING CHECK **CAUSE AND EFFECT**
Why did Shi Huangdi take power and land away from the nobles?

QIN DYNASTY
AND LEGALISM
221 B.C.–206 B.C.

HAN DYNASTY
AND CONFUCIANISM
202 B.C.–A.D. 220

› A Qin artisan casts standardized coins.

› A Han civil servant studies Confucianism.

› A Qin coin

› The official seal of a Han empress

Standardization

Shi Huangdi made other changes that helped unify his empire's people and economy. Before his rule, people in different parts of the empire paid for goods with different kinds of money. They also used different units for weights and measures. Lastly, the people of China did not share a common writing system.

To overcome these differences, Shi Huangdi began a policy of standardization. Standardization is making systems, such as money, weights and measures, and writing, the same for everyone.

To standardize writing, Shi Huangdi allowed only two kinds of Chinese writing. People had to use one kind for official documents and stone carvings and another, which was easier to write, for everyday uses. Standardized writing improved communication and recordkeeping.

To improve trade, Shi Huangdi standardized coins and the units for weights and measures. He also ordered the building of canals and roads to connect major cities within the empire. Shi Huangdi required that all roads, as well as the carts that traveled on the roads, have the same width.

Education became another focus of standardization. Shi Huangdi wanted tight control of all the books used to teach. His advisor Li Si said that too many books questioned Qin ideas. Because of this, Shi Huangdi ordered certain books, including many about Confucianism, to be burned.

Although some of Shi Huangdi's policies were harsh, most helped different groups in the empire think of themselves as one united people. This unification made the empire easier to control.

READING CHECK **SUMMARIZE**
What steps did Shi Huangdi take toward standardization? he unified the divides

Building a Great Wall

One of Shi Huangdi's best-known projects was a defensive wall. Invaders from the north who raided on horseback threatened the empire. Earlier rulers had built smaller walls to keep the invaders out. Shi Huangdi ordered workers to begin connecting the existing walls to make one long wall. The new wall was meant to protect all of the empire.

Clearly, Shi Huangdi wanted to take care of his empire. He did not, however, take care of the workers. For about ten years, he forced hundreds of thousands of workers to build the wall. Many workers did not have enough to eat. Some worked in freezing weather without warm clothing.

They were far away from their families, and they had no one to take care of them if they got sick. As a result, many workers died.

Depending on available materials, workers used stones, bricks, and dirt to build the wall. Under Shi Huangdi, the wall stood 25 feet high and 20 feet wide and stretched for more than 3,000 miles from east to west.

Along the wall, soldiers kept watch from 40-foot-high towers. If they saw enemies approaching, they used smoke or fire to signal soldiers in the next tower. These signals traveled from tower to tower along the wall, eventually reaching the capital. This system let the government know what was going on along the entire northern border of the empire.

Despite the wall, invaders from the north continued to attack the Qin Empire. Even after later emperors extended the wall, the raids continued.

READING CHECK SUMMARIZE
What was the purpose of Shi Huangdi's wall?

GEOGRAPHY

The Great Wall

Visitors to China marvel at the Great Wall. The Great Wall that exists today is a result of construction started in A.D. 1368. This Great Wall is much grander than Shi Huangdi's wall. Much of the Great Wall is 25 feet high and just as wide. It is made mostly from brick and stone and features tall watchtowers. It extends from the Bo Gulf of the Yellow Sea in the east to the Lop Nur region of western China. Its many sections and branches cover more than 4,500 miles.

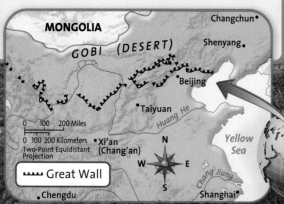

MONGOLIA

GOBI (DESERT)

Changchun

Shenyang

Beijing

Taiyuan

Huang He

0   100   200 Miles
0   100 200 Kilometers
Two-Point Equidistant
Projection

Xi'an
(Chang'an)

N
W   E
S

Yellow
Sea

Chang Jiang

⌐⌐⌐ Great Wall

Chengdu

Shanghai

The Emperor's Clay Army

Shi Huangdi planned a great burial place for himself. He ordered the building of a grand tomb as soon as he took the Qin throne, when he was only 13 years old. The tomb had been under construction for more than 30 years. It was still not finished at the time of his death.

By chance, some Chinese farmers discovered Shi Huangdi's tomb in the 1970s while drilling a water well. Archaeologists went on to excavate the site. Parts of the tomb had been robbed in ancient times, but much of it remained a secret for 2,000 years.

Shi Huangdi's tomb is one of the most amazing archaeological sites ever discovered. The most surprising thing about the tomb is its army of larger than life-size soldiers made of clay and holding real weapons. Each figure is remarkably lifelike and is different from all the others.

So far, more than 7,000 soldiers have been uncovered. The entire army faces east, the direction of other kingdoms that

❯ An army of clay soldiers, thousands strong, stands guard at the entrance of Shi Huangdi's tomb.

Shi Huangdi had conquered. The tomb also contains life-size clay horses and wood-and-bronze war chariots.

All these figures were originally painted with bright colors. Over the years in which the army has stood silent guard over the emperor's tomb, most of the paint has faded and worn off.

The tomb's site extends over a huge area and may have been designed to look like an imperial city. The work required to build such a tomb tells how important it was to Shi Huangdi. He made sure he would have everything and everyone he needed for the afterlife.

An artist (far right) makes a reproduction of clay soldiers buried with Shi Huangdi (right).

Shi Huangdi was buried in his tomb upon his death in 210 B.C. His son became emperor, but he could not keep control of the empire as his father had done. Power struggles broke out among government officials, who fought and killed one another. The people of the empire rebelled.

READING CHECK **DRAW CONCLUSIONS**
What kinds of information about the Qin might archaeologists gain from the discovery of Shi Huangdi's tomb?

Summary

Shi Huangdi unified northern China under the Qin dynasty, creating China's first empire. During his short reign, emperor Shi Huangdi made many policies and changes to strengthen the empire. He governed under the system of Legalism, created a bureaucracy, and used standardization. Shi Huangdi is also remembered for his contribution to the Great Wall and for his tomb.

REVIEW

1. What did Shi Huangdi do to unite northern China?

2. Use the terms **Legalism** and **bureaucracy** in a sentence.

3. What kind of ruler was Shi Huangdi?

4. What were the benefits of road building and of the standardization of money?

CRITICAL THINKING

5. **ANALYSIS SKILL** Shi Huangdi was able to gain power over northern China. Why might his son have been unable to keep that power?

6. **Make It Relevant** Do you think Shi Huangdi could be a successful leader in the United States today? Explain.

7. **Make a Model** Make a model of the Great Wall as it stands today out of construction paper, cardboard, or modeling clay. If these materials are not available, draw a picture of the wall. Label the wall with facts about its construction.

8. **Focus Skill** **COMPARE AND CONTRAST** On a separate sheet of paper, copy and complete the graphic organizer below.

Topic 1 — Feudalism | Similar | Topic 2 — Legalism

Shi Huangdi

Trustworthiness
Respect
Responsibility
Fairness
Caring
Patriotism

*"The reason why China suffers bitterly from endless wars is because of the existence of feudal lords and kings."**

Born with the name Chao Cheng, Shi Huangdi was the son of King Zhuang Xiang, ruler of the Qin kingdom. When Chao Cheng was only 13 years old, he became king of the Qin. However, Cheng's adviser, Lu Bu Wei, was the actual ruler until Cheng was 21.

In about 238 B.C., Chao Cheng began to defeat Qin's rival kingdoms. By 221 B.C., all of China was under his control. This made Chao Cheng the first supreme ruler of China. He took the name Shi Huangdi, which means "First Emperor," to show his new power.

Shi Huangdi's goals were to strengthen his empire and to unify its people. To accomplish these goals, Shi Huangdi tried to standardize Chinese language. He also tried to give the empire a single standard of measurement and a single standard of money. He hoped that these acts would bring people together and help the government rule more effectively. Shi Huangdi also began construction of the Great Wall. He believed it would protect China from invaders and preserve its glory for "10,000 generations."

Shi Huangdi was dedicated to making China powerful. However, he was not successful in his efforts. After his death, the empire fell apart. In the end, it was only Shi Huangdi's power and dedication that helped his ideas live on in China's history.

Shi Huangdi. *Records of the Grand Historian of China.* Ssu-ma Chi'en, author, Burton Watson, trans. Jacques Barzun, ed. Columbia University Press, 1961.

Why Character Counts

❓ **How did Shi Huangdi's actions reflect his patriotism?**

Bio Brief

259 B.C.
Born

246 B.C. Chao Cheng becomes king of the Qin

221 B.C. Chao Cheng unifies China under the Qin and renames himself Shi Huangdi

214 B.C. Shi Huangdi orders construction of the Great Wall to begin

210 B.C.
Died

GO ONLINE

Interactive Multimedia Biographies
Visit MULTIMEDIA BIOGRAPHIES at
www.harcourtschool.com/hss

439

Map and Globe Skills

Identify Changing Borders

▶ WHY IT MATTERS

Borders show what nation or group controls a region during a particular period of time. Seeing how borders change helps us better understand world history. Borders can change because of wars or invasions. They also can change because of natural disasters or large movements of people. Shifts in borders can even show the rise or decline of a country, kingdom, or empire. You can learn how the borders of countries have changed and how different parts of the world looked in the past by comparing maps from different time periods.

▶ WHAT YOU NEED TO KNOW

By looking at historical atlases or history books, you can find maps of different time periods. Titles or map keys usually identify the time period of a map. Color is often used to show which lands are controlled by different countries.

Most maps show geographical features as well as political borders. Sometimes political borders follow rivers or mountain ranges. They can be used to describe where borders begin and end.

Recall that borders that exist at one time in history may not exist at another time.

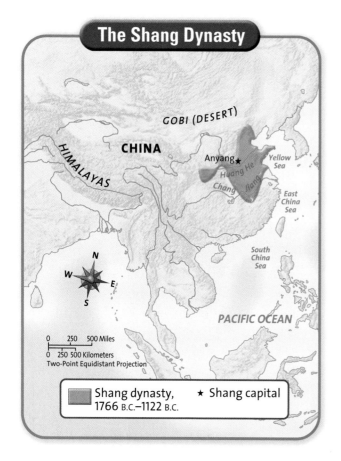

The Shang Dynasty

GOBI (DESERT)

CHINA

Anyang ★
Huang He
Yellow Sea
Chang Jiang
East China Sea

HIMALAYAS

South China Sea

N W E S

PACIFIC OCEAN

0   250   500 Miles
0 250 500 Kilometers
Two-Point Equidistant Projection

▨ Shang dynasty, 1766 B.C.–1122 B.C.   ★ Shang capital

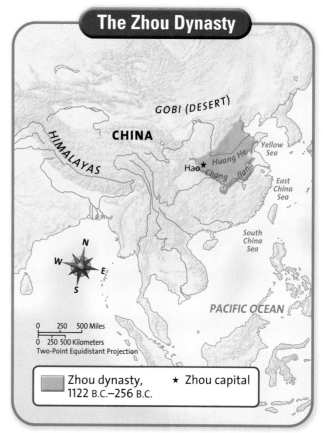

The Zhou Dynasty

GOBI (DESERT)

CHINA

Yellow Sea
Hao ★ Huang He
Chang Jiang
East China Sea

HIMALAYAS

South China Sea

N W E S

PACIFIC OCEAN

0   250   500 Miles
0 250 500 Kilometers
Two-Point Equidistant Projection

▨ Zhou dynasty, 1122 B.C.–256 B.C.   ★ Zhou capital

It is important to know exactly when each border was in effect. That way you can understand the change over time.

▶ PRACTICE THE SKILL

Use what you know about maps and changing borders to compare the Shang, Zhou, Qin, and Han dynasties.

1 Which dynasty's borders extended the farthest west?

2 Which natural features, if any, form the borders of each dynasty?

3 How would you describe each dynasty in terms of its borders?

▶ APPLY WHAT YOU LEARNED

Look at a map of present-day China. Compare its borders with the borders of China's ancient dynasties. Then write two questions about the differences for a classmate to answer.

Practice your map and globe skills with the **GeoSkills CD-ROM**.

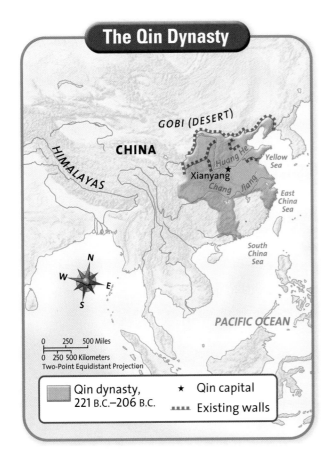

The Qin Dynasty

GOBI (DESERT)

HIMALAYAS

CHINA

Huang He
Xianyang ★
Chang Jiang

Yellow Sea

East China Sea

South China Sea

PACIFIC OCEAN

0   250   500 Miles
0 250 500 Kilometers
Two-Point Equidistant Projection

☐ Qin dynasty, 221 B.C.–206 B.C.
★ Qin capital
▪▪▪▪ Existing walls

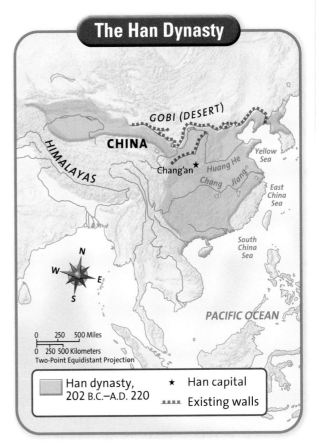

The Han Dynasty

GOBI (DESERT)

HIMALAYAS

CHINA

Chang'an ★ Huang He
Chang Jiang

Yellow Sea

East China Sea

South China Sea

PACIFIC OCEAN

0   250   500 Miles
0 250 500 Kilometers
Two-Point Equidistant Projection

☐ Han dynasty, 202 B.C.–A.D. 220
★ Han capital
▪▪▪▪ Existing walls

Map and Globe Skills

Time

3000 B.C.	1500 B.C.	B.C./A.D.

202 B.C.
The Han dynasty
begins in China

141 B.C.
Wu Di becomes
the Han emperor

101 B.C.
Wu Di conquers parts of
Korea and Vietnam

WHAT TO KNOW
What lasting impact
did the Han dynasty have
on China's culture and
government?

✓ Describe the Han's
Confucian government
and Wu Di's civil service.

✓ Summarize the political
contributions and the
cultural achievements
of the Han.

✓ Explain the importance
of the Silk Road.

VOCABULARY
civil service p. 444
ambassador p. 445
Silk Road p. 445

PEOPLE
Liu Bang
Gaozu
Wu Di
Sima Qian

PLACES
Chang'an
Xianyang
Xi'an

**COMPARE AND
CONTRAST**

California
Standards
HSS 6.6, 6.6.6, 6.6.7, 6.6.8

A Time of Achievement

YOU ARE THERE
The year is 100 B.C., and today you will take
the hardest and most important test of your
life. You've prepared for many years, reading the works
of Confucius so many times that you can recite the
Analects by heart. Still, you are very nervous because
your entire future may depend on whether you pass this
test. Only the best students will earn recom-
mendations for jobs in the government.

Your father worked for the government,
and so did his father before him. This
doesn't mean that you'll get a job. You
must prove your own skill by passing this
test. To pass would mean continued honor
for your family.

▶ This painting (below) from a later time shows students
on their way to take an exam. This clay statue (right) was
made during the Han dynasty.

The Han Dynasty

⏱ **TIME** 206 B.C.
🌐 **PLACE** Huang He Valley

The Qin dynasty fell in 206 B.C., and a period of civil war followed. Peasants, Qin generals and officials, and nobles fought one another for power. That same year, **Liu Bang**, a Qin official, claimed the title of king of Han, a state within the Qin Empire.

With the support of his army, Liu Bang had gained control over all the former Qin lands by 202 B.C. He declared himself emperor and was given the name of Han **Gaozu** (GOW•ZOO), or "High Ancestor."

Gaozu's rule began the Han dynasty, one of the most important dynasties in China's history. Even today, many Chinese call themselves *Han-ren*, or Han People. The long-lasting Han dynasty continued for more than 400 years, until A.D. 220.

The Han made their capital **Chang'an** (CHAHNG•AHN), near the old Qin capital of **Xianyang**. Chang'an later became known as **Xi'an** (SHEE•AHN).

As the first Han emperor, Gaozu was well-liked by the peasants. Because he came from a family of poor farmers, Gaozu understood how hard peasant life was. He helped the peasants by giving them land and reducing their taxes.

Gaozu, and later Han emperors, built on the Qin achievement of uniting China. Like the Qin, the Han accepted the idea of a strong central government and an all-powerful leader. Unlike the Qin, the Han followed some of the teachings of Confucius. Han rule became known for mixing Confucian and Legalist ideas.

The Han dynasty emperors came to be as feared and respected as Shi Huangdi had been, yet they did not use the many laws of the Qin. Instead, they depended

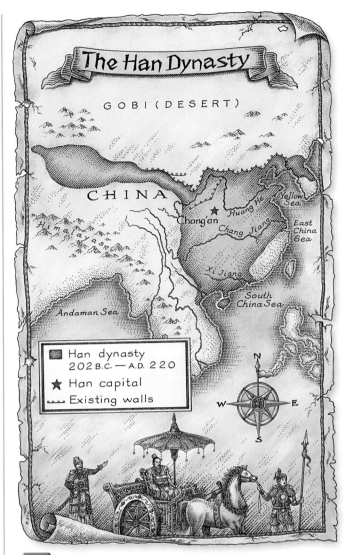

ANALYSIS SKILL **Analyze Maps** The Han dynasty continued to expand the borders of China by conquering new lands.
❖ **Regions** Which natural features may have slowed the Han's expansion of the empire?

on the Confucian idea that people should obey their rulers in the same way that children obey their parents.

The use of both Legalist and Confucian ideas helped the Han rulers make important political contributions that changed the course of China's history. They led to expansion of China's empire. At the same time, they brought about development of an imperial bureaucratic state, which lasted more than 2,000 years.

READING CHECK ⏱ **COMPARE AND CONTRAST**
How did Han rule compare to that of the Qin?

Wu Di and Civil Service

In 141 B.C., **Wu Di** (WOO DEE) rose to the Han throne. The name Wu Di, or "Warlike Emperor," suited him well. He formed large armies, some with as many as 300,000 soldiers, to protect and expand the empire.

Wu Di sent soldiers north to drive back tribes who tried to attack the empire. He also used armies to add more lands to the empire. By 101 B.C., Wu Di's expansion of the empire included western China and parts of ancient Korea and Vietnam.

Wu Di's military wins had a price. To pay for his troops and growing empire, the emperor created new taxes. These new taxes were not popular with the people.

Wu Di had a deep respect for the ideas of Confucius. The Qin had burned books about Confucianism. Wu Di started a university to teach Confucian ideas. He also made Confucianism the empire's official religion.

Wu Di even founded China's first civil service on Confucian ideals. A **civil service** is a part of a bureaucracy that does the day-to-day running of a government. According to Confucius, only skilled people should govern a state.

Wu Di helped start a system in which civil servants could be picked based on their abilities and achievements. Before, government jobs had been filled through family ties and loyalty to the emperor. Under the Han, educated people could become civil servants by passing written tests.

The civil service that Wu Di set up had many benefits. It placed educated people in government jobs. It also let people who did well on these tests receive jobs and social status. This meant that education became more important than ever in China.

READING CHECK Ŏ**COMPARE AND CONTRAST**
What made the Han civil service different from earlier methods of running the government?

❯ Chinese merchants frequently traveled the Silk Road in camel caravans. Often, Buddhist monks traveled with the merchants to spread the ideas of their religion.

Cultural Achievements

Beginning in about 200 B.C., China entered a Golden Age. Success in war, economic growth, and education led to good times for the Han Empire.

Art also flourished under the Han. Artists made China's first major stone sculptures. They also became skilled at painting land and people as well as at silk weaving and pottery making.

The Han also took giant steps in science. They improved the way they made paper and built the first seismograph, an instrument that shows the location and strength of an earthquake. They also invented sundials and water clocks to measure time.

Han writers enjoyed great success as well. Many poems written during the Han dynasty are still read in China today. One writer, **Sima Qian** (SOO•MAH CHIH•YIHN), contributed to Chinese culture by writing the first history of China.

READING CHECK **SUMMARIZE**
In what areas did the Han make advances during the Golden Age?

The Silk Road and Trade

In 139 B.C., Wu Di sent an **ambassador**, or government representative, to western Asia to find people to help him fight against invaders. The ambassador found no allies, but he did learn about civilizations west of China. In time, Wu Di's armies gained control of these lands and the trade routes that crossed through them.

The most-traveled trade routes became known as the **Silk Road**. These trans-Eurasian "silk roads" stretched 4,000 miles from the Han capital through the deserts and high plains of central Asia to the Mediterranean Sea. They connected China and Europe.

Chinese traders traveled west along the Silk Road with silk and other goods. They traded for horses, glass, spices, unusual fruits, musical instruments, and other items not found in China. Those who bought the Chinese goods, in turn, traded them to others. Some Chinese goods traveled as far away as what is now the country of Italy.

Han Children

In ancient China, children were expected to do chores, such as gather pillows and mats to take outside to air out. When all their chores were done, Han children were free to play. A favorite toy of children of all ages was the kite. Kites were made from brightly colored silk and paper attached to a bamboo frame. Some kites even had special hollow bamboo sticks on them that made sounds as they flew through the air.

Make It Relevant How does your life in the present-day United States differ from life in Han China?

The Silk Road was also significant to the diffusion, or spread, of Buddhism northward from India to China. Accompanying the merchants traveling the Silk Road were Buddhist monks who set up monasteries. Through their teachings, Buddhism began to spread.

READING CHECK SUMMARIZE
What was the significance of the Silk Road?

Summary

Han rulers such as Gaozu governed by combining Legalist and Confucian ideas. Wu Di expanded the empire's borders and developed a civil service system. Under the Han, merchants and Buddhists traveled a trans-Eurasian trade route called the Silk Road.

REVIEW

1. What lasting impact did the Han dynasty have on China's culture and government?

2. Use the term **ambassador** in a sentence about the **Silk Road**.

3. How did Buddhism spread to China?

4. What conditions led to China's Golden Age under the Han?

CRITICAL THINKING

5. **ANALYSIS SKILL** What were the benefits of Wu Di's military successes? What were the costs?

6. **ANALYSIS SKILL** How do you think the Silk Road trade affected Chinese culture?

7. **Make a Map** Imagine that you are a Chinese trader on the Silk Road during the Han dynasty. Using maps in this textbook as references, make your own map of the Silk Road.

8. **Focus Skill** COMPARE AND CONTRAST
On a separate sheet of paper, copy and complete the graphic organizer below.

Topic 1
Qin dynasty

Similar

Topic 2
Han dynasty

Ban Zhao

*"When you have done well, do not boast. When you have done wrong, do not deny your mistake."** *

These words are from a book called *Instruction for Chinese Women and Girls*. The author was Ban Zhao, the most important female scholar of the Han dynasty.

Ban Zhao's father and brother were imperial historians. They had the important task of recording the history of the Han dynasty. However, it was Ban Zhao's mother who provided her with a basic

▶ A historical illustration of Ban Zhao

education. After receiving her education, Ban Zhao married young. However, her husband died shortly after the marriage. She then placed her focus on writing.

Like most people of the Han dynasty, Ban Zhao followed the teachings of Confucius. Yet Confucius wrote little about women. Because of this, Ban Zhao wrote *Instruction for Chinese Women and Girls* to apply Confucianism to the role of women. Her book provided a set of rules to help Han women live responsible and meaningful lives. It also emphasized traditional Confucian ideals such as respect for parents and for governmental authority.

After the death of her brother, Ban Zhao followed in his footsteps to become an imperial historian. The work that Ban Zhao did on the history of the Han dynasty is considered some of the best ever written.

*Ban Zhao. *The Chinese Book of Etiquette and Conduct for Women and Girls Entitled: Instruction for Chinese Women and Girls.* S.L. Baldwin, trans. Editions Thanh-Long, 1988.

Biography

Trustworthiness

Respect

Responsibility

Fairness

Caring

Patriotism

Why Character Counts

❓ **What do Ban Zhao's writings tell about her sense of responsibility?**

Bio Brief

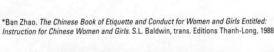

A.D.45
Born

A.D.115
Died

A.D. 59
Ban Zhao marries at age 14. Her husband dies a short time later

A.D. 106
Ban Zhao writes *Instruction for Chinese Women and Girls*

GO ONLINE

Interactive Multimedia Biographies
Visit MULTIMEDIA BIOGRAPHIES at
www.harcourtschool.com/hss

Chinese Designs

The ancient Chinese developed ways to work with bronze and other natural resources to create many beautiful objects. During the Shang dynasty, more than 3,000 years ago, artists learned to carve jade—a green stone—into fine jewelry. They also developed new ways of casting bronze to create elaborate designs. The artists of the Zhou dynasty developed these skills further. In 1977, archaeologists found a tomb belonging to a Marquis Yi of the Zeng state, who died in 433 B.C. Among many fine bronze and jade objects, they found a set of 65 bronze bells. Scientists were amazed to discover that each perfectly tuned bell can sound either of two tones, depending on where it is struck.

▶ The hammers held by this Chinese musician are used to play bronze bells.

This rack of 65 bronze bells from Yi's tomb is the heaviest musical instrument in the world.

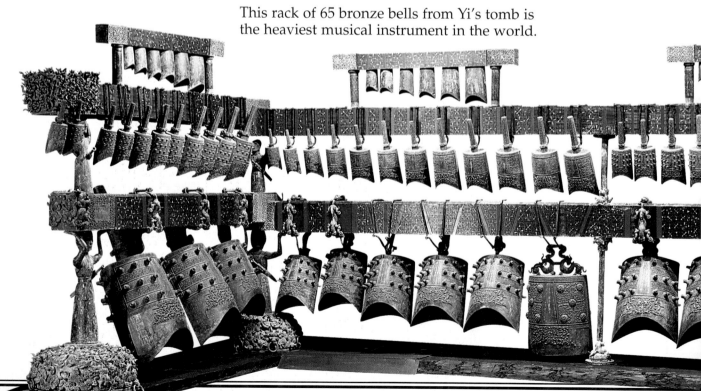

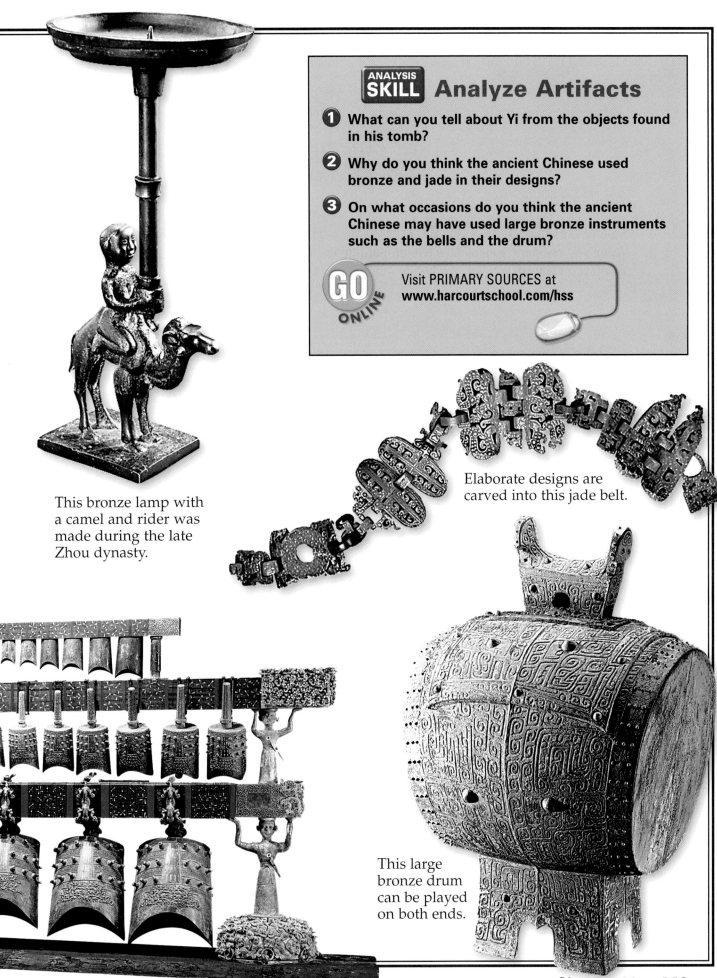

ANALYSIS SKILL Analyze Artifacts

1 What can you tell about Yi from the objects found in his tomb?

2 Why do you think the ancient Chinese used bronze and jade in their designs?

3 On what occasions do you think the ancient Chinese may have used large bronze instruments such as the bells and the drum?

GO ONLINE

Visit PRIMARY SOURCES at www.harcourtschool.com/hss

This bronze lamp with a camel and rider was made during the late Zhou dynasty.

Elaborate designs are carved into this jade belt.

This large bronze drum can be played on both ends.

1766 B.C.
The Shang
dynasty begins

1122 B.C.
The Zhou
dynasty
begins

Reading Social Studies

When you **compare**, you tell how two or more things are alike.
When you **contrast**, you tell how two or more things are different.

Compare and Contrast

Complete this graphic organizer to compare and contrast
the dynasties of ancient China. A copy of this graphic organizer
appears on page 121 of the Homework and Practice Book.

Dynasties of Ancient China

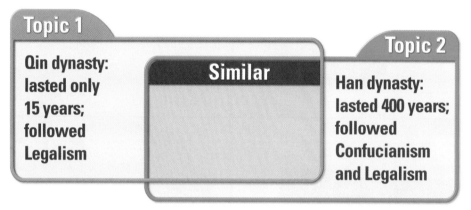

Topic 1

Qin dynasty:
lasted only
15 years;
followed
Legalism

Similar

Topic 2

Han dynasty:
lasted 400 years;
followed
Confucianism
and Legalism

California Writing Prompts

Write a Narrative Recall what you read about
the legend of Yu the Great and the Great Flood.
Write a narrative that tells your version of this
legend. Write the story using your own ideas, but
base your ideas on what you have read about
ancient China.

Write a Response to Literature Read
Confucius' proverbs on page 427. Write an essay
that interprets the meanings of these proverbs.
Discuss what Confucius' proverbs meant to the
people of ancient China and how the wisdom of
these proverbs can relate to today's world.

221 B.C.
The Qin dynasty
unites China

202 B.C.
The Han dynasty
begins

Use Vocabulary

Use one of the terms in the box to complete each sentence.

steppe, p. 416

dialect, p. 417

feudalism, p. 425

province, p. 434

Silk Road, p. 445

1. In northern China, there are treeless grasslands called _____ .

2. A _____ is an administrative region.

3. A different _____ was spoken in each region of ancient China.

4. The _____ connected China and Europe.

5. The Zhou rulers used the political system known as _____ .

Use the Time Line

 Use the summary time line above to answer these questions.

6. List the first four Chinese dynasties in chronological order.

7. In what year was China united?

Apply Skills

Read a Climograph

8. Look at the climographs on pages 420 and 421. Which city has a higher average monthly precipitation in June, July, and August?

Recall Facts

Answer these questions.

9. What geographic barriers kept ancient China isolated from the rest of the world?

10. What were two achievements of the Shang dynasty?

11. During what dynasty did Confucius live?

12. What advances in science were made under the Han dynasty?

Write the letter of the best choice.

13. Who controlled the land and taxes during the Qin dynasty?
    A feudal lords
    B appointed officials
    C elected leaders
    D foreign soldiers

14. Where did the Silk Road that began in China end?
    A at the Mediterranean Sea
    B at the Indus River
    C in Athens
    D in Rome

Think Critically

15. Why is the Han dynasty known as one of the most important dynasties in China's history?

16. **ANALYSIS SKILL** How did Wu Di's introduction of civil service affect education in China?

Xi'an, China

GET READY

The city of Xi'an (SHEE•AHN), formerly Chang'an, is located in the center of China. Xi'an was once the capital of China and a major trade center along the Silk Road. Inside the old city walls, visitors can see many historic places. There are also modern universities and museums.

One popular site is the Big Wild Goose Pagoda, the most famous pagoda in China. Built in A.D. 589, it is seven stories tall. The Bell Tower and Drum Tower, in the center of the city, also attract visitors. The bell and the drum once marked the hours of the day for monks to worship.

LOCATE IT

Xi'an

CHINA

WHAT TO SEE

In Xi'an today, people can buy items made from silk at markets just as they did in ancient times when the city was a trade center along the Silk Road.

The Forest of Stone Steles Museum contains about 3,000 steles, or carved stones, dating from the Han dynasty to the Qing dynasty. These steles are carved with Chinese teachings, books, and poetry.

Many Chinese rulers encouraged the arts, including poetry, painting, and music. These musicians perform Chinese music for visitors to Xi'an.

The Bell Tower was built during the Ming dynasty. It holds a huge bell once used for ringing out the time.

The location of Xi'an served as the capital of 11 dynasties, including the Tang. These Chinese dancers perform in the style of clothing worn during Tang rule.

A VIRTUAL TOUR

GO ONLINE

Visit VIRTUAL TOURS at
www.harcourtschool.com/hss

Review

Culture The people of ancient India and China had many new ideas about society, religion, and government.

Summary

Early Civilizations of India and China

Civilization in India developed in the Indus River valley by about 2500 B.C. The Aryan peoples from the north brought great changes. Hinduism and the caste system grew from Aryan beliefs. The teachings of the Buddha laid the groundwork for the religion of Buddhism, which spread throughout much of Asia.

Maurya rulers built an empire based on warfare. Then Emperor Ashoka changed his ways and became a kind, peaceful leader. Later, the Gupta Empire brought a Golden Age of peace, wealth, and cultural achievement.

Chinese civilization began in the Huang He Valley with the Shang dynasty. Confucius taught a way of life based on duty, kindness, and tradition. His teachings, known as Confucianism, are still practiced today.

In 221 B.C., Shi Huangdi united China to form the Qin dynasty. He began to build a bureaucracy that became a key element of ancient Chinese government.

The later Han dynasty was a time of long-distance trade along the Silk Road. The dynasty also encouraged many cultural accomplishments.

Main Ideas and Vocabulary

Read the summary above. Then answer the questions that follow.

1. What is Hinduism?
   A a language
   B a form of government
   C a religion
   D a social class

2. Which word best describes the Maurya rulers before Ashoka?
   A violent
   B fair
   C weak
   D wise

3. What is a bureaucracy?
   A a capital city
   B a form of punishment
   C a specially trained army
   D a large group of appointed officials

4. Which of the following occurred during the Han dynasty?
   A a return to the policies of Shi Huangdi
   B increased contacts with other civilizations
   C an attempt to wipe out Confucianism
   D China's first democratic government

Recall Facts

Answer these questions.

5. The Vedas led to the development of what religion?

6. What were the four classes in the Indian class system?

7. Who was Siddhartha Gautama?

8. What is one medical advance made by ancient Indian doctors that is still important today?

9. In what part of China is the Huang He Valley located?

10. How do the teachings of Daoism differ from those of Confucianism?

Write the letter of the best choice.

11. Which religion began in India and spread to China and other parts of Asia?
    A Buddhism
    B Confucianism
    C Daoism
    D Hinduism

12. How did the ideas and inventions of ancient India and China reach the rest of the world?
    A through conquest
    B through meetings of rulers
    C through the settling of colonies
    D through trade

13. Which of the following helped Shi Huangdi unify China?
    A feudalism and social classes
    B bureaucracy and standardization
    C agriculture and metalworking
    D trade with Europe and conquest of India

Think Critically

14. **ANALYSIS SKILL** How are the beginning of Indian civilization and the beginning of Chinese civilization related in time?

15. During which dynasty was ancient China's economy strongest? Explain how you arrived at your answer.

Apply Skills

Identify Changing Borders

ANALYSIS SKILL Use the maps to answer the questions.

16. Which empire controlled a larger area?

17. Which mountain range made up part of the northern border of both empires?

18. Which empire controlled part of present-day Afghanistan?

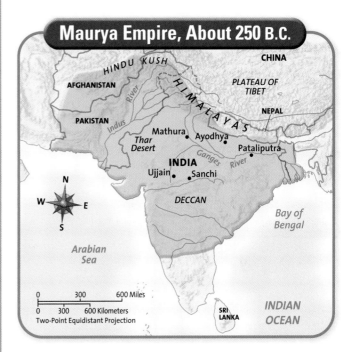

Maurya Empire, About 250 B.C.

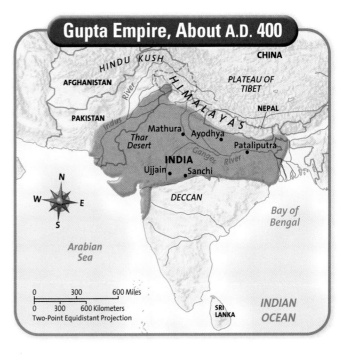

Gupta Empire, About A.D. 400

Read More

■ *Three Rivers of Asia* by Richie Chevat.

■ *The Silk Road* by Lisa Jo Rudy.

■ *Timekeepers: The History of Calendars* by Richie Chevat.

Show What You Know

Unit Writing Activity

Write a Comparison-Contrast Essay Compare and contrast Hinduism and Buddhism. Tell how the religions are similar and different. Also, compare and contrast the people who played a role in the development of the two religions.

Unit Project

Make an Illustrated Map Gather information about the geography and cultures of India and China. Research the natural regions and the early people who lived there. Then make an illustrated map of the region. Include important land features and cities. Also include written information and pictures about achievements, history, and ideas of the early people, and attach these to your map.

Visit ACTIVITIES at
www.harcourtschool.com/hss

The Development of Rome

START WITH THE STANDARDS

California History-Social Science Standards

6.7 Students analyze the geographic, political, economic, religious, and social structures during the development of Rome.

The Big Idea

INDIVIDUALISM

The actions of individuals affected the development of Rome as it changed from a monarchy to a republic to an empire.

What to Know

✔ How did the Roman Republic's government work?

✔ What influence did Julius Caesar and Augustus have in Rome's transition from republic to empire?

✔ Who and what led to the spread of Christianity in Europe and other Roman territories?

Show What You Know

★ Unit 6 Test

✐ Writing: A Research Report

✏ Unit Project: An Ancient Newspaper

Time

800 B.C.

400 B.C.

At the Same Time

 300 B.C. The Hopewell civilization develops in what is now the central United States

The Development of Rome

27 B.C. Rome becomes an empire, p. 509

A.D. 313 Christianity becomes an accepted religion in the Roman Empire, p. 552

A.D. 391 Christianity becomes the official religion of the Roman Empire, p. 553

B.C./A.D.

A.D. 400

 50 B.C. Mayan writing first appears on public monuments

 A.D. 300 The Mayan classical period begins

 A.D. 500 Tikal, the first great Mayan city, is built

Cincinnatus
519 B.C. – 430 B.C.
- Leader who took control of Rome when he was needed
- Example of the Roman idea of civic duty

Hannibal
247 B.C. – 183 B.C.
- Led Carthage's forces against Rome in the Second Punic War
- Successful military leader who had a great love for his city of Carthage

People

600 B.C. **300 B.C.**

519 B.C. – 430 B.C. • Cincinnatus

247 B.C. – 183 B.C. • Hannibal

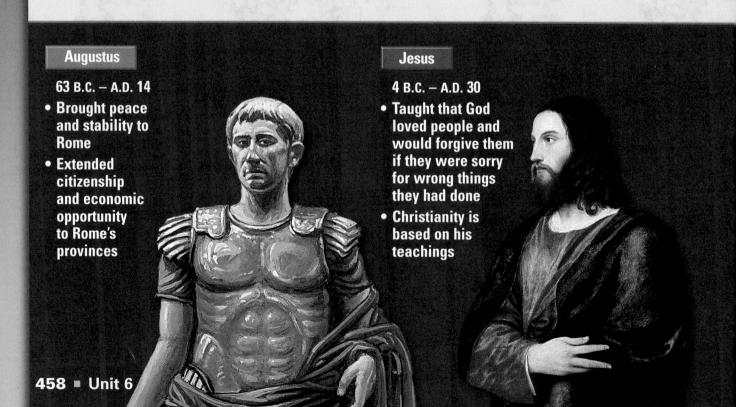

Augustus
63 B.C. – A.D. 14
- Brought peace and stability to Rome
- Extended citizenship and economic opportunity to Rome's provinces

Jesus
4 B.C. – A.D. 30
- Taught that God loved people and would forgive them if they were sorry for wrong things they had done
- Christianity is based on his teachings

Julius Caesar

100 B.C. – 44 B.C.
- Wanted to rule Rome and all its lands
- Declared himself dictator in 44 B.C.

Cleopatra VII

69 B.C. – 30 B.C.
- Lost power over Egypt after Augustus defeated her navy
- Last Macedonian ruler of Egypt

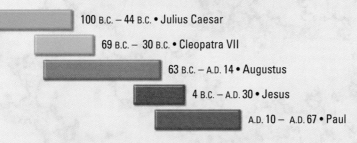

B.C./A.D.   A.D. 300

100 B.C. – 44 B.C. • Julius Caesar

69 B.C. – 30 B.C. • Cleopatra VII

63 B.C. – A.D. 14 • Augustus

4 B.C. – A.D. 30 • Jesus

A.D. 10 – A.D. 67 • Paul

A.D. 280 – A.D. 337 • Constantine

Paul

A.D. 10 – A.D. 67
- One of Jesus' apostles
- Spent his later life spreading Jesus' teachings

Constantine

A.D. 280 – A.D. 337
- Issued the Edict of Milan, which granted Christians the right to practice their religion in the Roman Empire
- Had the Church of the Holy Sepulchre built in Jerusalem

Unit 6

Place — The Roman Empire

BRITAIN

Londinium (London)

EUROPE

Danube River

GAUL

ALPS

Milan

Adriatic Sea

The Roman Forum, about A.D. 100

ATLANTIC OCEAN

Tagus River

Corsica

Rome

SPAIN

Toledo

Sardinia

Tyrrhenian Sea

New Carthage (Cartagena)

Carthage

Sicily

Syracuse

Ionian Sea

Zama

Mediterranean

NORTH AMERICA

ATLANTIC OCEAN

At The Same Time

Hopewell Indian Village, Ohio Valley, about A.D. 400

AFRICA

PACIFIC OCEAN

SOUTH AMERICA

0   250   500 Miles
0   250   500 Kilometers
Lambert Azimuthal Equal-Area Projection

Roman lands, by 274 B.C.
Lands added by 133 B.C.
Lands added by 44 B.C.
Lands added by A.D. 117
Major road

ASIA

DACIA

Black Sea

Caspian Sea

Byzantium

Pergamum

GREECE

Aegean Sea

Athens

Antioch

Euphrates

Tigris

River

River

Crete

Cyprus

JUDAEA

Babylon

Sea

Persian Gulf

Cyrene

Jerusalem

Alexandria

EGYPT

Nile River

Red Sea

Church of the Holy Sepulchre, Jerusalem, about A.D. 350

The lighthouse in Alexandria, about A.D. 100

(Focus Skill) Draw Conclusions

A **conclusion** is an understanding reached after careful thinking. To **draw a conclusion,** you use what you already know along with what you read about a subject to make a general statement about an idea or an event.

Why It Matters

Drawing conclusions can help you understand the deeper meaning of what you read.

Evidence		Knowledge

Conclusion

✓ To draw a conclusion, ask yourself, "How does what I am reading connect to what I know?"

✓ Drawing conclusions is like being a detective. Look for clues, and try to figure out what they mean.

Practice the Skill

Read the paragraphs. Draw a conclusion for the second paragraph.

Evidence
Knowledge
Conclusion

By the beginning of the first century A.D., trade routes linked three of the world's six inhabited continents. Products traveled from China as far west as Italy. As civilizations traded goods, they also influenced one another's cultures. (China is in Asia, and Italy is in Europe. The three linked continents must be Europe, Asia, and Africa.)

The influence of trade on cultures is especially true of the Silk Road, the trade route that started in China. Chinese traders easily found buyers for their goods. Many of these goods ended up in the far west, though the Chinese never traveled this far.

Apply What You Learned

⭐ **Draw Conclusions** Read the paragraphs, and answer the questions.

An Alternate Route from the East

Recently, archaeologists have learned about a link between ancient India and Rome that was much like the link between ancient China and Rome created by the Silk Road. The main site of the research is the Red Sea port of Berenike, in southern Egypt. In the first few centuries A.D., Egypt was part of the Roman Empire, and Berenike was a busy shipping center. Cargo moved from India, across the Indian Ocean, and over the Red Sea to Egypt.

At Berenike, archaeologists have dug down to the ruins of a port and a town that date back to the first century A.D. They were surprised to find that many buildings were made of teak. Teak is the wood from a kind of tree that does not grow in Africa or Europe. The scientists think that the teak must have arrived in Berenike in the form of ships' hulls.

Berenike features many ancient Indian goods that are no longer found in India itself. Egypt's dry climate has preserved objects that did not survive the centuries in India's wet climate. Some goods found in Berenike may have come from even farther east than India. These finds show just how wide trading was among the civilizations of Asia, Africa, and Europe.

The sea trade between India and the Roman Empire grew, most likely because enemies of Rome controlled the western sections of the Silk Road. The sea route from India has, until now, been much less well known. However, it may have been just as important as the Silk Road to the people of ancient Rome.

❱ A Roman tablet found in Berenike

Draw Conclusions

1. **What conclusions can you draw about the source of teak in Berenike and how it came to be used for building?**

2. **What conclusion can you draw about why objects that did not survive in India did survive in Egypt?**

3. **After Indian goods arrived in Egypt, in which direction do you think they were then carried? How did you reach your conclusion?**

463

Study Skills

WRITE TO LEARN

Writing about what you read can help you understand and remember information.

▶ Many students write about what they read in a learning log. Writing in a learning log can be both creative and personal.

▶ Writing about the text leads you to think about it more.

▶ Writing your reactions to the text makes it more meaningful to you.

Lesson 1: The Founding of Rome

What I Learned	My Response
Early Latins settled in Italy among seven hills south of the Tiber River. The people borrowed ideas from their neighbors, including the Etruscans and the Greeks.	The hills may have helped protect the Latins. They probably used the river for transportation and trade. Borrowing ideas seems to help cultures grow.

Apply As You Read

As you read this chapter, write entries in a learning log. Include your thoughts and feelings about what you read.

California History-Social Science Standards, Grade 6

6.7 Students analyze the geographic, political, economic, religious, and social structures during the development of Rome.

The Early Romans

▶ Ruins of the Roman Forum in Rome

WHO WERE THE ROMANS?

written by Phil Roxbee Cox   illustrated by Annabel Spenceley

Life in ancient Rome was very different from life in the United States today. One major difference is that not all children went to school in ancient Rome. Only the richest Roman families could afford to pay for their children's education. Read on to learn more about early Roman education.

Did Roman children go to school?

In the early days, rich Roman families paid private tutors to teach their children at home. Later, boys' schools were set up, but parents still had to pay to send their boys to them. This meant that poorer children never went to school, so they never learned to read or write. Very few girls were sent to school. Some were taught by their mothers.

What were the schools like?

Most schools had only one room and only one class. There were about twelve pupils. Schools were often above or behind a store.

This school is called a "ludus." It is for six to eleven year old boys.

This teacher is Greek. Many teachers were from Greece.

This is a "paedagogus." He has been sent by this boy's parents to make sure he works hard.

A scroll

This boy writes by scratching onto pieces of broken pottery.

What did they write on?

Not paper. The Romans did have a kind of paper made from reeds, and wrote on animal skins, but this was too expensive for children to write on. Schoolboys would usually write on wax tablets with a pointed stick called a stylus. They could then rub the wax smooth and start again.

Stylus

Wax tablet

What else did they learn at school?

As well as reading, writing and numbers, boys were also expected to learn Greek. When they were older, boys could learn to speak in public if they wanted to be a politician or a lawyer. This could take years and was very expensive.

This boy is learning public speaking with a special teacher called a "rhetor."

Did they read books?

Yes. A school would have had a few books, but not like this one you are reading now. Printing had not been invented, so books had to be written by hand. They were usually made from one long piece of paper rolled around a stick. This was called a scroll. Later, a new type of book called a codex was invented. A codex was shaped more like a book today.

This is a scroll. It is 10 m (over 30 ft) long. The writing is in columns.

This is a codex. It is also written by hand and in columns like a newspaper.

What did the girls learn at home?

Girls in the richer Roman families were taught how to read and write, and run a household. Some of them had private tutors and music teachers.

This girl is being taught to play the lyre. It is made from a tortoise shell.

A very old music teacher

This is an abacus. People slide the wooden balls along the wires as they count.

Did they do arithmetic?

Yes, and they didn't have electronic calculators. Roman numbers looked different from ours. They were written as capital letters. The Roman numbers from one to twelve are shown below.

Response Corner

1 Why do you think many of the teachers in ancient Rome were from ancient Greece?

2 What kind of books do you think students in ancient Rome would have read at school?

About 1000 B.C.
Latins settle on seven hills near the Tiber River

About 750 B.C.
Latin villages begin uniting to form Rome

About 616 B.C.
Etruscans begin to rule Rome

WHAT TO KNOW
How did the city of Rome develop?

✓ Explain how Rome was founded.

✓ Describe the advantages of Rome's location.

VOCABULARY
arable p. 469
forum p. 471
confederation p. 472

PEOPLE
Romulus
Remus
Aeneas
Ancus Marcius
Tarquinius Priscus

PLACES
Italian Peninsula
Rome

DRAW CONCLUSIONS

California
Standards
HSS 6.7, 6.7.1

The Founding of Rome

YOU ARE THERE

It's 1000 B.C. on the **Italian Peninsula**, and you're picking grapes in your family's vineyard. As you gaze down at the river valley, you can just make out the people trading and talking on the open field where the villagers meet. You wish you were down there because you like to look at all the goods people bring to trade. Suddenly, your father interrupts your daydream. He says, "We must work hard to finish picking the grapes, so we can go down to the market this afternoon." You smile as you hurriedly reach for a cluster of grapes on the vine.

▶ Early farmers harvested olives (above) and other crops along the Tiber River (below).

Settling the Seven Hills

Like all peninsulas, the Italian Peninsula is surrounded on three sides by water. Shaped like a boot, it juts from southern Europe into the Mediterranean Sea.

A mountain range called the Apennines (A•puh•nynz) extends along the length of the Italian Peninsula. Some of the mountains in this range were once volcanoes. When they erupted, the ash they created enriched the soil. It is no wonder that **arable** (AR•uh•buhl) land, or land that is good for growing crops, is plentiful in this region. Also, the climate on the peninsula is mild, creating a long growing season.

These favorable conditions tempted many people to settle on the Italian Peninsula long ago. Some came from the north to escape the harsher climate there. Many Greeks also settled there, preferring areas in the peninsula's southern region.

In about 1000 B.C., people from central Europe began migrating to the Italian Peninsula. These people, who became known as the Latins, settled on seven hills south of the Tiber River, about 15 miles from the Tyrrhenian (tuh•REE•nee•uhn) Sea. These seven hills would one day become the city of **Rome**, the heart of a mighty empire.

The early Latins were herders and farmers. They raised cattle, sheep, goats, and pigs and grew wheat, olives, grapes, and many other crops. For protection, they often built their villages on hillsides so that they could see people approaching. If danger threatened, they could climb to even higher ground to better protect themselves from attack. The hilly area also provided resources such as wood and stones for building.

READING CHECK ⟡ **DRAW CONCLUSIONS**

What attracted the Latins to the hills near the Tiber River? It was good for growing crops

GEOGRAPHY

The Tiber River

The early settlement that became Rome was located on the Tiber River. The Tiber begins in the Apennines and flows south for 251 miles to the Tyrrhenian Sea. Along the way, it collects a lot of silt and carries it to the sea.

Later, when Rome became a great city, the Tiber linked Rome with the port of Ostia at the mouth of the river. Ostia became a major center of trade and military power.

Over the years, the Tiber River has deposited a great amount of silt at its mouth. The port of Ostia built in Roman times is now located 4 miles inland!

ITALY

Pisa • Florence
Arno River
Siena
Lake Trasimeno
Perugia
Nera River
Ancona
TIBER RIVER
Adriatic Sea
Pescara
Pescara River
Tyrrhenian Sea
Aniene R.
Ostia ⊗ Rome
0 25 50 Miles
0 25 50 Kilometers
N E S W

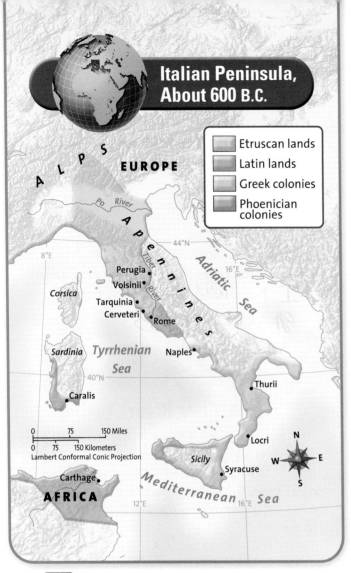

Italian Peninsula, About 600 B.C.

Etruscan lands
Latin lands
Greek colonies
Phoenician colonies

EUROPE
ALPS
Po River
Apennines
44°N
8°E
16°E
Perugia
Volsinii
Corsica
Tarquinia
Cerveteri
Rome
Adriatic Sea
Tiber River
Sardinia
Tyrrhenian Sea
Naples
40°N
Thurii
Caralis
0   75   150 Miles
0   75   150 Kilometers
Lambert Conformal Conic Projection
Locri
Sicily
Syracuse
N
W   E
S
Carthage
AFRICA
Mediterranean Sea
12°E
16°E

ANALYSIS SKILL **Analyze Maps** Different cultures existed on the Italian Peninsula in 600 B.C. The ruins of the Roman Forum (below) remain there today.

Regions Which culture controlled the most lands on the peninsula?

A Cultural Mix

To the north and south of the Latin villages on the seven hills, other peoples flourished in the region. Living just north of the Latins, the Etruscans were traders, ironworkers, and artists. Etruscan artwork included sculpture, pottery, and paintings.

Within 50 years of settling on the Italian Peninsula, the Greeks controlled large areas of the southern part of the peninsula. They spread Greek culture and achievements across much of the region.

The Etruscans and the Greeks set up trade routes between their settlements. Sandwiched between the two groups, the Latins frequently encountered Greeks and Etruscans passing through their land.

In about 750 B.C., the Latin villages on the seven hills began to unite. From this union, the villages would become the city of Rome, and the people would be known as Romans.

The Romans adopted the Greek religion, giving Latin names to Greek gods and goddesses. The Etruscans had borrowed the Greek alphabet and adapted it to their own needs. The Romans, in turn, borrowed it from the Etruscans. From both groups, the Romans learned about architecture.

READING CHECK **SUMMARIZE**
What two cultures influenced the Romans?

▶ Romulus and Remus are shown on a mosaic (left) with the mother wolf who saved them and on a relief (above).

The City of Rome

 **TIME** Mid-600s B.C.

PLACE Rome

Romans told legends to explain Rome's beginnings. One told how a Latin king's cruel brother took the throne by force. When the rightful king's daughter gave birth to twin boys, **Romulus** and **Remus,** the new king feared the boys would grow up to take back the throne. The legend says the twins were descendants of **Aeneas,** a hero of the Trojan War.

The king ordered the babies drowned in the Tiber River. According to the legend, a mother wolf saved the twins, and later, a farmer took them home. When the twins grew up, they won back the throne.

The legend says that the twins set out to build a settlement along the Tiber River, near where they had been rescued years before. However, they argued about which hill to build on, and Remus was killed. Romulus became the first ruler of the new city, which was named Rome in his honor.

The seven hills that became Rome surrounded a flat piece of land, which became known as the Roman Forum. A **forum** was a public square in ancient Roman cities where the Romans exchanged goods and ideas.

In the mid-600s B.C., the Romans began to move down from the hills and onto the flat land around the Forum. As Rome grew, kings, who were elected by an assembly of Rome's leading men, began to rule the Romans. Under the kings' leadership, the Romans started new building projects, such as roads and stone temples.

Rome's central location was ideal for trade with the rest of the peninsula. The Tiber River gave the Romans a route to the sea, where they traded with other cultures in the Mediterranean. In time, Rome would gain control of sea routes linking Europe, Asia, and Africa. "Not without good reason did gods and men choose this spot as the site of a city,"* a Roman historian wrote.

READING CHECK **SUMMARIZE**

Who was the first legendary ruler of Rome?

*Titus Livius. *The History of Rome*. Ernest Rhys, ed. Canon Roberts, tr. E.P. Dutton and Co., 1912.

Etruscan Rule

The earliest rulers of Rome were kings descended from the Latins, the first settlers of the seven hills. However, Etruscan rule was growing to the north. The Etruscans were wealthier and more advanced than the early Romans. They also had more experience with long-distance trade and with governing large areas.

Like the Greeks, the Etruscans formed independent city-states. The Etruscan city-states not only shared their cultural identity but also used the same system of government.

A king governed each city-state. Unlike most monarchs, Etruscan kings did not inherit their thrones. The leaders within each city-state elected their king. Having similar governments helped the Etruscans create a confederation of 12 city-states. A **confederation** is a group of governments joined together for a common purpose.

Eventually, the Etruscan confederation expanded into the territory of the Romans. Their takeover of Rome was peaceful because the Romans had already accepted much Etruscan influence. According to legend, when the Roman king **Ancus Marcius** died in about 616 B.C., an Etruscan, **Tarquinius Priscus**, took his place.

Tarquinius and the next king, also an Etruscan, served Rome well. First, they completed many large building projects. They added to the walls that protected the city, paved Rome's streets, and built a sewer system. Second, the Etruscan kings expanded Rome by conquest. They brought other Latin tribes, who lived in settlements around Rome, under Etruscan control.

The Etruscans were experienced at ruling large areas. They organized Rome's territory into districts that were easier to manage. An organized territory is easier to govern and more difficult to defeat. The Etruscans also organized the army.

▶ The Etruscans left many artifacts, such as this pottery (below) and this sarcophagus carved into the shape of a man and a woman (below right).

Under the Etruscan kings, Rome now possessed some of the strengths that would help it grow. It occupied an ideal location. It had built on the achievements of nearby civilizations and had begun to add to its territory. Rome's power was just beginning.

READING CHECK **GENERALIZE**
What influence did the Etruscan kings have on the development of Rome?

Summary

Latins founded the city of Rome in about 750 B.C. Legend says that the twins Romulus and Remus founded the city. According to history, Rome began as small villages, which joined together and grew. The city's location was ideal for farming and was easy to defend. The neighboring cultures of the Etruscans and the Greeks greatly influenced early Roman culture. In time, Etruscan kings ruled over the Romans.

❯ This section of wall art comes from the Tomb of the Leopards in Rome. It shows a flutist playing his instrument. The artist created this painting during the time that the Etruscans ruled Rome.

REVIEW

1. How did the city of Rome develop?

2. Explain the role that the **forum** played in the development of Rome.

3. What three geographical features contributed to the growth of Rome? Describe the role that each one played.

4. In what way was the power of the early Roman kings limited?

CRITICAL THINKING

5. **ANALYSIS SKILL** How did the Etruscan and Greek cultures influence the culture of early Rome?

6. **ANALYSIS SKILL** What might be some of the advantages of having a capital located in the center of a country?

7. **Write a Letter** Imagine that you live in Rome at the time of the Etruscan kings. Write a letter to a friend. Explain how you feel about having an Etruscan as your king even though Rome is a Latin city.

8. **Focus Skill** **DRAW CONCLUSIONS**
On a separate sheet of paper, copy and complete the graphic organizer below.

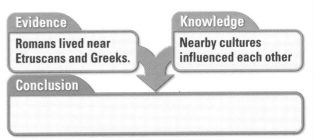

Evidence	Knowledge
Romans lived near Etruscans and Greeks.	Nearby cultures influenced each other

Conclusion

Compare Maps with Different Scales

▶ WHY IT MATTERS

In order to read a map, you need to understand the scale it uses. The scale tells you how distance on the map is related to distance in the real world. For example, 1 inch on a map might stand for 1 mile, 10 miles, or 100 miles.

Once you understand the scale, you can estimate the real-world distances between the places that are shown on the map. For example, you could use the scale on a historical map of the Italian Peninsula to calculate the actual distances between Rome and other ancient cities there.

The scale to which a map is drawn determines how much area and detail the map can show. Drawing places large allows more details to be shown. For example, more cities and towns can be shown. It is important to choose a map whose scale allows it to show the information you want.

▶ WHAT YOU NEED TO KNOW

Look at the map below and the maps on the next page. As you can see, the scale determines whether a map shows a close-up view or a faraway view.

Map A uses a small scale to show a large area of land with few details. Map C uses a large scale to show a small area of land with many details. Map B's scale is larger than Map A's and smaller than Map C's.

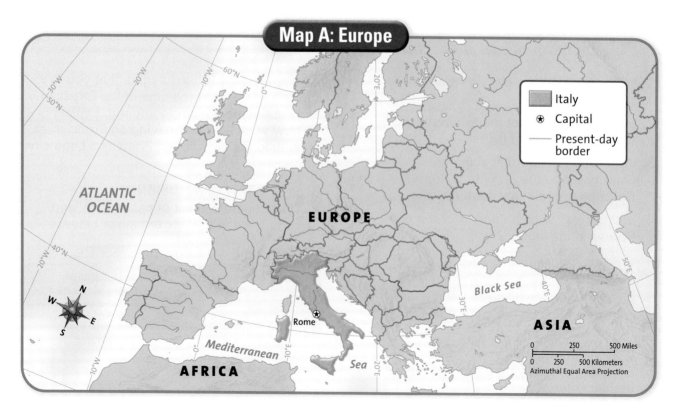

Map A: Europe

Italy
⊛ Capital
— Present-day border

ATLANTIC OCEAN

EUROPE

ASIA

Black Sea

Rome

Mediterranean Sea

AFRICA

0   250   500 Miles
0   250   500 Kilometers
Azimuthal Equal Area Projection

Map B: Italy

EUROPE

ALPS

Turin • Milan Padua •
Venice •
• Trieste

Genoa •
Bologna •
Pisa • Florence
8°E *Ligurian Sea*
Perugia •
Elba

Po River
Apennines
Tiber River
44°N
Ancona •
16°E
Adriatic Sea

Rome ⊛ **ITALY**
Foggia •
Bari •

Sassari •
Tyrrhenian Sea
Naples • ▲Mt. Vesuvius
Salerno •
Capri
Taranto •
Sardinia
40°N

Cagliari •

Palermo •
Messina •
Sicily ▲Mt. Etna
12°E
Syracuse •
16°E
36°N

Mediterranean Sea

⊛ Capital
• Major city
— Present-day border

0   75   150 Miles
0   75   150 Kilometers
Lambert Conformal Conic Projection

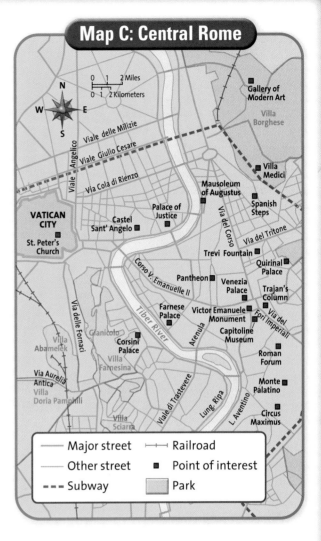

Map C: Central Rome

0   1   2 Miles
0   1   2 Kilometers

Gallery of Modern Art
Villa Borghese

Viale delle Milizie
Viale Giulio Cesare
Via Cola di Rienzo

Viale Angelico

Villa Medici

VATICAN CITY
St. Peter's Church

Castel Sant' Angelo ■
Mausoleum of Augustus ■
Palace of Justice ■
Spanish Steps ■
Via del Corso

Via del Tritone
Trevi Fountain ■
Quirinal Palace ■

Corso V. Emanuelle II
Pantheon ■
Venezia Palace ■
Trajan's Column ■
Via del Fori Imperiali

Via delle Fornaci
Farnese Palace ■
Victor Emanuele Monument ■
Capitoline Museum ■

Arenula
Tiber River

Villa Abamelek
Gianicolo
Corsini Palace ■
Villa Farnesina
Roman Forum ■

Via Aurelia Antica
Villa Doria Pamphili
Monte Palatino ■
Viale di Trastevere
Lung. Ripa
L. Aventino
Circus Maximus ■

Villa Sciarra

— Major street   ⊢⊣ Railroad
— Other street   ■ Point of interest
- - - Subway   ▨ Park

Map and Globe Skills

▶ PRACTICE THE SKILL

ANALYSIS SKILL Use the maps to answer the questions.

① Which map shows the most cities in Italy?

② Suppose you wanted to travel from Rome to the island of Sicily. Which map would be best to use for finding the distance between those two places? Explain your choice.

③ Which map would you use if you wanted to find historical sites in the city of Rome? Explain your choice.

▶ APPLY WHAT YOU LEARNED

ANALYSIS SKILL Find two maps that show the city or town where you live and that have different scales. Which areas and details appear on both maps? Which appear on only one map? Use both maps to find the actual distance between your city or town and another place that is shown on both maps.

Practice your map and globe skills with the **GeoSkills CD-ROM**.

Time

| 1000 B.C. | 500 B.C. | B.C./A.D. | A.D. 500 |

509 B.C.
The Roman Republic
begins

494 B.C.
The plebeians rebel
against the patricians

About 450 B.C.
The Twelve Tables are
displayed in the Forum

WHAT TO KNOW
How was the Roman
Republic different from
earlier governments?

✓ Explain the different
circumstances that led
to the rise of the Roman
Republic.

✓ Describe the features
of the government of
the Roman Republic.

VOCABULARY
republic p. 478
tripartite p. 478
consul p. 478
Senate p. 478
dictator p. 478
patrician p. 480
plebeian p. 480
tribune p. 481

PEOPLE
Tarquinius Superbus
Cincinnatus

PLACES
Rome

**DRAW
CONCLUSIONS**

California
Standards
HSS 6.7. 6.7.1, 6.7.2

The Roman Republic

YOU ARE THERE
You're living in unhappy times in 509 B.C. Years before your birth, the king of **Rome** was murdered. The dead king's son then took the throne. That was 25 years ago, and **Tarquinius Superbus** is still king. His name means "Tarquinius the Proud," but he should not be proud. He and his family ignore the law and steal from the people. No one is safe from them. "Tomorrow," your father whispers to you, "the senators will order that criminal out of Rome, and life will get better for us."

▶ This painting shows the twin gods Castor and Pollux helping the Romans at the battle of Rome.

▶ These columns (left) were once part of the temple that honored Castor and Pollux. The bust (above) shows Brutus.

The Last King

 TIME 509 B.C.

PLACE Rome

The Romans discovered that the third Etruscan king, Tarquinius Superbus, was different from the earlier kings. This one ignored the needs of the people. The king and his sons also committed terrible crimes against the Romans. For more than 20 years, no one dared to stand up to them.

Finally, in 509 B.C., two Romans—Brutus and Collatinus—led an effort to overthrow the king. They forced Tarquinius Superbus and his family to leave Rome.

The Romans had suffered long under a tyrant and did not want another king. They wanted a government in which no individual could gain total power. As a start, they elected Brutus and Collatinus to lead them for one year.

Meanwhile, Tarquinius plotted to regain the throne. The sons of Brutus planned to betray their father to help Tarquinius, but Brutus discovered the plot and sentenced his sons to death. This action showed how determined Brutus was to protect Rome from tyranny.

Next, an army of Etruscan soldiers attacked Rome to return Tarquinius to the throne. The Romans defeated them, but Brutus died in battle.

Finally, Tarquinius allied himself with 30 Latin cities in the area around Rome and attacked again. The Romans won once again. According to legend, twin gods, Castor and Pollux, mounted white horses and saved the day for the Romans. The Romans built a temple in their honor in the Forum.

READING CHECK ⊘ DRAW CONCLUSIONS
Why was Tarquinius Superbus overthrown?

The Republic Is Born

With Tarquinius no longer in power, the Romans started a new form of government. In 509 B.C., they ended the monarchy and created a republic. In a **republic**, citizens elect leaders to represent them.

The new Roman government was **tripartite**, meaning that it had three parts. By dividing the government into parts, there was a system of checks and balances, or separation of powers, that limited the power of each part of the government.

The first part was the **consuls**, who replaced the king. The Romans decided to have two consuls so that no one person would have too much power. They also decided that they would elect consuls every year.

The consuls were the most powerful leaders in the Republic, yet they did not have as much power as the kings had held. The authority of the consuls was limited and clearly defined. They led the army, carried out the laws, and acted as judges.

The second part of Rome's republican government was the Senate. The **Senate** was a group of 300 leading Roman men who advised the consuls. The Senate had existed at the time of the kings, but it became more important during the Republic. A king who ruled for life could afford to ignore the Senate's advice. However, a consul who faced election every year had to keep the support of Rome's citizens—especially the senators, who were the most powerful of these citizens.

▶ A Roman consul seated among symbols of authority

The third part of the new Roman government was the assemblies. Assemblies, too, became more important in the Roman Republic than they had been before. The assemblies were made up of all the adult male citizens of Rome, and every Roman man who had the right to vote was a member of an assembly. Together, the assemblies made laws for Rome and elected the consuls.

Rome's republican government had some things in common with the government of ancient Athens. Both had assemblies made up of male citizens. However, the government of Athens did not have consuls or a senate.

In emergencies, the Romans could appoint one leader—a dictator. A **dictator** had complete power during his time in office, which was limited to six months.

The story of **Cincinnatus** is a good example of what the Romans expected of a dictator. It also illustrates the Romans' idea of civic duty, that every citizen had a duty to serve Rome.

By 458 B.C., Cincinnatus had retired from the army and had become a farmer. The Romans were then at war with a tribe called the Aequi, who trapped the Roman army in the mountains. With the situation seemingly hopeless, the consuls appointed Cincinnatus dictator. Cincinnatus defeated the Aequi tribe in a single day, celebrated in Rome, resigned as dictator, and returned to his farm.

READING CHECK MAIN IDEA AND DETAILS
What were the three parts of the new Roman government?

ROMAN TRIPARTITE GOVERNMENT

▷ Roman consuls took the place of the king. Two consuls were elected every year. Consuls commanded military forces, proposed laws, and acted as judges.

▷ Composed of upper-class men, the Senate gave advice to the consuls.

▷ The assemblies helped make laws for Rome. They gathered in circular open-air structures.

Democratic Values

A written constitution is as important to United States citizens today as it was to the people of the Roman Republic.

In the early Republic, Roman laws were based on unwritten customs. In 451 B.C. and 450 B.C., the common people called for the laws to be recorded so that they could be applied equally to all citizens. The laws were posted in Rome's Forum on tablets called the Twelve Tables. Some of the laws stated citizens' rights, such as the right to own property. Other laws stated duties of citizens, such as military service. The Roman Republic did not begin with a written constitution. However, the tradition of recording laws provided a model for later constitutional governments.

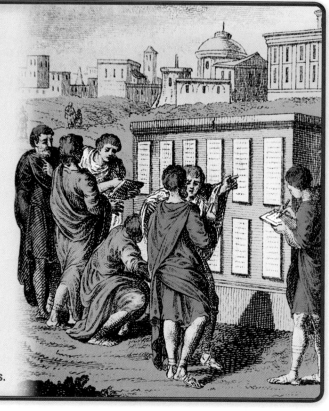

▶ Roman citizens read the Twelve Tables.

Social Classes

The Roman Republic had two main social classes, the patricians (puh•TRIH•shuhnz) and the plebeians (plih•BEE•uhnz). The **patricians** were wealthy landowners descended from the earliest settlers of Rome. Under Roman law, only patricians could be senators. Patricians also held the most important positions in the army and in Roman religious life.

The **plebeians** included all Roman citizens except the patricians. For the most part, plebeians were soldiers, farmers, craftworkers, and merchants. Slaves and those people born outside of Rome could not be part of either class.

Wars against the hostile tribes that surrounded Rome filled the republic's early years. Many plebeians had to leave their farms to fight. When and if they returned, they often found their homes and crops ruined by enemies. To start over, they had to borrow money from the wealthy patricians and if they could not repay their debts, they were imprisoned or enslaved.

Imagine how the plebeians felt. They had risked their lives in battle to save land for Rome, yet they ended up poorer than before. In 494 B.C., the plebeians took peaceful action by refusing to fight in the Roman army.

It was a wise strategy, or plan, because the patricians soon realized that Rome could not survive without its plebeian farmers and soldiers. They canceled the debts of plebeians who could not afford to pay.

▶ A patrician woman

▶ This Roman relief shows plebeians working as merchants selling pillows.

The plebeians also gained the right to elect leaders called **tribunes**. The tribunes could veto any law unfair to the plebeians. In Latin, *veto* means "I say no."

In about 450 B.C., the laws were recorded on bronze tablets and displayed in the Forum. These tablets became known as the Twelve Tables.

READING CHECK SUMMARIZE

What kind of protest did the plebeians use to make the patricians change the government?

Summary

In 509 B.C., the Romans forced their cruel king to leave the city. They created a new form of government, a republic. The Roman Republic had three parts—the consuls, the Senate, and the assemblies—to limit the power of each part. In the Republic, the plebeians began to gain more power. In about 450 B.C., the Twelve Tables were posted in the Forum.

REVIEW

1. How was the Roman Republic different from earlier governments?

2. Write a paragraph explaining the differences between the **patricians** and the **plebeians**.

3. What role did the assemblies play in the Roman Republic?

4. Why is Cincinnatus a good example of the Roman idea of civic duty?

CRITICAL THINKING

5. **ANALYSIS SKILL** **Make It Relevant** In what ways was the government of the Roman Republic like the government of the United States?

6. **ANALYSIS SKILL** Only patricians could be leaders in the early Roman Republic. How might a patrician have felt about this rule? Why might a plebeian have felt differently?

7. **Design a Graphic Organizer** The Roman Republic had a tripartite government. Design a graphic organizer that represents the Roman government.

8. **Focus Skill** DRAW CONCLUSIONS On a separate sheet of paper, copy and complete the graphic organizer below.

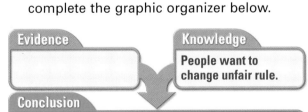

Evidence	Knowledge
	People want to change unfair rule.

Conclusion

The Romans created a republic.

WORKING FOR EQUALITY

"As there was no legal way to redress [set right] their wrongs, they decided that they would no longer serve in the army, but leave the patricians to fight their own battles."*

— from *Outlines of Roman History* by William C. Morey, 1901.

The painting above shows a celebration of plebeian leadership. Cato the Elder (right) was a plebeian who rose to become an important leader in Rome.

In the early years of the Roman Republic, plebeians had few rights. Patricians controlled government, religion, land, and wealth. However, plebeians made up the great majority of Roman citizens. Without plebeian workers, Rome's economy could not have grown. Without plebeian soldiers, Rome's army could not have conquered surrounding lands or defended itself.

In 494 B.C., plebeian soldiers realized that they had the power to win greater equality. They deserted the army and refused to fight for Rome until they had more rights. Their withdrawal strategy worked, and the plebeians continued to use it. Gradually, they

*William C. Morey. *Outlines of Roman History.* American Book Company, 1901.

gained equal rights in Roman society. They won the right to a share of public lands and the right to hold political offices. In 367 B.C., a plebeian was elected as consul for the first time.

Throughout history and all over the world, many groups have struggled for equality. In the United States, African Americans were granted freedom from slavery in 1863. From then on, they struggled for equal rights. The Civil Rights movement of the 1950s and 1960s brought many victories. Dr. Martin Luther King, Jr., led his fellow African Americans in the fight for civil rights. Through his protests, speeches, and strict rule of nonviolence, King made it clear to the world that there must be equality among its people. He helped pave the way for civil rights in the United States. African Americans are not the only ones who have had to struggle for equal rights. At different times, women, Latinos, American Indians, and other groups have struggled for equality in American society.

In the early 1900s, many women (above) in the United States fought for the right to vote. In the 1950s and 1960s, many Americans (below), such as Dr. Martin Luther King, Jr., were working to gain equal rights for African Americans.

Think About It!

Make It Relevant How has working for equality changed life in the United States today?

STUDENT NONVIOLENT COORDINATING COMMITTEE

WE SHALL OVERCOME

I HAVE A DREAM
LET FREEDOM RING
JAN. 15, 1929
APRIL 4, 1968
REV. MARTIN LUTHER KING
A GREAT AMERICAN

Time

1000 B.C.   500 B.C.   B.C./A.D.   A.D. 500

341 B.C.
Roman expansion
begins

272 B.C.
Rome controls all
of the Italian Peninsula

133 B.C.
Rome controls the
Mediterranean region

Roman Expansion

WHAT TO KNOW
How and why did the
Roman Republic expand?

✓ Explain why Rome fought
wars to expand its
territory.

✓ Identify the locations
of Rome's overseas
provinces.

VOCABULARY
romanize p. 485

PEOPLE
Hannibal
Scipio
Philip V
Mummius
Pausanias
Attalus III

PLACES
Rome
Carthage
Macedonia
Corinth
Achaea
Pergamum

**DRAW
CONCLUSIONS**

California
Standards
HSS 6.7, 6.7.3

YOU ARE THERE
It is 341 B.C., and you can tell that war is about
to begin. The streets of **Rome** echo with the
sound of metalworkers forging swords. Workers
carry food and supplies into the city, where they
will be safe from plunder. Lookouts watch from
the walls of the city day and night while scouts
come and go through the gates.

Until recently, Rome's neighbors on
the Italian Peninsula were its allies. Now
they fear Rome's growing power and are
seeking alliances with each other to fight
against Rome.

▶ This statue (right) shows a well-equipped Roman
soldier. The Romans originally built this bridge (below)
in Verona, Italy.

▶ The construction of roads and bridges helped the Romans control conquered territories. This art relief shows workers building a bridge.

Conquest of the Italian Peninsula

In 341 B.C., Rome began to expand its territory on the Italian Peninsula. The first cities to fall to Rome were the 30 cities called the Latin League, which were allied together against Rome. Next, the Romans defeated the Etruscans to the north and the Samnites to the east. Then, the Romans conquered the Greek colonies in the southern part. By 272 B.C., Rome's power extended across the Italian Peninsula.

Why was Rome so eager to expand? One reason was that Rome's neighbors were enemies who would attack Rome if Rome did not attack them first.

In ancient Rome, war was a path to economic growth. Victory in war added new land, which could be farmed, and slaves, who could either provide free labor or be sold. In addition, the Romans collected taxes from the conquered peoples.

The Roman rulers governed the conquered peoples, setting up colonies in defeated territories. These colonies were centers of Roman culture and Roman control, which helped **romanize** the conquered people, or make them Roman in character.

The Romans' skills as builders also helped them govern. The Romans built roads and bridges connecting Rome to conquered lands so that Roman soldiers could reach any place that Rome controlled. All across the Republic, the Romans built temples to Roman gods and goddesses to serve as another reminder of Roman rule. Often, the Romans enslaved conquered peoples and forced them to do the hard work of building.

READING CHECK ⭮ DRAW CONCLUSIONS
Why might it have been important for the Roman rulers to romanize their conquered peoples?

The Punic Wars

Roman soldiers had almost no time to rest before Rome faced another conflict. Two forces had been fighting for control of trade in the Mediterranean, the Greek cities in the southern part of the Italian Peninsula and the Phoenician city-state of **Carthage** in northern Africa. With the Greeks on the peninsula already defeated, only the Carthaginians, the people of Carthage, stood in Rome's way of controlling the trading routes.

Between 264 B.C. and 146 B.C., Rome and Carthage fought three wars. These wars are known as the Punic (PYOO•nik) Wars, from the Roman word for *Phoenician—Punicus.*

Rome won the First Punic War. To succeed, the Romans built a fleet of ships to fight the Carthaginians at sea. One story says that the Romans built 100 ships in 60 days. They defeated the Carthaginians, even though the Carthaginians were much more experienced sailors.

The Second Punic War nearly destroyed Rome. Carthaginian general **Hannibal** was a tireless soldier. An expert of surprise attacks, he crossed over the Mediterranean Sea into what is now Spain. Then he marched his army over the Alps to Rome. The Romans were not prepared, and Hannibal came close to victory.

The Romans would not give up. The Roman general **Scipio** (SIH•pee•oh) invaded northern Africa, forcing Hannibal to leave Rome to defend his homeland. In 202 B.C., Scipio's army defeated Hannibal in the Battle of Zama, near Carthage.

In the Third Punic War, Rome destroyed Carthage in 146 B.C. and sold many of its people into slavery. With the destruction of Carthage, Rome gained new provinces, or self-governing regions, in Africa, which had been controlled by Carthage.

READING CHECK **MAIN IDEA AND DETAILS**
In which Punic War was the city of Rome almost destroyed?

> This wall painting shows how an artist in the A.D. 1500s thought Hannibal's army might have looked.

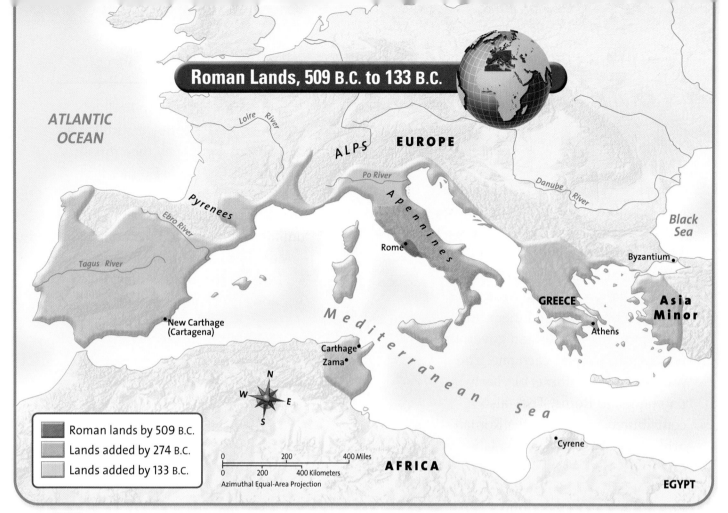

Roman Lands, 509 B.C. to 133 B.C.

ATLANTIC OCEAN

Loire River

EUROPE

ALPS

Po River

Danube River

Apennines

Pyrenees

Ebro River

Rome

Black Sea

Byzantium

Tagus River

GREECE

Asia Minor

New Carthage (Cartagena)

Mediterranean

Athens

Carthage

Zama

Sea

N
W   E
S

Cyrene

Roman lands by 509 B.C.

Lands added by 274 B.C.

Lands added by 133 B.C.

0   200   400 Miles
0   200   400 Kilometers
Azimuthal Equal-Area Projection

AFRICA

EGYPT

ANALYSIS SKILL **Analyze Maps** By 133 B.C., the Romans had gained control of lands in Europe, Asia, and Africa. Roman conquests continued to expand Roman lands over the years.

❖ **Regions** By what year did the Romans control most of the Italian Peninsula?

A "Roman Lake"

TIME By 133 B.C.

PLACE Eastern Mediterranean

Rome spread its power throughout the eastern Mediterranean. Rome conquered many of the Hellenistic, or Greek-like, kingdoms in this region that had once been part of Alexander the Great's empire.

First, the Romans defeated **Macedonia**. The Romans disliked the Macedonians because their leader, **Philip V**, had been an ally of Hannibal in the Second Punic War. After years of fighting, the Romans crushed Philip's army and made his kingdom a Roman province.

In 146 B.C., the Roman general **Mummius** (MUHM•ee•uhs) defeated

Corinth, an important city-state in Greece. **Pausanias**, a Greek historian, wrote, "The majority [of Corinth's men] were put to the sword by the Romans, but the women and children Mummius sold into slavery."* Mummius also tore down the city and took everything of value back to Rome. Greece later would become a Roman province known as **Achaea** (uh•KEE•uh).

The Romans did not have to fight for every new territory. One example of peaceful expansion is the small kingdom of **Pergamum** (PER•guh•muhm), which was located in Asia Minor. In 133 B.C., the king of Pergamum, **Attalus III**, was about to die and had no heirs to take over his throne. He had watched Roman soldiers defeat the much larger kingdoms all around his own.

*Chris Scarre. *The Penguin Historical Atlas of Ancient Rome.* Penguin, 1995.

As his death neared, Attalus arranged to turn Pergamum over to the Romans. Perhaps he did this to spare his people a hopeless war. He may have known that Rome would soon govern them, one way or another.

By this time, Rome controlled the Mediterranean Sea by ruling nearly all of the lands surrounding it. The sea even became known as the "Roman Lake."

To rule all their new lands outside the Italian Peninsula, the Roman leaders divided them into eight provinces. A Roman governor was sent to oversee each one. The provinces paid tribute, or yearly payments, to Rome. They also contributed soldiers to the Roman army and slaves to do hard labor on many building projects. Rome was now the most powerful state in the world.

READING CHECK **SUMMARIZE**
What three territories did Rome acquire in the eastern Mediterranean region?

Summary

The Romans conquered neighboring peoples until, in 272 B.C., they controlled all of the Italian Peninsula. They then fought the Punic Wars to win Rome's first overseas province, in northern Africa. Roman conquest continued until Rome controlled the entire Mediterranean region. Rome became the world's most powerful state at that time.

⚡ FAST FACT

This statue shows a Roman provincial governor seated on a curule (KYUR•ool) chair. In ancient Rome, only important officials had the privilege to sit on the chair.

REVIEW

1. 💡 How and why did the Roman Republic expand?

2. Use the word **romanize** to explain one purpose of Roman colonies.

3. Why did the Romans destroy Carthage?

4. How did war lead to economic growth for ancient Rome?

CRITICAL THINKING

5. **ANALYSIS SKILL** What were the roles of Hannibal and Scipio in Roman history?

6. **ANALYSIS SKILL** **Make It Relevant** Like the Roman Republic, the United States is a land of many cultures. What unites the people of the United States?

7. 🖌 **Make a Time Line** Make a time line that shows the important events of Rome's expansion. Write a caption for each event. Give the time line a title.

8. **Focus Skill** **DRAW CONCLUSIONS**
On a separate sheet of paper, copy and complete the graphic organizer below.

Evidence	Knowledge
The Romans built 100 ships in 60 days.	

Conclusion
The Romans had many resources.

Hannibal

"O Carthage, I see thy fate!" *

Hannibal was the son of a general. After his father died, Hannibal became commander of Carthage's army in Africa. Some say that Hannibal was one of the most brilliant generals in history.

Hannibal loved Carthage. He spent his career fighting to keep the Romans from conquering his city. Through slyness and bravery, Hannibal won several victories against Rome. In 216 B.C., his small army of 20,000 men defeated 50,000 or more Romans at the Battle of Cannae, in Italy. However, this victory over Rome did not last long.

Two events led to Hannibal's defeat. First, the Romans crushed the army of Hannibal's brother Hasdrubal. Hasdrubal was killed in battle, and that is when Hannibal cried, "O Carthage, I see thy fate!"*

▶ **Hannibal and his army cross the snow-covered Alps.**

Next, the Romans attacked Carthage while Hannibal was in Italy. Hannibal was forced to return to Carthage to defend it. At the battle of Zama, near Carthage, Hannibal's army was defeated.

Hannibal had given his all in service to his beloved Carthage, but he had failed to save it. The Romans banished Hannibal from Roman lands—which then included Carthage.

*Hannibal. *The History of Rome.* Vol. 4. Titus Livius, author, William Masfen Roberts, trans. E.P. Dutton, 1924.

Biography

Trustworthiness
Respect
Responsibility
Fairness
Caring
Patriotism

Why Character Counts

❓ **How did Hannibal's actions demonstrate his patriotism?**

Bio Brief

247 B.C.
Born

183 B.C.
Died

218 B.C.
Hannibal invades Italy

216 B.C.
Hannibal defeats the Romans at Cannae

202 B.C.
The Roman general Scipio defeats Hannibal at Zama

GO ONLINE

Interactive Multimedia Biographies
Visit MULTIMEDIA BIOGRAPHIES at
www.harcourtschool.com/hss

Read a Cartogram

▶ WHY IT MATTERS

Some areas have very few people living there, and other areas are very crowded. Factors such as resources and historical events affect the size of an area's population. For example, lands conquered by the ancient Romans grew in population as the Romans set up colonies there.

One way to compare places is to use a cartogram. A **cartogram** is a diagram that shows information about places by showing them in different sizes. A population cartogram shows which countries have many people and which have few people.

▶ WHAT YOU NEED TO KNOW

On most maps, the size of each country or continent is based on the size of its land area. On a cartogram, the size of a country or continent is based on a statistic, such as population. A population cartogram shows the size of each country according to the size of its population. A country with a large population is shown larger than a country with a small population. When countries are shown in this way, you can quickly compare their populations.

The map on this page is a political map of the world. The size of each country is

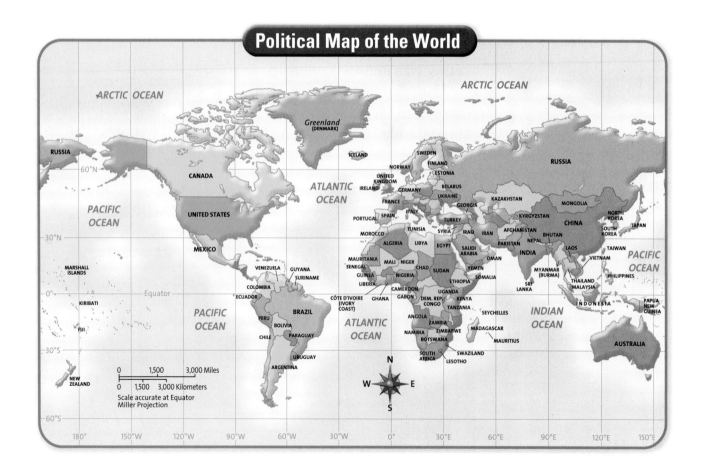

Political Map of the World

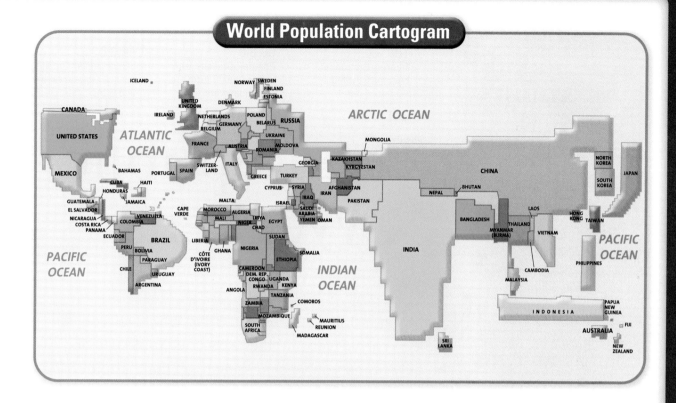

World Population Cartogram

based on the size of its land area. The diagram on this page is a population cartogram. On this diagram, the size of each country is based on the size of its population. Compare the sizes of China and Russia. Although China has a much smaller land area than Russia, it is shown larger than Russia on the cartogram because it has more people.

PRACTICE THE SKILL

ANALYSIS SKILL Use the political map and the cartogram to answer these questions.

1. Compare the country of Italy to the country of Australia. Which country has the larger land area? Which country has the larger population?

2. Which region has countries with larger populations, southern Europe or southeastern Asia?

3. Which continent on the cartogram has the largest population? Which continent has the smallest population? Explain.

APPLY WHAT YOU LEARNED

ANALYSIS SKILL Use atlases, the Internet, and other sources to make a population cartogram of the region of the United States that you live in. Show at least five states on your cartogram. Then compare the sizes of the states on your cartogram with their sizes on a political map.

Chart and Graph Skills

133 B.C.
Tiberius Gracchus
becomes a tribune

60 B.C.
Pompey, Crassus, and
Julius Caesar form the
first triumvirate

44 B.C.
Julius Caesar declares
himself dictator for life
and is then murdered

WHAT TO KNOW
**What problems weakened
the Roman Republic?**

✓ State the problems that
the Roman Republic
faced.

✓ Discuss how Julius
Caesar influenced the
Roman Republic.

VOCABULARY
triumvirate p. 495
assassinate p. 496

PEOPLE
Tiberius Gracchus
Gaius Gracchus
Gauis Marius
Sulla
Pompey
Crassus
Julius Caesar
Cato
Cicero

PLACES
Gaul

DRAW
CONCLUSIONS

California
Standards
HSS 6.7, 6.7.1, 6.7.2, 6.7.3, 6.7.4

The Republic Weakens

YOU ARE THERE It is 133 B.C. "You can bring whatever you can carry," your mother tells you. You're leaving the only home you've ever known, a small farm outside Rome. Your father has sold the farm because it cannot support your family anymore. All around you, enslaved people from conquered lands provide labor for wealthy landowners. The wealthy landowners no longer need the crops your parents grow. "What will we do when the money from the land runs out?" your father asks your mother.

Trouble in Rome

Just when the Romans' power in the Mediterranean world was almost complete, they began having serious problems at home. Many of the problems were of their own making. Historian William C. Morey put it well, when he wrote that the Romans came "to love power for its own sake, and to . . . love wealth more than honor."*

The Romans brought enslaved people from conquered lands to the Italian Peninsula to provide free labor. With no way to earn a living, Roman farmers sold their land to the wealthy and moved to the cities. Slaves were doing much of the work there, too. Many former farmers became beggars.

The wealthy and powerful people in Rome ignored the problems of the poor. They were either unwilling or unable to share their wealth and power with the less fortunate. Instead of taking action, they allowed the problem to get worse.

The greed of wealthy Romans caused problems in conquered lands as well as on the Italian Peninsula. Roman governors forced the conquered people to pay high taxes and spent the money on luxuries for themselves and on weapons for the army. They did little or nothing for the common people, who fell deeper and deeper into debt and had little opportunity to take part in government.

Rome's poor had some voice in government, but they had little power to change things. Over the years, wealthy senators had slowly added to their own power. The tribunes were supposed to protect the rights of the plebeians, but many tribunes had become political allies of the Senate. The gap between the rich and poor continued to grow, but two people were about to stand up for the poor, creating conflict in Rome.

READING CHECK ⭕DRAW CONCLUSIONS
Were Rome's problems caused by outside enemies or by Rome's own policies?

*William C. Morey. *Outlines of Roman History.* American Book Co., 1901.

▶ Daily life in Rome differed according to class. The patricians worked until lunchtime and then relaxed with friends during the afternoon. The plebeians were farmers and craftworkers who worked until dusk.

Attempts at Reform

When **Tiberius Gracchus** (GRA•kuhs) won election as a tribune in 133 B.C., he drew up a plan to give land to the poor. The Senate plotted to block any plan that took wealth from the powerful. It arranged for another tribune, named Octavius, to veto Gracchus's plan. Gracchus then asked the people to force Octavius from office. This action was against the law, but the people did it anyway.

The senators decided to kill Gracchus. When Gracchus was about to be reelected, senators started a riot that killed not only Gracchus but also 300 others.

Gaius (GAY•uhs) **Gracchus**, Tiberius's brother, became a tribune in 123 B.C. He tried to carry out and continue his brother's reforms. In 121 B.C., Gaius Gracchus, too, was killed, along with his followers, because of his political beliefs.

The peace and stability of Rome were broken by the Senate's use of violence to keep its power and wealth. For years to come, force, not law, would rule Rome.

Rome's outside enemies tried to make the most of its weakness. Roman general **Gaius Marius** put down a rebellion in Africa, saved Rome by defeating Germanic tribes who were attacking the city, and crushed a slave revolt. Another Roman general, **Sulla**, had defeated rebels on the Italian Peninsula and elsewhere.

In time, both Marius and Sulla set their sights on ruling Rome. From 88 B.C. to 82 B.C., the two fought a civil war. According to the early writer Plutarch, "No place remained undefiled by murder—neither temple of god, nor friendly home of hospitable hearth, nor ancestral home."*

Sulla won the war and had himself declared dictator—without the six-month limit that the law required. Sulla held absolute power in Rome for three years.

READING CHECK **GENERALIZE**
What kind of government did Rome have after the civil war?

*Plutarch. *Fall of the Roman Republic.* Rex Warner, trans. Penguin Books, 1972.

❯ There was a difference in political beliefs among Gaius Gracchus and the senators. This painting shows the confrontation that ultimately led to Gracchus's death.

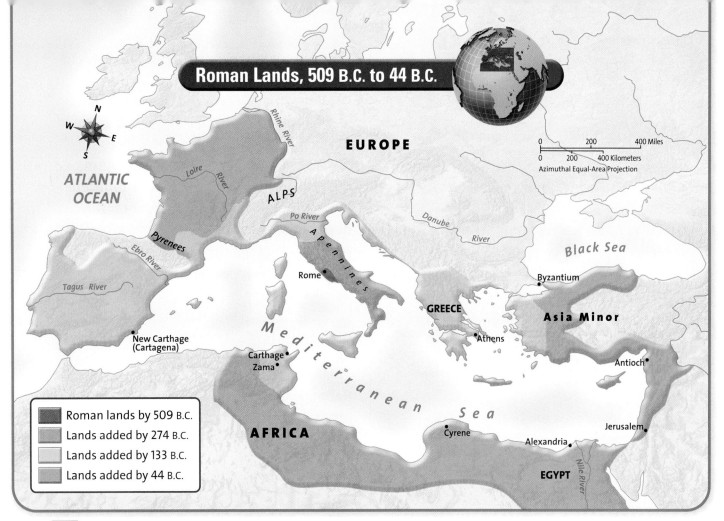

Roman Lands, 509 B.C. to 44 B.C.

EUROPE

ATLANTIC OCEAN

Rhine River

Loire River

ALPS

Pyrenees

Ebro River

Po River

Apennines

Danube River

Black Sea

Tagus River

Rome

Byzantium

GREECE

Asia Minor

New Carthage (Cartagena)

Carthage
Zama

Mediterranean Sea

Athens

Antioch

AFRICA

Cyrene

Alexandria

Jerusalem

Nile River

EGYPT

0   200   400 Miles
0   200   400 Kilometers
Azimuthal Equal-Area Projection

- Roman lands by 509 B.C.
- Lands added by 274 B.C.
- Lands added by 133 B.C.
- Lands added by 44 B.C.

ANALYSIS SKILL **Analyze Maps** Even though the Republic faced internal weaknesses, the Romans continued to conquer new lands in Asia, Europe, and Africa.

◆ **Regions** By what year had Rome conquered lands along the Black Sea?

The Rise of Caesar

After Sulla retired, generals continued to rule. In name, Rome was still a republic. In fact, power was held by one leader who used his army to gain and hold power.

In 60 B.C., three Roman men agreed to share power in an arrangement called a **triumvirate** (try•UHM•vuh•ruht), which simply means "a group of three rulers." All three were powerful generals. **Pompey** (PAHM•pee) and **Crassus** were older men, skilled in battle and in politics. **Julius Caesar** was young and ambitious.

Caesar became consul in 59 B.C. Soon he took action to win the people's favor. For one thing, he gave free grain to all who needed it. For another, he provided land to poor people.

Caesar put together a careful plan to rule all Roman lands. First, he formed an army and captured **Gaul** (GAWL), the region that is now France, then settled by Celtic peoples. He made Gaul a Roman province and became its governor. As governor of Gaul, Caesar kept a close watch on Rome.

While in Gaul, Caesar arranged to get rid of two powerful senators. He did not want anyone in Rome to challenge his power while he was gone. Caesar made one senator, **Cato,** governor of a province in Africa. He forced out the other senator, **Cicero** (SIH•suh•roh). With these senators gone, the Senate had little power.

▶ Enemy soldiers surrender their weapons to Julius Caesar in this painting created at a later time.

Now Caesar was ready to meet his highest goal—to rule Rome and all its lands. Under Roman law, no governor could lead his army outside his own province. The Rubicon River formed the border between Gaul and the Italian Peninsula. When Caesar and his army crossed the Rubicon toward Rome in 49 B.C., his plans were clear.

Caesar's army crushed all his enemies. In 44 B.C., Caesar declared himself dictator for life of Rome and all its provinces. A month later, on March 15, a group of senators **assassinated** Caesar, or murdered him for political reasons. The Roman Republic was about to end.

READING CHECK CAUSE AND EFFECT
What led to Caesar's murder?

Summary

After successful conquests, the Roman Republic began to have problems. Some problems were caused by slavery, the greed of the wealthy, and high taxes. Attempts at reform failed, leading to civil war. Eventually, three powerful generals shared power. One general, Julius Caesar, defeated the other two generals, only to be assassinated shortly afterward.

REVIEW

1. What problems weakened the Roman Republic?

2. Use the word **triumvirate** in a sentence about Julius Caesar.

3. What kind of government did Rome have before and after the civil war between Gaius Marius and Sulla?

4. What role did land ownership play in Rome's problems?

CRITICAL THINKING

5. **ANALYSIS SKILL** **Make It Relevant** In ancient Rome, people who did not own land were likely to become or remain poor. Why is this not always true in the United States today?

6. **ANALYSIS SKILL** What three questions do you have about Julius Caesar that you think can be answered by doing research about his life?

7. **Write an Obituary** An obituary is a notice that tells of a person's death. Obituaries usually include the date of the person's death, how the person died, and important information about the person's life. Write an obituary about Julius Caesar.

8. **Focus Skill** **DRAW CONCLUSIONS** On a separate sheet of paper, copy and complete the graphic organizer below.

Evidence	Knowledge
Poor Romans' problems were ignored.	Ignoring a problem makes it worse.

Conclusion

Julius Caesar

Biography

Trustworthiness
Respect
Responsibility
Fairness
Caring
Patriotism

*"Take we the course which the signs of the gods and false dealing of our foes point out. The die is cast!"** *

These were Julius Caesar's words as he led his army across the Rubicon River into Italy. His ultimate goal was to rule all of Rome, and he was close to achieving this goal. He was also much closer than he knew to his own violent death.

Caesar was a patrician, but he had close ties to the plebeians. He understood the importance of the plebeians' support and made an effort to gain it. Early in his career, Caesar pushed through many reforms that improved the plebeians' lives. He also provided expensive entertainment for the people, such as chariot races and circuses. When he crossed the Rubicon River, the plebeians' tribunes were there to welcome him. The plebeians knew that Caesar planned to make himself dictator and maybe even king. However, they trusted him more than they trusted the Senate or Caesar's other rivals.

It was the senators, not the people, who most resented Caesar's power. A group of senators stabbed him to death on March 15, 44 B.C. Two of the killers were men whom Caesar had pardoned for fighting against him.

> Julius Caesar crosses the Rubicon River.

*Julius Caesar. *Suetonius*. John Carew Rolfe, trans. Putnam, 1920.

Why Character Counts

❓ How did Caesar take responsibility for Rome's people?

Bio Brief

100 B.C.		44 B.C.
Born		Died

59 B.C.
Caesar becomes consul

49 B.C.
Caesar crosses the Rubicon River

44 B.C.
Caesar declares himself dictator for life and is murdered in the Senate

GO ONLINE
Interactive Multimedia Biographies
Visit **MULTIMEDIA BIOGRAPHIES** at
www.harcourtschool.com/hss

750 B.C.
Latin villages
unite to form Rome

450 B.C.
The Twelve
Tables are
written

Reading Social Studies

A **conclusion** is an understanding reached after careful thinking. To **draw a conclusion,** you use what you already know along with what you read about a subject to make a general statement about an idea or an event.

(Focus Skill) Draw a Conclusion

Complete this graphic organizer to show that you can draw conclusions about ancient Rome. A copy of this graphic organizer appears on page 133 of the Homework and Practice Book.

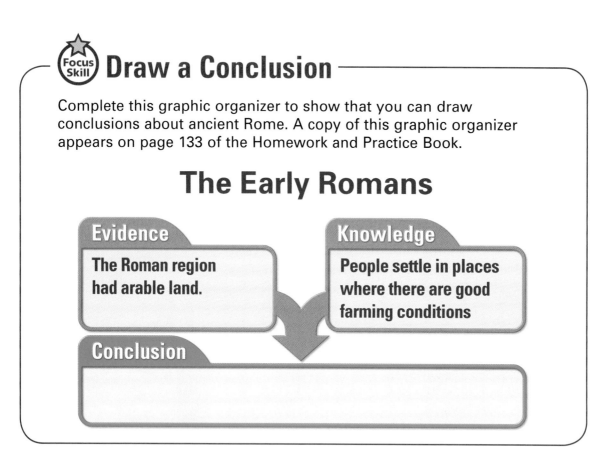

The Early Romans

Evidence

The Roman region had arable land.

Knowledge

People settle in places where there are good farming conditions

Conclusion

California Writing Prompts

Write a Persuasive Speech Imagine that you are a Roman tribune. Write a speech that you will give before the Senate. In your speech, try to persuade senators to support reforms to help the poor.

Write an Expository Paragraph Imagine that you live in a Latin village just before the city of Rome was founded. Write a paragraph that describes your surroundings and your day-to-day life.

300 B.C.	B.C./A.D.	A.D. 300

341 B.C.
Roman expansion
begins

264 B.C.
The Punic
Wars begin

44 B.C.
Julius Caesar
declares himself
dictator for life

Use Vocabulary

Write a sentence explaining the role of each of the following in the Roman Republic.

1. **consul** (p. 478)
2. **Senate** (p. 478)
3. **dictator** (p. 478)
4. **tribune** (p. 481)

Use the Time Line

 Use the summary time line above to answer these questions.

5. How long after Rome was formed were the Twelve Tables written?
6. What happened in 44 B.C.?

Apply Skills

Compare Maps with Different Scales

7. **ANALYSIS SKILL** Suppose that you want to find a map that shows where in Rome the Forum is located. Would you look for a map with a small scale or a large scale? Explain your answer.

Read a Cartogram

8. **ANALYSIS SKILL** Explain what you can learn about Italy today from a political map and what you can learn from a population cartogram.

Recall Facts

Answer these questions.

9. How did the Romans first come into contact with Greek culture, and how did it influence them?
10. What were the Twelve Tables, and why were they important?
11. Why did the Romans create a tripartite government?

Write the letter of the best choice.

12. Which of these men was *not* a Roman?
    A Cicero
    B Cincinnatus
    C Hannibal
    D Pompey
13. Which of the following civilizations influenced early Rome?
    A the Etruscans
    B the Egyptians
    C the Gauls
    D the Phoenicians

Think Critically

14. **ANALYSIS SKILL** Caesar wrote a book about his conquests in Gaul. How reliable do you think this book is? Explain your answer.
15. Of all the Roman leaders whom you have read about, which one do you think benefited Rome the most? Explain your answer.

Study Skills

UNDERSTAND VOCABULARY

Using a dictionary can help you learn new words that you encounter as you read.

➤ **A dictionary identifies all the meanings of a word.**

➤ **It may also describe the word's origin, and that information can help you better understand the meanings of the word.**

➤ **If you have never heard someone say the word, a dictionary can help you pronounce it.**

le•gion (lē′•jən) *n.* **1.** The principal unit of the ancient Roman army **2.** a large military force **3.** a very large number **4.** a national organization of retired military personnel [from the Latin *legion-*, a form of *legere*, to gather].

Word	Syllables	Origin	Definition
legion	le•gion	Latin	The principal unit of the Roman army

Apply As You Read

As you read this chapter, use a dictionary to learn about the unfamiliar words you encounter.

California History-Social Science Standards, Grade 6

6.7 Students analyze the geographic, political, economic, religious, and social structures during the development of Rome.

The Roman Empire

❯ Ruins of the Colosseum in Rome

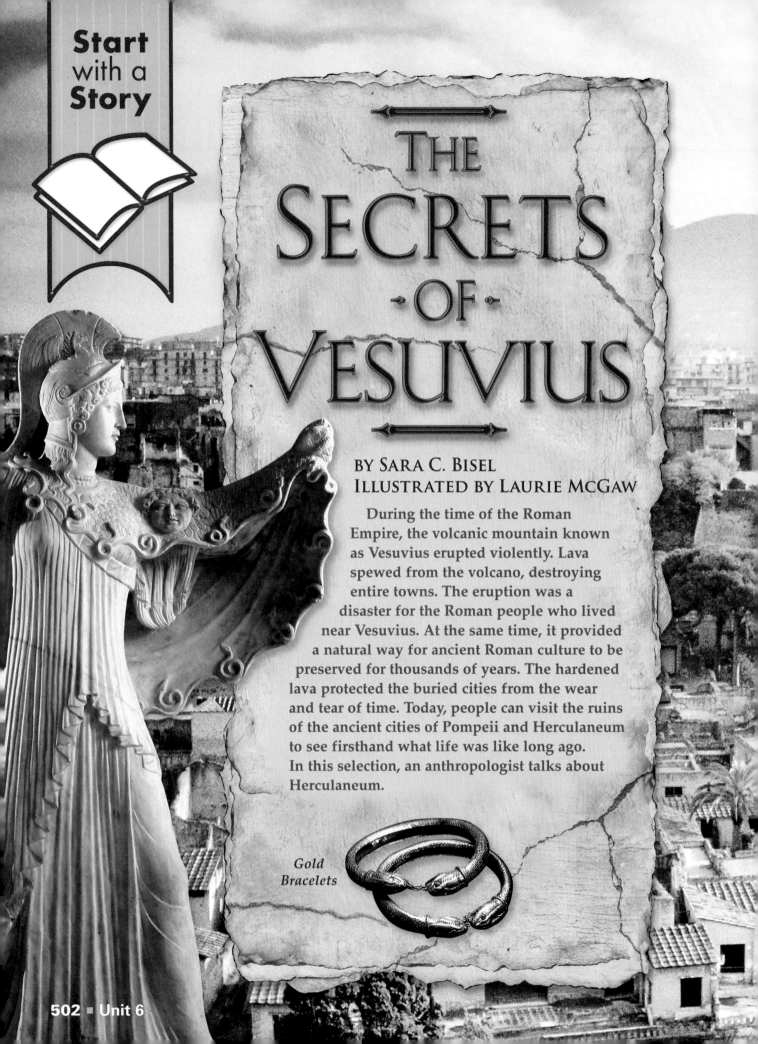

THE SECRETS OF VESUVIUS

BY SARA C. BISEL
ILLUSTRATED BY LAURIE MCGAW

During the time of the Roman Empire, the volcanic mountain known as Vesuvius erupted violently. Lava spewed from the volcano, destroying entire towns. The eruption was a disaster for the Roman people who lived near Vesuvius. At the same time, it provided a natural way for ancient Roman culture to be preserved for thousands of years. The hardened lava protected the buried cities from the wear and tear of time. Today, people can visit the ruins of the ancient cities of Pompeii and Herculaneum to see firsthand what life was like long ago. In this selection, an anthropologist talks about Herculaneum.

*Gold
Bracelets*

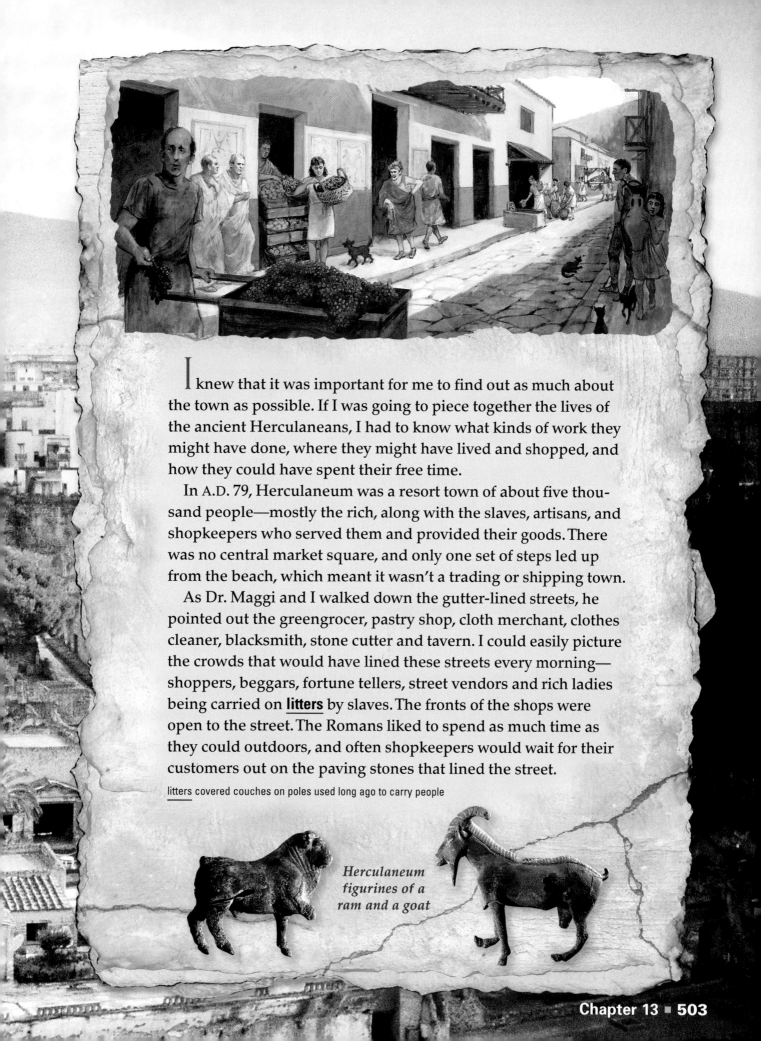

I knew that it was important for me to find out as much about the town as possible. If I was going to piece together the lives of the ancient Herculaneans, I had to know what kinds of work they might have done, where they might have lived and shopped, and how they could have spent their free time.

In A.D. 79, Herculaneum was a resort town of about five thousand people—mostly the rich, along with the slaves, artisans, and shopkeepers who served them and provided their goods. There was no central market square, and only one set of steps led up from the beach, which meant it wasn't a trading or shipping town.

As Dr. Maggi and I walked down the gutter-lined streets, he pointed out the greengrocer, pastry shop, cloth merchant, clothes cleaner, blacksmith, stone cutter and tavern. I could easily picture the crowds that would have lined these streets every morning—shoppers, beggars, fortune tellers, street vendors and rich ladies being carried on **litters** by slaves. The fronts of the shops were open to the street. The Romans liked to spend as much time as they could outdoors, and often shopkeepers would wait for their customers out on the paving stones that lined the street.

litters covered couches on poles used long ago to carry people

Herculaneum figurines of a ram and a goat

We stopped at one of the many *thermopolia*—take-out restaurants where people could buy bread, dried fish, cheese, wine and hot food to take home. Eating take-out food was more of a necessity than a treat, though, since only wealthy homes had full kitchens. I could see a jar of walnuts still sitting on the counter, and a small peep hole in the wall behind, which would have been useful for keeping an eye out for shoplifters or listening in on a juicy bit of gossip. . . .

Inside the *pistrinum*, or bakery, stood round millstones that were powered by slaves or blindfolded donkeys who walked in an endless circle to turn the stone and grind flour. This flour was used to bake breads, cakes, a kind of pizza (but without tomato sauce), and even dog biscuits! When the bakery was dug out, the bones of the donkeys were found still harnessed to the mills.

Beaded necklace with faces painted on beads

The tour of the main streets reminded me how little ordinary people have changed in two thousand years. Our lives today are not much different. We still have to shop, eat, and earn a living. As I poked my head into each shop, I could almost hear the voices of the people who had worked there, complaining about unpaid bills, yelling at their children, shooing a stray dog out of the store. . . .

Many of the poorer residents of Herculaneum lived in rooms behind or above their shops, or in larger buildings that had been divided into small apartments. These cramped, dark, low-ceilinged quarters were very different from the houses Dr. Maggi and I toured next—the homes of the rich.

I would love to have a house like one of these Roman villas. They were airy, beautifully laid out and comfortable, with lots of rooms.

Red quartz ring

Response Corner

1. Why do you think the anthropologist wanted to learn all about the town of Herculaneum?

2. What are three things you learned about the ancient Romans from the writer's description?

42 B.C.
Octavian and Antony defeat Brutus and Cassius at Philippi

31 B.C.
Octavian defeats Antony and Cleopatra and rules all of Rome's lands

27 B.C.
Octavian is given the title *Augustus*

From Republic to Empire

YOU ARE THERE

You and your neighbor **Octavian** (ahk•TAY•vee•uhn) live in **Rome** in 44 B.C. You used to envy Octavian because he is related to **Julius Caesar**, Rome's most powerful leader. For once, you're glad you're not Octavian. He's not even 20 years old, and the future of Rome depends on him now that Caesar has been assassinated. If Octavian wants to rule Rome, though, he will have to fight. In fact, he is eager to fight—as much to avenge Caesar as to win power for himself.

⚡ FAST FACT

The month of July is named for Julius Caesar. The month of August is named for Augustus Caesar, the title Octavian (right) took in 27 B.C.

WHAT TO KNOW
How did Rome make the transition from a republic to an empire?

✓ Identify the political and geographical reasons for the expansion of the empire.

✓ Discuss the influence of Augustus on Rome's transition from republic to empire.

VOCABULARY
heir p. 507

PEOPLE
Octavian/Augustus
Julius Caesar
Mark Antony
Lepidus
Brutus
Cassius
Cleopatra VII
Tacitus

PLACES
Rome
Philippi
Actium
Alexandria

DRAW CONCLUSIONS

California Standards
HSS 6.7, 6.7.3, 6.7.4

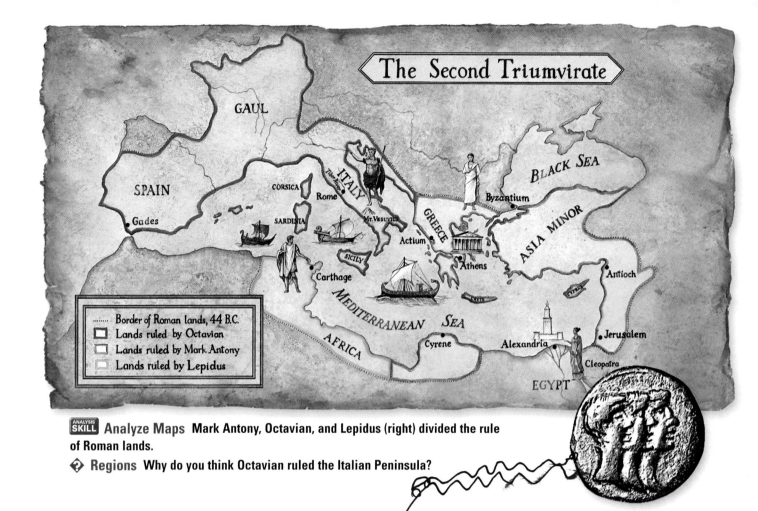

The Second Triumvirate

GAUL

SPAIN

Gades

CORSICA

Rome

SARDINIA

Mt. Vesuvius

ITALY

SICILY

Carthage

MEDITERRANEAN SEA

AFRICA

Cyrene

BLACK SEA

Byzantium

GREECE

Actium

Athens

ASIA MINOR

Antioch

CYPRUS

Jerusalem

Alexandria

Cleopatra

EGYPT

.... Border of Roman lands, 44 B.C.
☐ Lands ruled by Octavian
☐ Lands ruled by Mark Antony
☐ Lands ruled by Lepidus

ANALYSIS SKILL **Analyze Maps** Mark Antony, Octavian, and Lepidus (right) divided the rule of Roman lands.

◈ **Regions** Why do you think Octavian ruled the Italian Peninsula?

Civil War Again

The assassination of Julius Caesar led to another civil war in Rome. None of the senators who killed Caesar had the power or the support to rule Rome alone.

In addition, Caesar's young heir, Octavian, was determined to take revenge for Caesar's death. An **heir** (AIR) is a person entitled to receive the money or property of a person who has died. Octavian was Caesar's great-nephew, the grandson of Caesar's sister, but Caesar had adopted him as a son.

Octavian was a strong and intelligent leader who worked to win the support of the people. He agreed to share the leadership of Rome with **Mark Antony** and **Lepidus** (LEH•puh•duhs), two of Caesar's supporters. Together, they formed the Second Triumvirate and divided the

western provinces. **Brutus** and **Cassius**, the senators who had led the attack on Caesar, occupied the lands to the east.

In 42 B.C., Octavian and Antony won a civil war against Brutus and Cassius in **Philippi**, a hill town in Greece. Afterward, Antony ruled the eastern provinces, while Octavian took charge of the Italian Peninsula and the western provinces. Lepidus governed Roman lands in Africa.

In 36 B.C., Lepidus tried to overthrow Octavian. According to legend, Octavian heard about the plot, walked into Lepidus's army camp, and asked the soldiers not to rebel against him. The whole army agreed. This may not have really happened, but Octavian did take away Lepidus's role in the Triumvirate.

READING CHECK ☼ **DRAW CONCLUSIONS**
Why did Octavian and Mark Antony go to war against Brutus and Cassius?

▶ Cleopatra retreats from the Battle of Actium in a small ship.

Octavian Defeats Antony

TIME 31 B.C.

PLACE Actium, Greece

Antony and Octavian soon ended their alliance as they struggled to control Roman lands. Afterward, Antony met with **Cleopatra VII,** the queen of Egypt, the only land left on the Mediterranean Sea not under Roman control. Antony decided to share his power with Cleopatra. In exchange, she provided Antony with money, supplies, and food for his troops.

The Roman people were unhappy with the idea that a foreign queen had power over their lands. Back in Rome, Octavian used this ill will to gain support for a war against Antony and Cleopatra.

In 31 B.C., Antony and Cleopatra's forces clashed with Octavian's forces off the coast of Greece in a crucial sea battle called the Battle of **Actium.** Outnumbered and facing certain defeat, Antony and Cleopatra set sail for Egypt. Octavian set fire to the warships they left behind.

Octavian followed Antony and Cleopatra to **Alexandria,** Egypt. Within a year, both Antony and Cleopatra would be dead. Despite all of Cleopatra's efforts, Octavian conquered Egypt and made it a province of Rome. Now the entire Mediterranean world was part of the Roman world, and it was all under Octavian's control.

READING CHECK CAUSE AND EFFECT
How did Egypt become a Roman province?

▶ Cleopatra, ruler of Egypt

Rome Becomes an Empire

Octavian returned to a hero's welcome in Rome. In 27 B.C., the Senate gave him the title **Augustus**, which means "Respected One" or "Holy One." Octavian has been known ever since as Augustus Caesar, or simply Augustus.

Augustus was Rome's first emperor, although he did not call himself that. He took the title *Princeps Civitatis*, which means "first citizen of the state" in Latin.

Augustus tried to preserve for Rome's citizens the idea that they still lived in a republic. For many years, the Senate, assemblies, and tribunes still existed, but they did not function the way they once had. The idea behind the Republic's tripartite government had been to limit the power of any one person. By contrast, Augustus held absolute power over vast lands. No longer a republic, Rome had, in fact, become an empire.

Tacitus (TA•suh•tuhs), a Roman historian who lived shortly after Augustus, wrote:

> 66 The character of the government thus totally changed; no traces were to be found of the spirit of ancient institutions. The system by which every citizen shared in the government being thrown aside, all men regarded the orders of the prince as the only rule of conduct and obedience. 99 *

For centuries to come, emperors ruled Rome. Some, like Augustus, were wise leaders who strengthened the empire and ruled the people well. Others were poor leaders who were hated by the Roman people.

READING CHECK COMPARE AND CONTRAST
How did the Roman Empire differ from the Roman Republic?

*Cornelius Tacitus, from *The Works of Tacitus: The Oxford Translation, Revised, with Notes.* G. Bell, 1914.

ANALYSIS SKILL Analyze Time Lines The time line focuses on events that changed Rome's government.

Did Julius Caesar's successor become known as Augustus or conquer Egypt first?

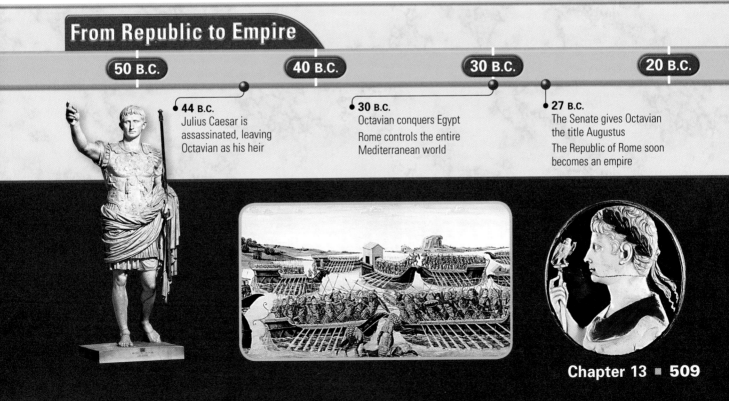

From Republic to Empire

50 B.C.   40 B.C.   30 B.C.   20 B.C.

44 B.C.
Julius Caesar is assassinated, leaving Octavian as his heir

30 B.C.
Octavian conquers Egypt
Rome controls the entire Mediterranean world

27 B.C.
The Senate gives Octavian the title Augustus
The Republic of Rome soon becomes an empire

Diversity and Unity

Augustus brought peace and stability to Rome. Because he was both strong and wise, he won widespread support. Wars over the leadership of Rome ended at last.

The empire that Augustus ruled was vast and diverse, made up of many cultures. As different as the cultures of ancient Greece and Egypt were, both were now part of the Roman Empire. So, too, were parts of western Europe and Asia.

Rome under Augustus achieved balance in ruling the provinces. On the one hand, Rome allowed for diversity by letting those that it conquered keep their own cultures. For example, conquered peoples continued to practice their own religions and speak their own languages.

On the other hand, Rome took steps to unite the various peoples in its empire. The Romans spread the use of Latin across the empire and made it the official language in Rome's western lands. In the east, Greek was the official language. The Romans did not force people to speak only the official languages. However, having the ability to speak Greek or Latin helped people communicate across the empire.

Augustus helped unify the empire by granting citizenship to free men in the provinces. Over time, men from the provinces could even serve in the Senate. Although the Senate had little real power, being a senator still brought wealth and honor. More important, the provinces now had a stake and a voice in the government of the empire.

Cultures and Languages in the Roman Empire

REGION	CULTURES	LANGUAGES
Northern Africa	Berbers Phoenicians Greeks	Berber languages Phoenician languages Greek
Egypt	Egyptians	Egyptian
Southwestern Asia	Hebrews Persians	Hebrew, Aramaic languages Persian, Aramaic languages
Greece	Greeks	Greek Koine
Rome, Italy	Romans	Latin
Northwestern Italy	Etruscans	Etruscan, Latin
Northeastern Europe	Germanic peoples	Germanic languages
Western Europe	Celtic peoples	Celtic languages

ANALYSIS SKILL **Analyze Tables** The Roman Empire included an astonishing diversity of lands, cultures, and languages. This diversity inspired Roman artists to create this tile mosaic (below) of the Nile River.

❓ **How might having official languages have helped the Romans rule?**

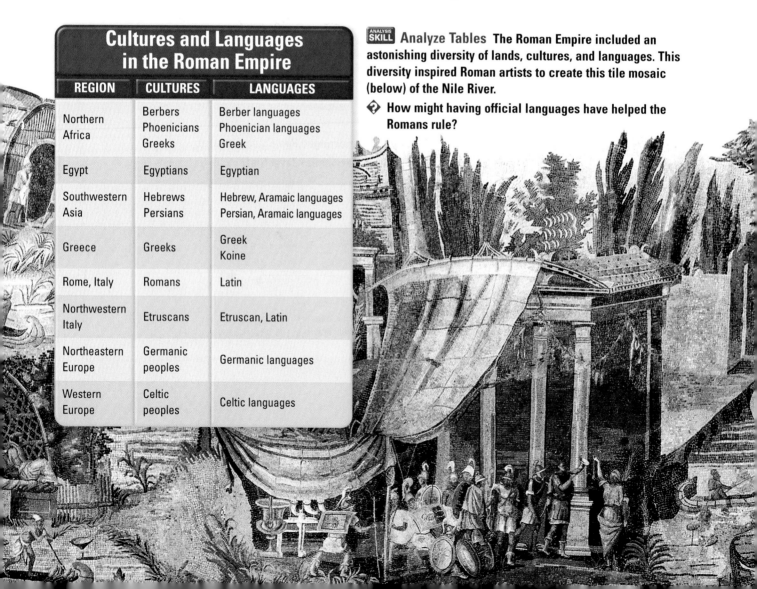

▶ Citizens of Rome line up to be counted for tax payments and military service.

Augustus also tried to improve the lives of the poor and to make taxation fairer. The peace that began with Augustus's reign helped increase trade. Merchants could trade with little fear of attack.

The people who lived in Rome's provinces were not free. Under Augustus, however, there were rewards for being part of the Roman Empire. Augustus spent many years extending both his empire and the benefits it granted.

READING CHECK **SUMMARIZE**
What steps did Augustus take to unite the various peoples in his empire?

Summary

After Caesar's murder, civil war broke out in Rome. Caesar's heir, Octavian, and Antony defeated Brutus and Cassius. Later, Antony allied himself with Cleopatra, queen of Egypt. Octavian defeated both of them to become the sole ruler of the Roman Empire. In 27 B.C., the Senate gave Octavian the title of Augustus, which means "Respected One." Afterward, Octavian became known as Augustus Caesar, or simply Augustus. Under the rule of Augustus, Rome became a diverse and united empire.

REVIEW

1. How did Rome make the transition from a republic to an empire?

2. Use the word **heir** in a sentence about Octavian.

3. How did the government of Rome change after Rome became an empire?

4. How did Octavian get the name *Augustus*, and what does it mean?

CRITICAL THINKING

5. **ANALYSIS SKILL** How might the history of Rome have been different if Mark Antony and Cleopatra had defeated Octavian?

6. **ANALYSIS SKILL** **Make It Relevant** How does the power that Augustus had as emperor compare to the power held by the President of the United States?

7. **Write a Newspaper Article** Write the first paragraph of a newspaper article for an event described in this lesson. Include *who*, *what*, *when*, *where*, and *how*.

8. **Focus Skill** **DRAW CONCLUSIONS**
On a separate sheet of paper, copy and complete the graphic organizer below.

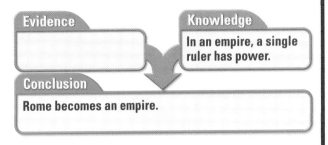

Evidence

Knowledge
In an empire, a single ruler has power.

Conclusion
Rome becomes an empire.

Map and Globe Skills

Compare Historical Maps

▶ WHY IT MATTERS

Historical maps show what places were like in the past. They may show what the borders and place names were at certain times. Comparing historical maps that show the same places at different times can help you understand how those places have changed.

▶ WHAT YOU NEED TO KNOW

Look at Map A on this page. The title tells you that the map shows lands controlled by Rome in 274 B.C. By reading the map key, you learn that Roman lands are shown in purple. The cream-colored areas show the lands that were outside of Rome's control.

Now look at Map B on page 513. First, read the title to find out what period of time it shows. Next, look at the map key. Purple shows Roman lands, just as it does on Map A.

These two maps use colors in the same way. However, many times you will compare maps that use different colors and symbols. You might also compare more than two maps. Map C on page 513 shows the Roman Empire at its greatest size, under Emperor Trajan.

▶ PRACTICE THE SKILL

ANALYSIS SKILL Use the maps on these pages to answer the following questions.

1 Which map shows what lands Rome controlled by 44 B.C.?

2 By what year did Rome control the cities of Antioch and Jerusalem?

3 How did Rome's borders change between 274 B.C. and A.D. 117?

▶ Trajan's Column in Rome

Map A: Rome in 274 B.C.

Roman lands

ATLANTIC OCEAN

0 400 800 Miles
0 400 800 Kilometers
Azimuthal Equal-Area Projection

BRITAIN
EUROPE
ASIA
Danube River
ALPS
Aral Sea
Tagus River
Rome
Black Sea
Caspian Sea
New Carthage (Cartagena)
GREECE
Byzantium
Zama
Carthage
Athens
Antioch
Tigris
Mediterranean Sea
Euphrates River
Cyrene
Alexandria
Jerusalem
EGYPT
Nile River
Red Sea
Persian Gulf
AFRICA

Map B: Rome in A.D. 117

Roman lands

ATLANTIC OCEAN

BRITAIN

EUROPE

ASIA

Aral Sea

Danube River

ALPS

Black Sea

Caspian Sea

Tagus River

Rome

Byzantium

GREECE

Athens

Antioch

Mediterranean Sea

Euphrates River

Tigris River

New Carthage (Cartagena)

Zama

Carthage

Cyrene

Alexandria

Jerusalem

EGYPT

Persian Gulf

AFRICA

Nile River

Red Sea

0   400   800 Miles
0   400   800 Kilometers
Azimuthal Equal-Area Projection

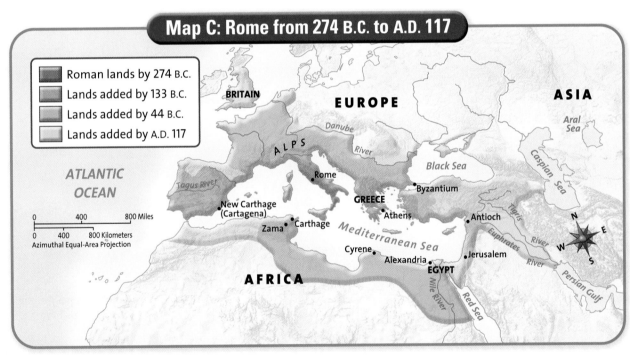

Map C: Rome from 274 B.C. to A.D. 117

Roman lands by 274 B.C.
Lands added by 133 B.C.
Lands added by 44 B.C.
Lands added by A.D. 117

ATLANTIC OCEAN

BRITAIN

EUROPE

ASIA

Aral Sea

Danube River

ALPS

Black Sea

Caspian Sea

Tagus River

Rome

Byzantium

GREECE

Athens

Antioch

Mediterranean Sea

Euphrates River

Tigris River

New Carthage (Cartagena)

Zama

Carthage

Cyrene

Alexandria

Jerusalem

EGYPT

Persian Gulf

AFRICA

Nile River

Red Sea

0   400   800 Miles
0   400   800 Kilometers
Azimuthal Equal-Area Projection

❯ APPLY WHAT YOU LEARNED

Use an atlas to find historical maps that show the political expansion of the United States. Then draw a map that shows this growth. Use different colors to indicate the size of the nation at different times in history. Write a paragraph describing the border changes shown on your map.

Practice your map and globe skills with the **GeoSkills CD-ROM**.

Map and Globe Skills

Time

1000 B.C.	500 B.C.	B.C./A.D.	A.D. 500

A.D. 14
Augustus dies

A.D. 64
Fire destroys much of Rome

A.D. 180
Marcus Aurelius dies

Times of Peace

WHAT TO KNOW
How did the Roman rulers strengthen their empire in times of peace?

✓ Explain the role Augustus played in strengthening the Roman Empire.

✓ Describe how the use of currency and trade routes helped the Roman economy grow.

VOCABULARY
legion p. 515
currency p. 516

PEOPLE
Augustus
Tiberius
Caligula
Claudius
Nero
Nerva
Trajan
Hadrian
Antoninus Pius
Marcus Aurelius

DRAW CONCLUSIONS

California Standards
HSS 6.7, 6.7.3, 6.7.4

YOU ARE THERE
The year is A.D. 7. You have never seen your parents as happy as they are today. Your father has been a Roman soldier for a long time. For much of your life, he has been away at war.

Now there is wonderful news—**Augustus** is reducing the size of the army. Many soldiers are being asked to become colonists instead of warriors. The army has offered your father free land if he will help start a Roman colony in the provinces. For your father, there will be no more fighting. Your family will be together.

"The place where we're going is beautiful," your father says. "We can live a quiet life on our own land." Both of your parents have tears in their eyes, but you know they are happy, not sad.

▶ For many Roman soldiers, Augustus's rule brought citizenship, pay, and land.

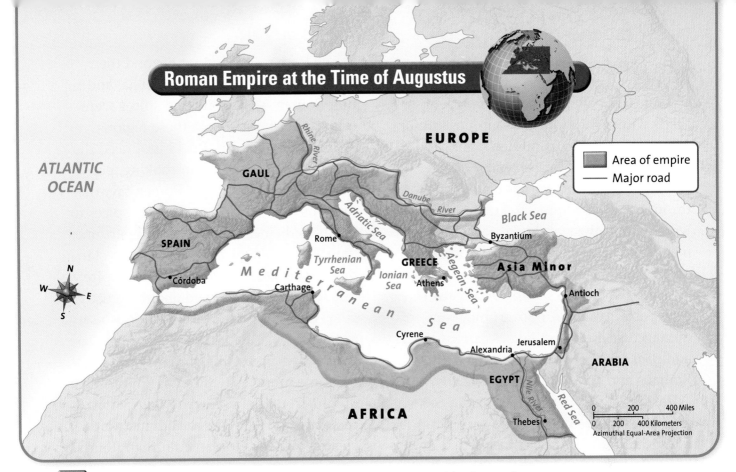

Roman Empire at the Time of Augustus

EUROPE

ATLANTIC OCEAN

GAUL

Rhine River

Danube River

Black Sea

Byzantium

SPAIN

Rome

Adriatic Sea

GREECE

Aegean Sea

Asia Minor

Córdoba

Tyrrhenian Sea

Ionian Sea

Athens

Antioch

M e d i t e r r a n e a n   S e a

Carthage

Cyrene

Alexandria

Jerusalem

ARABIA

EGYPT

Nile River

Red Sea

AFRICA

Thebes

Area of empire

Major road

0   200   400 Miles

0   200   400 Kilometers

Azimuthal Equal-Area Projection

ANALYSIS SKILL **Analyze Maps** Under Augustus's rule, the Roman Empire stretched for thousands of miles and included lands in Europe, Asia, and Africa.

❖ **Regions** How do you think Romans traveled to Alexandria, by land or by water?

The Reign of Augustus

Augustus ruled the Roman Empire for more than 40 years. Under his leadership, the empire grew and prospered. By the end of his reign, Rome controlled people and lands in Africa, Asia, and Europe.

Augustus gained much of his success at leadership by enacting reforms, or changes. He dramatically reformed Rome's army. Augustus cut the size of the army in half and organized it into 28 legions. A **legion** (LEE•juhn) was a group of a few thousand soldiers. Augustus's army had about 160,000 soldiers.

In the past, soldiers had not been paid with money, but with valuables from those they conquered. Instead, Augustus taxed rich Romans to give soldiers regular pay and created a retirement program for the

soldiers. After completing a set period of service, a soldier got land or money. Many became colonists in the provinces. Soldiers who were not Romans could become Roman citizens. Because of these changes, more soldiers made the army a career. The army became more professional—and more loyal to Rome than to any one army leader.

Augustus also reformed the organization of Rome's provinces by establishing two kinds of provinces. The senatorial provinces were governed by the Senate. The emperor controlled the imperial provinces, taking charge of troublesome ones by having the army enforce Roman control. By controlling these provinces, the emperor controlled the army as well.

READING CHECK ⊙DRAW CONCLUSIONS
How did Augustus's reforms improve the army?

Trade and Currency

Augustus believed that a network of roads within the empire was important for conquests, defense, communication, and trade. He repaired and extended roads so that soldiers and traders could travel throughout the empire. The main highways were wide, paved, and built to last. They made the exchange of goods and ideas across long distances easier.

Using the empire's roads, Augustus set up a postal system for government and military use. Relays of horses carried letters and packages between towns for wealthy Romans and government officials.

Besides roads, the Mediterranean Sea and the empire's major rivers served as important trade routes. Ships carried millions of sacks of grain from Egypt to Rome each year. Spain exported olive oil to other parts of the empire.

The Romans traded far beyond their empire—with China, India, Persia, and non-Roman Africa. Silk and spices were important imports from these regions. Asian and African traders introduced the Romans to new spices. In cooking, pepper from India became a Roman favorite. Romans also learned how to use spices to make medicines, cosmetics, and perfumes.

In 24 B.C., Augustus established a standard **currency**, or money, for the empire. The Romans had learned about the use of coins from the Greeks. Augustus also set a standard value for each kind of coin so that traders across the empire could use the same money. The Roman Empire's use of trade routes and currency supported economic growth. The wealth that trade created allowed Roman culture to flourish.

READING CHECK MAIN IDEA AND DETAILS
Why was road building important to the Roman Empire?

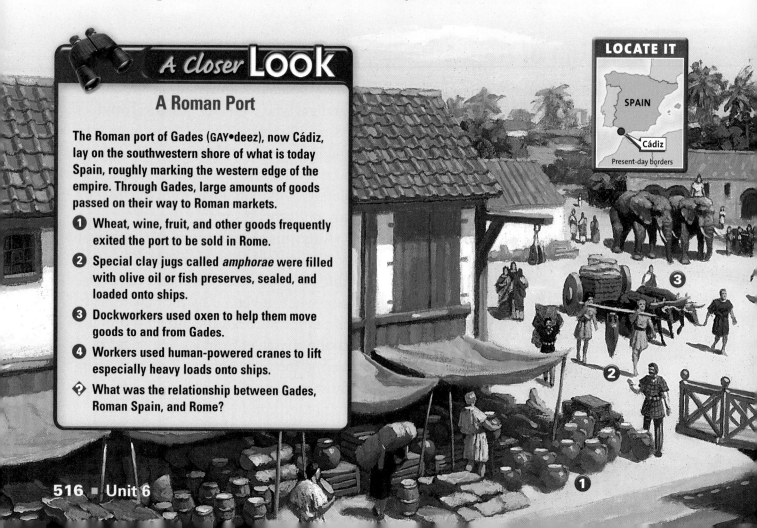

A Closer Look

A Roman Port

The Roman port of Gades (GAY•deez), now Cádiz, lay on the southwestern shore of what is today Spain, roughly marking the western edge of the empire. Through Gades, large amounts of goods passed on their way to Roman markets.

❶ Wheat, wine, fruit, and other goods frequently exited the port to be sold in Rome.

❷ Special clay jugs called *amphorae* were filled with olive oil or fish preserves, sealed, and loaded onto ships.

❸ Dockworkers used oxen to help them move goods to and from Gades.

❹ Workers used human-powered cranes to lift especially heavy loads onto ships.

◆ What was the relationship between Gades, Roman Spain, and Rome?

LOCATE IT

SPAIN

Cádiz

Present-day borders

The *Pax Romana*

Augustus took Rome from republic to empire. His rule also marked the beginning of the *Pax Romana*, or Roman Peace, which lasted for more than 200 years. Augustus died in A.D. 14. According to legend, his last words were "Have I played my part well?"*

Tiberius, Augustus's adopted son, became Rome's next emperor. In the provinces, little changed when Tiberius took power. In Rome, Tiberius took more political rights away from people and even made it a crime to criticize the emperor. Tiberius had to rely on bodyguards because he made so many enemies.

When Tiberius died, the Senate chose **Caligula** (kuh•LIH•gyuh•luh) to rule. Like Augustus and Tiberius, Caligula

*Allen M. Ward, Fritz M. Heichelheim, and Cedric E. Yeo. *A History of the Roman People.* Prentice Hall, 1999.

was related to Julius Caesar. The new emperor soon became ill. He could not rule, yet there was no legal way to remove him from power. After four years of poor rule, assassins killed Caligula.

The army and the Senate then named Tiberius's nephew **Claudius** as emperor. He is remembered for bringing part of Britain into the Roman Empire in A.D. 43.

The next emperor was **Nero**, a stepson of Claudius. The people grew to hate Nero and rebelled against him. In A.D. 64, much of Rome burned in a huge fire, and this disaster added to Nero's unpopularity.

READING CHECK Ŏ **DRAW CONCLUSIONS**
How is Claudius remembered as an emperor of Rome?

Five Good Emperors

In A.D. 69, Rome had a series of four emperors, all of whom were generals. They were also the first rulers outside of Caesar's family to become emperors. The first three took power only to be overthrown by another within months. The fourth one, Vespasian (veh•SPAY•zhuhn), took power

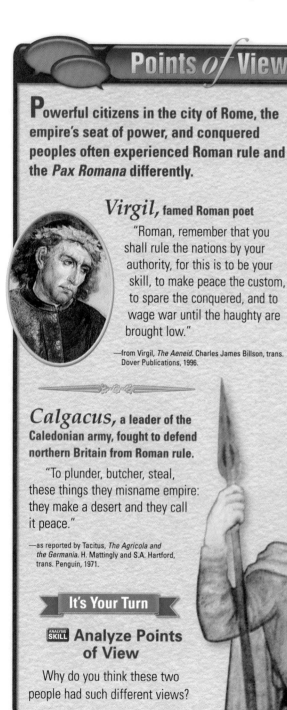

Points of View

Powerful citizens in the city of Rome, the empire's seat of power, and conquered peoples often experienced Roman rule and the *Pax Romana* differently.

Virgil, famed Roman poet

"Roman, remember that you shall rule the nations by your authority, for this is to be your skill, to make peace the custom, to spare the conquered, and to wage war until the haughty are brought low."

—from Virgil, *The Aeneid.* Charles James Billson, trans. Dover Publications, 1996.

Calgacus, a leader of the Caledonian army, fought to defend northern Britain from Roman rule.

"To plunder, butcher, steal, these things they misname empire: they make a desert and they call it peace."

—as reported by Tacitus, *The Agricola and the Germania.* H. Mattingly and S.A. Hartford, trans. Penguin, 1971.

It's Your Turn

ANALYSIS SKILL **Analyze Points of View**

Why do you think these two people had such different views?

and then held it for ten years. His sons Titus and Domitian (duh•MIH•shuhn) followed him as emperor.

Vespasian and Titus were, for the most part, successful rulers. Under their rule, the empire remained mostly at peace. Vespasian and Titus did, however, face a Jewish revolt in Judaea, at that time a province of Rome. Titus destroyed Jerusalem and the Temple in A.D. 70.

The people were unhappy under the leadership of Domitian, the next ruler. Domitian was a tyrant, and in A.D. 96, he was assassinated.

The next period, from A.D. 96 to A.D. 180, is known as the time of the Five Good Emperors. During this time, the empire was at its peak.

Nerva (NER•vuh) was tolerant of non-Roman religions such as Judaism and Christianity. He also provided land for the poor and education for their children. After a brief reign, he died of natural causes.

Trajan (TRAY•juhn), who had been adopted by Nerva, was the first emperor born outside of the Italian Peninsula—in Spain, which was then a Roman province. Trajan was a wise and generous ruler, and the people loved him. He was also the first emperor since Claudius to conquer new territories. The Roman Empire grew to its largest size under Trajan.

Hadrian, the adopted son of Trajan, ruled in much the same way as his father had. However, he concentrated on defending lands, rather than on trying to take more. Hadrian was succeeded by **Antoninus Pius** (an•tuh•NY•nuhs PY•uhs), his own adopted

> Bronze coin of emperor Nerva

> Gold coin of emperor Antoninus Pius

> Silver coin of emperor Trajan and empress Plotina

> Gold coin of emperor Hadrian

son. Antoninus ruled over a long period of peace and prosperity.

In A.D. 161, **Marcus Aurelius** (MAR•kuhs aw•REEL•yuhs) began his rule. He was a wise leader who faced new problems. First, a plague swept across the empire, killing millions. Then, invaders threatened the empire's borders. Aurelius turned back the invaders but died shortly after, in A.D. 180.

READING CHECK SUMMARIZE
What was the period from A.D. 96 to A.D. 180 like for the Roman Empire?

Summary

Augustus ruled the Roman Empire for 40 years. He reformed the military, reorganized the provinces, and set up a postal system. He also expanded Roman trade far beyond the empire. His reign set the stage for the *Pax Romana*. After a period of instability, Rome prospered from A.D. 96 to A.D. 180 under the rule of the Five Good Emperors. During their reign, the Roman Empire grew to its largest size.

REVIEW

1. How did the Roman rulers strengthen their empire in times of peace?

2. Write a paragraph about the rule of Augustus using the words **legion** and **currency**.

3. How did the empire's use of trade routes and currency foster, or support, economic growth?

CRITICAL THINKING

4. What steps did Augustus take to make Rome strong and stable?

5. **ANALYSIS SKILL** How might Augustus's reforms of the Roman army have helped increase Rome's control over its provinces?

6. **ANALYSIS SKILL** **Make It Relevant** What effects do you think war and peace have on countries today?

7. **Design a Coin** Design a coin that might have been used in the Roman Empire. Think about what images would have been good symbols for Rome. Write a caption that explains the symbols you drew.

8. **Focus Skill** **DRAW CONCLUSIONS** On a separate sheet of paper, copy and complete the graphic organizer below.

Evidence

Knowledge
Organized systems help economic growth.

Conclusion
The Roman Empire's economy grew.

Lesson 3 Everyday Life in Ancient Rome

WHAT TO KNOW
What was everyday life like in the Roman Empire?

✓ Describe what cities, farms, and daily life were like in the Roman Empire.

✓ Explain how the lives of the poor and the rich differed in ancient Rome.

VOCABULARY
census p. 522
aqueduct p. 522
gladiator p. 524

PEOPLE
Augustus

PLACES
Rome
Athens
Antioch
Alexandria
Carthage

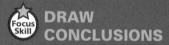

DRAW CONCLUSIONS

California Standards
HSS 6.7, 6.7.3, 6.7.8

YOU ARE THERE It's a hot day in 27 B.C., and this school day seems endless! All you want to do is go outside and play, but you force yourself to work on your math problem instead. Using a piece of pointed metal, you scratch numbers in the wax that covers your writing tablet. When you make a mistake, you rub the numbers out of the wax and start over.

Finally, you finish the problem, and your teacher says that you are finished for the day. As you leave the classroom, you think about children who are unable to go to school because their families are poor. While they work hard learning their parents' trades, you learn new ideas at school.

▶ Wealthy Romans could afford magnificent villas like this one, complete with an atrium (AY•tree•uhm), or central hall, a kitchen, and artwork.

Life at Home

Few ancient Romans who lived in cities could afford their own homes, so most lived in apartments. The city of **Rome** itself had more than 45,000 blocks of apartment buildings. Many were four or five stories tall and were crowded, noisy, and dirty. People threw their garbage out of their windows into the streets below. It was common for roofs or walls to cave in and for whole buildings to collapse. Fire was a constant danger, since many buildings were made at least partly of wood.

The apartments did not have running water, kitchens, or heat. People carried water from public fountains and bought their meals from food vendors on the street or cooked outdoors on small grills. People ate mostly bread, vegetables, fruit, and cheese. Meat was a luxury that people rarely ate.

Many wealthy families had large homes in the city and the country. These homes usually had many rooms built around a central courtyard, with running water and private gardens. Slaves did the cooking and other chores. Wealthy people ate foods imported from all over the empire, including deer, pork, ostrich, and flamingo.

Rich people entertained their friends at banquets, or feasts. Slaves prepared and served expensive foods and drinks. Often, the hosts hired professional musicians, singers, and dancers to entertain their guests.

READING CHECK Ŏ **DRAW CONCLUSIONS**
How did living in a large empire affect the home life of wealthy Romans?

Children IN HISTORY

Roman Children

Roman education started at home when the children were very young. Women taught small boys and girls. When a boy was old enough, he spent time with his father and learned to do his father's job. A girl would remain in the home, where she learned crafts and household chores from her mother. As Rome's power and wealth grew, tutors became more common, especially among the richer families.

Children also liked to play games. They played with toys including balls, dolls, marbles, stilts, and kites. They built models, and they played board games such as tic-tac-toe. Dogs and birds were the most common pets.

Make It Relevant How were the lives of Roman children similar to the lives of children in the United States today?

City Life and Country Life

At the time of **Augustus,** Rome was the largest city in the empire. The Roman census shows that about 1 million people lived there at that time. A **census** is a count of the people in a certain place. The empire's other large cities—**Athens, Antioch, Alexandria,** and **Carthage**—had populations of about 100,000 to about 200,000 people.

Many cities in the empire were modeled after Rome. Each one had a forum, which served as a marketplace and meeting place. Public buildings lined the forum. A building called the basilica (buh•SIH•lih•kuh) held government offices and courtrooms. A town's most important temples were also located near the forum.

Large cities and towns had streets and sidewalks paved with stone while smaller towns had roads of gravel or dirt. Cities also had public baths. Since most people did not have running water at home, these were an important public service. The baths were also important areas for conducting business and exchanging ideas.

Water came from wells or aqueducts. An **aqueduct** is a system of bridges and canals that carries water from a natural source, such as a river, to a town. The well-built Roman aqueducts supplied water for public baths and drinking fountains. For a fee, wealthy Romans could pipe water from the aqueducts into their homes.

Across the empire, life in the countryside was simple and often hard. People farmed with only simple tools, such as shovels and hoes, and used oxen to pull their plows. People grew or made nearly everything they needed.

> **READING CHECK** SUMMARIZE
> **Why did Roman cities have public baths?**

A Closer LOOK

Ancient Rome

Rome grew from a village into one of the grandest cities the world has ever known. These pictures show some of the major buildings of Rome in about A.D. 320.

❖ How did the buildings of ancient Rome influence architecture of today's world?

> **Circus Maximus**

Slavery

In the countryside and the cities, the day-to-day running of the Roman Empire depended on slavery. Historians estimate that during the time of Augustus, about 3 million slaves and about 5 million free people lived on the Italian Peninsula.

The Twelve Tables offer clues about slavery in Rome's early days. They state that a person who failed to pay a debt could be sold into slavery. This practice was later

Arch of Constantine

Pantheon

Aqueduct of Claudius

Colosseum

outlawed, but prisoners of war could be enslaved and many were. The Romans also bought some of their slaves from traders and pirates.

Slaves did many different kinds of jobs in Roman society. Many worked on farms, in mines, and as household servants. Towns and cities owned slaves and put them to work on public building projects. Some slaves even worked as doctors, teachers, and architects, and these slaves often lived better than many free citizens.

Slaves had few rights, and their treatment varied. Sometimes slaves were chained in the fields while others were locked in prisons at night. Yet some slave owners treated their slaves well because they risked losing money if the slave could not work. Some slaves were freed upon their owner's death. Others earned enough money to buy freedom.

READING CHECK **SUMMARIZE**

How was daily life in the Roman Empire dependent on slavery?

Entertainment

Roman rulers had a long tradition of providing "bread and circuses" for the people. The phrase refers to free grain for the poor and free entertainment for all. Rulers knew they could count on these gifts to help win the people's support.

In ancient Rome, the word *circus* referred to a building in which sports events were held. Rome's first circus was a huge stadium called the Circus Maximus. It was about 2,000 feet long and 600 feet wide.

The most popular event was the dangerous sport of chariot racing. Chariots crashed into each other as they jockeyed for the winning position. Drivers could be thrown onto the track and trampled by the horses. Winning drivers became wealthy and were heroes. Other sporting events at the circus included footraces, boxing, wrestling, and javelin throwing.

Gladiators provided another popular form of entertainment. **Gladiators** were trained at special schools and then forced to fight to the death. They fought each other, and they fought wild animals. Most gladiators were criminals, slaves, or prisoners of war. A few were women.

A gladiator show lasted all day and had many events. Often, several battles were fought at once. It was common for criminals to be killed as part of the show. The largest arena for these "games" was the Colosseum (kah•luh•SEE•uhm).

Some Romans preferred theater. The Romans learned about theater from the Greeks and enjoyed Greek plays. Most actors were slaves, and all were men. Women's roles were played by men.

> In Rome, thousands of spectators packed the Circus Maximus to watch thrilling and dangerous sporting events such as the chariot races shown below.

➤ The Romans enjoyed music and dance (left). They also liked to laugh, as seen in this depiction of a comedy being performed (above).

Pantomime, or the art of telling a story only through movements of the body and facial expressions, was also a popular form of entertainment. Performances combined dancing, acting, and music. Women were allowed to play roles in pantomime.

READING CHECK ♂ **DRAW CONCLUSIONS**
Why do you think some Romans were tempted to move from the country to the city?

Summary

Most Romans were poor, but wealthy Romans lived in luxury. Slaves worked many kinds of jobs. Cities in the empire were modeled after Rome, with paved roads, forums, and temples. Romans enjoyed entertainment, such as gladiator battles and plays.

REVIEW

1. 💡 What was everyday life like in the Roman Empire?

2. Write a paragraph that explains the role of **gladiators** in ancient Rome.

3. Why were aqueducts important to the people of Rome?

CRITICAL THINKING

4. **ANALYSIS SKILL** How might life in ancient Rome have been different if slavery had not existed?

5. **ANALYSIS SKILL** How might daily life have changed for a wealthy Roman if he or she had to live as a slave?

6. **ANALYSIS SKILL** **Make It Relevant** What similarities exist in home life between the ancient Romans and present-day Americans?

7. 🖌 **Plan a Roman City** Imagine that you have been asked to plan and build a new Roman city. Draw a simple city plan showing the main structures that you will build.

8. (Focus Skill) **DRAW CONCLUSIONS**
On a separate sheet of paper, copy and complete the graphic organizer below.

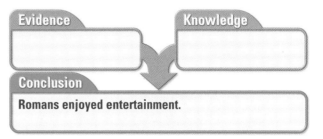

Evidence	Knowledge

Conclusion
Romans enjoyed entertainment.

Read Editorial Cartoons

▶ WHY IT MATTERS

Some cartoons are created to make people laugh. Others present a serious message to make people think. The kind of cartoon that appears on the editorial page of a newspaper is called an editorial cartoon. **Editorial cartoons** present the artist's point of view about people, current events, or politics. Knowing how to read editorial cartoons can help you understand political and cultural issues and opinions about them.

▶ WHAT YOU NEED TO KNOW

Some drawings from early Rome used images to criticize Roman leadership and government. These drawings are the ancestors of editorial cartoons. The first editorial cartoons that were printed on paper were created in Germany in the early 1500s.

Benjamin Franklin published one of the first American editorial cartoons in 1754. As political changes happened in the Americas and in Europe, drawing editorial cartoons became a common way for artists to express their views.

The American cartoon on this page expresses an opinion about the American Revolution. The French cartoon on the next page offers a view on the many revolutions that were taking place in the world by the late 1700s.

In the American cartoon, the horse stands for Britain's American colonies in the late 1700s. The "master" riding the horse is King George III, ruler of Britain and Britain's colonies. The horse is throwing off the master, an action that represents the Declaration of Independence. In the French cartoon, electricity is the "spark"

▶ This ancient Roman drawing criticizes elections.

▶ This political cartoon from early American history makes a statement about the American Revolution.

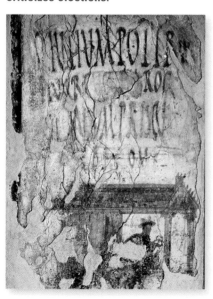

Electricité Républicaine donnant aux Despotes une Commotion qui renverse leurs Trônes.

l'Espiegle Joseph

Le Courou de Sardaigne

Le Despoto Espagnol

Le Petit Papa

La grosse Catherin

le Stathouder

Le Tyran de Prusse

La Chûte en Masse

Ainsi l'Etincelle électrique de la Liberté, renversera tous les Trônes des Brigands Couronnés.

❯ The artist drew this cartoon to show the effect of new ideas on the people of the world.

of new ideas that were causing revolutions across the world.

To help you understand the meaning of an editorial cartoon, ask yourself these questions:

1 When was the cartoon created? What do I know about that time in history?

2 Do I recognize any people, or types of people, who are shown?

3 What symbols are shown? What do the symbols stand for?

4 What issue is the cartoon about?

5 What opinion did the cartoonist express about the issue?

❯ **PRACTICE THE SKILL**

Answer the following questions.

1 What do you think was the American artist's opinion of the British? What symbols or details helped you decide?

2 Why do think the colonies are represented by a horse?

3 Do you think the artist supported the American Revolution? Explain.

4 In the French cartoon, what did the artist represent by showing people being knocked down by electricity?

5 Do you think the French artist supported the political revolutions of the time? Explain.

❯ **APPLY WHAT YOU LEARNED**

Choose a current event that you have a strong opinion about. Write a paragraph that tells your opinion. Then draw your own editorial cartoon.

Roman Writing

Much of what the Romans wrote, as well as what they wrote on and with, survives today. From history to bedtime stories, from love poems to declarations of war, the Romans wrote about everything.

The words recorded on stone and parchment give us information about Roman life that would otherwise be lost forever. Because the Romans wrote things down, their thoughts, beliefs, and feelings are known to us.

▶ In this fresco titled *The Poetess of Pompeii*, the subject holds a stylus and tablet.

Students used writing tablets, blocks of wax, and styluses like these.

This tablet fragment contains a line from the poet Virgil. It was probably a student's writing exercise.

This scrap of parchment contains words from one of Cicero's speeches.

ANALYSIS SKILL **Analyze Artifacts**

1 What is the value of scraps of Roman writing for a historian? For an archaeologist?

2 What can ancient writings tell us that other ancient primary sources cannot?

3 Why might great emperors have ordered their deeds to be written on stone?

GO ONLINE Visit PRIMARY SOURCES at www.harcourtschool.com/hss

Hammer and chisel have spoken through centuries about people and deeds that would otherwise be forgotten.

The Romans kept their styluses in jars for convenience.

C·PLINIOLF
QVI CAECILIO
SE VNDO COS
AVG CVR ALVEI TIBER
ET RIPAR ET CLOACAR VRB

31 B.C.
Octavian defeats Antony and Cleopatra

27 B.C.
Octavian is given the title *Augustus*

Reading Social Studies

A **conclusion** is an understanding reached after careful thinking. To **draw a conclusion,** you use what you already know along with what you read about a subject to make a general statement about an idea or an event.

 ## Draw a Conclusion

Complete this graphic organizer to show that you can draw conclusions about the Roman Empire. A copy of this graphic organizer appears on page 144 of the Homework and Practice Book.

The Roman Empire

Evidence

Roman officials made Latin the official language of the Roman Empire.

Knowledge

Conclusion

Communication across the Roman Empire grew.

 ## California Writing Prompts

Write a Narrative Poem Imagine you are a poet living in the Roman Empire. Write a poem that tells the story of how the Roman Republic became the Roman Empire.

Write a Proposal Think about one of the problems that the Roman Empire faced. Think of a solution to the problem and write a proposal to try to persuade a Roman leader to try your solution.

A.D. 75

A.D. 150

A.D. 225

A.D. 70
Emperor Titus
destroys Jerusalem

A.D. 161
Marcus Aurelius
begins his
rule of Rome

Use Vocabulary

Use a term from this list to complete each of the following sentences.

heir, p. 507

legion, p. 515

currency, p. 516

census, p. 522

gladiator, p. 524

1. Augustus created a standard system of _____.

2. In many cases an emperor's _____ ruled after his death.

3. A _____ fought to the death to entertain spectators.

4. A _____ was a unit of Roman soldiers.

5. The Roman government used information from the _____ to help it collect all the taxes that citizens owed.

Use the Time Line

 Use the summary time line above to answer these questions.

6. When was Octavian given the title *Augustus*?

7. What happened in A.D. 161?

Apply Skills

Read Editorial Cartoons

8. Write a short paragraph for each of the editorial cartoons on pages 526 and 527 to show you understand their meaning.

Recall Facts

Answer these questions.

9. Why did Octavian attack Cleopatra's navy?

10. Who established a standard currency for the Roman Empire?

11. Who were the Five Good Emperors?

12. What was the Roman tradition of providing "bread and circuses"?

Write the letter of the best choice.

13. Which of the following contributed to the economic growth of the Roman Empire?
    A walls and fortresses
    B soldiers
    C trade routes and currency
    D civil wars

14. Which emperor brought part of Britain into the Roman Empire?
    A Augustus
    B Claudius
    C Nero
    D Aurelius

Think Critically

15. **ANALYSIS SKILL** Based on the primary source quotes you have read in this chapter, what conclusions can you draw about the Roman Empire?

16. **ANALYSIS SKILL** What events led up to the Roman Republic becoming an empire?

Study Skills

POSE QUESTIONS

Asking questions as you read can help you better understand the text.

> **Form questions as you read. Think about how and why events happened and how the events are related.**

> **Use the questions to guide your reading. Looking for the answers as you read will improve your understanding.**

| Chapter 14: Christianity and the Legacies of Rome ||
Questions	Answers
Which religions did the people under Roman rule follow?	Most Romans followed the Roman religion. In Judaea, many people practiced Judaism. In that same area, the religion of Christianity began to grow.

Apply As You Read

As you read this chapter, write down any questions you have about the events, ideas, primary sources, people, or places discussed. Then read on to look for the answers.

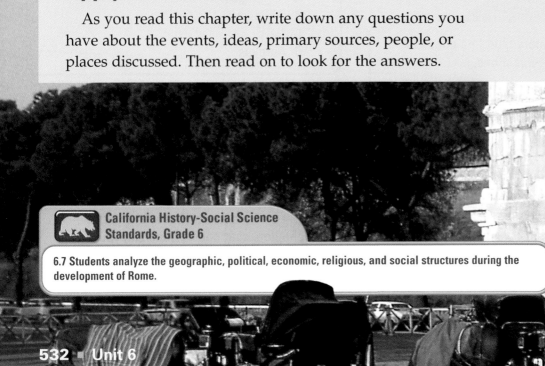

California History-Social Science Standards, Grade 6

6.7 Students analyze the geographic, political, economic, religious, and social structures during the development of Rome.

The Arch of Constantine in Rome

Christianity and the Legacies of Rome

CHAPTER

14

THE PRODIGAL SON

from The Parables of Jesus
retold from the Bible
and illustrated by Tomie dePaola

During the time of the ancient Romans, a new religion came into being. The Christian religion was based on the ideas of Jesus. Living in the Roman-controlled land of Judaea, Jesus taught new ideas about love and compassion. One way he did this was through parables. A parable is a short story based on everyday life that teaches a moral or spiritual lesson. The following parable tells the story of two very different brothers and the important lessons they learn.

There was a man with two sons, and the younger one said to his father, "Father, I would like my share of the property. Will you give it to me?" So the father divided the estate between the two sons.

Shortly after, the younger son turned his share into cash and went off to a distant land where he soon spent it all in wild and reckless living.

A severe famine came upon the land and the young man was in desperate need.

So, he went and attached himself to a local landowner who sent him into the fields to tend pigs.

The young man would have gladly eaten the husks that the pigs were eating, as no one gave him anything to eat.

But suddenly, he came to his senses. "My father has hired servants that have more than enough to eat, and here I am starving to death.

"I will go back home to my father and say to him, 'Father, I have sinned against God and against you.

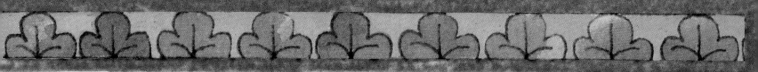

'I'm no longer worthy to be called your son. Treat me as one of your paid servants.'"

So, he started for home, to his father's house. While he was still a ways off, his father saw him coming and was so happy that he ran to meet him. He threw his arms around his son and kissed him.

The young man said, "Father, I have sinned against God and against you. I'm no longer worthy to be called your son."

But the father called his servants and said, "Quickly, fetch the best robe and put it on my son. Put rings on his fingers and shoes on his feet.

"Bring the fatted calf and kill it, for we will have a feast today.

"My son was dead and has come back to life. He was lost and is now found." And the celebration began.

Now, the older son had been out in the fields and as he came near the house, he heard the sound of music and dancing.

He called to one of the servants and asked what was going on.

The servant answered, "Your brother has come home, and your father has killed the fatted calf because he is safe and sound. There is a celebration."

The older brother was angry and refused to go in to the party. The father came out and pleaded with the young man to join the celebration.

"I have slaved for you all these years," the older brother said. "I have never disobeyed you, yet you have never even given me a baby goat for a feast with my friends.

"But my brother comes home after spending all his money on wild and reckless living, and you kill the fatted calf for him."

"My son," the father said, "you are always with me and everything I have is yours.

"But how could we help but celebrate this happy day, for your brother was dead and is now alive. He was lost and now at last is found."

Response Corner

1. What lessons did the two brothers learn?

2. Why was the older brother angry that his father was having a party for the younger son?

Lesson 1

Time

| 1000 B.C. | 500 B.C. | B.C./A.D. | A.D. 500 |

63 B.C.
Judaea becomes part of the Roman Empire

A.D. 70
Romans destroy the Temple in Jerusalem

A.D. 135
The third Jewish rebellion ends, and Jews are expelled from Jerusalem

WHAT TO KNOW

What were the religious beliefs of the people of the Roman Empire?

✓ Describe ancient Roman religious beliefs and practices.

✓ Explain how conflicts with the Romans affected the Jewish people.

✓ Trace the migration of the Jewish people during the time of the Roman Empire.

VOCABULARY

mystery religion p. 539
sect p. 541

PEOPLE

Augustus
Herod the Great
Titus
Hadrian

PLACES

Judaea
Syria
Greece
Egypt
Cyprus

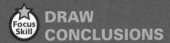

DRAW CONCLUSIONS

California Standards
HSS 6.7, 6.7.5, 6.7.6

Religion in the Roman Empire

YOU ARE THERE

The year is 25 B.C., and March 19 has finally come again! Today's the first day of the ancient Roman holiday Quinquatria (kwin•KWAH•tree•uh), a five-day festival honoring the goddess of wisdom, Minerva. The aroma of honey cakes, roasted chicken, and pear pudding fills the air, but this is no time to eat! Running alongside the street, you see poets reciting their latest verses to eager crowds. You join your friends by the public well and talk about the gifts you'll give the teacher when classes start again.

▶ Mars, the Roman god of war, drives his chariot across the sky in this engraving from the A.D. 1500s.

Jupiter, king of the Roman gods

Zeus

Hera

Juno, queen of the Roman gods

GREEK GODS & GODDESSES

Minerva, goddess of wisdom and war

Athena

Apollo

Venus, goddess of love

Aphrodite

ROMAN GODS & GODDESSES

Apollo, god of music and poetry

ANALYSIS SKILL Analyze Charts The Romans adopted religious beliefs from the Greeks and other cultures.

❖ Why do you think the Greeks had such a strong influence on Roman religion?

The Roman Gods

Just as they influenced other parts of Roman culture, the Greeks influenced Roman religion. The earliest Romans thought of their gods as spirits or powerful forces of nature. This view changed when the Romans came into contact with the Greeks. The Greeks believed that their gods had human forms. The Romans borrowed this idea, giving their own gods human characteristics. They even adopted some of the Greek gods as their own.

Jupiter, the most powerful Roman god, was the Roman version of the Greek god Zeus. The Romans based Jupiter's wife, Juno, on the Greek goddess Hera.

The Greeks' beliefs about their goddess Demeter influenced Roman beliefs about a goddess called Ceres (SIR•eez). The Romans believed that Ceres ruled over agriculture and grain. The English word *cereal* comes from her name. Mars, the Roman god of farming, took on the traits of Ares, the Greek god of war. His wife, Venus, was the Roman version of the Greek goddess of love, Aphrodite.

Other cultures also influenced Roman gods. The Romans borrowed some gods from the Etruscans. Minerva was originally an Etruscan goddess of crafts. She took on the traits of the Greek goddess Athena and became the goddess of wisdom and war. In the northern part of the empire, Roman gods took on the qualities of local Celtic gods. In the eastern part, Egyptian deities influenced Roman gods.

READING CHECK ☼ DRAW CONCLUSIONS
What can you conclude about how religion may spread from one culture to another?

Roman Beliefs

The Romans built temples to honor their gods. Each temple contained a statue of the god it honored. A Roman temple was not a place where people gathered to worship. It was a place where priests made offerings and sacrifices. Offerings might be cakes, honey, or incense, a substance that makes a pleasing smell when burned. Often the priests would sacrifice animals to the gods.

The Romans made these offerings on special days called festivals. Because Rome had many gods, it had many festivals—more than 100 each year. Some lasted for several days. On festival days, priests performed rituals outside the temple of the god being honored.

Until the late A.D. 300s, the religion of the Romans was the state religion, which meant that religion was part of the government. Roman law required citizens to honor the Roman gods. For example, they had to bow or pray to statues of the gods or make offerings to them on altars in their homes. The Romans believed that they could win favor with the gods by honoring them. They thought that the gods kept the empire safe and allowed it to expand, and that any punishment by the gods would end the empire.

Since religion in Rome was part of the government, the emperor was also a religious leader. For example, **Augustus** built and repaired many temples. He made sure that priests performed rituals. He also told the people to attend public rituals and to make offerings to the gods.

Augustus believed that observing the state religion would help unite the Roman people. In time, Romans began to worship their emperors as gods. Refusal to worship the emperor as a god could mean death.

READING CHECK SUMMARIZE
Why was the Roman emperor also a religious leader?

▶ This painting shows Romans celebrating a festival of the grape harvest. Most Roman festivals were happy occasions, with feasting, music, rest, and reflection.

▶ The Egyptian goddess Isis (far left) was popular among many Greeks and Romans. Ahura Mazda (center), or "Wise Lord," was the main god of a Persian religion. Ruins of Roman temples for the Persian god Mithras (above) have been found in Britain.

Other Religions in Rome

Rome was a huge empire with people of many different cultures. For the most part, the Roman government let people practice any religion they chose. The only rule was that they also had to take part in Rome's state religion.

Many people living in the Roman Empire followed **mystery religions**. These religions featured ceremonies celebrating the seasons—the "death" of autumn and the "rebirth" of spring. One such mystery religion developed around Isis, a powerful mother goddess who was first worshipped by the Egyptians. Another example was Mithraism, a warlike religion that worshipped the Persian sun god Mithras.

Still others practiced philosophies that did not have to do with the worship of gods. The Epicureans believed that the key to a happy or good life was to seek and achieve balance in life. Stoics believed that fate decided everything, but that people were still responsible for their actions. They believed that people should try to live a virtuous life.

Jews lived in all parts of the Roman Empire. The Jewish people refused to worship Roman gods, but they did not discourage others from following the Roman religion. For this reason, the Romans allowed the Jews to practice their religion for many years. Still, many people in the empire treated Jews badly. Over time, conflicts grew between the Jewish people and the Roman government.

READING CHECK ŏDRAW CONCLUSIONS
How might Rome's policy toward religions have helped spread Roman culture?

Under Roman Rule

⏱ **TIME** 63 B.C. – A.D. 135

🌐 **PLACE** Judaea

Judaea and **Syria** became part of the Roman Empire in 63 B.C. Many Jews still lived in Judaea, their ancient homeland. Yet, because of past conquests and exiles, Jews lived in many parts of the Roman world. Some experts think that as many as 100,000 Jews lived in the city of Rome. **Greece**, Syria, and **Egypt** also had large Jewish communities.

Before Judaea was a Roman province, it was ruled by a local king who was loyal to Rome. From 37 B.C. to 4 B.C., **Herod the Great** ruled as the king of Judaea, delivering to Rome the taxes paid by the Judaeans. In return, the Roman rulers allowed the Judaeans to practice their religion in peace. Herod was able to save enough tax money to rebuild the Jewish Temple in Jerusalem.

The Temple became the cause of Jewish conflict with Rome. When Caligula became emperor, he demanded that his statue be placed in the Temple. This upset the Jews. Other insults to the Jewish religion followed, and in A.D. 66, the Jewish people revolted. In A.D. 70, **Titus** crushed the revolt and destroyed the Temple.

The Jews revolted again in A.D. 115. This time, the rebellion was not just in Judaea. Jews living in Egypt, **Cyprus**, and other regions attacked Roman soldiers and towns because they were tired of suffering at the hands of the Romans. It took the Romans two years to put down the second rebellion. Many Jews were killed, especially in Egypt.

In A.D. 132, Jews in Judaea rebelled a third time. The Romans' response was even more brutal than in the past. One ancient writer reported that more than half a million Jews were killed. The emperor, **Hadrian,** expelled all Jews from Jerusalem, and the Romans changed the name of Judaea to Syria Palaestina. Many Jews moved to other parts of the empire.

▶ After Jerusalem fell to the Romans in A.D. 70, a group of Jewish people resisted the Romans from the Masada fortress (below). It was located on top of a mountain (left) near the Dead Sea.

LOCATE IT

ISRAEL

Masada

About this time, missionaries from a little-known religion called Christianity began traveling outside of Judaea. Christianity had begun as a **sect**, or a division, of Judaism. By A.D. 135, when the third Jewish rebellion ended, Christianity was a separate religion. The Romans did not suspect how much it would change their world.

READING CHECK ⟲ DRAW CONCLUSIONS
What conclusions can you make about the Jews' relationship with Rome by A.D. 135?

Summary

The Romans borrowed gods from other religions. The Romans honored their gods with offerings at temples. People in the empire were allowed to follow their own religions as long as they also honored Roman gods. In the first century A.D., conflict increased between the Jews and the Romans. Finally, the Romans expelled all Jews from Jerusalem.

⚡ **FAST FACT**

It took nearly 15,000 Roman soldiers almost two years to conquer the fewer than 1,000 Jewish defenders at Masada.

REVIEW

1. 💡 What were the religious beliefs of the people of the Roman Empire?

2. Write a sentence that describes the term **sect**.

3. Why did many Jews move from Judaea to other parts of the Mediterranean region?

CRITICAL THINKING

4. **ANALYSIS SKILL** How did the Roman government's acceptance of Judaism change over time, and what effects did this have on the Jewish people?

5. **Make It Relevant** What do you think might happen if the United States adopted the Roman government's policy of having a state religion?

6. 🖊 **Make a Map** Use resources from the library and the Internet to make a map of the many different religions in the Roman Empire. Show the areas in which each religion could be found.

7. ⭐ Focus Skill **DRAW CONCLUSIONS**
On a separate sheet of paper, copy and complete the graphic organizer below.

Evidence	Knowledge

Conclusion
Rome was no longer accepting of Judaism.

Lesson 2

Time

1000 B.C.	500 B.C.	B.C./A.D.	A.D. 500

4 B.C.
Jesus is born
in Bethlehem

About A.D. 30
Jesus is crucified

About A.D. 33
Paul becomes a
Christian

The Beginnings of Christianity

YOU ARE THERE

The year is A.D. 6. It will soon be morning, and you are sitting on a hilltop overlooking the port of Caesarea, named for Augustus Caesar. Caesarea has been made the new capital of **Judaea**, replacing **Jerusalem**. Judaea is now a Roman province. Roman soldiers patrol the streets, and taxes are paid to Rome.

People have been whispering that in years ahead a leader will come who will become the king of the Jews. What might the Romans think about a revived Jewish kingship?

You see the faint outlines of Roman ships as they approach the harbor to unload more troops. You wonder what the future holds.

▶ A painting of Jesus being held by his mother, Mary

WHAT TO KNOW

How did Christianity develop in the Roman Empire?

✓ Tell about the life and teachings of Jesus of Nazareth.

✓ Describe the origins and spread of Christianity.

✓ Discuss Paul's contributions to Christianity.

VOCABULARY

disciple p. 544
parable p. 544
messiah p. 544
resurrection p. 546
apostle p. 546
persecution p. 546
martyr p. 547

PEOPLE

Jesus
Herod the Great
Pontius Pilate
Saul/Paul

PLACES

Judaea
Jerusalem
Bethlehem
Nazareth

DRAW CONCLUSIONS

California
Standards
HSS 6.7, 6.7.6, 6.7.7

PRIMARY SOURCES

The Gospel of Mark

ANALYSIS SKILL Analyze Documents

Historians believe that Mark's Gospel was first written down in Jerusalem some time in the A.D. 60s, just before the Temple was destroyed. This page from the Gospel of Mark was created in Constantinople, the capital of the Byzantine Empire, and dates to the late A.D. 1000s.

❶ The picture shows Mark writing his Gospel in Jerusalem. The halo, or circle of light, surrounding his head is a symbol of holiness.

❷ The heavily decorated border and the use of bright colors and gold tell us that this book was created in the style of an "illuminated manuscript." These eye-catching details were thought to illuminate, or light up, the page.

❸ The text is written in Greek, the language in which the New Testament was written.

◈ How is this page similar to and different from books that you are familiar with?

The Early Life of Jesus

Four main sources tell of the life of **Jesus** and the beginning of Christianity. These sources are the first four books of the New Testament, and they are called the Gospels. The New Testament is part of the Bible, a text sacred to followers of the Christian religion.

Two of the Gospels, those of **Matthew** and **Luke**, tell about the early life of Jesus. They do not tell exactly when he was born. From clues in these books, experts think that Jesus was born in 4 B.C. in the small town of **Bethlehem** at a time when **Herod the Great** ruled Judaea.

The Gospel of **Matthew** reports that Herod tried to have Jesus killed when Jesus was a baby. According to the Gospel, when Herod heard that some people believed that Jesus would grow up to be the king of the Jews, he sent soldiers to find and kill Jesus. Jesus' parents fled to Egypt and stayed there until Herod died. Then they returned to Judaea and lived in the town of **Nazareth**.

The Gospel of **Luke** explains that Jesus' parents raised him in the Jewish religion. Jesus learned Jewish law, and on special occasions, his parents took him to the Temple in Jerusalem.

When Jesus was 12 years old, his family traveled to Jerusalem for the feast of Passover. According to the Gospel of Luke, while there, Jesus impressed the teachers in the Temple courts with the questions he asked. Luke says that everyone at the Passover seder was amazed at his understanding and his questions.

READING CHECK ⟳ DRAW CONCLUSIONS
What conclusions about Judaea can you draw from the early life of Jesus?

The Teachings of Jesus

When Jesus grew up, he began to travel around Judaea and to teach in synagogues and outdoors. He reminded people of basic Jewish beliefs, such as believing in one God and following the Ten Commandments. Jesus also spoke of the kingdom of God. He told people that if they turned away from sin, God would forgive them. He assured his listeners that God loved them, and he urged them to love one another.

Soon large crowds of people came to hear Jesus teach. Even people who were not Jewish were interested in the ideas he taught. Eventually, Jesus gathered a group of **disciples**, or followers, made up of 12 men who traveled with him.

Jesus told **parables**, or simple stories that teach lessons about life. Jesus used the parable of the Good Samaritan to teach people what it means to be a good neighbor. In this story, a man is robbed, beaten, and left lying by the road. All those who pass him on the road ignore him. Finally, a stranger from an unfriendly land stops to help. Jesus made it clear that the man who stopped to help was the good neighbor.

For centuries, many Jews had been expecting the arrival of a **messiah**, or savior. According to the Gospels, some believed that Jesus was the Messiah. However, most Jewish leaders did not. As a result, Jesus became a source of conflict among the Jews.

The idea that Jesus might be the Messiah worried the Romans. For one thing, *Messiah* means "anointed one," which usually refers to a king. The Romans were not about to allow the Jews to have their own king. The Romans also knew that the Jews believed their Messiah would free them from Roman rule. The more followers

The Life of Jesus

> The birth of Jesus

> Jesus helps Joseph with his work as a carpenter.

> Jesus delivers the Sermon on the Mount.

4 B.C.

Jesus attracted, the more worried the Romans became.

According to the Gospels, Jesus had no interest in rebelling against the Romans. He even told people to pay their taxes to Rome, but the Romans still saw Jesus as a threat as well as his teachings.

In about A.D. 30, **Pontius Pilate**, the Roman governor of Judaea, ordered that Jesus be put to death by crucifixion (kroo•suh•FIK•shuhn). Crucifixion was a way of putting someone to death by tying or nailing the person to a cross.

When Jesus was put to death, it seemed that the conflict was over. According to the Gospels, an amazing event happened. Jesus' disciples said that he had come back to life and that they had seen him.

READING CHECK SUMMARIZE
What basic Jewish beliefs did Jesus teach?

> **Jesus before Pilate (below) and Jesus' crucifixion (right)**

A.D. 30

THE BEATITUDES

The Beatitudes (bee•A•tuh•toodz) are a group of statements made by Jesus. The Beatitudes appear in the New Testament as a part of Jesus' Sermon on the Mount (Matthew 5:3–12).*

Blessed are the poor in spirit, for theirs is the kingdom of heaven.

Blessed are those who mourn, for they will be comforted.

Blessed are the meek, for they will inherit the earth.

Blessed are those who hunger and thirst for righteousness, for they will be filled.

Blessed are the merciful, for they will receive mercy.

Blessed are the pure in heart, for they will see God.

Blessed are the peacemakers, for they will be called children of God.

Blessed are those who are persecuted for righteousness' sake, for theirs is the kingdom of heaven.

Blessed are you when people revile you and persecute you and utter all kinds of evil against you falsely on my account.

Rejoice and be glad, for your reward is great in heaven.

*Holy Bible: New Revised Standard Version. Zondervan Bible Publishers, 1990.

The Conflict Continues

The story of Jesus' **resurrection**, or return to life, spread. The New Testament book of Acts tells how a group of men called **apostles** (ah•PAH•salz) traveled all over the Roman Empire teaching people about Jesus and proclaiming that Jesus was the Messiah.

Most of the apostles had been Jesus' disciples before his death. One of them was a man named Peter. According to Acts, Peter told a crowd in Jerusalem, "This Jesus God raised up, and of that all of us are witnesses."*

One man who became an apostle had not been a disciple of Jesus. He was a Jewish man named **Saul**. At first, Saul tried to stop the apostles from claiming that Jesus was the Messiah. Then one day, Saul is said to have had a vision of Jesus. He became convinced that the apostles were right, and he joined them in about A.D. 33. Soon after this, Saul's name was changed to **Paul**. He spent the rest of his life spreading the teachings of Jesus.

*Acts 2:32. *Holy Bible: New Revised Standard Version.* Zondervan Bible Publishers, 1990.

No one knows exactly when the followers of Jesus became known as Christians. The followers of Jesus came from many lands and spoke many different languages, but most could speak Greek. Paul, for example, wrote letters about Christianity in Greek. *Christos* is the Greek word for "Messiah." The Greek-speaking followers of Jesus called him Jesus Christ, meaning "Jesus the Messiah." People began to call Jesus' followers *Christians* and their new religion *Christianity.*

As the apostles traveled around Judaea and beyond, Christianity grew. Just as the Romans had worried about Jesus, they worried about the new religion. One reason was that Christians refused to worship the Roman gods. Like Jews, Christians believed that it was wrong to worship any god except their own. Unlike Jews, however, Christians urged other people to give up the Roman religion.

The Romans viewed this act as a form of rebellion against Rome. It led to the **persecution**, or punishment for having different beliefs, of Christians. When Rome

❯ This painting shows Jesus with the apostles. The word *apostle* comes from the Greek word *apostolos,* which means "[person] sent."

burned in A.D. 64, the Roman Emperor Nero falsely blamed Christians for starting the fire. In the following years, the Romans killed thousands of Christians. These Christians were **martyrs** (MAR•turz), people who chose to die rather than give up their religion.

READING CHECK SUMMARIZE
Why did the Romans view Christianity as a form of rebellion against Rome?

Summary

Jesus was a Jewish teacher who was born in 4 B.C. in Judaea. He attracted large crowds, and the idea that he might be the Messiah threatened some Roman leaders. Jesus was put to death, but his followers said that he rose from the dead. The apostles spread his teachings, which became the basis of Christianity.

▶ Polycarp was a religious leader who became one of the earliest Christian martyrs.

REVIEW

1. How did Christianity develop in the Roman Empire?

2. In a sentence, explain the difference between a **disciple** and an **apostle**.

3. What were the roles of Herod the Great and Pontius Pilate in the government of Judaea?

4. Why did the followers of Jesus refer to him by the Greek title of *Christ*, rather than a Hebrew or Latin title?

CRITICAL THINKING

5. **Make It Relevant** In what ways is being a good neighbor important in your community today?

6. **ANALYSIS SKILL** Why do you think Nero blamed Christians, rather than some other group, for the great fire in Rome?

7. **Using a Newspaper** For a week, look for newspaper articles that show how religion affects modern society. Read the articles, and take notes about how the events affect people's lives.

8. **Focus Skill** DRAW CONCLUSIONS
On a separate sheet of paper, copy and complete the graphic organizer below.

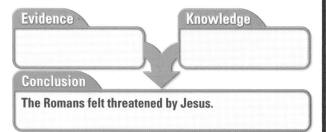

Evidence	Knowledge

Conclusion
The Romans felt threatened by Jesus.

Compare Graphs

❯ WHY IT MATTERS

After the fall of the Roman Empire, Christianity continued to grow and, in many parts of the world, it is still growing. For example, the religion has grown at a very fast rate in Africa.

Suppose you want to prepare a report on the growth of Christianity across time. One way you might do this is by making graphs. Knowing how to read graphs and how to make different kinds of graphs can help you compare large amounts of information.

❯ WHAT YOU NEED TO KNOW

Different kinds of graphs show information in different ways. A line graph is particularly useful for showing a **trend**, or the way something changes over time. The line graph on page 549 shows the growth of Christianity in Africa from 1900 to 2000.

A bar graph is especially useful for comparing quantities quickly. The bar graph on page 549 shows the growth of Christianity in the world from 1900 to 2000.

❯ Christians gather for a religious holiday at the Church of Mary of Zion in Aksum, Ethiopia.

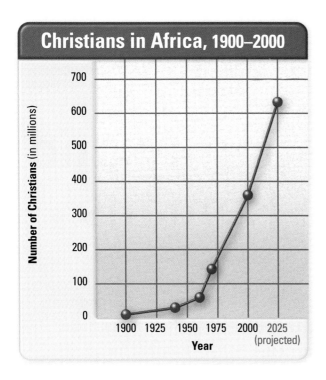

Christians in Africa, 1900–2000

Number of Christians (in millions)

700
600
500
400
300
200
100
0

1900 1925 1950 1975 2000 2025 (projected)

Year

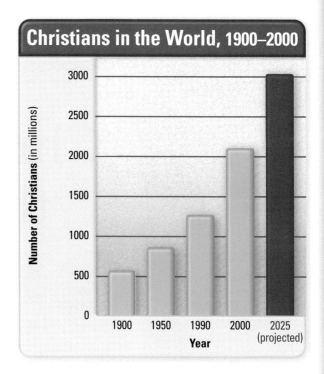

Christians in the World, 1900–2000

Number of Christians (in millions)

3000
2500
2000
1500
1000
500
0

1900 1950 1990 2000 2025 (projected)

Year

◗ PRACTICE THE SKILL

Compare the values in the graphs by answering the following questions.

1 About how many Christians were there in the world in 1900?

2 About how many Christians were living in Africa in 2000?

3 In which years shown on the bar graph were there fewer than 1 billion Christians in the world?

4 About how many Christians are there projected to be in Africa by 2025?

◗ APPLY WHAT YOU LEARNED

Use reliable Internet sources or other references to find out how the population of your state or community has changed in recent decades. Find population numbers for at least three different years. Make a bar graph showing your data.

Chart and Graph Skills

A.D. **312**
Constantine has a
vision and accepts
Christianity

A.D. **324**
Constantine rules
all Roman lands

A.D. **391**
Theodosius I
makes Christianity
the state religion

WHAT TO KNOW
What led to the growth
of Christianity in the Roman
Empire?

✓ Explain the spread of
Christianity throughout
the Roman Empire.

✓ Tell how the support of
Roman leaders affected
Christianity.

VOCABULARY
salvation p. 551
Trinity p. 552
baptize p. 552
pope p. 554

PEOPLE
Theodosius I
Pliny the Younger
Trajan
Constantine the Great

PLACES
Rome

**DRAW
CONCLUSIONS**

California
Standards
HSS 6.7, 6.7.6, 6.7.7

Christianity and the Romans

YOU ARE THERE
The year is A.D. 395. You've just learned that
Emperor **Theodosius I**, who made Christianity
the official religion of the Roman Empire, has died.
With his death, the empire has once again split into two
parts—Eastern and Western—each controlled by one of
Theodosius's sons. How much the empire has changed
since the days of Augustus! You think back to all you
have learned about Roman history and are saddened by
a feeling of loss. It hardly seems like the same empire.

FAST FACT

Early Christians fleeing persecution
carved houses and churches into
the rock formations of the Goreme
Valley, in present-day Turkey.

▶ The Santa Francesca Romana church (far right) was built within the ruins of the Roman Forum.

The Appeal of Christianity

Until the A.D. 300s, Christians were a small but slowly growing group in the Roman Empire. During this time, Roman treatment of Christians varied. Some emperors ordered Christians killed. Others made it a policy to ignore them. One Roman official, **Pliny the Younger**, wrote to Emperor **Trajan** to ask what to do about Christians. Here is part of Trajan's reply:

> **They are not to be sought out; if they are denounced and proved to be guilty, they are to be punished, with this reservation, that whoever denies that he is a Christian and quite clearly proves it—that is, by worshipping our gods— he shall gain pardon.** *

Even though Christians suffered persecution, the new religion spread. Christianity grew fastest

▶ Emperor Trajan

*Pliny, "Letters," in *The Romans: From Village to Empire.* M.T. Boatwright, D.J. Gargola, and R.J. Talbert, eds. Oxford University Press, 2004.

in the eastern part of the empire, where it had begun. Large cities in the western part also had Christian churches. These churches started as small groups that met secretly in members' homes. By A.D. 50, only about 20 years after Jesus' death, the apostle Paul had started a Christian church in the city of **Rome**.

Christianity appealed to people from many walks of life. One reason was that it reached out to everyone, including women, the poor, and enslaved people.

Another reason was that Christianity gave people hope for a better life after death. Christianity promised **salvation**, or the saving of the human soul from evil with a promise of happiness after death. For many, life was hard, and Christianity's promise of a joyful life after death was very attractive.

READING CHECK ⟳ DRAW CONCLUSIONS
What made the appeal of Christianity stronger than the threat of persecution?

Constantine the Great

Christianity soon won a strong supporter. In A.D. 312, **Constantine the Great** set out to conquer the Italian Peninsula and unite the empire under his rule. Before a battle for the city of Rome, Constantine claimed to have had a vision. He said he saw the Greek sign for Christ, *chi rho*, appear in the sky with the words: "In this sign, conquer."* Believing this to be a sign from God, Constantine ordered his soldiers to paint Christian symbols on their shields. Constantine won the battle and, as a result, became a Christian.

The next year, Constantine issued the Edict of Milan, an order giving Christians and all others the right to follow their religion. By A.D. 324, Constantine controlled all Roman lands. Christianity and all others soon became accepted across the empire.

In A.D. 325, Constantine called for the Christian Council of Nicaea to meet and settle a disagreement about what Jesus' role was. The council declared that Jesus was part of a **Trinity**, or one God made of a Father, a Son, and a Holy Spirit.

Constantine's support of Christianity helped make the Roman Empire a Christian state. Constantine was **baptized**, or symbolically purified of sins, before he died. He died in A.D. 337 and was buried in the Church of the Apostles, a church he built in Constantinople.

READING CHECK ⏀DRAW CONCLUSIONS
What effect did Constantine's actions have on Christianity?

*Eusebius of Caesarea in *Life of Constantine*. Averil Cameron and Stuart George Hall, ed., trans. Clarendon Press and Oxford University Press, 1999.

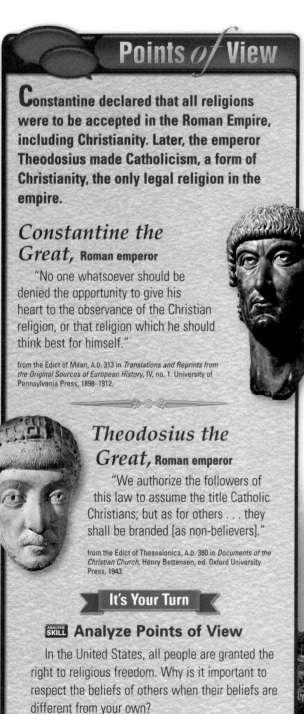

Points *of* View

Constantine declared that all religions were to be accepted in the Roman Empire, including Christianity. Later, the emperor Theodosius made Catholicism, a form of Christianity, the only legal religion in the empire.

Constantine the Great, Roman emperor

"No one whatsoever should be denied the opportunity to give his heart to the observance of the Christian religion, or that religion which he should think best for himself."

from the Edict of Milan, A.D. 313 in *Translations and Reprints from the Original Sources of European History*, IV, no. 1. University of Pennsylvania Press, 1898–1912.

Theodosius the Great, Roman emperor

"We authorize the followers of this law to assume the title Catholic Christians; but as for others . . . they shall be branded [as non-believers]."

from the Edict of Thessalonica, A.D. 380 in *Documents of the Christian Church*, Henry Bettensen, ed. Oxford University Press, 1943.

It's Your Turn

ANALYSIS SKILL Analyze Points of View

In the United States, all people are granted the right to religious freedom. Why is it important to respect the beliefs of others when their beliefs are different from your own?

❯ **The Arch of Constantine**

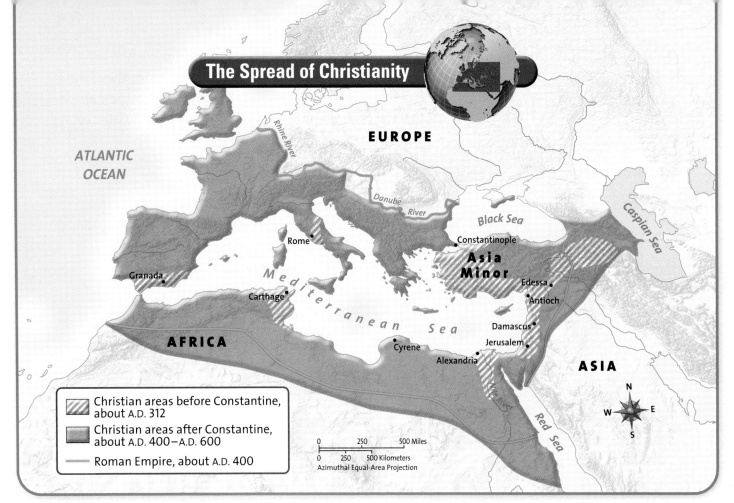

The Spread of Christianity

EUROPE

ATLANTIC OCEAN

Rhine River

Danube River

Black Sea

Constantinople

Asia Minor

Edessa

Antioch

Rome

Granada

Mediterranean Sea

Carthage

Damascus

AFRICA

Cyrene

Jerusalem

Alexandria

Caspian Sea

ASIA

Nile River

Red Sea

- ▨ Christian areas before Constantine, about A.D. 312
- ▬ Christian areas after Constantine, about A.D. 400–A.D. 600
- ── Roman Empire, about A.D. 400

0   250   500 Miles
0   250   500 Kilometers
Azimuthal Equal-Area Projection

SKILL **Analyze Maps** Constantine helped Christianity grow by making it an accepted religion of the Roman Empire.

◈ **Regions** How many continents had Christianity reached by A.D. 400?

The Power of the Bishops

TIME A.D. 391

PLACE Roman Empire

Christianity's role in Roman culture grew quickly. In A.D. 391, Emperor Theodosius I made Christianity the official religion of the Roman Empire. Christianity replaced the old state religion, with its many gods and goddesses. Theodosius banned the practice of the old religion and closed its temples.

Official favor brought changes to Christianity. Churches had been small, informal groups without much money. Now the Roman government built large churches to replace the old temples. Church leaders managed these large churches and the money the government provided for them. The most powerful of these leaders were the bishops.

Each large city had a church along with a bishop to take care of church business. Since they controlled money given to the churches, bishops often became rich and powerful. Christians looked up to the bishops as leaders who explained Christianity and told them what was right and what was wrong. This gave the bishops political power. Rulers knew that if they displeased the bishops, the bishops could turn the people against them.

In the beginning, all bishops had equal authority. Some bishops had more money and power than others, but each bishop was the supreme church leader in his city.

➤ According to Roman Catholic tradition, Jesus gave Peter "the keys to the kingdom," making him the first pope.

The bishop of Rome became known as the **pope**, a name that came from the Latin word for *father*. Over time, the pope gained more authority and became the leader of the Christian churches.

By A.D. 395, the empire had once again split into eastern and western regions, never to unite again. Invaders from the north soon conquered the western region. Meanwhile, Christianity began to spread outside the empire.

READING CHECK **SUMMARIZE**
What role did Theodosius I have in the spread of Christianity in the Roman Empire?

Summary

In spite of persecution, Christianity spread throughout the Roman Empire. Its promise of a better life after death appealed to many people. When Constantine the Great became a Christian, Christianity gained official acceptance. Official favor brought changes to the churches, including more money and power to the bishops.

REVIEW

1. What led to the growth of Christianity in the Roman Empire?

2. Describe how the terms **salvation** and **Trinity** relate to Christianity.

3. When did Christianity's status in the empire change greatly?

4. How were the bishops able to influence the Roman government?

CRITICAL THINKING

5. **ANALYSIS SKILL** What conclusions can you draw about Roman leaders' views on Christianity from the quotations you have read in this lesson?

6. **Make It Relevant** Why is freedom of religion important in the United States?

7. **Write a Newspaper Story** The Edict of Milan was important to the growth of Christianity in the Roman Empire. Write a short newspaper story that describes the edict.

8. **(Focus Skill) DRAW CONCLUSIONS**
On a separate sheet of paper, copy and complete the graphic organizer below.

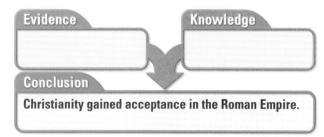

Evidence	Knowledge

Conclusion
Christianity gained acceptance in the Roman Empire.

The Apostle Paul

Biography

Trustworthiness
Respect
Responsibility
Fairness
Caring
Patriotism

"*My brothers, I have fulfilled my duty to God in all good conscience to this day.*"*

According to the New Testament of the Christian Bible, Paul spoke these words when he was on trial for starting a riot. Paul had been telling people about Jesus and his teachings, and both Jewish and Roman leaders objected to his words and actions. Still, Paul believed that he had a duty to keep his faith in God and to spread the teachings of Jesus. Because of his sense of duty, Paul was a trusted follower of Jesus from his early adulthood to the end of his life.

Paul was born in Tarsus, in what is now Turkey. He was a Roman citizen and a Jew, and he was well educated. In Paul's earlier years, Paul worked with the Jewish priests to try to stop the growth of Christianity. However, in about A.D. 33, Paul had a vision of Jesus. This caused him to become a Christian. He spent about 15 years studying the teachings of Jesus and then became a teacher himself.

Paul started the first Christian churches in many cities. As Paul moved from place to place, he wrote letters to the churches he had started. Some of these letters are now part of the New Testament. The letters gave Paul's views on Christianity and often helped settle differences between members of the Christian community.

Why Character Counts

❓ **How did Paul demonstrate trustworthiness in his actions as a Christian leader?**

*Paul. Acts 23:1. *The Holy Bible: New International Version, Containing the Old Testament and the New Testament.* Zondervan Bible Publishers, 1986.

Bio Brief

A.D. 10	A.D. 67
Born	Died

A.D. 33
Paul has a vision of Jesus and becomes a Christian

A.D. 48
Paul begins spreading the teachings of Jesus

A.D. 60
Paul is put in prison in Rome

Interactive Multimedia Biographies
Visit **MULTIMEDIA BIOGRAPHIES** at
www.harcourtschool.com/hss

Identify Causes and Effects

WHY IT MATTERS

To find links between events in the past, you need to understand cause and effect. A **cause** is an event or action that makes something else happen. What happens is the **effect**. Learning about cause-and-effect relationships is important for understanding both history and current events. It can also help you think about possible consequences before you make decisions.

WHAT YOU NEED TO KNOW

The following tips can help you identify cause-and-effect relationships when you read.

- A cause-and-effect relationship can be simple—one cause leads to one effect.

This painting by an Italian artist shows the baptism of Constantine.

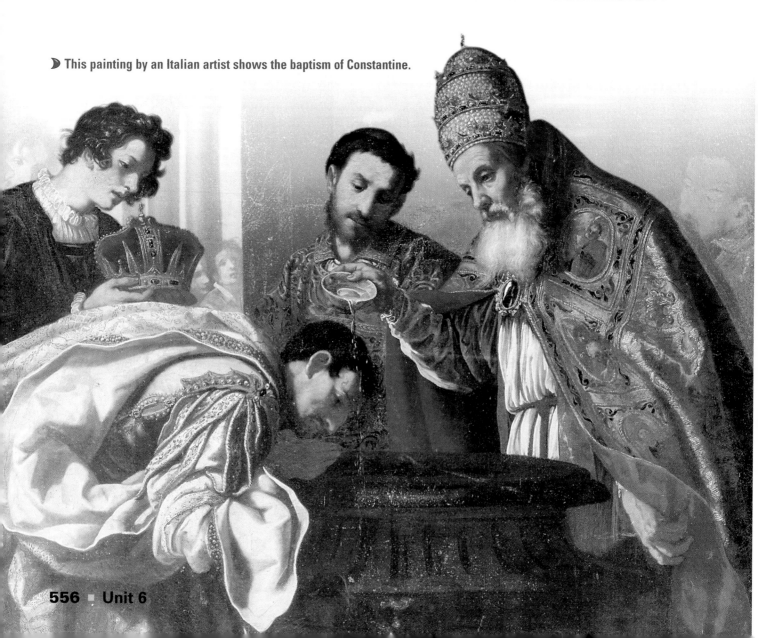

- In some cause-and-effect relationships, one cause may lead to two or more effects. In others, two or more causes may lead to one effect.

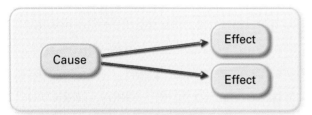

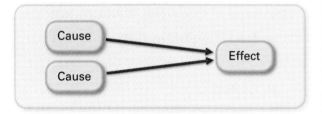

- In some cases, a single cause may lead to a chain of linked effects. Each effect is the cause of another effect.

- When you read, look for words and phrases that signal cause-and-effect relationships. Examples include *because, as a result, since, consequently, for this reason,* and *in response.* Words such as *also* and *in addition* often signal relationships that have multiple causes or multiple effects.

▶ PRACTICE THE SKILL

ANALYSIS SKILL Use the cause-and-effect chart on this page to answer these questions.

1 What kind of cause-and-effect relationship does the chart show?

2 What caused Constantine to become a Christian?

3 What were the two main effects of the Edict of Milan?

▶ APPLY WHAT YOU LEARNED

ANALYSIS SKILL Identify multiple causes and effects of a recent historical event, and show them in a cause-and-effect chart.

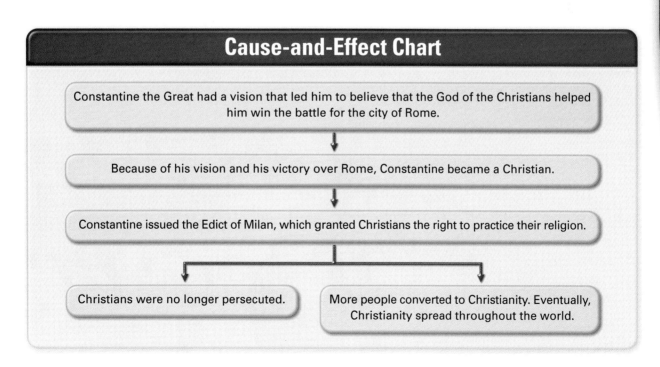

Cause-and-Effect Chart

Constantine the Great had a vision that led him to believe that the God of the Christians helped him win the battle for the city of Rome.

Because of his vision and his victory over Rome, Constantine became a Christian.

Constantine issued the Edict of Milan, which granted Christians the right to practice their religion.

Christians were no longer persecuted.

More people converted to Christianity. Eventually, Christianity spread throughout the world.

Lesson  Rome's Legacy

WHAT TO KNOW
Which achievements of ancient Rome are important today?

✓ Explain how modern civilizations have been influenced by Roman language, literature, and law.

✓ Describe the legacies of Roman science, technology, architecture, and art.

VOCABULARY
patriotism p. 561

PEOPLE
Cicero
Tacitus
Virgil
Horace
Ovid
Ulpian
Ptolemy
Galen

PLACES
Alexandria

DRAW CONCLUSIONS

California Standards
HSS 6.7, 6.7.2, 6.7.8

YOU ARE THERE It is A.D. 150, and you live in Rome. You and your family are going to the stadium to see a track meet. Along the way, you pass a large statue of one of your country's former rulers. It reminds you of the coin your father gave you to spend today. The coin has a picture on it of the same ruler.

The streets and walkways outside the stadium are newly paved with concrete. The stadium itself is huge. Hundreds of arches hold up row after row of seats, where thousands of fans eagerly wait the start of the events. As you enter the stadium, the roar of the crowd gives you goose bumps.

❯ The Roman Senate (below) has inspired modern democracies and other forms of government, including the United States Senate (left).

Language and Law

People study ancient Rome as history now, but its accomplishments live on. Many legacies from Roman art and architecture, technology and science, literature, language, and law survive today. Almost every part of our modern life builds on a Roman achievement.

Latin, the language of the Romans, is the basis of several modern languages, including Italian, Spanish, French, and Portuguese. Almost half of all English words come from Latin.

Modern world literature has also been shaped by ancient Romans. The speeches of the Roman leader **Cicero** are still used as models of public speaking. **Tacitus** remains a respected author of ancient history. Students still study the poems of **Virgil**, **Horace**, and **Ovid**.

Every modern republic, including the United States, owes much to the early Romans. The Romans created this form of government, in which power is shared among different leaders and groups.

Roman law is the basis of legal systems in many parts of the world. The Roman judge **Ulpian** explained, "Justice is a steady

Development of the Latin Alphabet			
PHOENICIAN (About 1000 B.C.)	GREEK (About 600 B.C.)	ETRUSCAN (About 500 B.C.)	LATIN (Present Day)
K	A	A	A
゛	M	M	M
7	Γ	Γ	P
≢	S	S	S
+	T	T	T

ANALYSIS SKILL **Analyze Tables** Today, use of the Latin alphabet has spread worldwide.

❖ Why do you think the Romans adapted letters from the Greeks and Etruscans?

and enduring desire to give every man his due. The basic principles of law are these: to live honorably, not to injure any other person, and to render to each his own."* Modern ideas of equal rights and justice are rooted in these ideas.

READING CHECK ⏱ **DRAW CONCLUSIONS**
In what ways have Roman government and law influenced modern societies?

*Ulpian. "Digest" in *The Romans: From Village to Empire*. M.T. Boatwright, D.J. Gargola, and R.J. Talbert, eds. Oxford University Press, 2004.

Science and Art

The work of scientists in the Roman Empire provided a foundation for those who came after them. **Ptolemy** (TAH•luh•mee) was a Greek who lived in **Alexandria**, Egypt, under Roman rule. Ptolemy's understanding of astronomy guided sailors for almost 1,500 years. **Galen**, a Greek subject of the empire, was a doctor to Emperor Marcus Aurelius. He understood that blood circulated in the body. Doctors used his teachings for hundreds of years.

Roman engineers used new technologies to plan cities and equip them with systems that made life easier and healthier.

They built aqueducts to bring clean water to cities and built sewer systems to remove waste. Their roads and bridges were so well built that some are still used today.

Roman architects improved on the ideas of builders from other cultures. From the Etruscans, the Romans learned to build arches. They were the first to use arches to make a hollow dome, a key feature of Roman architecture. From the Greeks, the Romans adopted the use of columns to support walls and roofs. They changed the designs of the Greek columns to create new styles.

The Romans created a kind of building called a basilica. The design was originally used for city halls. Later, the

▶ The Jefferson Memorial (left) in Washington, D.C., features a Roman hollow-dome design as seen on the ancient Pantheon (below) in Rome.

M·AGRIPPA·L·F·COS·TERTIVM·FECIT

> Rome's spectacular mosaics have stood the test of time. This mosaic (right) from the 100s B.C. was found in Pompeii.

basilica became a common style for Christian churches.

The Romans invented concrete, one of today's most widely used building materials. Concrete is made in much the same way today as it was in ancient Rome.

Roman artists, too, were influenced by the Greeks. The mosaics for which Rome is famous were made using ideas learned from the Greeks.

Many Roman artists made sculptures and other paintings of the emperors. Their work encouraged **patriotism**, or loyalty to one's home country. The Roman custom of minting coins with the portraits of leaders on them survives all around the world today.

READING CHECK SUMMARIZE
How did Roman engineers improve the design of cities?

Summary

The legacy of ancient Rome continues to influence modern civilizations. Almost half of English words come from Latin. Rome's principles of government and law have spread around the world. Roman styles in architecture and art can be seen in today's buildings and artworks.

REVIEW

1. Which achievements of ancient Rome are important today?

2. Write a sentence explaining how the ancient Romans encouraged **patriotism**.

3. What architectural feature did the Romans borrow from the Greeks?

CRITICAL THINKING

4. **ANALYSIS SKILL** How do you think historians know that the Romans borrowed the use of arches and columns from other cultures?

5. **Make It Relevant** How might modern European languages be different today, if Rome had not built an empire?

6. **Make It Relevant** What evidence of Roman influence have you seen in your state or community?

7. **Create a Newspaper Picture with a Caption** Think about the many Roman achievements in art, architecture, and science. Then draw a picture that represents one of them. Write a caption announcing the achievement to go with your picture.

8. **Focus Skill** DRAW CONCLUSIONS
On a separate sheet of paper, copy and complete the graphic organizer below.

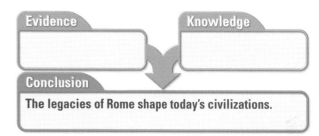

Evidence	Knowledge

Conclusion
The legacies of Rome shape today's civilizations.

Time

150 B.C.   B.C./A.D.

• **63 B.C.**
Judaea becomes part
of the Roman Empire

A.D. 30
Jesus is put
on trial and
crucified

Reading Social Studies

A **conclusion** is an understanding reached after careful thinking. To **draw a conclusion**, you use what you already know along with what you read about a subject to make a general statement about an idea or an event.

 Draw a Conclusion

Complete this graphic organizer to show that you can draw conclusions about the legacies of Rome. A copy of this graphic organizer appears on page 156 of the Homework and Practice Book.

The Legacies of Rome

Evidence
The Romans invented concrete.

Knowledge

Conclusion
The legacy of Rome lives on in today's society.

 ## California Writing Prompts

Write a Myth Write a myth in narrative form with one of the Roman gods or goddesses as the main character. Build your story around the parts of nature that your main character has power over.

Write an Expository Paragraph Write a paragraph that compares and contrasts the various religions that existed in the Roman Empire. Use a Venn diagram to help organize your thinking before you begin to write.

A.D. 313
Emperor Constantine
grants everyone in
Rome religious freedom

A.D. 391
Emperor Theodosius
makes Christianity
the official religion of
the Roman Empire

Use Vocabulary

Use each term in a sentence or two to explain both what the term means and how that meaning relates to religion in the Roman Empire.

1. **mystery religion** (p. 539)
2. **sect** (p. 541)
3. **disciple** (p. 544)
4. **parable** (p. 544)
5. **apostle** (p. 546)
6. **persecution** (p. 546)
7. **pope** (p. 554)

Use the Time Line

 ANALYSIS SKILL Use the summary time line above to answer these questions.

8. What happened in 63 B.C.?
9. What did Constantine do in A.D. 313?
10. How long after Jesus was crucified did Christianity become the official religion of the Roman Empire?

Apply Skills

Identify Causes and Effects

11. **ANALYSIS SKILL** Make a chart showing the causes and effects of one of the events you read about in this chapter.

Recall Facts

Answer these questions.

12. In which other places were Jewish people living at the time of Rome's conquest of Judaea?
13. What lessons did Jesus teach with parables?
14. What did Roman engineers contribute to the legacy of Rome?

Write the letter of the best choice.

15. Where did Jewish people move to after Emperor Hadrian expelled them from Jerusalem?
    A the Americas
    B other parts of the Roman Empire
    C southern Africa
    D eastern China

16. Which Roman leaders helped the spread of Christianity?
    A Constantine and Theodosius I
    B Hadrian and Trajan
    C Julius Caesar and Augustus
    D Marcus Aurelius and Pliny the Younger

Think Critically

17. **ANALYSIS SKILL** What different points of view are expressed in the paintings showing Jesus in Lesson 2?

18. **ANALYSIS SKILL** Explain how the beginning of Christianity and the fire that burned Rome are related to each other in time. Why do you think Nero blamed Christians for the fire?

Rome, Italy

GET READY

Rome is home to more than 2,700,000 people and thousands of monuments and other well-known sites. Often called the Eternal City, Rome's streets and plazas are filled with layer upon layer of history.

Rome is also home to the Vatican, the seat of the Roman Catholic Church. With a population of fewer than 1,000, the Vatican is the world's smallest independent country.

Rome is famous for its more than 300 public fountains. They are great for keeping cool under the hot Italian sun, and millions of people toss coins into them every year for good luck.

WHAT TO SEE

The Colosseum (above) still attracts crowds 1,900 years after its completion. However, these spectators come to admire the structure itself, rather than to cheer gladiators.

LOCATE IT

ITALY
Rome

Decorative figures line the Bridge of Sant'Angelo, which spans the Tiber River.

Tens of thousands of Catholics gather in Saint Peter's Square to listen to the Pope speak (top). The ceiling of the Sistine Chapel (above), painted by Michaelangelo, is one of the Vatican's many historic treasures.

Another of Rome's many religious buildings is the Pantheon (top). The name *pantheon* means "house of all gods." About 500 years after its construction, it became a Christian church. It overlooks a plaza (above) that has cafes and a fountain.

A VIRTUAL TOUR

GO ONLINE

Visit VIRTUAL TOURS at
www.harcourtschool.com/hss

Unit 6 Review

THE BIG IDEA

Individualism The actions of individuals affected the development of Rome as it changed from a monarchy to a republic to an empire.

Summary

The Development of Rome

Latin villagers, influenced by the Etruscans and the Greeks, built the city of Rome at the foot of the Seven Hills. Rome was ruled by kings until 509 B.C., when Romans created the first republic. During the Roman Republic, Romans conquered the Italian Peninsula and the lands around the Mediterranean. Later the Republic weakened and Julius Caesar ruled as dictator until he was killed.

Caesar's heir, Octavius, and Mark Antony defeated Caesar's killers. When Mark Antony allied himself with Cleopatra, Octavius defeated them to become sole ruler of an empire. Known as Augustus, he ruled for 40 years and set the stage for the *Pax Romana*.

People in the Roman Empire were allowed to follow their own religion. However, they were required to honor Roman gods.

In about 4 B.C., Jesus was born in Judaea. As a young man, he attracted large crowds, and his claim to be the Messiah made him a threat to Roman leaders. He was put to death, but his followers claimed that he rose from the dead. The apostles spread his teachings, which became the basis of Christianity. In spite of persecution, Christianity spread across the empire. After Constantine the Great became a Christian, Christianity became an accepted religion in the Roman Empire.

Main Ideas and Vocabulary

Read the summary above. Then answer the questions that follow.

1. Who were the first Romans?
   A Etruscans
   B Greeks
   C Latins
   D Hebrews

2. Who leads a republic?
   A a king or a queen
   B elected leaders
   C a foreign conqueror
   D a military dictator

3. Where did Christianity begin?
   A in Italy
   B in Greece
   C in Judaea
   D in Egypt

4. Who is the heir of a person most likely to be?
   A his or her ancestor
   B his or her ruler
   C his or her father
   D his or her child

566 ▪ Unit 6

Answer these questions.

5. Why did the Romans start a republic form of government?

6. What three parts made up the Roman tripartite government?

7. How did standard currency benefit the Roman Empire?

8. What lesson did Jesus teach with the parable of the Good Samaritan?

9. What features of Roman architecture can be seen in many modern buildings?

Write the letter of the best choice.

10. What were the two main social classes of the Roman Republic?
   - **A** kings and their subjects
   - **B** consuls and senators
   - **C** plebeians and patricians
   - **D** dictators and soldiers

11. Who was the first emperor of Rome?
   - **A** Augustus
   - **B** Julius Caesar
   - **C** Nero
   - **D** Trajan

12. Which of the following served as important trade routes for the Roman Empire?
   - **A** paths through the forests
   - **B** irrigation canals
   - **C** migration paths of birds
   - **D** roads, rivers, and the Mediterranean Sea

Think Critically

13. **ANALYSIS SKILL** Identify the three main kinds of government that existed in ancient Rome. Then construct a time line showing when each kind of government came about and the key events and people that changed how Rome was governed.

14. **ANALYSIS SKILL** Write five facts you learned about the Roman Empire. Then create five statements that represent opinions about the Roman Empire.

Apply Skills

Compare Historical Maps

ANALYSIS SKILL Use the maps to answer the questions.

15. How did the area that was the Western Roman Empire change by A.D. 1000?

16. What empire controlled part of Europe in A.D. 1000?

Western Roman Empire, A.D. 395

European Kingdoms, A.D. 1000

Unit 6 Activities

Read More

■ *Daily Life in a Roman City* by Stefan Petrucha.

■ *Roman Leaders* by Miranda Barry.

■ *Discovering Pompeii* by Jeffrey Nelson.

Show What You Know

Unit Writing Activity

Write a Research Report Search the library and the Internet for information about the founding of Rome. Take notes on what you have read and organize them in an outline. Next, write a rough draft, revise it, and prepare a final version.

Unit Project

Publish an Ancient Newspaper Put together a newspaper that tells about important people, places, and events of ancient Rome. Decide on a clever name for your paper. Then choose people, places, and events that you will include in the paper, and decide how you will show them. You could show them in a weather report, an obituary, a biography, and in stories. Illustrate your newspaper with drawings and advertisements that relate to that time.

Visit ACTIVITIES at
www.harcourtschool.com/hss

For Your Reference

LOCAL OPTIONS

ATLAS/ ALMANAC

RESEARCH HANDBOOK

BIOGRAPHICAL DICTIONARY

GAZETTEER

GLOSSARY

INDEX

LOCAL
OPTIONS

ATLAS/
ALMANAC

RESEARCH
HANDBOOK

BIOGRAPHICAL
DICTIONARY

GAZETTEER

GLOSSARY

INDEX

Time Marches On

California History-Social Science
Standards, Grade 6

7.1 Students analyze the causes and effects of the vast expansion and ultimate disintegration of the Roman Empire.

Changes for the Roman Empire

► Roman ruins in Palmyra, Syria

Time

B.C./A.D.   A.D. 500   A.D. 1000

A.D. 167
A rebellion leads the Roman Empire into war

A.D. 253
Valerian divides the empire into two parts

The Roman Empire Faces Problems

WHAT TO KNOW
What problems did the Roman Empire face during the A.D. 200s?

✔ Describe the events that led to the end of the *Pax Romana*.

✔ Explain how conflicts within the Roman Empire and with outside groups weakened the empire.

VOCABULARY
frontier p. R6
barbarian p. R7
inflation p. R8

PEOPLE
Marcus Aurelius
Dio Cassius
Commodus
Valerian
Shapur I

PLACES
Roman Empire
Rome
Persia

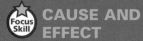

CAUSE AND EFFECT

California Standards
HSS 7.1, 7.1.1, 7.1.2

YOU ARE THERE

The year is A.D. 251. You live in a northeastern province of the **Roman Empire** called Dacia (DAY•shuh). Your family has farmed this land for generations. Both of your brothers are Roman soldiers, yet neither of them has ever been to **Rome**.

You've listened to them talking late into the night. Why, they ask, should they be sent hundreds of miles away to fight the Persians? All they have to do is look across the Danube River to see Germanic tribes getting ready to attack. Why should they obey an emperor in Rome who has never even seen their homeland?

▶ Ancient Roman ruins in what is now Turkey

▶ This oil painting titled *The Course of Empire: Destruction* illustrates the decline of Rome. It was painted by the artist Thomas Cole in A.D. 1836.

A Vast Empire

Under the rule of Augustus, the Roman Empire grew strong. Augustus's ideas, reforms, and building projects set the stage for the more than 200 years of peace and growth of the *Pax Romana.*

During this time, Romans continued to enjoy the benefits of citizenship and of their rights under Roman law. Romans also made lasting contributions in art, architecture, engineering, and philosophy. In addition, they spread Christianity.

The size of the Roman Empire continued to grow, too. Each new conquest increased Rome's wealth by bringing more land, taxes, and slaves under its control. At its height, in A.D. 117, the borders of the empire stretched east from what is now England to lands that are today part of Iraq. Rome controlled all lands that surrounded the Mediterranean, including the northern coast of Africa.

Today, historians agree that the great size of the Roman Empire was one of many causes that led to its end. The empire was too big to control and to defend.

Signs of trouble came about during the rule of **Marcus Aurelius**, the last of the Five Good Emperors. In A.D. 167, a rebellion led the empire into war. At the same time, Aurelius had to defend the empire against attacks along its borders.

During the A.D. 200s, the Roman Empire continued to face problems both inside and outside its borders. Enemies made repeated attacks on Roman lands. From within, political disorder, dishonesty, and civil war weakened the empire. As a result, Rome's people faced difficult social and economic problems. The *Pax Romana* was over. The Roman historian **Dio Cassius** wrote, "Our history now descends from a kingdom of gold to one of iron and rust."*

READING CHECK ⭕CAUSE AND EFFECT
How did the Roman Empire's great size affect it?

*Dio Cassius, from *Dio's Roman History: With an English Translation.* Earnest Cary and Herbert Baldwin Foster, trans. The Macmillan Co., 1927.

Challenges in the Empire

The cultures of the Roman Empire were varied. Rome did not force those under its rule to give up their cultures. Romans, of all cultural backgrounds, were expected to follow Roman law and pay their taxes. In return, the empire promised peace and a good life.

Over time, the empire's promise was hard to keep because of weaknesses that formed in the empire. Disorder within the empire grew under the rule of **Commodus**, the son of Marcus Aurelius.

GEOGRAPHY

Roman Britain

For many years, only the English Channel separated the Britons from Roman rule. In time, Roman armies crossed the channel from Gaul to conquer the Britons. After years of fighting, Roman Britain included only Britannia, which is today England and Wales. Hibernia, present-day Ireland, and Caledonia, present-day Scotland, never became part of the Roman Empire. The Irish Sea shielded Hibernia from Roman invasion, while the mountainous land of Caledonia made marching and fighting too hard for Roman soldiers.

ATLANTIC OCEAN
CALEDONIA — Hadrian's Wall
ROMAN EMPIRE
Luguvallium (Carlisle)
HIBERNIA
Eburacum (York)
North Sea
Deva (Chester)
Lindum (Lincoln)
Camulodunum (Colchester)
BRITANNIA
English Channel
Isca (Caerleon)
Aquae Sulis (Bath)
Londinium (London)
Isca Dumnoniorum (Exeter)
Irish Sea
0   50   100 Miles
0 50 100 Kilometers

- City
- Roman Legion fortress
- Roman fort
- Roman road

After Aurelius's rule, political conflicts caused the government of Rome to weaken. Independent military powers arose in the empire. Roman leaders fought one another in civil wars, with the winners claiming the throne. Most of these leaders ruled only a short time before being forced out. From A.D. 235 to A.D. 284, more than 60 leaders held the title of emperor.

These emperors had, at best, a loose grip on the empire. News traveled slowly between the provinces and the city of Rome. In addition, Roman citizens were losing respect for their government. Even the soldiers who defended the empire's **frontiers**, or borderlands, from invaders felt little loyalty toward the empire. Instead, they supported their generals, who often acted independently of Rome's wishes.

The political conflicts within the Roman Empire caused its economy to suffer. Trade decreased. Roman money lost value. Prices rose, bringing hardships to the Roman people.

READING CHECK ○ **CAUSE AND EFFECT**
What caused Rome's leadership to weaken?

Attacks on the Empire

During much of the A.D. 200s, outsiders threatened the Roman Empire from three directions. From the east, the Persians invaded Roman provinces in Asia. From the south, an African people called the Berbers (BER•berz) attacked Roman lands in northern Africa. Germanic tribes attacked the empire's edges from the north.

In A.D. 253, the emperor **Valerian** tried to make the empire stronger. Believing that the empire was too large for one leader to rule and to defend, he divided it into two parts. Valerian put his son Gallienus (ga•lee•EE•nuhs) in charge of the western part. Valerian ruled the eastern part.

In A.D. 256, King **Shapur I** (shah•PUR) of **Persia** took advantage of Rome's weakness and attacked its eastern lands. Shapur captured Valerian and put him in prison, but Valerian died a year later.

In northern Africa, the Berbers fought against a weak Roman army. The Berbers raided Roman cities all along the coast of northern Africa.

❯ This medallion shows the Persian king Shapur I and the Roman emperor Valerian in battle.

A Germanic people called the Goths repeatedly claimed lands along the northern border of the Roman Empire. Before, Germanic peoples had lived peacefully alongside and within the empire. Many had fought in the Roman army, and some had become military leaders. Still, the Romans called these Germanic people "barbarians" because they were not educated in Roman ways. Today, a **barbarian** is a person who is considered to be rough-mannered.

READING CHECK SUMMARIZE
Why did Valerian divide the Roman Empire?

⚡**FAST FACT**

In A.D. 122, the emperor Hadrian ordered his soldiers to build an 80-mile-long wall to protect the Roman Empire's northern border in Britannia. The wall, which became known as Hadrian's Wall, took about 10,000 soldiers and six years to build. Today, ruins of Hadrian's Wall stand along the border between England and Scotland.

Inflation in Rome

PRODUCT	COST IN ROMAN DENARII (in about A.D. 300)	COST IN ROMAN DENARII (in about A.D. 307)
1 chicken	60	120
1 egg	1	2
1 lemon	24	48
1 quart of honey	80	160
1 modius (about 8 quarts) of wheat	100	200
1 pair of women's boots	60	120
1 pair of farm-worker's boots	120	240
1 pound of silk	12,000	24,000

ANALYSIS SKILL **Analyze Tables** The Roman mosaic shows Romans bringing their products to market. The table shows how the prices of products increased over a 7-year period.

❓ About how much did prices for products increase over this period of time?

Ways of Life Change

A border about 3,000 miles long enclosed the lands claimed by the Roman Empire. In time, the burden of defending this large empire fell on Roman citizens. The government collected tax money from its citizens to pay the army.

Many farmers could not afford to pay the heavy taxes and had to leave their farms. Some farmers sold their land to large landowners. Others turned to robbery or joined the invading armies.

To raise more money, in A.D. 212 Rome gave citizenship to all free people living in the empire. Soon, the rights of citizenship began to weaken. Dishonest leaders began to give wealthy citizens more rights, while taking away the rights of other citizens. Even the growing number of slaves meant that more and more people lacked citizenship.

With no more wealth flowing into the empire from newly conquered lands, Rome faced a shortage in silver, the main metal used in Roman coins. To make more coins, the government began to mix silver with less-valuable metals. Because the new coins were less valuable than the old ones, merchants raised their prices. In this way, they got the same amount of silver. A rise in prices caused by a decrease in the value of money is called **inflation**. The price of food rose dramatically, bringing more troubles for the Roman people.

Rising prices, political chaos, and invasions disrupted almost all parts of Roman life. The empire's problems even affected education. There was no longer money for the few public schools that had opened during the *Pax Romana*. Once again, only Rome's wealthiest families could afford to send their sons to school.

Trade decreased between the cities and the countryside. Armies on the move made transporting goods to the cities too dangerous. The Roman urban centers began losing their food supplies, creating food shortages. Poverty and the gap between rich and poor grew sharply. The wealthy fled the cities. When possible, poor Romans fled too. Some went to the frontier to work on the farms of large landowners. Others joined the army. For those who remained in the cities, Rome's once glorious city life was now filled with crime, hunger, and disease.

READING CHECK **SUMMARIZE**
What weakened citizenship in the Roman Empire?

▶ A Roman citizen pays taxes to a tax collector.

Summary

By the third century A.D., the Roman Empire had become difficult to rule and to defend. Political struggles and invasions weakened the empire. These problems changed the Roman way of life and caused decreased trade, high taxes, and poverty.

REVIEW

1. What problems did the Roman Empire face during the A.D. 200s?

2. Write a paragraph describing **inflation** in the Roman Empire.

3. How did soldiers' loss of loyalty toward Rome hurt the empire in the A.D. 200s?

CRITICAL THINKING

4. How did the invasions along the Roman frontiers change life in Roman cities?

5. **ANALYSIS SKILL** Why do you think some free people might have been unhappy with Rome's decision to make them citizens in A.D. 212?

6. **Make It Relevant** What problems faced by countries today are similar to those faced by the Roman Empire?

7. **Write a Newspaper Article** Imagine that you are a news reporter in Rome in the A.D. 200s. Write a newspaper article announcing attacks along the Roman Empire's borders. Be sure to include the directions from which the attacks come and the identities of the attackers.

8. **Focus Skill** **CAUSE AND EFFECT**
On a separate sheet of paper, copy and complete the graphic organizer below.

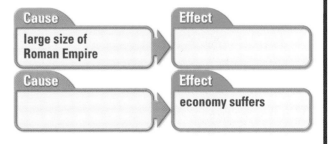

Cause	Effect
large size of Roman Empire	
Cause	Effect
	economy suffers

Time

B.C./A.D.   A.D. 500   A.D. 1000

A.D. 330
Constantine moves the Roman capital to Byzantium

A.D. 395
The Roman Empire officially splits into two empires

A.D. 476
The Western Roman Empire ends

WHAT TO KNOW
What events led to the fall of Rome and the end of the Western Roman Empire?

✓ Describe how the Roman Empire split into two empires.

✓ Explain what brought the Western Roman Empire to an end.

✓ Describe how Roman culture lived on after the fall of the Western Roman Empire.

VOCABULARY
vandal p. R12
convert p. R13

PEOPLE
Diocletian
Constantine the Great
Alaric
Odoacer
Clovis
Justinian I
Theodora

PLACES
Rome
Byzantium
Constantinople/Istanbul

CAUSE AND EFFECT

California Standards
HSS 7.1, 7.1.1, 7.1.2, 7.1.3

Decline of the Western Roman Empire

YOU ARE THERE

The year is A.D. 284. You're standing in the middle of the Forum in **Rome**. The new emperor, **Diocletian**, has just announced that he is dividing the leadership of the Roman Empire. You worry that his decision will tear the empire apart.

You try to imagine the northern forests of Gaul, filled with Germanic tribes. Looking east, you recall the Persians, who have defeated Roman troops many times. Turning south, you think of Africa's huge deserts, and to the west, the miles of ocean and wilderness.

Perhaps Diocletian is right. The empire and its problems are too large for any one person to handle.

FAST FACT

This statue, called the Tetrarchs, represents the Rule of Four during the time of Diocletian. To show their equality, all four rulers have the same height, the same clothing, and the same sword. The rulers' embrace shows their unity.

The Roman Empire Splits in Two, A.D. 395

ATLANTIC OCEAN

Londinium (London)

Colonia Agrippina (Cologne)

EUROPE

Caspian Sea

Burdigala (Bordeaux)

Mediolanum (Milan)

Aquincum (Budapest)

Viminiacium

Black Sea

WESTERN ROMAN EMPIRE

Massilia (Marseilles)

Rome

Adriatic Sea

Thessalonika

Constantinople (Istanbul)

EASTERN ROMAN EMPIRE

Ephesus

Antioch

Córdoba

Tyrrhenian Sea

Ionian Sea

Aegean Sea

Athens

New Carthage (Cartagena)

Gades (Cadiz)

Carthage

Syracuse

Tyre

Tingi (Tangier)

Caesarea

Mediterranean Sea

Cyrene

Alexandria

Memphis

Red Sea

Capital
Other city

0   200   400 Miles
0   200   400 Kilometers
Azimuthal Equal-Area Projection

N W E S

AFRICA

ANALYSIS SKILL **Analyze Maps** After Diocletian's division of the Roman Empire, Constantine reunited it. Even so, the empire officially split in A.D. 395.

Regions What was the capital of the Eastern Roman Empire?

A Divided Empire

In the late A.D. 200s, better times briefly returned to the Roman Empire. In A.D. 284, the Roman general Diocletian (dy•uh•KLEE•shuhn) became emperor. Like Valerian, Diocletian believed that one person could not rule the empire alone, so he divided it. He ruled the eastern part and put a loyal officer named Maximian in charge of the western part.

In A.D. 293, Diocletian made a bold reform that created what is now called the Rule of Four. He appointed two generals, Constantius (kuhn•STAN•chee•uhs) and Galerius (guh•LIR•ee•uhs), to serve under himself and Maximian as rulers. Under the Rule of Four, the size of the Roman army increased. The army was now able to put down rebellions and to push back invaders.

To control inflation, Diocletian made economic reforms in A.D. 301. He passed a law that set price limits on goods and services across the empire. He also had new coins made from good-quality metal.

Diocletian's reforms only stopped the empire's decline for a time. Eventually, the Rule of Four collapsed. Once again, civil wars divided Rome. Then, in A.D. 324, the emperor **Constantine the Great** managed to unite the whole empire under his rule.

READING CHECK **CAUSE AND EFFECT**
What caused Diocletian to reorganize the empire?

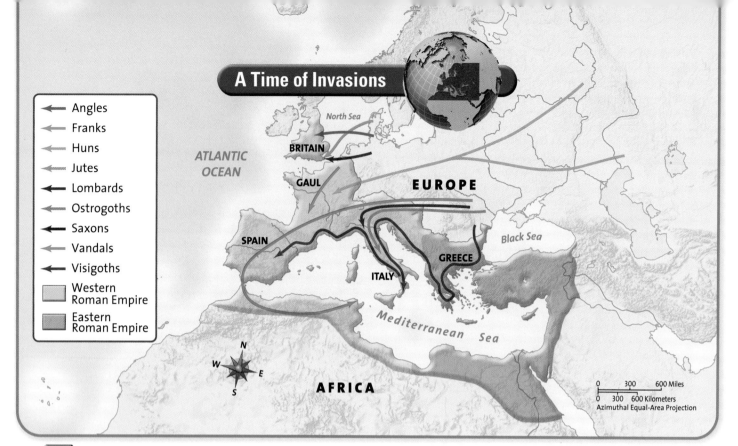

A Time of Invasions

Legend:
- Angles
- Franks
- Huns
- Jutes
- Lombards
- Ostrogoths
- Saxons
- Vandals
- Visigoths
- Western Roman Empire
- Eastern Roman Empire

ANALYSIS SKILL Analyze Maps Many different Germanic tribes invaded the Western Roman Empire.

❖ **Regions** Which tribes invaded Britain? Northern Africa? Italy?

The Western Empire Ends

Constantine moved the empire's capital eastward from Rome to **Byzantium** (buh•ZAN•tee•uhm) in A.D. 330. Nearly surrounded by water, the city was well located for trade and easy to defend.

Soon Byzantium replaced Rome as the empire's most important city. In honor of Constantine, the city was renamed **Constantinople** (kahn•stan•tuhn•OH•puhl). Today, Constantinople is known as **Istanbul** (is•tuhn•BUL), Turkey.

In A.D. 395, the Roman Empire officially split into two empires, one in the east and one in the west. Cities and trade grew in the Eastern Roman Empire. The Western Roman Empire began to decline.

Beginning in the A.D. 300s, Germanic tribes invaded both empires. They came in search of new lands on which to settle.

Their own lands were being taken by the Huns, a people from central Asia.

In A.D. 410, the Visigoths, led by **Alaric** (A•luh•rik), captured Rome. In A.D. 455, Rome was attacked again, this time by the Vandals. They stole items of value and destroyed monuments. Today, we use the word **vandal** to describe someone who damages property on purpose.

After many attacks, Rome finally fell in A.D. 476 to a Germanic chief named **Odoacer** (OH•duh•way•ser). After overthrowing the Roman emperor Romulus Augustus in the Western Roman Empire, Odoacer became the first Germanic king of the Italian Peninsula. Many historians consider this event the end of the Western Roman Empire.

READING CHECK **DRAW CONCLUSIONS**
What message might Alaric's attack on Rome have sent to other Germanic tribes?

New Germanic Kingdoms

Germanic tribes continued to conquer lands of the former Western Roman Empire and to form kingdoms. The Angles and the Saxons ruled Britain. The Lombards took control of the Italian Peninsula.

In A.D. 486, **Clovis,** a leader of the Franks, captured the last Roman territory in Gaul and set up his own kingdom. By A.D. 511, Clovis ruled lands from the Rhine River to the Pyrenees. Gaul came to be called France in honor of the Franks.

As new Germanic kingdoms formed, the Christian Church grew. The Church fed and clothed its poorer members. This charity brought many new **converts** (KAHN•verts), or people who change their religion, to Christianity. Also, missionaries traveled through Europe teaching Christianity. Some of them were able to convert kings, who, in turn, spread their new religion to their people. In A.D. 496, Clovis became a Christian, bringing all of Gaul into the Church.

With no other organized institution controlling Europe, the Church's power grew. Each city had its own bishop, or religious leader. The Roman bishop became the pope, or the leader of all bishops.

For many years, the pope held power in matters of both the Church and the Germanic states, or governments. This relationship between the Church and states greatly influenced the European civilization that developed in the former empire. Through the Church's influence, Roman culture, including the Latin language, lived on in Europe.

READING CHECK ☼ **CAUSE AND EFFECT**
What allowed the Church's power to grow in Europe?

❯ This nineteenth century wood engraving shows the last Roman emperor of the Western Roman Empire surrendering to Odoacer in A.D. 476.

Christianity and the Byzantine Empire

As the Western Roman Empire crumbled, the Eastern Roman Empire, which became known as the Byzantine Empire, thrived. The Byzantine Empire would continue for almost 1,000 years.

In A.D. 527, **Justinian I** became emperor of the Byzantine Empire. Justinian wanted to make the empire as powerful as the Roman Empire had once been.

Justinian used many Roman ideas to build the Byzantine Empire. He gathered Roman laws into one book called the *Justinian Code.* This code still forms the foundation for the laws of many countries of the world today. He used money from trade and taxes to make Constantinople

a "New Rome." He ordered the construction of buildings, roads, and aqueducts throughout the city. Constantinople became a crossroads for travel, trade, and cultural exchange in the region.

Under Justinian's rule, the Byzantine Empire reached its greatest size. The intelligence and political skills of Empress **Theodora**, Justinian's wife and most trusted adviser, helped the empire succeed.

In the Byzantine Empire, Christianity was important to the people, just as it was to the people of the Germanic kingdoms. However, the Christians in the Byzantine Empire held a different view on Church-state relations than did the Christians of the Germanic kingdoms. They believed that the state had the highest power in government matters, not religious leaders. These two distinct, or different, views on Church-state relations led to conflicts between Christians in the Byzantine Empire and Christians in the Germanic kingdoms.

ANALYSIS SKILL Analyze Maps The Christian Church split because of differing views on Church-state relations.

Regions After the split, which Church dominated Europe?

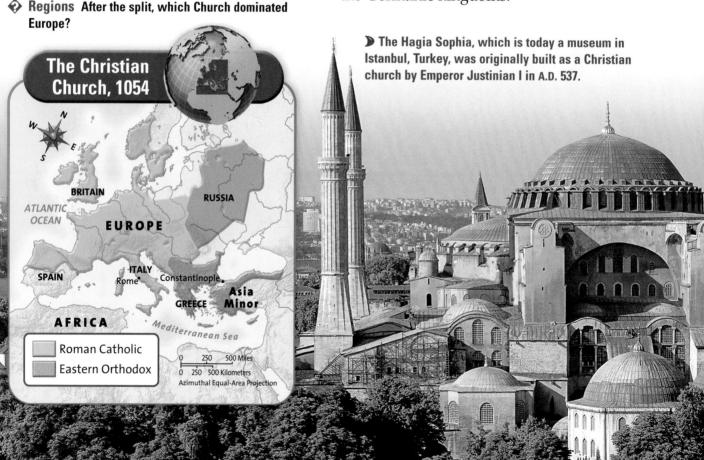

The Christian Church, 1054

W N E S

BRITAIN
ATLANTIC OCEAN
EUROPE
RUSSIA
SPAIN
ITALY
Rome
Constantinople
GREECE
Asia Minor
AFRICA
Mediterranean Sea

Roman Catholic
Eastern Orthodox

0 250 500 Miles
0 250 500 Kilometers
Azimuthal Equal-Area Projection

The Hagia Sophia, which is today a museum in Istanbul, Turkey, was originally built as a Christian church by Emperor Justinian I in A.D. 537.

These conflicts eventually caused the Christian Church to split in A.D. 1054. The Church in the Byzantine Empire became the Eastern Orthodox Church, based in Constantinople. The Christian Church in western Europe became the Roman Catholic Church, based in Rome.

READING CHECK **MAIN IDEA AND DETAILS**
Why did the Christian Church split in A.D. 1054?

Summary

Because the Roman Empire had grown too large for one person to govern, Diocletian divided the rule of the empire. In A.D. 395, the empire split into two empires, one in the west and one in the east. In time, the Western Roman Empire fell to Germanic tribes, but the Church survived and grew. Roman culture lived on in the Eastern Roman Empire, later called the Byzantine Empire, which lasted for another 1,000 years.

REVIEW

1. What events led to the fall of Rome and the end of the Western Roman Empire?

2. Write two sentences, using the word **convert** as a verb and as a noun.

3. Why did Constantine move the empire's capital to Byzantium?

CRITICAL THINKING

4. **ANALYSIS SKILL** Why might people of the Byzantine Empire have considered themselves to be Romans after Rome's fall?

5. **ANALYSIS SKILL** In what ways did the Roman Empire's influence continue for centuries after the empire's political decline?

6. **Draw a Map** Draw a map that shows the Roman Empire at its height. Then use a differently colored pencil to draw the boundaries of Roman lands after the fall of the Western Roman Empire in A.D. 476. Be sure to label major cities, places, and bodies of water.

7. **Focus Skill** **CAUSE AND EFFECT** On a separate sheet of paper, copy and complete the graphic organizer below.

Cause	Effect
	Byzantium replaces Rome as the empire's most important city.
Cause	Effect
	The Western Roman Empire ends.

California History-Social Science
Standards, Grade 6

7.7 Students compare and contrast the geographic, political, economic, religious, and social structures of the Meso-American and Andean civilizations.

Early Civilizations of the Americas

Ruins of the Mayan city of Tikal in Guatemala

Time

2000 B.C.   1000 B.C.   B.C./A.D.

About 1900 B.C.
Early people in
South America
build El Paraíso

1500 B.C.
People in Mesoamerica
form the beginnings of
the Olmec civilization

400 B.C.
Olmec culture ends

Early Cultures of the Americas

WHAT TO KNOW
How did the climate and geography of the Americas affect the development of culture there?

✔ Describe the climates and landforms of the Americas.

✔ Explain how the early people of the Americas had to adapt to changing environments.

VOCABULARY
tropical zone p. R19
temperate zone p. R19
cordillera p. R19
Mesoamerica p. R20

PLACES
Poverty Point
El Paraíso
Chavín
La Venta
San Lorenzo
Oaxaca

 **CAUSE AND EFFECT**

 **California Standards**
HSS 7.7, 7.7.1, 7.7.2, 7.7.5

YOU ARE THERE

It is 1500 B.C. You're sitting cross-legged on the dirt floor of your home, watching your father finish the jaguar he's been carving from black stone. Your father polishes the stone, making it shine like the coat of a real jaguar.

Jaguars are admired by your people. You've seen this magnificent animal in the rain forest. Safely hidden with your father in a tree, you watched a jaguar on its midnight hunt.

Today, your father let you use some of the tools of his craft. It will be a long time before you can carve a jaguar that will equal the beauty of his.

▶ People have lived in the Cascade Mountains (below) of North America for more than 8,000 years. The figurine (above) was important to the ancient Olmec people of Mexico.

The Land of the Americas

The Americas—made up of North America and South America—stretch over a large area. Many different climates and landforms exist within this area.

The Americas are mainly in two climate zones. The **tropical zone** contains all land within 1,600 miles of the equator. There, the temperature is hot. Large amounts of rain fall in every season. North and south of the tropical zone is the **temperate zone**, where climate varies with the season.

In both North America and South America, groups of mountain ranges called **cordilleras** (kawr•duhl•YAIR•uhs) run through the western regions. The North American cordillera is made up of many ranges. These include the Sierra Madre, the Rockies, the Sierra Nevada, the Cascade Range, and the Coast Ranges. The South American cordillera includes the Andes.

To the east of these cordilleras lie grassy plains within river basins. Some of the best farmland on both continents is found there. East of the plains are lower mountains.

In Central America, which is part of North America, many mountains are active volcanoes. Surrounding these mountains are lowlands of rain forests and swamps. These conditions make farming difficult.

READING CHECK ⚬ CAUSE AND EFFECT
What causes farming to be difficult in the lowlands of Central America?

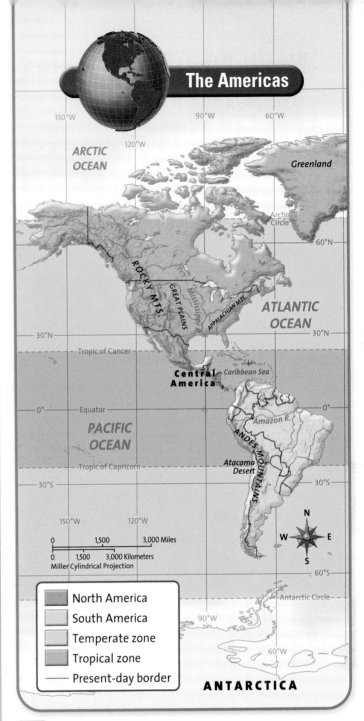

ANALYSIS SKILL Analyze Maps

◈ **Regions** What mountain range runs along the western coast of South America?

North American Cultures

The end of the last Ice Age brought changes to the climate of North America. As glaciers melted, temperatures became warmer farther north. By about 6000 B.C., the climate was about what it is today.

Early people adapted to these changes. In general, their lives depended on the search for food. They began to make new tools, such as bows and arrows, to help in hunting. Some groups continued traveling as hunters and gatherers. Others made the most of the warmer climate, setting up permanent villages and learning to farm. By about 2000 B.C., many societies were planting crops and raising herds of animals.

Between 2000 B.C. and 1000 B.C., some early people of the Americas developed complex societies that involved social classes and ceremonies. The remains of one of these early cultures have been found at **Poverty Point**, in what is now Louisiana. Huge earthen ridges and smaller earthen mounds are found at the site. The people who built them used baskets to carry the soil. Historians think these features were the bases for homes.

Built near several rivers, Poverty Point was a perfect place for trade. Archaeologists have found goods there that came from more than 600 miles away.

The ancient lands of Mexico and Central America are called **Mesoamerica**. There, villages with surrounding farmlands were common by 2000 B.C. The early people of Mesoamerica planted beans, squash, and maize, or corn, which was their main crop. These communities may have formed earlier than those in other parts of North America because of the local environment.

READING CHECK **SUMMARIZE**
What evidence suggests that the people of Poverty Point carried out trade?

LOCATE IT

OHIO

Miamisburg

▶ Evidence of Ohio's first farming culture includes this carving (above) and the Miamisburg Mound (below).

▶ Artists from the Chavín culture, Peru's earliest-known civilization, crafted this clay flute player (left), these hammered gold pendants (center), and this jaguar vase (right).

South American Cultures

In South America, farmers did well in the western highlands, the area on the western lower slopes of the Andes. They planted maize and cotton as their main crops. Highland farming communities traded with people along the coast for dried fish and salt. The two peoples enjoyed a long-lasting relationship.

The oldest-known ruins along the South American coast are at **El Paraíso** (el pah•rah•EE•soh), in what is now central Peru. These ruins date from about 1900 B.C. El Paraíso is a U-shaped group of square buildings made of mud and rock. They were built around what seems to have been a religious center. The people of El Paraíso had strong religious ideas, believing they could communicate with the spirit world.

In about 900 B.C., another culture, the Chavín (chah•VEEN), formed in central South America, in the Andes. The Chavín people came up with a style of religious art that spread over the northern and central parts of what is now Peru.

The city of **Chavín** was a religious and trading center. In its grand temple, a group of narrow halls led to a large central room. In this room stood a statue of a human figure with a jaguar's face.

The statue of the jaguar shows that the people's religious beliefs were connected with the animals they saw in their environment. In fact, the environment was important to all the early cultures in the Americas.

READING CHECK ▶ SUMMARIZE
What were the main crops in the western highlands of South America?

Olmec Lands

El Viejón
Tlatilco • Tlapacoya
Chalcatzinco • Tres Zapotes
Las Bocas
Oxtotitán •
Juxtlahuaca •
PACIFIC OCEAN
MEXICO
Gulf of Mexico
La Venta
Laguna de los Cerros • San Lorenzo
Balancán
Xoc
Padre Piedra •
Pijijiapan •
Izapa •
La Blanca •
MESOAMERICA

☐ Olmec homeland
● Olmec ceremonial center
• Other Olmec city

0   50   100 Miles
0   50   100 Kilometers

ANALYSIS SKILL **Analyze Maps** The Olmec and other ancient civilizations built cities throughout Mesoamerica.

Regions The land that was once the Olmec homeland lies in what present-day country?

The Olmec

By 1500 B.C., the Olmec had built the first real urban center in the Americas, in what is now southern Mexico. The Olmec society was divided into classes. The ruling class ordered the construction of large building projects. Their strong religious beliefs led them to build ceremonial plazas, mounds of earth, and temples at two locations—**La Venta** and **San Lorenzo**.

The Olmec based their religion on the forces of nature. They worshipped many gods. Their most important god was the rain god, which had the form of a jaguar. In much Olmec religious art, the gods take on both animal and human features. For example, many statues are of humans with noses and mouths like cats.

The Olmec carved huge stone heads out of single blocks of basalt (buh•SAWLT) rock. Experts believe that the heads may represent their rulers. The basalt came from places far away, either from the area of the Balsas River or from the mountains in **Oaxaca** (wuh•HAH•kuh).

The Olmec introduced writing to the Americas. They developed a writing script that they carved on pottery, pillars, monuments, slabs of stone, and sculptures.

Olmec farmers depended on flooding to water their crops and to make the soil rich. They developed a number system and a calendar to keep track of the flood season. They grew maize, beans, squash, avocados, and peppers. They planted their maize, beans, and squash together. In this way, farmers made the best possible use of the soil.

The Olmec made use of the resources around them. They built their houses with reeds from the rivers and grasses from the savannas. Coastal waters and rivers provided them with fish.

One of the resources that the Olmec traded was rubber. They also used rubber to make balls needed for a game called *pelota* (puh•LOH•tuh).

Olmec ideas spread throughout Mesoamerica. *Pelota* was played by other peoples. Other groups also used the Olmec calendar and continued the Olmec number and writing systems.

There are no traces of the Olmec after 400 B.C. However, their achievements lived on through later Mesoamerican civilizations. That is why experts call the Olmec culture the "mother civilization" of the Americas.

READING CHECK GENERALIZE

How were the Olmec able to keep track of the flood season?

⚡ **FAST FACT**

The Olmec carved large heads from basalt rock. To date, 17 heads have been found. This one stands about 8 feet tall and weighs more than 20 tons. It appears to be wearing a helmet.

Summary

The land and climate of the Americas are varied. At the end of the last Ice Age, the early people adapted to climate changes. Many groups gave up their nomadic way of life and settled as farmers. The Olmec developed the first real urban society in the Americas.

REVIEW

1. 💡 How did the climate and geography of the Americas affect the development of culture there?

2. Use the terms **tropical zone** and **temperate zone** to describe the climates of the Americas.

3. How did the religious beliefs of the Olmec affect their building projects?

4. How did the farmers of the South American western highlands obtain food they could not produce for themselves?

CRITICAL THINKING

5. **ANALYSIS SKILL** In what ways did the Olmec affect later civilizations in Mesoamerica?

6. **ANALYSIS SKILL** Why might it have been important for the Olmec to develop a writing system?

7. 🖌 **Make a Time Line** Make a time line that shows events from the end of the Ice Age to the end of the Olmec civilization.

8. **Focus Skill** **CAUSE AND EFFECT**
On a separate sheet of paper, copy and complete the graphic organizer below.

Cause	Effect
	The climate of North America changes.

Cause	Effect
People take advantage of the warmer climate.	

Lesson 2

500 B.C.   B.C./A.D.   A.D. 500

About 500 B.C.
The Maya begin building cities near Olmec centers

About 50 B.C.
Mayan glyphs first appear on public monuments

A.D. 300–A.D. 900
The Mayan civilization reaches its peak

The Maya

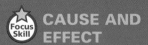

WHAT TO KNOW
What cultural achievements were made by the Mayan civilization?

- Explain how the environment affected the development and achievements of the Mayan civilization.

- Describe Mayan achievements in astronomy and mathematics and in the development of the calendar.

VOCABULARY
codex p. R29

PLACES
Tikal
Palenque
Copán
Chichén Itzá

CAUSE AND EFFECT

California Standards
HSS 7.7, 7.7.1, 7.7.2, 7.7.4, 7.7.5

YOU ARE THERE

The year is 500 B.C. The village priest has seen good fortune in the calendar. Today, all the 14-year-old boys and 12-year-old girls are gathering at the elders' house to receive a blessing.

The elders have purified the patio, covering it with leaves and mats. The priest places a white cloth on everyone's head and prays. Another priest walks down the line, tapping each young person nine times on the forehead. Then each boy and girl presents an offering of feathers and cacao beans to the priests. When everyone is back in line, the priest cuts out the white bead braided in each boy's hair. The mothers remove the red shells their daughters have worn around their waists since infancy. Today, the boys and girls will celebrate and feast. Tomorrow, they will be eligible to marry.

▶ Mayan ruins in Tulum, Mexico

The Mayan Civilization

CHICHÉN ITZÁ
UXMAL
TULUM
GULF OF MEXICO
YUCATÁN PENINSULA
MEXICO
Usumacinta River
BONAMPAK
TIKAL
BELIZE
CARIBBEAN SEA
GUATEMALA
COPÁN
HONDURAS
PACIFIC OCEAN
EL SALVADOR

Mayan lands

N
W   E
S

ANALYSIS SKILL **Analyze Maps** This map shows the major cities and ceremonial centers of the ancient Maya.

Regions On what peninsula were many Mayan cities located?

Mayan Beginnings

The civilization of the Maya was one of the longest-lasting civilizations of the ancient Americas. The Maya began as a simple farming society in the hot and steamy rain forests of Mesoamerica. They lived in the area that today includes southern Mexico, Belize, Guatemala, western Honduras, and El Salvador.

As early as 1000 B.C., the Maya had settled in farming villages in the lowlands of northern Guatemala, bringing with them clay containers and plants. The Maya probably came from the highlands to the west and south, in search of fertile land. In time, they raised crops, gathered food from the forests, and hunted small game.

By about 600 B.C., Mayan farming settlements were growing into thriving cities. Families lived in clusters of one-room, mud-plastered huts framed with wooden poles and vines. High roofs were made of thatched grasses and sloped steeply for protection against heavy rains.

Religious ceremonial centers made of stone were set apart from the farmers' huts. The Maya built flat-topped pyramids and carved stone monuments. On top of the pyramids, the Maya erected temples that looked like the peasants' huts. Over time, religious architecture became more complex and decorative.

By about 500 B.C., Mayan cities were developing near Olmec urban centers. The Maya probably traded with the Olmec. The Maya borrowed many Olmec cultural traits and innovations, such as the calendar and writing system. By building on Olmec ideas, the Mayan civilization grew strong.

READING CHECK **CAUSE AND EFFECT**
What caused the Maya to leave the highlands?

A Farming Economy

Since the Maya lived in the lowlands, the temperature did not change much throughout the year. The Maya divided the year into a rainy season and a dry season. These two seasons shaped the Mayan farming economy. The dry season lasted from November through April.

The lowlands were not a good location for farming. The soil was thin, and it washed away during the rainy season. In addition, there were only a few rivers and lakes for a year-round water supply. To survive the dry season, Mayan farmers who lived far from a river or lake dug canals and reservoirs. The canals were wide enough for canoes, providing a transportation route as well as a water supply. The reservoirs stored enough water for farming during the dry season.

In the rainy season, the land flooded. The Mayan solution was to raise the fields by digging trenches and then piling the dirt from the trenches in the fields. On hillsides, they made terraces, or ledges, that they used for farmland.

The Maya grew enough food for a rapidly growing population, with maize as the main crop. Like the Olmec farmers, Mayan farmers grew maize, beans, and squash in the same field. They also grew avocados and cacao beans.

To plant crops, farmers walked through the fields carrying seed bags and pointed sticks. They used the sticks to make holes and then dropped the seeds into the holes. In the warm climate, many farmers were able to get two harvests every year.

To clear the land, the Maya used stone tools to cut down vines and saplings. They also used slash-and-burn farming. At the end of the dry season, they cut down the dry plants and then set fire to the fields. This cleared the fields and fertilized them.

READING CHECK ⟳ **CAUSE AND EFFECT**
What effect did the cycle of the seasons have on the Maya's methods of farming?

2

Mayan Way of Life

The Maya were skilled architects and builders, who constructed more than 100 cities and towns. Their cities had ceremonial centers that included temples, plazas, pyramids, palaces, and ball courts.

The Maya worshipped many gods. They believed in gods of the sun, the rain, and other features of nature. By honoring their gods, they believed that harmony and balance could be maintained.

Mayan civilization had no central government. Instead, powerful kings reigned in cities and controlled the surrounding areas. All Maya were required to pay tribute to their king. They could do this by giving gifts or by working on temples, palaces, and homes for the ruling class.

Mayan society was made up of four social classes. The rulers were the upper class. Then came the middle class of stonemasons, merchants, and artisans. Below the middle class were the commoners, who were mostly farmers. Ranking below the commoners were the slaves, criminals, and war captives.

Cities were constantly at war to take captives. Many of the captives became slaves. The king led the war. Women prepared meals for the warriors to carry on their backs. The warriors also carried shields and short spears and had slings for hurling rocks.

The largest ancient Mayan city was **Tikal** (tih•KAHL), which had as many as 100,000 people. Two other Mayan cities, **Palenque** (puh•LENG•kay) and **Copán** (koh•PAHN), were centers of religion and art.

READING CHECK SUMMARIZE
What were the religious beliefs of the Maya?

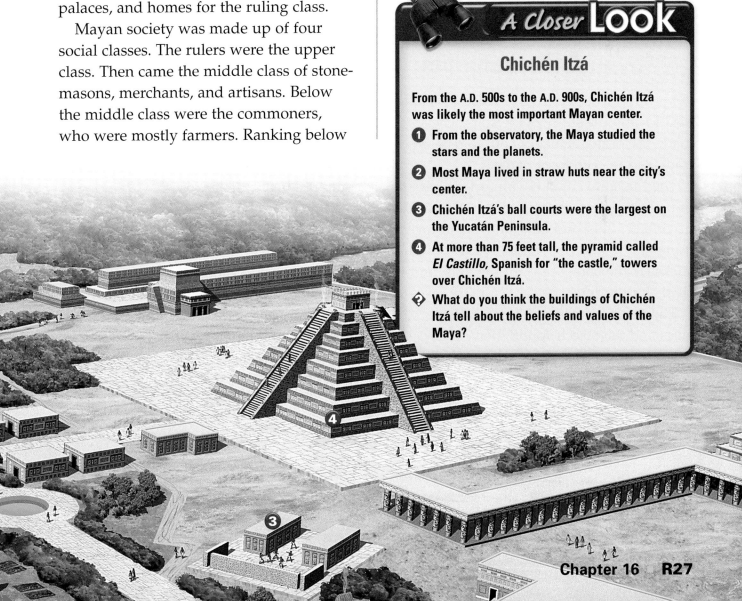

A Closer LOOK

Chichén Itzá

From the A.D. 500s to the A.D. 900s, Chichén Itzá was likely the most important Mayan center.

1. From the observatory, the Maya studied the stars and the planets.
2. Most Maya lived in straw huts near the city's center.
3. Chichén Itzá's ball courts were the largest on the Yucatán Peninsula.
4. At more than 75 feet tall, the pyramid called *El Castillo,* Spanish for "the castle," towers over Chichén Itzá.
   - What do you think the buildings of Chichén Itzá tell about the beliefs and values of the Maya?

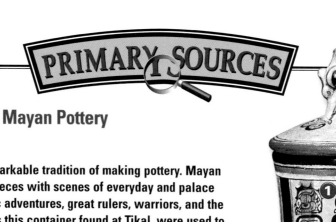

PRIMARY SOURCES

Mayan Pottery

ANALYSIS SKILL Analyze Artifacts

The Maya developed a remarkable tradition of making pottery. Mayan artists decorated pottery pieces with scenes of everyday and palace life, animals, plants, mythic adventures, great rulers, warriors, and the gods. Other pieces, such as this container found at Tikal, were used to record events.

1 This container is painted with the symbols representing five days of the Mayan calendar. The name of each of the five days is written in its own column. The symbols in each column are read from bottom to top.

2 The use of more than three colors and a shiny glaze is typical of pottery made in the Early Classic period of Mayan civilization, which lasted from about A.D. 250 to A.D. 650.

3 Containers dating to the Early Classic period often had 3 feet.

4 The handle of the lid is shaped like a bird.

◆ Why do you think containers such as this one had lids?

Mayan Achievements

Mayan priests led lives devoted to mathematics and the study of the stars. They made use of mathematics both to record trade and to keep track of days.

The Maya invented the important idea of using the zero. They used a system made up of bars, dots, and an oval to stand for numbers. To add or subtract, traders used sticks for the bars, beans for the dots, and shells for the zeros.

The Maya were also interested in the skies and the objects found there. They watched the sky closely, following the movements of stars and planets. The Maya carefully tracked the planet Venus, which they worshipped as a god. They could see Venus in the morning and at night. Also, by watching the sky, Mayan astronomers could predict future eclipses.

From their study of the skies, the Maya made two calendars that worked together. One calendar had a 365-day year, which the Maya used to keep track of planting, harvesting, and flooding. The other one was a 260-day calendar that was used to keep track of religious events.

▶ Some Mayan families still farm the land of Guatemala.

The Maya also had a writing system based on pictures. Writing first appeared on Mayan public monuments in about 50 B.C. as single glyphs, or picture-symbols. As the system formed, some glyphs stood for sounds. Others stood for ideas or people. The symbols could be put together in different ways. The few Mayan **codices** (KOH•duh•seez), or hand-drawn books, that have survived tell about such subjects as religion and the stars.

The Maya also carved their writings on the walls of temples, monuments, and altars. Most of these glyphs are records of events in Mayan history.

The Mayan civilization grew from A.D. 300 to A.D. 900. Afterward, the Maya left some of their cities. During the A.D. 900s, a new Mayan civilization formed on the Yucatán Peninsula, in what is now Mexico. **Chichén Itzá** (chih•CHEN it•SAH) became the Maya's new capital.

READING CHECK **DRAW CONCLUSIONS**
Why did the Maya use different calendars?

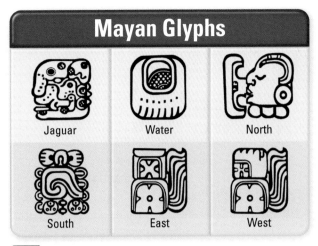

Mayan Glyphs

| Jaguar | Water | North |
| South | East | West |

ANALYSIS SKILL **Analyze Charts** Some Mayan glyphs represent sounds, while others stand for objects, people, and ideas.

❔ Which two glyphs look most alike?

Summary

By about 600 B.C., the Mayan civilization began to take shape in thriving cities. The Maya borrowed and adapted the Olmec calendar and writing system. They also made cultural achievements in both mathematics and astronomy.

REVIEW

1. What cultural achievements were made by the Mayan civilization?

2. Write two or three sentences to explain the Mayan **codices**.

3. What was the architecture of Mayan religious buildings like?

4. What advances in astronomy did the Maya make?

CRITICAL THINKING

5. **ANALYSIS SKILL** What might the ability to complete large building projects say about the performance of the Mayan economy?

6. **ANALYSIS SKILL** **Make It Relevant** In what ways are taxes today similar to the tribute that the Maya paid their kings?

7. **Research** Research the kinds of stone that the Maya used to build their temples and carve their statues. Write a paragraph, describing stone as a Mayan natural resource.

8. **Focus Skill** **CAUSE AND EFFECT** On a separate sheet of paper, copy and complete the graphic organizer below.

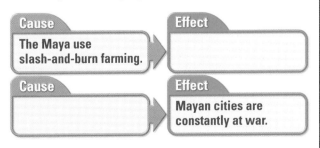

Cause	Effect
The Maya use slash-and-burn farming.	
Cause	Effect
	Mayan cities are constantly at war.

Local Options Review

Summary

Local Options: Time Marches On

During the A.D. 200s, the Roman Empire continued to face problems. Rebellion within and foreign invasions brought constant warfare. War led to economic problems, including inflation and a decline in trade. Diocletian split the empire into two parts to make it easier to rule. This and other reforms strengthened the empire for a time. However, in A.D. 476, Germanic soldiers took over Rome and ended the Western Roman Empire. The empire's language, religion, and laws lived on as many new rulers adopted elements of Roman culture.

In the Americas, people had established farming settlements in Mesoamerica by about 2000 B.C. Five hundred years later, in present-day Mexico, the Olmec built the first city and the first civilization in the Americas. The Olmec were farmers who had a writing system, a number system, and a calendar. Building on Olmec accomplishments, the Maya built a long-lasting civilization beginning in about 600 B.C. The Maya built several cities, each ruled by a king. They made advances in writing, architecture, mathematics, and astronomy.

Main Ideas and Vocabulary

Read the summary above. Then answer the questions that follow.

1. What is inflation?
   A an increase in trade
   B a decrease in the value of money
   C an attack by foreign soldiers
   D a tax collected from defeated peoples

2. What was the short-term effect of Diocletian's reforms?
   A They caused economic problems.
   B They increased the empire's territory.
   C They led to civil war.
   D They strengthened the empire.

3. Which of the following did the ancient region of Mesoamerica include?
   A Mexico
   B Canada
   C North America
   D South America

4. Who ruled the Mayan civilization?
   A priests
   B kings
   C an emperor
   D a dictator

Middle America

Gulf of Mexico

90°W

Tropic of Cancer

PACIFIC OCEAN

110°W

20°N

MEXICO

SIERRA MADRE ORIENTAL

SIERRA MADRE OCCIDENTAL

VALLEY OF MEXICO

SIERRA MADRE DEL SUR

Gulf of Tehuantepec

100°W

N

W E

S

Yucatán Peninsula

20°N

Caribbean Sea

BELIZE

GUATEMALA

HONDURAS

EL SALVADOR

NICARAGUA

0 150 300 Miles
0 150 300 Kilometers
Albers Equal-Area Projection

Olmec homeland
Mayan homeland
Present-day border
Olmec site
Mayan site

Recall Facts

Answer these questions.

5. Which three groups attacked the Roman Empire from beyond its borders?

6. Who was Clovis?

7. How did the people of Poverty Point build the mounds that still exist there?

8. Where did the Chavín culture develop?

9. What innovations did the Maya borrow from the Olmec?

10. Into what two seasons did the Maya divide the year?

Write the letter of the best choice.

11. Which city did Constantine make the capital of the Roman Empire?
    A Alexandria
    B Byzantium
    C Córdoba
    D Carthage

12. In Mayan society, who studied mathematics and the stars?
    A kings
    B traders
    C slaves
    D priests

Think Critically

13. In what ways did leaders of the Roman Empire contribute to its economic problems?

14. How did the Christian Church contribute to the spread of Roman culture after the end of the Western Roman Empire?

15. **ANALYSIS SKILL** What caused the Christian Church to split in A.D. 1054?

Apply Skills

Map Skills Review

ANALYSIS SKILL Use the map on this page to answer these questions.

16. What major mountain ranges are located in Mexico?

17. Which Middle American culture had a larger homeland?

18. Which present-day countries have lands that were once part of the Mayan homeland?

19. According to the map, which present-day countries have both Olmec and Maya sites?

20. At what latitude can you find the Yucatán Peninsula?

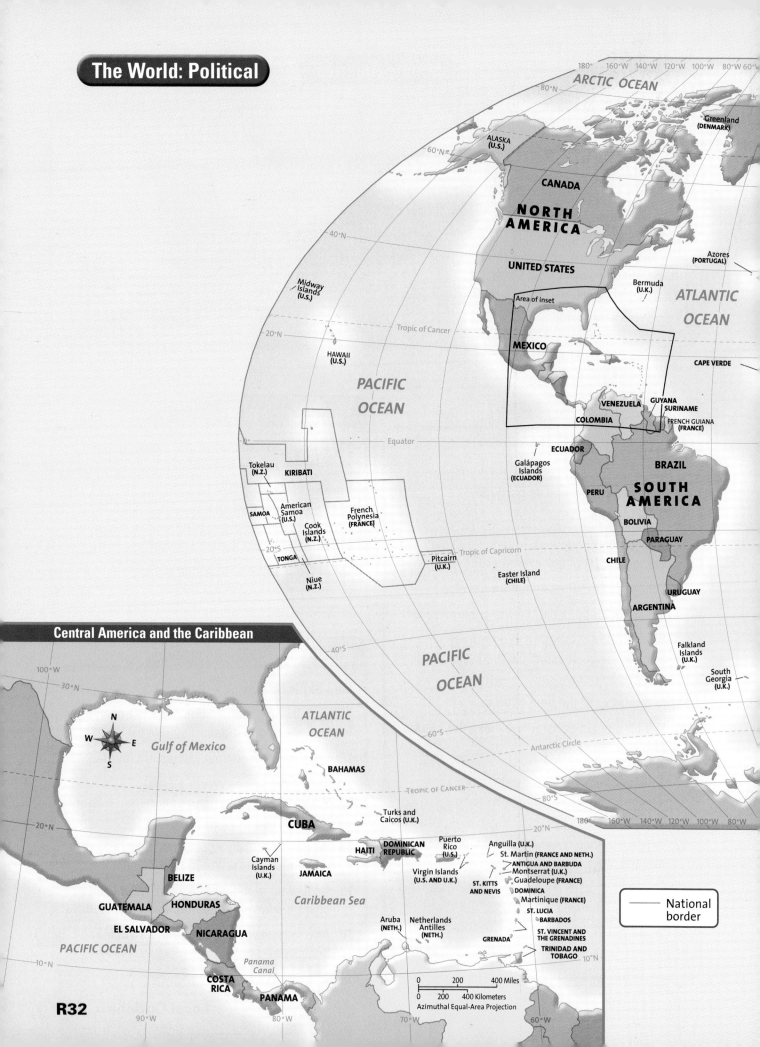

The World: Political

ARCTIC OCEAN

Greenland (DENMARK)

ALASKA (U.S.)

CANADA

NORTH AMERICA

UNITED STATES

Azores (PORTUGAL)

Midway Islands (U.S.)

Bermuda (U.K.)

ATLANTIC OCEAN

Tropic of Cancer

HAWAII (U.S.)

MEXICO

CAPE VERDE

Area of inset

PACIFIC OCEAN

VENEZUELA   GUYANA
                        SURINAME
COLOMBIA   FRENCH GUIANA (FRANCE)

Equator

ECUADOR

BRAZIL

Galápagos Islands (ECUADOR)

Tokelau (N.Z.)   KIRIBATI

SOUTH AMERICA

PERU

SAMOA   American Samoa (U.S.)

French Polynesia (FRANCE)

Cook Islands (N.Z.)

BOLIVIA

PARAGUAY

20°S   TONGA

Pitcairn (U.K.)

Tropic of Capricorn

CHILE

URUGUAY

Niue (N.Z.)

Easter Island (CHILE)

ARGENTINA

40°S   PACIFIC OCEAN

Falkland Islands (U.K.)

South Georgia (U.K.)

60°S   Antarctic Circle

80°S

180°   160°W   140°W   120°W   100°W   80°W

Central America and the Caribbean

100°W

30°N

W N E S

Gulf of Mexico

ATLANTIC OCEAN

BAHAMAS

Tropic of Cancer

20°N

CUBA

Turks and Caicos (U.K.)

Cayman Islands (U.K.)

HAITI   DOMINICAN REPUBLIC

Puerto Rico (U.S.)

Anguilla (U.K.)
St. Martin (FRANCE AND NETH.)
ANTIGUA AND BARBUDA
Montserrat (U.K.)

BELIZE

JAMAICA

Virgin Islands (U.S. AND U.K.)

ST. KITTS AND NEVIS

Guadeloupe (FRANCE)

DOMINICA

GUATEMALA   HONDURAS

Caribbean Sea

Martinique (FRANCE)

ST. LUCIA

EL SALVADOR   NICARAGUA

Aruba (NETH.)

Netherlands Antilles (NETH.)

BARBADOS

ST. VINCENT AND THE GRENADINES

PACIFIC OCEAN

GRENADA

TRINIDAD AND TOBAGO

10°N

COSTA RICA

Panama Canal

PANAMA

90°W   80°W   70°W   60°W

0   200   400 Miles
0   200   400 Kilometers
Azimuthal Equal-Area Projection

—— National border

R32

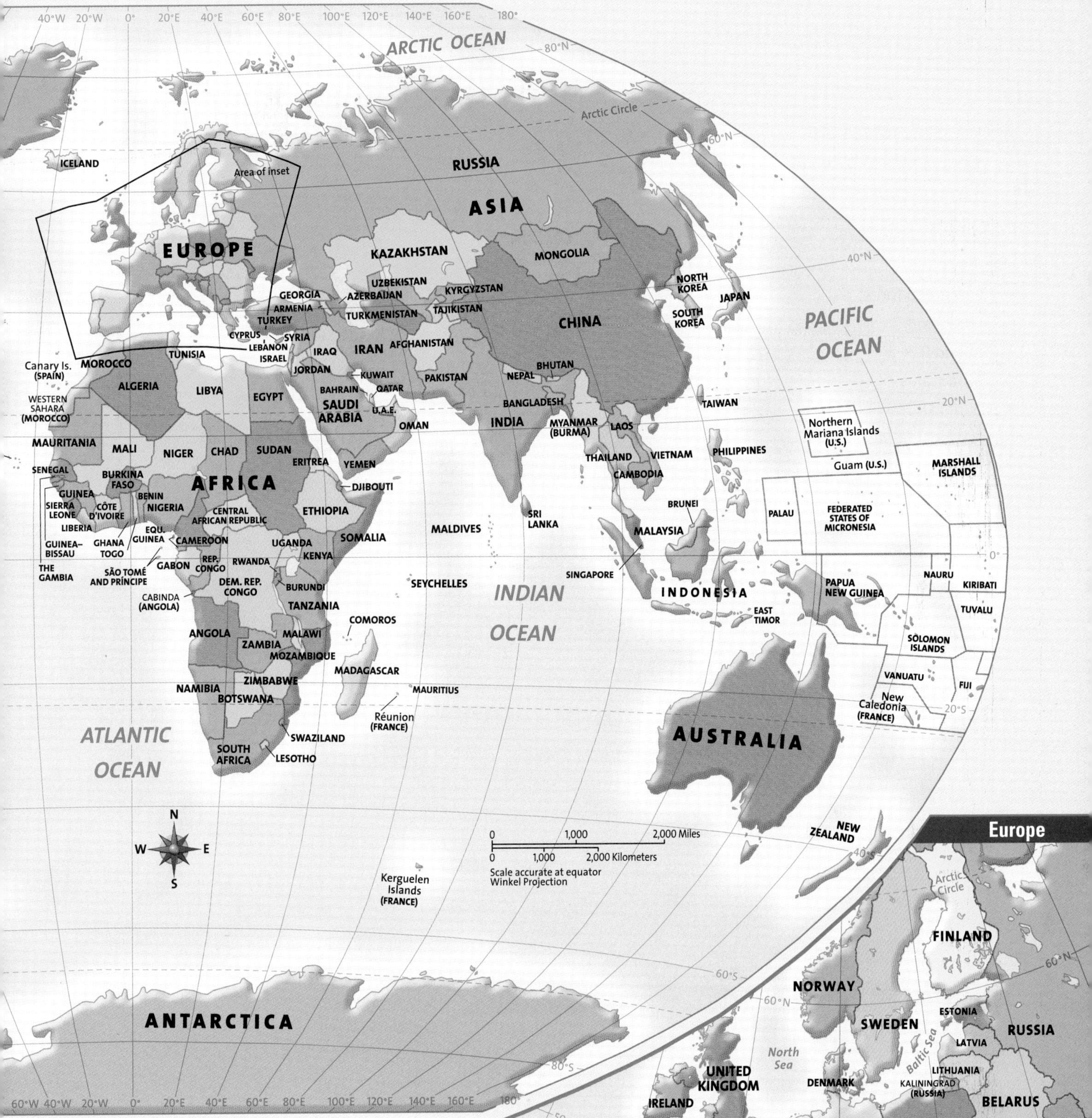
ARCTIC OCEAN
Arctic Circle
PACIFIC OCEAN
INDIAN OCEAN
ATLANTIC OCEAN
ICELAND
Area of inset
EUROPE
RUSSIA
ASIA
KAZAKHSTAN
MONGOLIA
UZBEKISTAN
KYRGYZSTAN
GEORGIA
ARMENIA
AZERBAIJAN
TURKMENISTAN
TAJIKISTAN
TURKEY
CYPRUS
SYRIA
LEBANON
ISRAEL
IRAQ
IRAN
AFGHANISTAN
JORDAN
KUWAIT
BAHRAIN
QATAR
SAUDI ARABIA
U.A.E.
OMAN
YEMEN
PAKISTAN
NEPAL
BHUTAN
INDIA
BANGLADESH
CHINA
NORTH KOREA
SOUTH KOREA
JAPAN
TAIWAN
MYANMAR (BURMA)
LAOS
THAILAND
VIETNAM
CAMBODIA
PHILIPPINES
SRI LANKA
MALDIVES
MALAYSIA
BRUNEI
SINGAPORE
INDONESIA
EAST TIMOR
PAPUA NEW GUINEA
Northern Mariana Islands (U.S.)
Guam (U.S.)
MARSHALL ISLANDS
PALAU
FEDERATED STATES OF MICRONESIA
NAURU
KIRIBATI
TUVALU
SOLOMON ISLANDS
VANUATU
FIJI
New Caledonia (FRANCE)
AUSTRALIA
NEW ZEALAND
Canary Is. (SPAIN)
MOROCCO
TUNISIA
ALGERIA
LIBYA
EGYPT
WESTERN SAHARA (MOROCCO)
MAURITANIA
MALI
NIGER
CHAD
SUDAN
ERITREA
DJIBOUTI
SENEGAL
BURKINA FASO
AFRICA
GUINEA
BENIN
SIERRA LEONE
CÔTE D'IVOIRE
NIGERIA
CENTRAL AFRICAN REPUBLIC
ETHIOPIA
LIBERIA
EQU. GUINEA
SOMALIA
GUINEA-BISSAU
GHANA
TOGO
CAMEROON
UGANDA
KENYA
THE GAMBIA
SÃO TOMÉ AND PRÍNCIPE
GABON
REP. CONGO
RWANDA
DEM. REP. CONGO
BURUNDI
SEYCHELLES
CABINDA (ANGOLA)
TANZANIA
COMOROS
ANGOLA
MALAWI
ZAMBIA
MOZAMBIQUE
MADAGASCAR
ZIMBABWE
MAURITIUS
NAMIBIA
BOTSWANA
Réunion (FRANCE)
SWAZILAND
SOUTH AFRICA
LESOTHO
N
S
E
W
0 1,000 2,000 Miles
0 1,000 2,000 Kilometers
Scale accurate at equator
Winkel Projection
Kerguelen Islands (FRANCE)
ANTARCTICA
80°N
60°N
40°N
20°N
0°
20°S
40°S
60°S
80°S
60°W 40°W 20°W 0° 20°E 40°E 60°E 80°E 100°E 120°E 140°E 160°E 180°

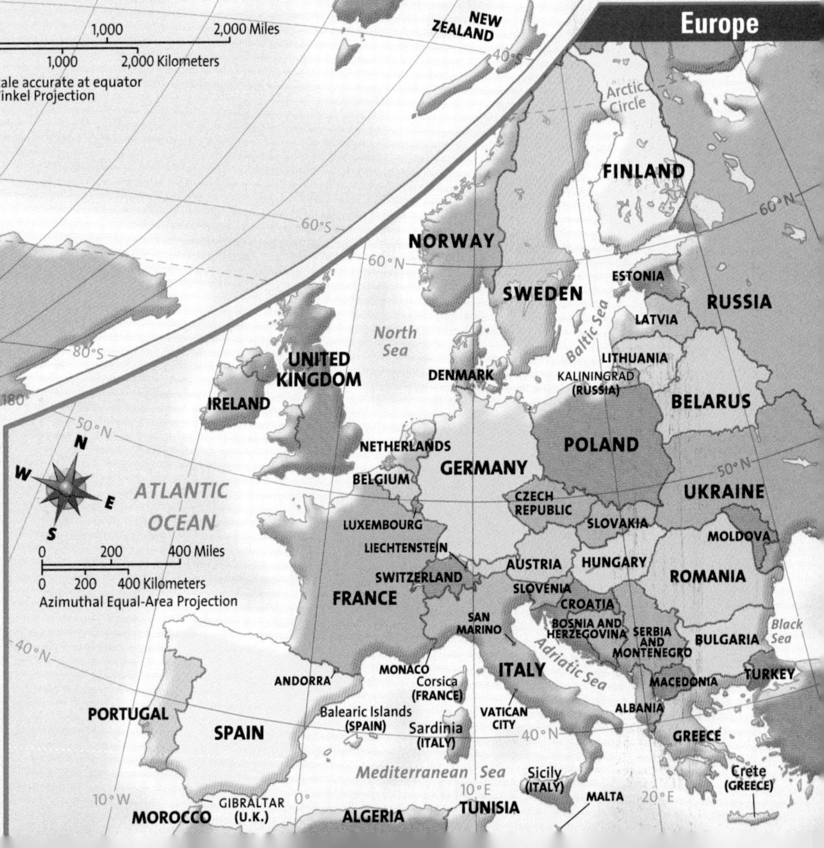
Europe
Arctic Circle
FINLAND
NORWAY
ESTONIA
SWEDEN
RUSSIA
LATVIA
North Sea
Baltic Sea
LITHUANIA
UNITED KINGDOM
DENMARK
KALININGRAD (RUSSIA)
BELARUS
IRELAND
NETHERLANDS
POLAND
GERMANY
BELGIUM
UKRAINE
CZECH REPUBLIC
LUXEMBOURG
SLOVAKIA
MOLDOVA
LIECHTENSTEIN
AUSTRIA
HUNGARY
ROMANIA
SWITZERLAND
SLOVENIA
FRANCE
CROATIA
SAN MARINO
BOSNIA AND HERZEGOVINA
SERBIA AND MONTENEGRO
BULGARIA
Black Sea
Adriatic Sea
MONACO
ITALY
ANDORRA
Corsica (FRANCE)
MACEDONIA
TURKEY
ALBANIA
PORTUGAL
Balearic Islands (SPAIN)
VATICAN CITY
SPAIN
Sardinia (ITALY)
GREECE
Mediterranean Sea
Sicily (ITALY)
Crete (GREECE)
MALTA
MOROCCO
GIBRALTAR (U.K.)
ALGERIA
TUNISIA
ATLANTIC OCEAN
N
E
S
W
0 200 400 Miles
0 200 400 Kilometers
Azimuthal Equal-Area Projection
60°N
50°N
40°N
10°W
0°
10°E
20°E

Abbreviations

DEM. REP. CONGO	DEMOCRATIC REPUBLIC OF THE CONGO
EQU. GUINEA	EQUATORIAL GUINEA
NETH.	NETHERLANDS
N.Z.	NEW ZEALAND
REP. CONGO	REPUBLIC OF THE CONGO
U.A.E.	UNITED ARAB EMIRATES
U.K.	UNITED KINGDOM
U.S.	UNITED STATES

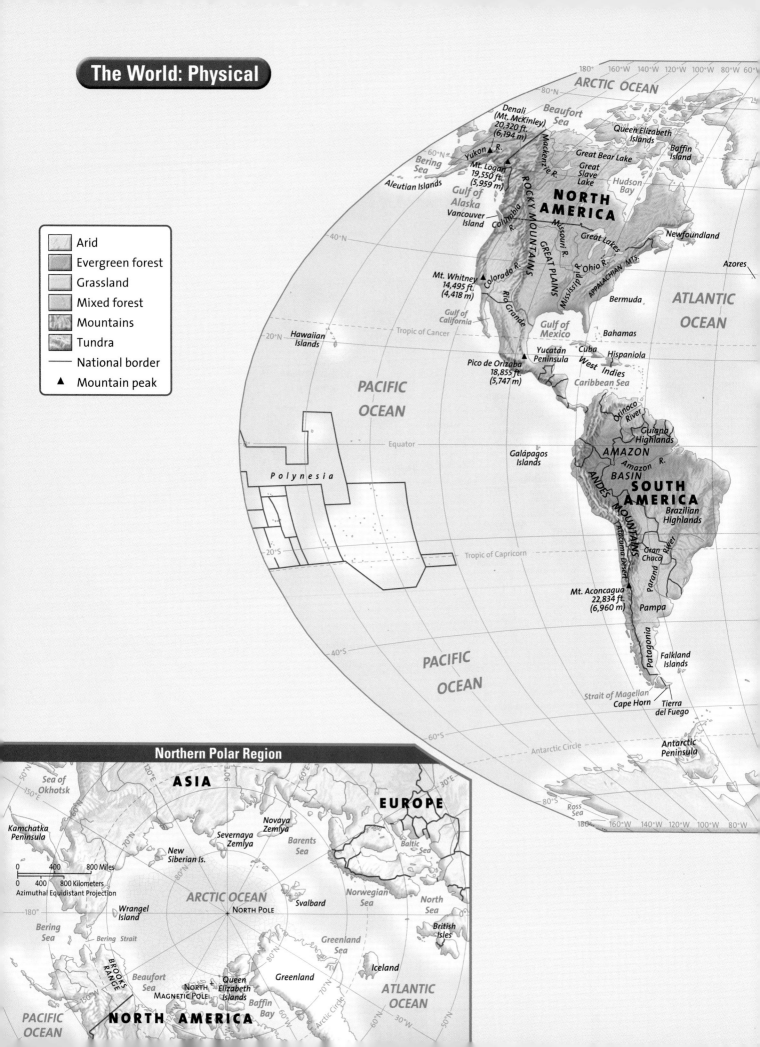

The World: Physical

Legend:
- Arid
- Evergreen forest
- Grassland
- Mixed forest
- Mountains
- Tundra
- National border
- ▲ Mountain peak

North America / South America map labels:

ARCTIC OCEAN

180° 160°W 140°W 120°W 100°W 80°W 60°

80°N

Beaufort Sea

Denali (Mt. McKinley) 20,320 ft. (6,194 m)

Queen Elizabeth Islands

Baffin Island

60°N

Bering Sea

Yukon R.

Mt. Logan 19,550 ft. (5,959 m)

Mackenzie R.

Great Bear Lake

Great Slave Lake

Hudson Bay

NORTH AMERICA

Aleutian Islands

Gulf of Alaska

ROCKY MOUNTAINS

Vancouver Island

Columbia R.

Missouri R.

Great Lakes

Newfoundland

40°N

GREAT PLAINS

Azores

Mt. Whitney 14,495 ft. (4,418 m)

Colorado R.

Mississippi R. Ohio R.

APPALACHIAN MTS.

Rio Grande

Bermuda

ATLANTIC OCEAN

20°N

Hawaiian Islands

Tropic of Cancer

Gulf of California

Gulf of Mexico

Bahamas

Yucatán Peninsula

Cuba

Hispaniola

Pico de Orizaba 18,855 ft. (5,747 m)

West Indies

Caribbean Sea

PACIFIC OCEAN

Equator

Galápagos Islands

Orinoco River

Guiana Highlands

AMAZON BASIN

Amazon R.

Polynesia

SOUTH AMERICA

ANDES MOUNTAINS

Brazilian Highlands

Atacama Desert

Gran Chaco

20°S

Tropic of Capricorn

Paraná River

Mt. Aconcagua 22,834 ft. (6,960 m)

Pampa

40°S

PACIFIC OCEAN

Patagonia

Falkland Islands

Strait of Magellan

Cape Horn

Tierra del Fuego

60°S

Antarctic Circle

Antarctic Peninsula

80°S

Ross Sea

180° 160°W 140°W 120°W 100°W 80°W

Northern Polar Region

Sea of Okhotsk

ASIA

EUROPE

120°E

150°E

90°E

60°E

30°E

Kamchatka Peninsula

Novaya Zemlya

Severnaya Zemlya

Barents Sea

Baltic Sea

New Siberian Is.

70°N

80°N

ARCTIC OCEAN

NORTH POLE

Svalbard

Norwegian Sea

North Sea

0   400   800 Miles
0   400   800 Kilometers
Azimuthal Equidistant Projection

Wrangel Island

180°

Bering Sea

Bering Strait

Beaufort Sea

NORTH MAGNETIC POLE

Queen Elizabeth Islands

Greenland

British Isles

Iceland

Greenland Sea

30°E

BROOKS RANGE

Baffin Bay

Arctic Circle

ATLANTIC OCEAN

PACIFIC OCEAN

NORTH AMERICA

30°W

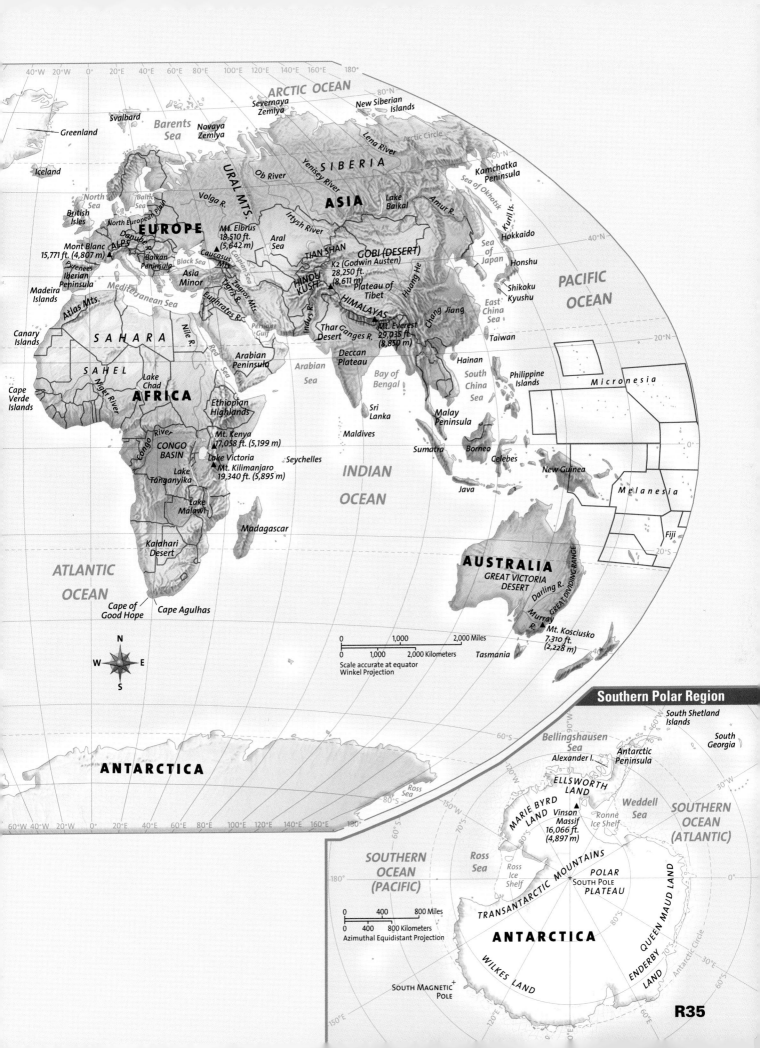

ARCTIC OCEAN

80°N

Svalbard
Greenland
Severnaya Zemlya
New Siberian Islands
Barents Sea
Novaya Zemlya
60°N
Iceland
British Isles
North Sea
Baltic Sea
North European Plain
URAL MTS.
Ob River
Yenisey River
SIBERIA
Lena River
Arctic Circle
Kamchatka Peninsula
Sea of Okhotsk
ASIA
40°N
EUROPE
Volga R.
Irtysh River
Aral Sea
Lake Baikal
Amur R.
Kuril Is.
Mont Blanc 15,771 ft. (4,807 m)
ALPS
Danube R.
Balkan Peninsula
Black Sea
Mt. Elbrus 18,510 ft. (5,642 m)
Caucasus Mts.
Caspian Sea
TIAN SHAN
GOBI (DESERT)
K2 (Godwin Austen) 28,250 ft. (8,611 m)
Huang He
Hokkaido
Sea of Japan
Honshu
Shikoku
Kyushu
PACIFIC OCEAN
Pyrenees
Iberian Peninsula
Asia Minor
Zagros Mts.
HINDU KUSH
Plateau of Tibet
Chang Jiang
East China Sea
Taiwan
20°N
Madeira Islands
Mediterranean Sea
Tigris R.
Euphrates R.
Indus R.
HIMALAYAS
Mt. Everest 29,035 ft. (8,850 m)
ATLAS MTS.
Nile R.
Red Sea
Persian Gulf
Thar Desert
Ganges R.
Deccan Plateau
Hainan
South China Sea
Philippine Islands
Micronesia
Canary Islands
SAHARA
Arabian Peninsula
Arabian Sea
Bay of Bengal
Cape Verde Islands
SAHEL
Lake Chad
Niger River
AFRICA
Ethiopian Highlands
Sri Lanka
Maldives
Malay Peninsula
Congo River
CONGO BASIN
Mt. Kenya 17,058 ft. (5,199 m)
Lake Victoria
Mt. Kilimanjaro 19,340 ft. (5,895 m)
Seychelles
INDIAN OCEAN
Sumatra
Borneo
Celebes
New Guinea
Fiji
Melanesia
Lake Tanganyika
Lake Malawi
Madagascar
Java
ATLANTIC OCEAN
Kalahari Desert
AUSTRALIA
GREAT VICTORIA DESERT
Darling R.
GREAT DIVIDING RANGE
Cape of Good Hope
Cape Agulhas
N
W E
S

0   1,000   2,000 Miles
0   1,000   2,000 Kilometers
Scale accurate at equator
Winkel Projection

Murray R.
Mt. Kosciusko 7,310 ft. (2,228 m)
Tasmania
20°S

40°W 20°W 0° 20°E 40°E 60°E 80°E 100°E 120°E 140°E 160°E 180°

60°S
80°S

ANTARCTICA

60°W 40°W 20°W 0° 20°E 40°E 60°E 80°E 100°E 120°E 140°E 160°E 180°

Southern Polar Region

South Shetland Islands
Bellingshausen Sea
Alexander I.
Antarctic Peninsula
South Georgia
60°S
90°W
30°W
ELLSWORTH LAND
Weddell Sea
SOUTHERN OCEAN (ATLANTIC)
MARIE BYRD LAND
Vinson Massif 16,066 ft. (4,897 m)
Ronne Ice Shelf
SOUTHERN OCEAN (PACIFIC)
Ross Sea
Ross Ice Shelf
TRANSANTARCTIC MOUNTAINS
POLAR PLATEAU
SOUTH POLE
QUEEN MAUD LAND
0°
80°S
180°
ANTARCTICA
WILKES LAND
ENDERBY LAND
SOUTH MAGNETIC POLE
Antarctic Circle
60°S
30°E
60°E
90°E
120°E
150°E

0   400   800 Miles
0   400   800 Kilometers
Azimuthal Equidistant Projection

R35

Africa: Political

EUROPE

ASIA

ATLANTIC OCEAN

Mediterranean Sea

Madeira Islands (PORTUGAL)

Ceuta (SPAIN)
Algiers • Tunis
Tangier • Constantine
Rabat • Oran • Sfax
Melilla (SPAIN) • TUNISIA
Casablanca • Fès
Marrakech • Tripoli
MOROCCO • Benghazi

Canary Islands (SPAIN)

WESTERN SAHARA (Occupied by Morocco) • El Aaiún

Alexandria • Port Said
Tanta • Suez Canal
Giza • Suez
Cairo

ALGERIA

LIBYA

EGYPT

Aswan

Tropic of Cancer

MAURITANIA

Nouakchott

Timbuktu
MALI • Gao

NIGER

CHAD

Port Sudan

Omdurman
SUDAN • Khartoum

ERITREA
Asmara

Dakar
SENEGAL
GAMBIA
Banjul
Bissau
GUINEA-BISSAU
Conakry
GUINEA
SIERRA LEONE
Freetown
Monrovia
LIBERIA

Bamako
BURKINA FASO
Ouagadougou
Niamey
BENIN
TOGO
GHANA
CÔTE D'IVOIRE
Yamoussoukro
Lomé
Accra
Abidjan
Porto-Novo

Kano
NIGERIA
Abuja
Ogbomosho
Ibadan
Lagos

N'Djamena

Lake Chad

DJIBOUTI
Djibouti

Addis Ababa
ETHIOPIA
Dire Dawa

Gulf of Aden

Red Sea

CAMEROON
Douala
Malabo
EQUATORIAL GUINEA
SÃO TOMÉ AND PRÍNCIPE
São Tomé
Yaoundé

CENTRAL AFRICAN REPUBLIC
Bangui

Kisangani
UGANDA
Kampala
KENYA
Kisumu
Nairobi
Mogadishu
SOMALIA
Kismaayo

INDIAN OCEAN

Annobón (EQUATORIAL GUINEA)

Libreville
GABON
Brazzaville
REPUBLIC OF THE CONGO
Kinshasa
CABINDA (ANGOLA)

DEMOCRATIC REPUBLIC OF THE CONGO

Kigali
RWANDA
Bujumbura
BURUNDI

Lake Victoria
Mwanza

Kananga
Mbuji-Mayi

Dodoma
TANZANIA
Dar es Salaam

Lake Tanganyika

Luanda

ATLANTIC OCEAN

Acsension (UNITED KINGDOM)

Lobito
ANGOLA
Huambo

Kolwezi
Lubumbashi
Kitwe
ZAMBIA
Lusaka

Lake Malawi
MALAWI
Lilongwe
Blantyre

COMOROS
Moroni

St. Helena (UNITED KINGDOM)

Harare
ZIMBABWE
Bulawayo

MOZAMBIQUE
Beira

Mozambique Channel
Antananarivo
MADAGASCAR

Tropic of Capricorn

NAMIBIA
Windhoek

BOTSWANA
Gaborone

Pretoria
Johannesburg
Kimberley
Bloemfontein
Maseru
LESOTHO

Maputo
Mbabane
Lobamba
SWAZILAND
Durban

SOUTH AFRICA

Cape Town
Port Elizabeth

N
W E
S

— National border
⊛ National capital
• Major city

0 500 1,000 Miles
0 500 1,000 Kilometers
Azimuthal Equal-Area Projection

R36

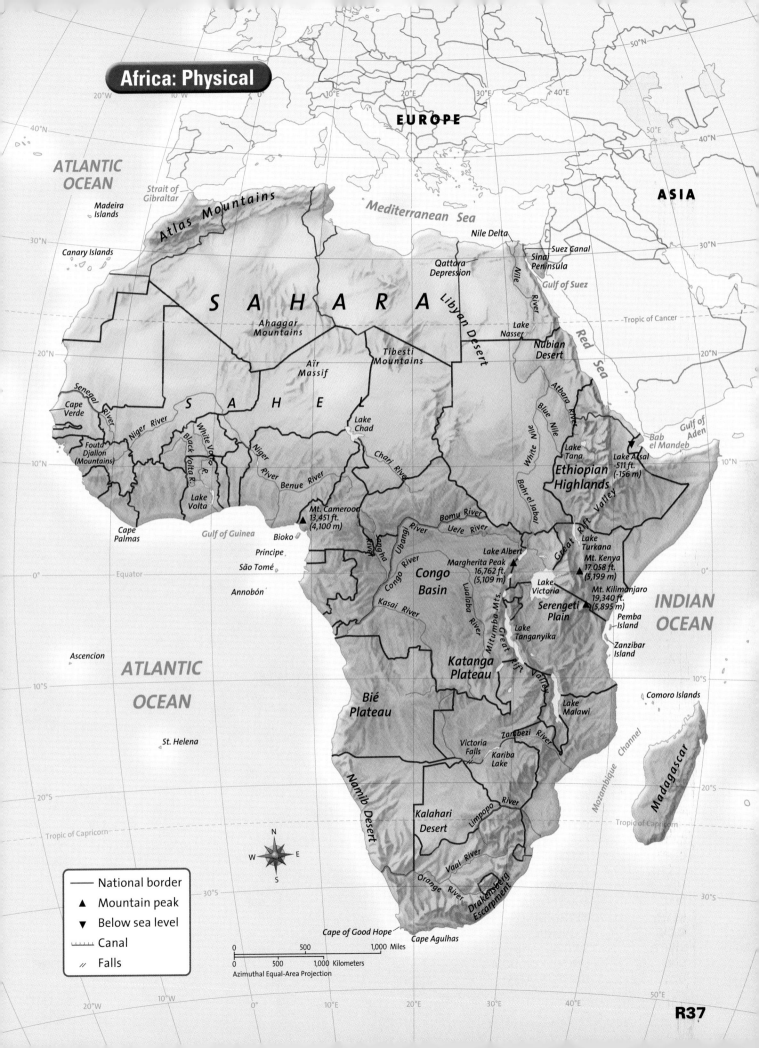

Africa: Physical

EUROPE

ASIA

ATLANTIC OCEAN

Strait of Gibraltar

Madeira Islands

Canary Islands

Mediterranean Sea

Atlas Mountains

S A H A R A

Ahaggar Mountains

Tibesti Mountains

Aïr Massif

Nile Delta

Suez Canal

Sinai Peninsula

Gulf of Suez

Qattara Depression

Libyan Desert

Lake Nasser

Nubian Desert

Nile River

Tropic of Cancer

Red Sea

Gulf of Aden

Bab el Mandeb

S A H E L

Lake Chad

Senegal River

Cape Verde

Niger River

Fouta Djallon (Mountains)

White Volta R.

Black Volta R.

Lake Volta

Niger River

Benue River

Chari River

Atbara River

Blue Nile

White Nile

Bahr el Jabal

Lake Tana

Ethiopian Highlands

Lake Assal -511 ft. (-156 m)

Cape Palmas

Gulf of Guinea

Bioko

Mt. Cameroon 13,451 ft. (4,100 m)

Sangha River

Bomu River

Uele River

Lake Albert

Margherita Peak 16,762 ft. (5,109 m)

Lake Turkana

Mt. Kenya 17,058 ft. (5,199 m)

Great Rift Valley

Príncipe

São Tomé

Congo River

Ubangi River

Congo Basin

Lake Victoria

Mt. Kilimanjaro 19,340 ft. (5,895 m)

Equator

Annobón

Kasai River

Lualaba River

Mitumba Mts.

Lake Tanganyika

Serengeti Plain

Pemba Island

Zanzibar Island

INDIAN OCEAN

Ascencion

ATLANTIC OCEAN

Katanga Plateau

Great Rift Valley

Lake Malawi

Comoro Islands

Bié Plateau

St. Helena

Victoria Falls

Zambezi River

Kariba Lake

Mozambique Channel

Madagascar

Namib Desert

Kalahari Desert

Limpopo River

Vaal River

Orange River

Drakensberg Escarpment

Tropic of Capricorn

Cape of Good Hope

Cape Agulhas

N
W   E
S

Legend

— National border
▲ Mountain peak
▼ Below sea level
⊣⊢ Canal
// Falls

0   500   1,000 Miles
0   500   1,000 Kilometers
Azimuthal Equal-Area Projection

R37

Europe and Asia: Political

NORTH AMERICA

ICELAND
Reykjavík

ATLANTIC OCEAN

Glasgow

Dublin
IRELAND
Birmingham
London

UNITED KINGDOM

The Hague
Amsterdam
NETH.
Brussels
BELG.
Luxembourg
LUX.
Paris

FRANCE
Lyon
Turin
Marseille

ANDORRA
Porto
Madrid
Barcelona
Valencia
PORTUGAL
Lisbon
Gibraltar (U.K.)
Balearic Is.

SPAIN

Bergen
Oslo
Stockholm
Göteborg
NORWAY
SWEDEN
DENMARK
Copenhagen

North Sea

GERMANY
Hamburg
Berlin
Prague
CZECH REP.
Munich
Vienna
AUST.
Bern
SWITZ.
LIECHT.
Ljubljana
SLOV.
Milan
SAN MARINO
MONACO
Corsica
Rome
Naples
Sardinia
ITALY
Zagreb
CRO.
BOS. & HERZ.
Sarajevo
SERBIA AND MONTENEGRO
Tiranë
ALBANIA
MAC.
Skopje
Sofia

Sicily

MALTA
Valletta

Crete

Mediterranean Sea

Warsaw
Kraków
POLAND
Budapest
HUNGARY
SLOVAKIA
Bratislava
ROMANIA
Belgrade
Bucharest
BULGARIA

Helsinki
FINLAND
Tallinn
ESTONIA
Riga
LATVIA
LITHUANIA
Vilnius
Minsk
BELARUS
RUSSIA

Baltic Sea

St. Petersburg
Arctic Circle
Norwegian Sea

Murmansk

Arkhangel'sk

RUSSIA

Lake Onega
Lake Ladoga

Nizhniy Novgorod
Moscow
Kazan

Perm
Yekaterinburg
Chelyabinsk
Ufa
Omsk

Samara

Volgograd
Saratov
Rostov
Donetsk
Dnipropetrovsk
Kharkiv
Kiev
UKRAINE
MOLDOVA
Chisinau
Odessa

Black Sea

Istanbul
GEORGIA
Tbilisi
Ankara
ARMENIA
Izmir
Yerevan
TURKEY
AZERBAIJAN
Baku

Athens
GREECE

Nicosia
CYPRUS
Beirut
SYRIA
Damascus
LEBANON
WEST BANK
ISRAEL
Jerusalem
Amman
GAZA STRIP
JORDAN
EGYPT

Euphrates R.
Tigris R.
Baghdad
IRAQ
Al Basrah
KUWAIT
Kuwait

Manama
BAHRAIN
QATAR
Doha
UNITED ARAB EMIRATES

Medina
Riyadh
Abu Dhabi
Muscat
OMAN

Jiddah
Mecca

Red Sea

SAUDI ARABIA

YEMEN
Sanaa

Gulf of Aden

Tehran
IRAN
Esfahan

Mashhad

Astana
Qaraghandy

KAZAKHSTAN

Aral Sea

Lake Balkhash

Bishkek
Almaty
UZBEKISTAN
KYRGYZSTAN
Tashkent
TURKMENISTAN
Ashgabat
Dushanbe
TAJIKISTAN

Herat
Kabul
AFGHANISTAN
Islamabad
Lahore

PAKISTAN

Delhi
New Delhi
Kanpur

Karachi
Ahmadabad
INDIA

Arabian Sea

Mumbai (Bombay)
Hyderabad

Bangalore
Chennai (Madras)

Colombo
SRI LANKA

MALDIVES
Male

INDIAN OCEAN

Caspian Sea

Bay of Biscay

Don River
Volga River
Kama River
Irtysh River
Ob River

Novaya Zemlya
Kara Sea
Barents Sea

Indus River
Ganges R.

Socotra (YEMEN)

Tropic of Cancer

AFRICA

Diego Garcia (U.K.)

N
W E
S

Legend

— National border
- - - Disputed border
⊛ National capital
• Major city

Abbreviations

AUST.	AUSTRIA
BELG.	BELGIUM
BOS. & HERZ.	BOSNIA AND HERZEGOVINA
CRO.	CROATIA
CZECH REP.	CZECH REPUBLIC
LIECHT.	LIECHTENSTEIN
LUX.	LUXEMBOURG
MAC.	MACEDONIA
NETH.	NETHERLANDS
SLOV.	SLOVENIA
SWITZ.	SWITZERLAND
U.K.	UNITED KINGDOM
U.S.	UNITED STATES

0   500   1,000 Miles
0   500   1,000 Kilometers
Robinson Projection

ARCTIC OCEAN

Severnaya Zemlya

Laptev Sea

New Siberian Islands

East Siberian Sea

Wrangel Island

ALASKA (U.S.)

Arctic Circle

Bering Strait

RUSSIA

Lena River

Magadan

Bering Sea

•Novosibirsk

•Krasnoyarsk

Angara River

Yenisey River

Irkutsk•

Lake Baikal

Sea of Okhotsk

Petropavlovsk-Kamchatskiy

MONGOLIA

⊛Ulaanbaatar

Khabarovsk

Sakhalin

•Ürümqi

Harbin•

Changchun•

Vladivostok•

Sapporo•

Kuril Islands

Shenyang•

Beijing⊛

Tianjin⊛

Taiyuan•

P'yongyang⊛

NORTH KOREA

Sea of Japan

JAPAN

Tokyo⊛

Nagoya•

Yokohama

Seoul⊛

SOUTH KOREA

Osaka•

Xi'an•

Huang He

Pusan•

Yellow Sea

CHINA

Chengdu•

Wuhan•

Nanjing•

Shanghai•

East China Sea

PACIFIC OCEAN

Lhasa•

Kathmandu⊛

Thimphu⊛

Chongqing•

Chang Jiang

Tropic of Cancer

NEPAL

BHUTAN

BANGLADESH

Dhaka•

Kunming•

Ryukyu Islands

Taipei⊛

Okinawa

Chittagong•

Kolkata (Calcutta)•

MYANMAR (BURMA)

Mekong R.

Guangzhou•

Macao•

Hong Kong•

TAIWAN

Hanoi•

LAOS

Bay of Bengal

Chiang Mai•

Vientiane⊛

Hainan

South China Sea

Philippine Sea

Yangon (Rangoon)⊛

Hue•

THAILAND

VIETNAM

Quezon City⊛

Bangkok•

CAMBODIA

Manila•

Andaman Islands (INDIA)

Phnom Penh⊛

Ho Chi Minh City•

PHILIPPINES

Nicobar Islands (INDIA)

Sulu Sea

Davao•

Bandar Seri Begawan⊛

BRUNEI

Kuala Lumpur•

Celebes Sea

Medan•

MALAYSIA

Halmahera

SINGAPORE

Singapore•

Borneo

0° Equator

Sumatra

Celebes

Java Sea

INDONESIA

Banda Sea

New Guinea

Jakarta⊛

Bandung•

Java

Surabaya•

EAST TIMOR

Timor

Arafura Sea

Timor Sea

AUSTRALIA

Europe and Asia: Physical

Kara Sea

Novaya Zemlya

Gulf of Ob

Norwegian Sea

Kjølen Mountains

Lapland

Kola Peninsula

Mt. Narodnaya
6,217 ft.
(1,895 m)

West Siberian Plain

Iceland

Faeroe Islands

Galdhøpiggen
8,100 ft.
(2,469 m)

Scandinavian Peninsula

White Sea

URAL MOUNTAINS

Ob River

Arctic Circle

ATLANTIC OCEAN

Highlands

British Isles

Ireland

Great Britain

Celtic Sea

English Channel

North Sea

Jutland

Baltic Sea

Gulf of Bothnia

Gulf of Finland

Lake Onega

Lake Ladoga

NORTHERN EUROPEAN PLAIN

Central Russian Upland

Lake Onega

Volga River

Kama River

Irtysh River

Rhone R.

Carpathian Mountains

Danube River

Oka-Don Lowland

Volga Upland

Ural River

Kazakh Upland

The Steppes

Lake Balkhash

Mt. Blanc
15,771 ft.
(4,807 m)

ALPS

Massif Central (Plateau)

Pyrenees

Dinaric Alps

Balkan Mts.

Donets Basin

Don River

Sea of Azov

Caspian Lowland

Aral Sea

Turan Lowland

Syr Darya

TIAN SHAN

Bay of Biscay

Apennines

Adriatic Sea

Balkan Peninsula

Crimea

Black Sea

Mt. Elbrus
18,510 ft.
(5,642 m)

Caucasus Mts.

Caspian Sea
-92 ft.
(-28 m)

Kyzyl Kum (Desert)

Amu Darya

Takla Makan (Desert)

Pamirs

Kunlun

Iberian Peninsula

Corsica

Balearic Islands

Sardinia

Tyrrhenian Sea

Sicily

Ionian Sea

Pindus Mts.

Aegean Sea

Dardanelles

Bosporus

Pontic Mountains

Plateau of Anatolia

Mt. Ararat
16,854 ft.
(5,137 m)

Tigris River

Mt. Elburz Mts.

Mt. Damavand
18,606 ft.
(5,671 m)

Kara Kum (Desert)

Dasht-e Kavir (Desert)

HINDU KUSH

K2
(Godwin Austen)
28,250 ft.
(8,611 m)

HIMALAYAS

Strait of Gibraltar

Crete

Cyprus

Taurus Mts.

Mediterranean Sea

Mesopotamia

Euphrates R.

Syrian Desert

Zagros Mountains

Plateau of Iran

Indus River

Thar Desert

Ganges River

Dead Sea
-1,339 ft.
(-408 m)

Sinai Peninsula

Strait of Hormuz

Persian Gulf

Gulf of Oman

Tropic of Cancer

AFRICA

Red Sea

Arabian Peninsula

Rub' al Khali Desert

Gulf of Aden

Socotra

Gulf of Oman

Arabian Sea

Narmada R.

Deccan

Godavari R.

Plateau

Western Ghats

Eastern Ghats

Palk Strait

Sri Lanka

INDIAN OCEAN

Legend

— National border
----- Disputed border
▲ Mountain peak
▼ Point below sea level

Compass: N, S, E, W

0   500   1,000 Miles
0   500   1,000 Kilometers
Robinson Projection

R40

ARCTIC OCEAN

Taymyr Peninsula
Laptev Sea
New Siberian Islands
East Siberian Sea
Wrangel Island
Chukchi Sea

North Siberian Lowland
Kolyma Lowland
Arctic Circle
Chukchi Peninsula

Central Siberian Plateau
Verkhoyansk Range
Kolyma R.
Kolyma Mountains
Bering Strait

S I B E R I A
Korya Range

Yenisey River
Lena River
Central Range

Angara River
Stanovoy Range
Dzhugdzhur Range
Kamchatka Peninsula
Bering Sea

Sayan Mountains
Lake Baikal
Yablonovy Range
Amur River
Sea of Okhotsk
Sakhalin
Kuril Islands

Yenisey R.
Greater Khingan Range
Sikhote Alin Range

Ob River
Altai Mountains
Plateau of Mongolia
Manchurian Plain
Hokkaido

Junggar Basin
▼ Turpan Depression
-505 ft.
(-154 m)
Gobi (Desert)

Tarim Basin
Qilian Shan
Korean Peninsula
Sea of Japan

Shan
North China
Yellow Sea
Honshu
▲ Mt. Fuji
12,388 ft.
(3,776 m)

NORTH PACIFIC OCEAN

Plateau of Tibet
Huang He
Plain
Kyushu
Shikoku

▲ Mt. Everest
29,028 ft.
(8,848 m)
Kanchenjunga
28,208 ft.
(8,598 m)
Chang Jiang
Sichuan Basin

East China Sea

Ganges R.
Irrawaddy River
Ryukyu Islands
Tropic of Cancer

Taiwan
Philippine Sea

Bay of Bengal
Mekong R.
Gulf of Tonkin
Hainan

Khorat Plateau
Indochina Peninsula
South China Sea
Luzon

Andaman Islands
Philippine Islands

Andaman Sea
Gulf of Thailand
Palawan
Sulu Sea

Nicobar Islands
Mindanao

Malay Peninsula
Celebes Sea

Strait of Malacca
Halmahera

Sumatra
Borneo
Moluccas
0° Equator

SOUTH PACIFIC OCEAN

G r e a t e r   S u n d a
Celebes
▲ Rantekombola
11,335 ft.
(3,455 m)
Ceram
Banda Sea

Java Sea
I s l a n d s
New Guinea

Java
Bali
Lombok
Sumbawa
Flores
Timor
Arafura Sea
Lesser Sunda Islands
Timor Sea
Sumba

AUSTRALIA

The Americas: Political

ARCTIC OCEAN

Beaufort Sea

Bering Strait

Viscount Melville Sound

Baffin Bay

Greenland
(DENMARK)

ALASKA
(U.S.)

Fairbanks

Anchorage

Whitehorse

Juneau

Gulf of
Alaska

Bering
Sea

Yukon River

Mackenzie River

Great Bear
Lake

Liard River

Great Slave Lake

Yellowknife

CANADA

Peace River

Athabasca R.

Lake Athabasca

Saskatchewan R.

Lake Winnipeg

Edmonton

Calgary

Saskatoon

Regina

Winnipeg

Vancouver

Seattle

Portland

Puget Sound

Columbia R.

Snake R.

UNITED STATES

Boise

Great Salt Lake

Salt Lake City

Reno

San Francisco

Las Vegas

Colorado R.

Los Angeles

San Diego

Phoenix

Tucson

Hermosillo

El Paso

Rio Grande

Denver

Missouri R.

Mississippi R.

Chicago

Detroit

St. Louis

Memphis

Dallas

Houston

San Antonio

New Orleans

Tampico

Arctic Circle

Davis Strait

Foxe Basin

Hudson Strait

Labrador Sea

Hudson Bay

James Bay

St. Lawrence River

Great Lakes

Gulf of St. Lawrence

Thunder Bay

Ottawa

Quebec

St. John's

Toronto

Albany

Montreal

St. John

Halifax

Cleveland

Boston

Indianapolis

New York City

Philadelphia

Washington, D.C.

Richmond

Norfolk

Atlanta

Raleigh

Charleston

Savannah

Jacksonville

Orlando

Tampa

Miami

BAHAMAS

Nassau

Havana

CUBA

HAITI

Port-au-Prince

Santo Domingo

Puerto Rico (U.S.)

DOMINICAN REPUBLIC

JAMAICA

Kingston

ATLANTIC OCEAN

Honolulu

HAWAII
(U.S.)

PACIFIC OCEAN

Tropic of Cancer

MEXICO

Durango

León

Guadalajara

Puebla

Acapulco

Chihuahua

Monterrey

Mexico City

Veracruz

Gulf of California

Gulf of Mexico

BELIZE

Belmopan

GUATEMALA

Guatemala City

HONDURAS

San Salvador

Tegucigalpa

EL SALVADOR

Managua

NICARAGUA

San José

COSTA RICA

PANAMA

Panama City

Maracaibo

Caracas

VENEZUELA

GUYANA

SURINAME

Paramaribo

Georgetown

Cayenne

FRENCH GUIANA (FRANCE)

Medellín

Cali

Bogotá

COLOMBIA

Caribbean Sea

0°

Equator

Galápagos Islands
(ECUADOR)

Quito

Guayaquil

ECUADOR

Iquitos

Trujillo

PERU

Lima

Cuzco

Manaus

Río Negro

Amazon R.

Belém

Fortaleza

Recife

Tapajós River

Xingu R.

Tocantins R.

BRAZIL

São Francisco R.

French Polynesia
(FRANCE)

Papeete

PACIFIC OCEAN

Lake Titicaca

La Paz

Arequipa

BOLIVIA

Sucre

Brasília

Goiânia

Salvador

Belo Horizonte

Rio de Janeiro

Tropic of Capricorn

Antofagasta

Campo Grande

Paraguay R.

Paraná R.

PARAGUAY

Salta

Asunción

São Paulo

Curitiba

30°S

CHILE

San Miguel de Tucumán

Córdoba

Pôrto Alegre

URUGUAY

Valparaíso

Santiago

Rosario

Buenos Aires

La Plata

Río de la Plata

Montevideo

Mar del Plata

Concepción

Bahía Blanca

Valdivia

ARGENTINA

0   1,000   2,000 Miles

0   1,000   2,000 Kilometers

Miller Cylindrical Projection

—— National border

⊛ National capital

• City

N
W   E
S

Punta Arenas

Falkland Islands
(U.K.)

South Georgia
(U.K.)

150°W   120°W   90°W   60°W   30°W

60°N

30°N

R42

The Americas: Physical

ARCTIC OCEAN

NORTH MAGNETIC POLE +
Queen Elizabeth Islands

Ellesmere Island

Melville Island

Devon Island

Viscount Melville Sound

Baffin Bay

Greenland

Beaufort Sea

Banks Island

Victoria Island

Baffin Island

Bering Strait
Point Barrow

Brooks   Range

Foxe Basin

Davis Strait

Arctic Circle

60°N

Mt. McKinley
20,320 ft.
(6,194 m)

Yukon   River

Yukon

Plateau

Mackenzie Mts.

Mackenzie River

Liard R.

Great Bear Lake

Great Slave Lake

Hudson Strait

Cape Farewell

Alaska Range

Mt. Logan
19,550 ft.
(5,959 m)

Coast Mountains

Peace River

Athabasca R.

Lake Athabasca

Hudson Bay

Labrador

Labrador Sea

Gulf of Alaska

Kodiak Island

Alaska Peninsula

Bering Sea

Aleutian Islands

Queen Charlotte Islands

Vancouver Island

Puget Sound

Coast Ranges

Cascade Range

Snake R.

ROCKY   MOUNTAINS

GREAT   PLAINS

Saskatchewan River

Lake Winnipeg

CANADIAN   SHIELD

James Bay

NORTH AMERICA

Great Lakes

Niagara Falls

St. Lawrence R.

Gulf of St. Lawrence

Newfoundland

Nova Scotia

Bay of Fundy

Sierra Nevada

Great Salt Lake

GREAT BASIN

Colorado R.

Black Hills

Missouri R.

Platte R.

Mississippi

INTERIOR PLAINS

Ohio R.

Ozark Plateau

Arkansas R.

APPALACHIAN MTS.

Cape Cod

Long Island

Chesapeake Bay

Cape Hatteras

Mt. Whitney
14,495 ft. (4,418 m)

Death Valley
(lowest point in N.A.)
-282 ft. (-86 m)

Sonoran Desert

Rio Grande

Sierra Madre Occidental

Sierra Madre Oriental

COASTAL PLAIN

ATLANTIC OCEAN

30°N

Baja California

Gulf of California

Gulf of Mexico

Bahamas

Cuba

Hispaniola

Puerto Rico

Lesser Antilles

Tropic of Cancer

Hawaiian Islands

PACIFIC OCEAN

Yucatán Peninsula

Greater Antilles

Caribbean Sea

Pico de Orizaba
18,855 ft.
(5,747 m)

Lake Maracaibo

Lake Nicaragua

Isthmus of Panama

Galápagos Islands

Llanos

Orinoco R.

Angel Falls

Guiana Highlands

Chimborazo
20,702 ft.
(6,310 m)

Rio Negro

Amazon R.

Cape São Roque

Equator

Line   Islands

Marquesas Islands

AMAZON BASIN

ANDES

Tapajós River

Xingu River

Tocantins R.

São Francisco River

Huascarán
22,205 ft.
(6,768 m)

Mato Grosso Plateau

Brazilian

Cook Islands

Tuamotu Archipelago

Society Islands

Lake Titicaca

Altiplano

Atacama Desert

Paraguay R.

Highlands

SOUTH AMERICA

Tropic of Capricorn

MOUNTAINS

Gran Chaco

Paraná R.

Iguazú Falls

30°S

0   1,000   2,000 Miles

0   1,000   2,000 Kilometers

Miller Cylindrical Projection

Mt. Aconcagua
22,834 ft.
(6,960 m)

Uruguay R.

Rio de la Plata

Pampa

▲ Mountain peak

▼ Point below sea level

— National border

≈ Waterfall

N
W   E
S

Patagonia

Valdés Peninsula
(lowest point in S.A.)
-131 ft. (-40 m)

Strait of Magellan

Tierra del Fuego

Cape Horn

Falkland Islands

South Georgia

150°W   120°W   90°W   60°W   30°W

The Pacific Rim: Political

ARCTIC OCEAN

Arctic Circle

RUSSIA

60°N

Magadan

Sea of Okhotsk

Bering Sea

Bering Strait

Alaska (U.S.)

Gulf of Alaska

CANADA

Hudson Bay

Aleutian Islands

Kuril Islands

MONGOLIA

Ulaanbaatar

Beijing

P'yongyang

Sapporo

Sea of Japan

NORTH KOREA

JAPAN

Tokyo

SOUTH KOREA

Seoul

CHINA

Shanghai

30°N

East China Sea

Hanoi

Taipei

TAIWAN

Hong Kong

VIETNAM

THAILAND

Bangkok

CAMBODIA

Phnom Penh

Kuala Lumpur

MALAYSIA

Singapore

Manila

PHILIPPINES

Philippine Sea

South China Sea

Northern Mariana Islands (U.S.)

PACIFIC OCEAN

Vancouver

Seattle

Portland

San Francisco

Los Angeles

UNITED STATES

Washington, D.C.

Ottawa

Tropic of Cancer

Honolulu

Hawaii (U.S.)

MEXICO

Gulf of Mexico

Mexico City

BELIZE

GUATEMALA

EL SALVADOR

HONDURAS

NICARAGUA

COSTA RICA

PANAMA

COLOMBIA

Bogotá

Quito

ECUADOR

Koror

PALAU

Palikir

FEDERATED STATES OF MICRONESIA

MARSHALL ISLANDS

Majuro

Tarawa

Yaren

NAURU

Equator

0°

Galápagos Islands (ECUADOR)

PERU

Lima

PAPUA NEW GUINEA

Jakarta

INDONESIA

EAST TIMOR

Port Moresby

SOLOMON ISLANDS

Honiara

TUVALU

Funafuti

KIRIBATI

SAMOA

Apia

American Samoa (U.S.)

French Polynesia (FR.)

Coral Sea

VANUATU

FIJI

Suva

Port-Vila

New Caledonia (FR.)

TONGA

Nuku'alofa

Cook Islands (N.Z.)

Papeete

Tahiti

Tropic of Capricorn

AUSTRALIA

Brisbane

30°S

Sydney

Canberra

Melbourne

Tasmania

Auckland

Tasman Sea

NEW ZEALAND

Wellington

PACIFIC OCEAN

Pitcairn Island (U.K.)

Easter Island (CHILE)

Santiago

CHILE

INDIAN OCEAN

60°S

Antarctic Circle

0   1,000   2,000 Miles

0   1,000   2,000 Kilometers

Miller Cylindrical Projection

N

W   E

S

ANTARCTICA

R44

120°E   150°E   180   150°W   120°W   90°W

Legend

— National border

⍟ National capital

• Major city

Abbreviations

FR.	FRANCE
N.Z.	NEW ZEALAND
U.K.	UNITED KINGDOM
U.S.	UNITED STATES

The Pacific Rim: Physical

ARCTIC OCEAN

Severnaya Zemlya

Laptev Sea

Taymyr Peninsula

New Siberian Islands

East Siberian Sea

Wrangel Island

Chukchi Sea

Chukchi Peninsula

Ellesmere Island

Melville Island

Banks Island

Beaufort Sea

Amundsen Gulf

Victoria Island

Baffin Island

Melville Peninsula

Kolyma Lowland

Kolyma R.

Chukchi Range

Bering Strait

Brooks Range

Yukon River

Mackenzie River

Great Bear Lake

Great Slave Lake

SIBERIA

Arctic Circle

Kolyma Range

Central Range

Korya Range

60°N

Bering Sea

Denali (Mt. McKinley) 20,320 ft. (6,194 m)

Mt. Logan 19,550 ft. 5,959 m)

R.

Ungava Peninsula

Hudson Bay

Lena River

Coast Mountains

Peace

Saskatchewan R.

NORTH AMERICA

ASIA

Sea of Okhotsk

Kamchatka Peninsula

Aleutian Islands

Alaska Peninsula

Gulf of Alaska

ROCKY MOUNTAINS

Missouri R.

Great Lakes

Lake Baikal

Amur R.

Greater Khingan Range

Sikhote Alin Range

Sakhalin

Kuril Islands

Manchurian Plain

Hokkaido

PACIFIC OCEAN

Vancouver Island

Columbia R.

GREAT PLAINS

Mississippi R.

APPALACHIAN MTS.

Gobi (Desert)

Huang He

Sea of Japan

Honshu

Mt. Fuji 12,388 ft. (3,776 m)

Colorado R.

North China Plain

Yellow Sea

Shikoku

Kyushu

30°N

Mt. Whitney 14,495 ft. (4,418 m)

Sierra Madre

Chang Jiang

East China Sea

Tropic of Cancer

Baja California

Gulf of Mexico

Yucatán Peninsula

Cuba

Caribbean Sea

Taiwan

Northern Mariana Islands

Hawaiian Islands

PHILIPPINE IS.

Philippine Sea

MARSHALL ISLANDS

Indochina Peninsula

South China Sea

Mt. Kinabalu 13,455 ft. (4,101 m)

MICRONESIA

CAROLINE ISLANDS

Gulf of Panama

SOUTH AMERICA

Malay Peninsula

Celebes Sea

0°

MELANESIA

POLYNESIA

Equator

Galápagos Islands

Sumatra

INDONESIA

New Guinea

Huascarán 22,205 ft. (6,768 m)

Greater Sunda Islands

Java

Timor

Great Barrier Reef

Coral Sea

American Samoa

Cook Islands

Tahiti

TUAMOTU ARCHIPELAGO

French Polynesia

ANDES

GREAT SANDY DESERT

New Caledonia

Pitcairn Island

Tropic of Capricorn

Easter Island

AUSTRALIA

GREAT VICTORIA DESERT

Great Dividing Range

Darling R.

Mt. Kosciusko 7,310 ft. (2,228 m)

30°S

Aconcagua 22,834 ft. (6,960 m)

INDIAN OCEAN

Tasmania

Mt. Cook 12,349 ft. (3,764 m)

New Zealand

Tasman Sea

PACIFIC OCEAN

60°S

0   1,000   2,000 Miles

0   1,000   2,000 Kilometers

Miller Cylindrical Projection

Cape Horn

Antarctic Circle

Alexander Island

N

W   E

S

Amundsen Sea

Thurston Island

Bellingshausen Sea

Ross Sea

—— National border

▲ Mountain peak

ANTARCTICA

120°E   150°E   180°   150°W   120°W   90°W

United States: Political

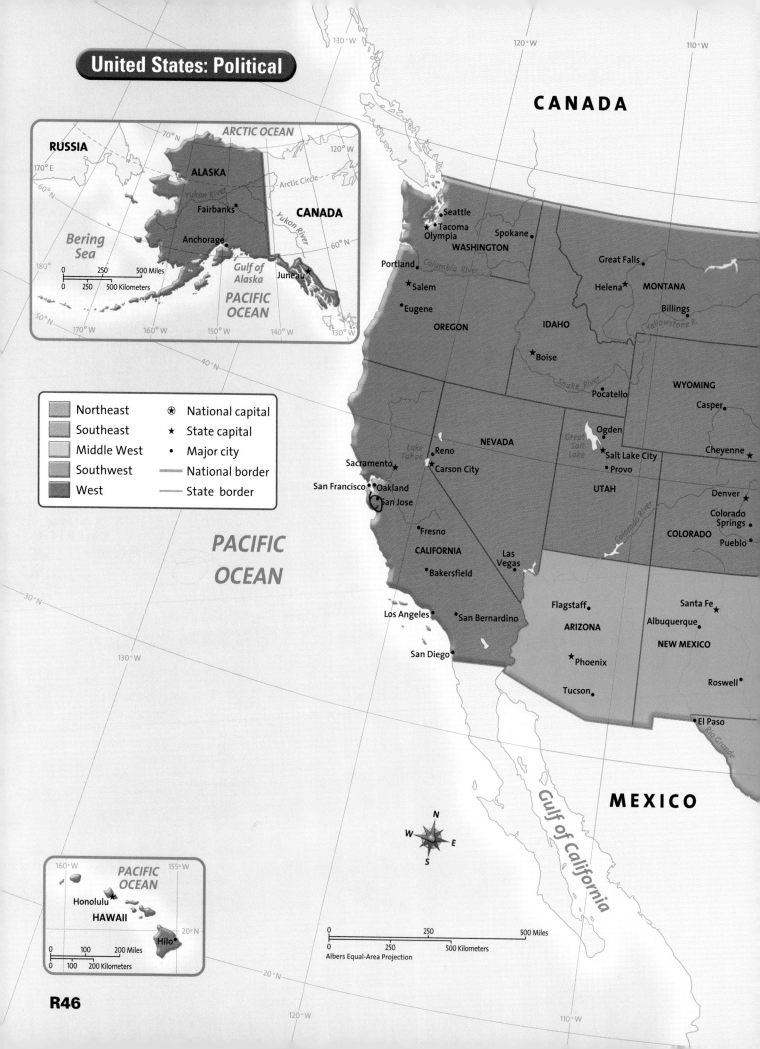

CANADA

Legend

- Northeast
- Southeast
- Middle West
- Southwest
- West
- ✹ National capital
- ★ State capital
- • Major city
- National border
- State border

Alaska inset
RUSSIA
ARCTIC OCEAN
170° E
70° N
ALASKA
CANADA
Arctic Circle
Yukon River
60° N
Fairbanks
Bering Sea
Anchorage
Yukon River
Gulf of Alaska
Juneau
PACIFIC OCEAN
180°
170° W
160° W
150° W
140° W
130° W
50° N
60° N
40° N
0 250 500 Miles
0 250 500 Kilometers

Hawaii inset
160° W
155° W
PACIFIC OCEAN
Honolulu
HAWAII
Hilo
20° N
0 100 200 Miles
0 100 200 Kilometers

Main map

CANADA
130° W
120° W
110° W

Seattle
Tacoma
Olympia ★
Spokane
WASHINGTON
Portland
Columbia River
Great Falls
Helena ★
MONTANA
Salem ★
Billings
Eugene
OREGON
IDAHO
Yellowstone R.
Boise ★
Snake River
WYOMING
Pocatello
Casper
Reno
NEVADA
Great Salt Lake
Ogden
Cheyenne ★
Lake Tahoe
Sacramento ★
Carson City ★
Salt Lake City ★
Provo
San Francisco
Oakland
San Jose
UTAH
Denver ★
Colorado Springs
COLORADO
Fresno
Pueblo
Colorado River
CALIFORNIA
Las Vegas
Bakersfield
Flagstaff
Santa Fe ★
Albuquerque
Los Angeles
San Bernardino
ARIZONA
NEW MEXICO
San Diego
Phoenix ★
Roswell
Tucson
El Paso
Rio Grande

PACIFIC OCEAN

MEXICO
Gulf of California

30° N
130° W
120° W
110° W
20° N
40° N

N
W E
S

0 250 500 Miles
0 250 500 Kilometers
Albers Equal-Area Projection

R46

CANADA

Lake of the Woods

Lake Superior

Lake Michigan

Lake Huron

Lake St. Clair

Lake Erie

Lake Ontario

Lake Champlain

St. Lawrence River

NORTH DAKOTA
Grand Forks
• Duluth
Fargo •
★ Bismarck

MINNESOTA

Sault Sainte Marie •

MICHIGAN

MAINE
• Augusta ★

VERMONT
Burlington • ★
Montpelier ★

NEW HAMPSHIRE
• Portland

NEW YORK
Manchester • • Concord
★ ★
Worcester • Boston •

SOUTH DAKOTA
Rapid City •
St. Paul ★
Minneapolis •

Green Bay •

Grand Rapids •
Flint •

Lansing ★
Detroit •

Cleveland •

Syracuse •
Albany ★
Rochester •

Hartford ★

MASSACHUSETTS
Providence ★

RHODE ISLAND

CONNECTICUT
• Bridgeport

★ Pierre

WISCONSIN
Madison ★

Milwaukee •

• Rockford
Chicago •

South Bend •
Gary •

Toledo •
Akron •

OHIO
Columbus ★

Wheeling •

Buffalo •

Pittsburgh •

PENNSYLVANIA
Harrisburg ★

Newark •
★ Trenton

NEW JERSEY
• New York City
• Philadelphia

Sioux Falls •

IOWA
Cedar Rapids •
Davenport •

Sioux City •

NEBRASKA
Omaha •

Des Moines ★

ILLINOIS
• Peoria
Decatur •

INDIANA
Indianapolis ★

• Dayton
Cincinnati •

Baltimore •

WEST VIRGINIA
Annapolis ★
Washington, ✪
D.C.

MARYLAND

Wilmington •
Dover ★

DELAWARE

Platte River

Missouri River

Lincoln ★

Springfield ★

Louisville •
Frankfort ★
Lexington •

Charleston •

VIRGINIA
Richmond •

• Newport News
Norfolk •

Chesapeake Bay

Virginia Beach •

KANSAS
Topeka ★

Kansas City •

St. Louis •

Evansville •

Ohio River

KENTUCKY

Roanoke •

Greensboro •
★ Raleigh

Wichita •

Jefferson City ★

MISSOURI
Springfield •

Knoxville •
★ Nashville

Winston-Salem •
Charlotte •

NORTH CAROLINA

Missouri River

Arkansas River

TENNESSEE
Chattanooga •

OKLAHOMA
• Tulsa

ARKANSAS

Memphis •

Huntsville •

SOUTH CAROLINA
Columbia ★

• Charleston

ATLANTIC OCEAN

Amarillo •

Oklahoma City ★

Fort Smith •

Little Rock ★

Birmingham •

★ Atlanta

GEORGIA
Macon •

Savannah •

Arkansas River

Lake Texoma

Red River

MISSISSIPPI

ALABAMA

Columbus •

Lubbock •

Fort Worth •
Dallas •

Shreveport •

Meridian •
Jackson ★

Montgomery ★

Jacksonville •

Abilene •

LOUISIANA

★ Tallahassee

Odessa •

TEXAS

Biloxi •
Mobile •

FLORIDA

Orlando •

Austin ★
Beaumont •

Baton Rouge ★

New Orleans •

Tampa •
West Palm Beach •

Houston •

Lake Okeechobee

San Antonio •

St. Petersburg •

Rio Grande

Miami •

Laredo •
Corpus Christi •

BAHAMAS

Gulf of Mexico

CUBA

R47

United States: Physical

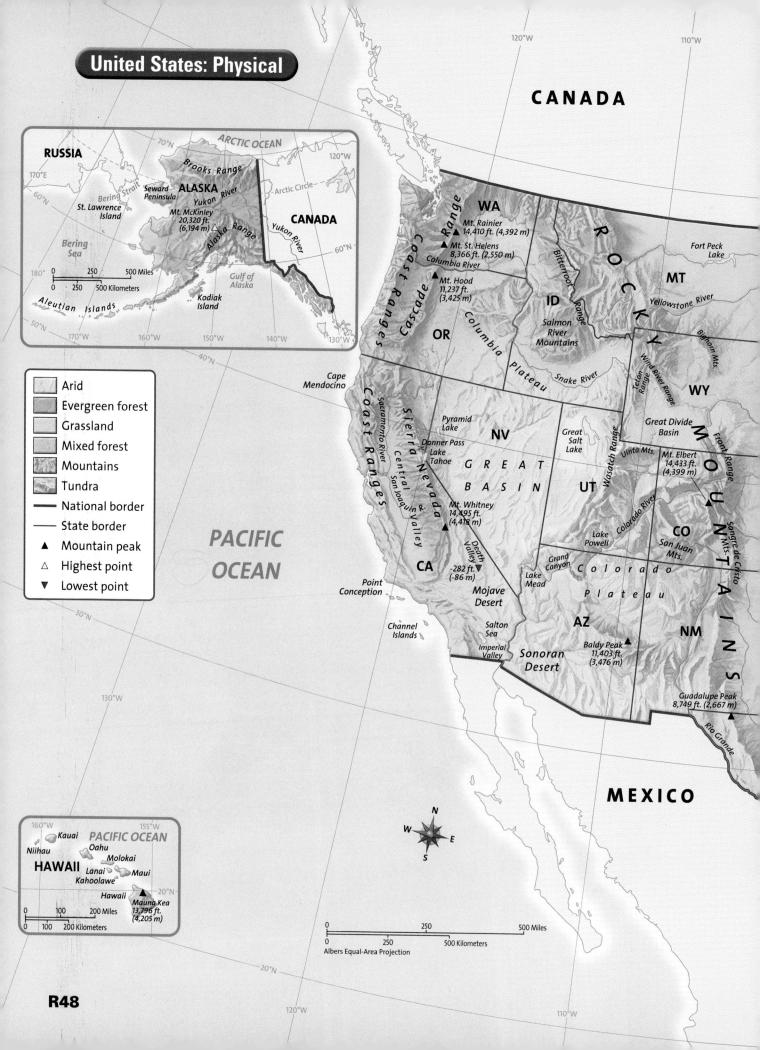

RUSSIA

ARCTIC OCEAN

Brooks Range

ALASKA

Seward Peninsula

St. Lawrence Island

Mt. McKinley 20,320 ft. (6,194 m)

Yukon River

Alaska Range

Bering Strait

Bering Sea

Aleutian Islands

Gulf of Alaska

Kodiak Island

CANADA

Yukon River

Arctic Circle

70°N

60°N

50°N

40°N

170°E

180°

170°W

160°W

150°W

140°W

130°W

120°W

250   500 Miles
250   500 Kilometers

Legend

	Arid
	Evergreen forest
	Grassland
	Mixed forest
	Mountains
	Tundra
▬	National border
—	State border
▲	Mountain peak
△	Highest point
▽	Lowest point

PACIFIC OCEAN

CANADA

120°W   110°W

Coast Ranges

Cascade Range

Mt. Rainier 14,410 ft. (4,392 m)

Mt. St. Helens 8,366 ft. (2,550 m)

Columbia River

Mt. Hood 11,237 ft. (3,425 m)

WA

Bitterroot Range

ID

Salmon River Mountains

Columbia Plateau

Snake River

OR

Cape Mendocino

Coast Ranges

Sacramento River

Sierra Nevada

Central San Joaquin Valley

Pyramid Lake

Donner Pass Lake Tahoe

NV

GREAT BASIN

Mt. Whitney 14,495 ft. (4,418 m)

Death Valley -282 ft. (-86 m) ▽

Mojave Desert

CA

Point Conception

Channel Islands

Salton Sea

Imperial Valley

Sonoran Desert

Great Salt Lake

UT

Wasatch Range

Uinta Mts.

Lake Powell

Colorado River

Grand Canyon

Lake Mead

AZ

Colorado Plateau

Baldy Peak 11,403 ft. (3,476 m)

ROCKY

Fort Peck Lake

MT

Yellowstone River

Bighorn Mts.

Teton Range

Wind River Range

WY

Great Divide Basin

Mt. Elbert 14,433 ft. (4,399 m)

Front Range

CO

San Juan Mts.

Sangre de Cristo Mts.

M O U N T A I N S

NM

Guadalupe Peak 8,749 ft. (2,667 m)

Rio Grande

MEXICO

160°W   155°W

PACIFIC OCEAN

Kauai

Niihau

Oahu

Molokai

HAWAII

Lanai   Maui

Kahoolawe

Hawaii

Mauna Kea 13,796 ft. (4,205 m)

20°N

0   100   200 Miles
0   100   200 Kilometers

N
W   E
S

0   250   500 Miles
0   250   500 Kilometers

Albers Equal-Area Projection

30°N

20°N

130°W   120°W   110°W

100°W   90°W   80°W   70°W

50°N

CANADA

ME
Mt. Katahdin
5,269 ft.
(1,606 m)
Moosehead
Lake

Lake of
the Woods
Upper
Red Lake
Lower
Red Lake   Isle
Royale
Lake Superior
Keweenaw
Peninsula

G R E A T

Lake Sakakawea

ND

Mesabi
Range
Leech
Lake
Mille
Lacs
Lake

Upper Peninsula

Lake Huron

VT
Lake
Champlain   White Mts.
Mt. Washington
6,288 ft.
(1,917 m)

MN

NY
Adirondack
Mountains
Green Mts.

NH
Cape Ann

Lake
Oahe

SD

Missouri
River

WI

Wisconsin River

Lake Michigan

MA
Cape
Cod

MI
Lake
St. Clair

Finger
Lakes
Lake Ontario
Connecticut R.
Hudson R.

RI
CT

Black
Hills

Lake
Winnebago

Niagara
Falls

Lower Peninsula

Lake Erie

40°N

Long
Island

P L A I N S

Sand Hills

North Platte R.

IA

Illinois River

OH

PA
Allegheny Mts.

NJ

70°N

NE

Platte River

I N T E R I O R

Wabash River

MD
Potomac R.

DE
Delaware
Bay

South Platte R.

P L A I N S

IL

IN

CENTRAL PLAINS

Ohio River

WV

VA
James R.
Roanoke

Cape
Charles
Chesapeake
Bay

Smoky Hills

Missouri River

MO

Lake of
the Ozarks

KY

Albemarle
Sound

KS

Harry S. Truman
Reservoir

Lake
Barkley
Cumberland
Gap

APPALACHIAN MOUNTAINS
PIEDMONT

NC
Cape Fear River

Cape
Hatteras

Red Hills

Ozark Plateau

Mt. Mitchell
6,684 ft.
(2,037 m)

Arkansas

OK

Canadian River

Cumberland R.

TN

Tennessee R.

Cape
Fear

River

Ouachita
Mountains

AR

Mississippi River

SC

Savannah River

Red River

Lake
Texoma

Cape
Canaveral

Llano
Estacado

MS

Tombigbee R.

Stone
Mountain

Clark
Hill Lake
Oconee R.

Pecos River

Sabine River

Toledo
Bend
Reservoir

LA

AL

Alabama R.

GA

Chattahoochee R.

Ocmulgee R.
Altamaha R.

30°N

TX

Brazos River

C O A S T A L

Okefenokee
Swamp

St. Johns River

Edwards
Plateau

Colorado River

Sam
Rayburn
Reservoir

Lake
Maurepas

Mobile
Bay

P L A I N

ATLANTIC
OCEAN

Rio Grande

Galveston
Bay

Lake
Pontchartrain

Mississippi
Delta

Tampa
Bay

FL

Lake
Okeechobee

BAHAMAS

Gulf of Mexico

Everglades
Cape
Sable
Florida Keys
Straits of Florida

CUBA

California: Political

IDAHO

42°N

Crescent City
DEL NORTE
Yreka
SISKIYOU
Goose Lake
MODOC
Alturas

Klamath River

Pit River

41°N

HUMBOLDT

Eureka
Trinity River
SHASTA
Shasta Lake
LASSEN
Susanville

Weaverville
TRINITY
Redding

Eel River

40°N

Red Bluff
TEHAMA
Sacramento River

PLUMAS
Quincy

MENDOCINO
GLENN
Willows
Chico
BUTTE

SIERRA
Downieville

Feather R.

Oroville
Nevada City
NEVADA

Ukiah
LAKE
COLUSA
Colusa
YUBA
Yuba City
Marysville
PLACER
Truckee

39°N

Lakeport
SUTTER
Auburn
Lake Tahoe

Russian River

YOLO
Woodland
Placerville
Markleeville

SONOMA
NAPA
EL DORADO

Santa Rosa
Napa
SACRAMENTO
Sacramento
AMADOR

Sonoma
Fairfield
Jackson
ALPINE

Petaluma
SOLANO
Martinez
CALAVERAS

MARIN
Berkeley
CONTRA COSTA
San Andreas
Bridgeport

38°N
San Rafael
Stockton
TUOLUMNE
NEVADA

San Francisco
Oakland
SAN JOAQUIN
Sonora

124°W
SAN FRANCISCO
ALAMEDA
Mono Lake

San Francisco Bay
Modesto
STANISLAUS
MONO

Redwood City
San Jose
STANISLAUS
MARIPOSA

SAN MATEO
SANTA CLARA
Mariposa

37°N
SANTA CRUZ
MERCED
Merced
MADERA

Santa Cruz
Madera
FRESNO

Monterey Bay
Hollister
Joaquin River
Kings River
Independence

Salinas
SAN BENITO
Fresno

Monterey
INYO

MONTEREY
Hanford
Visalia

36°N
Salinas River
KINGS
Tulare
TULARE

Lake Mead

SAN LUIS OBISPO
Kern River
Ridgecrest

35°N
San Luis Obispo
Bakersfield
KERN
Cuyama R.

W N E S

Santa Maria
SANTA BARBARA
Barstow
Needles

Lompoc
Santa Ynez River
SAN BERNARDINO

VENTURA
Santa Clarita

Santa Barbara
Santa Clara R.
LOS ANGELES

34°N
Ventura
Oxnard
Glendale
Pasadena
San Bernardino

PACIFIC OCEAN
Los Angeles
Riverside
Palm Springs

Torrance
Anaheim
Blythe

Long Beach
Santa Ana
RIVERSIDE

Huntington Beach
ORANGE

Colorado River

33°N
Oceanside
Escondido
Salton Sea
ARIZONA

SAN DIEGO
IMPERIAL

San Diego
El Centro

San Diego Bay

0   75   150 Miles
0   75   150 Kilometers
Albers Equal-Area Projection

123°W

R50

32°N

122°W   121°W   120°W   119°W   118°W

MEXICO

Legend
★ State capital
• County seat
• Other city
━ National border
━ State border
━ County border

California: Physical

OREGON

IDAHO

NEVADA

ARIZONA

MEXICO

PACIFIC OCEAN

Legend
— National border
— State border
▲ Mountain peak
▲ Highest point
▽ Lowest point

Klamath River
Klamath Mountains
Cascade Range
Mount Shasta 14,162 ft. (4,317 m)
Goose Lake
Warner Mts.
River
Pit
Clair Engle Lake
Trinity River
Trinity Mts.
Shasta Lake
Lassen Peak 10,457 ft. (3,187 m)
Eagle Lake
Humboldt Bay
Coast Ranges
Eel River
Sacramento River
Lake Oroville
Lake Almanor
Pyramid Lake
Feather River
Clear Lake
Russian River
Sacramento Valley
Yuba River
American River
Sierra
Lake Tahoe
Folsom Lake
Lake Berryessa
Napa Valley
Farallon Islands
San Francisco Bay
San Joaquin River
Stanislaus River
Mono Lake
Nevada
White Mountain Peak 14,246 ft. (4,342 m)
Santa Cruz Range
San Joaquin Valley
Merced River
Lake McClure
San Joaquin River
Pine Flat Reservoir
North Palisade Peak 14,242 ft. (4,341 m)
San Luis Reservoir
Monterey Bay
Coast Ranges
Diablo Range
Kings River
Mount Whitney 14,495 ft. (4,418 m)
Mount Williamson 14,370 ft. (4,380 m)
Panamint Range
Death Valley
Lake Mead
Salinas Valley
Salinas River
Santa Lucia Range
Lake Nacimiento
Temblor Range
Kern River
Isabella Lake
-282 ft. (-86 m)
Lake Mohave
Mount Pinos 8,831 ft. (2,692 m)
Cuyama R.
Tehachapi Mountains
Mojave Desert
Lake Havasu
Santa Ynez River
Santa Clara Valley
Santa Clara R.
San Gabriel Mountains
San Bernardino Mts.
Coachella Valley
Colorado River
Santa Barbara Channel
Channel Islands
San Jacinto Mts.
Colorado Desert
Salton Sea
Alamo R.
Laguna Mts.
New R.
Imperial Valley
San Diego Bay

N
W E
S

0 ——— 75 ——— 150 Miles
0 ——— 75 ——— 150 Kilometers
Albers Equal-Area Projection

Oceans and Rivers of the World

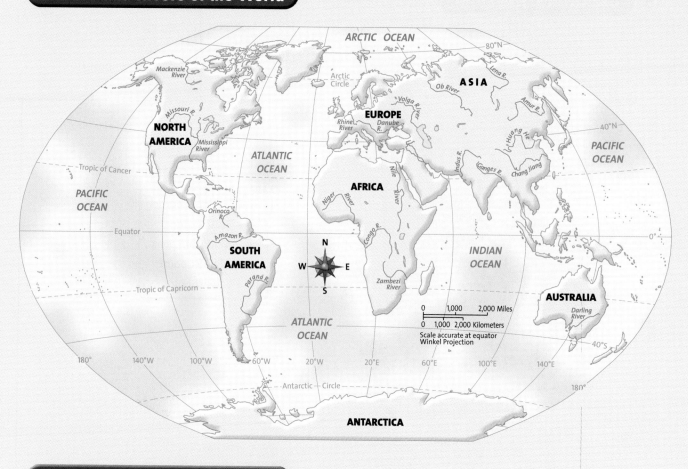

Mountain Ranges of the World

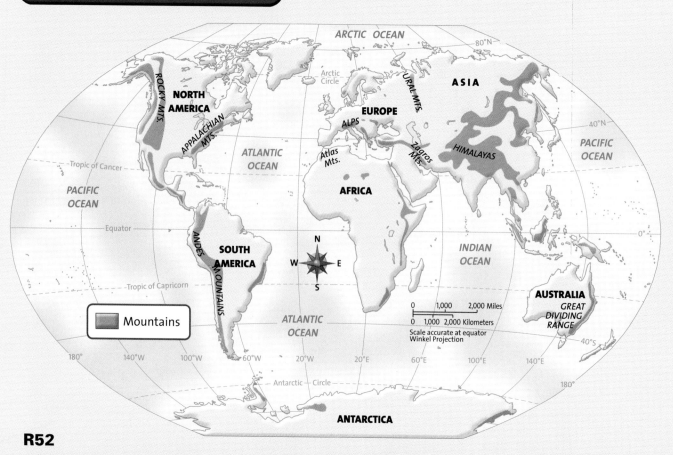

Plains of the World

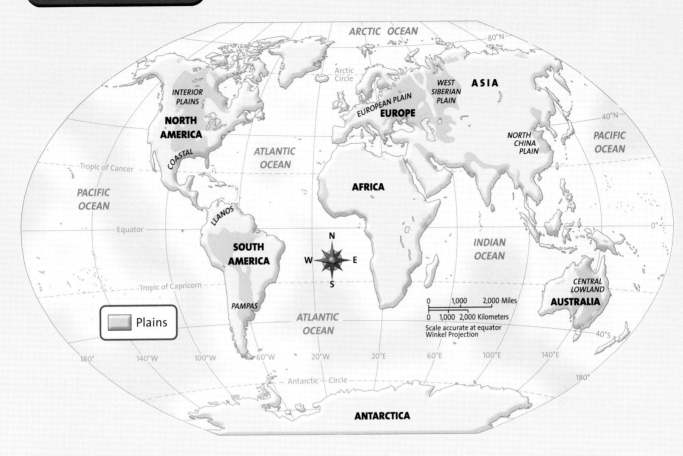

ARCTIC OCEAN
80°N
Arctic Circle
INTERIOR PLAINS
NORTH AMERICA
COASTAL
ATLANTIC OCEAN
Tropic of Cancer
PACIFIC OCEAN
Equator
LLANOS
SOUTH AMERICA
Tropic of Capricorn
PAMPAS
EUROPEAN PLAIN
EUROPE
WEST SIBERIAN PLAIN
ASIA
40°N
NORTH CHINA PLAIN
PACIFIC OCEAN
AFRICA
INDIAN OCEAN
0°
CENTRAL LOWLAND
AUSTRALIA
40°S

N
W   E
S

0   1,000   2,000 Miles
0 1,000 2,000 Kilometers
Scale accurate at equator
Winkel Projection

ATLANTIC OCEAN

Plains

180° 140°W 100°W 60°W 20°W 20°E 60°E 100°E 140°E 180°

Antarctic Circle

ANTARCTICA

Deserts of the World

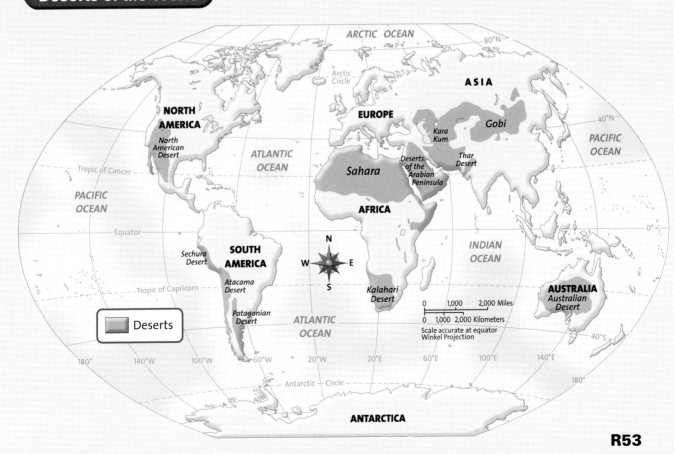

ARCTIC OCEAN
80°N
Arctic Circle
NORTH AMERICA
North American Desert
ATLANTIC OCEAN
Tropic of Cancer
PACIFIC OCEAN
Equator
Sechura Desert
SOUTH AMERICA
Atacama Desert
Tropic of Capricorn
Patagonian Desert
EUROPE
ASIA
Kara Kum
Gobi
40°N
Sahara
Deserts of the Arabian Peninsula
Thar Desert
PACIFIC OCEAN
AFRICA
INDIAN OCEAN
Kalahari Desert
AUSTRALIA
Australian Desert
40°S

N
W   E
S

0   1,000   2,000 Miles
0 1,000 2,000 Kilometers
Scale accurate at equator
Winkel Projection

ATLANTIC OCEAN

Deserts

180° 140°W 100°W 60°W 20°W 20°E 60°E 100°E 140°E 180°

Antarctic Circle

ANTARCTICA

Almanac
Facts About the World

ATLAS/ALMANAC

Country Flag	Country	Capital	Population*	Area (sq. mi.)	Economy
Africa					
	Algeria	Algiers	32,818,500	919,590	oil, natural gas, light industry, food processing, grains, iron mining, petrochemical
	Angola	Luanda	10,766,471	481,351	textiles, coffee, sugarcane, bananas, iron, diamonds, cement, fish processing, phosphates
	Benin	Porto-Novo	7,041,490	43,483	palm products, peanuts, cotton, corn, oil, construction materials, petroleum
	Botswana	Gaborone	1,573,267	231,803	livestock processing, corn, coal, copper, tourism, diamonds, salt, silver
	Burkina Faso	Ouagadougou	13,228,460	105,869	agricultural processing, textiles, millet, sorghum, manganese, soap, gold, beverages
	Burundi	Bujumbura	6,096,156	10,745	food processing, coffee, cotton, tea, nickel, soap, shoes
	Cameroon	Yaoundé	15,746,179	183,567	oil products, food processing, cocoa, coffee, lumber, textiles
	Cape Verde	Praia	412,137	1,557	bananas, coffee, sweet potatoes, salt, fish processing, ship repair
	Central African Republic	Bangui	3,683,538	240,534	textiles, cotton, coffee, diamonds, sawmills, footwear, assembly of bicycles and motorcycles

Country Flag	Country	Capital	Population*	Area (sq. mi.)	Economy
	Chad	N'Djamena	9,253,493	495,752	cotton, sorghum, millet, uranium, meatpacking, soap, construction materials
	Comoros	Moroni	632,948	838	perfume, textiles, vanilla, coconut oil, plants, fruits, furniture, jewelry, construction materials
	Republic of the Congo	Brazzaville	2,954,258	132,046	oil, wood products, cocoa, coffee, potash, soap, sugar milling
	Côte d'Ivorie (Ivory Coast)	Yamoussoukro	16,962,491	124,502	food processing, coffee, cocoa, oil, diamonds, textiles, fertilizer, construction materials
	Democratic Republic of the Congo	Kinshasa	56,625,039	905,563	mining, food processing, sugar, rice, cobalt, cement, diamonds, textiles
	Djibouti	Djibouti	457,130	8,880	mainly service activities, dairy products, mineral water bottling
	Egypt	Cairo	74,718,797	386,660	textiles, tourism, chemicals, cotton, rice, beans, oil, gas, construction, cement, metals
	Equatorial Guinea	Malabo	510,473	10,830	fish, cocoa, coffee, bananas, oil, saw milling, natural gas
	Eritrea	Asmara	4,362,254	46,842	food processing, cotton, coffee, tobacco, gold, potash, textiles
	Ethiopia	Addis Ababa	66,557,553	435,184	food processing, textiles, coffee, grains, platinum, gold

* These population figures are from the most recent available statistics.

Country Flag	Country	Capital	Population*	Area (sq. mi.)	Economy
	Gabon	Libreville	1,321,560	103,346	textiles, cocoa, coffee, oil, manganese, uranium, cement
	Gambia	Banjul	1,501,050	4,363	tourism, peanuts, rice, fish, woodworking, metalworking
	Ghana	Accra	20,467,747	92,456	aluminum, cocoa, gold, manganese, food processing, lumbering
	Guinea	Conakry	9,030,220	94,925	mining, bananas, pineapples, iron, bauxite, diamonds
	Guinea-Bissau	Bissau	1,360,827	13,946	peanuts, cashews, cotton, rice, bauxite, agricultural processing
	Kenya	Nairobi	31,639,091	224,961	tourism, oil refining, coffee, corn, gold, limestone, cement, soap, textiles
	Lesotho	Maseru	1,861,959	11,720	food processing, textiles, corn, grains, diamonds, construction, tourism
	Liberia	Monrovia	3,317,176	43,000	mining, rice, cassava, coffee, iron, diamonds, gold, rubber, timber
	Libya	Tripoli	5,449,074	679,358	oil, food processing, dates, olives, gypsum, handicrafts, textiles, cement
	Madagascar	Antananarivo	16,979,744	226,656	textiles, meat processing, coffee, cloves, vanilla, chromite, graphite, soap, paper, petroleum, tourism
	Malawi	Lilongwe	11,651,239	45,745	agricultural processing, sugar, tea, tobacco, coffee

Country Flag	Country	Capital	Population*	Area (sq. mi.)	Economy
	Mali	Bamako	11,626,219	478,764	millet, rice, peanuts, cotton, gold, phosphates, construction
	Mauritania	Nouakchott	2,912,584	397,953	fish processing, dates, grains, iron ore, gypsum
	Mauritius	Port Louis	1,210,447	788	tourism, textiles, sugarcane, tea, metal products
	Morocco	Rabat	31,689,265	172,413	carpets, clothing, leather goods, grains, fruits, phosphates, iron ore, tourism
	Mozambique	Maputo	17,479,226	309,494	chemicals, petroleum products, cashews, cotton, sugar, coal, titanium, textiles, glass, cement
	Namibia	Windhoek	1,927,447	318,694	diamonds, copper, gold, fish, meatpacking, dairy products
	Niger	Niamey	11,058,590	489,189	peanuts, cotton, uranium, coal, iron, gold, petroleum
	Nigeria	Abuja	133,881,703	356,667	oil, gas, textiles, cocoa, palm products, construction materials, chemicals, ceramics, steel
	Rwanda	Kigali	7,810,056	10,169	coffee, tea, tin, cement, soap, furniture, shoes, textiles
	São Tomé and Príncipe	São Tomé	175,883	386	cocoa, coconuts, textiles, soap, fish processing, timber
	Senegal	Dakar	10,580,307	75,749	food processing, fishing, peanuts, millet, phosphates, construction materials, fertilizer production

* These population figures are from the most recent available statistics.

ATLAS/ALMANAC

Country Flag	Country	Capital	Population*	Area (sq. mi.)	Economy
	Seychelles	Victoria	80,469	176	food processing, tourism, coconut products, cinnamon, vanilla, fishing, boat building, printing
	Sierra Leone	Freetown	5,732,681	27,699	mining, cocoa, coffee, diamonds, titanium, textiles, footwear
	Somalia	Mogadishu	8,025,190	246,199	sugar, bananas, iron, tin, textiles
	South Africa	Cape Town/ Pretoria	42,768,678	471,008	steel, automobiles, corn, other grains, gold, diamonds, platinum, metalworking, textiles, chemicals
	Sudan	Khartoum	38,114,160	967,493	textiles, gum arabic, cotton, chromium, copper, cement, sugar, shoes, petroleum refining
	Swaziland	Mbabane	1,161,219	6,704	wood pulp, sugar, corn, cotton, asbestos, clay, coal
	Tanzania	Dar es Salaam	35,922,454	364,898	agricultural processing, cotton, tin, diamonds, textiles, fertilizer, salt
	Togo	Lomé	5,429,299	21,925	textiles, coffee, cocoa, yams, phosphates, handicrafts
	Tunisia	Tunis	9,924,742	63,170	food processing, textiles, oil products, grains, olives, dates, phosphates, tourism
	Uganda	Kampala	25,632,794	91,135	textiles, cement, coffee, cotton, tea, copper, cobalt, sugar

Country Flag	Country	Capital	Population*	Area (sq. mi.)	Economy
	Zambia	Lusaka	10,307,333	290,584	corn, cassava, sugar, cobalt, copper, zinc, emeralds, gold, silver, construction, chemicals
	Zimbabwe	Harare	12,576,742	150,803	clothing, steel, chemicals, tobacco, sugar, chromium, gold, nickel, wood products, steel

Asia

Country Flag	Country	Capital	Population*	Area (sq. mi.)	Economy
	Afghanistan	Kabul	28,717,213	250,000	textiles, furniture, wheat, fruits, copper, coal, wool, natural gas, oil, soap
	Armenia	Yerevan	3,326,448	11,506	vegetables, grapes, copper, gold, electric motors, tires, chemicals, trucks, watches, microelectronics
	Azerbaijan	Baku	7,830,764	33,436	oil, grains, cotton, iron, cattle, cement, textiles
	Bahrain	Manama	667,238	257	oil, gas, fruits, vegetables, ship repairing, tourism
	Bangladesh	Dhaka	138,448,210	55,598	jute, textiles, fertilizers, rice, tea, cement, chemical fertilizer
	Bhutan	Thimphu	2,139,549	18,147	rice, corn, timber, cement, processed fruits
	Brunei	Bandar Seri Begawan	358,098	2,228	petroleum, rice, bananas, cassava, construction

* These population figures are from the most recent available statistics.

Country Flag	Country	Capital	Population*	Area (sq. mi.)	Economy
	Cambodia	Phnom Penh	13,124,764	69,900	rice, wood, rubber, corn, gemstones, garments, wood and wood products, cement
	China	Beijing	1,286,975,468	3,705,386	iron, steel, textiles, tea, rice and other grains, cotton, coal, petroleum, cement, food processing, toys, footwear
	Cyprus	Nicosia	771,657	3,571	barley, grapes, olives, copper, tourism, metal products, wood products
	East Timor	Dili	997,853	5,814	coffee, mining, marble, fishing, tourism
	Georgia	Tbilisi	4,934,413	26,911	manganese, citrus fruits, potatoes, corn, steel, aircraft, machine tools, textiles
	India	New Delhi	1,049,700,118	1,269,338	textiles, steel, rice and other grains, tea, spices, coal, iron, chemicals, cement, mining, petroleum
	Indonesia	Jakarta	234,893,453	741,096	textiles, rice, cocoa, peanuts, nickel, tin, oil, petroleum, plywood, chemical fertilizers, rubber, tourism
	Iran	Tehran	68,278,826	636,293	sugar refining, carpets, rice and other grains, oil, gas, textiles, cement, construction materials
	Iraq	Baghdad	24,683,313	168,753	textiles, grains, dates, oil, chemicals, construction materials
	Israel	Jerusalem	6,116,533	8,019	diamond cutting, textiles, electronics, citrus fruits, copper, phosphates, tourism, chemicals, metal products
	Japan	Tokyo	127,214,499	145,882	electronics, automobiles, fishing, rice, potatoes, machine tools, ships, textiles

Country Flag	Country	Capital	Population*	Area (sq. mi.)	Economy
	Jordan	Amman	5,460,265	35,687	oil refining, cement, grains, olives, phosphates, tourism, potash
	Kazakhstan	Astana	16,763,795	1,049,150	steel, grains, cotton, oil, coal, phosphates, electric motors, construction materials
	Kuwait	Kuwait	2,183,161	6,880	oil, oil products, gas, food processing, construction materials
	Kyrgyzstan	Bishkek	4,892,808	76,641	textiles, mining, tobacco, cotton, sugar beets, gold, refrigerators, furniture, electric motors
	Laos	Vientiane	5,921,545	91,428	wood products, mining, sweet potatoes, corn, cotton, gypsum, construction
	Lebanon	Beirut	3,727,703	4,015	banking, textiles, oil refining, fruits, olives, vegetables, jewelry, wood and furniture products, metal fabricating
	Malaysia	Kuala Lumpur	23,092,940	127,316	rubber goods, logging, steel, electronics, palm oil, tin, iron, petroleum production
	Maldives	Male	329,684	116	fish processing, tourism, coconuts, sweet potatoes, corn, shipping, boatbuilding, garments, handicrafts
	Mongolia	Ulaanbaatar	2,712,315	604,247	food processing, mining, grains, coal, oil, construction materials, copper
	Myanmar (Burma)	Yangon (Rangoon)	42,510,537	261,969	textiles, petroleum, rice, sugarcane, lead, gemstones, pharmaceuticals, copper, tin, fertilizer, construction materials

* These population figures are from the most recent available statistics.

Country Flag	Country	Capital	Population*	Area (sq. mi.)	Economy
	Nepal	Kathmandu	26,469,569	54,363	sugar, jute, tourism, rice and other grains, quartz, carpet, textiles, cement and brick production
	North Korea	P'yongyang	22,466,481	46,540	textiles, corn, potatoes, coal, lead, machine building, chemicals, mining, tourism
	Oman	Muscat	2,807,125	82,031	dates, vegetables, limes, oil, gas, construction, cement, copper
	Pakistan	Islamabad	150,694,740	310,401	textiles, petroleum products, rice, wheat, natural gas, iron ore, paper products, clothing
	Palau	Koror	19,717	177	tourism, fish, coconuts, copra, cassava, sweet potatoes, garment making
	Philippines	Manila	84,619,974	115,830	textiles, clothing, wood products, sugar, cobalt, copper, food processing, electronics, fishing
	Qatar	Doha	817,052	4,416	oil, petroleum products, fertilizers, cement
	Saudi Arabia	Riyadh	24,293,844	756,981	oil, oil products, gas, dates, wheat, cement, construction, fertilizer
	Singapore	Singapore	4,608,595	267	shipbuilding, oil refining, electronics, banking, tourism, rubber processing, biotechnology
	South Korea	Seoul	48,289,037	38,023	electronics, automobiles, textiles, clothing, rice, barley, tungsten, shipbuilding, footwear
	Sri Lanka	Colombo	19,742,439	25,332	clothing, textiles, tea, coconuts, rice, graphite, limestone, processing of rubber, cement, petroleum refining

Country Flag	Country	Capital	Population*	Area (sq. mi.)	Economy
	Syria	Damascus	17,585,540	71,498	oil products, textiles, cotton, grains, olives, phosphate, rock mining
	Taiwan	Taipei	22,603,000	13,892	textiles, clothing, electronics, rice, fruits, coal, marble, iron, steel, cement, machinery
	Tajikistan	Dushanbe	6,863,752	55,251	aluminum, cement, barley, coal, lead, chemicals and fertilizers, machine tools
	Thailand	Bangkok	64,265,276	198,455	textiles, tourism, rice, corn, tapioca, sugarcane, cement, furniture, plastics, tungsten, tin
	Turkey**	Ankara	68,109,469	301,382	steel, textiles, grains, mercury, food processing, mining, petroleum, lumber, paper
	Turkmenistan	Ashgabat	4,775,544	188,455	oil, mining, textiles, grains, cotton, coal, sulfur, salt, natural gas
	United Arab Emirates	Abu Dhabi	2,484,818	32,000	oil, vegetables, dates, fishing, construction materials, handicrafts
	Uzbekistan	Tashkent	25,981,647	172,741	machinery, natural gas, vegetables, cotton, textiles, food processing
	Vietnam	Hanoi	81,624,716	127,243	food processing, textiles, rice, sugar, phosphates, cement, fertilizer, steel, paper, oil, coal
	Yemen	Sanaa	19,349,881	203,849	oil, grains, fruits, salt, food processing, handicrafts

** in both Asia and Europe
* These population figures are from the most recent available statistics.

Country Flag	Country	Capital	Population*	Area (sq. mi.)	Economy
Australia and Oceania					
	Australia	Canberra	19,731,894	2,967,893	iron, steel, textiles, electrical equipment, wheat, cotton, fruits, bauxite, coal, mining, food processing
	Fiji	Suva	868,531	7,054	tourism, sugar, bananas, gold, timber, clothing, silver
	Kiribati	Tarawa	98,549	313	fishing, coconut oil, breadfruit, sweet potatoes, handicrafts
	Marshall Islands	Majuro	56,429	70	agriculture, tourism, fish, crafts from shells, wood and pearls
	Federated States of Micronesia	Palikir	136,973	271	tourism, tropical fruits, vegetables, pepper, construction, fish processing
	Nauru	Yaren	12,570	8.11	phosphates, coconut products
	New Zealand	Wellington	3,951,307	103,737	food processing, textiles, machinery, fish, forest products, grains, potatoes, gold, gas, iron, coal, tourism
	Papua New Guinea	Port Moresby	5,295,816	178,703	coffee, coconuts, cocoa, gold, copper, silver, plywood production, construction, tourism
	Samoa	Apia	178,173	1,104	timber, tourism, coconuts, yams, hardwoods, fish

Country Flag	Country	Capital	Population*	Area (sq. mi.)	Economy
	Solomon Islands	Honiara	509,190	10,985	fishing, coconuts, rice, gold, bauxite, mining, timber
	Tonga	Nuku'alofa	108,141	289	tourism, fishing, coconut products, bananas
	Tuvalu	Funafuti	11,305	10	coconut products, coconuts, fishing, tourism
	Vanuatu	Port-Vila	199,414	5,700	fish processing, meat canneries, tourism, coconut products, manganese, wood processing

Europe

Country Flag	Country	Capital	Population*	Area (sq. mi.)	Economy
	Albania	Tiranë	3,582,205	11,100	cement, textiles, food processing, corn, wheat, chromium, coal, lumber, chemicals, mining
	Andorra	Andorra la Vella	69,150	181	tourism, sheep, tobacco products, iron, lead, timber
	Austria	Vienna	8,188,207	32,378	steel, machinery, automobiles, grains, iron ore, construction, lumber and wood processing, tourism
	Belarus	Minsk	10,322,151	80,154	manufacturing, chemicals, grains, vegetables, tractors, fertilizer, textiles
	Belgium	Brussels	10,298,088	11,780	steel, glassware, diamond cutting, automobiles, wheat, coal, engineering, textiles, petroleum
	Bosnia and Herzegovina	Sarajevo	3,989,018	19,741	steel, mining, textiles, timber, corn, wheat, berries, bauxite, iron, coal, vehicle assembly

* These population figures are from the most recent available statistics.

Country Flag	Country	Capital	Population*	Area (sq. mi.)	Economy
	Bulgaria	Sofia	7,537,929	42,822	chemicals, machinery, metals, textiles, grains, fruits, bauxite, copper, zinc, construction materials
	Croatia	Zagreb	4,422,248	21,831	chemicals, plastics, steel, paper, olives, wheat, oil, bauxite, electronics, aluminum, textiles, petroleum, shipbuilding
	Czech Republic	Prague	10,249,216	30,450	machinery, oil products, glass, wheat, sugar beets, rye, coal, kaolin, motor vehicles, metal crafting
	Denmark	Copenhagen	5,384,384	16,639	food processing, machinery, textiles, furniture, grains, potatoes, dairy products, oil, salt, electronics, construction
	Estonia	Tallinn	1,408,556	17,462	shipbuilding, electric motors, potatoes, oil, phosphates, cement, furniture, paper, shoes
	Finland	Helsinki	5,190,785	130,127	metal, wood products, grains, copper, iron, paper, food stuffs, chemicals
	France	Paris	60,180,529	211,208	steel, textiles, tourism, wine, perfume, grains, fruits, vegetables, bauxite, iron, automobiles, electronics, mining
	Germany	Berlin	82,398,326	137,846	shipbuilding, automobiles, grains, potatoes, coal, potash, steel, iron, cement, machinery, electronics, food and beverages, textiles
	Greece	Athens	10,665,989	50,942	textiles, tourism, chemicals, wine, grains, olives, grapes, citrus fruits, bauxite, mining, petroleum
	Hungary	Budapest	10,045,407	35,919	iron, steel, wheat, corn, sunflowers, bauxite, coal, mining, construction materials, motor vehicles

Country Flag	Country	Capital	Population*	Area (sq. mi.)	Economy
	Iceland	Reykjavik	280,798	39,768	fish, aluminum, potatoes, tourism
	Ireland	Dublin	3,924,140	27,135	food processing, textiles, chemicals, tourism, potatoes, grains, zinc, lead, pharmaceuticals, machinery
	Italy	Rome	57,998,353	116,305	tourism, steel, machinery, automobiles, textiles, shoes, grapes, olives and olive oil, mercury, potash, sulfur, iron, food processing
	Latvia	Riga	2,348,784	24,938	machinery, train cars, sugar beets, fertilizer, electronics, pharmaceuticals, processed foods
	Liechtenstein	Vaduz	33,145	62	electronics, textiles, ceramics, vegetables, wheat, metal manufacturing, tourism
	Lithuania	Vilnius	3,592,561	25,174	machinery, shipbuilding, grains, potatoes, vegetables, electric motors, petroleum refining, fertilizer
	Luxembourg	Luxembourg	454,157	998	steel, chemicals, food processing, grains, potatoes, grapes, metal products, tires, glass, aluminum
	Macedonia	Skopje	2,063,122	9,781	mining, textiles, wheat, rice, chromium, lead, coal, wood products
	Malta	Valletta	400,420	122	textiles, tourism, potatoes, tomatoes, electronics, shipbuilding and repair, construction
	Moldova	Chisinau	4,439,502	13,067	canning, wine, textiles, grains, lignite, gypsum, sugar, shoes, refrigerators and freezers

* These population figures are from the most recent available statistics.

Country Flag	Country	Capital	Population*	Area (sq. mi.)	Economy
	Monaco	Monaco	32,130	465 acres	tourism, chemicals, plastics
	Netherlands	Amsterdam	16,150,511	16,033	metals, machinery, chemicals, grains, potatoes, flowers, oil, gas, fishing
	Norway	Oslo	4,546,123	125,181	paper, shipbuilding, grains, potatoes, copper, petroleum, chemicals, timber, mining, textiles
	Poland	Warsaw	38,622,660	120,728	shipbuilding, chemicals, grains, potatoes, sugar beets, coal, copper, silver, iron, steel, food processing, glass
	Portugal	Lisbon	10,102,022	35,672	textiles, footwear, cork, fish, grains, potatoes, tungsten, uranium, iron, metalworking, oil refining, chemicals, tourism
	Romania	Bucharest	22,271,839	91,699	mining, machinery, oil, oil products, grains, grapes, gas, coal, timber, chemicals, food processing
	Russia**	Moscow	144,526,278	6,592,735	steel, machinery, motor vehicles, chemicals, textiles, grains, sugar beets, mercury, cobalt, shipbuilding, handicrafts
	San Marino	San Marino	28,119	24	tourism, postage stamps, woolen goods, wheat, grapes, ceramics, cement, wine
	Serbia and Montenegro	Belgrade	10,655,774	39,517	steel, machinery, corn and other grains, oil, gas, coal, mining, footwear, chemicals, pharmaceuticals
	Slovakia	Bratislava	5,430,033	18,859	iron, steel, glass, grains, potatoes, chemicals, textiles, rubber products

** in both Asia and Europe

Country Flag	Country	Capital	Population*	Area (sq. mi.)	Economy
	Slovenia	Ljubljana	1,935,677	7,827	electronics, vehicles, coal, lead, zinc, wood products, chemicals, machine tools
	Spain	Madrid	40,217,413	194,896	machinery, textiles, grains, olives, grapes, lignite, uranium, lead, chemicals, shipbuilding, tourism
	Sweden	Stockholm	8,878,085	173,731	steel, machinery, vehicles, grains, potatoes, zinc, iron, lead, paper products, processed foods, motor vehicles
	Switzerland	Bern	7,318,638	15,943	machinery, chemicals, watches, cheese, chocolate products, tourism, salt
	Ukraine	Kiev	48,055,439	233,089	chemicals, machinery, grains, sugar beets, potatoes, iron, manganese, coal, food processing
	United Kingdom	London	60,094,648	94,525	steel, vehicles, shipbuilding, banking, textiles, grains, sugar beets, coal, tin, oil, gas, limestone, chemicals, petroleum, paper and paper products
	Vatican City	—	900	109 acres	tourism, postage stamps

North America

Country Flag	Country	Capital	Population*	Area (sq. mi.)	Economy
	Antigua and Barbuda	St. John's	67,897	171	manufacturing, tourism, construction
	Bahamas	Nassau	297,477	5,382	tourism, rum, banking, pharmaceuticals, fishing
	Barbados	Bridgetown	277,264	166	sugar, tourism, manufacturing

* These population figures are from the most recent available statistics.

Country Flag	Country	Capital	Population*	Area (sq. mi.)	Economy
	Belize	Belmopan	266,440	8,867	sugar, garment production, food processing, tourism
	Canada	Ottawa	32,207,113	3,851,788	nickel, zinc, copper, gold, livestock, fish, chemicals, wood and paper products, petroleum
	Costa Rica	San José	3,896,092	19,730	furniture, aluminum, textiles, fertilizers, coffee, gold, construction materials, plastic products
	Cuba	Havana	11,263,429	42,803	food processing, tobacco, sugar, rice, coffee, cobalt, nickel, iron, copper, salt, textiles, chemicals, petroleum
	Dominica	Roseau	69,655	291	tourism, bananas, citrus fruits, pumice, soap, furniture, cement blocks
	Dominican Republic	Santo Domingo	8,715,602	18,815	cement, tourism, sugar, cocoa, coffee, nickel, bauxite, gold
	El Salvador	San Salvador	6,470,379	8,124	food products, tobacco, coffee, corn, sugar, chemicals, fertilizer, textiles
	Grenada	St. George's	89,258	133	textiles, spices, bananas, cocoa, tourism, construction
	Guatemala	Guatemala City	13,909,384	42,042	furniture, rubber, textiles, coffee, sugar, bananas, oil, chemicals, petroleum, metals
	Haiti	Port-au-Prince	7,527,817	10,714	textiles, coffee, sugar, bananas, bauxite, tourism, cement

ATLAS/ALMANAC

Country Flag	Country	Capital	Population*	Area (sq. mi.)	Economy
	Honduras	Tegucigalpa	6,669,789	43,278	textiles, wood products, bananas, sugar, gold, silver, copper, lead
	Jamaica	Kingston	2,695,867	4,244	tourism, sugar, coffee, bananas, potatoes, bauxite, limestone, textiles, rum, food processing
	Mexico	Mexico City	104,907,991	761,602	steel, chemicals, textiles, rubber, petroleum, tourism, cotton, coffee, wheat, silver, lead, zinc, gold, oil, gas, mining, motor vehicles
	Nicaragua	Managua	5,128,517	49,998	food processing, chemicals, textiles, cotton, fruits, coffee, gold, silver, copper, petroleum refining, beverages, footwear
	Panama	Panama City	2,960,784	30,193	oil refining, international banking, bananas, rice, copper, mahogany, shrimp, cement, sugar milling
	Saint Kitts and Nevis	Basseterre	38,763	101	sugar, tourism, cotton, salt, clothing, footwear
	Saint Lucia	Castries	162,157	239	clothing, tourism, bananas, coconuts, forests, beverages, cardboard boxes
	Saint Vincent and the Grenadines	Kingstown	116,812	150	tourism, bananas, arrowroot, coconuts, food processing, clothing, furniture
	Trinidad and Tobago	Port-of-Spain	1,104,209	1,980	oil products, chemicals, tourism, sugar, cocoa, asphalt, oil, gas, cotton, textiles
	United States of America	Washington, D.C.	290,342,554	3,794,083	wheat, corn, coal, lead, uranium, iron, copper, gold, computers, electronics, machinery, motor vehicles, chemicals, lumber, mining

ATLAS/ALMANAC

* These population figures are from the most recent available statistics.

Country Flag	Country	Capital	Population*	Area (sq. mi.)	Economy
South America					
	Argentina	Buenos Aires	38,740,807	1,068,296	food processing, automobiles, chemicals, grains, oil, lead, textiles, printing, steel
	Bolivia	La Paz/Sucre	8,586,443	424,162	mining, tobacco, coffee, sugar, potatoes, soybeans, tin, tungsten, handicrafts, clothing
	Brazil	Brasília	182,032,604	3,286,470	steel, automobiles, textiles, coffee, soybeans, sugar, iron, manganese, shoes, chemicals, cement, lumber, aircraft
	Chile	Santiago	15,665,216	292,258	fish, wood, grains, grapes, beans, copper, cement, textiles
	Colombia	Bogotá	41,662,073	439,733	textiles, food processing, coffee, rice, bananas, emeralds, oil, gas, cement, gold
	Ecuador	Quito	13,710,234	109,483	food processing, bananas, coffee, oil, gas, copper, zinc, silver, gold, textiles, metalwork, fishing
	Guyana	Georgetown	702,100	83,000	mining, textiles, sugar, bauxite, diamonds, gold, rice, fishing
	Paraguay	Asunción	6,036,900	157,046	food processing, textiles, cement, corn, cotton, iron, manganese, limestone, sugar, wood products
	Peru	Lima	28,409,897	496,223	fishing, mining, textiles, cotton, sugar, coffee, rice, copper, silver, gold, oil, auto assembly, cement, shipbuilding

ATLAS/ALMANAC

Country Flag	Country	Capital	Population*	Area (sq. mi.)	Economy
	Suriname	Paramaribo	435,449	63,039	aluminum, food processing, rice, sugar, fruits, bauxite, iron, lumbering, fishing
	Uruguay	Montevideo	3,413,329	68,039	meatpacking, textiles, wine, corn, wheat, oil refining, food processing, chemicals
	Venezuela	Caracas	24,654,694	352,143	steel, textiles, coffee, rice, corn, oil, gas, iron, petroleum, mining, motor vehicle assembly

ATLAS/ALMANAC

* These population figures are from the most recent available statistics.

Research Handbook

Before you can write a report or complete a project, you must gather information about your topic. You can find some information in your textbook. Other sources of information are technology resources, print resources, and community resources.

Technology Resources

- Internet
- Computer disk
- Television and radio

Print Resources

- Almanac
- Atlas
- Dictionary
- Encyclopedia
- Nonfiction book
- Periodical
- Thesaurus

Community Resources

- Teacher
- Museum curator
- Community leader
- Older citizen

Technology Resources

The main technology resources you can use for researching information are the Internet and computer disks. Your school or local library may have CD-ROMs or DVDs that contain information about your topic. Other media, such as television and radio, can also be good sources of current information.

Using the Internet

The Internet contains vast amounts of information. By using a computer to go online, you can read documents, see pictures and artworks, listen to music, take a virtual tour of a museum, and read about current events.

Information that you find online is always changing. Keep in mind that some websites that you find might contain mistakes or incorrect information. To get accurate information, be sure to visit only trusted websites, such as museum and government sites. Also, try to find two or more websites that give the same facts.

❱ Plan Your Search

- Identify the topic to be researched.
- Make a list of questions that you want to answer about your topic.
- List key words or groups of words that can be used to write or talk about your topic.
- Look for good online resources to find answers to your questions.
- Choose the steps you will take to find the information you need.

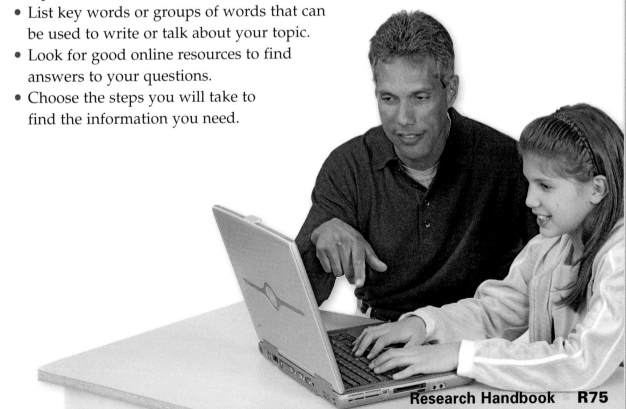

Use a Search Engine

A search engine is an online collection of websites that can be sorted by entering a key word or group of words. There are many different search engines available. You may want to ask a librarian, a teacher, or a parent for suggestions on which search engine to use.

> **Search by Subject** To search by subject, or topic, use a search engine. Choose from the list of key words that you made while planning your search, and enter a key word or group of words in the search engine field on your screen. Then click SEARCH or GO. You will see a list of websites that have to do with your topic. Click on the site or sites you think will be most helpful. If you do not find enough websites listed, think of other key words or related words, and search again.

> **Search by Address** Each website has its own address, called a Uniform Resource Locator, or URL for short. To get to a website using a URL, simply type the URL in the LOCATION/GO TO box on your screen and hit ENTER or click GO.

> **Use Bookmarks** The bookmark feature is an Internet tool for keeping and organizing URLs. If you find a website that seems especially helpful, you can save the URL so that you can quickly and easily return to it later. Click BOOKMARKS or FAVORITES at the top of your screen, and choose ADD. Your computer makes a copy of the URL and keeps a record of it.

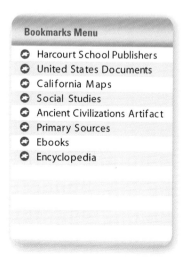

Print Resources

Books in libraries are organized through a system of numbers. Every book has its own call number. This call number tells where in the library the book can be found. Some reference books, such as encyclopedias, are usually kept in a separate section of a library. Each book there has R or RE—for *reference*—on its spine. Most reference books can only be used in the library. Most libraries also have a special section for periodicals, which include magazines and newspapers.

❱ Almanac

An almanac is a book or electronic resource that contains facts about different subjects. The subjects are listed in alphabetical order in an index. Many facts that involve numbers and dates are shown in tables or charts. New almanacs are published each year, so they have the most current information.

❱ Atlas

An atlas is a book of maps. It gives information about places. Different kinds of atlases show different places at different times. Your teacher or librarian can help you find the kind of atlas you need for your research.

❱ Dictionary

A dictionary gives the correct spelling of words and their definitions, or meanings. It also gives the words' pronunciations, or how to say the words aloud. In addition, many dictionaries have lists of foreign words, abbreviations, well-known people, and place names.

\-ˌgäg-ē, -ˌgäj-ē\ *n*
de•mand\di-´mand** *n* **1: to ask with authority **2:** the desire or need for a product or service
de•pend\di-´pend** *vi* **1: to be undecided **2:** to rely on for help
de•pos•it\di-´pä-zit** *vb* **1: to put money into a bank account **2:** to place for safekeeping or as a pledge

Dictionary entry

◗ Encyclopedia

An encyclopedia is a book or set of books that gives information about many different topics. The topics are arranged alphabetically. An encyclopedia is a good source to use when beginning your research. In addition to words, electronic encyclopedias often have sound and video clips.

◗ Nonfiction Books

A nonfiction book gives facts about real people, places, and things. All nonfiction books in a library are arranged in order and by category according to their call numbers. To find a book's call number, you use a library's card file or computer catalog. You can search for a book in the catalog by subject, author, or title.

Encyclopedia article

◗ Periodicals

A periodical is published each day, each week, or each month. Periodicals are good resources for current information on topics not yet found in books. Many libraries have a guide that lists magazine articles by subject. Two such guides are the *Children's Magazine Guide* and the *Readers' Guide to Periodical Literature*. The entries in guides are usually in alphabetical order by subject, author, or title.

◗ Thesaurus

A thesaurus (thih•SAWR•uhs) gives synonyms, or words that mean the same or nearly the same as another word. A thesaurus also gives antonyms, or words that have the opposite meanings. Using a thesaurus can help you find words that better describe your topic and make your writing more interesting.

Community Resources

Many times, people in your community can tell you information about your research topic. You can learn facts, opinions, or points of view by asking these people thoughtful questions. Before you talk to any of them, always ask a teacher or a parent for permission.

Listening to Find Information

It is important to plan ahead whenever you talk with people as part of your research. Planning ahead will help you gather the information you need. Follow these tips as you gather information from people in your community.

▶ Before
- Find out more about the topic you want to discuss.
- Think about the kind of information you still need.
- Consider the best way to gather the information you need.
- List the people you want to talk to.
- Make a list of useful questions you want to ask. Make sure your questions are clear and relevant.

▶ During
- Speak clearly and loudly enough when asking questions.
- Listen carefully. Make sure you are getting the information you need, and revise your questions based on what you hear. You may also think of new questions to ask.
- Think about the speaker's point of view, tone of voice, and word choice. Use these clues to evaluate whether the speaker is a good source of information about your topic.
- Be polite. Do not interrupt or argue with the person who is speaking.
- Take notes to help you remember important ideas and details.
- Write down the person's exact words if you think you will want to quote them in your report. If possible, use a tape recorder. Be sure to ask the speaker for permission in advance.

▶ After
- Thank the person you spoke with.
- Follow up by writing a thank-you note.

Writing to Get Information

You can also write to people in your community to gather information. You can write an e-mail or a letter. Keep these ideas in mind as you write:

- Write neatly or use a computer.
- Say who you are and why you are writing. Be clear and specific about what you want to know.
- Carefully check your spelling and punctuation.
- If you are writing a letter, provide a self-addressed, stamped envelope for the person to send you a response.
- Thank the person.

222 Central Avenue
Bakersfield, CA 93301
October 25, 20- -

Northern Regional Tourism Division
Attn: Ms. Stephanie Nguyen
123 Main Street
Sacramento, CA 94211

Dear Ms. Nguyen:

My name is David Thomas, and I am writing this letter to see if you can send me some information about scenic attractions in the state of California. My family is planning a vacation next month, and we would like to visit some of the attractions in the northern part of the state. Please send a brochure listing the scenic attractions and a highway map. I understand this is a service you provide for those planning vacations in the area. I am excited about visiting your part of the state.

Thank you for your help.

Sincerely,

David Thomas

David Thomas
222 Central Avenue
Bakersfield, CA 93301

Bureau of Tourism
Attn: Stephanie Nguyen
123 Main Street
Sacramento, CA 94211

Reporting

❯ Written Reports

Your teacher may ask you to write a report about the information you find. Knowing how to write a report will help you make good use of the information. The following tips will help you write your report.

❯ Before Writing

- Choose a main idea or topic.
- Think of questions about your topic. Questions should be clear and focus on specific ideas.
- Gather information from more than one source. You may use print resources, technology resources, or community resources. Be sure to look for answers to your questions.
- Take notes on the information you find.
- Review your notes to be sure you have the information you need. Write down ideas and details about your topic to put in your report.
- Use your notes to make an outline of the information you found. Organize your ideas in a way that is easy to understand.

❯ Citing Sources

An important part of research and writing is citing or listing sources. When you cite a source, you keep a written record of where you got your information. The list of sources will make up a bibliography. A bibliography is a list of the books, periodicals, and other sources that you used to find the information in your report.

Outline

The California Capitol Building

I. Where, when, and why the capitol building was constructed

    A. The capitol building was built in Sacramento.

        1. In 1849, the capital was in San Jose.

        2. In 1852, the capital moved from San Jose to Vallejo.

        3. Since Vallejo was not a good place for a capitol building, the capital moved to Sacramento.

    B. The population of California increased, creating a need for a capitol building.

        1. People wanted a symbol to represent the state of California.

        2. In 1854, Sacramento's statehouse became the new capitol building.

    C. Many important decisions are made in the capitol building.

        1. Government representatives make new laws.

        2. Government officials meet to talk about California issues.

    D. Knowing about the state capitol is important for good citizenship.

        1. The building includes information everyone should know.

        2. Citizens vote for people who represent them.

Bibliography

Hernandez, Elizabeth. *Sacramento Through the Years*. San Antonio, Texas: Old Alamo Press, 2004

Wyatt, Adam. *The History of California*. Philadelphia, Pennsylvania: Scenic River Publishing, 2003

Bibliography Card

Wyatt, Adam. *The History of California*. Philadelphia, Pennsylvania: Scenic River Publishing, 2003, page 25.

San Jose was the first state capital of California. Eventually the state government moved to Sacramento in 1854.

THE CALIFORNIA CAPITOL BUILDING	
Reading Notes	**Class Notes**
• The California Legislature first met at the Capitol building in 1869	• Visitors can tour the offices of the California attorney general, secretary of state, treasurer, and governor
• Government representatives make laws in the Capitol building	• Outside the building is a statue of Junipero Serra
• Government representatives vote on issues there	• Around the building are 40 acres of garden
• The capital of California was San Jose in 1849	• The capital moved from San Jose to Vallejo to Sacramento, when the statehouse became the Capitol building
• In 1852, the capital moved to Vallejo	• The Capitol building is a symbol for the people of California
• The Sacramento statehouse became the new Capitol building	• The Capitol building was built out of the statehouse and took four more years to complete

▶ Write a First Draft

- Use your notes and your outline to write a draft of your report. Keep in mind that your purpose is to share information.
- Write in paragraph form. Develop your topic with facts, details, examples, and explanations. Each paragraph should focus on one new idea.
- Get all your ideas down on paper. You can revise your draft and correct errors in the next step.

▶ Revise

- Read over your draft. Does it make sense? Does your report have a beginning, a middle, and an end? Have you answered all your questions about your topic?
- Rewrite sentences that are unclear or poorly worded. Move sentences that seem out of place.
- Add details when needed to support your ideas.
- If too many sentences are alike, make some sentences shorter or longer to keep your report interesting.
- Check any quotations to be sure you have shown someone's exact words and that you have noted the source correctly.

▶ Proofread and Edit

- Proofread your report, checking for errors.
- Correct any errors in spelling, capitalization, or punctuation. If you are writing your report on a computer, use the spell-check feature.
- Use a thesaurus to find words that better describe your topic or that make your report more interesting.

▶ Publish

- Make a neat, clean copy of your report.
- Include illustrations, maps, or other drawings to help explain your topic.

Rough draft

Allison Cesareo
Social Studies

A History of the Capitol Building in Sacramento, California

The capitol Building in Sacramento, California, is a very important place. The capitol building is the place where our state government works on making new laws. It is also where our government officials meet to talk about important issues happening in California. Many people do not know about the history of the capitol building because it was built before many of today's California citizens were born. There are many interesting historical facts about the Capital building in Sacramento, California. It is important to know who made the decision to build it, where it was built, when it was built, and what happens in the capitol building today.

The capitol Building in Sacramento was not always the location of our state's government offices. A long time ago, the capitol of California was located in San Jose. In 1849, In 1852 the capital of California moved from San jose to Vallejo, California. At that time, Vallejo was not a good place for the capitol building. The work on the building took a long time and it was very expensive. Then In 1853, the capital moved to Benicia where it remained until the city of Sacramento offered its courthouse as the new capitol building. In 1854, Sacramento's courthouse became the new statehouse. The building that the first session held its meeting in, is not the same building that serves as today's capitol building. When the capital first moved to Sacramento, members of the legislature were happy to have a place to meet that would stand as a symbol of the great State of California. But, soon after, the city began to grow. As the population increased, so did the need for a new Capitol building.

Final draft

Allison Cesareo
Social Studies

A History of the Capitol Building in Sacramento, California

The capitol building in Sacramento, California, is a very important place. The capitol building is the place where our government representatives make new laws. It is also where our government officials meet to talk about important issues happening in California. Many people do not know about the history of the capitol building because it was built before many of today's California citizens were born. There are many interesting historical facts about the capitol building, which is located in Sacramento, California. It is important to know where it was built, when it was built, and what happens in the capitol building today.

The capitol building in Sacramento was not always the location of our state's government offices. In 1849, the capitol of California was located in San Jose. In 1852, California's capital moved from San Jose to Vallejo, California. At that time, Vallejo was not a good place for the capitol building because work on the building took a long time and it was very expensive. In 1853, the capital of California moved to Benicia where it remained until the city of Sacramento offered its courthouse as the new capitol building. In 1854, Sacramento's courthouse became the new statehouse. The building in Sacramento that held the first state sesssion in 1854 is not the same building that serves as today's California capitol building.

When the state capital was first moved to Sacramento, members of the legislature were happy to have a nice place to meet that would serve as a symbol of the great state of California. But, soon after, the city began to grow. As the population increased, so did the need for a new Capitol building.

Proofreading marks and their meanings	
Mark	**Meaning**
∧	Insert word.
∧ (comma)	Insert comma.
¶	Start a new paragraph.
═ (cap)	Use capital letter.
ℯ	Delete.
(lc)	Use lowercase letter.

Oral Presentations

Sometimes in class you may be asked to give an oral presentation. Like a written report, the purpose of an oral presentation is to share information. These tips will help you prepare an oral presentation:

- Follow the steps described in Before Writing to gather and organize information.
- Use your notes to plan and organize your presentation. Include an introduction and a conclusion in your report.
- Prepare note cards that you can refer to as you speak.
- Prepare visuals such as illustrations, diagrams, maps, or other graphics to help listeners better understand your topic.
- Give your audience a controlling idea about your topic. A controlling idea is the main idea that you support with facts and details.
- Practice your presentation.
- Be sure to speak clearly and loudly enough. Keep your listeners interested in your report by using facial expressions and hand movements.

Biographical Dictionary

The Biographical Dictionary provides information about many of the people introduced in this book. Names are listed alphabetically by last name. Pronunciation guides are provided for hard-to-pronounce names. After each name are the birth and death dates, if known, of that person. If the person is still alive, only the year of birth appears. A brief description of the person's main achievement is then given. The page number that follows tells where the main discussion of that person appears in this book. (You can check the Index for other page references.) Guide names at the top of each page help you quickly locate the name you need to find.

A

Abraham *c. 1900s B.C.* Earliest ancestor of the Israelites. p. 205

Aesop (EE•sahp) *c. 500s B.C.* Author of fables that use animal characters to teach a lesson. p. 301

Agamemnon *c. 1200s B.C.* Brother of the king of Mycenea. Led the Myceneans against the Trojans. Thought up the Trojan Horse. p. 267

Akhenaton (ahk•NAH•tuhn) *c. 1300s B.C.* Egyptian ruler who changed his name from Amenhotep IV. He and Nefertiti, his wife, urged the Egyptians to worship only one god, the Aton. p. 160

Alara *700s B.C.* Leader who began the Kushite dynasty of the land once known as Nubia, in Africa. p. 179

Alaric (AL•uh•rik) *c. A.D. 370–A.D. 410* King of the Visigoths, who crossed the Alps and attacked Rome in 410. p. R12

Alexander the Great *356 B.C.–323 B.C.* Son of Philip. He was tutored by Aristotle and became king of Macedonia in 336 B.C. As ruler, Alexander built a huge empire. p. 346

Amani-Shakete (uh•MAN•uh•shuh•KAY•tay) *first century B.C.* Queen of ancient Meroë, in Nubia. p. 181

Amenemhet I (AHM•uhn•em•het) *1991 B.C.–1962 B.C.* Vizier who made Egypt an empire. His rule began the period called the Middle Kingdom, which lasted for 200 years. p. 151

Amenhotep IV *c. 1300s B.C.* Egyptian ruler who changed his name to Akhenaton. He and Nefertiti, his wife, urged the Egyptians to worship only one god, the Aton. p. 160

Antoninus Pius (an•tuh•NY•nuhs PY•uhs) *A.D. 86–A.D. 161* Emperor whose reign brought peace and prosperity to Rome. p. 518

Archimedes (ar•kuh•MEE•deez) *c. 287 B.C.–212 B.C.* Greek teacher and inventor who used mathematics to build many useful machines. p. 349

Aristarchus (a•ruh•STAR•kuhs) *c. 200s B.C.* Greek teacher who used mathematics to discover that Earth moves in a path around the sun. p. 349

Aristophanes (air•uh•STAH•fuh•neez) *c. 450 B.C.–c. 388 B.C.* Ancient Greek writer of comedies, or humorous plays. p. 327

Aristotle (AIR•uh•staht•uhl) *384 B.C.–322 B.C.* Greek philosopher and tutor of Alexander the Great. He is considered one of the greatest thinkers of all time. p. 331

Ashoka (uh•SHOH•kuh) *c. 200s B.C.* Maurya emperor remembered as "the greatest and noblest ruler India has known." p. 399

Ashvaghosa Indian poet who wrote *Life of the Buddha.* p. 394

Attalus III *?–133 B.C.* Last king of Pergamum. He gave the city to the Romans upon his death. p. 487

Augustus *63 B.C.–A.D. 14* Julius Caesar's grandnephew and adopted son Octavian, later known as Augustus. By defeating Mark Antony, he gained rule of all Roman lands. He was Rome's first true emperor. p. 509

B

Ban Zhao *A.D. 45–A.D. 115* The most important female scholar of the Han dynasty. p. 447

Bar Kokhba, Simon (BAR KAWK•bah) Jewish leader who led an unsuccessful revolt against the Romans, resulting in the exile of nearly all the Jews of Judah. p. 245

Brutus *85 B.C.–42 B.C.* Roman politician who helped plan and carry out Caesar's assassination. p. 507

Buddha *563 B.C.–c. 483 B.C.* Known as the "Enlightened One," he founded the religion of Buddhism in India. Originally named Siddhartha Gautama. p. 391

C

Caesar, Julius *100 B.C.–44 B.C.* Roman general and statesperson. He was dictator of Rome until he was murdered by a group of nobles. p. 495

Caligula *A.D. 12–A.D. 41* Roman emperor who demanded that his statue be placed in the Jewish Temple in Jerusalem. p. 517

Cassius *?–42 B.C.* Roman general and conspirator who helped plan and carry out Caesar's assassination. p. 507

Chandragupta I (chuhn•druh•GUP•tuh) *c. A.D. 300s* Gupta emperor of India. He gave up his throne to his son Samudragupta. p. 400

Chandragupta II (chuhn•druh•GUP•tuh) *reigned A.D. 375–A.D. 415* Gupta emperor who encouraged learning during his reign. p. 400

Chandragupta Maurya (chuhn•druh•GUP•tuh MOWR•yuh) *?–c. 297 B.C.* Emperor who united India. He gave up the throne to his son in 297 B.C. p. 397

Chavez, Cesar *1927–1993* Mexican American labor leader and organizer of the United Farm Workers. p. 318

Cicero (SI•suh•roh) *106 B.C.–43 B.C.* Roman orator, statesperson, and philosopher. He served as a consul of Rome. p. 559

Cincinnatus *c. 519 B.C.–430 B.C.* Roman general and statesperson. p. 478

Claudius *10 B.C.–A.D. 54* Roman emperor who added Britain to the Roman Empire. p. 517

Cleisthenes (KLYS•thuh•neez) *c. 570 B.C.–508 B.C.* Athenian leader who is regarded as the founder of democracy. p. 318

Cleopatra VII *69 B.C.–30 B.C.* Egyptian queen who, with Mark Antony, planned to set up an independent empire until the Roman leader Octavian defeated them. p. 508

Clovis *c. A.D. 466–A.D. 511* Leader of the Franks who captured the last Roman territory in Gaul. p. R13

Commodus *A.D. 161–A.D. 192* Roman emperor; son and successor of Marcus Aurelius. p. R6

Confucius *551 B.C.–479 B.C.* Philosopher considered the most revered person in Chinese history. His philosophy, known as Confucianism, became a guide for the way people lived. p. 427

Constantine (KAHN•stuhn•teen) *A.D. 280–A.D. 337* Roman general and emperor. The Edict of Milan, which was issued in 313 (during his reign), made Christianity an accepted religion within the Roman Empire. pp. 552, R11

Constantius (kuhn•STAN•chee•uhs) *c. A.D. 250–A.D. 306* Roman general and later emperor of Rome. Appointed by Diocletian to rule as part of the Rule of Four. p. R11

Cyrus II *c. 585 B.C.–529 B.C.* Also called Cyrus the Great. Leader who built the Persian Empire and conquered Babylon. p. 302

D

Darius I (duh•RY•uhs) *550 B.C.–486 B.C.* Persian ruler who brought order to the Persian Empire. He also built roads, established a postal system, and standardized weights, measures, and coinage. p. 302, 315

David *1025 B.C.–967 B.C.* Second king of Israel. He led the defeat of the Philistines. p. 214

Deborah *1100s B.C.* Hebrew prophet who rallied the Israelites in their struggles against Sisera. p. 225

Democritus (dih•MAH•kruh•tuhs) *c. 460 B.C.– c. 370 B.C.* Greek scientist and philosopher. p. 329

Dio Cassius *c. A.D. 155–A.D. 235?* Roman historian and administrator. p. R5

Diocletian (dy•uh•KLEE•shuhn) *c. A.D. 245–c. A.D. 313* As Roman emperor, he tried to strengthen the struggling empire. p. R11

Domitian *A.D. 51–A.D. 96* Roman emperor and son of Vespasian. p. 519

Draco *600s B.C.* Lawmaker who wrote the first recorded laws for Athens. p. 299

E

Eratosthenes (eh•ruh•TAHS•thuh•neez) *c. 275 B.C.–195 B.C.* Greek scholar. He is credited with measuring the circumference and diameter of Earth and the size of and distance from Earth to the sun and the moon. p. 348

Euclid (YOO•kluhd) *c. 300s B.C.* Greek teacher who began the study of geometry. p. 348

Ezra *400s B.C.* A Hebrew high priest who led many Jewish people back to Jerusalem after their Babylonian exile. p. 238

G

Galen *c. A.D. 130–c. A.D. 200* Greek physician whose medical findings include how blood flows through arteries and veins. p. 560

Galerius (guh•LIR•ee•uhs) *d. A.D. 310* Roman general and later emperor of Rome. Appointed by Diocletian to rule the eastern part of the empire as part of the Rule of Four. p. R11

Gandhi, Mohandas (GAHN•dee, moh•HAHN•dahs) *1869–1948* Indian nationalist and spiritual leader. He was called Mahatma, or "Great Soul," by his followers and is considered the founder of independent India. p. 393

Gautama, Siddhartha (GOW•tuh•muh, sih•DAR•tuh) *563 B.C.–c. 483 B.C.* Known as Buddha, or the "Enlightened One," he gave up worldly goods to search for enlightenment and truth. He founded the religion of Buddhism in India. p. 390

Gilgamesh *c. 2700s B.C.* King of the ancient Sumerian city-state of Uruk. He is the subject of one of the world's oldest stories. pp. 90, 113

Gracchus, Tiberius *163 B.C.–133 B.C.* Ancient Roman who, like his brother Gaius, died while working to change Roman law to help the plebeian class. p. 494

H

Hadrian *A.D. 76–A.D. 138* Adopted son of Trajan. He built a wall, called Hadrian's Wall, to mark the northernmost boundary of Roman Britain. pp. 518, R7

Hammurabi (ha•muh•RAH•bee) *1700s B.C.* King of the city-state of Babylon. He compiled the set of laws known as the Code of Hammurabi. pp. 120, 122

Han Gaozu (GOW•ZOO) *256 B.C.–195 B.C.* Founded the Han dynasty of China. He was a respected leader who combined ideas from Legalism and Confucianism. p. 443

Hannibal *247 B.C.–183 B.C.* Carthaginian general who attacked Rome during the Second Punic War. p. 486

Hatshepsut (hat•SHEP•soot) *1504 B.C.–1458 B.C.* Female Egyptian pharaoh who expanded Egyptian trade routes. p. 159

Herod the Great *73 B.C.–4 B.C.?* King of Judaea when Jesus was born. pp. 540, 543

Herodotus (hih•RAH•duh•tuhs) *c. 484 B.C.– 430 B.C.* Greek historian who traveled throughout most of the world known to the Greeks during his time. p. 329

Hesiod *c. 700s B.C.* Greek poet and author. pp. 293, 326

Hezekiah King of Judah who saved Jerusalem from an Assyrian invasion in 701 B.C. p. 223

BIOGRAPHICAL DICTIONARY

Hillel, Rabbi *30 B.C.–A.D. 10* Jewish scholar and the founder of *Beit Hillel* school. His interpretations of Jewish law were recorded in the Mishnah and Talmud. p. 246

Hippocrates (hih•PAH•kruh•teez) *c. 460 B.C.–377 B.C.* Greek physician known as the Father of Medicine. p. 328

Homer *c. 700s B.C.* Greek poet and author of the *Iliad* and the *Odyssey*. Much of what we know about the Mycenaeans comes from his stories. p. 279, 282, 292

Horace *65 B.C.–A.D. 8* Roman poet. p. 559

Huang Di (SHWAHNG•DEE) *c. 200s B.C.* Chinese ruler who ordered the invention of Chinese writing. p. 418

Hypatia (hy•PAY•shuh) *A.D. 370–A.D. 415* Greek philosopher, mathematician, and astronomer. She headed a school of philosophy in Alexandria, Egypt. pp. 348, 351

Isaac *c. 1900s B.C.* Son of Abraham; considered to be the ancestor of the Jewish people. p. 205

Ishmael *c. 1900s B.C.* Son of Abraham; considered to be the ancestor of the Arab people. p. 247

Jacob *c. 1900s B.C.* Early leader of the descendants of the Israelites. Later called Israel, he was the son of Isaac and grandson of Abraham. p. 206

Jeremiah *c. 600s B.C.* A Hebrew prophet of the seventh and sixth centuries B.C. p. 235

Jesus *c. 4 B.C.–c. A.D. 30* The person whose life and teachings are the basis of Christianity. Believing him to be the Son of God, his disciples proclaimed him the Messiah and savior of humankind. pp. 247, 543

Johanson, Donald *1943–* Paleoanthropologist who, along with Tim White, discovered the australopithecine nicknamed Lucy. p. 17

Joseph A son of Jacob who rose to high political office in Egypt and helped his family. p. 206

Justinian I *A.D. 483–A.D. 565* Byzantine emperor. His set of laws, known as the Justinian Code, is the basis of law in Europe today. p. R14

Kalidasa (kah•lih•DAH•suh) *A.D. 400–A.D. 455* An author during India's Golden Age. He is considered to be among India's greatest writers. p. 400

Kashta (KAHSH•tuh) *700s B.C.* King of ancient Kush; father of Piye. p. 179

Khafre *2000s B.C.* Son of King Khufu. During his reign, two more pyramids were built at Giza, as well as the Sphinx. p. 145

Khufu *c. 2500s B.C.* Egyptian king who built the Great Pyramid at Giza, the most famous of Egypt's pyramids. p. 145

King, Dr. Martin Luther, Jr. *1929–1968* African American civil rights leader who worked for equal rights in nonviolent ways. He won the Nobel Peace Prize in 1964. pp. 393, 483

King Minos *c. 2000s B.C.* According to legend, the ruler of ancient Crete during the years of its greatest success. p. 279

King Omri *800s B.C.* Self-proclaimed king of Israel. He founded the ancient city of Samaria and made it the capital of the northern kingdom of Israel in the early ninth century B.C. p. 223

Leakey, Louis *1903–1972* Scientist well known for his discoveries relating to early hominids. p. 14

Leakey, Mary *1913–1996* A scientist whose discovery of an early hominid in Tanzania, Africa, changed many scientists' ideas about the ancient past. pp. 14, 21

Lepidus *?–152 B.C.* Consul of Rome who, with Julius Caesar and Mark Antony, formed the Second Triumvirate. p. 507

Li Si (LEE SUH) *c. 260 B.C.* Adviser to Emperor Shi Huangdi of the ancient Qin dynasty in China. p. 433

Luke *first century A.D.* One of the twelve apostles, the group of men who were Jesus' closest followers; author of the third Gospel and the Acts of the Apostles. p. 543

M

Maccabee, Judah (MAK•uh•bee) *d. 160 B.C.* Jewish military leader who led a revolt against the Greeks, called the Revolt of the Maccabees. This revolt brought about a restoration of Jewish political and religious life. p. 245

Mahavira, Vardhamana *c. 600s B.C.* Founded the religion of Jainism. p. 393

Marcus Aurelius *A.D. 121–A.D. 180* Roman emperor and last of the "Five Good Emperors." The end of his reign brought the *Pax Romana* to an end. pp. 519, R5

Mark Antony *c. 82 B.C.–30 B.C.* Roman orator and general. He lost control of Roman lands when he was defeated by Octavian in 31 B.C. p. 507

Matthew *first century A.D.* One of the 12 apostles, the group of men who were Jesus' closest followers; author of the first book of the New Testament. p. 543

Maximian *?–A.D. 310* Roman general and later emperor of Rome. Appointed by Diocletian to rule the western part of the empire as part of the Rule of Four. p. R11

Moses *c. 1200s B.C.* Prophet and lawgiver who led the Israelites out of Egypt and received the Ten Commandments. p. 207

Muhammad *c. 570–632* Prophet who brought the message of Islam to the world. p. 247

Mummius *?–146 B.C.* Roman statesperson and general who put down a rebellion against Roman rule in Greece. p. 487

N

Naomi Mother-in-law of Ruth, of the Bible. p. 246

Narmer *c. 3000s B.C.* Ruler who united the Two Lands of Egypt. p. 143

Nebuchadnezzar (neb•uh•kuhd•NEZ•er) *d. 562 B.C.* King of Babylonian Empire. p. 124

Neferti Egyptian scribe who wrote of the hardships of famine in Egypt. p. 151

Nefertiti (neh•fer•TEE•tee) *c. 1300s B.C.* Wife of Akhenaton. p. 160

Nero *A.D. 37–A.D. 68* Roman emperor who was blamed for the burning of Rome. p. 517

Nerva *c. A.D. 30–A.D. 98* One of the "Five Good Emperors of Rome." p. 518

O

Octavian (ahk•TAY•vee•uhn) *63 B.C.–A.D. 14* Julius Caesar's great-nephew, later known as Augustus. By defeating Mark Antony, he gained rule of all Roman lands. He was Rome's first true emperor. p. 506

Odoacer (OH•duh•way•ser) *A.D. 433–A.D. 493* Germanic chief who overthrew the Roman emperor in the west. p. R12

Ovid *43 B.C.–A.D. 18* Roman poet. p. 559

P

Paul *c. A.D. 10–c. A.D. 67* Born a Jew, he converted to Christianity and became an apostle; formerly known as Saul, he founded new churches and wrote many epistles, or letters, about Jesus to church members. pp. 546, 555

BIOGRAPHICAL DICTIONARY

Pericles (PAIR•uh•kleez) *c. 495 B.C.–429 B.C.* Leader who ruled Athens during its Golden Age. pp. 318, 321

Peter *?–A.D. 64* One of the twelve apostles, the group of men who were Jesus' closest followers. p. 546

Philip II *382 B.C.–336 B.C.* King of Macedonia and father of Alexander the Great. p. 345

Pilate, Pontius *? B.C.–c. A.D. 36* Roman governor of Judaea. He was the judge at Jesus' trial and condemned Jesus to death by crucifixion. p. 545

Piye (PEE•yeh) *reigned 747 B.C.–716 B.C.* King of Kush and son of Kashta. He conquered Lower Egypt. Also known as Piankhi. p. 179

Plato *c. 428 B.C.–c. 348 B.C.* Greek philosopher, student of Socrates, and teacher of Aristotle. p. 331

Pliny the Younger (PLIH•nee) *c. A.D. 61–c. A.D. 113* Roman government official in Asia Minor. He is perhaps best remembered for his account of the volcanic eruption of Vesuvius. p. 551

Ptolemy (TAHL•luh•may) *300s B.C.* Greek astronomer in Alexandria, Egypt. p. 560

Pythagoras (puh•THAG•uh•rus) *c. 580 B.C.–500 B.C.* Greek philosopher and mathematician; the inventor of geometry. p. 328

R

Ramses II also **Ramses the Great** (RAM•seez) *1200s B.C.* Egyptian pharaoh perhaps best known for the temples he ordered built. p. 160

Rehoboam (ree•uh•BOH•uhm) The first king of Judah and son of Solomon. p. 220

Remus A descendent of Aeneas and twin brother to Romulus. p. 471

Romulus A descendent of Aeneas and twin brother to Remus; according to legend, the founder of Rome. p. 471

Ruth *1100s B.C.* Biblical figure known for her loyalty. p. 246

S

Samudragupta (suh•MUH•druh•GUP•tuh) *c. A.D. 300* Son of Chandragupta I of India's Gupta dynasty. He extended the empire. p. 400

Samuel *c. 1000s B.C.* Hebrew judge who appointed Saul as the first ruler of Israel. p. 213

Sargon *2000s B.C.* Warrior who founded the Akkadian Empire and so became the first ruler of an empire in the Fertile Crescent. p. 121

Saul *c. 1000s B.C.* First king of Israel. p. 213

Scipio (SIH•pee•oh) *c. 237 B.C.–183 B.C.* Roman general who defeated Hannibal of Carthage. p. 486

Senwosret I Son of Egyptian ruler Amenemhet I. p. 157

Shabaka (SHA•buh•kuh) *?–695 B.C.* Piye's brother and the pharaoh who firmly established the Kushite dynasty. p. 179

Shanakdakhete Kushite queen of ancient Meroë. p. 181

Shapur I (shah•PUR) *A.D. 241–A.D. 272* King of Persia. He attacked Rome's eastern provinces and defeated emperor Valerian. p. R7

Shen Nong *c. 200s B.C.* Chinese ruler who brought agriculture to the people of China. p. 418

Shi Huangdi (SHIR HWAHNG•DEE) *c. 259 B.C.–210 B.C.* Founder of the Qin dynasty and unifier of China. p. 432

Sima Qian (SOO•MAH CHIH•YIHN) *c. 100s B.C.* Scholar who recorded China's history during the Han dynasty. p. 445

Socrates (SAH•kruh•teez) *c. 470 B.C.–c. 399 B.C.* Greek philosopher who taught by asking questions. pp. 324, 330

Solomon *c. 900s B.C.* David's son and king of Israel. Under Solomon's rule, Israel rose to the height of its greatness. p. 215

BIOGRAPHICAL DICTIONARY

BIOGRAPHICAL DICTIONARY

Solon *c. 630 B.C.–c. 560 B.C.* Poet and statesperson who helped bring democracy to the Greek city-state of Athens. p. 299

Sophocles (SAH•fuh•kleez) *c. 496 B.C.–c. 406 B.C.* Ancient Greek writer of tragedies, or serious plays. p. 327

Taharqa (tuh•HAR•kuh) *c. 600s B.C.* Kushite pharaoh remembered for the many temples and pyramids he ordered built. p. 179

Tarquinius Priscus *616 B.C.–578 B.C.* Etruscan king of Rome. He carried out building projects, including paved streets and a sewer system in Rome. p. 472

Tarquinius Superbus *534 B.C.–510 B.C.* The last Etruscan king of Rome, who was expelled for his cruelty. p. 476

Theodosius I (thee•uh•DOH•shuhs) *c. A.D. 347–A.D. 395* Roman emperor who in 391 made Christianity the official religion of the Roman Empire. p. 550

Thucydides (thoo•SIH•duh•deez) *471 B.C.–c. 400 B.C.* Greek teacher who is considered the greatest historian of ancient times. p. 329

Thutmose III *c. 1500s B.C.* Son of Thutmose II. He continued Egypt's conquests after Pharaoh Hatshepsut. During his rule, the Egyptian Empire grew to its largest size and was its wealthiest. p. 159

Trajan *A.D. 53–A.D. 117* Adopted son of Nerva. During his reign as emperor, the Roman Empire grew to its largest size. pp. 518, 551

Tutankhamen (too•tahng•KAH•muhn) *c. 1370 B.C.–1352 B.C.* During his brief reign as pharaoh, his ministers restored the old religion of Egypt. Tutankhamen is perhaps best known for the discovery of his gold-filled tomb. p. 160

Urakagina *c. 2300s B.C.* Ruler of the city-state of Lagash, in Mesopotamia. He created laws to protect the poor. p. 116

Ur-Nammu *c. 2000 B.C.* Ruler of the ancient city-state of Ur, in Mesopotamia. p. 116

Valerian *A.D. 200–A.D. 260* Roman emperor who divided the Roman Empire into two parts. p. R7

Vespasian *A.D. 9–A.D. 79* Roman emperor who restored peace and stability to Rome following the death of Nero. p. 518

Virgil (VER•juhl) *70 B.C.–19 B.C.* Roman poet who wrote the epic poem Aeneid, which is about the founding of Rome. p. 518

White, Tim *1950–* Paleoanthropologist who, with Donald Johanson, discovered the australopithecine nicknamed Lucy. p. 17

Woolley, Leonard *1880–1960* Archaeologist who oversaw the excavation of the ancient city of Ur, in Mesopotamia. p. 106

Wu Di (WOO DEE) *?–86 B.C.* Han ruler who established a civil service administration to run the daily business of government in China. p. 444

Xerxes (ZERK•seez) *c. 519 B.C.–c. 465 B.C.* King of Persia and son of Darius I. p. 316

Yohanan ben Zaccai (yoh•HAN•uhn ben ZAK•ay•eye) *15 B.C.–A.D. 85* Founder of the Jewish academy at Yavneh. p. 245

Zoser *c. 2600s B.C.* King of Egypt. p. 145

Gazetteer

The Gazetteer is a geographical dictionary that can help you locate places discussed in this book. Place-names are listed alphabetically. Hard-to-pronounce names are followed by pronunciation guides. A description of the place is then given. The absolute location, or latitude and longitude, of each city is provided. The page number that follows tells where each place is shown on a map. Guide words at the top of each page help you locate the place-name you need to find.

A

Abu Hureyra Site of an ancient settlement in present-day northern Syria. p. 67

Adriatic Sea An extension of the Mediterranean Sea; located east of Italy and west of the Balkan Peninsula. p. 271

Afghanistan A country in central Asia; located between Pakistan and Iran. p. 375

Africa One of the world's seven continents. p. 26

Akkad (AH•kahd) The capital of the ancient Akkadian Empire; located in southwestern Asia. p. 123

Akkadian Empire An area in ancient Mesopotamia located between the Tigris and Euphrates Rivers; ruled by Sargon in about 2300 B.C. p. 123

Alexandria (a•lig•ZAN•dree•uh) A port on the Mediterranean Sea; located on the northern coast of Egypt on the Nile Delta. (31°N, 30°E) p. 346

Alps The largest group of mountains in Europe; located in France, Switzerland, Italy, Austria, Slovenia, Bosnia and Herzegovina, Serbia and Montenegro, Croatia, and Albania. p. 271

Amazon River The largest river in the world; flows across northern Brazil into the Atlantic Ocean. p. R19

Anchorage A coastal city in southern Alaska. (61°N, 150°W) p. 353

Andes A mountain system in South America that extends along the western coast. p. 36

Antarctica One of the world's seven continents. p. 26

Appalachian Mountains (a•puh•LAY•chee •uhn) A large chain of mountains in the United States that extends from Maine to northern Georgia and central Alabama. p. R19

Arabia The historic name for the lands now known as the Arabian Peninsula, the Sinai Peninsula, Syria, and Mesopotamia. p. 238

Arabian Peninsula A peninsula bordered by the Red Sea, the Persian Gulf, and the Arabian Sea in southwestern Asia; location of the countries of Saudi Arabia, Yemen, Oman, the United Arab Emirates, Qatar, and Kuwait. p. 206

Arabian Sea The sea located west of India and east of the Arabian Peninsula; forms the southern border of southwestern Asia. p. 238

Aral Sea (AR•uhl) A large inland body of water located in the countries of Kazakhstan and Uzbekistan in central Asia. p. 238

Arctic Ocean One of the world's oceans. p. 26

Argos An ancient Greek city-state. (38°N, 23°E) p. 291

Asia One of the world's seven continents. p. 26

Asia Minor A peninsula at the western end of Asia; located between the Black Sea and the Mediterranean Sea; now occupied by Turkey. p. 103

Assur (AH•soor) An ancient Mesopotamian city on the Tigris River. (36°N, 43°E) p. 123

Assyrian Empire (uh•SIR•ee•uhn) An ancient empire in southwestern Asia. p. 123

Aswan An ancient trade center and a present-day city; located in south-eastern Egypt on the Nile River, near Lake Nasser and the Aswan Dam. (24°N, 33°E) p. 136

Aswan High Dam An embankment dam across the Nile River, at Aswan, Egypt, measuring 364 feet high. p. 136

Atacama Desert (ah•tah•KAH•mah) A desert in the north-central part of Chile in South America. p. R19

Athens An ancient Greek city-state; the capital of present-day Greece; located near the southeastern coast of Greece. (38°N, 24°E) p. 291

Atlantic Ocean One of the world's oceans. p. 26

Atlas Mountains A mountain system in northern Africa. p. 271

Attica (A•tih•kuh) An ancient region in the southeastern part of the Greek mainland; home of the ancient Greek city-state of Athens. p. 291

Australia One of the world's seven continents; a present-day country filling the continent of Australia. p. 26

B

Babylon The capital of the ancient Babylonian Empire; located on the Euphrates River in central Iraq. (33°N, 44°E) p. 103

Babylonian Empire (ba•buh•LOH•nyuhn) An ancient kingdom in the lower Tigris–Euphrates River valley in southwestern Asia. p. 123

Balkan Peninsula A peninsula extending from mainland Europe into the Mediterranean Sea; occupied by Greece, Albania, Slovenia, Croatia, Bosnia and Herzegovina, Serbia and Montenegro, Romania, Macedonia, Bulgaria, and part of Turkey. p. 271

Bangladesh (bahn•gluh•DESH) A country in southern Asia on the coast of the Bay of Bengal. p. 375

Bay of Bengal An inlet of the Indian Ocean that runs alongside eastern India. p. 375

Beijing (BAY•JING) The capital of China; located in northeastern China. (40°N, 116°E) p. 436

Belize (buh•LEEZ) A country in Central America. p. R25

Black Sea A sea between Europe and Asia, surrounded by Bulgaria, Romania, Moldova, Ukraine, Russia, Georgia, and Turkey. p. 96

Britain A western European kingdom; includes England, Scotland, Wales, and northern Ireland. p. R12

Britannia Name given by the Romans to the portion of the island of Great Britain that they occupied. p. R6

C

Caledonia The ancient Roman name for present-day Scotland. p. R6

Caribbean Sea (kar•uh•BEE•uhn) The sea bordered by Central America, South America, and the West Indies. p. R19

Cartagena (kar•tah•HAY•nah) An ancient and present-day city in southeastern Spain. (38°N, 1°W) p. 487

Carthage (KAR•thij) An ancient Phoenician city-state; located on the northern coast of present-day Tunisia. (37°N, 10°E) p. 487

Caspian Sea A salt lake between Europe and Asia, east of the Black Sea. p. 95

Çatal Hüyük (CHAH•tahl HOO•yook) One of the earliest human agricultural settlements discovered, dating from c. 7000 B.C. to 5600 B.C.; located in central Turkey. (38°N, 33°E) p. 67

Central America The southernmost part of the continent of North America. p. R19

Chang Jiang (CHAHNG JYAHNG) A river in eastern China; flows from the Plateau of Tibet to the East China Sea. p. 415

Chang'an (CHAHNG•AHN) An ancient capital of the Han dynasty of China; now known as Xi'an, or Sian; located in central China on the Wei River. (34°N, 109°E) p. 443

Chichén Itzá (chee•CHAYN it•SAH) An ancient Mayan city in what is now Mexico. (21°N, 88°W) p. R25

Chongqing The largest city of Szechwan Province, China. The leading river port and industrial center in southwestern China. (105°E, 32°N) p. 63

Constantinople (kahn•stan•tuh•NOH•puhl) Formerly the ancient city of Byzantium; rebuilt, renamed, and made the capital of the Byzantine Empire by Constantine I in A.D. 330; present-day Istanbul, Turkey. (41°N, 29°E) p. R11

Corinth An ancient city-state and a present-day Greek city; located on the isthmus between the Peloponnesus and the Greek mainland. (38°N, 23°E) p. 281

Corsica A French island in the Mediterranean Sea; located west of Italy. p. 470

Crete The largest Greek island; located southeast of the Balkan Peninsula; separates the Mediterranean and Aegean Seas. p. 271

Cyclades Islands (SIH•kluh•deez) A group of islands in the southern Aegean Sea, between the Peloponnesus and the Dodecanese. p. 274

Cyprus (SY•pruhs) An island country in the eastern Mediterranean Sea. p. 271

Cyrene (sy•REE•nee) An ancient city in northern Africa; located in Libya on the Mediterranean Sea. (33°N, 22°E) p. 487

Dallas A city in northeastern Texas. (33°N, 97°W) p. 353

Dead Sea A salt lake in Israel and Jordan; the world's lowest place at 1,302 feet below sea level. p. 206

Deccan Plateau (DEH•kuhn) A triangle-shaped plateau in central India, between the Western and Eastern Ghats. p. 400

Delphi (DEL•fy) A place sacred to the ancient Greeks; located in central Greece, near the Gulf of Corinth. (38°N, 22°E) p. 281

East China Sea The part of the China Sea north of Taiwan. p. 415

Eridu (AIR•uh•doo) The earliest-known Sumerian city in Mesopotamia; located on the Euphrates River in present-day Iraq. (31°N, 46°E) p. 67

Euphrates River (yoo•FRAY•teez) A river that begins in Turkey, flows through Syria and Iraq, and empties into the Persian Gulf. p. 67

Europe One of the world's seven continents. p. 26

Fertile Crescent An area of land in southwestern Asia; extends from present-day Israel through Lebanon, Syria, Turkey, and Iraq to the Persian Gulf. p. 67

France A country in western Europe. p. 29

Ganges River (GAN•jeez) A river regarded as holy in India; flows from the Himalayas into the Bay of Bengal. p. 375

Gaul An ancient land that included most of the present-day countries of France and Belgium; once part of the Roman Empire. p. 507

Germany A country located in north-central Europe. p. 29

Gobi A desert in eastern Asia; located in Mongolia and China. p. 415

Great Plains The western part of the Interior Plains in North America. p. R19

Greenland The largest island in the world; located off northeastern North America; a territory of Denmark. p. R19

GAZETTEER

Greenwich (GREH•nich) Part of the city of London, England; the meridian it lies on serves as the center for time zones around the world. (52°N, 0°) p. 353

Guatemala A country in Central America; formerly part of the region controlled by the Maya and later a colony of Spain. p. R25

Gulf of Mexico A gulf located south of the United States, east of Mexico, and west of Cuba. p. R25

Harappa (huh•RA•puh) An ancient center of Indus civilization; located in the Indus Valley, in present-day Pakistan. (32°N, 73°E) p. 375

Harbin The capital of Heilungkiang province; located in northeastern China. (46°N, 127°E) p. 63

Himalayas (hih•muh•LAY•uhz) A mountain system on the northern edge of southern Asia; runs through Nepal, Bhutan, southern Tibet, and northern India. p. 375

Hittite Empire An ancient empire in Asia Minor; stretched from Mesopotamia to Syria and Palestine and included present-day Turkey. p. 206

Honduras A country in Central America; located between the Caribbean Sea and Guatemala. p. R25

Huang He (HWAHNG HUH) A river in China that flows east from the Plateau of Tibet. p. 415

Iberian Peninsula A peninsula that forms southwestern Europe; extends into the Atlantic Ocean and the Mediterranean Sea; occupied by the countries of Portugal and Spain. p. 271

India A country in southern Asia; occupies much of a large peninsula extending from central Asia into the Indian Ocean; the name given to the ancient land that is present-day Pakistan and India. p. 375

Indian Ocean One of the world's four oceans. p. 26

Indus River A river in southern Asia; flows from Tibet, through northern India and Pakistan, and into the Arabian Sea. p. 375

Ionian Sea A sea located east of Italy and west of Greece. p. 271

Iran A country in southwestern Asia; formerly known as Persia; located on the Persian Gulf. p. 375

Israel An ancient kingdom and present-day country in southwestern Asia; a holy land for Jews, Christians, and Muslims; located on the eastern coast of the Mediterranean Sea. p. 221

Italian Peninsula A boot-shaped peninsula that extends from south-central Europe into the Mediterranean Sea. p. 271

Ithaca (IH•thi•kuh) An ancient and present-day Greek island and its chief town. (38°N, 21°W) p. 281

J

Jarmo Site of the ancient agricultural village of Qalat Jarmo; located in northern Iraq. (36°N, 45°E) p. 67

Jericho (JAIR•ih•koh) The oldest known city in the world; located north of the Dead Sea, in present-day Jordan. (32°N, 35°E) p. 67

Jerusalem The capital of Israel; a holy city for Jews, Christians, and Muslims. (32°N, 35°E) p. 206

Judah An ancient kingdom in southwestern Asia; located between the Mediterranean and Dead Seas. p. 221

GAZETTEER

Kenya A country in eastern Africa. p. 29

Kerma A capital of the ancient kingdom of Kush; located on the Nile River in Sudan. (20°N, 31°E) p. 135

Kish An ancient Sumerian city-state on the Euphrates River, located in present-day Iraq. (32°N, 45°E) p. 103

Knossos (NAHS•uhs) A city and capital of ancient Crete located near the north coast of the island. (35°N, 35°E) p. 281

Kush An ancient Nubian kingdom; located in the Nile Valley in the northern part of present-day Sudan. p. 179

La Venta An ancient Olmec city in what is now Mexico. (I8°N, 94°W) p. R22

Lima (LEE•mah) The capital of Peru, in South America; an ancient Inca city. (12°S, 77°W) p. 353

Lower Egypt The northernmost section of Egypt, stretching from just south of present-day Cairo to the Nile Delta at Alexandria. p. 135

Lydia An ancient land located on the western end of Asia Minor, in present-day Turkey in southwestern Asia. p. 238

M

Macedonia A present-day Balkan country; an ancient kingdom near the Aegean Sea, located on lands that are part of present-day Greece and Turkey. p. 238

Marathon (MA•ruh•thahn) An ancient Greek town in eastern Attica; the site of an ancient Greek victory during the Persian Wars. (38°N, 24°E) p. 281

Mediterranean Sea The sea south of Europe, north of Africa, and west of Asia; connects to the Atlantic Ocean, the Red Sea, and the Black Sea. p. 67

Memphis An ancient Egyptian capital; located along the Nile River in northern Egypt. (30°N, 31°E) p. 135

Meroë (MAIR•oh•wee) A capital of the ancient kingdom of Kush; located on the eastern bank of the Nile River in northern Sudan. (17°N, 34°E) p. 135

Mexico A country in southern North America; located between the United States and Central America. p. R22

Mississippi River The largest river in the United States; flows from Minnesota to the Gulf of Mexico. p. R19

Mount Olympus A mountain believed to be the home of the gods and goddesses of ancient Greek mythology; located on the eastern coast of Greece. p. 271

Mycenae (my•SEE•nee) A city-state and empire in ancient Greece; located on the eastern side of the Peloponnesus. (38°N, 23°E) p. 271

Napata (NA•puh•tuh) A capital of the ancient kingdom of Kush; located on the east bank of the Nile River, in northern Sudan. (19°, 32°E) p. 135

Nazareth (NA•zuh•ruhth) A city in northern Israel. (33°N, 35°E) p. 221

Nile River A river in northeastern Africa; flows from Lake Victoria to the Mediterranean Sea on the northeastern coast of Egypt. p. 95

Nippur (ni•PUR) An ancient Sumerian and Babylonian city in what is today called southwestern Asia, in present-day central Iraq. (32°N, 45°E) p. 103

North America One of the world's seven continents. p. 26

Nubia (NOO•bee•uh) An ancient land in Africa that extended along the Nile River from Egypt's southern border near present-day Khartoum, Sudan. p. 173

Nubian Desert A desert region in Sudan, Africa; east of the Nile River. p. 173

GAZETTEER

O

Olympia A plain in the northwestern Peloponnesus; an ancient Greek religious center and site of the ancient Olympic Games. (38°N, 22°E) p. 281

Oman (oh•MAHN) A country in southwestern Asia; located on the Arabian Peninsula. p. 241

P

Pacific Ocean The largest of the world's oceans. p. 26

Pakistan A country in southern Asia. p. 375

Peloponnesus (peh•luh•puh•NEE•suhs) A wide peninsula on the southern end of Greece; home of the ancient city-states of Sparta and Corinth. p. 271

Persepolis (per•SEH•puh•luhs) The capital of the ancient Persian Empire; located near Shiraz in present-day Iran. (30°N, 53°E) p. 238

Persia The core of the Persian Empire; former name of present-day Iraq. p. 238

Persian Gulf A gulf in southwestern Asia; connected to the Gulf of Oman and the Arabian Sea. p. 96

Philistia (fih•LIS•tee•uh) An ancient land in southwestern Asia. p. 214

Phoenicia (fuh•NEE•shuh) An ancient land; located in present-day Syria and Lebanon. p. 214

Pindus Mountains A mountain range in northwestern Greece. p. 271

Po River A river in northern Italy; flows from Mount Viso into the northern Adriatic Sea. p. 487

Pyrenees (PIR•uh•neez) The mountain range that separates the Iberian Peninsula from Europe; forms the border between Spain and France. p. 487

R

Red Sea The sea between northeastern Africa and the Arabian Peninsula; connected to the Mediterranean Sea by the Suez Canal and to the Arabian Sea by the Gulf of Aden. p. 95

Rocky Mountains A range of mountains in North America extending from Alaska to New Mexico; this range divides rivers that flow east from those that flow west. p. R19

Rome The capital of the ancient Roman Empire and of present-day Italy; located on the Tiber River. (42°N, 12°E) p. 469

Russia A historic empire and the largest republic of the former Soviet Union; a present-day country in northeastern Europe and northern Asia. p. R14

S

Sahara A desert covering the northern third of Africa. p. 135

Samaria An ancient area of southwestern Asia; located between Judaea and Galilee. p. 223

Saudi Arabia A country that occupies most of the Arabian Peninsula in southwestern Asia. p. 96

Sea of Galilee A freshwater lake in northern Israel, also known as Lake Tiberias. p. 221

Shechem (SHEH•kuhm) An ancient town located north of Jerusalem, Israel. (32°N, 35°E) p. 206

South Africa A country located on the southern tip of Africa, between the Atlantic and Indian Oceans. p. 29

South America One of the world's seven continents. p. 26

GAZETTEER

South China Sea The part of the China Sea south of Taiwan. p. 394

Spain A country in southwestern Europe; located on the Iberian Peninsula. p. 507

Sparta An ancient Greek city-state and rival of Athens; located on the southern end of the Peloponnesus. (37°N, 22°E) p. 291

Sumer (SOO•mer) An ancient region in southern Mesopotamia; located on the Persian Gulf, in what is today southeastern Iraq. p. 96

Syria A country located on the eastern end of the Mediterranean Sea. p. 346

Taurus Mountains A mountain range in southern Turkey; runs parallel to the southern Mediterranean coast and the border between Turkey and Syria. p. 67

Thar Desert Also called the Great Indian Desert; located in India and Pakistan. p. 400

Thebes The capital of ancient Egypt during the Middle Kingdom; located in southern Egypt. (26°N, 33°E) p. 135

Thermopylae (ther•MAH•puh•lee) The site of an ancient Greek defeat during the Persian Wars; a mountain pass in southern Greece. (39°N, 23°E) p. 316

Thrace An ancient land; located in what are now the countries of Turkey, Bulgaria, Macedonia, and much of northwestern Greece. p. 238

Tiber River A river in central Italy; flows from the Apennine Mountains, through Rome, and into the Tyrrhenian Sea. p. 469

Tigris River A river in southwestern Asia; begins in eastern Turkey and joins the Euphrates River. p. 67

Tikal (tih•KAHL) An ancient Mayan city in what is now Guatemala. (17°N, 89°W) p. R25

Troy An ancient city in northwestern Asia Minor. (40°N, 26°E) p. 271

Turkey A country located in southeastern Europe and southwestern Asia. p. 241

Tyrrhenian Sea (tuh•REE•nee•uhn) The sea located west of the Italian Peninsula, north of Sicily, and east of Sardinia and Corsica. p. 271

United Arab Emirates A country on the eastern Arabian Peninsula. p. 241

Upper Egypt A narrow strip of land that extends from present-day Aswan to the area south of present-day Cairo. p. 135

Ur (UR) A city in ancient Sumer; located on the Euphrates River, near present-day southeastern Iraq. (31°N, 46°E) p. 67

Uruk An ancient Sumerian city in southwestern Asia; located near the eastern bank of the Euphrates River, in present-day southeastern Iraq. (31°N, 46°E) p. 103

Wei River A river in north-central China; flows across Shaanxi to the Huang He. p. 415

Yellow Sea The sea west of the Korean Peninsula and east of China. p. 415

Yemen (YEH•muhn) A country on the Arabian Peninsula in southwestern Asia. p. 241

Yucatán Peninsula (yoo•kah•TAHN) A peninsula extending from the eastern coast of Central America; occupied by the countries of Mexico, Belize, and Guatemala. p. R25

Glossary

The Glossary contains important history and social science words and their definitions, listed in alphabetical order. Each word is respelled as it would be in a dictionary. When you see the mark ´ after a syllable, pronounce that syllable with more force. The page number at the end of the definition tells where the word is first used in this book. Guide words at the top of each page help you quickly locate the word you need to find.

add, āce, câre, pälm; end, ēqual; it, īce; odd, ōpen, ôrder; tŏŏk, pōōl; up, bûrn; yōō as *u* in *fuse*; oil; pout; ə as *a* in *above*, *e* in *sicken*, *i* in *possible*, *o* in *melon*, *u* in *circus*; check; ring; thin; this; zh as in *vision*

A

acropolis (ə•krä´pə•ləs) A fort built on top of a large hill. p. 289

adapt (ə•dapt´) To change to fit the surroundings. p. 24

aesthetic (es•the´tik) Relating to beauty. p. 400

afterlife (af´tər līf) Life after death. p. 137

agora (a´gə•rə) An open-air market where people gathered to trade and discuss the news of the day in Greek city-states. p. 289

agriculture (a´gri•kul•chər) The knowledge of raising plants and animals. p. 51

alluvial plain (ə•lōō´vē•əl plān) A low, flat land formed from fine soil left behind by streams. p. 96

almanac (ôl´mə•nak) Writings that include information that describes the best way to plant, irrigate land, and care for crops. p. 109

ambassador (am•ba´sə•dər) A government representative. p. 445

annex (ə•neks´) To add on. p. 175

apostle (ə•pä´səl) A person who traveled throughout the Roman Empire, teaching people about Jesus and that he was the Messiah. p. 546

aqueduct (a´kwə•dəkt) A system of bridges and canals that carry water from a natural source, such as a river, to a town. p. 522

arable (ar´ə•bəl) Good for growing crops. p. 469

archaeology (är•kē•ä´lə•jē) The study of things that earlier people left behind. p. 15

architecture (är•kə•tek´chər) A style of building. p. 106

arid (ar´əd) Very dry. p. 135

artifact (är´ti•fakt) A human-made object, especially from long ago; artifacts include art, clothing, pottery, tools, and weapons. p. 15

Aryan (ar´ē•ən) A warrior and herder from central Asia who migrated to India beginning in about 1500 B.C. p. 385

assassinate (ə•sa´sən•āt) To murder a leader for political reasons. p. 496

assembly (ə•sem´blē) A lawmaking group. p. 297

authority (ə•thôr´ə•tē) The right to rule. p. 104

B

baptize (bap´tīz) To symbolically purify of one's sins. p. 552

barbarian (bär•ber´ē•ən) A Germanic invader who was not fully educated in Roman ways. p. R7

bard (bärd) A professional storyteller who traveled from town to town, telling stories and singing songs about Greek gods, goddesses, and heroes. p. 282

barter (bär´tər) To trade for things people want. p. 60

Buddhism (bōō´di•zəm) A religion based on the teachings of Siddhartha Gautama, who became known as the Buddha. p. 391

bureaucracy (byōō•rok´rə•sē) A network consisting of appointed officials. p. 434

canonize (kan´ə•nīz) To become an official part of a certain teaching. p. 238

caravan (kar´ə•van) A group of traders traveling together on a long journey. p. 105

cartogram (kär´tə•gram) A diagram that gives information about places by showing them in different sizes. p. 490

caste (kast) A group of people in a particular social class. p. 387

cataract (ka´tə•rakt) Rapids, or waterfalls. p. 135

cause (côz) An event or action that makes something else happen. p. 556

census (sen´səs) A count of the people in a certain place. p. 522

character (kar´ik•tər) A symbol that represents whole words. p. 424

Christianity (kris•chē•an´ə•tē) The religion based on the life and teachings of Jesus Christ. p. 247

circle graph (sûr´kəl graf) A graph that shows information by means of a circle divided into parts. p. 322

citadel (sit´ə•dəl) A fortlike structure. p. 377

city-state (sit´ē•stāt) A city and the farmlands around it. p. 103

civil service (siv´əl sûr´vəs) A part of a bureaucracy that oversees the day-to-day running of a government. p. 444

civil war (siv´əl wôr) A war between two groups in the same nation. p. 151

civilization (siv•ə•lī•zā´shən) A society with developed forms of religion and ways of governing. p. 70

classify (kla´sə•fī) To group items of information. p. 126

climograph (klī´mə•graf) A kind of graph that shows both the average monthly temperature and the average monthly precipitation for a place. p. 420

Code of Hammurabi (kōd əv ha•mə•rä´bē) The collection of laws that Hammurabi organized for the people of Babylon to follow. p. 122

codex (kō´deks) A hand-lettered book of glyphs, or other writing, that contains a record of such matters as religion and learning. p. R29

colony (kä´lə•nē) A new settlement separated from but ruled by a homeland. p. 291

comedy (kom´ə•dē) A humorous play. p. 327

commerce (kä´mûrs) Large-scale trade. p. 291

commercial (kə•mər´shəl) Related to large-scale trading. p. 173

compromise (käm´prə•mīz) An agreement reached when each person in a conflict gives up some of what he or she wants. p. 342

confederation (kən•fe•də•rā´shən) A group of governments joined together for a common purpose. p. 472

conflict (kän´flikt) A disagreement. p. 342

conformal projection (kən•fôr´məl prə•jek´shən) A map projection that shows directions correctly but distorts the sizes of places, especially near the poles. p. 140

Confucianism (kən•fyoo´shə•ni•zəm) The ideas of the Chinese philosopher Confucius, which are used as a guide for the way people should live. p. 427

conquer (käng´kər) To take over. p. 121

consequence (kän´sə•kwens) A result of an action. p. 25

consul (kän´səl) One of two chief officials who held office in the ancient Roman Republic in place of a king. p. 478

contour line (kän´toor līn) A line on a relief map that connects all points of equal elevation. p. 62

convert (kən´vərt) A person who changed his or her religion. p. R13

cordillera (kôr•dəl•yer´ə) A group of mountain ranges. p. R19

cost-benefit analysis (kost•be´nə•fit ə•na´lə•səs) An examination made to decide whether to carry on trade. p. 152

covenant (kəv´ə•nənt) A special agreement. p. 205

cultural borrowing (kulch´rəl bär´ə•wing) The process by which a culture takes ideas from other cultures. p. 281

culture (kul´chər) A way of life shared by members of a group. p. 31

cuneiform (kyoo•nē´ə•fôrm) A writing system based on wedge-shaped symbols. p. 112

currency (kə´rən•sē) Money. p. 516

D

decipher (dē•sī´fər) To figure out the meaning of something. p. 181

deity (dē´ə•tē) One exalted or revered as supremely good or powerful, such as a god. p. 118

delta (del´tə) A triangle-shaped piece of fertile land formed from soil deposited at the mouth of a river. p. 135

demagogue (de´mə•gäg) A weak leader who is popular because he tells people what they want to hear, even if it is not true. p. 336

democracy (di•mä´krə•sē) Rule by the people. p. 290

dharma (dər´mə) A religious duty. p. 389

dialect (dī´ə•lekt) A way of speaking. p. 417

Diaspora (dī•as´pə•rə) The scattering of Jews outside their homeland. p. 237

dictator (dik´tā•tər) A ruler with complete power. p. 478

dictatorship (dik•tā´tər•ship) A governing system in which absolute power is held by one person or a small group. p. 337

diplomacy (də•plō´mə•sē) The skill of conducting negotiations. p. 143

direct democracy (də•rekt´ di•mä´krə•sē) A system in which all citizens make decisions about their government. p. 318

disciple (di•sī´pəl) A follower of a religion. p. 544

distortion (di•stôr´shən) An area that is not accurate on a map projection. p. 140

diviner (də•vī´nər) A person who could speak to the gods and to ancestors. p. 424

division of labor (də•vi´zhən əv lā´bər) A system in which people do different jobs according to their abilities and the needs of the group. p. 69

domesticate (də•mes´tə•kāt) To tame plants or animals for human use. p. 50

drought (drout) A long period of time with little or no rain. p. 49

dynasty (dī´nəs•tē) A series of rulers from the same family. p. 143

E

editorial cartoon (e•də•tōr´ē•əl kär•tōōn´) A cartoon that represents the artist's point of view about people, current events, or politics. p. 526

effect (i•fekt´) The result of an event or action. p. 556

elevation map (el•ə•vā´shən map) A map that shows the elevation of the land in relation to sea level. p. 62

emperor (em´pər•ər) The ruler of an empire. p. 121

empire (em´pīr) Vast lands and varied people under the control of a single government. p. 121

enlightenment (in•lī´tən•mənt) The complete understanding of truth. p. 392

environment (en•vī´rən•mənt) Surroundings. p. 24

epic (e´pik) A long poem. p. 282

equal-area projection (ē´kwəl âr´ē•ə prə•jek´shən) A map projection that shows an equal area on either side of the prime meridian and on either side of the equator; it shows the sizes of regions in correct relation to one another but distorts shapes. p. 140

essential (i•sen´shəl) Needed to understand a subject fully. p. 156

exile (eg•zīl) The act of being forced to leave one's homeland. p. 235

Exodus (ek´sə•dəs) The mass departure of the Israelites from Egypt to escape slavery. p. 207

export (ek´spōrt) To send out goods for sale to other places. p. 175

extinct (ik•stingt´) No longer found on Earth. p. 24

F

fable (fā´bəl) A short story that uses animal characters to teach a lesson. p. 301

GLOSSARY

fact (fakt) A statement that can be proved to be true. p. 72

famine (fā´mən) A food shortage. p. 151

feudalism (fyōō´dəl•i•zəm) A political system of exchanging land for loyalty and protection. p. 425

filial piety (fi´lē•əl pī´ə•tē) Treating parents with honor and respect. p. 427

flowchart (flō´chärt) A diagram that shows the order in which things happen. p. 380

forum (fōr´əm) A public square in ancient Roman cities. p. 471

fossil (fä´səl) The remains, such as bones, of humans and animals that were once alive. p. 15

frontier (frən•tir´) Borderlands. p. R6

G

gladiator (gla´dē•ā•tər) A criminal, slave, or prisoner of war of ancient Rome who was trained at a special school and then forced to fight to the death for entertainment. p. 524

government (gə´vərn•mənt) An organized system of leaders and laws. p. 69

granary (grā´nə•rē) A place for storing grain. p. 377

H

harbor (här´bər) A sheltered place with deep water close to shore. p. 273

heir (âr) A person entitled to receive the money or property of a person who has died. p. 507

Hellenistic Age (he•lə•nis´tik āj) A Greek-like age. p. 347

helot (he´lət) A person conquered by Sparta who became a slave. p. 297

heritage (hâr´ə•tij) A set of ideas that have been passed down from one generation to another. p. 417

hieroglyph (hī´rə•glif) Pictures or symbols that stand for sounds, words, or ideas. p. 144

Hindu-Arabic numeral (hin´dōō ar´ə•bik nōōm´rəl) A numeral in a system of mathematics based on nine numerals and a zero. p. 401

Hinduism (hin´dōō•i•zəm) A religion that developed from the Aryans' religious beliefs and the beliefs of the ancient people of India. p. 388

hominid (hä´mə•nəd) Any member of different species with humanlike features. p. 17

humankind (hyōō´mən•kind) The human race. p. 23

hunters and gatherers (hən´tərz and ga´thər•ərz) Members of *Homo sapiens* who spent many hours a day searching for food. p. 25

I

import (im´pōrt) To bring in goods from other places. p. 175

incidental (in•sə•dən´təl) Not needed to gain knowledge of a subject. p. 156

independence (in•də•pen´dəns) Freedom. p. 176

inflation (in•flā´shən) A rise in prices caused by a decrease in the value of money. p. R8

innovation (i•nə•vā´shən) A new way of doing things. p. 109

interest (in´tə•rəst) The extra money that a bank pays a person to let the bank use that person's funds. p. 218

international date line (in•tər•na´shə•nəl dāt līn) The meridian where the eastern and western time zones meet. p. 352

irrelevant (i•re´lə•vənt) Unrelated to a subject. p. 156

irrigation (ir•ə•gā´shən) Ways to move water to land. p. 59

Islam (is•läm´) The religion of Muslims, based on belief in one God, or Allah. p. 247

isthmus (is´məs) A small strip of land connecting larger land areas. p. 271

Judaism (jōōˊdə•i•zəm) The religion of the Jewish people. p. 205

karma (kärˊmə) Actions that determine the caste into which a person will be reborn. p. 389

land use (land yōōs) What is done with most of the land in a particular place or region. p. 100

latitude (laˊtə•tōōd) The distance north or south of the equator. p. 28

league (lēg) A group of allies. p. 303

Legalism (lēˊgə•li•zəm) A way of governing that gives absolute power to the ruler. p. 433

legend (leˊjənd) A story handed down from earlier times that explains the past. p. 282

legion (lēˊjən) A group of a few thousand soldiers, particularly in ancient Roman times. p. 515

livestock (līvˊstäk) Domesticated animals that provide resources. p. 51

loess (les) A deposit of yellow silt. p. 415

longitude (länˊjə•tōōd) The distance east or west of the equator. p. 28

M

majority rule (mə•jorˊə•tē rōōl) A system in which every member has one vote, and in which the person or idea that receives the most votes is chosen. p. 300

Mandate of Heaven (manˊdāt əv heˊvən) An order given by the god Tian to the Zhou kings to rule over China. p. 425

martyr (märˊtər) A person who chooses to die rather than to give up his or her religion. p. 547

meditate (meˊdə•tāt) To concentrate so deeply that the mind becomes clear and calm. p. 391

mercenary (mərˊsən•er•ē) A soldier who is willing to fight in the army of a foreign country for pay. p. 339

merchant (mərˊchənt) A person who sells goods bought from traders. p. 69

Mesoamerica (meˊzō•ə•mer•i•kə) The ancient lands of Mexico and Central America. p. R20

messiah (mə•sīˊə) A savior. p. 544

metallurgy (meˊtəl•ər•jē) The science and technology of metals. p. 401

migrate (mīˊgrātˊ) To move from one place to another. p. 20

missionary (miˊshə•ner•ē) A person who takes his or her religious ideas to other parts of the world. p. 399

monarchy (monˊər•kē) The governing system in which a king or a queen rules. p. 104

monk (mənk) A man who devotes his life to studying and teaching religious beliefs. p. 394

monotheism (mäˊnə•thē•i•zəm) The concept of one God. p. 205

monsoon (män•sōōnˊ) A seasonal wind. p. 376

multicultural (məl•tē•kəlch´rəl) Relating to many different peoples and cultures. p. 348

mummy (məˊmē) A preserved body. p. 146

mystery religion (misˊtər•ē ri•liˊjən) A religion that featured ceremonies celebrating the seasons, the "death" of autumn, and the "rebirth" of spring. p. 539

myth (mith) A story about how the actions of gods and goddesses affected the lives of people. p. 283

mythology (mith•äˊlə•jē) A collection of myths passed down from generation to generation. p. 283

GLOSSARY

nation-state (nā´shən•stāt) A region with a united group of people and a single government. p. 143

nirvana (nir•vä´nə) In Buddhism, the highest state of the human mind, free from the desires that lead to human suffering and ignorance. p. 392

nomad (nō´mad) A person with no settled home. p. 31

oligarchy (ä´lə•gär•kē) Rule by a few. p. 290

opinion (ə•pin´yən) A statement that cannot be proved. p. 72

opportunity cost (ä•pər•tōō´nə•tē kôst) What is given up because of an economic choice. p. 218

oracle bone (ôr´ə•kəl bōn) An animal bone or turtle shell used by the ancient Chinese to find out about the future. p. 424

Paleolithic era (pā•lē•ə•li´thik ər´a) The earliest period of the Stone Age. p. 18

papyrus (pə•pī´rəs) A paperlike material on which ancient Egyptians wrote. p. 144

parable (pa´rə•bəl) A simple story that teaches lessons about life. p. 544

parallel time line (par´ə•lel tīm līn) A time line that is made up of two or more time lines. p. 54

pastoral society (pas´tə•rəl sə•sī´ə•tē) A group of people living as nomads with herds of animals. p. 61

patrician (pə•tri´shən) A wealthy landowner descended from the earliest settlers of Rome. p. 480

patriotism (pā´trē•ə•ti•zəm) Loyalty to one's country. p. 561

peasant (pe´zənt) A poor farmer. p. 281

peninsula (pə•nin´sə•lə) A stretch of land almost completely surrounded by water. p. 271

persecution (pər•si•kyōō´shən) Punishment for having beliefs that differ from those of others. p. 546

personal finances (pər´sən•əl fī´nan•səs) Individual money matters. p. 218

pharaoh (fer´ō) A ruler of ancient Egypt. p. 159

plague (plāg) A disaster. p. 207

plateau (pla•tō´) A high, flat area of land. p. 96

plebeian (pli•bē´ən) A Roman citizen who was not a patrician. p. 480

plow (plou) A tool used to cut, lift, and turn over soil. p. 59

polis (pä´ləs) A Greek city-state that connected a city and the farms, towns, and villages around it. p. 289

polytheism (pä´lē•thē•i•zəm) A belief in many gods. p. 104

pope (pōp) The leader of the Roman Catholic Church. p. 554

population density (po•pyə•lā´shən den´sə•tē) The number of people who live in 1 square mile or 1 square kilometer of land. p. 276

predict (pri•dikt´) To tell in advance. p. 137

prehistory (prē•his´tə•rē) The period of time before people began to write. p. 15

primary source (prī´mer•ē sôrs) A record made by someone who saw or took part in an event. p. 286

prime meridian (prīm mə•ri´dē•ən) The line that runs from north to south through Greenwich, England, near the city of London. p. 28

projection (prə•jek´shən) One of many different views showing the round Earth on a flat map. p. 140

prophet (prä´fət) A person who is believed to receive messages from God. p. 236

GLOSSARY

proverb (prä´vərb) A short saying that expresses a truth about life. p. 216

province (prä´vəns) An administrative region of a country. p. 434

pyramid (pir´ə•mid) A structure that served as tombs for Egyptian rulers. p. 145

R

rabbi (ra´bī) A person who teaches the history and laws of Judaism. p. 236

raw material (rô mə•tir´ē•əl) A natural resource that can be made into a valuable product. p. 174

reform (ri•form´) A change. p. 299

reign (rān) A time of rule. p. 159

reincarnation (rē•in•kär•nā´shən) The belief that souls are reborn into other beings after death. p. 389

relevant (re´lə•vənt) Directly related to a subject. p. 156

relief map (ri•lēf´ map) A map that shows the different heights or depths of hills, valleys, and other physical features. p. 62

representative democracy (re•pri•zen´tə•tiv di•mä´krə•sē) A democracy in which citizens elect other people to make decisions for them. p. 318

republic (ri•pu´blik) A form of government in which citizens elect leaders to represent them. p. 478

resurrection (re•zə•rek´shən) Return to life. p. 546

role (rōl) The part a person plays in society; responsibility. p. 31

romanize (rō´mə•nīz) To make Roman in character. p. 485

rural (roor´əl) Relating to the country. p. 161

S

salvation (sal•vā´shən) The saving of the human soul from evil with a promise of happiness after death. p. 551

Sanskrit (san´skrit) A language of India first spoken by the ancient Aryans. p. 386

scribe (skrīb) A person who records things for others. p. 112

secondary source (se´kən•der•ē sôrs) A source that provides information about an event by someone who was not an eyewitness. p. 287

sect (sekt) A group within a religion that has a different set of teachings. p. 541

Senate (se´nət) A group of 300 leading men in Rome who advised the consuls. p. 478

Silk Road (silk rōd) The most heavily traveled trade routes that stretched 4,000 miles from the Han capital through the deserts and high plains of central Asia to the Mediterranean Sea. p. 445

silt (silt) Soil and tiny rocks carried or deposited on the land by floodwaters. p. 96

slash-and-burn farming (slash•and•bərn fär´ming) A system of farming in which thick forestlands are cut and burned to prepare the soil for planting. p. 52

social class (sō´shəl klas) A group that has a specific level of importance in a society. p. 69

society (sə•sī´ə•tē) A group of people living and working under a set of rules and traditions. p. 31

standardization (stan•dər•də•zā´shən) Making systems, such as money, weights and measures, and writing, the same for everyone. p. 435

standing army (stan´ding är´mē) A permanent army. p. 121

steppe (step) A dry, treeless grassland. p. 416

subcontinent (sub•kän´tən•ənt) A large area of land isolated from the rest of a continent by geographic features. p. 375

subsist (səb•sist´) To survive. p. 57

surplus (sər´pləs) An extra supply. p. 52

synagogue (si´nə•gäg) A Jewish place of worship. p. 236

taxation (tak•sā´shən) A system in which people pay taxes to support a government. p. 70

technology (tek•nə•lä•jē) The proper application of knowledge to develop new tools or ways to make and do things. p. 23

temperate zone (tem´pə•rət zōn) The areas north and south of the tropical zone. p. R19

Ten Commandments (ten kə•mand´mənts) A set of laws for responsible behavior given to Moses by God. p. 208

terrace (ter´əs) Flat areas built on the slopes of hills and mountains. p. 58

terrace farming (ter´əs fär´ming) Growing crops in terraces dug into the slopes of hills and mountains. p. 416

territory (ter´ə•tôr•ē) A region. p. 214

theocracy (thē•ä´krə•sē) A state ruled by religious law. p. 238

theory (thē´ə•rē) A proposed explanation about life. p. 15

time zone (tīm zōn) A division of Earth in which all places have the same time. p. 352

Torah (tōr´ə) The oldest religious writings of the Jewish people. p. 205

trade-off (trād´ôf) The giving up of one thing to get another. p. 218

trade network (trād net´wərk) A group of buyers and sellers. p. 181

tragedy (tra´jə•dē) A serious play in which the main characters come to an unhappy end. p. 327

trend (trend) A way something changes over time. p. 548

tribune (tri´byoōn) In ancient Rome, a leader elected to protect the plebeians' interests. p. 481

tributary (tri´byə•ter•ē) A river that flows into a larger river. p. 96

tribute (tri´byoōt) A required payment from one ruler to a more powerful ruler. p. 120

Trinity (tri´nə•tē) One God made up of a Father, a Son, and a Holy Spirit. p. 552

tripartite (trī•pär´tīt) Having three parts. p. 478

triumvirate (trī•əm´və•rət) A group of three rulers. p. 495

tropical zone (trä´pi•kəl zōn) An area in which all land falls within 1,600 miles of the equator. p. R19

turning point (tûrn´ing point) A point at which a sudden change occurs. p. 399

tyrant (tī´rənt) A person who takes control of a government by force. p. 290

unverifiable (ən•ver•ə•fī´ə•bəl) Cannot be proved. p. 156

urban (ûr´bən) Relating to a city or cities. p. 70

vandal (van´dəl) Someone who purposely damages property. p. R12

Vedas (vā´dəz) Sacred texts that formed the foundation of ancient civilizations of India and that are some of the oldest texts in the world. p. 386

verifiable (ver•ə•fī´ə•bəl) Can be proved. p. 156

veto (vē´tō) To reject. p. 318

virtue (vər´choō) A good quality. p. 425

vizier (və•zir´) The chief adviser to an ancient Egyptian king. p. 143

ziggurat (zi´gə•rat) The largest and tallest temple in every Sumerian city-state. p. 111

GLOSSARY

Index

The Index lets you know where information about important people, places, and events appear in the book. All entries are listed in alphabetical order. For each entry, the page reference indicates where information about that entry can be found in the text. Page references for illustrations are set in italic type. An italic *m* indicates a map. Page references set in boldface type indicate the pages on which vocabulary terms are defined. Guide words at the top of each page help you identify which words appear on which page.

INDEX

INDEX

INDEX

INDEX

INDEX

INDEX

Sites. *See* Archaeological sites

Skills. *See* Chart and Graph Skills; Critical Thinking Skills; Focus Skills; Map and Globe Skills; Participation Skills; Study Skills

Skimming, 408

Slash-and-burn farming, 52, R26

Slavery
  Africans and, 237
  in Egypt, 161, 206, 207, 210
  in Greek city-states, 297, 299, 313, 339
  in Mesoamerica, R27
  in Rome, 480, 485, 486, 487, 493, 494, 521, 522–523, 524, 551, R8
  in Sumerian city-states, 118, *118*

Sloths, giant, 24, *25*

Smithsonian Institute, *15*

Snow, in China, *420*

Social class, 69
  in China, 423, 425, 434, *434*, 443
  in early towns, 69
  in Egypt, 161
  in Greece, 281, 300
  in India, 387, *388*, 389
  in Mesoamerica, R22, R27
  in Olmec culture, R22
  in Rome, 480–481, *480*, *481*, 482–483, *482*, *483*, 492, *492–493*, 493
  in Sumer, 118–119, *118*

Social Studies. *See* Reading Social Studies

Society, 31
  complex, 56–61, *57*, *58–59*, 69
  pastoral, *2*, **61**, *61*

Socrates, *258*, 324, *329*, 330, 341, *341*, R89

Socratic Method, 330

Solomon
  as king of Israel, *194*, 215–217, *216*, 220, 221, 246, R89
  proverbs of, 216, *216*
  temple of, *196*, *214–215*, 215, *218*, 245

Solon (Greek leader), 299, 300, *300*, 305, *305*, R90

Sophocles, *259*, 327, R90

Sounion, Cape, *m273*

Sources
  citing, R81
  primary vs. secondary, 286–287, 307. *See also* Primary Sources

South America
  agriculture in, 36, 51, *54*, R21
  Andes Mountains in, 36, *36–37*, *m36*, 51

art of, R21, *R21*
climate in, R19, *mR19*
cultures of, R21, *R21*
hunters and gatherers in, 36–37, *36–37*, *m36*
mountain ranges in, R19, *mR19*
religion in, R21

Southern Hemisphere, 28

Southwestern Asia, 2
  agriculture in, 34, 48, *48–49*, *m49*, 50, 51, *51*, 52, *58–59*, 59, 70
  climate changes in, 49
  early river valley civilizations in, 95, *m95*
  farming villages in, 57, *57*, 58, *58–59*
  land use and products map of, 100–101, *m101*, 129
  languages of, *m241*
  religion in, 67, 68, 69
  settlements in, 66, *66*, 67, *m67*
  trade in, 67, 68, 69
  See also Mesopotamia

Southwestern United States, Anasazi in, *361*

Spain
  Hannibal's army in, 486
  trade in, 516

Sparta (Greek city-state), *261*, 289, *m291*, *m297*, 310
  Athens under control of, 337
  concerns about Persia in, 303
  education in, 296, *296–297*, 298, *298*
  government of, 297
  life in, 298, *298*
  in Persian Wars, 315, 316, 317
  population of, 297
  population density around, 359, *m359*
  rivalry with Athens, 317, 329
  ruins of theater in, *338*
  slavery in, 297, 339
  trade in, 339
  at war with Athens, 334–337, *334*, *m335*, *336–337*
  women in, 298

Spear(s), 23, 33, 35, *35*, *39*, *294*

Spear throwers, 23

Specialized workers, *3*, 70, *70*, 117

Speeches, persuasive, 40, 228, 354, 498

Sphinx (Egypt), 142, *142*, *144*, 145, *148*, 160

Spices, 175, 516

Squash, 36, R20, R22, R26

Staffs, royal (Egyptian), *165*

Stamp, *73*

Standard of Ur, *107*, *108*

Standardization, *363*, 435, *435*, 439

Standing army, 121

Stanford, Dr. Dennis, *15*

Statues, *66*, *71*, *87*, 113, 155, *161*, 162, *162*, *180*, 325, *325*, 340, *386*, 432, *442*, 484, *488*, 506, *R10*, R22

Step Pyramid at Saqqara, 145

Steppes, 416

Stone Age News, The (MacDonald), 44–47

Stone tools, *2*, 18, *m18–19*, 20, 23, 34, *39*, R26

Stories, writing, 139

Storytelling, Greek, *278*, *278*, 282–283, 285

Study Skills, 8, 42, 88, 130, 168, 200, 230, 264, 308, 368, 408, 464, 500, 532

Stylus, *320*, *528*, *529*

Subcontinent, 375, *m375*

Subsist, 57

Sudan, *169*, 173, 176, *177*, 180, 188, *189*

Sudras (Indian class), 387, *388*

Sulla (Roman general), 494, 495

Sumer, 96, *m96*, 99
  art of, 87, *87*, 113, *114*
  building blocks of civilization in, 199
  daily life in, 114–119, *115*, *116–117*, *119*
  legends of, 90–93
  number system in, 110
  political systems in, 199
  writing in, 103, 105, 109, 112–113, *112*

Sumerian Achievements (Odom), 192

Sumerian city-states, 102–107
  architecture in, 106, *110–111*, 111, 115
  children in, 119
  commerce in, *104–105*, 105
  conquest of, *120–121*, 121
  culture of, 103
  Eridu, 103, *m103*
  government of, 104, 116
  Kish, 103, *m103*, 112, 121
  law in, 104, 116
  life in, 115
  literature of, 113
  marketplace in, 115, *116–117*
  measurements in, 110
  metalworking in, 109, 114, *115*, 117
  population of, 103
  religion in, 104, 106, 118
  size of, 103
  slavery in, 118, *118*
  social structure in, 118–119, *118*
  trade in, *104–105*, 105, 117
  Ur, 102, *102*, 103, *m103*, 106–107, *106–107*, 111
  Uruk, 70, 90–93, 99, 103, *m103*, 112

women in, 119

Summaries, writing, 80, 360

Summarizing, 86–87, 99, 107, 113, 119, 124, 128, 139, 147, 154, 163, 166, 177, 182, 186

Sun god
  Egyptian, 137, 145
  Persian, 539, *539*

Sundials, 445

Sunzi, 430, 431, *431*

Surplus, 52
  of food, 52–53, 57, 60, 67, 69, 78, 95, 97, 98, 103, 105, 117, 136, 138
  trade and, *3*, 53, 60, 67, 117

Symbols
  of authority in Rome, *478*
  of Christ, 552

Synagogue, 236, *236–237*

Syria, 34, 44–47, 152, 540. *See also* Abu Hureyra

Syrian Desert, 67

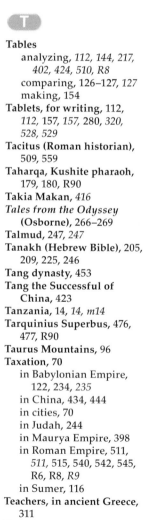

Tables
  analyzing, *112*, *144*, *217*, *402*, *424*, *510*, *R8*
  comparing, 126–127, *127*
  making, 154

Tablets, for writing, 112, *112*, 157, *157*, 280, *320*, *528*, *529*

Tacitus (Roman historian), 509, 559

Taharqa, Kushite pharaoh, 179, 180, R90

Takia Makan, *416*

Tales from the Odyssey (Osborne), 266–269

Talmud, 247, *247*

Tanakh (Hebrew Bible), 205, 209, 225, 246

Tang dynasty, 453

Tang the Successful of China, 423

Tanzania, 14, *14*, *m14*

Tarquinius Superbus, 476, 477, R90

Taurus Mountains, 96

Taxation, 70
  in Babylonian Empire, 122, 234, *235*
  in China, 434, 444
  in cities, 70
  in Judah, 244
  in Maurya Empire, 398
  in Roman Empire, 511, *511*, 515, 540, 542, 545, R6, R8, *R9*
  in Sumer, 116

Teachers, in ancient Greece, 311

Technology, 23
  agricultural, 59, 109
  aqueducts, 522, *523*, 560, R14
  bridges, *484*, 485, *485*, 560, *564*

INDEX

INDEX

Vedas, 386, *386,* 388
Vegetarianism, 393
Verifiable information, 156, *156*
Verner, Miroslav, 149, *149*
Vespasian (Roman emperor), 518, R90
Vesuvius, Mount (Roman Empire), 502–505
Veto, 318
Villa, Roman, *520–521*
Villages, farming, 57–58, *58–59*
Virgil (Roman poet), 518, *518, 529,* 559, R90
Virtue, 425, *434*
Vishnu the Preserver (Hindu god), *386,* 388
Visigoths, R12, *mR12*
Vizier, 143
Volcanoes
  in Central America, R19
  on Italian Peninsula, 469, 502–505
Voting rights
  in Greece, 318
  in Rome, 478
  in United States, *483*

Wall(s)
  around cities, 70, 91, 103, 223, 334, 335, 336, 337, 377, 378, 423, 484
  Great Wall of China, *363, 409,* 436, *436–437, m436,* 439
  Hadrian's Wall, *R6–R7,* R7
  around houses, 68
  around palace, 104
  around towns, 67
  Western Wall (Jerusalem), *231, 252*
Wall paintings
  in Egypt, *134, 150,* 151
  in Greece, 280, *286*
  of Hannibal's army, *486*
  in India, 401
  in Rome, *473, 528*
Wall relief, *126, 334,* 485, 511, *525,* R9
War(s)
  civil, 151, 494, 507, R6
  Greek, 294–295, *294, 295*
  Peloponnesian, *257,* 334–337, *334, m335, 336–337,* 342
  Persian, 315–317, *m316–317*
  Punic, *458,* 486, *486*
  Trojan, 267–268, 278, *278, 282, 282,* 285, 293
  See also Battles
Warring Kingdoms (States) Period, 426, 433
Warshaw, Robin, 80
Water buffalo, 58, 98
Water clocks, 445

Water supplies, in cities, 70
Waterfalls, 135, *m135. See also* Cataracts
Weather
  agriculture and, 57
  near Nile River, 135, 136
Wei River Valley, 425, 426, 433
Western Roman Empire
  decline of, R10–R15, *mR12*
  end of, R12, *R13*
  Germanic kingdoms in, R13
Western Wall (Jerusalem), *231,* 240, *252*
Wetlands, 98, *98–99*
Wheat, 44, 46, 49, *49, 57,* 58, 67, 98, 108, 110, 117, 135, 138, 181, 272, 274, 376, 385, 469
Wheel, *383*
Wheeled carts, *108,* 112, 199
White, Tim, 17, R90
Who Were the Romans? **(Cox),** 466–467
Women
  in agriculture, *50,* 52
  in art, 87, *87*
  Chinese, 447, *447*
  early modern humans, 24
  in Egypt, *82, 83,* 145, 155, *155,* 159, 161, *161, 259, 459,* 508, *508*
  as gatherers, 49
  as gladiators, 524
  in Greece, 298, 301, 318
  in Israel, 216
  in Kush, 181, *181*
  as leaders, *82, 83,* 155, *155,* 159, 181, *181,* 216, 508, *508*
  Mayan, R27
  men playing in theater, 327, 525
  in Rome, *480, 519,* 521, 524, 551
  as scholars, 348, *348,* 351, *351*
  in Sparta, 298
  in Sumerian city-states, 119
  voting rights of, *483*
Wood, uses of, *2,* 33
Woolley, Leonard, 106, 111, R90
Word web, 42
World
  political map of, *m490*
  population of, *m276–277, 491*
Writing
  in Americas, R22, R23, R29, *R29*
  Chinese, 367, 418, 423, 424, *424,* 435
  in civilizations, 71, 138
  cuneiform, 112–113, *112, 234*
  Egyptian, 132–133, *133,* 138, 144, *144,* 146, *147,* 154, *292*

  in Greece, 280, 281, 284, 292, *292, 320*
  Hebrew, *217*
  hieroglyphs, 132–133, *133,* 144, *144,* 146, *147,* 154, *164,* R29, *R29*
  Hindi, 367
  of Indus Valley civilization, 377
  for information, R80
  of Judaism, 246, *246,* 247, *247*
  Kushite, 181
  Nubian, 181
  Olmec, R22, R23, R25
  Persian, *331*
  Phoenician, 199, 292, *292*
  prehistory and, 15, 38
  Roman, 528–529, *528, 529*
  Sumerian, 103, 105, 109, 112–113, *112*
Writing activities
  advertisements, 128
  ballads, 354
  classroom code, 124
  comparison-contrast essay, 456
  editorials, 306
  explanations, 107
  expository writing, 74, 166, 228, 498, 562
  interpretations, 250
  journal entries, 20
  letters, 186, 303, 473, R80
  lists, 248
  myths, 562
  narrative, 74, 128, 166, 186, 192, 406, 450
  narrative poetry, 530
  newspaper articles, 340, 554, R9
  paragraphs, 74, 166, 228, 256, 275, 402, 428, 498, 562
  persuasive writing, 40, 186, 228, 306, 354, 498
  proposals, 530
  questions, 37
  research reports, 40, 250, 406
  Response to Literature, 306, 450
  stories, 139
  summaries, 80, 360
  travel narrative, 406
Written reports, 40, 250, 406, R81–R82
Wu, king of China (Zhou dynasty), 425
Wu Di, emperor of China, *362,* 444, 445, R90

Xerxes, emperor of Persia, 316–317, R90
Xia dynasty (China), 418–419
Xi'an, China, 443, 452, *452–453, m452*

Xianyang, China, 434, 443
Xilingshi, empress of China, 418, 422

Yangshao farming culture (China), 58
Yangtze (Chang Jiang) River, 415, *m415,* 416, 423
Yellow Sea, 415, *m415*
Yohanan ben Zaccai, *195,* 245, 249, *249,* R87
Yom Kippur, 247
Yu the Great, 414, 418, *418–419*

Zama, Battle of, 486, 489
Zealots, 249
Zeman, Ludmila, 90–93
Zengzhou, China, 423
Zeus, Greek god of thunder and lightning, 283, *283,* 293, 537, *537*
Zheng, king of China, 426
Zhou dynasty (China), 424–428, *m425,* 426, 433, 434, *434, m440,* 448
Ziggurats, *85, 110–111,* 111, 115
Zinc, 401
Zoser, king of Egypt, 145, R90

For permission to reprint copyrighted material, grateful acknowledgment is made to the following sources:

Atheneum Books for Young Readers, an imprint of Simon & Schuster Children's Publishing Division: From *The Shipwrecked Sailor: An Egyptian Tale with Hieroglyphs* by Tamara Bower. Copyright © 2000 by Tamara Bower.

David Barry and BookStop Literary Agency: The Rajah's Rice, adapted by David Barry. Text copyright © 1994 by David Barry.

Candlewick Press Inc., Cambridge, MA, on behalf of Walker Books Ltd., London: From *The Stone Age News* by Fiona Macdonald. Text copyright © 1998 by Fiona Macdonald; illustrations copyright © 1998 by Walker Books Ltd.

Children's Press, a Scholastic Library Publishing imprint: From *Modern Rhymes About Ancient Times: Ancient Africa* by Susan Altman and Susan Lechner. Text © 2001 by Children's Press®; a division of Scholastic Inc.

Clarion Books/Houghton Mifflin Company: "The Thaw" from *Maroo of the Winter Caves* by Ann Turnbull. Text copyright © 1984 by Ann Turnbull.

Eerdmans Books for Young Readers: From *Masada: The Last Fortress* by Gloria D. Miklowitz. Text © 1998 by Gloria D. Miklowitz.

Holiday House, Inc.: "The Prodigal Son" from *The Parables of Jesus,* retold by Tomie dePaola. Copyright © 1987 by Tomie dePaola.

Hyperion Books for Children: From *Tales from the Odyssey: The One-Eyed Giant* by Mary Pope Osborne. Text copyright © 2002 by Mary Pope Osborne.

Margaret K. McElderry Books, an imprint of Simon & Schuster Children's Publishing Division: "The Tower of Babel" from *God's People: Stories from the Old Testament,* retold by Geraldine McCaughrean. Text copyright © 1997 by Geraldine McCaughrean.

Donna Perrone: Illustrations by Donna Perrone from *The Rajah's Rice,* adapted by David Barry. Illustrations copyright © 1994 by Donna Perrone. Illustrations by Donna Perrone from *Modern Rhymes About Ancient Times: Ancient Africa* by Susan Altman and Susan Lechner. Published by Children's Press, a Scholastic Library Publishing imprint, 2001.

Scholastic Inc.: From *The Secrets of Vesuvius* by Sara C. Bisel, illustrations by Laurie McGaw. Text copyright © 1990 by Sara C. Bisel and family and The Madison Press Limited.

Tundra Books: From *Gilgamesh The King,* retold and illustrated by Ludmila Zeman. © 1992 by Ludmila Zeman. Published by Tundra Books, Toronto and in the United States by Tundra Books of Northern New York.

Usborne Publishing, 83-85 Saffron Hill, London EC1N 8RT, UK : From *Who Were the Romans?* by Phil Roxbee Cox, illustrated by Annabel Spenceley. Copyright © 2002 by Usborne Publishing Ltd. Distributed in the USA by EDC Publishing.

Viking Penguin, A Division of Penguin Young Readers Group, A Member of Penguin Group (USA) Inc., 345 Hudson St., New York, NY 10014: From *The Emperor's Silent Army: Terracotta Warriors of Ancient China* by Jane O'Connor. Text copyright © 2002 by Jane O'Connor.

David West Children's Books, 7 Princeton Court, 55 Felsham Road, London SW15 1AZ: From *All in a Day's Work: Athletes and Actors* by Anita Ganeri. Copyright © 1997 by David West Children's Books; text copyright © 1997 by Anita Ganeri.

All maps by MapQuest.com

PHOTO CREDITS

PLACEMENT KEY: (t) top; (b) bottom; (l) left; (r) right; (c) center; (bg) background; (fg) foreground; (i) inset.

COVER

Cover: Ian M Butterfield/Alamy Images (Statue of Queen Hatshepsut); Jon Arnold/DanitaDelimont.com (Pont du Gard, Provence, France); Jon Arnold/DanitaDelimont.com (Parthenon, Acropolis, Athens, Greece); Tibor Bognar/(Great Wall).

Endsheet imagery: Ian M Butterfield/Alamy Images (Statue of Queen Hatshepsut); Jon Arnold/DanitaDelimont.com (Pont du Gard, Provence, France); Keren Su/ DanitaDelimont.com (Landscape of Great Wall).

TITLE PAGE AND TABLE OF CONTENTS

ii-iii Panoramic Images; iv: Gianni Dagli Orti/Corbis; v (l) Scala/Art Resource, NY; v (r) Erich Lessing/Art Resource, NY; vi The Granger Collection, New York; vii (l) Jürgen Liepe; vii (r) Bode Museum, Berlin, Germany/Bridgeman Art Library; ix (l) Erich Lessing/Art Resource, NY; ix (r) National Gallery of Budapest/Dagli Orti (A)/The Art Archive; x (l) Mary Evans Picture Library; x (r) JFB/The Art Archive; xi Nimatallah/Art Resource, NY; xii (l) Doranne Jacobson/International Images; xii (r) By permission of The British Library; xii Laurent Lecat/akg-images; xiv (l) Araldo de Luca/Corbis; xiv (r) Erich Lessing/Art Resource, NY; xv (l) Réunion des Musées Nationaux/Art Resource, NY ; xv (r) Mary Evans Picture Library

UNIT 1

Opener 1-2 National Geographic Image Collection; 8-9 Richard A. Cooke/Corbis; 14 Bob Campbell/National Geographic Image Collection; 15 Kenneth Garrett/National Geographic Image Collection; 16 (t) Kenneth Garrett/National Geographic Image Collection; 16 (tl) Jonathan Blair/Corbis; 17 (b) Ferorelli Enterprises, Inc.; 17 (br) John Reader/Photo Researchers, Inc.;18 (tc) Robin Siegel/National Geographic Image Collection; 18 (tr) Pascal Goetgheluck/Photo Science Library/Photo Researchers, Inc.; 19 John Reader/Photo Researchers, Inc.; 20 AP/Wide World Photos; 21 (br) Kenneth Garrett/National Geographic Image Collection; 21 (tl) National Geographic Image Collection; 24 (b) Sisse Brimberg/ National Geographic Image Collection; 24 (bl) Sisse Brimberg/National Geographic Image Collection; 31 (tr) Archivo Iconografico, S.A./Corbis; 32 Roger De La Harpe; Gallo Images/Corbis; 36-37 Digital Vision; 38 Kenneth Garrett Photography; 39 (tl, cl, br) Musée des Antiquités St Germain en Laye /Dagli Orti/The Art Archive; 39 (t, bl, cr) Musée des Antiquités St Germain en Laye /Dagli Orti/The Art Archive; 42-43 Stuart Franklin/Magnum Photos; 48-49 Cover Image by G. C. Hillmann from VILLAGE ON THE EUPHRATES: THE EXCAVATION OF ABU HUREYRA by Andrew M. T. Moore and A. Legge, copyright 1999 by Oxford University Press, used by Permission of Oxford University Press, Inc./Oxford University Press; 49 Dorling Kindersley Ltd. Picture Library; 52 Francoise de Mulder/Corbis; 53 (c) AAAC/ Topham/The Image Works, Inc.; 53 (cr) The British Museum/Topham-HIP/The Image Works, Inc.; 54 (b) Caroline Penn/Corbis; 57 Courtesy of the Oriental Institute of the University of Chicago; 60 (b) James L. Otis/ Corbis; 60 (bl) James L. Amos/Corbis; 60 (br) Erich Lessing/Art Resource, NY; 64 Pictures of Record, Inc.; 65 (br) Richard Hutchings/ PhotoEdit; 65 (cr) Patrick Molnar/Taxi/Getty Images; 65 (t) Spencer Grant/PhotoEdit; 65 (tr) ChromoSohm/Photo Researchers, Inc.; 66 (b) Christine Osborne Pictures/MEP; 66 (br) Erich Lessing/Art Resource, NY; 70 (tl) Scala/Art Resource, NY; 70 (tr) Erich Lessing/Art Resource, NY; 70 (tr) Scala/Art Resource, NY; 71 Gianni Dagli Orti/Corbis; 72 Museum of Anatolian Civilisations Ankara / Dagli Orti/The Art Archive; 73 (tl) Ara Guler/Magnum Photos; 073 (tl) Pictures of Record, Inc.; 73 (tr) Pictures of Record, Inc.; 73 (itr) Pictures of Record, Inc.; 74 Christine Osborne Pictures/MEP; 75 (tr) Gianni Dagli Orti/Corbis; 76-77 (bg) Sisse Brimberg/National Geographic Image Collection; 76 (ic) Sisse Brimberg/National Geographic Image Collection; 76 (it) Gamma Press, Inc.; 77 (ic) AFP/Getty Images; 77 (icl) AFP/Getty Images; 77 (icr) Gamma Press, Inc.; 77 (t) Charles Walker/Topham/The Image Works, Inc.; 78 (bl) Jonathan Blair/ Corbis; 78 (tr) The British Museum/Topham-HIP/The Image Works, Inc.; 78 (tr) Archivo Iconografico, S.A./Corbis

UNIT 2

Opener 81-82 akg-images; 86-87 (bg) Michael S. Yamashita/Corbis; 87 (br) Erich Lessing/Art Resource, NY; 88-89 Charles & Josette Lenars/Corbis; 95-96 (b); Nik Wheeler; 96 (tl) The British Museum/Topham-HIP/The Image Works, Inc.;97 Gellie Yves/Gamma Press, Inc.; 98-99 (b) Nik Wheeler; 98 (tc) Réunion des Musées Nationaux./Art Resource, 100 Getty Images Editorial; 102 University of Pennsylvania Museum (neg# S4-141575); 106 (tc) Topham/The Image Works, Inc.; 106 (tr) Ashmolean Museum, University of Oxford, UK/Bridgeman Art Library; 107 (tc helmet) Scala/Art Resource, NY; 107 (tc) Erich Lessing/Art Resource, NY;

107 (tl) The British Museum/Topham-HIP/ The Image Works, Inc.; 107 (tr) The British Museum/Topham-HIP/The Image Works, Inc.; 107 (tr game) The British Museum/ Topham-HIP/The Image Works, Inc.; 108 Michael Holford Photographs; 109 Michael S. Yamashita/Corbis; 113 (tl) Mary Evans Picture Library; 113 (tr) Musée du Louvre Paris/ Dagli Orti/The Art Archive; 114 Courtesy of the Oriental Institute of the University of Chicago, photographed by Victor J. Boswell, Jr., National Geographic Society; 122 Erich Lessing/Art Resource, NY; 125 Erich Lessing/ Art Resource, NY; 127 British Museum/ Dagli Orti/The Art Archive; 129 The British Library/Topham/The Image Works, Inc.; 132-133 Steve Vidler/SuperStock; 134-135 A1PIX London Ltd; 134 Deir el-Medina, Thebes, Egypt/Bridgeman Art Library; 137 (tc) Giraudon/Art Resource, NY; 137 (tl) Christine Osborne/Corbis;137 akg-images;138 Bildarchiv Preussischer Kulturbesitz/Art Resource, NY; 139 (tl) Dagli Orti/The Art Archive; 139 (tr) The Granger Collection, New York; 142 Ben Mangor/SuperStock; 144 Archivo Iconografico, S.A./Corbis; 147 Explorer, Paris/SuperStock;148 C. F. Payne/ National Geographic Image Collection;149 (cr) A. Winston, courtesy of www.touregypt.net; 149 (tl) Bildarchiv Preussischer Kulturbesitz/ Art Resource, NY; 150 (b)The Metropolitan Museum of Art, Gift of Egypt Exploration Fund, 1907 (07.230.2) Photograph © 1994 The Metropolitan Museum of Art; 150 (c) Egyptian Museum Turin/Dagli Orti (A)/The Art Archive; 152 (br) The British Museum/ Topham-HIP/The Image Works, Inc.;152 (c) The British Museum/Topham-HIP/The Image Works, Inc.; 153 Scala/Art Resource, NY; 154 Egyptian National Museum, Cairo, Egypt/Bridgeman Art Library; 155 Scala/Art Resource, NY; 157 (t) Musée du Louvre Paris/ Dagli Orti/The Art Archive; 157 (tr) Giraudon/ Art Resource, NY; 158 Gavin Hellier/Stone/ Getty Images; 160 (bl) Stephen Studd/ Photographer's Choice/Getty Images; 160 (br) Reunion des Musees Nationaux/Art Resource, NY; 160 (c) Egyptian Museum Turin/Dagli Orti/The Art Archive; 161 (bl)Bildarchiv Preussischer Kulturbesitz/Art Resource, NY; 161 (bl Temple) Rohan/Stone/Getty Images; 161 (br) Giraudon/Art Resource, NY; 161 (br) Bode Museum, Berlin, Germany/Bridgeman Art Library; 161 (c) Egyptian Museum Cairo/Dagli Orti/The Art Archive; 162-163 (b) Bill Bachmann/Index Stock Imagery 162 (tc) Scala/Art Resource, NY; 163 (tr) Egyptian National Museum, Cairo, Egypt/Bridgeman Art Library;164 (br) Sandro Vannini/Corbis; 164 (tr)Araldo de Luca; 165 (bl) Araldo de Luca; 165 (br) Gianni Dagli Orti/Corbis; 165 (tl) Araldo de Luca; 168-169 (ChapOp) Le Tourneur D'Ison Cyril/Gamma Press, Inc.; 172 (br) Jürgen Liepe; 172-173 (b) Le Tourneur D'Ison Cyril/Gamma Press, Inc.; 175 (tc) The British Museum/Topham-HIP/ The Image Works, Inc.; 176 Jürgen Liepe; 177 Topham/The Image Works, Inc.;178 Douglas Waugh/Peter Arnold, Inc.; 179 The British Museum/Topham-HIP/The Image Works, Inc.; 180 Naga, Sudan/Bridgeman Art Library; 180 (tl) Statue of Khonsuiraa, Egyptian, Third Intermediate Period, Dynasty 25, about 760-660 B.C. Black diorite Height x width x depth: 43.5 x 12.6 x 13.5 cm (17 1/8 x 4 15/16 x 5 5/16 in.) Museum of Fine Arts, Boston: James Fund and Contribution 07.494/

Museum of Fine Arts, Boston; 181 Mask of Queen Malakaye. Nubian. Napatan Period, reign of Tanwetamani, 664-653 B.C. Sudan, Nubia, (Nuri) Gilt silver. Height x width x depth: 13 x 11.5 x 1.1 cm (5 1/8 x 4 1/2 x 7/16 in.) Museum of Fine Arts, Boston: Harvard University - Museum of Fine Arts Expedition 20.1059, Photo copyright 2003 Museum of Fine Arts; Boston/Museum of Fine Arts, Boston; 182 Kazuyoshi Nomachi/HAGA/The Image Works, Inc.; 184 Erich Lessing/Art Resource, NY; 185 James Gurney; 186 Jürgen Liepe; 187 Naga, Sudan/Bridgeman Art Library; 188-189 (bg) Le Tourneur D'Ison Cyril/Gamma Press, Inc.188 (br) Kenneth Garrett/National Geographic Image Collection; 188 (ib) John Elk III hotography;188 (ic) James Strachan/ Stone/Getty Images; 189 (tl) John Elk III Photography; 189 (tl) Le Tourneur D'Ison Cyril/Gamma Press, Inc.; 189 (tr) Saulnier Didier/Gamma Press, Inc.; 190 (bl) Egyptian National Museum, Cairo, Egypt/Bridgeman Art Library; 190 (tr)The British Museum/ Topham-HIP/The Image Works, Inc.

UNIT 3

Opener 193-194 Giraudon/Bridgeman Art Library; 194 (tl) Scala/Art Resource, NY; 194 (tr) Scala/Art Resource, NY; 195 (bl) Scala/Art Resource, NY; 195 (tl) SuperStock; 195 (tr) Gianni Dagli Orti/Corbis; 199 (br) The Granger Collection, New York; 200-201 Richard T. Nowitz/Corbis; 204 Erich Lessing/ Art Resource, NY; 204-205 (b) Steve Kaufman/ Corbis; 205 (tr) National Gallery Budapest/ Dagli Orti (A)/The Art Archive; 206 National Gallery Collection; By kind permission of the Trustees of the National Gallery, London/ Corbis; 207 Mary Evans Picture Library; 208 Ellen B. Senisi;209 (br) Ali Meyer/Corbis; 209 (cl) Dagli Orti/The Art Archive; 210 (b) Tissot, James Jacques Joseph (1836-1902), Moses Speaks to Pharaoh. 18.9 x 28.6 cm., The Jewish Museum, New York, NY, U.S.A./The Jewish Museum, NY/Art Resource, NY; 210 (tl)Zev Radovan/Land of the Bible Photo Archive; 211 (b) Bob Daemmrich/The Image Works, Inc.; 211 (br) Aaron Haupt/Photo Researchers, Inc.; 211 (tc) Henry Groskinsky/Time Life Pictures/Getty Images; 211 (tr) The Granger Collection, New York; 212-213 Richard T. Nowitz/Corbis; 213 The Pierpont Morgan Library/Art Resource, NY; 214 Musee Conde, Chantilly, France/Giraudon/Bridgeman Art Library; 216 Bibliothèque Municipale Valenciennes/Dagli Orti/The Art Archive; 217 The British Library/The Art Archive; NY; 219 Howard Kingsnorth/Stone/Getty Images;220 akg-images; 221 Erich Lessing/Art Resource, NY; 222 Erich Lessing/Art Resource, NY; 222 British Museum/Dagli Orti/The Art Archive; 223 Richard T. Nowitz/Corbis; 224 (tl) The Granger Collection, New York; 224 (tr) Hanan Isachar/Israelimages; 225 (tl) Courtesy of The British Library; 226 akg-images; 228 National Gallery Budapest/Dagli Orti (A)/The Art Archive; 229 British Museum/Dagli Orti/The Art Archive; 230-231 © Chase Swift/Corbis; 234 Yale University Babylonian Collection; 234-235 (b) Maynard Owen Williams/ National Geographic Image Collection; 239 Musée du Louvre Paris/Dagli Orti (A)/The Art Archive; 240 © Chase Swift/Corbis; 242 (bl) Torah Scroll. Nuremberg, 1700-1751. Johann Conrad Weiss, active 1699-after 1751 (staves and fittings). Ink on vellum; staves,

wood with silver, cast and engraved. Scroll: 6-9/16 in. Gift of Samuel and Lucille Lemberg/ The Jewish Museum, NY/Art Resource, NY; 242 (br) Mezuzah. Jerusalem, Bezalel School, Mid-late 20th c. Silver: cast, granulation, filigree. L. 2 7/16 x W 11/16 in. Gift of Mrs. William Linder. 1987-57/The Jewish Museum, NY/Art Resource, NY; 242 (tr) Zev Radovan/ Land of the Bible Photo Archive; 243 (bl) Amulets, 1)Amulet of Mass'udah, Morocco 19th-20th century, silver on brass, F 4965, Gift of Dr. Harry G. Friedman, 2) Amulet, Meknes early 20th c., silver: incised, enamel, JM 23-47, Gift of Dr. Harry Friedenwald, 3) Amulet Against Lilith, Morocco late 19th-early 20th c., silver, engraved, JM 29-47, Gift of Dr. Harry Friedenwald, Photo: John Parnell. The Jewish Museum, New York, NY, U.S.A./The Jewish Museum, NY/Art Resource, NY; 243 (br) Hanukkah Menorah for the Synagogue. Eastern Europe, 18th c. Brass: cast, cut and engraved./The Jewish Museum, NY/Art Resource, NY; 243 (cl) Purim Noisemaker. Western Europe, 19th century. Silver: cast openwork, chased; topaz; glass stones. Gift of Dr. Harry G. Friedman/The Jewish Museum, NY/Art Resource, NY; 243 (tl) Dreidls, Poland, 18th century Wood: carved. 2 1/8 x 1 in. The Rose and Benjamin Mintz Collection/The Jewish Museum, NY/Art Resource, NY; 244 (b) Erich Lessing/Art Resource, NY; 245 akg-images; 246 Tate Gallery, London/Art Resource, NY; 247 From "Arch Selden A 5 folio2v"/The Bodleian Library/The Art Archive; 248 Kevin Unger/Corbis/Sygma; 250 Yale University Babylonian Collection; 251 akg-images; 252 (ib) Steve Allen/Brand X/Alamy Images; 252 (it) Steve Allen/Brand X Pictures/Alamy Images; 252-253 (bg) Richard Nowitz Photography; 253 (ib) Zefa/Masterfile; 253 (itr) Richard T. Nowitz/Corbis; 253 (inset tl) Daniel Lainé/Corbis; 254 (t) From "Arch Selden A 5 folio2v"/The Bodleian Library/ The Art Archive; 254 (tr) Erich Lessing/Art Resource, NY

UNIT 4

Opener 257-258 Archives Charmet/Bridgeman Art Library; 258 (br) akg-images; 259 (bl) Peter Willi/Bridgeman Art Library; 262-263 (bg) Bibliothèque des Arts Décoratifs Paris /Dagli Orti/The Art Archive; 263 Steve Vidler/SuperStock; 264-265 Walter Bibikow/Taxi/Getty Images; 270 Jack Parsons/Omni Photo Communications; 272 (b) Charlie Waite/Stone/Getty Images; 272 (c) foodfolio/Alamy Images; 273 Miles Ertman/Masterfile; 274-275 Yann Arthus-Bertrand/Corbis; 278 Robert Harding Picture Library Ltd./Alamy Images; 280 (bc) Charles Walker/Topfoto/The Image Works, Inc.; 280 (t)Erich Lessing/Art Resource, NY; 282 (tc) Archaeological Museum Istanbul/Dagli Orti/ The Art Archive; 282 (tl) The British Museum/ Topham-HIP/The Image Works, Inc.; 282 (t) akg-images; 282 (tr)The Granger Collection, New York; 283 (tc) Museo Nazionale Taranto/ Dagli Orti/The Art Archive; 283 (tr) Erich Lessing/Art Resource, NY; 284 (tc) Musée du Louvre Paris/Dagli Orti/The Art Archive; 284 (tl)Réunion des Musées Nationaux/Art Resource, NY; 285 Réunion des Musées Nationaux/Art Resource, NY; 286 Wolfgang Kaehler/Corbis; 290 Erich Lessing/Art Resource, NY; 292-293 (b) Quememer Ym/ Corbis/Sygma; 293 Goulandris Foundation Athens/Dagli Orti/The Art Archive; 294

Peter Connolly/akg-images; 295 (tl); Erich Lessing/Art Resource, NY; 295 (tc) Ancient Art & Architecture Collection, Ltd.; 295 (tr) C. M. Dixon Colour Photo Library; 300 Erich Lessing/Art Resource, NY; 301 Images.com/Corbis; 302 Ronald Sheridan/Ancient Art & Architecture Collection, Ltd.; 304 akg-images; 305 (bl) Gerhard Rempel; 305 (tl) Erich Lessing/Art Resource, NY; 305 (tr) Christopher Blackwell; 306 Mahaux Photography/Image Bank/Getty Images; 307 Erich Lessing/Art Resource, NY; 310-311 Corbis; 314-315 Miles Ertman/Masterfile; 315 Dagli Orti/The Art Archive; 318 Najlah Feanny/Corbis;318 JFB/The Art Archive; 319 akg-images; 320 (tl) The British Museum; 320 (tr) Réunion des Musées Nationaux/Art Resource, NY; 321 Stock Montage; 322-323 (b) Birmingham Museums and Art Gallery/Bridgeman Art Library; 324-325 Marty Snortum Studio/Panoramic Images; 325 (tc) Nimatallah/Art Resource, NY; 326 Ruggero Vanni/Corbis; 327 Réunion des Musées Nationaux/Art Resource, NY; 328 (tl) Araldo de Luca/Corbis; 328 (itl) akg-images; 328 (tc) akg-images; 328 (itc) Science Museum, London/Topham-HIP/The Image Works, Inc.; 328 (tr) The Granger Collection, New York; 328 (itr) Corbis; 329 (tl) Nimatallah/Art Resource, NY; 329 (itl) Reproduced from the original held by the Department of Special Collections of the University Libraries of Notre Dame; 329 (tc) Scala/Art Resource, NY; 329 (itc) Northwestern Library; 329 (tr) Giraudon/Art Resource, NY; 329 (ir) Northwestern Library; 330 Scala/Art Resource, NY; 331 Giraudon/Art Resource, NY; 332 (b) Dagli Orti/The Art Archive; 332 (c) Dagli Orti/The Art Archive; 332 (cl) Archaeological Museum Corinth / Dagli Orti/The Art Archive; 332 (cr) Archaeological Museum Corinth / Dagli Orti/The Art Archive; 333 (bl) Michele Burgess/Index Stock Imagery; 333 (c) H. R. Goette (Neg 2001/1086 F)/DAI, Athens (Deutsches Archaologisches Institut); 333 (t) Nimatallah/Art Resource, NY; 334 (b) Archaeological Museum, Istanbul, Turkey/Bridgeman Art Library; 338 Bettmann/Corbis; 339 (bc) Bates Littlehales/National Geographic Image Collection; 339 (bl) Bates Littlehales/National Geographic Image Collection; 339 (r) Bates Littlehales/National Geographic Image Collection; 339 (itr) AFP/Getty Images; 340 Dagli Orti/The Art Archive; 341 (br) akg-images; 341 (cl) Scala/Art Resource, NY; 342 akg-images; 343 (b) Archives Charmet/Bridgeman Art Library;343 Nimatellah/Art Resource, NY; 344 Bettmann/Corbis; 348 (tc) Culver Pictures; 348 (tr) Scala/Art Resource, NY; 349 (bl) Jordan Anders Blomqvist/Lonely Planet Images; 349 (br) Brooklyn Museum of Art/Corbis; 350 akg-images; 351 akg-images; 352 (bc) John Turner/Corbis; 352 (bl) Agora Museum Athens/Dagli Orti/The Art Archive; 352 (br) SSPL/The Image Works, Inc.; 354 JFB/The Art Archive; 356-357 (bg) Vanni Archive/Corbis; 356 (i) Bill Bachman/Index Stock Imagery; 357 (b) Gail Mooney/Corbis; 357 (cl) Wolfgang Kaehler/Corbis; 357 (icr) Chris Hellier/Corbis; 357 (itr) Alamy Images; 357 (itr) Anders Blomqvist/Lonely Planet Images; 358 (bl) Ruggero Vanni/Corbis; 358 (bl) Réunion des Musées Nationaux/

Art Resource, NY; 358 (tr) Charles Walker/Topfoto/The Image Works, Inc.;

UNIT 5

Opener 361-362 Hongnian Zhang/National Geographic Image Collection; 366-367 (bg) Jia Guorong/Imaginechina.com; 367 (bl) Musee des Beaux-Arts, Orleans, France/Bridgeman Art Library; 368-369 SEF/Art Resource, NY; 374 T. Bognar/Art Directors & TRIP Photo Library; 376 (t) Ric Ergenbright/Corbis; 377 andy Olson/Aurora Photos; 380 (b) P. Koch/Robert Harding Picture Library; 381 (tl) Ancient Art and Architecture Collection, Ltd./Bridgeman Art Library; 382 (b) Corbis; 382 (tl) Copyright J.M. Kenoyer, Courtesy Dept. of Archaeology and Museums, Govt. of Pakistan/www.harappa.com; 383 (bl) James P. Blair/National Geographic Image Collection; 383 (bl) Jehangir Gazdar/Woodfin Camp & Associates; 383 (c) Scala/Art Resource, NY; 383 (cl) J.M. Kenoyer, Courtesy Department of Archaeology and Museums, Government of Pakistan/www.harappa.com; 386 The British Museum/Topham-HIP/The Image Works, Inc. 387 Oriental Museum, Durham University, UK/Bridgeman Art Library; 388-389 Gavriel Jecan/Corbis; 390 Angelo Hornak/Corbis; 391 By permission of The British Library; 392 (tc) Gilles Mermet/Art Resource, NY; 392 (tl) Michael Freeman/Corbis; 392 (tr) DPA / SOA/The Image Works, Inc.; 393 (tc) The British Museum/Topham-HIP/The Image Works, Inc.; 393 (tl) Musée Guimet Paris/Dagli Orti (A)/The Art Archive; 393 (tr) Hu Zhao/Alamy Images; 395 (tc) Bettmann/Corbis; 395 (tr) The Granger Collection, New York; 396-397 Brian A. Vikander/Corbis; 398 Courtesy of The British Library; 399 Dave Sarnath/Dinodia Picture Agency; 401 (b) Bridgeman Art Library; 401 (i) Doranne Jacobson/International Images; 403 Adam Woolfitt/Corbis; 404 (b) Dinodia Picture Agency; 404 (i) Hulton Archive/Getty Images; 405 (t) David Young-Wolff/PhotoEdit; 407 Michael Freeman/Corbis; 408-409 Daryl Benson/Masterfile; 410-411 (bg) O. Louis Mazzatenta/National Geographic Image Collection; 411 (i) Keren Su/China Span; 412 (i) Doug Stern/National Geographic Image Collection; 412-413 (bg) Keren Su/China Span; 413 (r) Glen Allison/Stone/Getty Images; 414 Robert Harding Picture Library Ltd./Alamy Images; 416 (il) Galen Rowell/Corbis; 416 (ir) Keren Su/China Span; 416-417 Bill Wassman/Lonely Planet Images; 417 (i) Keren Su/Lonely Planet Images; 417(ir) Imaginechina.com; 418 The Granger Collection, New York; 420 David Noton Photography/Alamy Images; 422 Giraudon/Bridgeman Art Library; 424 H. Rogers/Art Directors & TRIP Photo Library; 426 Imaginechina.com; 427 Vanni/Art Resource, NY; 428 C.Walker/Topham/The Image Works, Inc.; 428 ChinaStock, 429 National Palace Museum Taiwan/Art Archive; 430 ChinaStock; 431 (bl) ChinaStock; 431 (cr) ChinaStock; 431 (tl) Archives Charmet/Bridgeman Art Library; 432-433 Giraudon/Art Resource, NY; 434 (tl) Asian Art & Archaeology, Inc./Corbis; 434 (tr) Burstein Collection/Corbis; 435 (tl) American

Numismatic Society; 435 (tr) O. Louis Mazzatenta/National Geographic Image Collection; 436-437 Daryl Benson/Masterfile; 437 Nigel Hicks/SuperStock; 438 (tl) O. Louis Mazzatenta/National Geographic Image Collection; 438 (tr) O. Louis Mazzatenta/National Geographic Image Collection; 442 (b) Snark/Art Resource, NY; 442 (cr) Laurent Lecat/akg-images; 447 ChinaStock; 448-449 Asian Art & Archaeology, Inc./Corbis; 449 Asian Art & Archaeology, Inc./Corbis; 449 (c) Cultural Relics Publishing House; 449 (tl) Asian Art & Archaeology, Inc./Corbis; 451 Giraudon/Art Resource, NY; 452-453 (bg) Keren Su/Corbis; 452 (i) Dennis Cox/ChinaStock; 453 (bl) Wu hui/Imaginechina.com;453 (itr) Dennis Cox/ChinaStock; 453 (icr) ChinaStock; 454 (bl) Genius of China Exhibition/Art Resource, NY;454 (tr) Laurent Lecat/akg-images

UNIT 6

Opener 457-458 Scala/Art Resource, NY; 458 (br) Rabatti - Domingie/akg-images; 458 (tr) Langevin Jacques/Corbis/Sygma; 459 (bl) National Trust Photographic Library/John Hammond/The Image Works, Inc.; 459 (tr) Titian/Arte & Immagini srl/Corbis; 462-463 (bg) Willeke Wendrich/Photo Berenike Project; 463 (br) Archebase; 466-467 Gail Mooney/Masterfile; 468 (c) Gilles Mermet/akg-images; 468-469 (b) K. Yamashita/PanStock/Panoramic Images; 470 Christopher Groenhout/Lonely Planet Images; 471 (tl) Leeds Museums and Art Galleries (City Museum) UK/Bridgeman Art Library; 471 (tr) akg-images; 472 (b) Museo di Villa Giulia Rome/Dagli Orti (A)/The Art Archive; 472 (bc) The British Museum/Topham-HIP/The Image Works, Inc.; 472 (bl) Scala/Art Resource, NY; 473 (tr) Scala/Art Resource, NY; 476 Galleria degli Uffizi, Florence, Italy/Bridgeman Art Library; 477 (tl) Ric Ergenbright/Corbis; 477 (tr) Araldo de Luca/Corbis; 478 Erich Lessing/Art Resource, NY; 480 (b) Mary Evans Picture Library; 480 (tr) Bettmann/Corbis; 481 Scala/Art Resource, NY; 482 (r) Alinari/Art Resource, NY;482 (tl) Sotheby's/akg-images; 483 (b)Ivan Massar/Stock Photo; 483 (br) AP/Wide World Photos; 483 (c) David J. & Janice L. Frent Collection/Corbis; 483 (tr) Courtesy of Ronnie Lapinsky-Sax; 483 (tr photo) Security Pacific Collection/Los Angeles Public Library; 483 (tr banner) Social History Division/Smithsonian Institution, National Museum of American History; 484 (b)Art Kowalsky/Alamy Images; 484 (cr) Museo della Civilta Romana Rome/Dagli Orti/The Art Archive; 485 (t) Scala/Art Resource, NY; 486 (b) Museo Capitolino Rome/Dagli Orti/The Art Archive; 488 (t) Dagli Orti/The Art Archive; 488 (tr) Tim McCarthy/Art Resource, NY; 489 The Stapleton Collection/Bridgeman Art Library; 494 Giraudon/Art Resource, NY; 496 Giraudon/Art Resource, NY;498 Bettmann/Corbis;499 (tl) Museo Capitolino Rome/Dagli Orti/The Art Archive; 499 (tr) Giraudon/Art Resource, NY; 500-501 David Marshall/Index Stock Imagery; 502-503 (bg) Roger Ressmeyer/Corbis; 502 (l) Nimatallah/Art Resource, NY; 502 (b) O. Louis Mazzatenta/National Geographic Image Collection;

503 (b) O. Louis Mazzatenta/National Geographic Image Collection; 504-505 (bg) Roger Ressmeyer/Corbis; 505 O. Louis Mazzatenta/National Geographic Image Collection; 506 O. Louis Mazzatenta/National Geographic Image Collection; 506 ARPL/Topham/The Image Works, Inc.; 507 Antiqua, Inc.;508 (b) Sandro Vannini/Corbis; 508 (t) National Maritime Museum, London; 509 North Carolina Museum of Art/Corbis; 510 Sandro Vannini/Corbis; 511 Réunion des Musées Nationaux/Art Resource, NY; 512 Ancient Art & Architecture Collection, Ltd.; 514 Photo courtesy the Legion Six Historical Foundation, Los Angeles, CA. Also represented is Legio IX Hispan, San Diego, CA/David Michaels; 518 (bl) William Hole, Portrait of Calgacus from the Frieze at the Scottish National Portrait Gallery, The Scottish National Portrait Gallery; 518 Réunion des Musées Nationaux/Art Resource, NY; 519 (tl) American Numismatic Society; 519 (tc) akg-images; 519 (tc) Jan Vinchon Numismatist Paris/Dagli Orti/The Art Archive; 519 Araldo de Luca/Corbis; 522 Angelo Hornak/Corbis; 523 (b) Erich Lessing/Art Resource, NY; 523 (bc) Angelo Hornak/Corbis; 523 (ibl) Scala/Art Resource, NY; 523 (ibr) David Marshall/Index Stock Imagery; 523 (itl) Alinari/Art Resource, NY; 523 (itr) Scala/Art Resource, NY; 524 (b) Manchester Art Gallery, UK/Bridgeman Art Library; 525 (tl) Private Collection/Bridgeman Art Library; 525 (tr) Scala/Art Resource, NY; 526 (bl) Archaeological Museum Naples/Dagli Orti (A)/The Art Archive; 527 (br) Hulton Archive/Getty Images; 527 (t) Musée Carnavalet Paris /Dagli Orti/The Art Archive; 528 (b) Archaeological Museum Saintes/Dagli Orti/The Art Archive; 528 (tl)Scala/Art Resource, NY; 529 (bl) Archaeological Museum Rabat/Dagli Orti/The Art Archive; 529 (br) Museo della Civilta Romana Rome/Dagli Orti/The Art Archive; 529 (cl) Cicero, In Catilinam. 1, Rare Books, Manuscript and Special Collections Library/Duke University Libraries; 529 (t) The Trustees of The British Museum; 530 (t) SuperStock; 531 The Art Archive; 532-533 Mike Yamashita/Woodfin Camp & Associates; 536 akg-images; 537 (b) Scala/Art Resource, NY; 537 (bc-l) Erich Lessing/Art Resource, NY; 537 (tc-r) National Archaeological Museum Athens/Dagli Orti/The Art Archive; 53(bl) National Museum Damascus Syria/Dagli Orti/The Art Archive; 537 (br) The British Museum/Topham-HIP/The Image Works, Inc.; 537 (cl) The Granger Collection, New York; 537 (cr) Burstein Collection/Corbis; 537 (tl) Reunion des Musees Nationaux/Art Resource, NY; 537 (tl) The Granger Collection, New York; 537 (tr) Araldo de Luca/Corbis; 538 Miramare Palace Trieste/Dagli Orti (A)/The Art Archive; 539 (tc) Museum of Anatolian Civilisations Ankara/Dagli Orti/The Art Archive; 539 (tl) Araldo de Luca/Corbis; 539 (tr) Museum of Antiquities, Newcastle Upon Tyne, UK/Bridgeman Art Library; 540 (i) James L. Stanfield/National Geographic Image Collection; 540-541 Doron Horowitz/Israelimages; 542 Werner Forman/Art Resource, NY; 543 The Pierpont Morgan Library/Art Resource, NY; 544 (bc) Dagli Orti/The Art Archive; 544 (bl) Scrovegni Chapel Padua / Dagli Orti (A)/The Art Archive; 544 (br) Sant'Apollinare Nuovo, Ravenna, Italy/Bridgeman Art Library; 545 (bc) Victoria and Albert Museum London/Sally Chappell/The Art Archive; 545 (bl) Scuola Grande di San Rocco, Venice, Italy/Bridgeman Art Library; 546 Scala/Art Resource, NY; 547 The Crosiers/Gene Plaisted, OSC; 548 David Else/Lonely Planet Images; 550 Adam Woolfitt/Corbis; 551 (bc) Araldo de Luca/Corbis; 551 (t) Dallas and John Heaton/Corbis; 552 (b) Vanni Archive/Corbis; 552 (bl) Erich Lessing/Art Resource, NY; 552 (tc) Archivo Iconografico, S. A./Corbis; 554 Museo Civico Bolzano/Dagli Orti/The Art Archive; 555 National Trust Photographic Library/John Hammond/The Image Works, Inc.; 557 Scala/Art Resource, NY; 558-559 Scala/Art Resource, NY; 558 Bettmann/Corbis; 560 (b) Scala/Art Resource, NY; 560 (i) Mark Segal/Panoramic Images; 561 Scala/Art Resource, NY; 562 Scuola Grande di San Rocco, Venice, Italy/Bridgeman Art Library; 563 Erich Lessing/Art Resource, NY; 564-565 (bg) PhotoDisc ; 564 (tc) J. Lawrence/ImageState/Alamy Images; 564 (tr) Medioimages/Alamy Images; 565 (tr) Gail Mooney/Masterfile; 566 (bl) Araldo de Luca/Corbis; 566 (br) O. Louis Mazzatenta/National Geographic Image Collection; 566 (cl) Ferdinando Scianna/Magnum Photos; 566 (cr) Robert Frerck/Odyssey Productions, Chicago 566 (tl) Louis Grandadam/Stone/Getty Images; 566 (tr) Araldo de Luca/Corbis; 569-570 Richard T. Nowitz/National Geographic Image Collection; 571 (ct) Justin Kerr, K4224/Kerr Associates; 571 (tr) Lowe Art Museum, University of Miami; 572 Robert Frerck/Odyssey Productions, Chicago; 573 New York Historical Society, New York, USA/Bridgeman Art Library; 574-575 David Noton/Masterfile; 575 Erich Lessing/Art Resource, NY; 576 Erich Lessing/Art Resource, NY; 577 Musée Luxembourgeois Arlon Belgium/Dagli Orti/The Art Archive;578 Erich Lessing/Art Resource, NY; 581 The Granger Collection, New York; 582-583 Murat Ayra/SuperStock; 586-587 Ken Welsh/Alamy Images; 588-589 (b) K Yamashita/PanStock/Panoramic Images; 588 (cl) Museum of Mankind London / Eileen Tweedy/The Art Archive; 590 (b) Ohio Historical Society; 590 (tc) Ohio Historical Society; 591 (bc) Justin Kerr, K4226/Kerr Associates; 591 (tl) Werner Forman/Art Resource, NY; 592 Felipe Davalos/National Geographic Image Collection; 593 Yoshio Tomii/SuperStock; 594 Steve Vidler/SuperStock; 596 Sean Sexton Collection/Corbis; 598 (b)Frans Lemmens/Image Bank/Getty Images; 598 (tr) Justin Kerr, K5618/Kerr Associates; 602 (b) Erich Lessing/Art Resource, NY; 602 (t) Justin Kerr, K4226/Kerr Associates

REFERENCE

R1 Cosmo Condina/Stone/Getty Images

All other photos from Harcourt School Photo Library and Photographers: Ken Kinzie, April Riehm and Doug Dukane.

California
History–Social Science
Standards and
Analysis Skills

Source for California Standards: California Department of Education

History–Social Science Content Standards

World History and Geography: Ancient Civilizations

Students in grade six expand their understanding of history by studying the people and events that ushered in the dawn of the major Western and non-Western ancient civilizations. Geography is of special significance in the development of the human story. Continued emphasis is placed on the everyday lives, problems, and accomplishments of people, their role in developing social, economic, and political structures, as well as in establishing and spreading ideas that helped transform the world forever. Students develop higher levels of critical thinking by considering why civilizations developed where and when they did, why they became dominant, and why they declined. Students analyze the interactions among the various cultures, emphasizing their enduring contributions and the link, despite time, between the contemporary and ancient worlds.

6.1 Students describe what is known through archaeological studies of the early physical and cultural development of humankind from the Paleolithic era to the agricultural revolution.

6.1.1 Describe the hunter-gatherer societies, including the development of tools and the use of fire.

6.1.2 Identify the locations of human communities that populated the major regions of the world and describe how humans adapted to a variety of environments.

6.1.3 Discuss the climatic changes and human modifications of the physical environment that gave rise to the domestication of plants and animals and new sources of clothing and shelter.

(continued)

6.2 Students analyze the geographic, political, economic, religious, and social structures of the early civilizations of Mesopotamia, Egypt, and Kush.

6.2.1 Locate and describe the major river systems and discuss the physical settings that supported permanent settlement and early civilizations.

6.2.2 Trace the development of agricultural techniques that permitted the production of economic surplus and the emergence of cities as centers of culture and power.

6.2.3 Understand the relationship between religion and the social and political order in Mesopotamia and Egypt.

6.2.4 Know the significance of Hammurabi's Code.

6.2.5 Discuss the main features of Egyptian art and architecture.

6.2.6 Describe the role of Egyptian trade in the eastern Mediterranean and Nile valley.

6.2.7 Understand the significance of Queen Hatshepsut and Ramses the Great.

6.2.8 Identify the location of the Kush civilization and describe its political, commercial, and cultural relations with Egypt.

6.2.9 Trace the evolution of language and its written forms.

6.3 Students analyze the geographic, political, economic, religious, and social structures of the Ancient Hebrews.

6.3.1 Describe the origins and significance of Judaism as the first monotheistic religion based on the concept of one God who sets down moral laws for humanity.

6.3.2 Identify the sources of the ethical teachings and central beliefs of Judaism (the Hebrew Bible, the Commentaries): belief in God, observance of law, practice of the concepts of righteousness and justice, and importance of study; and describe how the ideas of the Hebrew traditions are reflected in the moral and ethical traditions of Western civilization.

6.3.3 Explain the significance of Abraham, Moses, Naomi, Ruth, David, and Yohanan ben Zaccai in the development of the Jewish religion.

6.3.4 Discuss the locations of the settlements and movements of Hebrew peoples, including the Exodus and their movement to and from Egypt, and outline the significance of the Exodus to the Jewish and other people.

6.3.5 Discuss how Judaism survived and developed despite the continuing dispersion of much of the Jewish population from Jerusalem and the rest of Israel after the destruction of the second Temple in A.D. 70.

(continued)

6.4 Students analyze the geographic, political, economic, religious, and social structures of the early civilizations of Ancient Greece.

6.4.1 Discuss the connections between geography and the development of city-states in the region of the Aegean Sea, including patterns of trade and commerce among Greek city-states and within the wider Mediterranean region.

6.4.2 Trace the transition from tyranny and oligarchy to early democratic forms of government and back to dictatorship in ancient Greece, including the significance of the invention of the idea of citizenship (e.g., from *Pericles' Funeral Oration*).

6.4.3 State the key differences between Athenian, or direct, democracy and representative democracy.

6.4.4 Explain the significance of Greek mythology to the everyday life of people in the region and how Greek literature continues to permeate our literature and language today, drawing from Greek mythology and epics, such as Homer's *Iliad* and *Odyssey*, and from *Aesop's Fables*.

6.4.5 Outline the founding, expansion, and political organization of the Persian Empire.

6.4.6 Compare and contrast life in Athens and Sparta, with emphasis on their roles in the Persian and Peloponnesian Wars.

6.4.7 Trace the rise of Alexander the Great and the spread of Greek culture eastward and into Egypt.

6.4.8 Describe the enduring contributions of important Greek figures in the arts and sciences (e.g., Hypatia, Socrates, Plato, Aristotle, Euclid, Thucydides).

6.5 Students analyze the geographic, political, economic, religious, and social structures of the early civilizations of India.

6.5.1 Locate and describe the major river system and discuss the physical setting that supported the rise of this civilization.

6.5.2 Discuss the significance of the Aryan invasions.

6.5.3 Explain the major beliefs and practices of Brahmanism in India and how they evolved into early Hinduism.

6.5.4 Outline the social structure of the caste system.

6.5.5 Know the life and moral teachings of Buddha and how Buddhism spread in India, Ceylon, and Central Asia.

6.5.6 Describe the growth of the Maurya empire and the political and moral achievements of the emperor Asoka.

6.5.7 Discuss important aesthetic and intellectual traditions (e.g., Sanskrit literature, including the *Bhagavad Gita*; medicine; metallurgy; and mathematics, including Hindu-Arabic numerals and the zero).

(continued)

6.6 Students analyze the geographic, political, economic, religious, and social structures of the early civilizations of China.

6.6.1 Locate and describe the origins of Chinese civilization in the Huang-He Valley during the Shang Dynasty.

6.6.2 Explain the geographic features of China that made governance and the spread of ideas and goods difficult and served to isolate the country from the rest of the world.

6.6.3 Know about the life of Confucius and the fundamental teachings of Confucianism and Taoism.

6.6.4 Identify the political and cultural problems prevalent in the time of Confucius and how he sought to solve them.

6.6.5 List the policies and achievements of the emperor Shi Huangdi in unifying northern China under the Qin Dynasty.

6.6.6 Detail the political contributions of the Han Dynasty to the development of the imperial bureaucratic state and the expansion of the empire.

6.6.7 Cite the significance of the trans-Eurasian "silk roads" in the period of the Han Dynasty and Roman Empire and their locations.

6.6.8 Describe the diffusion of Buddhism northward to China during the Han Dynasty.

(continued)

6.7 Students analyze the geographic, political, economic, religious, and social structures during the development of Rome.

6.7.1 Identify the location and describe the rise of the Roman Republic, including the importance of such mythical and historical figures as Aeneas, Romulus and Remus, Cincinnatus, Julius Caesar, and Cicero.

6.7.2 Describe the government of the Roman Republic and its significance (e.g., written constitution and tripartite government, checks and balances, civic duty).

6.7.3 Identify the location of and the political and geographic reasons for the growth of Roman territories and expansion of the empire, including how the empire fostered economic growth through the use of currency and trade routes.

6.7.4 Discuss the influence of Julius Caesar and Augustus in Rome's transition from republic to empire.

6.7.5 Trace the migration of Jews around the Mediterranean region and the effects of their conflict with the Romans, including the Romans' restrictions on their right to live in Jerusalem.

6.7.6 Note the origins of Christianity in the Jewish Messianic prophecies, the life and teachings of Jesus of Nazareth as described in the New Testament, and the contribution of St. Paul the Apostle to the definition and spread of Christian beliefs (e.g., belief in the Trinity, resurrection, salvation).

6.7.7 Describe the circumstances that led to the spread of Christianity in Europe and other Roman territories.

6.7.8 Discuss the legacies of Roman art and architecture, technology and science, literature, language, and law.

(continued)

History–Social Science Content Standards
Historical and Social Sciences Analysis Skills

The intellectual skills noted below are to be learned through, and applied to, the content standards for grades six through eight. They are to be assessed *only in conjunction with* the content standards in grades six through eight.

In addition to the standards for grades six through eight, students demonstrate the following intellectual reasoning, reflection, and research skills:

Chronological and Spatial Thinking

1. Students explain how major events are related to one another in time.

2. Students construct various time lines of key events, people, and periods of the historical era they are studying.

3. Students use a variety of maps and documents to identify physical and cultural features of neighborhoods, cities, states, and countries and to explain the historical migration of people, expansion and disintegration of empires, and the growth of economic systems.

(continued)

Research, Evidence, and Point of View

1. Students frame questions that can be answered by historical study and research.

2. Students distinguish fact from opinion in historical narratives and stories.

3. Students distinguish relevant from irrelevant information, essential from incidental information, and verifiable from unverifiable information in historical narratives and stories.

4. Students assess the credibility of primary and secondary sources and draw sound conclusions from them.

5. Students detect the different historical points of view on historical events and determine the context in which the historical statements were made (the questions asked, sources used, author's perspectives).

Historical Interpretation

1. Students explain the central issues and problems from the past, placing people and events in a matrix of time and place.

2. Students understand and distinguish cause, effect, sequence, and correlation in historical events, including the long- and short-term causal relations.

3. Students explain the sources of historical continuity and how the combination of ideas and events explains the emergence of new patterns.

4. Students recognize the role of chance, oversight, and error in history.

5. Students recognize that interpretations of history are subject to change as new information is uncovered.

6. Students interpret basic indicators of economic performance and conduct cost-benefit analyses of economic and political issues.

The Great Wall of China